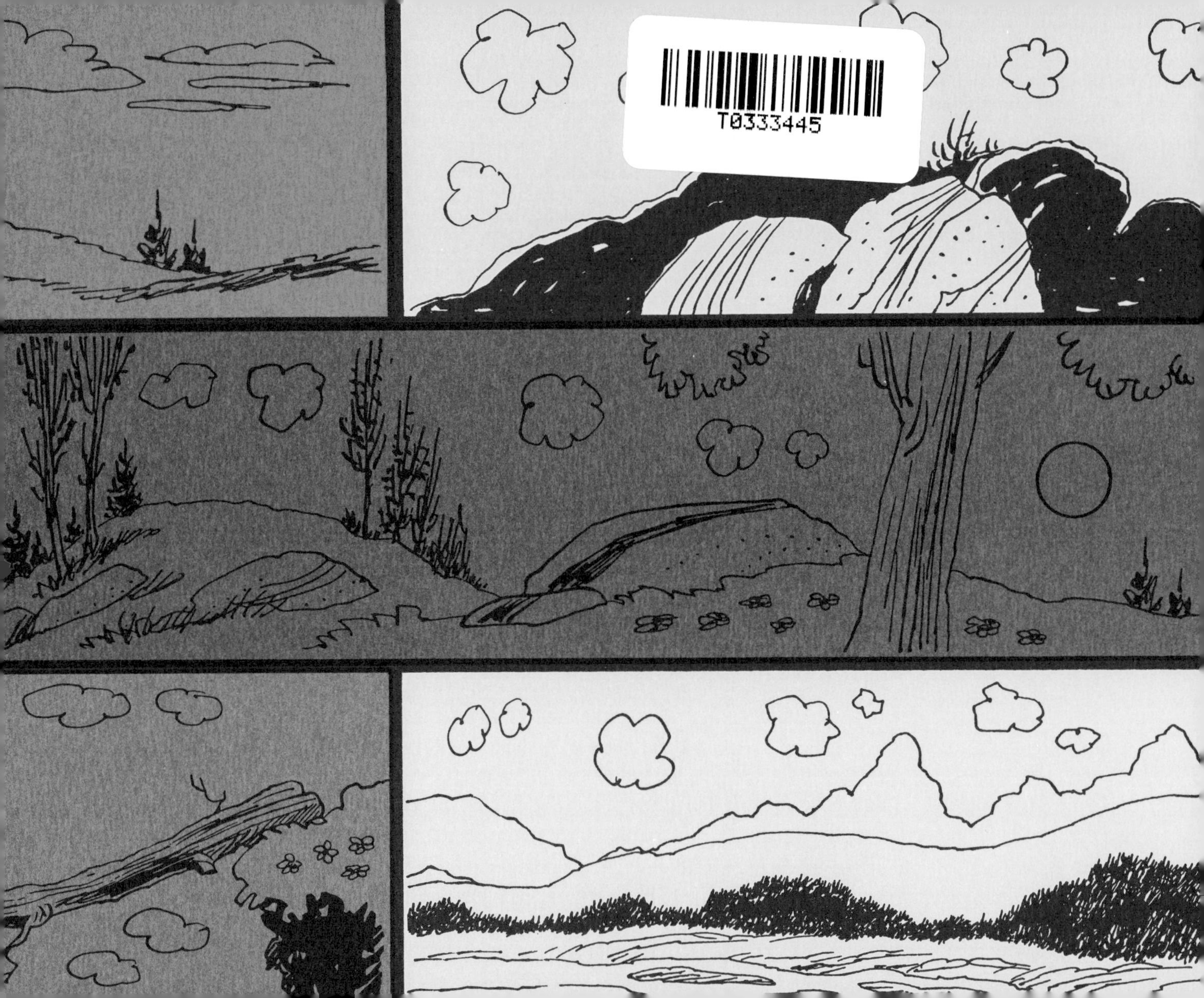

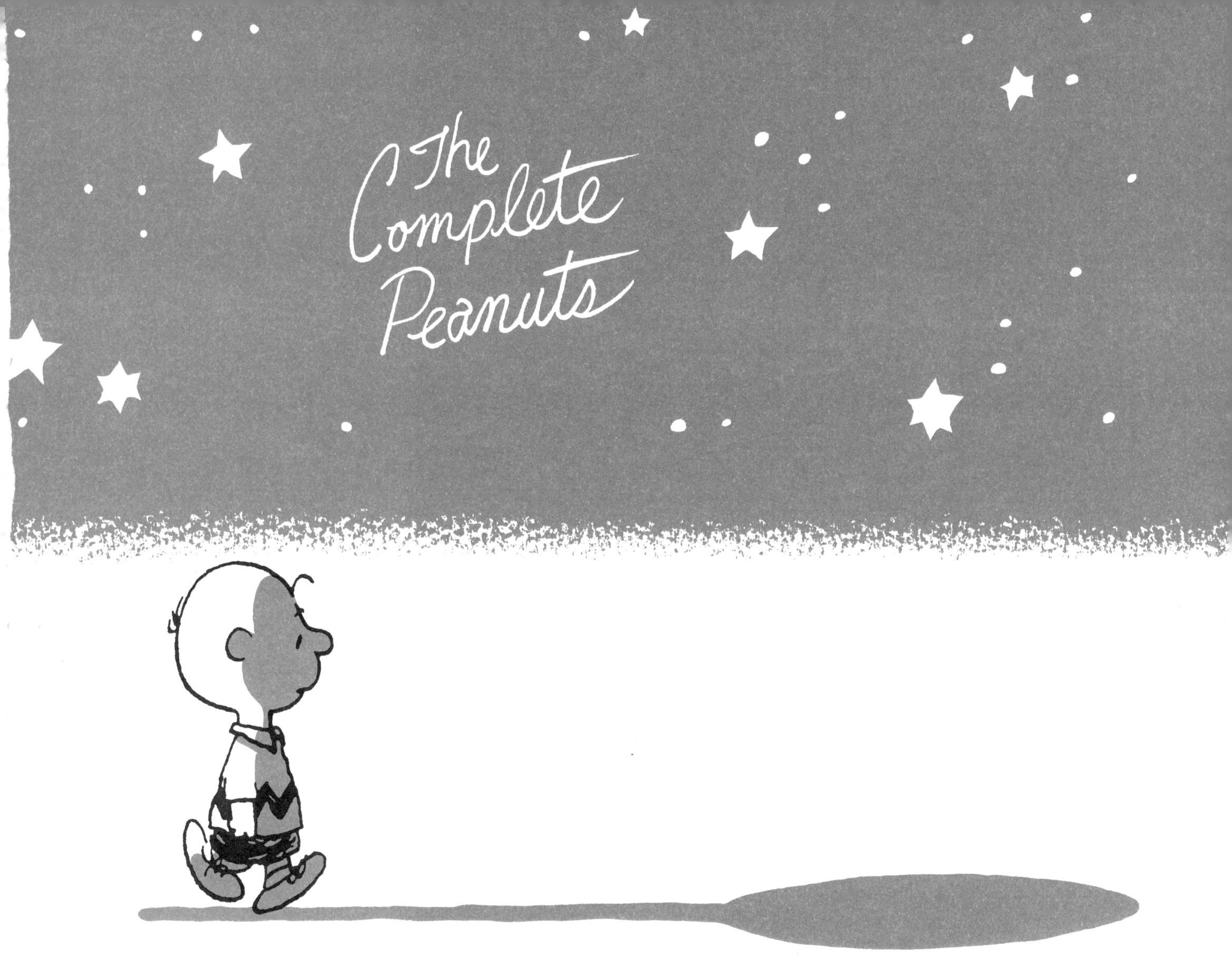
The Complete Peanuts

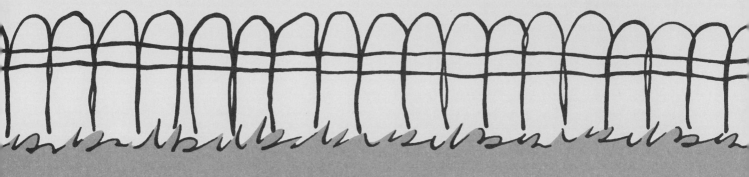

THE COMPLETE PEANUTS
by Charles M. Schulz

Editor: Gary Groth
Designer: Seth
Production Manager: Kim Thompson
Production, assembly and restoration: Paul Baresh
Archival assistance: Marcie Lee
Index compiled by Ben Horak, Janice Lee, and Madisen Smet
Associate Publisher: Eric Reynolds
Publishers: Gary Groth & Kim Thompson

Special thanks to Jeannie Schulz, without whom
this project would not have come to fruition.
Thanks also to John R. Troy and the
Charles M. Schulz Creative Associates,
especially Paige Braddock and Kim Towner.
Thanks for special support from Peanuts International, LLC.

First published in America in 2012 by Fantagraphics Books,
7563 Lake City Way, Seattle, WA 98115, USA

First published in Great Britain in 2014 by Canongate Books Ltd,
14 High Street, Edinburgh, EH1 1TE

1

British Library Cataloguing-in-Publication Data
A catalogue record for this book is available on request from the British Library.

ISBN 978 1 78211 515 1
Printed and bound in China
www.canongate.tv

CHARLES M. SCHULZ

THE COMPLETE PEANUTS

1985 TO 1986

" SUDDENLY, YOU'RE
REMINDED OF A
LOST LOVE... "

CANONGATE BOOKS

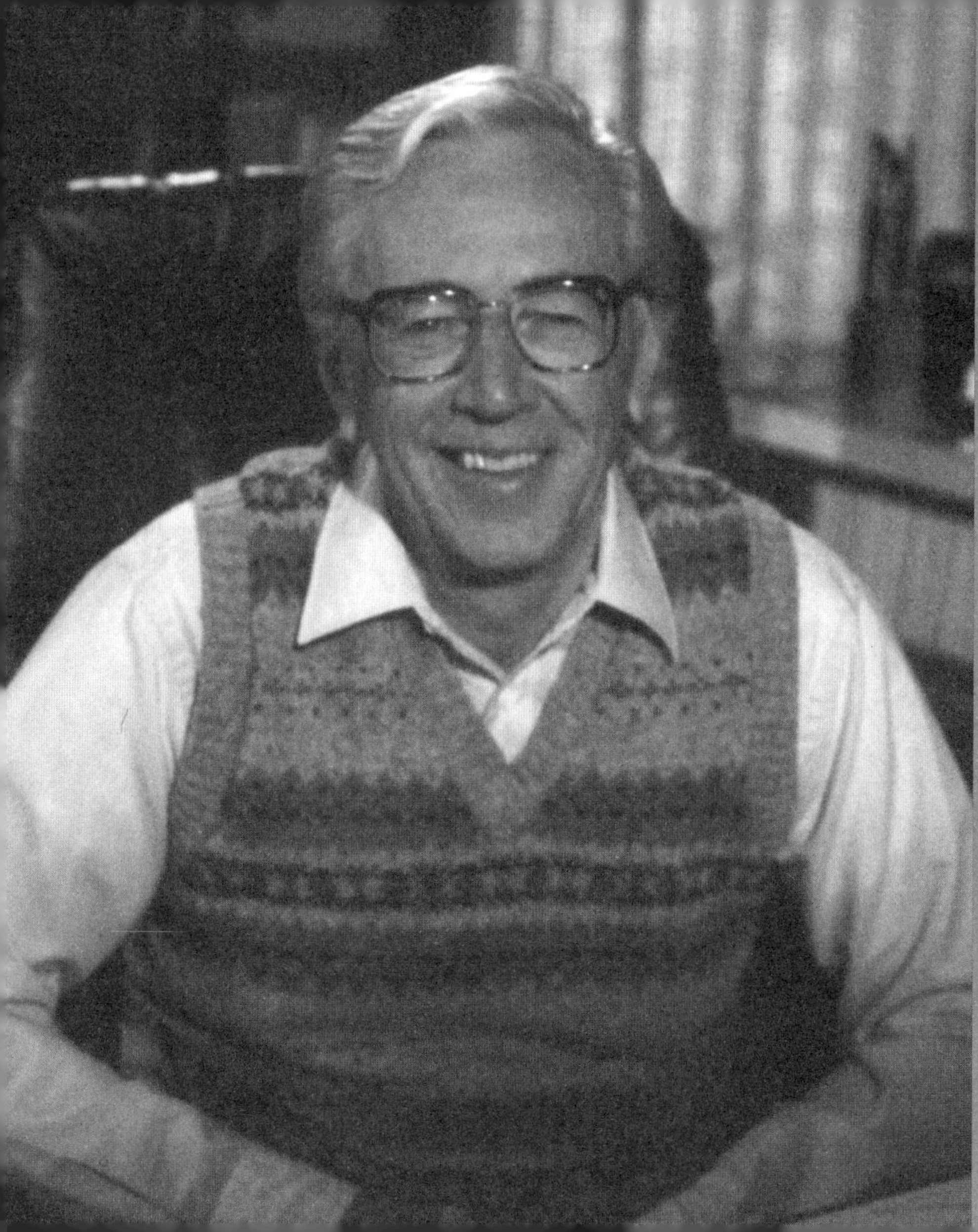

Charles M. Schulz in 1985 during the filming of *It's Your 20th Television Anniversary, Charlie Brown*. Courtesy of The Charles M. Schulz Museum and Research Center, Santa Rosa, California.

FOREWORD by **PATTON OSWALT**

The first Calvin and Hobbs collection I owned was the third one published — *The Essential Calvin and Hobbes*. Charles M. Schulz wrote the introduction. I've probably thought about it at least once a month since I read it, in 1988. It was the same year I started stand-up.

I can't quote you his exact phrasing. But the essence of the man, his quiet expertise and wordless knowledge, which he'd absorbed so deeply that he could only parcel it out in cryptic clues, was there.

The way he wrote about how Bill Watterson really knew how to draw splashes of water, and bedside tables, and how Calvin's shoes looked like "little dinner rolls." He said something to the effect that these small, throwaway details might not seem important, taken by themselves. But together, and without drawing any attention to the fact, they made up the crucial elements of any successful comic strip.

Reading these two years' worth of *Peanuts*, 1985 to 1986, I understand better what Schulz was talking about. At this point, Schulz had been drawing *Peanuts* for 35 years. He had another 15 to go before he capped his pen and said goodbye.

The existential angst of Charlie Brown, the philosophical curiosity of Linus, the brashness of Lucy, and the near-savant imagination and playfulness of Snoopy now had to contend with America staggering towards the millennium. Notice how the first strip in this collection has to do with answering machines. Keep in mind, this was a comic strip that, when it started, featured children using nib pens with desktop inkwells at school.

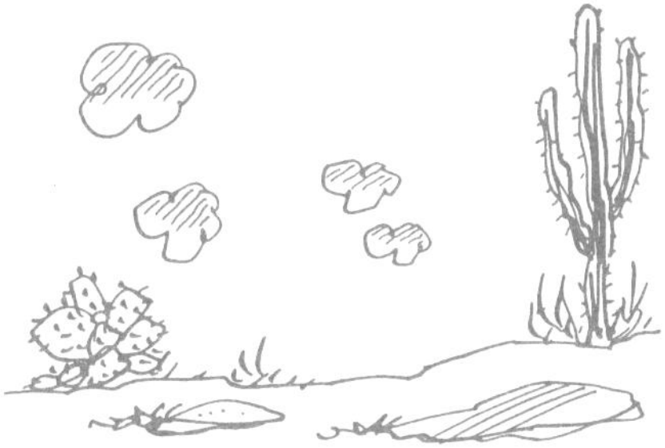

There are also references to "Baby on Board" signs, ghetto blasters (which become "Beagle blasters" in the *Peanuts* universe) and, most troubling, endless talk of attorneys and lawsuits. Snoopy even adds a new make-believe character to his repertoire which has, to this point, included the WWI Flying Ace, the passionate Unpublished Author, and Joe Cool. Sadly, his new imaginary persona is a bowtie-wearing, bowler-topped attorney. The one series of strips which *does* feature the WWI Flying Ace ominously mentions attorneys as well.

Shadow autobiography? How deep was Schulz mired, at this point in his career, in merchandising and broadcast rights and ancillary residuals? Like every other rock band whose first album is about struggle and survival, and whose subsequent works deal with excess, fame and the ennui of it all, even Schulz couldn't escape success.

But, just like he hinted in his Calvin and Hobbes intro, he still held firm to his basic principles. The bedside tables, water splashes, and shoes that look like dinner rolls are all there. Even Snoopy's "beagle blaster" has a spongy, blustering personality all its own.

Charles Schulz wrote a fifty year-long psychological autobiography starring a bald kid and a sentient dog. And he made the water splashes look great.

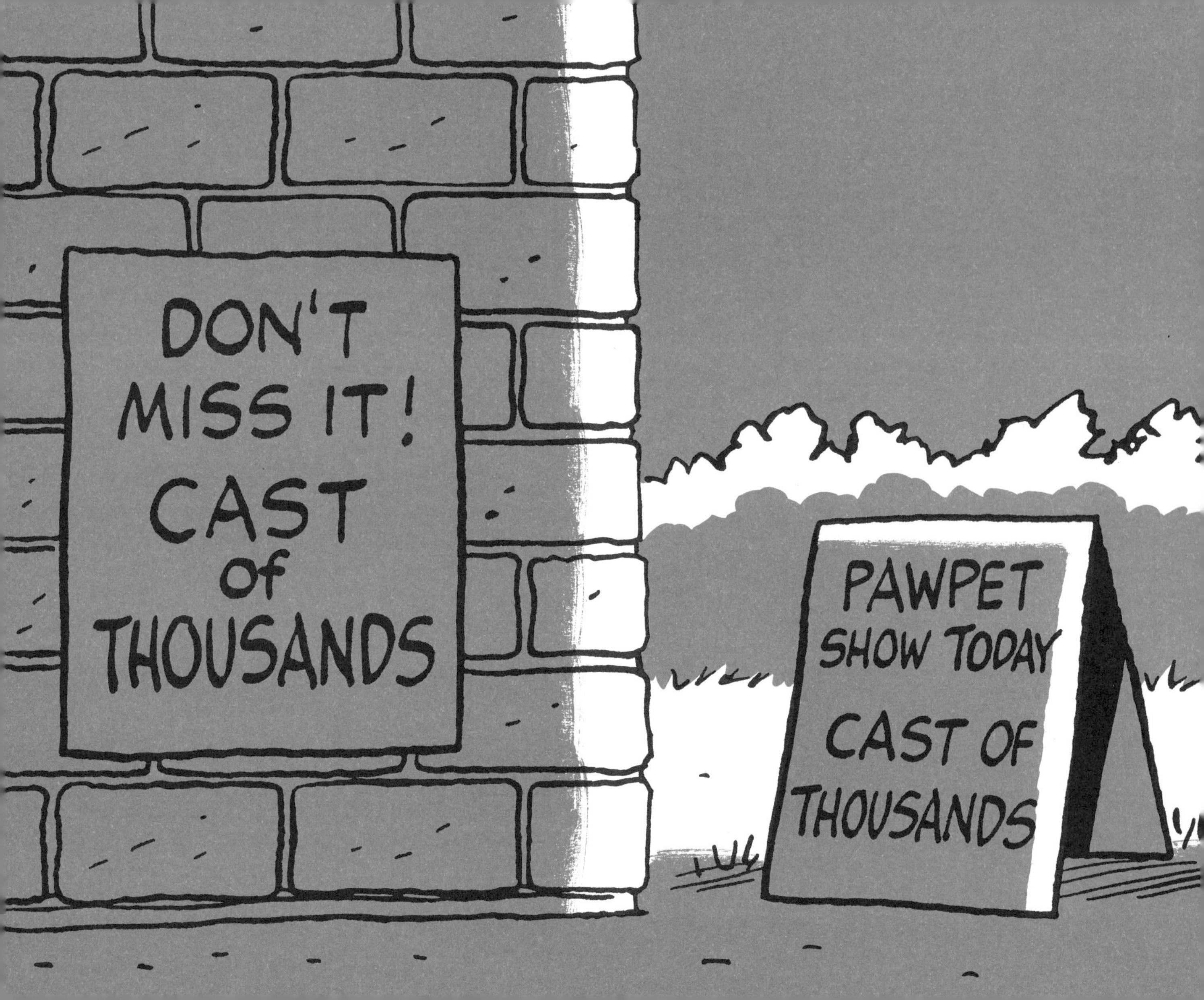
DON'T
MISS IT!
CAST
of
THOUSANDS
PAWPET
SHOW TODAY
CAST OF
THOUSANDS

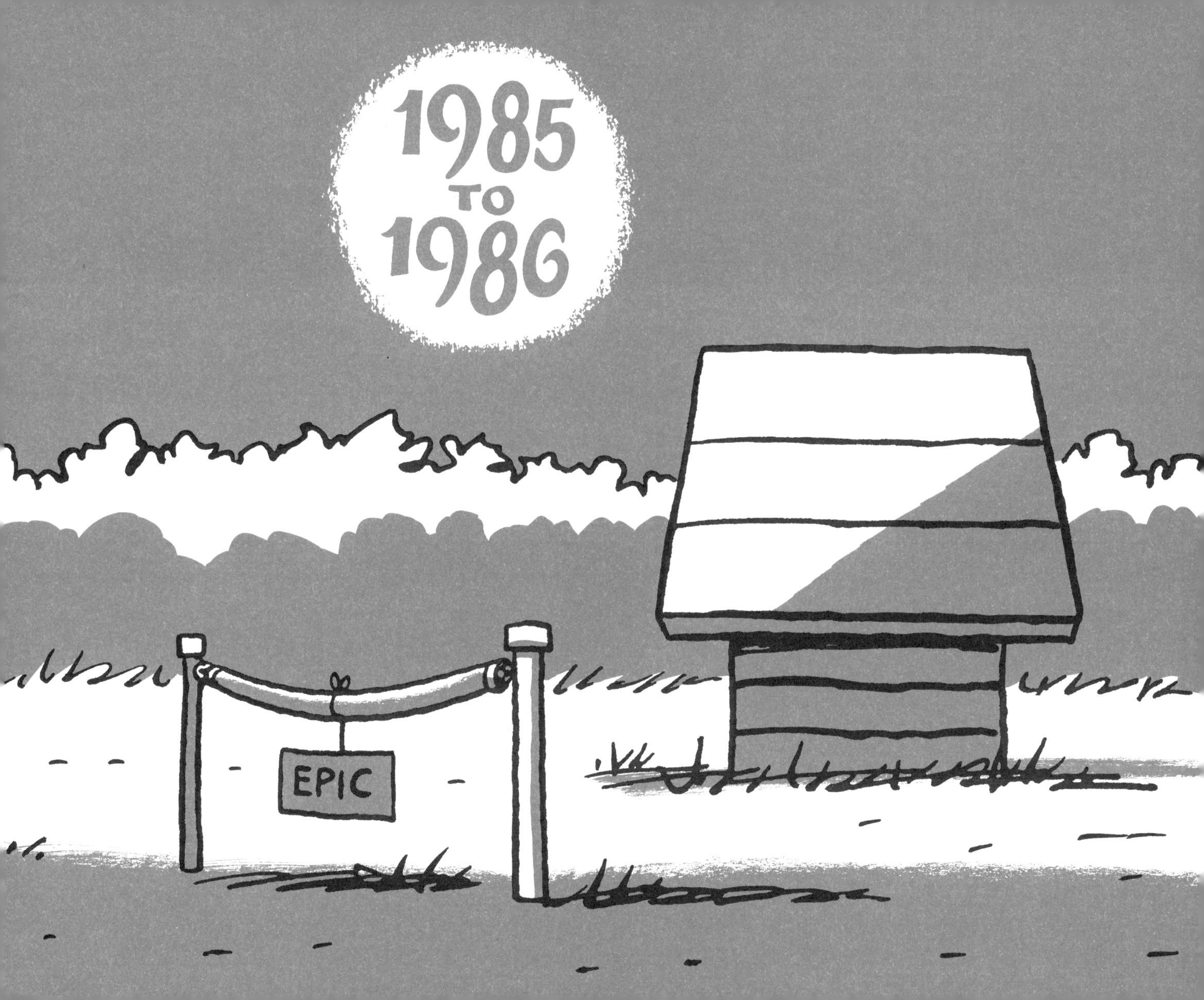
1985
TO
1986
EPIC

HI, CHUCK! WE JUST CALLED TO WISH YOU A HAPPY NEW YEAR
DO YOU STILL LOVE ME, CHUCK?
MARCIE WANTS TO KNOW IF YOU STILL LOVE HER, TOO, CHUCK...
I'M SORRY...I'M NOT HERE ANY MORE..I'VE SUDDENLY BECOME A RECORDING!
1-1-85

WHERE'S THE FOOTBALL GAME?
I THOUGHT THERE WAS FOOTBALL ON THURSDAY NIGHTS
THIS IS WEDNESDAY
THAT'S NO EXCUSE!
1-2-85

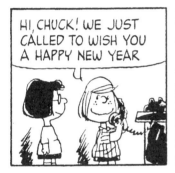

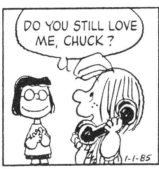

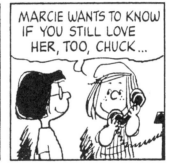

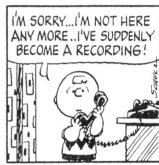

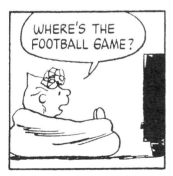

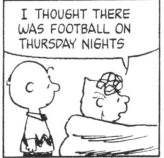

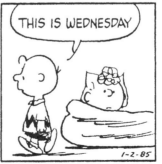

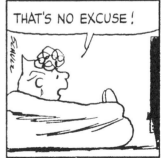

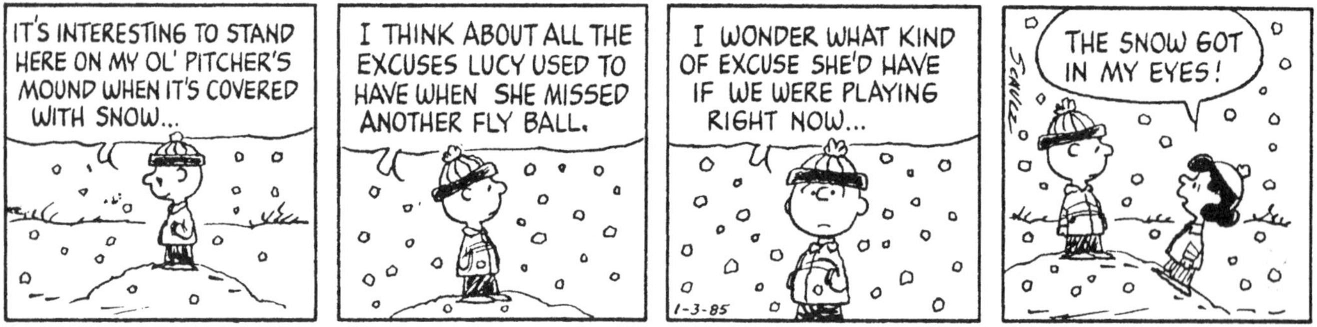
IT'S INTERESTING TO STAND HERE ON MY OL' PITCHER'S MOUND WHEN IT'S COVERED WITH SNOW...
I THINK ABOUT ALL THE EXCUSES LUCY USED TO HAVE WHEN SHE MISSED ANOTHER FLY BALL.
I WONDER WHAT KIND OF EXCUSE SHE'D HAVE IF WE WERE PLAYING RIGHT NOW...
1-3-85
THE SNOW GOT IN MY EYES!
SCHULZ

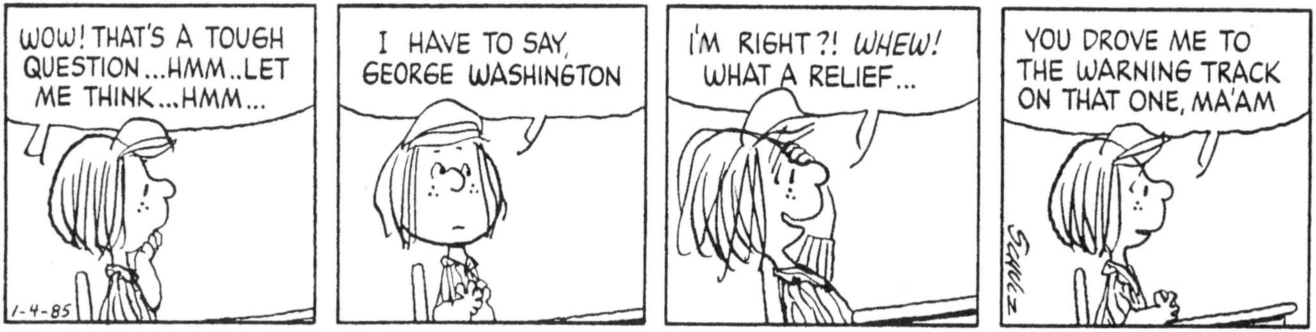
WOW! THAT'S A TOUGH QUESTION...HMM..LET ME THINK...HMM...
1-4-85
I HAVE TO SAY, GEORGE WASHINGTON
I'M RIGHT?! *WHEW!* WHAT A RELIEF...
YOU DROVE ME TO THE WARNING TRACK ON THAT ONE, MA'AM
SCHULZ

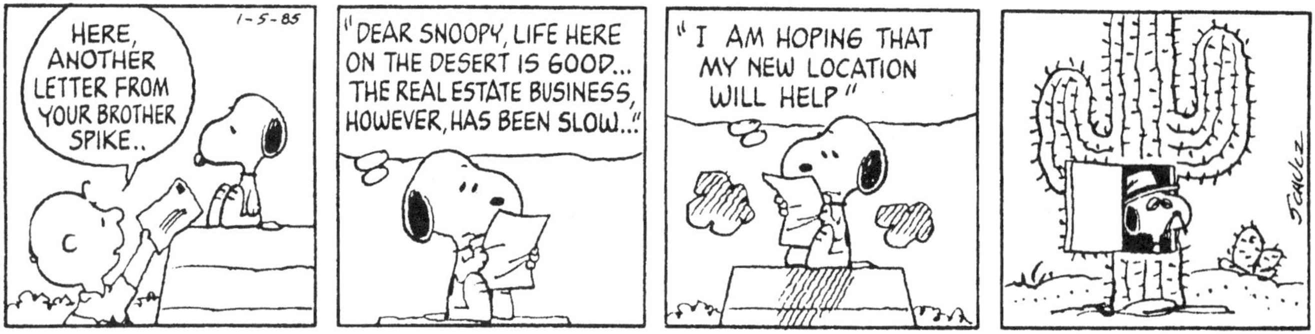
HERE, ANOTHER LETTER FROM YOUR BROTHER SPIKE..
1-5-85
"DEAR SNOOPY, LIFE HERE ON THE DESERT IS GOOD... THE REAL ESTATE BUSINESS, HOWEVER, HAS BEEN SLOW..."
"I AM HOPING THAT MY NEW LOCATION WILL HELP"
SCHULZ

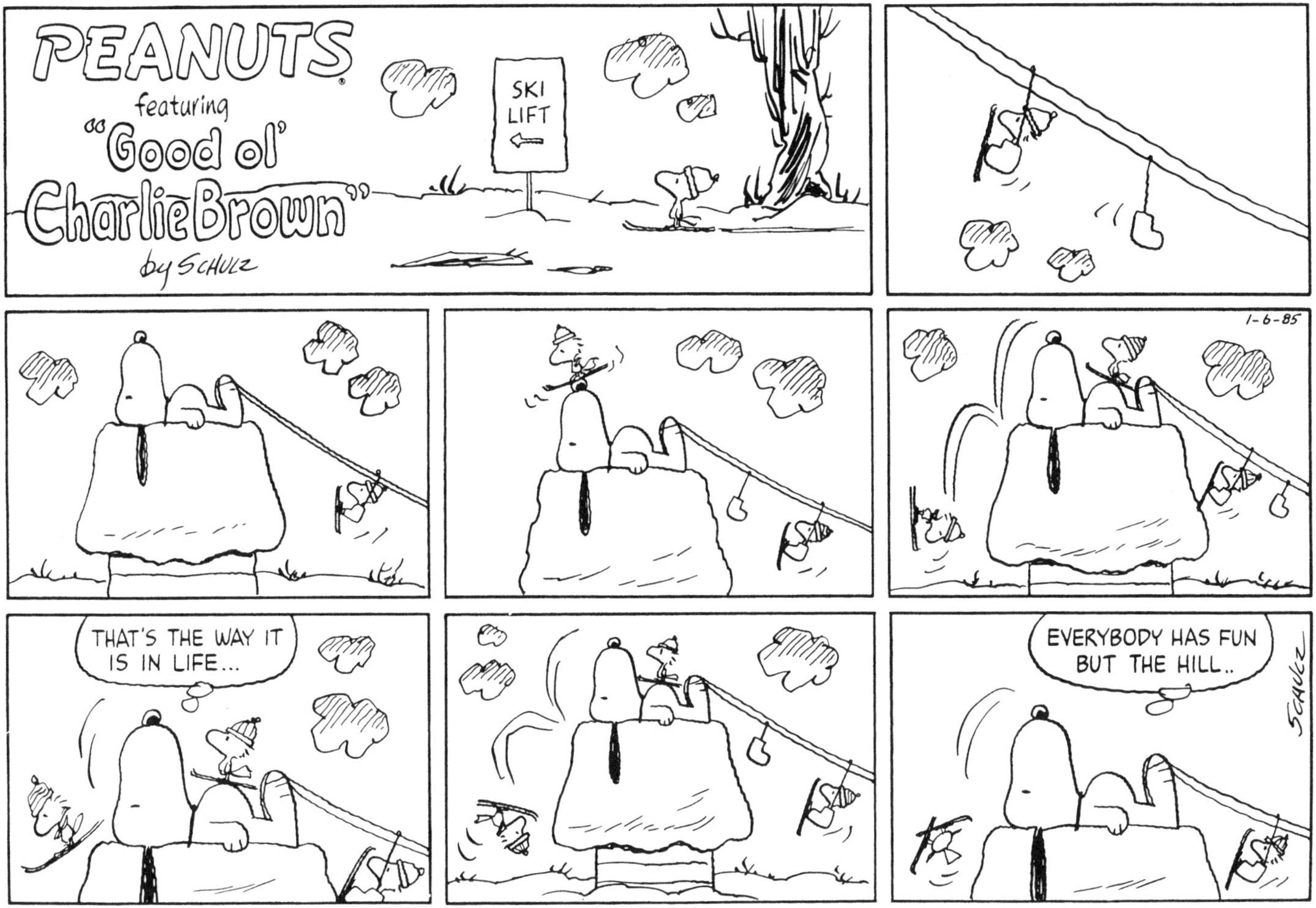
PEANUTS
featuring
"Good ol' Charlie Brown"
by SCHULZ
SKI LIFT
1-6-85
THAT'S THE WAY IT IS IN LIFE...
EVERYBODY HAS FUN BUT THE HILL..
SCHULZ

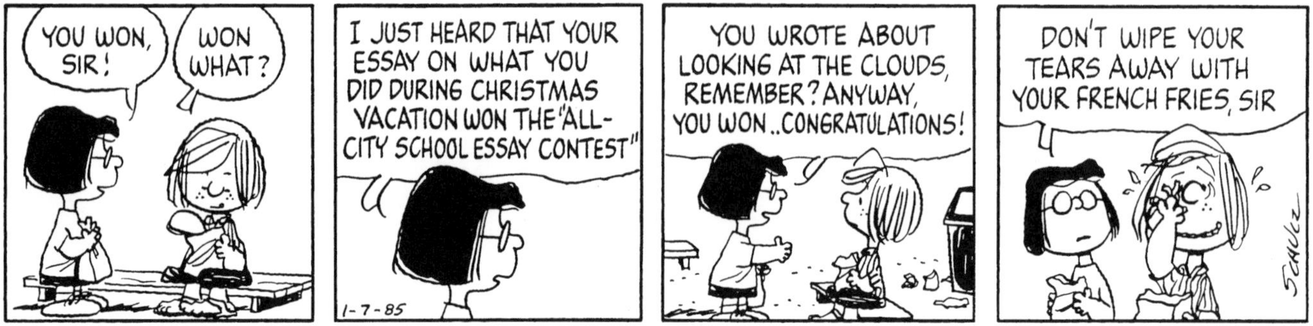
YOU WON, SIR!
WON WHAT?
I JUST HEARD THAT YOUR ESSAY ON WHAT YOU DID DURING CHRISTMAS VACATION WON THE "ALL-CITY SCHOOL ESSAY CONTEST"
1-7-85
YOU WROTE ABOUT LOOKING AT THE CLOUDS, REMEMBER? ANYWAY, YOU WON..CONGRATULATIONS!
DON'T WIPE YOUR TEARS AWAY WITH YOUR FRENCH FRIES, SIR
SCHULZ

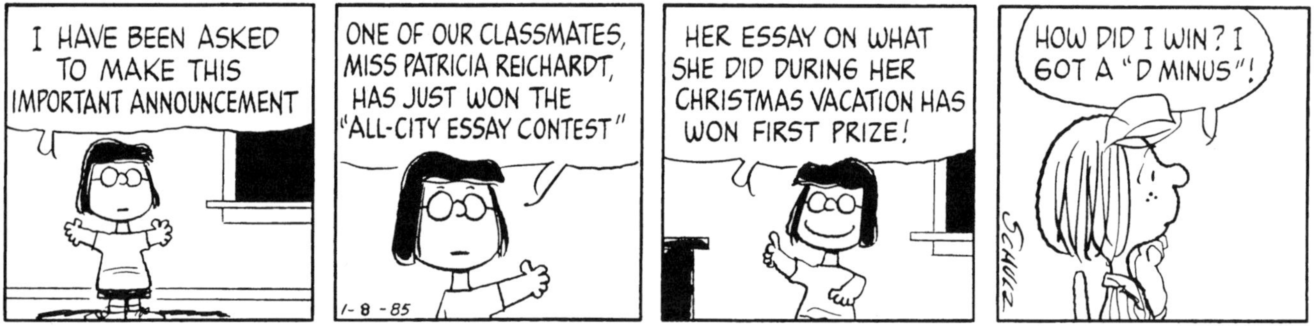
I HAVE BEEN ASKED TO MAKE THIS IMPORTANT ANNOUNCEMENT
ONE OF OUR CLASSMATES, MISS PATRICIA REICHARDT, HAS JUST WON THE "ALL-CITY ESSAY CONTEST"
1-8-85
HER ESSAY ON WHAT SHE DID DURING HER CHRISTMAS VACATION HAS WON FIRST PRIZE!
HOW DID I WIN? I GOT A "D MINUS"!
SCHULZ

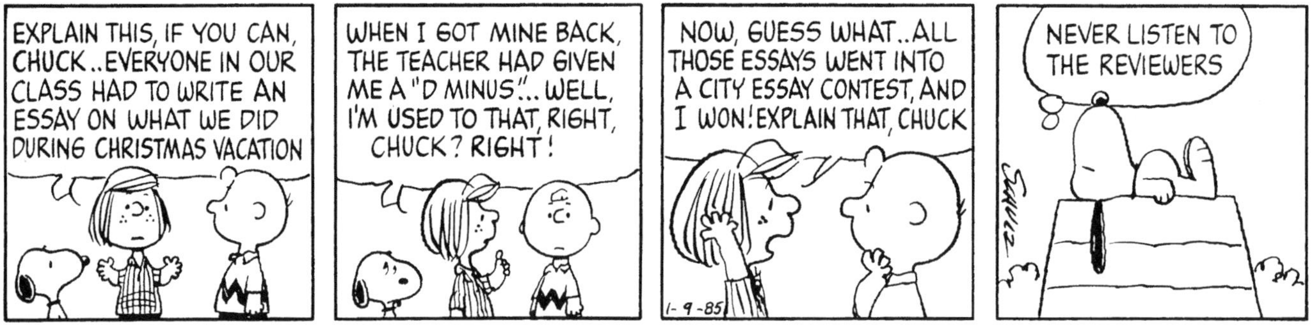
EXPLAIN THIS, IF YOU CAN, CHUCK..EVERYONE IN OUR CLASS HAD TO WRITE AN ESSAY ON WHAT WE DID DURING CHRISTMAS VACATION
WHEN I GOT MINE BACK, THE TEACHER HAD GIVEN ME A "D MINUS"... WELL, I'M USED TO THAT, RIGHT, CHUCK? RIGHT!
NOW, GUESS WHAT..ALL THOSE ESSAYS WENT INTO A CITY ESSAY CONTEST, AND I WON! EXPLAIN THAT, CHUCK
1-9-85
NEVER LISTEN TO THE REVIEWERS
SCHULZ

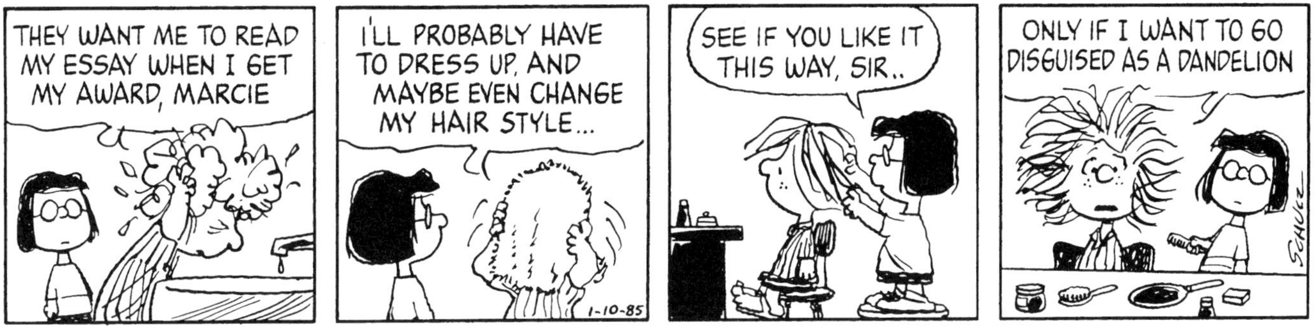
THEY WANT ME TO READ MY ESSAY WHEN I GET MY AWARD, MARCIE
I'LL PROBABLY HAVE TO DRESS UP, AND MAYBE EVEN CHANGE MY HAIR STYLE...
1-10-85
SEE IF YOU LIKE IT THIS WAY, SIR..
ONLY IF I WANT TO GO DISGUISED AS A DANDELION
SCHULZ

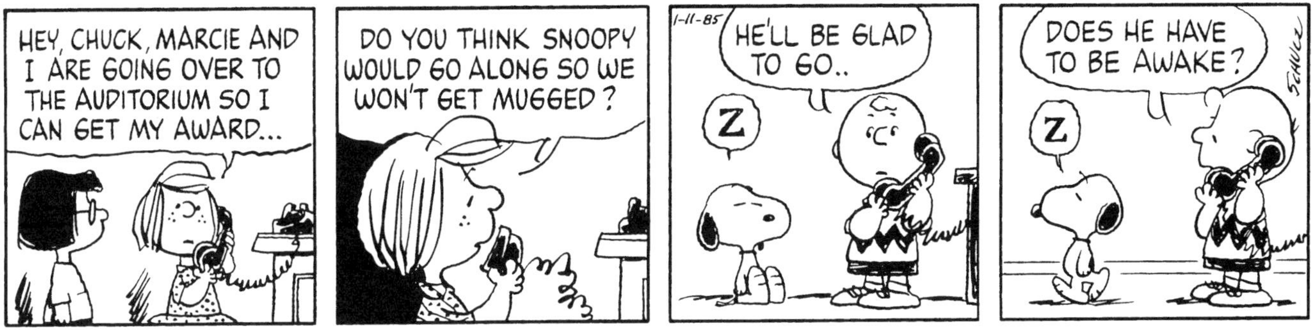
HEY, CHUCK, MARCIE AND I ARE GOING OVER TO THE AUDITORIUM SO I CAN GET MY AWARD...
DO YOU THINK SNOOPY WOULD GO ALONG SO WE WON'T GET MUGGED?
1-11-85
HE'LL BE GLAD TO GO..
Z
DOES HE HAVE TO BE AWAKE?
Z
SCHULZ

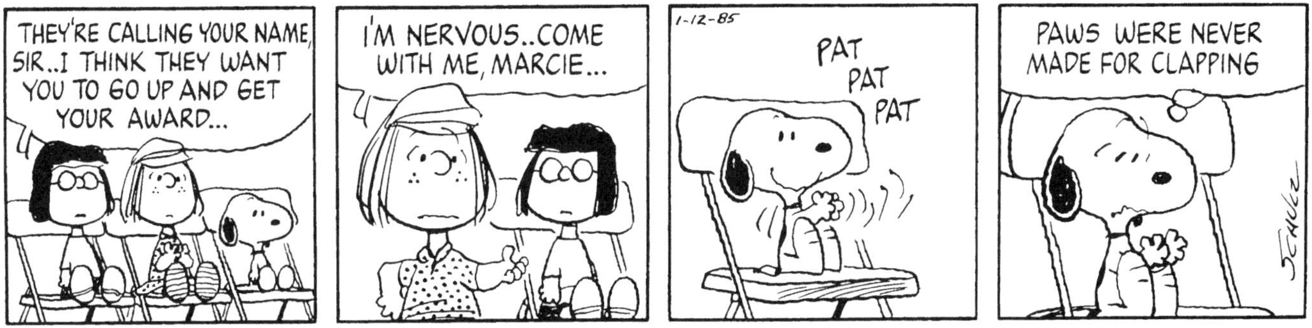
THEY'RE CALLING YOUR NAME, SIR..I THINK THEY WANT YOU TO GO UP AND GET YOUR AWARD...
I'M NERVOUS..COME WITH ME, MARCIE...
1-12-85
PAT
PAT
PAT
PAWS WERE NEVER MADE FOR CLAPPING
SCHULZ

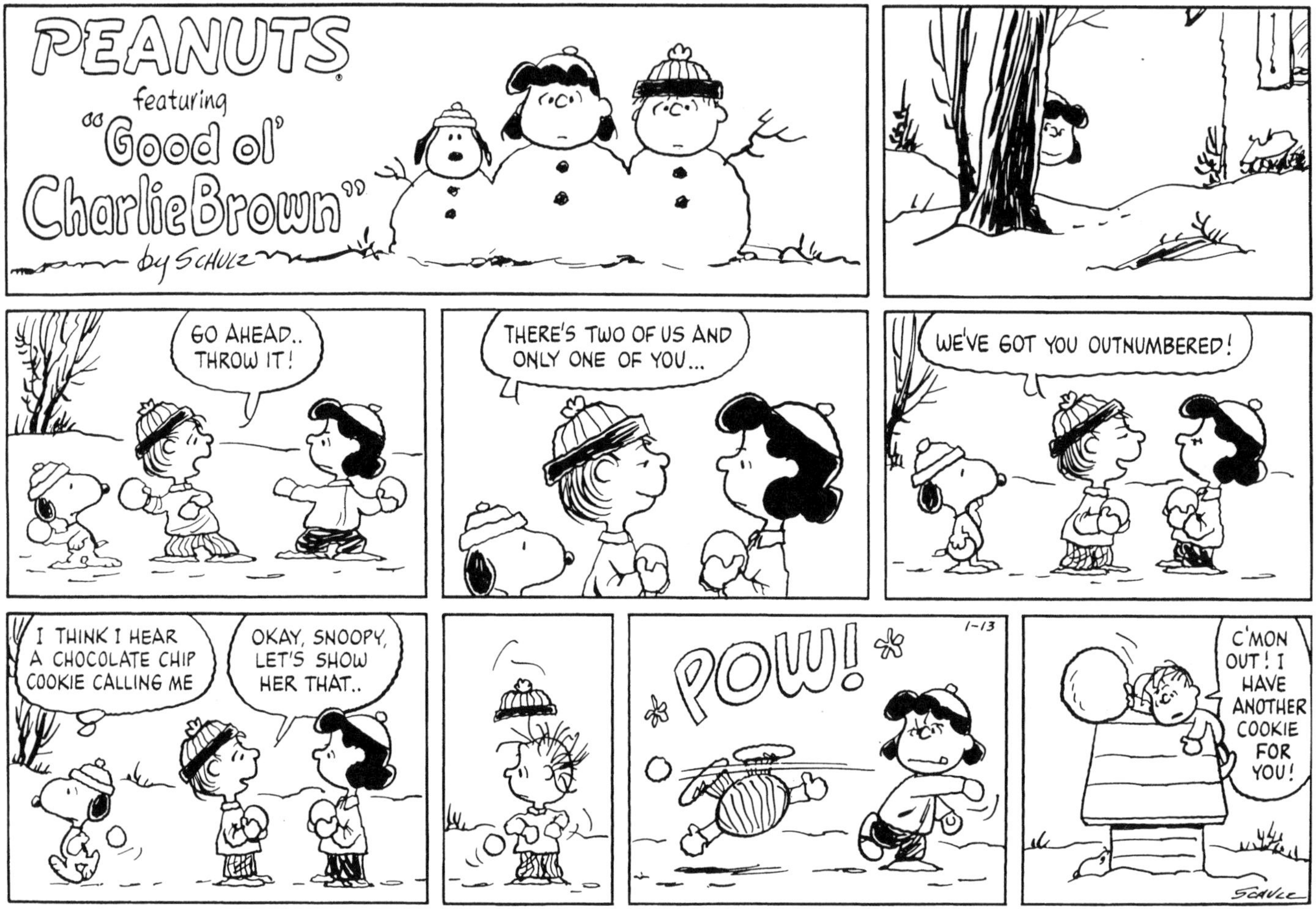
PEANUTS
featuring
"Good ol' CharlieBrown"
by SCHULZ
GO AHEAD.. THROW IT!
THERE'S TWO OF US AND ONLY ONE OF YOU...
WE'VE GOT YOU OUTNUMBERED!
I THINK I HEAR A CHOCOLATE CHIP COOKIE CALLING ME
OKAY, SNOOPY, LET'S SHOW HER THAT..
1-13
POW!
C'MON OUT! I HAVE ANOTHER COOKIE FOR YOU!
SCHULZ

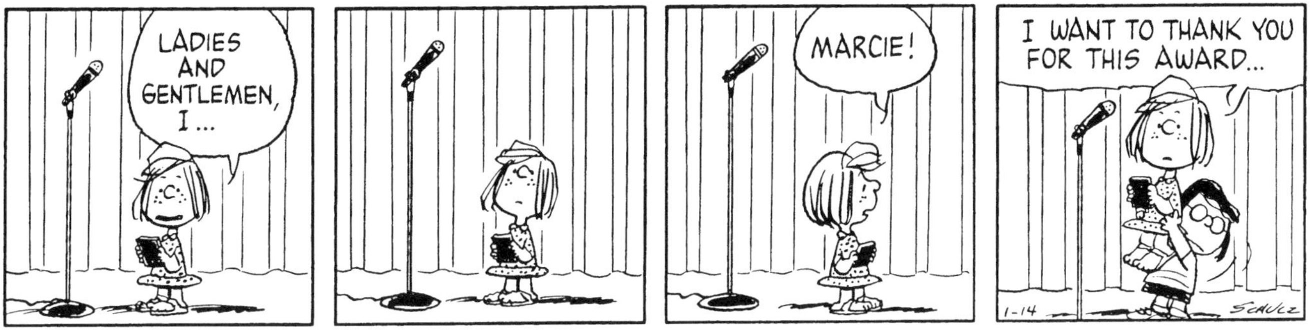
LADIES AND GENTLEMEN, I ...
MARCIE!
I WANT TO THANK YOU FOR THIS AWARD...
1-14
SCHULZ

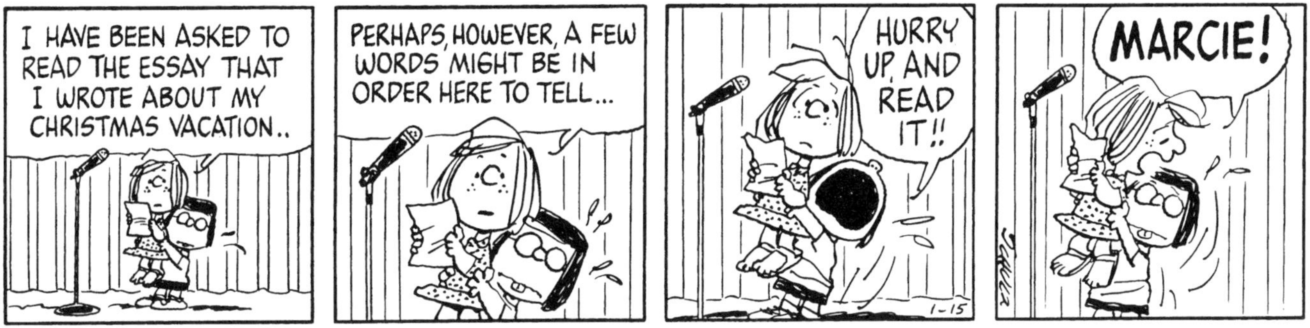
I HAVE BEEN ASKED TO READ THE ESSAY THAT I WROTE ABOUT MY CHRISTMAS VACATION..
PERHAPS, HOWEVER, A FEW WORDS MIGHT BE IN ORDER HERE TO TELL...
HURRY UP, AND READ IT!!
1-15
MARCIE!
SCHULZ

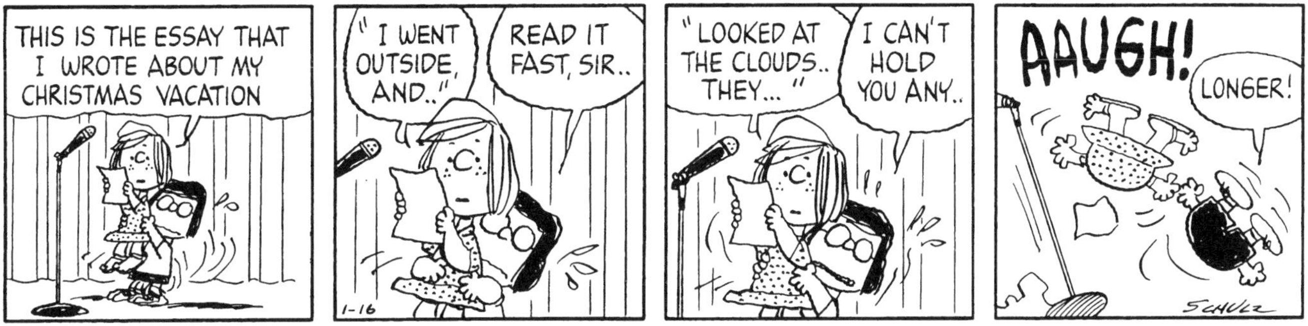
THIS IS THE ESSAY THAT I WROTE ABOUT MY CHRISTMAS VACATION
"I WENT OUTSIDE, AND.."
READ IT FAST, SIR..
1-16
"LOOKED AT THE CLOUDS.. THEY... "
I CAN'T HOLD YOU ANY..
AAUGH!
LONGER!
SCHULZ

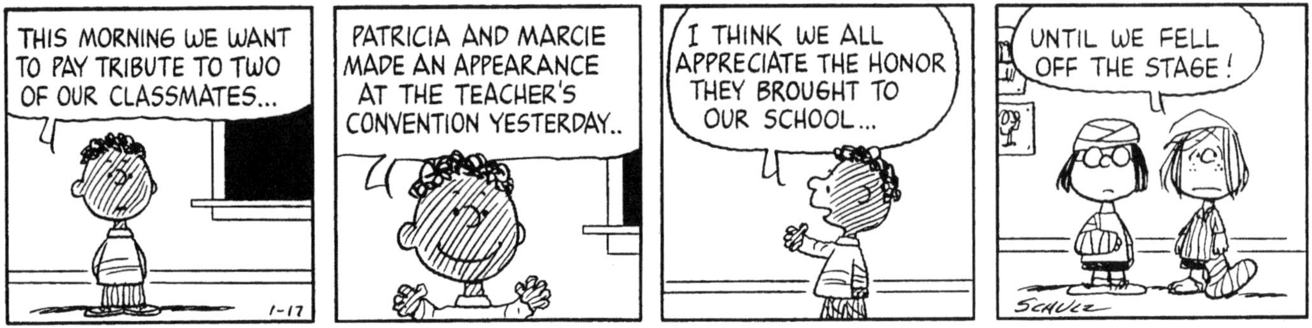
THIS MORNING WE WANT TO PAY TRIBUTE TO TWO OF OUR CLASSMATES...
PATRICIA AND MARCIE MADE AN APPEARANCE AT THE TEACHER'S CONVENTION YESTERDAY..
I THINK WE ALL APPRECIATE THE HONOR THEY BROUGHT TO OUR SCHOOL...
UNTIL WE FELL OFF THE STAGE!

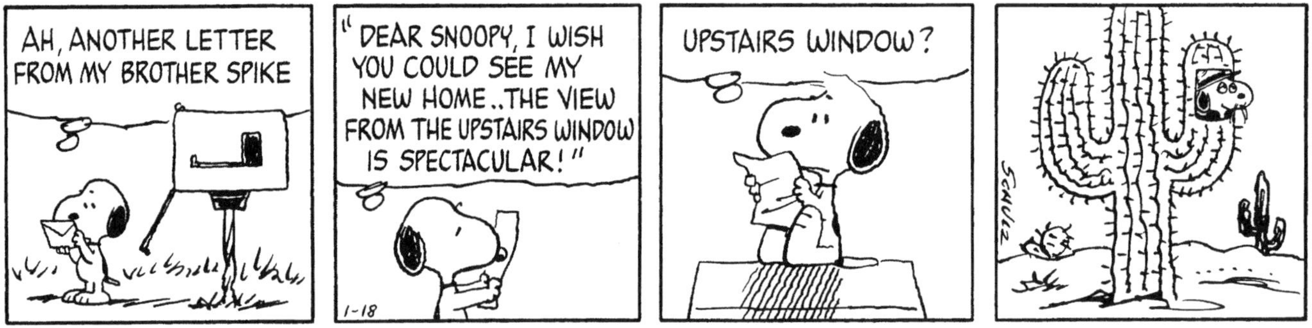
AH, ANOTHER LETTER FROM MY BROTHER SPIKE
"DEAR SNOOPY, I WISH YOU COULD SEE MY NEW HOME..THE VIEW FROM THE UPSTAIRS WINDOW IS SPECTACULAR!"
UPSTAIRS WINDOW?

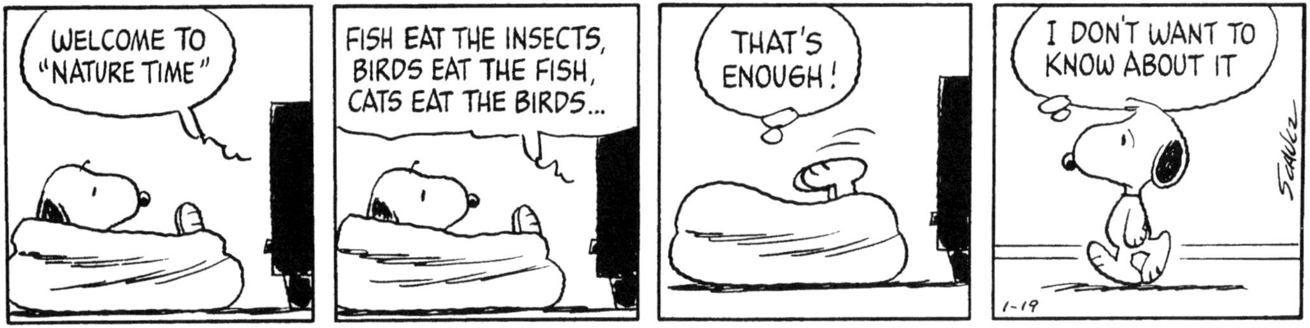
WELCOME TO "NATURE TIME"
FISH EAT THE INSECTS, BIRDS EAT THE FISH, CATS EAT THE BIRDS...
THAT'S ENOUGH!
I DON'T WANT TO KNOW ABOUT IT

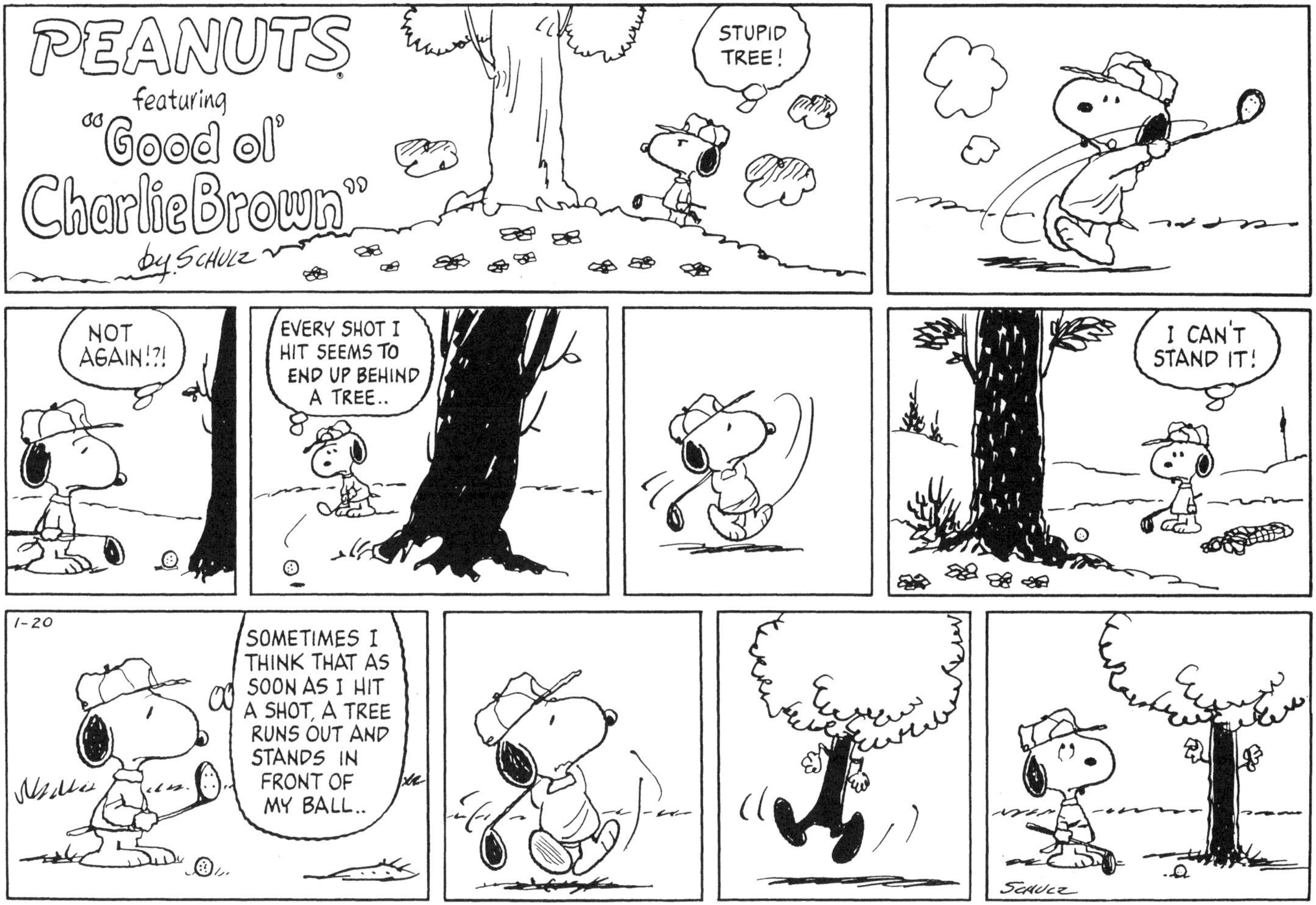
PEANUTS
featuring
"Good ol' CharlieBrown"
by SCHULZ
STUPID TREE!
NOT AGAIN!?!
EVERY SHOT I HIT SEEMS TO END UP BEHIND A TREE..
I CAN'T STAND IT!
1-20
SOMETIMES I THINK THAT AS SOON AS I HIT A SHOT, A TREE RUNS OUT AND STANDS IN FRONT OF MY BALL..
SCHULZ

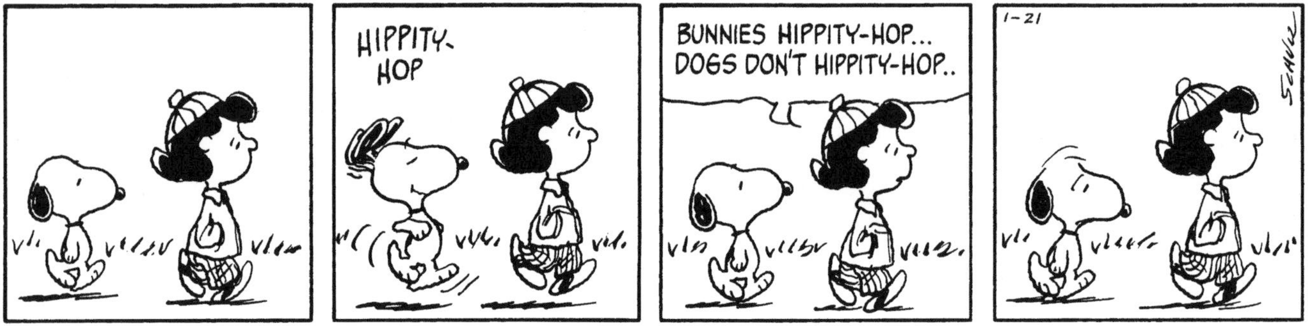
HIPPITY-HOP
BUNNIES HIPPITY-HOP... DOGS DON'T HIPPITY-HOP..
1-21

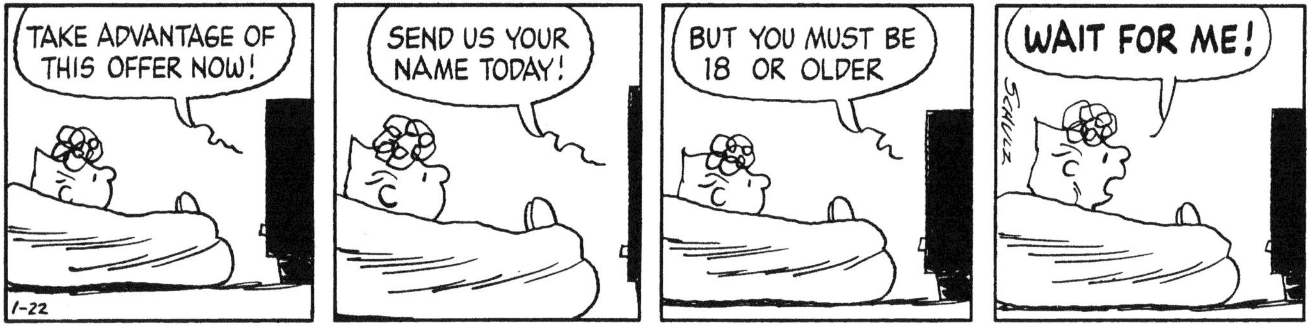
TAKE ADVANTAGE OF THIS OFFER NOW!
1-22
SEND US YOUR NAME TODAY!
BUT YOU MUST BE 18 OR OLDER
WAIT FOR ME!

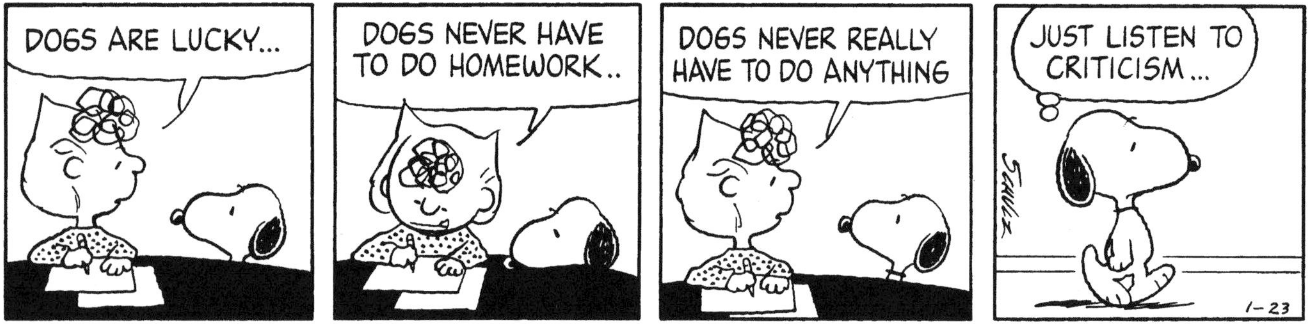
DOGS ARE LUCKY...
DOGS NEVER HAVE TO DO HOMEWORK..
DOGS NEVER REALLY HAVE TO DO ANYTHING
JUST LISTEN TO CRITICISM...
1-23

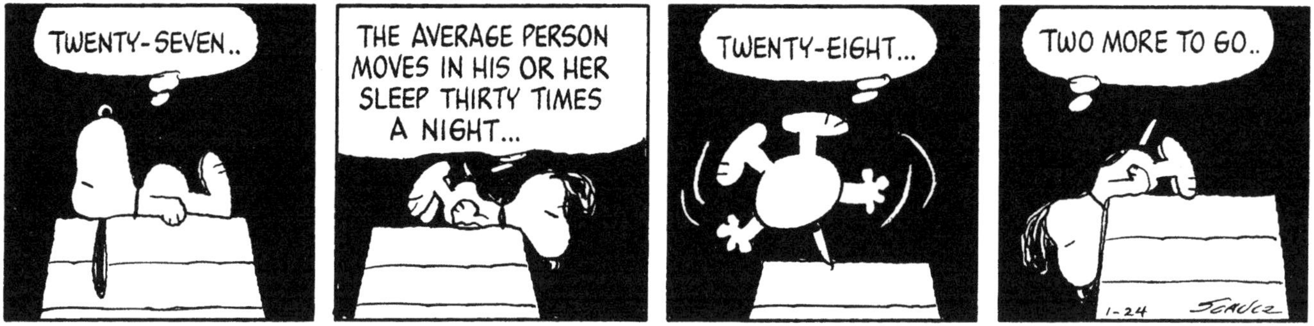
TWENTY-SEVEN..
THE AVERAGE PERSON MOVES IN HIS OR HER SLEEP THIRTY TIMES A NIGHT...
TWENTY-EIGHT...
TWO MORE TO GO..
1-24
SCHULZ

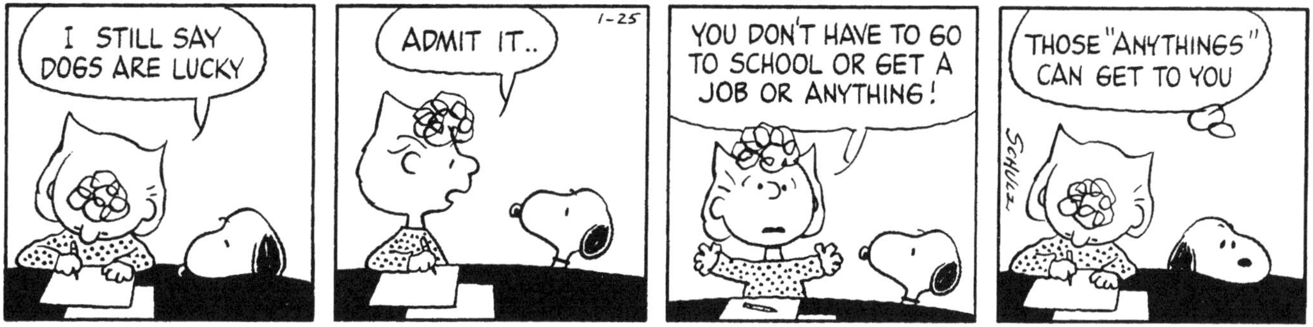
I STILL SAY DOGS ARE LUCKY
ADMIT IT..
1-25
YOU DON'T HAVE TO GO TO SCHOOL OR GET A JOB OR ANYTHING!
THOSE "ANYTHINGS" CAN GET TO YOU
SCHULZ

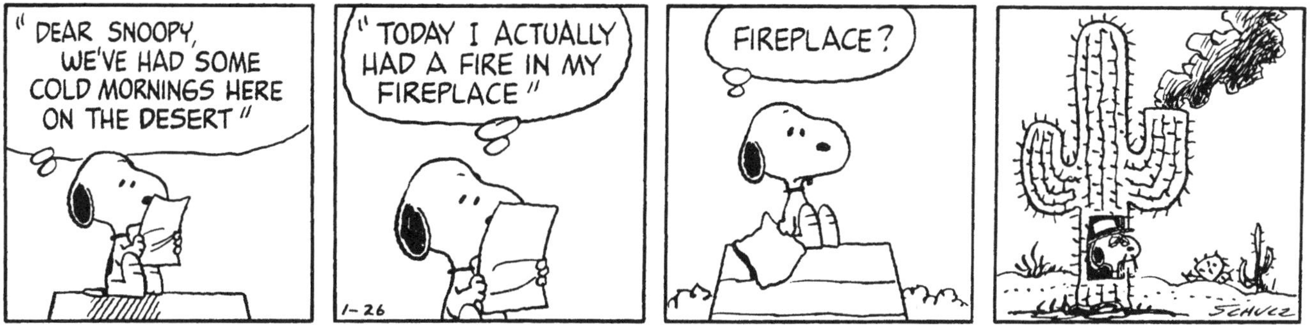
" DEAR SNOOPY, WE'VE HAD SOME COLD MORNINGS HERE ON THE DESERT "
" TODAY I ACTUALLY HAD A FIRE IN MY FIREPLACE "
1-26
FIREPLACE?
SCHULZ

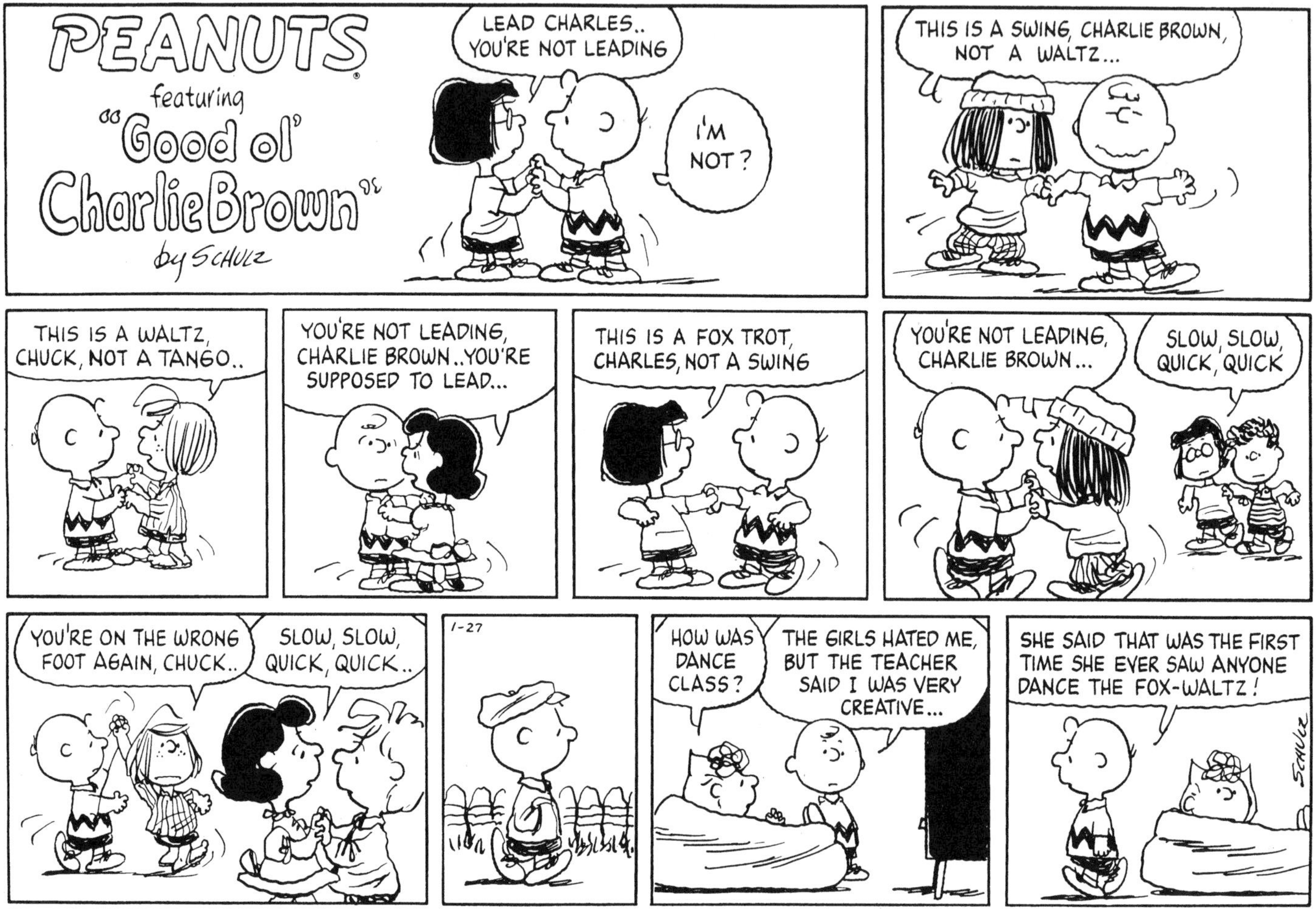
PEANUTS
featuring "Good ol' Charlie Brown"
by SCHULZ
LEAD CHARLES.. YOU'RE NOT LEADING
I'M NOT?
THIS IS A SWING, CHARLIE BROWN, NOT A WALTZ...
THIS IS A WALTZ, CHUCK, NOT A TANGO..
YOU'RE NOT LEADING, CHARLIE BROWN..YOU'RE SUPPOSED TO LEAD...
THIS IS A FOX TROT, CHARLES, NOT A SWING
YOU'RE NOT LEADING, CHARLIE BROWN...
SLOW, SLOW, QUICK, QUICK
YOU'RE ON THE WRONG FOOT AGAIN, CHUCK..
SLOW, SLOW, QUICK, QUICK..
1-27
HOW WAS DANCE CLASS?
THE GIRLS HATED ME, BUT THE TEACHER SAID I WAS VERY CREATIVE...
SHE SAID THAT WAS THE FIRST TIME SHE EVER SAW ANYONE DANCE THE FOX-WALTZ!
SCHULZ

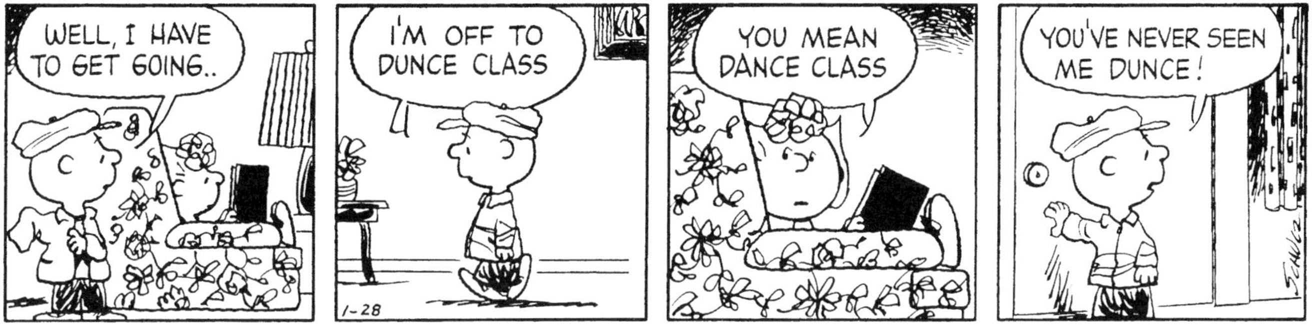
WELL, I HAVE TO GET GOING..
I'M OFF TO DUNCE CLASS
YOU MEAN DANCE CLASS
YOU'VE NEVER SEEN ME DUNCE!

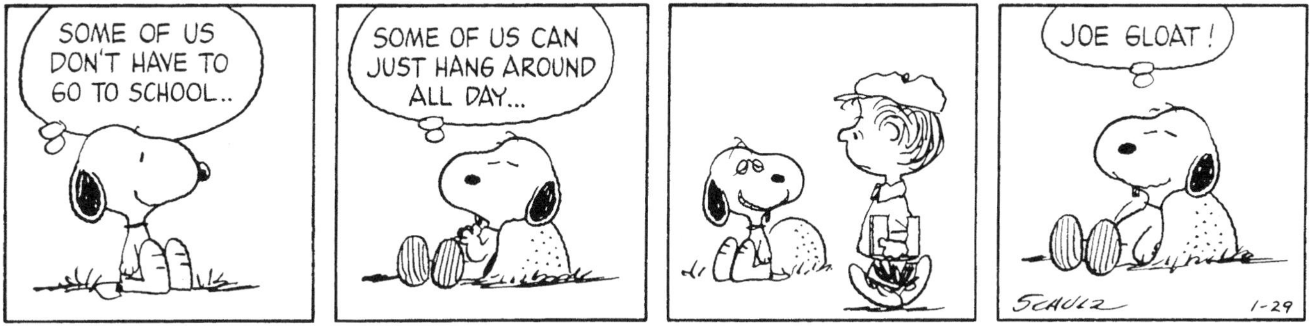
SOME OF US DON'T HAVE TO GO TO SCHOOL..
SOME OF US CAN JUST HANG AROUND ALL DAY...
JOE GLOAT!

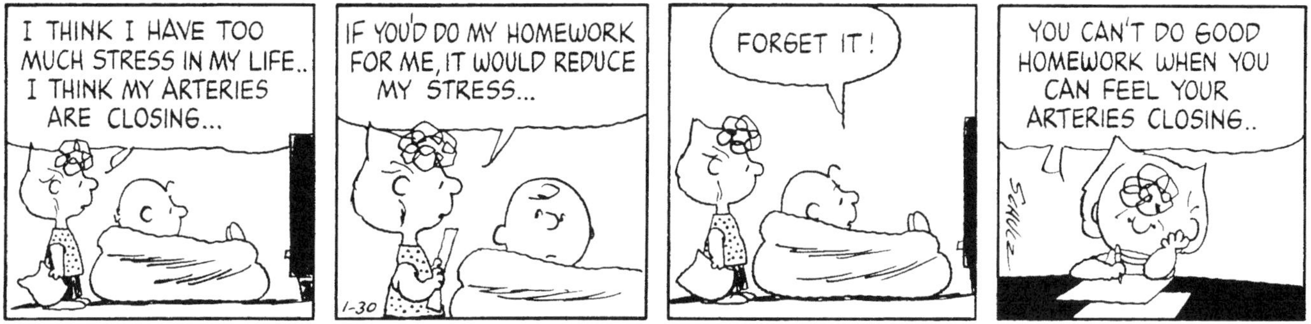
I THINK I HAVE TOO MUCH STRESS IN MY LIFE.. I THINK MY ARTERIES ARE CLOSING...
IF YOU'D DO MY HOMEWORK FOR ME, IT WOULD REDUCE MY STRESS...
FORGET IT!
YOU CAN'T DO GOOD HOMEWORK WHEN YOU CAN FEEL YOUR ARTERIES CLOSING..

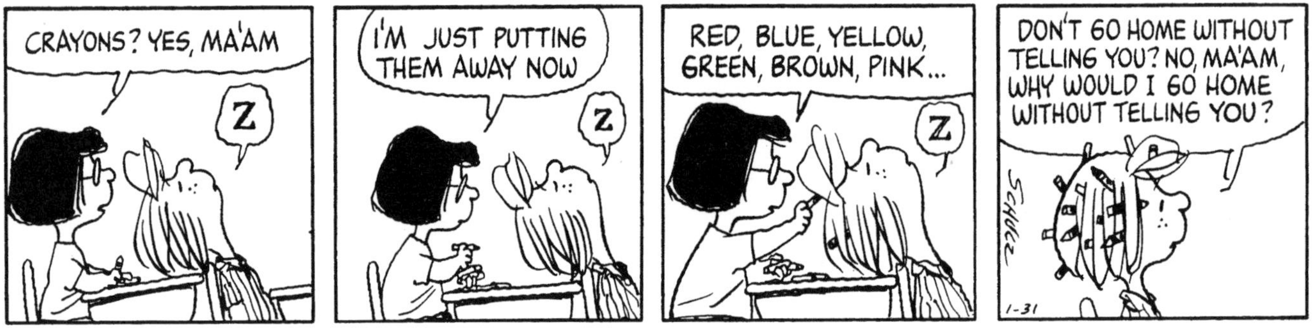

CRAYONS? YES, MA'AM
Z
I'M JUST PUTTING THEM AWAY NOW
Z
RED, BLUE, YELLOW, GREEN, BROWN, PINK...
Z
DON'T GO HOME WITHOUT TELLING YOU? NO, MA'AM, WHY WOULD I GO HOME WITHOUT TELLING YOU?
1-31

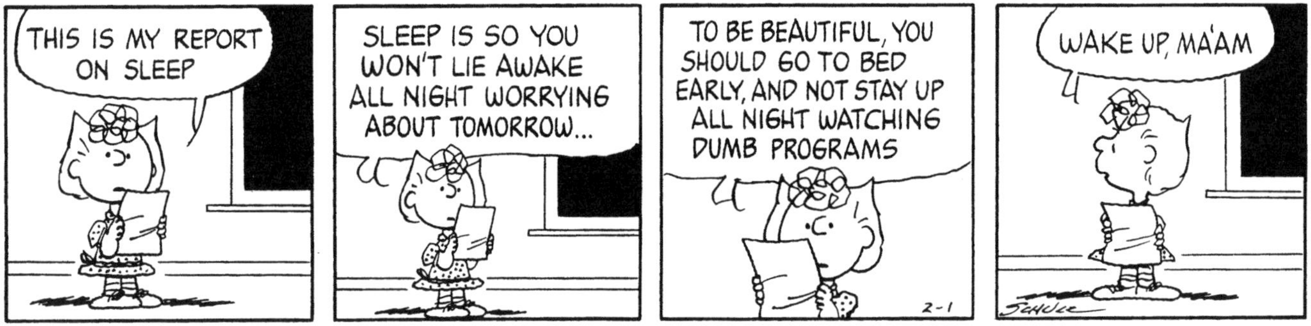

THIS IS MY REPORT ON SLEEP
SLEEP IS SO YOU WON'T LIE AWAKE ALL NIGHT WORRYING ABOUT TOMORROW...
TO BE BEAUTIFUL, YOU SHOULD GO TO BED EARLY, AND NOT STAY UP ALL NIGHT WATCHING DUMB PROGRAMS
2-1
WAKE UP, MA'AM

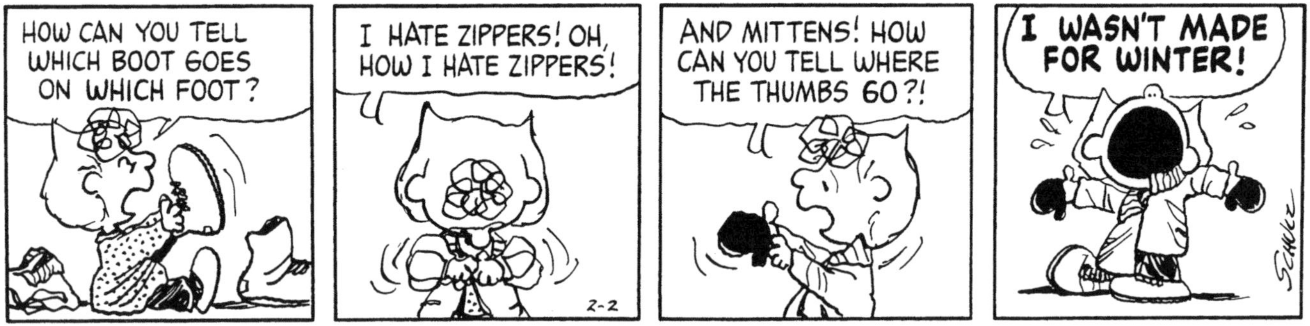

HOW CAN YOU TELL WHICH BOOT GOES ON WHICH FOOT?
I HATE ZIPPERS! OH, HOW I HATE ZIPPERS!
2-2
AND MITTENS! HOW CAN YOU TELL WHERE THE THUMBS GO?!
I WASN'T MADE FOR WINTER!

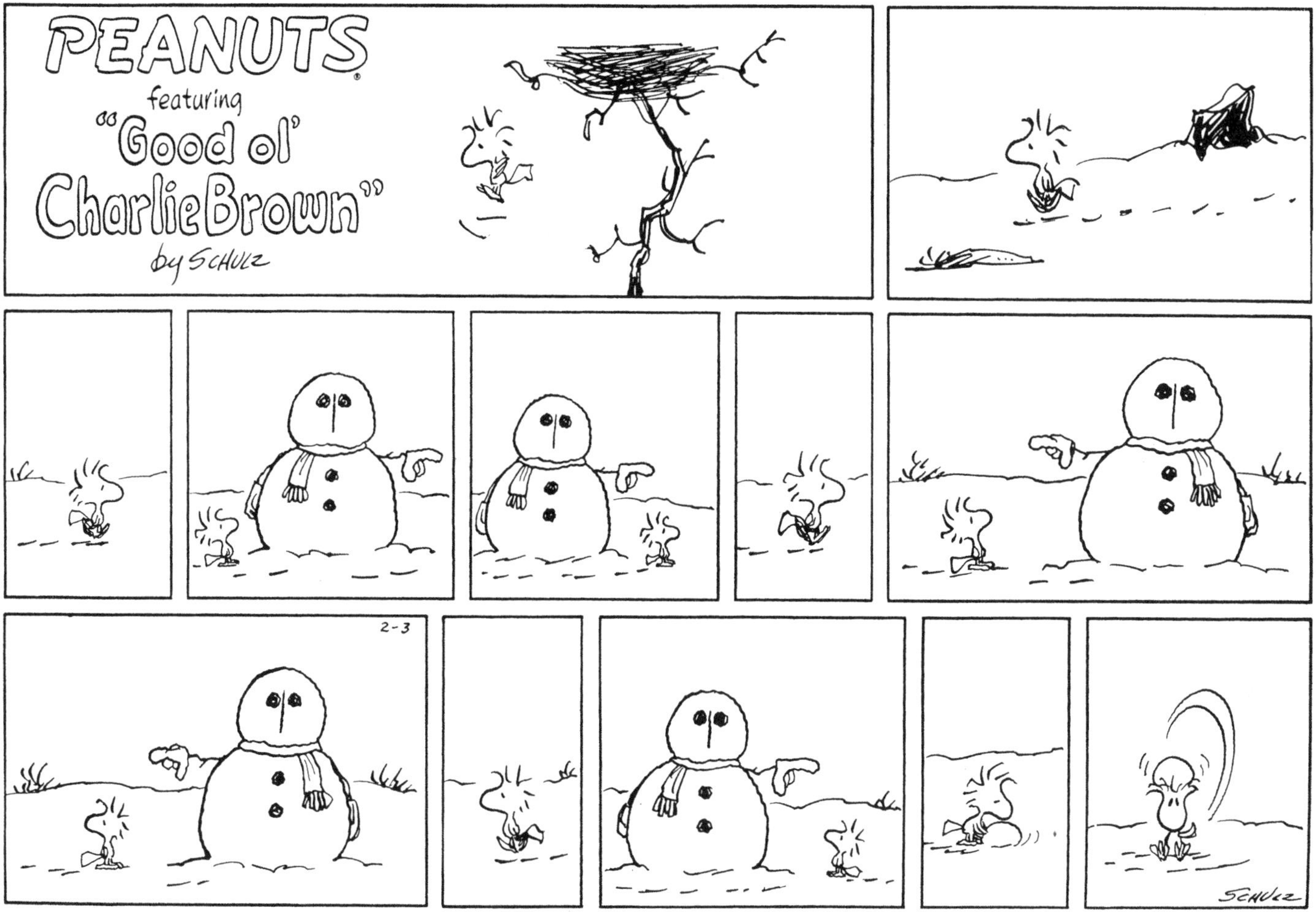
PEANUTS
featuring
"Good ol' Charlie Brown"
by SCHULZ
2-3
SCHULZ

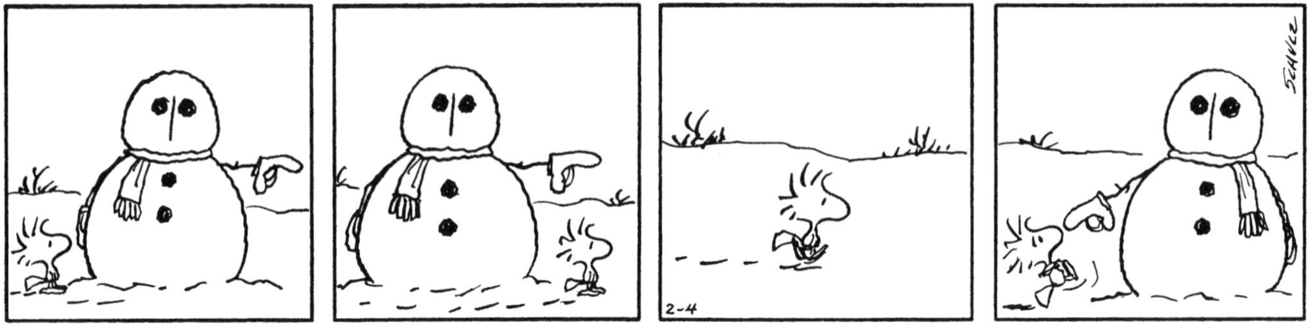

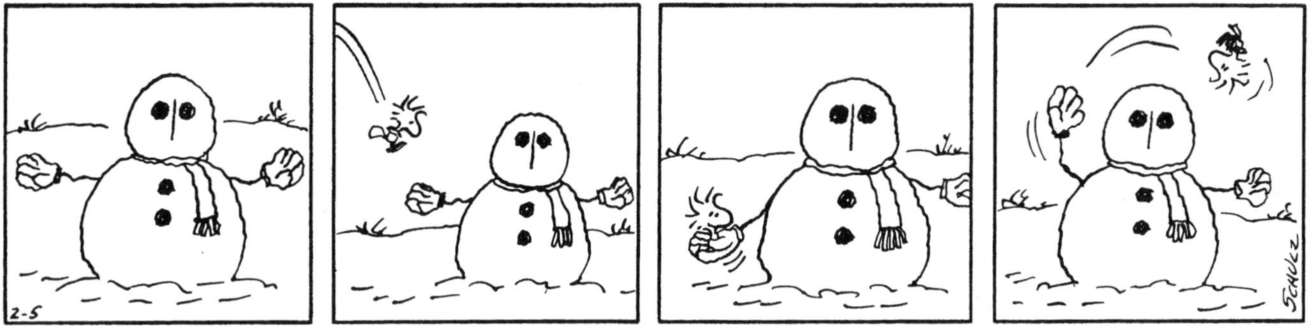

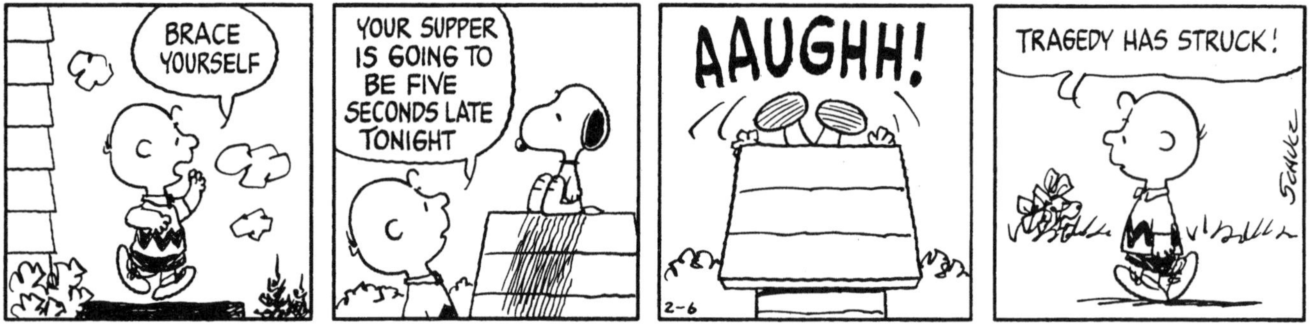

BRACE YOURSELF
YOUR SUPPER IS GOING TO BE FIVE SECONDS LATE TONIGHT
AAUGHH!
TRAGEDY HAS STRUCK!

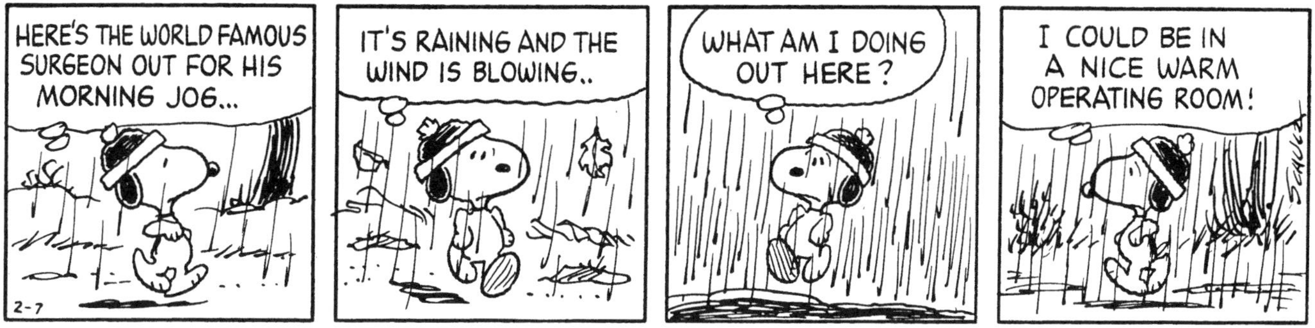
HERE'S THE WORLD FAMOUS SURGEON OUT FOR HIS MORNING JOG...
2-7
IT'S RAINING AND THE WIND IS BLOWING..
WHAT AM I DOING OUT HERE?
I COULD BE IN A NICE WARM OPERATING ROOM!

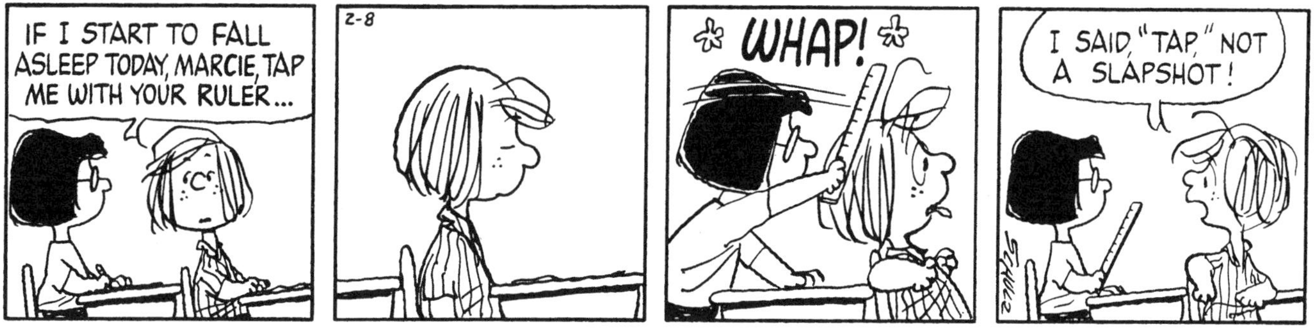
IF I START TO FALL ASLEEP TODAY, MARCIE, TAP ME WITH YOUR RULER...
2-8
WHAP!
I SAID, "TAP," NOT A SLAPSHOT!

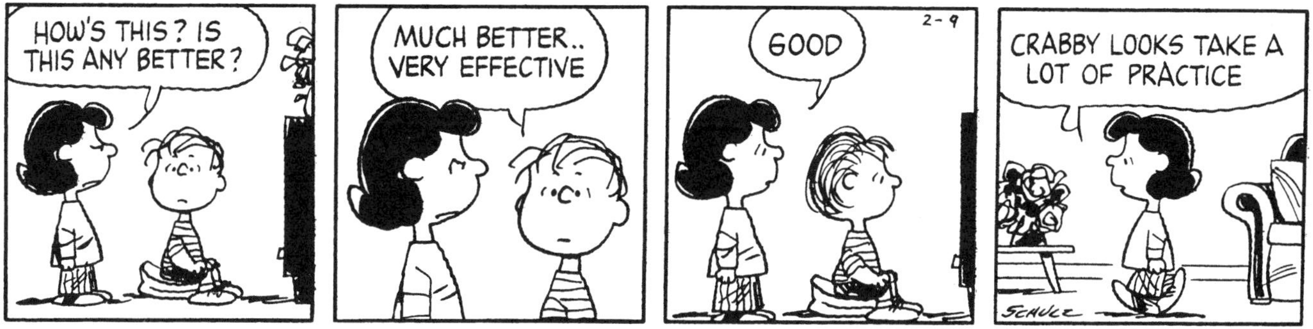
HOW'S THIS? IS THIS ANY BETTER?
MUCH BETTER.. VERY EFFECTIVE
2-9
GOOD
CRABBY LOOKS TAKE A LOT OF PRACTICE

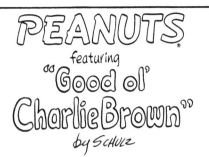

PEANUTS
featuring
"Good ol' Charlie Brown"
by Schulz

WHAT DO YOU THINK?

THIS IS A VALENTINE I BOUGHT FOR THAT LITTLE RED-HAIRED GIRL...

I WANT TO GO OVER TO HER HOUSE, AND GIVE IT TO HER, BUT I THINK I'D BE TOO NERVOUS TO DO IT WITHOUT PRACTICE...

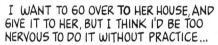

I'LL GO OUTSIDE AND RING THE DOORBELL, AND YOU PRETEND YOU'RE THE LITTLE RED-HAIRED GIRL, OKAY?

2-10

RING!

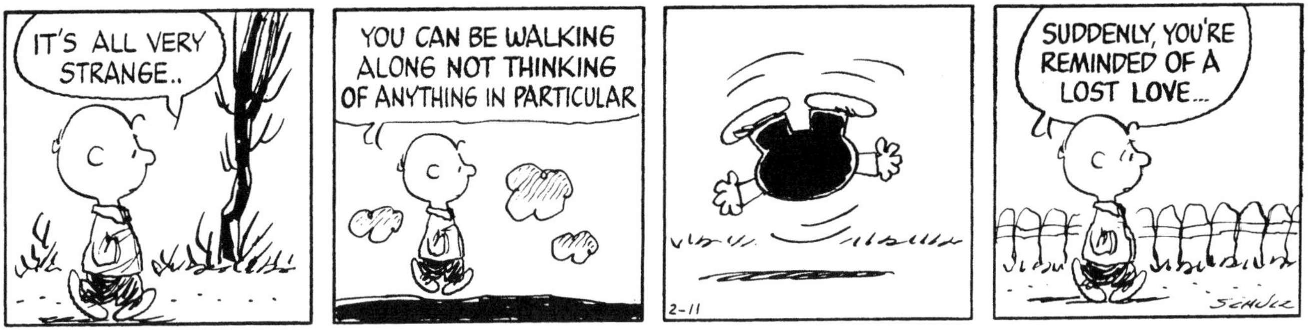
IT'S ALL VERY STRANGE..
YOU CAN BE WALKING ALONG NOT THINKING OF ANYTHING IN PARTICULAR
SUDDENLY, YOU'RE REMINDED OF A LOST LOVE...
2-11

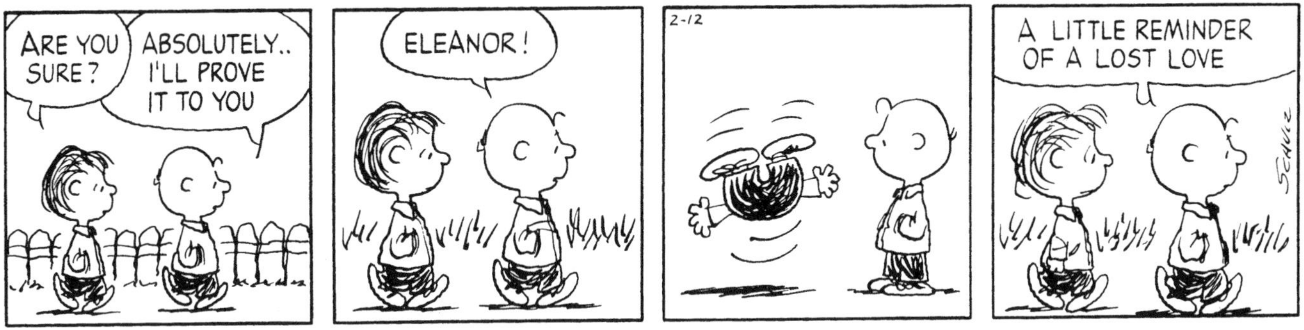
ARE YOU SURE?
ABSOLUTELY.. I'LL PROVE IT TO YOU
ELEANOR!
2-12
A LITTLE REMINDER OF A LOST LOVE

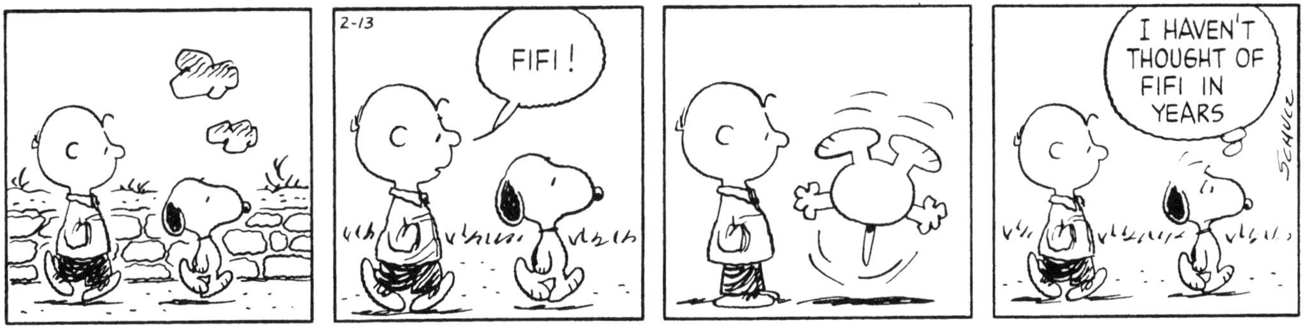
2-13
FIFI!
I HAVEN'T THOUGHT OF FIFI IN YEARS

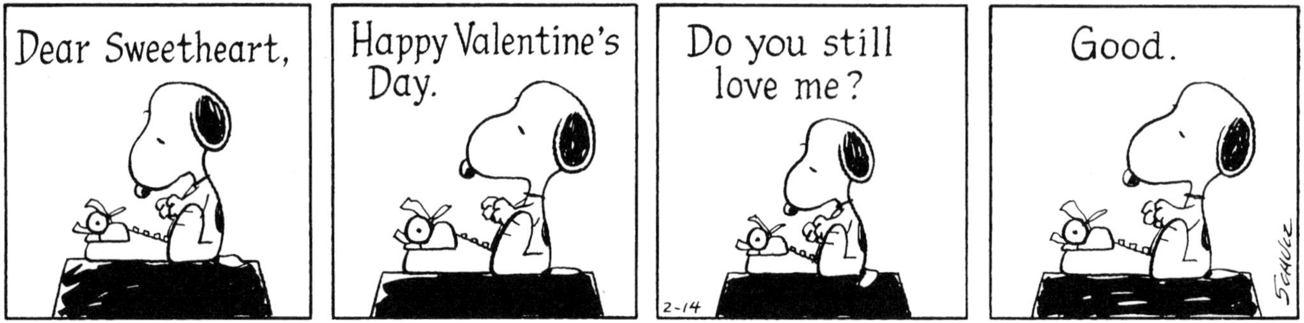
Dear Sweetheart,
Happy Valentine's Day.
Do you still love me?
Good.
2-14

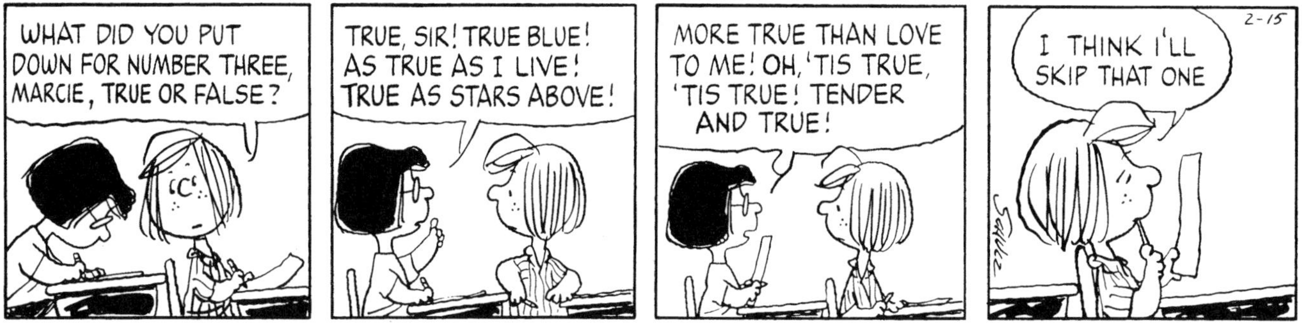
WHAT DID YOU PUT DOWN FOR NUMBER THREE, MARCIE, TRUE OR FALSE?
TRUE, SIR! TRUE BLUE! AS TRUE AS I LIVE! TRUE AS STARS ABOVE!
MORE TRUE THAN LOVE TO ME! OH, 'TIS TRUE, 'TIS TRUE! TENDER AND TRUE!
I THINK I'LL SKIP THAT ONE
2-15

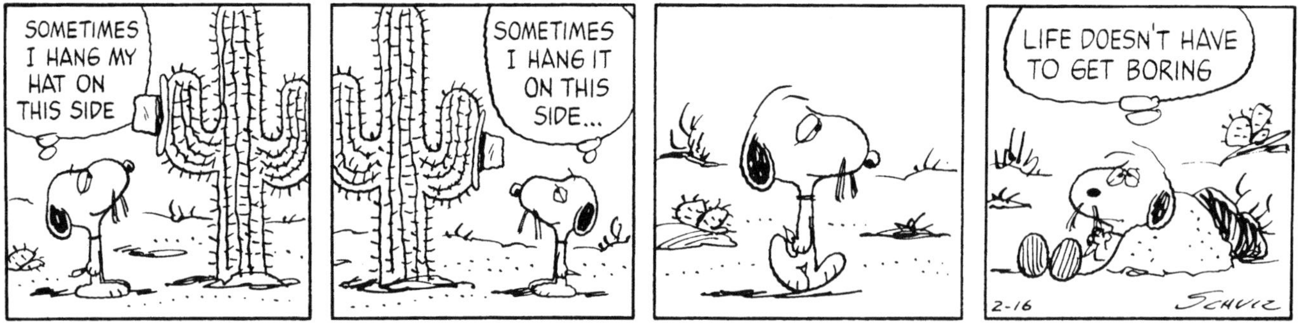
SOMETIMES I HANG MY HAT ON THIS SIDE
SOMETIMES I HANG IT ON THIS SIDE...
LIFE DOESN'T HAVE TO GET BORING
2-16

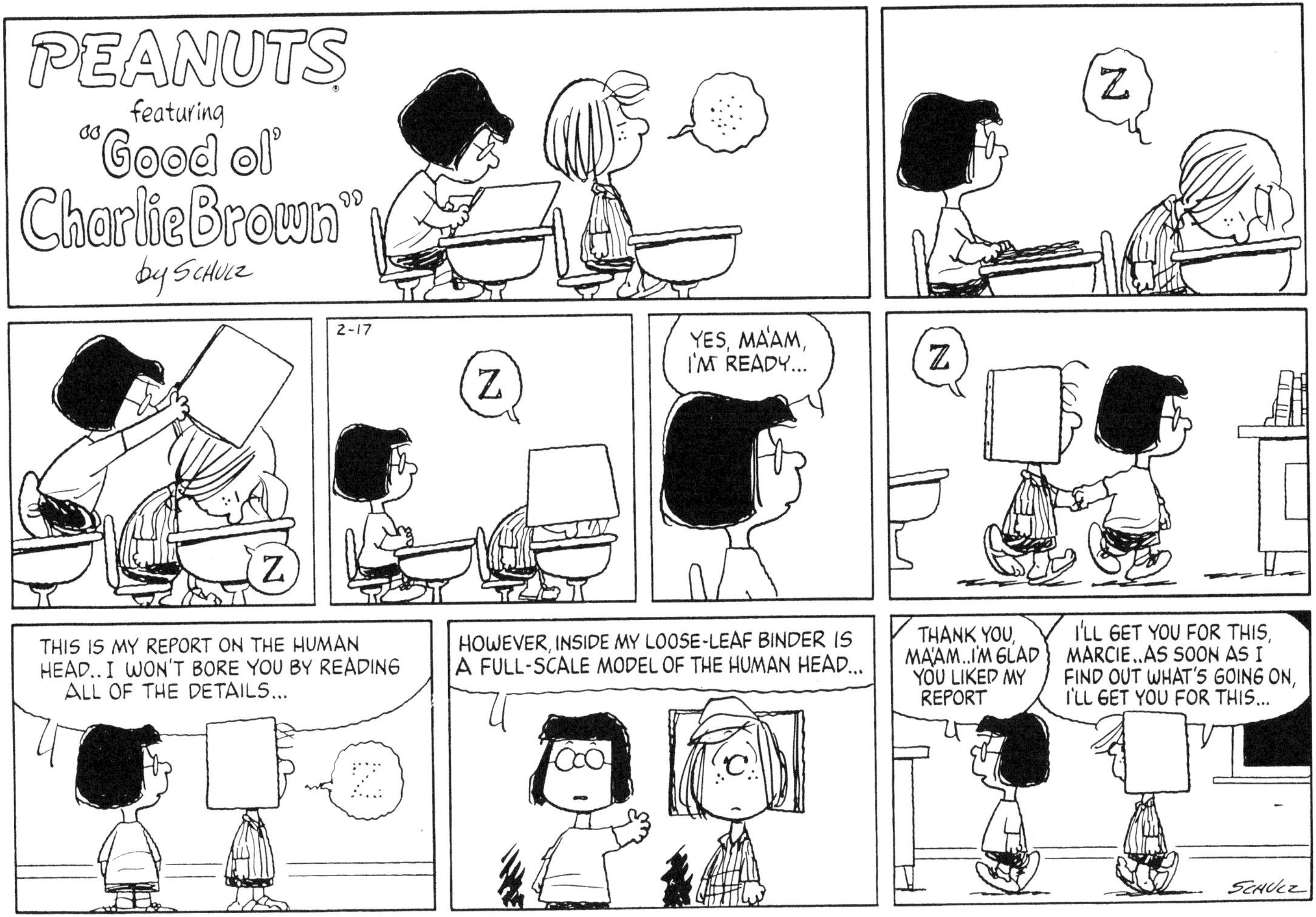
PEANUTS
featuring
"Good ol' Charlie Brown"
by SCHULZ
Z
2-17
Z
Z
YES, MA'AM, I'M READY...
Z
THIS IS MY REPORT ON THE HUMAN HEAD.. I WON'T BORE YOU BY READING ALL OF THE DETAILS...
HOWEVER, INSIDE MY LOOSE-LEAF BINDER IS A FULL-SCALE MODEL OF THE HUMAN HEAD...
THANK YOU, MA'AM..I'M GLAD YOU LIKED MY REPORT
I'LL GET YOU FOR THIS, MARCIE..AS SOON AS I FIND OUT WHAT'S GOING ON, I'LL GET YOU FOR THIS...
SCHULZ

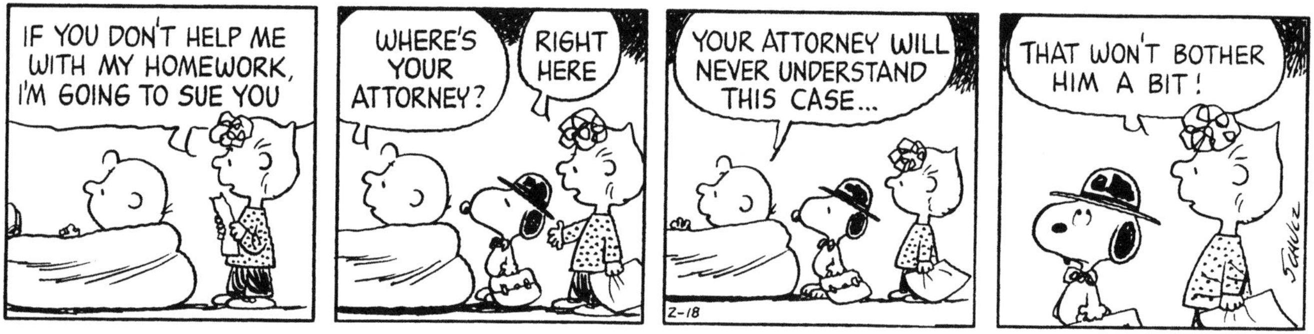
IF YOU DON'T HELP ME WITH MY HOMEWORK, I'M GOING TO SUE YOU
WHERE'S YOUR ATTORNEY?
RIGHT HERE
YOUR ATTORNEY WILL NEVER UNDERSTAND THIS CASE...
THAT WON'T BOTHER HIM A BIT!

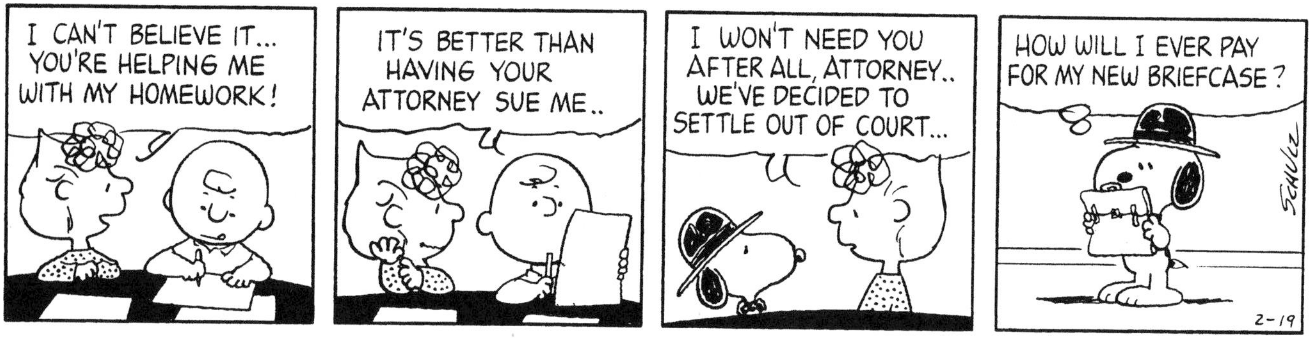
I CAN'T BELIEVE IT... YOU'RE HELPING ME WITH MY HOMEWORK!
IT'S BETTER THAN HAVING YOUR ATTORNEY SUE ME..
I WON'T NEED YOU AFTER ALL, ATTORNEY.. WE'VE DECIDED TO SETTLE OUT OF COURT...
HOW WILL I EVER PAY FOR MY NEW BRIEFCASE?

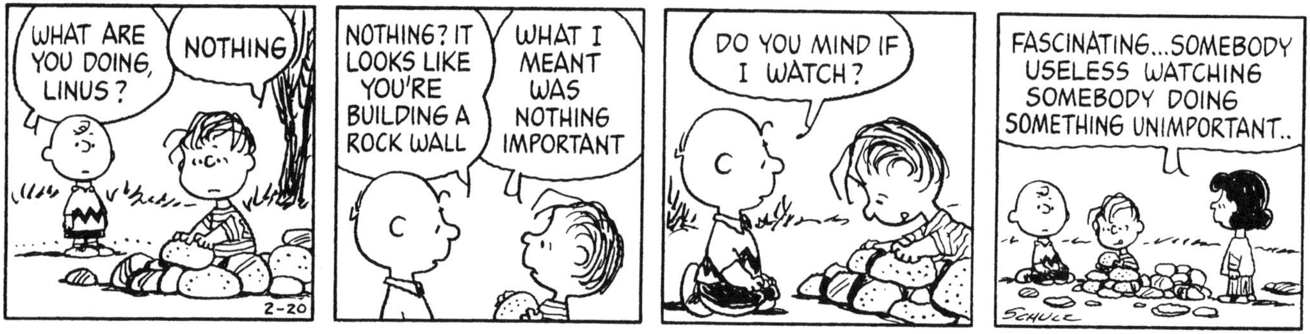
WHAT ARE YOU DOING, LINUS?
NOTHING
NOTHING? IT LOOKS LIKE YOU'RE BUILDING A ROCK WALL
WHAT I MEANT WAS NOTHING IMPORTANT
DO YOU MIND IF I WATCH?
FASCINATING...SOMEBODY USELESS WATCHING SOMEBODY DOING SOMETHING UNIMPORTANT..

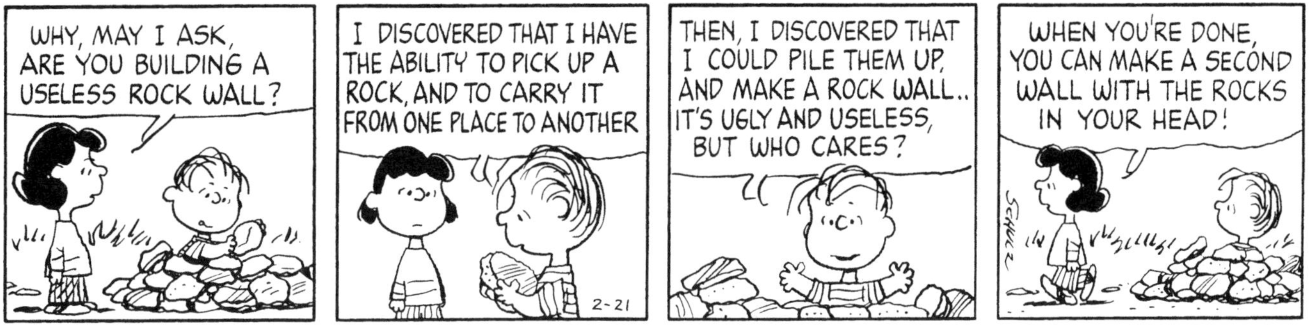
WHY, MAY I ASK, ARE YOU BUILDING A USELESS ROCK WALL?
I DISCOVERED THAT I HAVE THE ABILITY TO PICK UP A ROCK, AND TO CARRY IT FROM ONE PLACE TO ANOTHER
2-21
THEN, I DISCOVERED THAT I COULD PILE THEM UP, AND MAKE A ROCK WALL.. IT'S UGLY AND USELESS, BUT WHO CARES?
WHEN YOU'RE DONE, YOU CAN MAKE A SECOND WALL WITH THE ROCKS IN YOUR HEAD!
SCHULZ

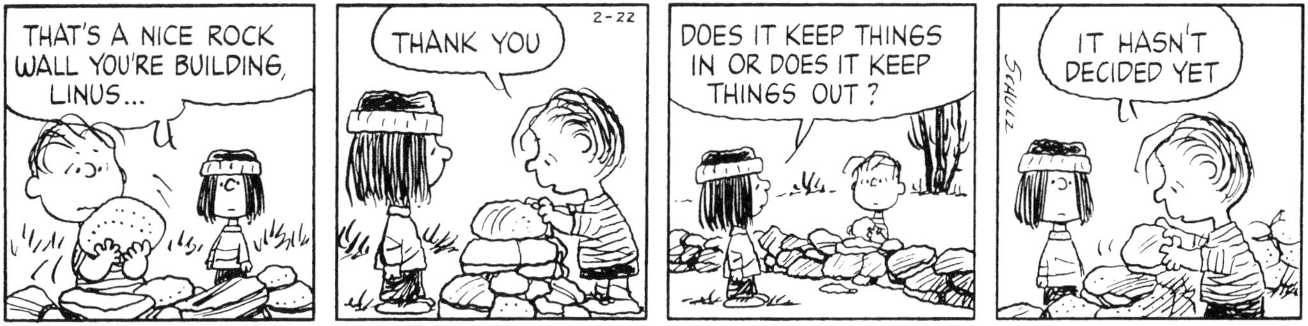
THAT'S A NICE ROCK WALL YOU'RE BUILDING, LINUS...
THANK YOU
2-22
DOES IT KEEP THINGS IN OR DOES IT KEEP THINGS OUT?
SCHULZ
IT HASN'T DECIDED YET

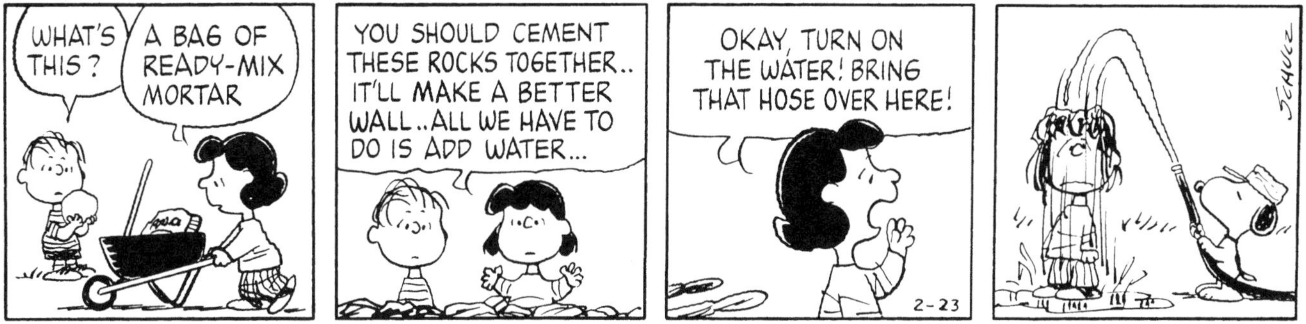
WHAT'S THIS?
A BAG OF READY-MIX MORTAR
YOU SHOULD CEMENT THESE ROCKS TOGETHER.. IT'LL MAKE A BETTER WALL..ALL WE HAVE TO DO IS ADD WATER...
OKAY, TURN ON THE WATER! BRING THAT HOSE OVER HERE!
2-23
SCHULZ

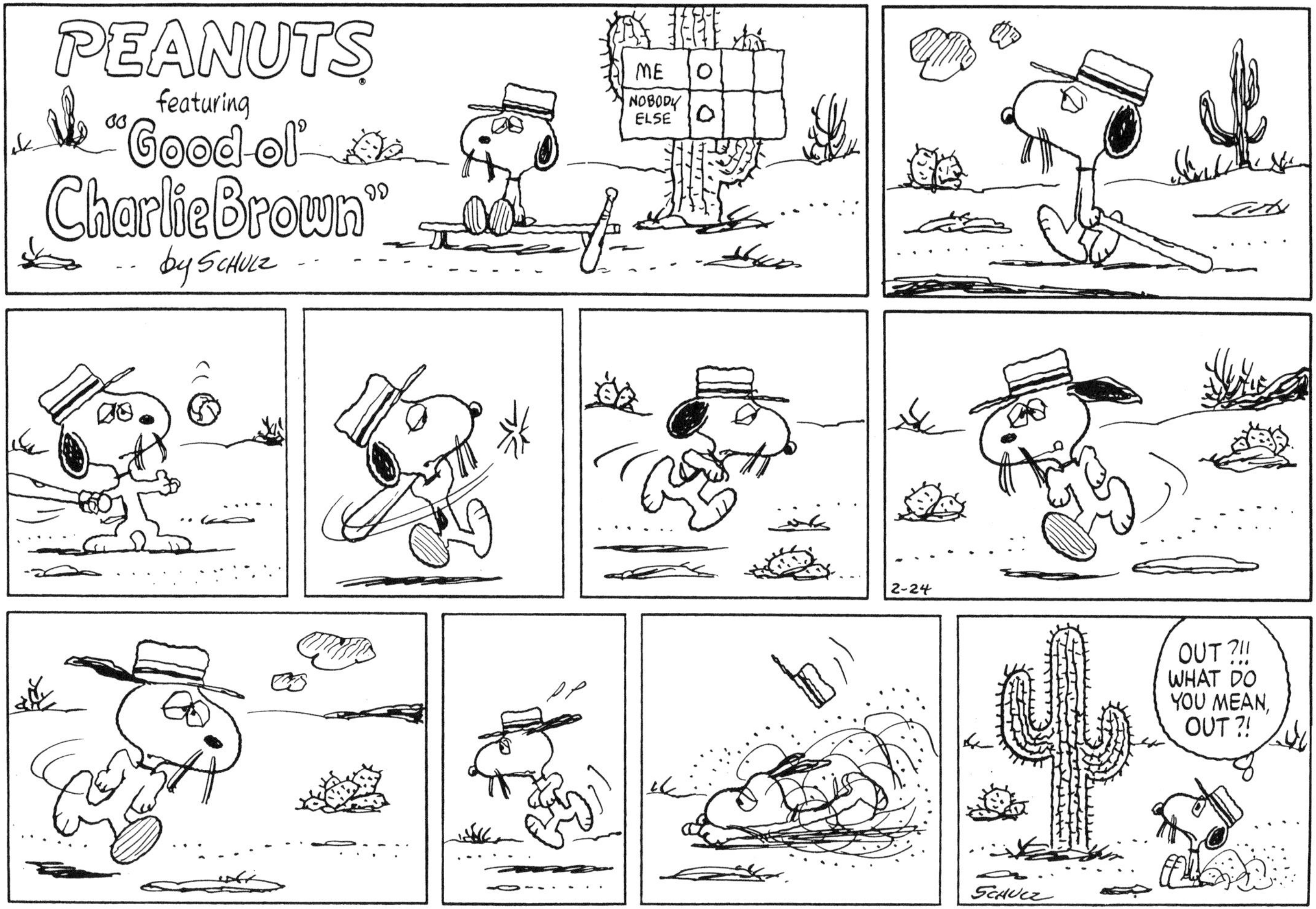
PEANUTS
featuring "Good ol' Charlie Brown"
by SCHULZ
ME
NOBODY ELSE
2-24
OUT ?!! WHAT DO YOU MEAN, OUT ?!
SCHULZ

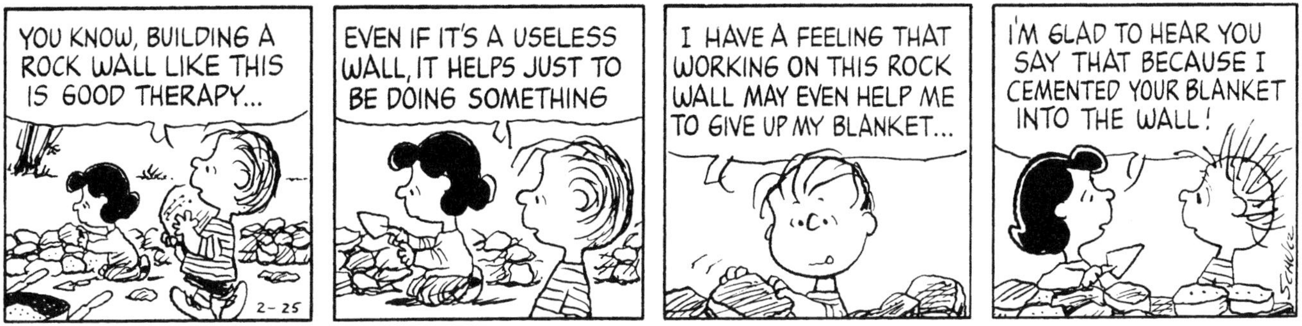
YOU KNOW, BUILDING A ROCK WALL LIKE THIS IS GOOD THERAPY...
EVEN IF IT'S A USELESS WALL, IT HELPS JUST TO BE DOING SOMETHING
I HAVE A FEELING THAT WORKING ON THIS ROCK WALL MAY EVEN HELP ME TO GIVE UP MY BLANKET...
I'M GLAD TO HEAR YOU SAY THAT BECAUSE I CEMENTED YOUR BLANKET INTO THE WALL!

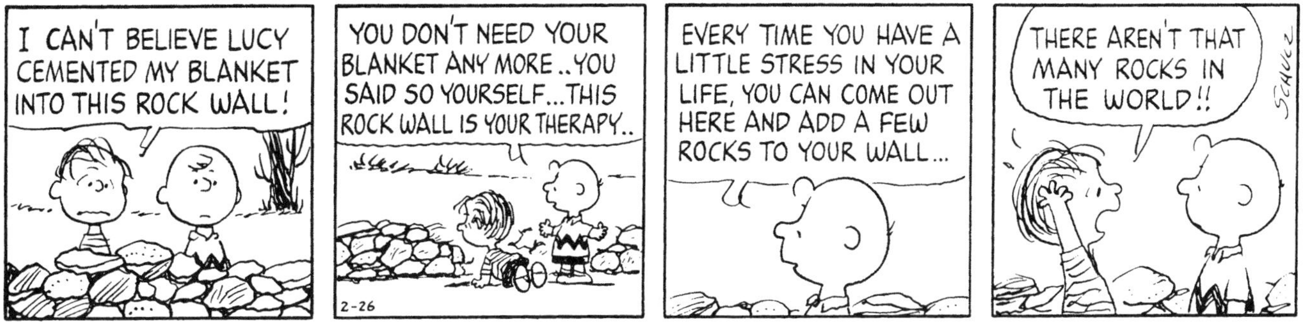
I CAN'T BELIEVE LUCY CEMENTED MY BLANKET INTO THIS ROCK WALL!
YOU DON'T NEED YOUR BLANKET ANY MORE..YOU SAID SO YOURSELF...THIS ROCK WALL IS YOUR THERAPY..
EVERY TIME YOU HAVE A LITTLE STRESS IN YOUR LIFE, YOU CAN COME OUT HERE AND ADD A FEW ROCKS TO YOUR WALL...
THERE AREN'T THAT MANY ROCKS IN THE WORLD!!

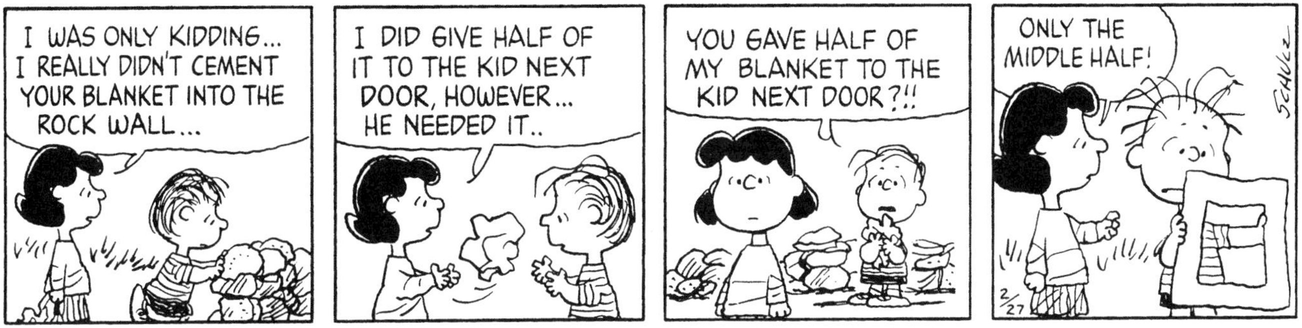
I WAS ONLY KIDDING... I REALLY DIDN'T CEMENT YOUR BLANKET INTO THE ROCK WALL...
I DID GIVE HALF OF IT TO THE KID NEXT DOOR, HOWEVER... HE NEEDED IT..
YOU GAVE HALF OF MY BLANKET TO THE KID NEXT DOOR?!!
ONLY THE MIDDLE HALF!

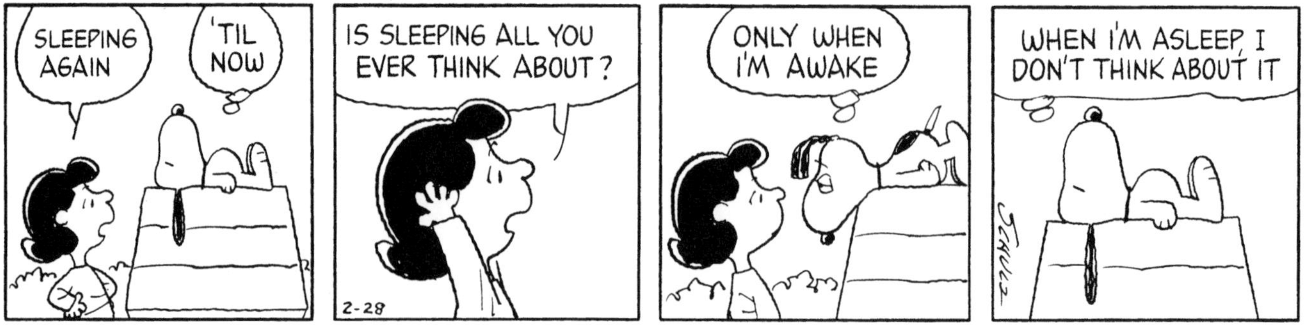
SLEEPING AGAIN
'TIL NOW
IS SLEEPING ALL YOU EVER THINK ABOUT?
2-28
ONLY WHEN I'M AWAKE
WHEN I'M ASLEEP, I DON'T THINK ABOUT IT
SCHULZ

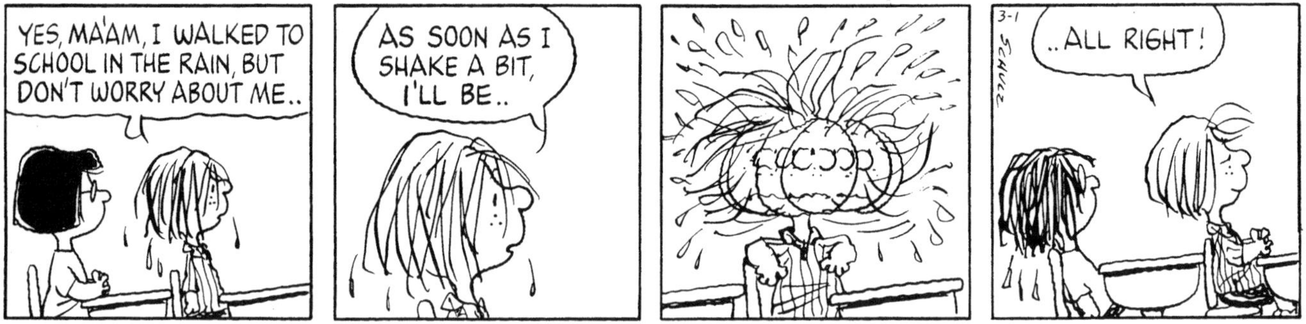
YES, MA'AM, I WALKED TO SCHOOL IN THE RAIN, BUT DON'T WORRY ABOUT ME..
AS SOON AS I SHAKE A BIT, I'LL BE..
3-1
SCHULZ
..ALL RIGHT!

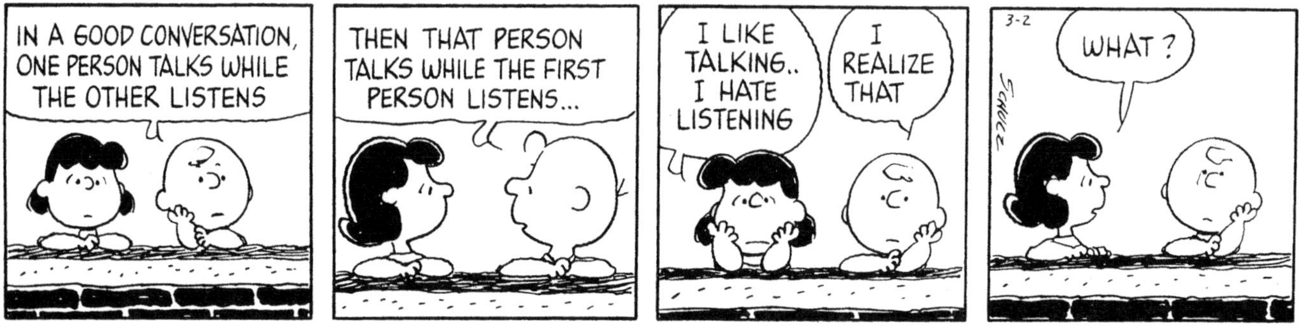
IN A GOOD CONVERSATION, ONE PERSON TALKS WHILE THE OTHER LISTENS
THEN THAT PERSON TALKS WHILE THE FIRST PERSON LISTENS...
I LIKE TALKING.. I HATE LISTENING
I REALIZE THAT
3-2
SCHULZ
WHAT?

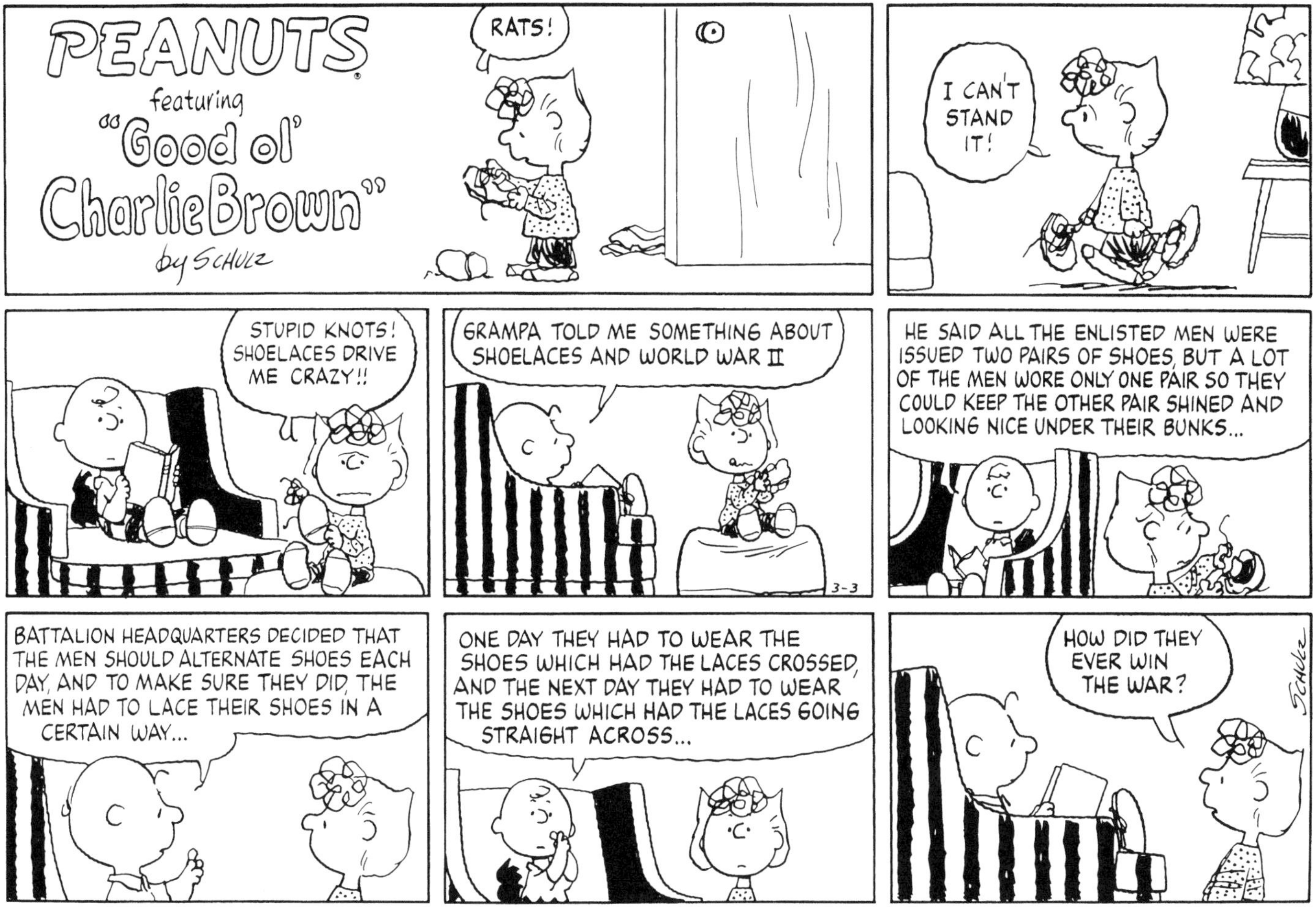
PEANUTS
featuring
"Good ol' CharlieBrown"
by SCHULZ
RATS!
I CAN'T STAND IT!
STUPID KNOTS! SHOELACES DRIVE ME CRAZY!!
GRAMPA TOLD ME SOMETHING ABOUT SHOELACES AND WORLD WAR II
3-3
HE SAID ALL THE ENLISTED MEN WERE ISSUED TWO PAIRS OF SHOES, BUT A LOT OF THE MEN WORE ONLY ONE PAIR SO THEY COULD KEEP THE OTHER PAIR SHINED AND LOOKING NICE UNDER THEIR BUNKS...
BATTALION HEADQUARTERS DECIDED THAT THE MEN SHOULD ALTERNATE SHOES EACH DAY, AND TO MAKE SURE THEY DID, THE MEN HAD TO LACE THEIR SHOES IN A CERTAIN WAY...
ONE DAY THEY HAD TO WEAR THE SHOES WHICH HAD THE LACES CROSSED, AND THE NEXT DAY THEY HAD TO WEAR THE SHOES WHICH HAD THE LACES GOING STRAIGHT ACROSS...
HOW DID THEY EVER WIN THE WAR?
SCHULZ

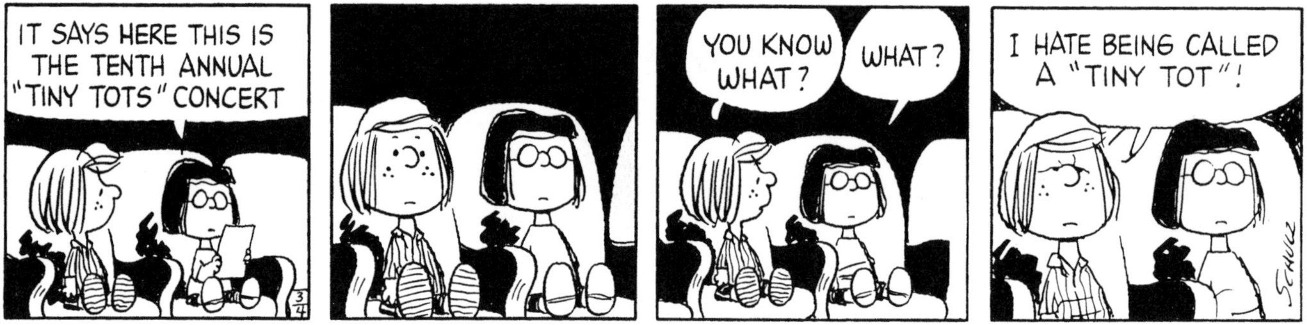

IT SAYS HERE THIS IS THE TENTH ANNUAL "TINY TOTS" CONCERT
YOU KNOW WHAT?
WHAT?
I HATE BEING CALLED A "TINY TOT"!

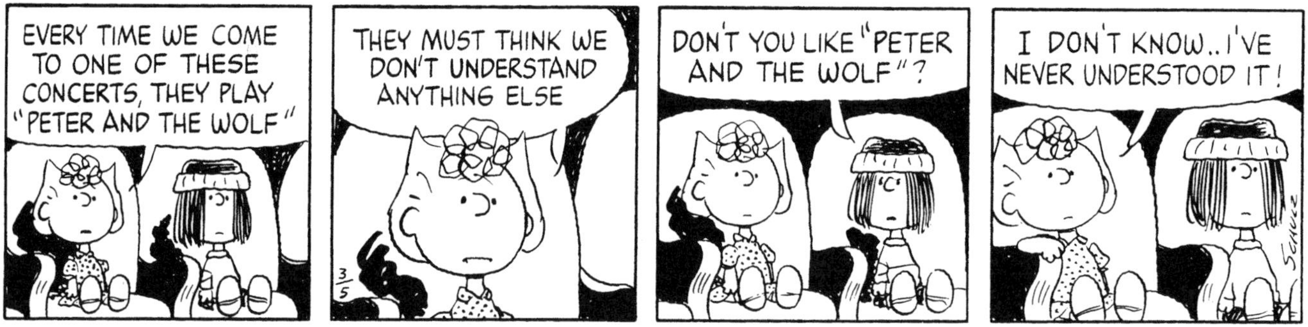

EVERY TIME WE COME TO ONE OF THESE CONCERTS, THEY PLAY "PETER AND THE WOLF"
THEY MUST THINK WE DON'T UNDERSTAND ANYTHING ELSE
DON'T YOU LIKE "PETER AND THE WOLF"?
I DON'T KNOW.. I'VE NEVER UNDERSTOOD IT!

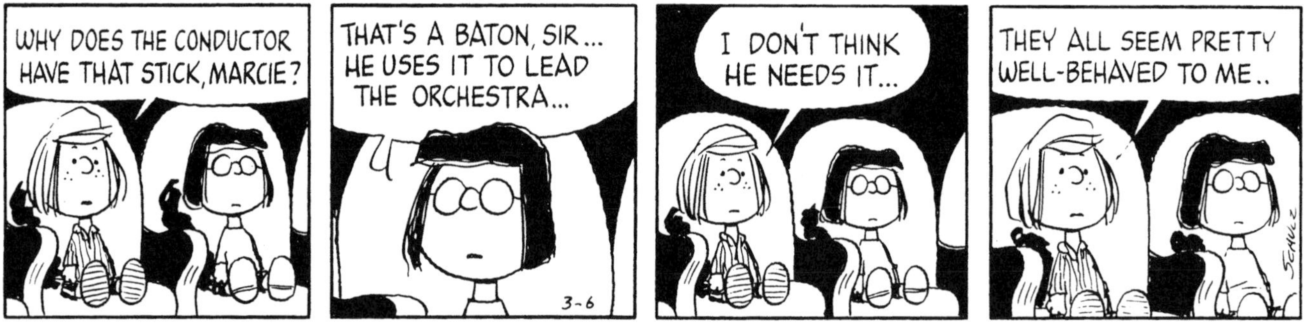

WHY DOES THE CONDUCTOR HAVE THAT STICK, MARCIE?
THAT'S A BATON, SIR... HE USES IT TO LEAD THE ORCHESTRA...
I DON'T THINK HE NEEDS IT...
THEY ALL SEEM PRETTY WELL-BEHAVED TO ME..

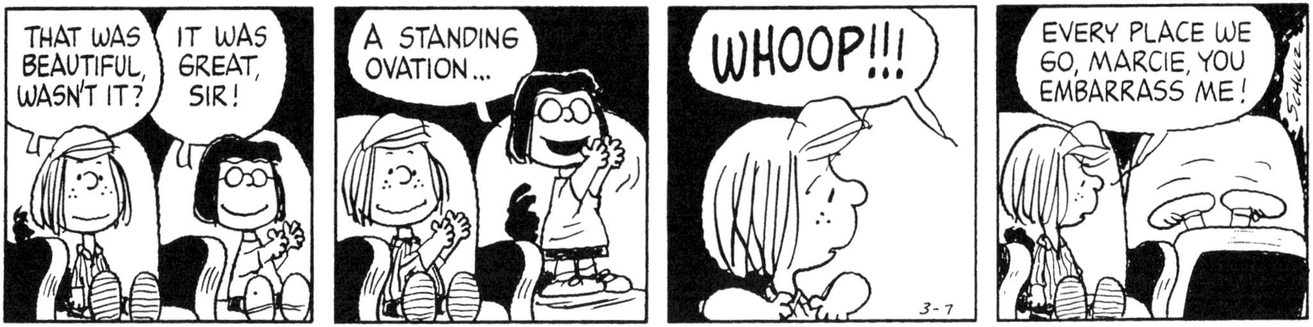
THAT WAS BEAUTIFUL, WASN'T IT?
IT WAS GREAT, SIR!
A STANDING OVATION...
WHOOP!!!
3-7
EVERY PLACE WE GO, MARCIE, YOU EMBARRASS ME!
SCHULZ

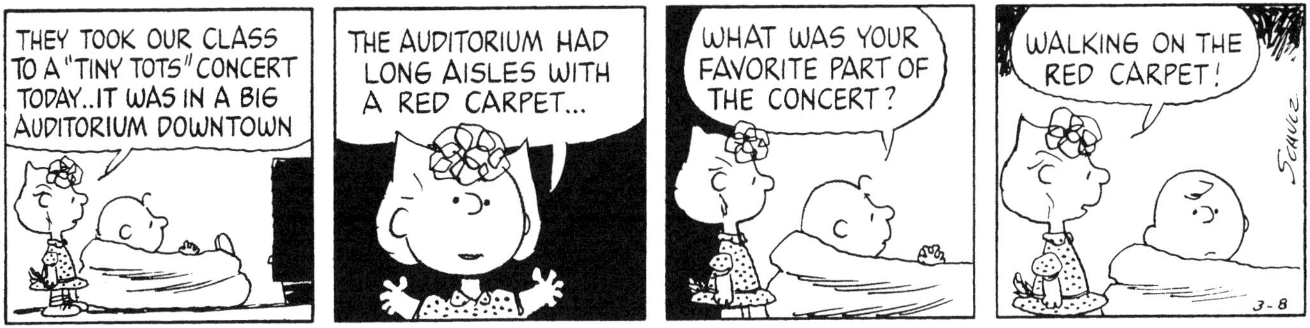
THEY TOOK OUR CLASS TO A "TINY TOTS" CONCERT TODAY..IT WAS IN A BIG AUDITORIUM DOWNTOWN
THE AUDITORIUM HAD LONG AISLES WITH A RED CARPET...
WHAT WAS YOUR FAVORITE PART OF THE CONCERT?
WALKING ON THE RED CARPET!
SCHULZ
3-8

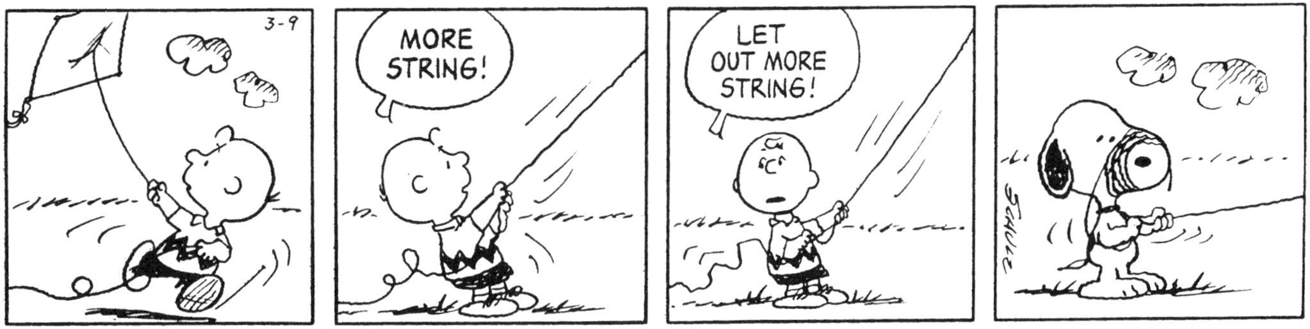
3-9
MORE STRING!
LET OUT MORE STRING!
SCHULZ

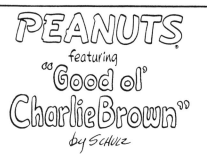

PEANUTS featuring *"Good ol' CharlieBrown"* by SCHULZ

A POP FLY!

I GOT IT! IT'S ALL MINE!

IF I CATCH THIS BALL, WE'LL WIN OUR FIRST GAME OF THE SEASON..

3-10

PLEASE LET ME CATCH IT! PLEASE LET ME BE THE HERO! PLEASE LET ME CATCH IT! PLEASE!

ON THE OTHER HAND, DO I THINK I DESERVE TO BE THE HERO?

THE KID WHO HIT IT DOESN'T WANT TO BE THE GOAT...

IS A BASEBALL GAME REALLY THIS IMPORTANT?

LOTS OF KIDS ALL OVER THE WORLD NEVER EVEN HEARD OF BASEBALL...

LOTS OF KIDS DON'T GET TO PLAY AT ALL, OR HAVE A PLACE TO SLEEP, OR..

BONK!

CHARLIE BROWN, HOW COULD YOU MISS SUCH AN EASY POP FLY?!

I PRAYED MYSELF OUT OF IT..

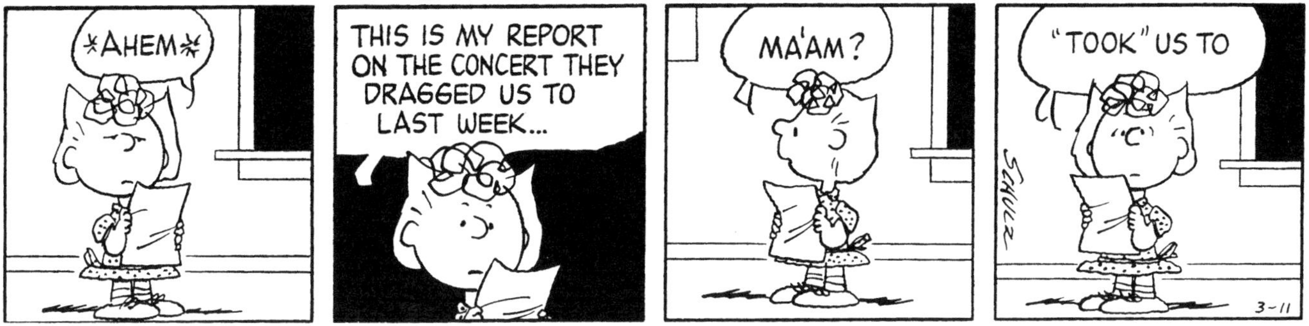
AHEM
THIS IS MY REPORT ON THE CONCERT THEY DRAGGED US TO LAST WEEK...
MA'AM?
"TOOK" US TO

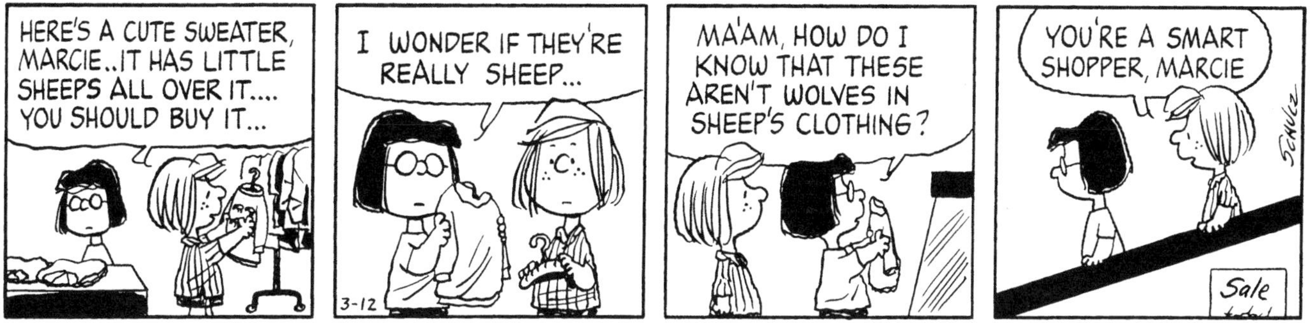
HERE'S A CUTE SWEATER, MARCIE..IT HAS LITTLE SHEEPS ALL OVER IT.... YOU SHOULD BUY IT...
I WONDER IF THEY'RE REALLY SHEEP...
MA'AM, HOW DO I KNOW THAT THESE AREN'T WOLVES IN SHEEP'S CLOTHING?
YOU'RE A SMART SHOPPER, MARCIE
Sale

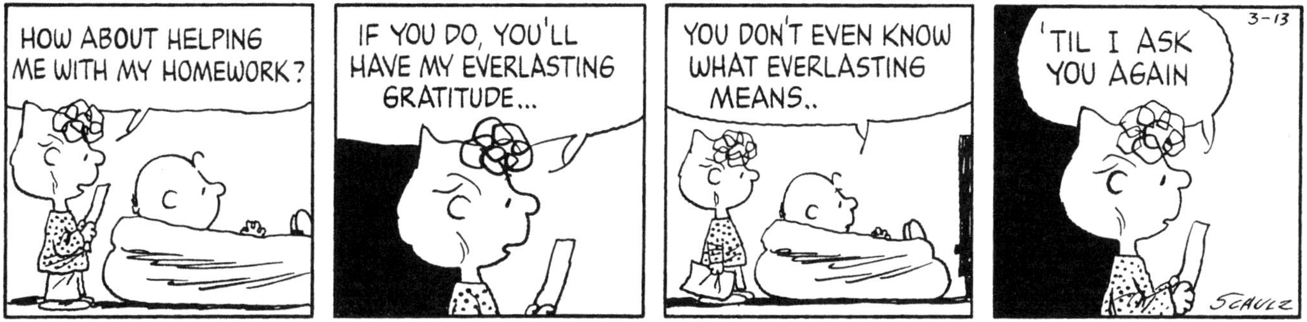
HOW ABOUT HELPING ME WITH MY HOMEWORK?
IF YOU DO, YOU'LL HAVE MY EVERLASTING GRATITUDE...
YOU DON'T EVEN KNOW WHAT EVERLASTING MEANS..
'TIL I ASK YOU AGAIN

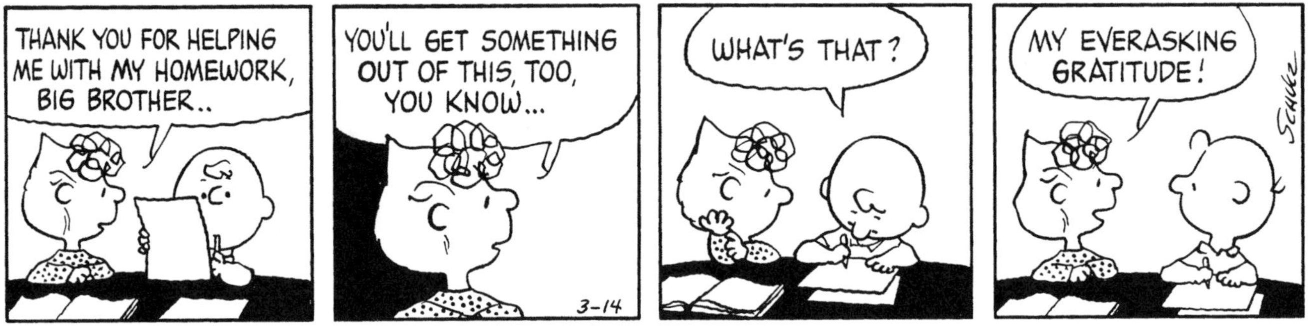
THANK YOU FOR HELPING ME WITH MY HOMEWORK, BIG BROTHER..
YOU'LL GET SOMETHING OUT OF THIS, TOO, YOU KNOW...
3-14
WHAT'S THAT?
MY EVERASKING GRATITUDE!
SCHULZ

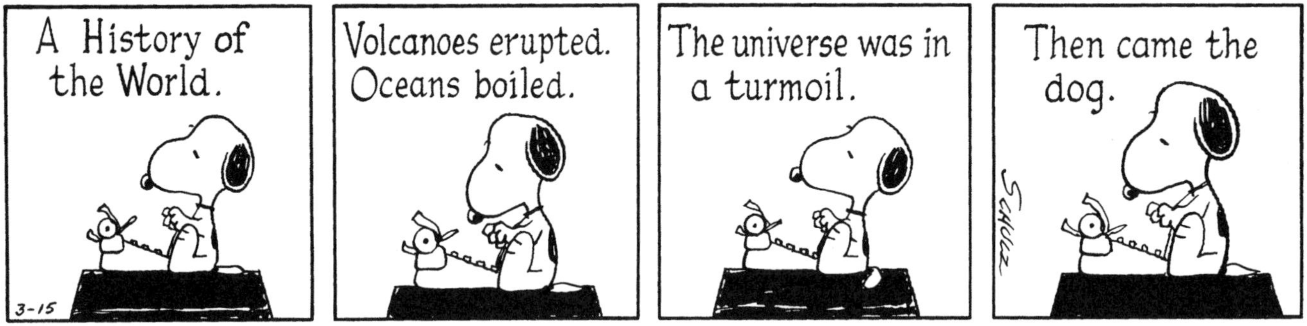
A History of the World.
3-15
Volcanoes erupted. Oceans boiled.
The universe was in a turmoil.
Then came the dog.
SCHULZ

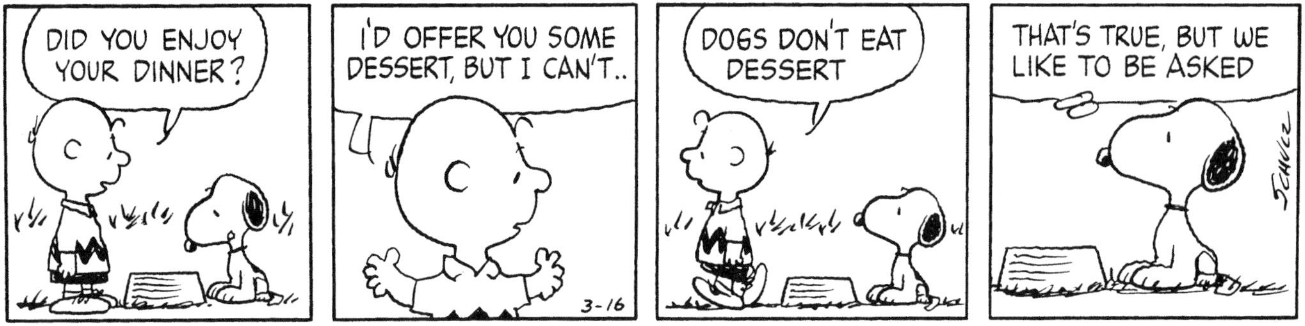
DID YOU ENJOY YOUR DINNER?
I'D OFFER YOU SOME DESSERT, BUT I CAN'T..
3-16
DOGS DON'T EAT DESSERT
THAT'S TRUE, BUT WE LIKE TO BE ASKED
SCHULZ

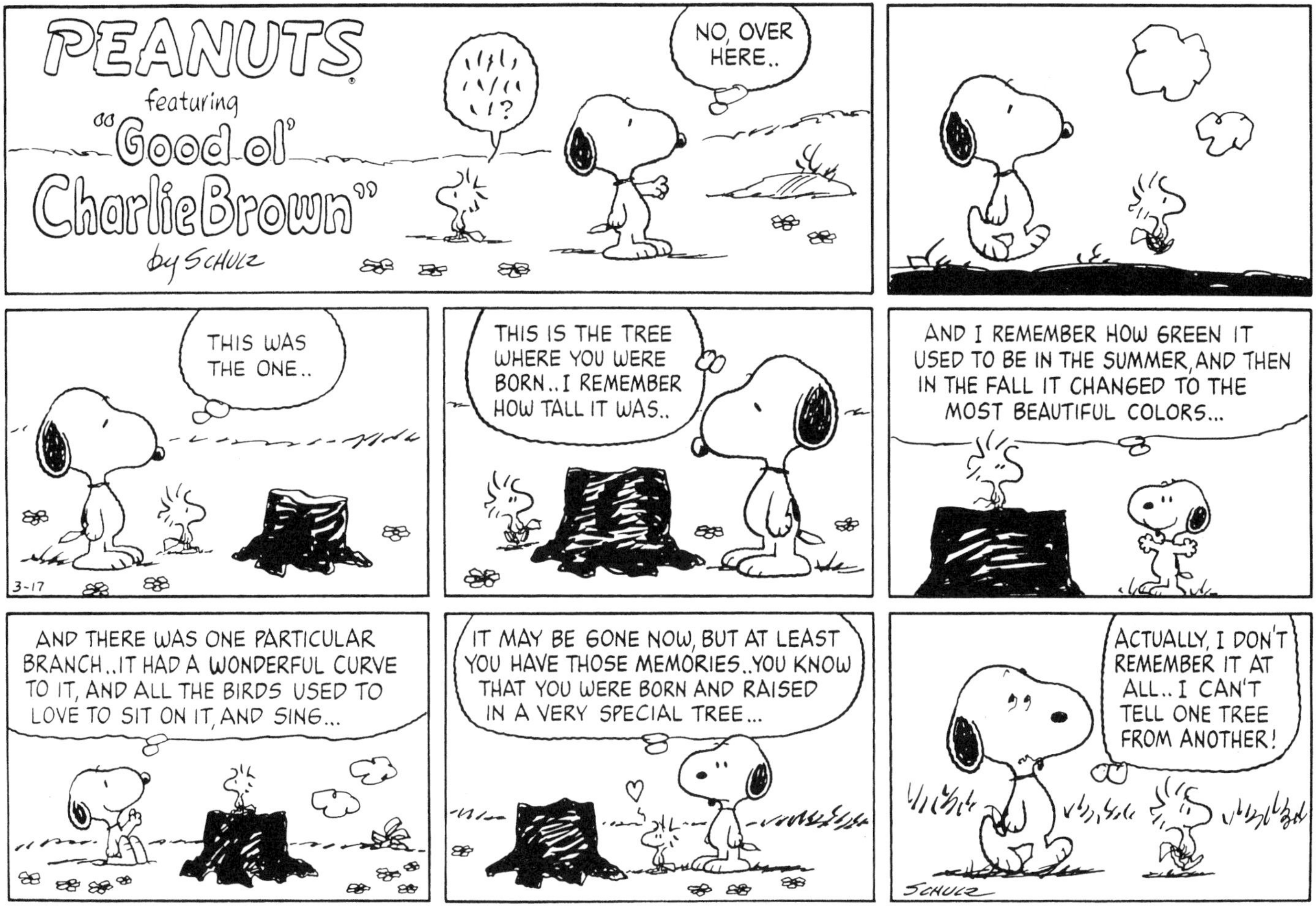
PEANUTS
featuring "Good ol' CharlieBrown"
by SCHULZ
!?
NO, OVER HERE..
THIS WAS THE ONE..
3-17
THIS IS THE TREE WHERE YOU WERE BORN..I REMEMBER HOW TALL IT WAS..
AND I REMEMBER HOW GREEN IT USED TO BE IN THE SUMMER, AND THEN IN THE FALL IT CHANGED TO THE MOST BEAUTIFUL COLORS...
AND THERE WAS ONE PARTICULAR BRANCH..IT HAD A WONDERFUL CURVE TO IT, AND ALL THE BIRDS USED TO LOVE TO SIT ON IT, AND SING...
IT MAY BE GONE NOW, BUT AT LEAST YOU HAVE THOSE MEMORIES..YOU KNOW THAT YOU WERE BORN AND RAISED IN A VERY SPECIAL TREE...
ACTUALLY, I DON'T REMEMBER IT AT ALL.. I CAN'T TELL ONE TREE FROM ANOTHER!
SCHULZ

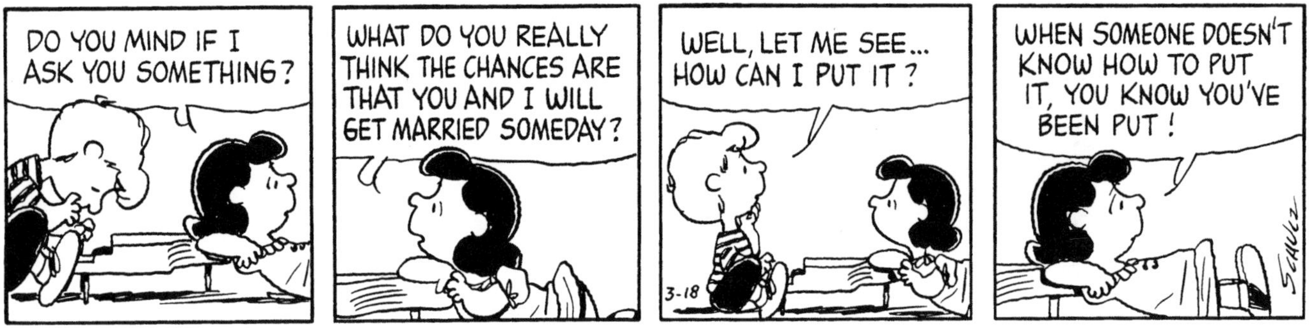
DO YOU MIND IF I ASK YOU SOMETHING?
WHAT DO YOU REALLY THINK THE CHANCES ARE THAT YOU AND I WILL GET MARRIED SOMEDAY?
WELL, LET ME SEE... HOW CAN I PUT IT?
3-18
WHEN SOMEONE DOESN'T KNOW HOW TO PUT IT, YOU KNOW YOU'VE BEEN PUT!
SCHULZ

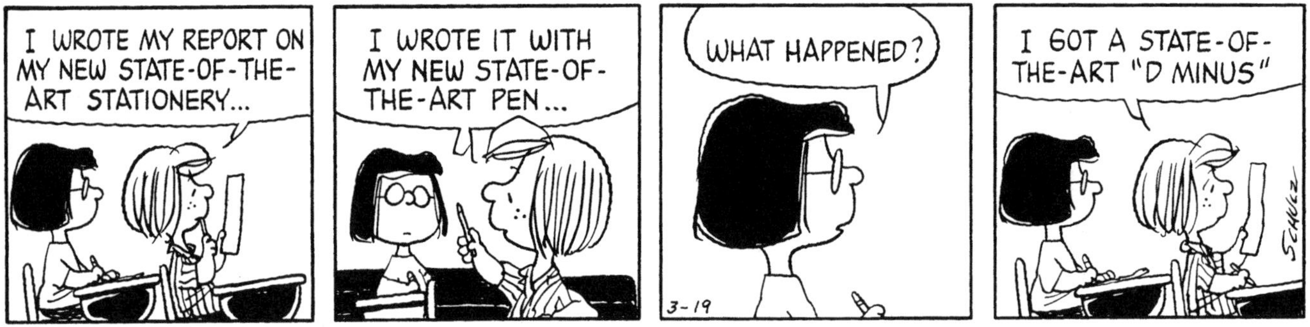
I WROTE MY REPORT ON MY NEW STATE-OF-THE-ART STATIONERY...
I WROTE IT WITH MY NEW STATE-OF-THE-ART PEN...
WHAT HAPPENED?
3-19
I GOT A STATE-OF-THE-ART "D MINUS"
SCHULZ

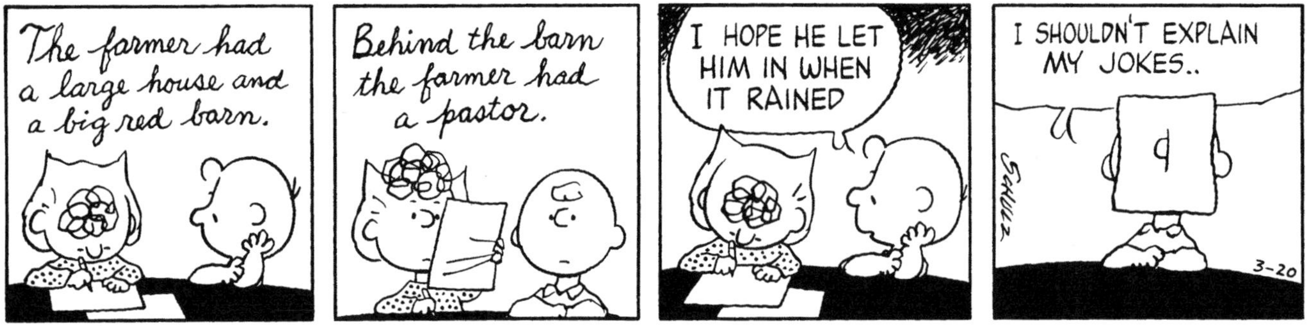
The farmer had a large house and a big red barn.
Behind the barn the farmer had a pastor.
I HOPE HE LET HIM IN WHEN IT RAINED
I SHOULDN'T EXPLAIN MY JOKES..
SCHULZ
3-20

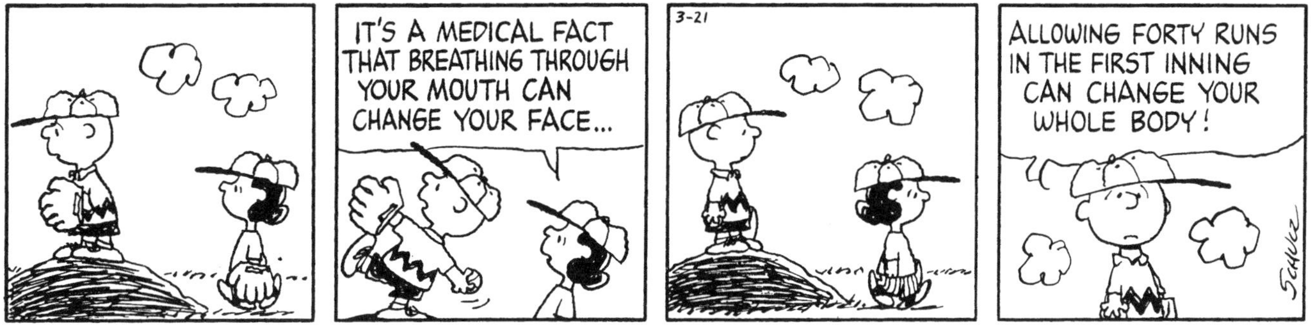
3-21
IT'S A MEDICAL FACT THAT BREATHING THROUGH YOUR MOUTH CAN CHANGE YOUR FACE...
ALLOWING FORTY RUNS IN THE FIRST INNING CAN CHANGE YOUR WHOLE BODY!

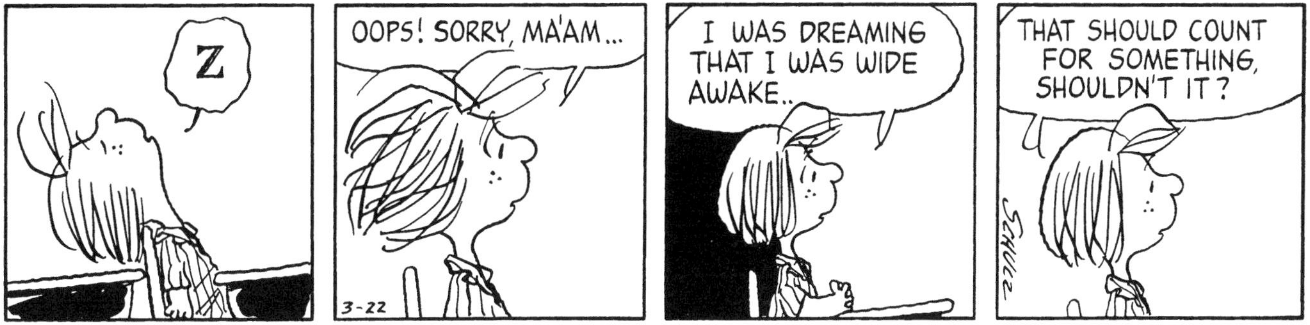
Z
OOPS! SORRY, MA'AM...
3-22
I WAS DREAMING THAT I WAS WIDE AWAKE..
THAT SHOULD COUNT FOR SOMETHING, SHOULDN'T IT?

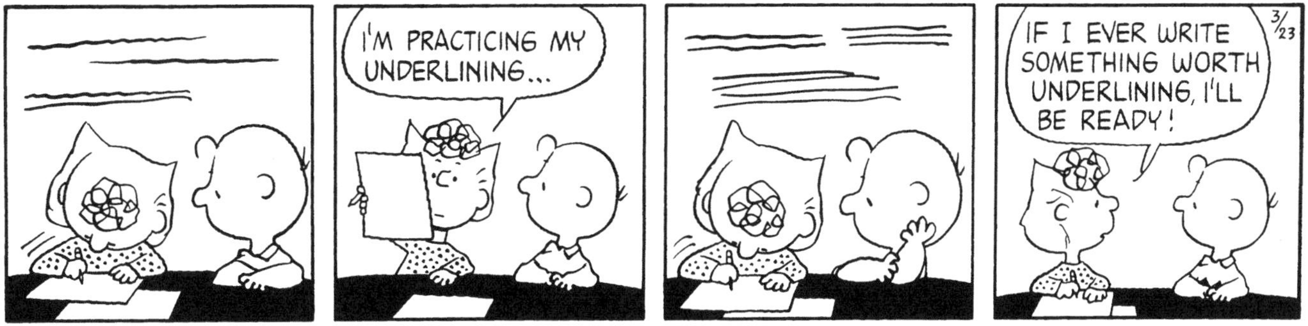
I'M PRACTICING MY UNDERLINING...
IF I EVER WRITE SOMETHING WORTH UNDERLINING, I'LL BE READY!

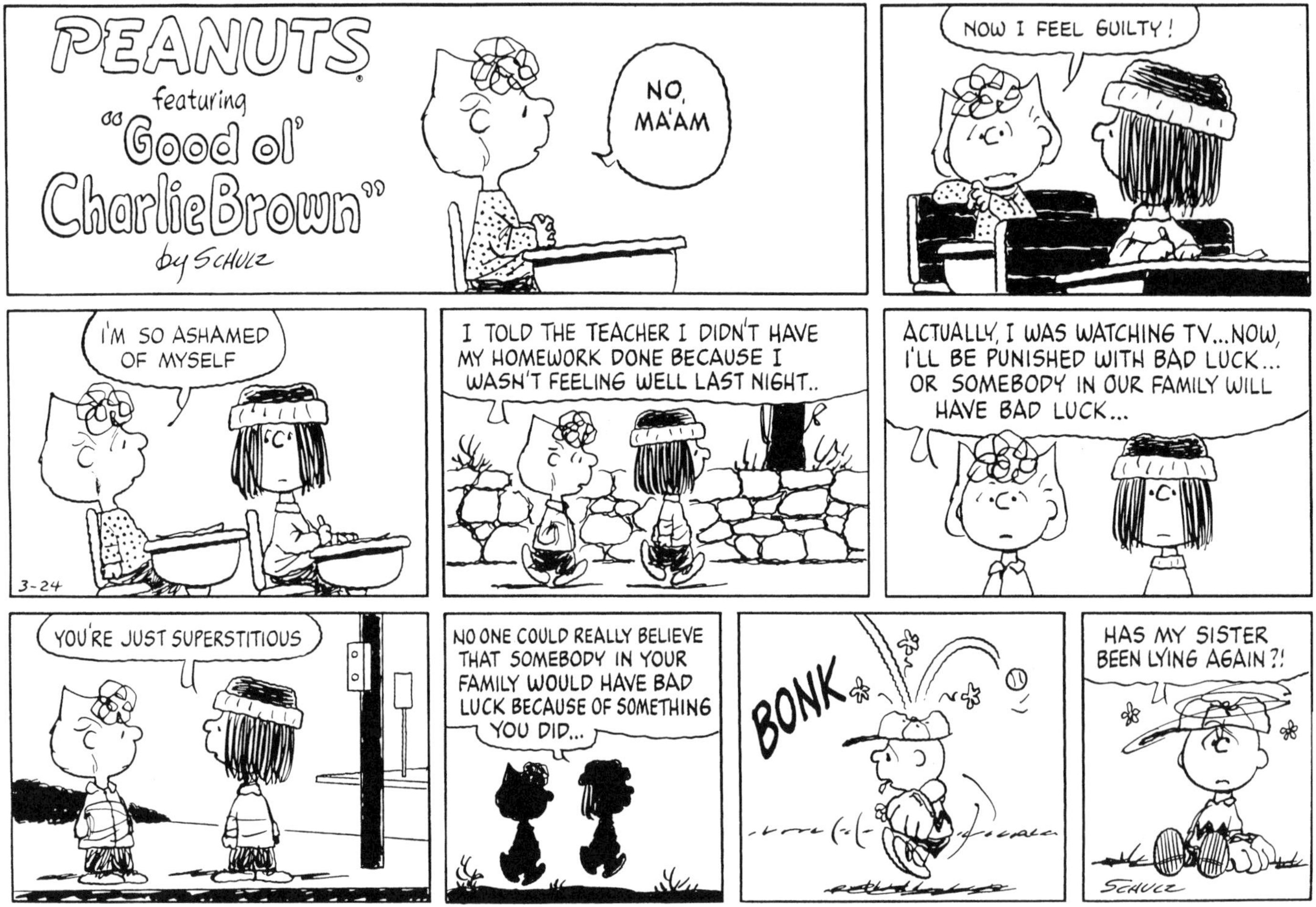
PEANUTS
featuring "Good ol' Charlie Brown"
by SCHULZ
NO, MA'AM
NOW I FEEL GUILTY!
I'M SO ASHAMED OF MYSELF
3-24
I TOLD THE TEACHER I DIDN'T HAVE MY HOMEWORK DONE BECAUSE I WASN'T FEELING WELL LAST NIGHT..
ACTUALLY, I WAS WATCHING TV...NOW, I'LL BE PUNISHED WITH BAD LUCK... OR SOMEBODY IN OUR FAMILY WILL HAVE BAD LUCK...
YOU'RE JUST SUPERSTITIOUS
NO ONE COULD REALLY BELIEVE THAT SOMEBODY IN YOUR FAMILY WOULD HAVE BAD LUCK BECAUSE OF SOMETHING YOU DID...
BONK
HAS MY SISTER BEEN LYING AGAIN?!
SCHULZ

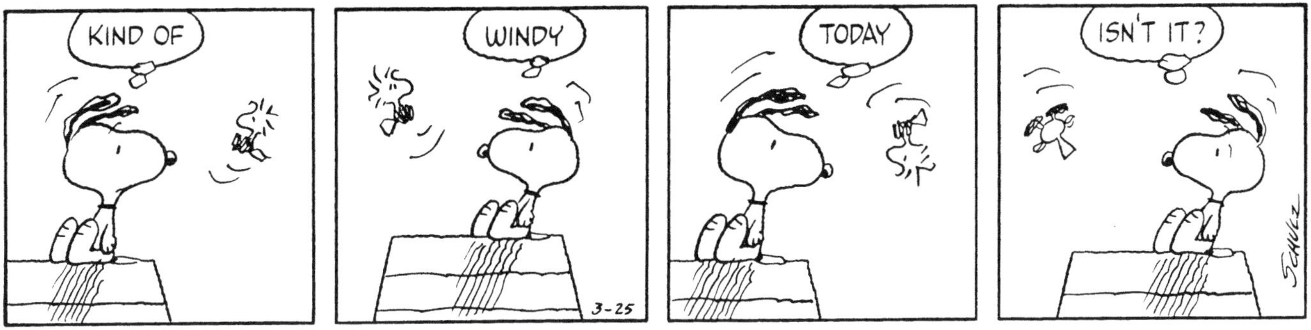
KIND OF
WINDY
TODAY
ISN'T IT?
3-25
SCHULZ

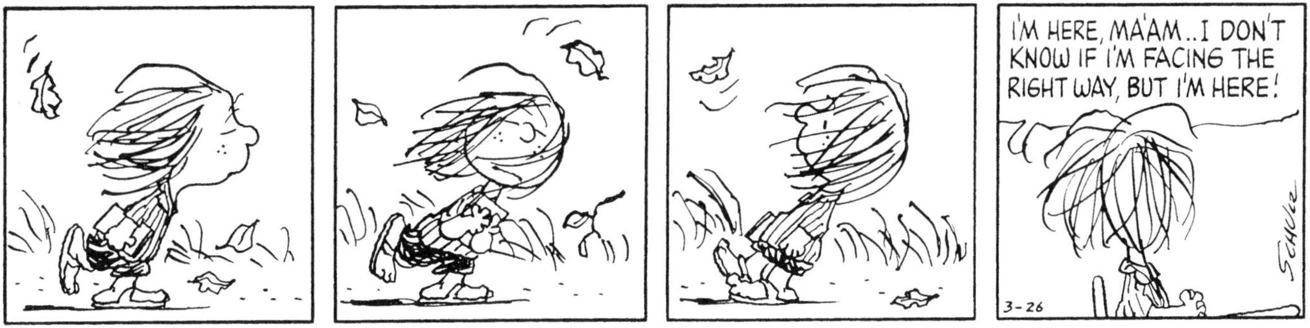
I'M HERE, MA'AM..I DON'T KNOW IF I'M FACING THE RIGHT WAY, BUT I'M HERE!
3-26
SCHULZ

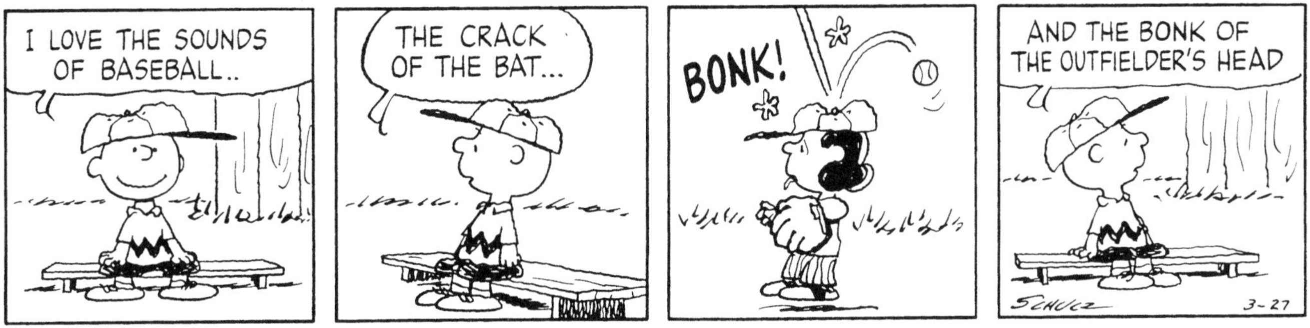
I LOVE THE SOUNDS OF BASEBALL..
THE CRACK OF THE BAT...
BONK!
AND THE BONK OF THE OUTFIELDER'S HEAD
SCHULZ
3-27

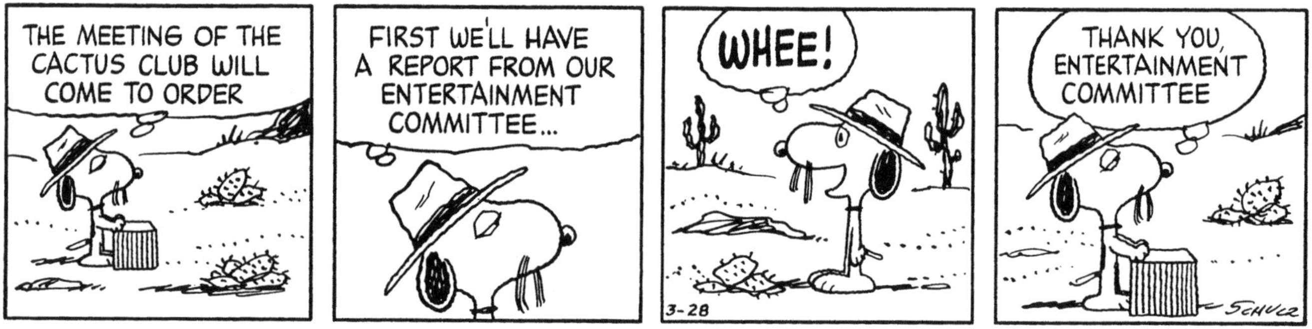
THE MEETING OF THE CACTUS CLUB WILL COME TO ORDER
FIRST WE'LL HAVE A REPORT FROM OUR ENTERTAINMENT COMMITTEE...
WHEE!
THANK YOU, ENTERTAINMENT COMMITTEE
3-28

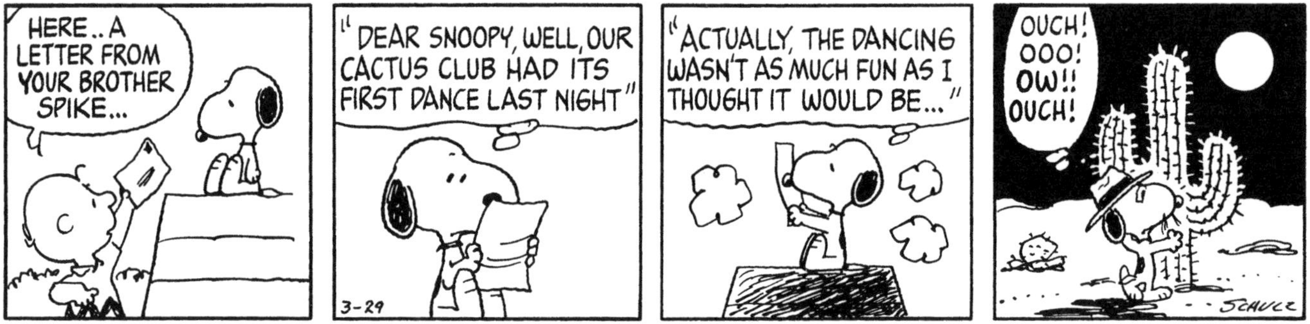
HERE.. A LETTER FROM YOUR BROTHER SPIKE...
"DEAR SNOOPY, WELL, OUR CACTUS CLUB HAD ITS FIRST DANCE LAST NIGHT"
"ACTUALLY, THE DANCING WASN'T AS MUCH FUN AS I THOUGHT IT WOULD BE..."
OUCH! OOO! OW!! OUCH!
3-29

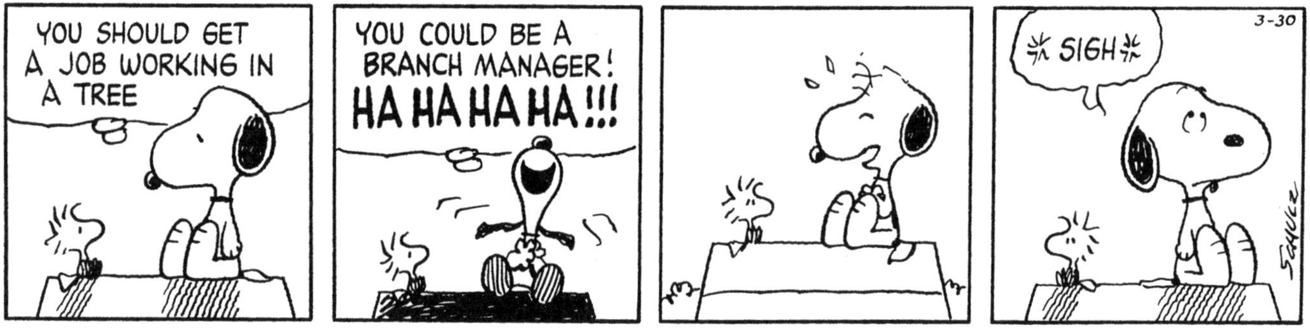
YOU SHOULD GET A JOB WORKING IN A TREE
YOU COULD BE A BRANCH MANAGER! HA HA HA HA!!!
SIGH
3-30

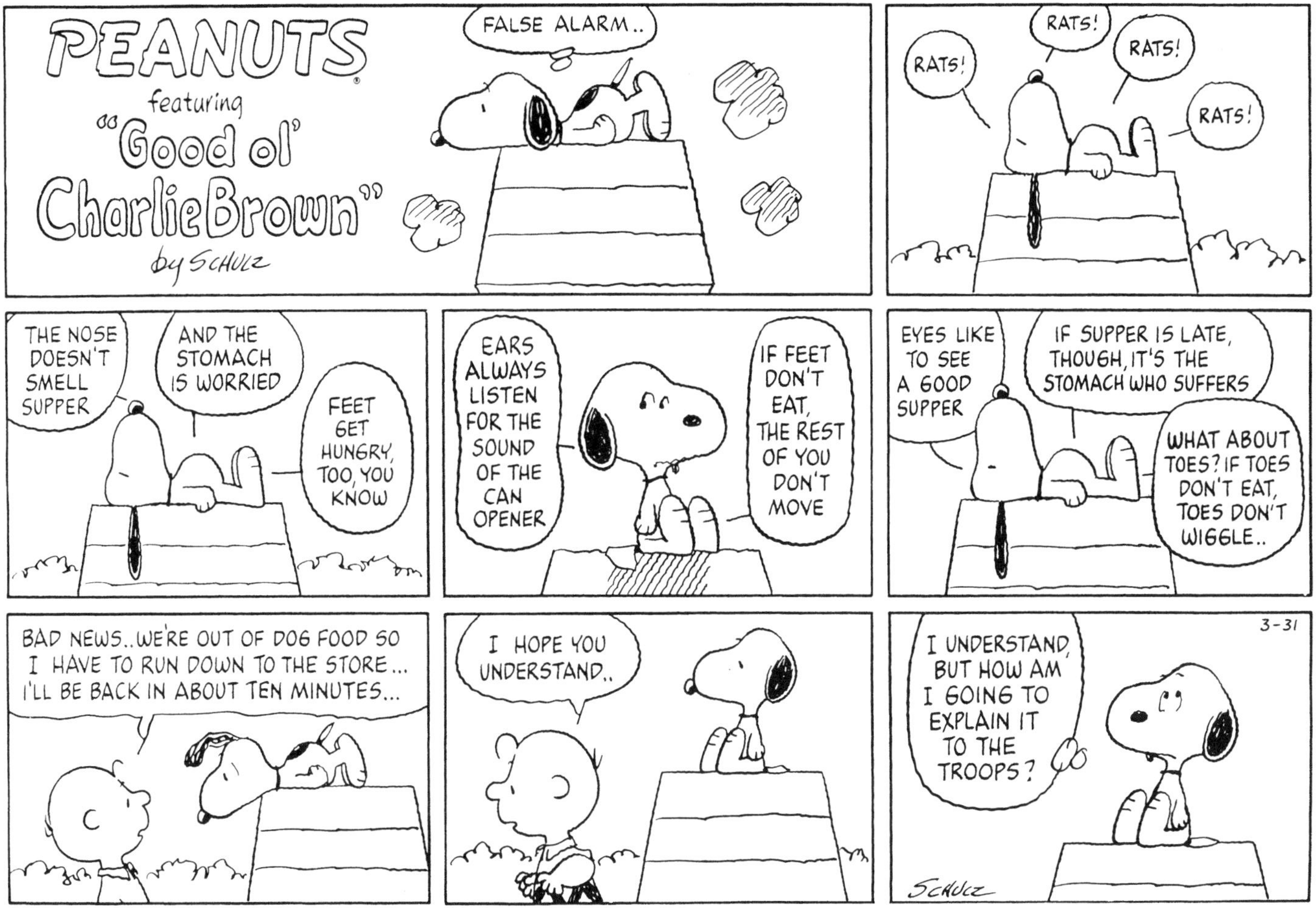
PEANUTS
featuring "Good ol' Charlie Brown"
by SCHULZ
FALSE ALARM..
RATS!
RATS!
RATS!
RATS!
THE NOSE DOESN'T SMELL SUPPER
AND THE STOMACH IS WORRIED
FEET GET HUNGRY, TOO, YOU KNOW
EARS ALWAYS LISTEN FOR THE SOUND OF THE CAN OPENER
IF FEET DON'T EAT, THE REST OF YOU DON'T MOVE
EYES LIKE TO SEE A GOOD SUPPER
IF SUPPER IS LATE, THOUGH, IT'S THE STOMACH WHO SUFFERS
WHAT ABOUT TOES? IF TOES DON'T EAT, TOES DON'T WIGGLE..
BAD NEWS..WE'RE OUT OF DOG FOOD SO I HAVE TO RUN DOWN TO THE STORE... I'LL BE BACK IN ABOUT TEN MINUTES...
I HOPE YOU UNDERSTAND..
3-31
I UNDERSTAND, BUT HOW AM I GOING TO EXPLAIN IT TO THE TROOPS?
SCHULZ

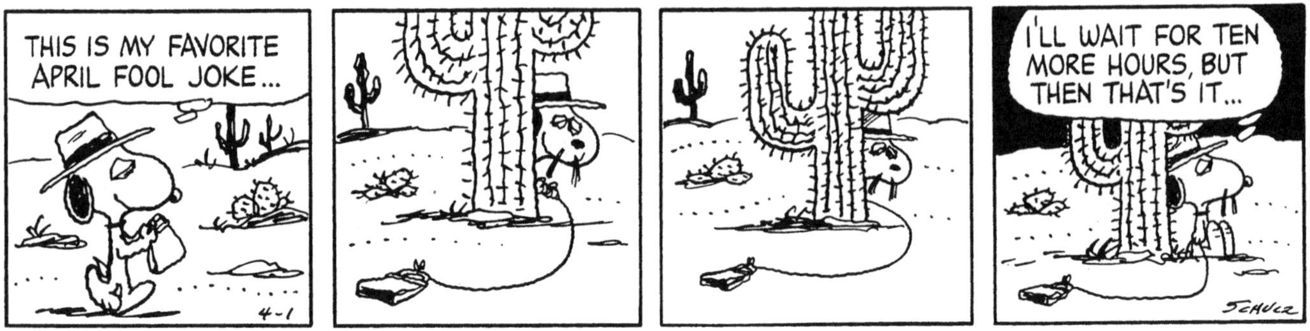
THIS IS MY FAVORITE APRIL FOOL JOKE...
4-1
I'LL WAIT FOR TEN MORE HOURS, BUT THEN THAT'S IT...
SCHULZ

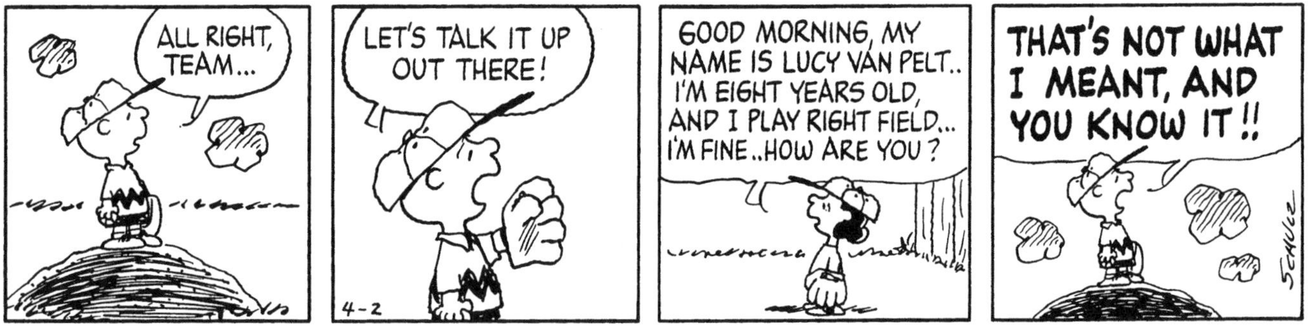
ALL RIGHT, TEAM...
LET'S TALK IT UP OUT THERE!
4-2
GOOD MORNING, MY NAME IS LUCY VAN PELT.. I'M EIGHT YEARS OLD, AND I PLAY RIGHT FIELD... I'M FINE..HOW ARE YOU?
THAT'S NOT WHAT I MEANT, AND YOU KNOW IT!!
SCHULZ

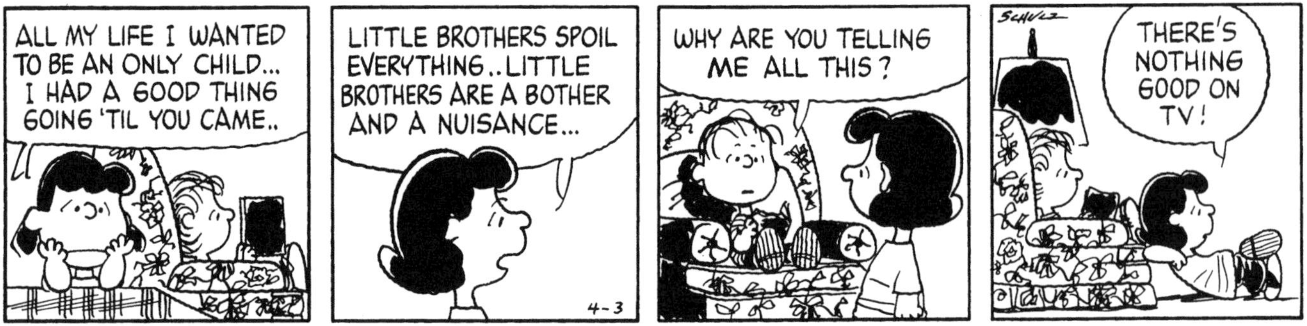
ALL MY LIFE I WANTED TO BE AN ONLY CHILD... I HAD A GOOD THING GOING 'TIL YOU CAME..
LITTLE BROTHERS SPOIL EVERYTHING..LITTLE BROTHERS ARE A BOTHER AND A NUISANCE...
4-3
WHY ARE YOU TELLING ME ALL THIS?
SCHULZ
THERE'S NOTHING GOOD ON TV!

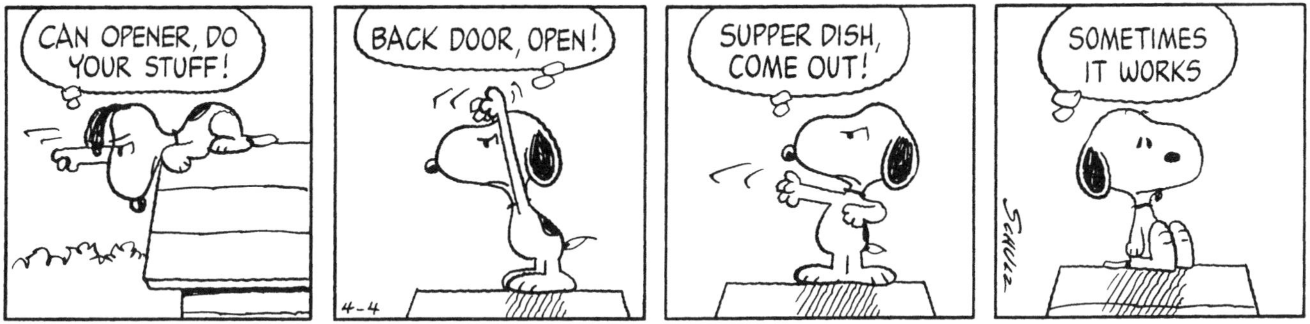
CAN OPENER, DO YOUR STUFF!
BACK DOOR, OPEN!
SUPPER DISH, COME OUT!
SOMETIMES IT WORKS

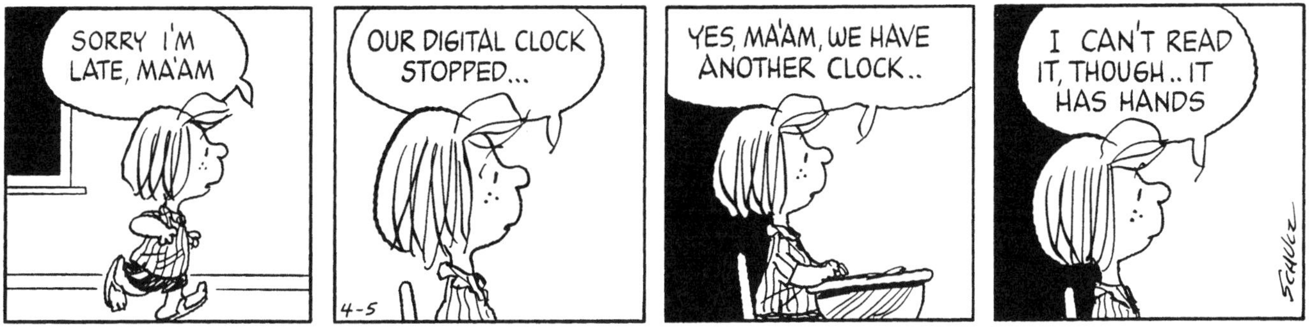
SORRY I'M LATE, MA'AM
OUR DIGITAL CLOCK STOPPED...
YES, MA'AM, WE HAVE ANOTHER CLOCK..
I CAN'T READ IT, THOUGH.. IT HAS HANDS

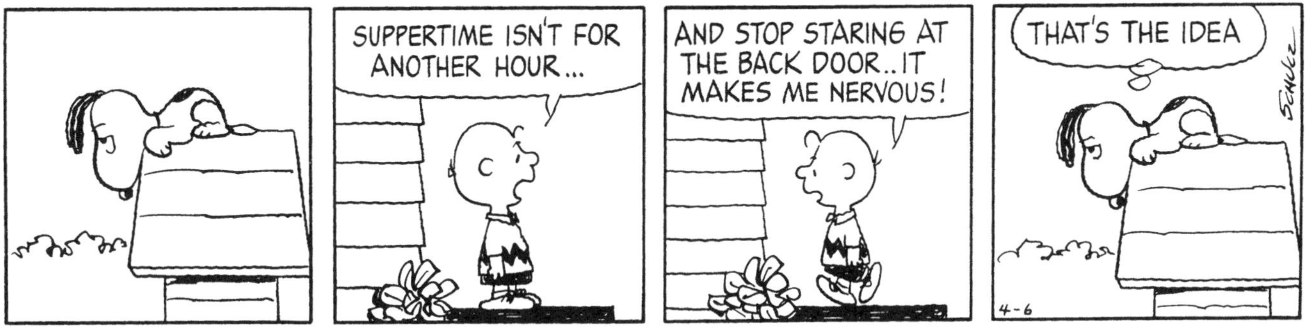
SUPPERTIME ISN'T FOR ANOTHER HOUR...
AND STOP STARING AT THE BACK DOOR.. IT MAKES ME NERVOUS!
THAT'S THE IDEA

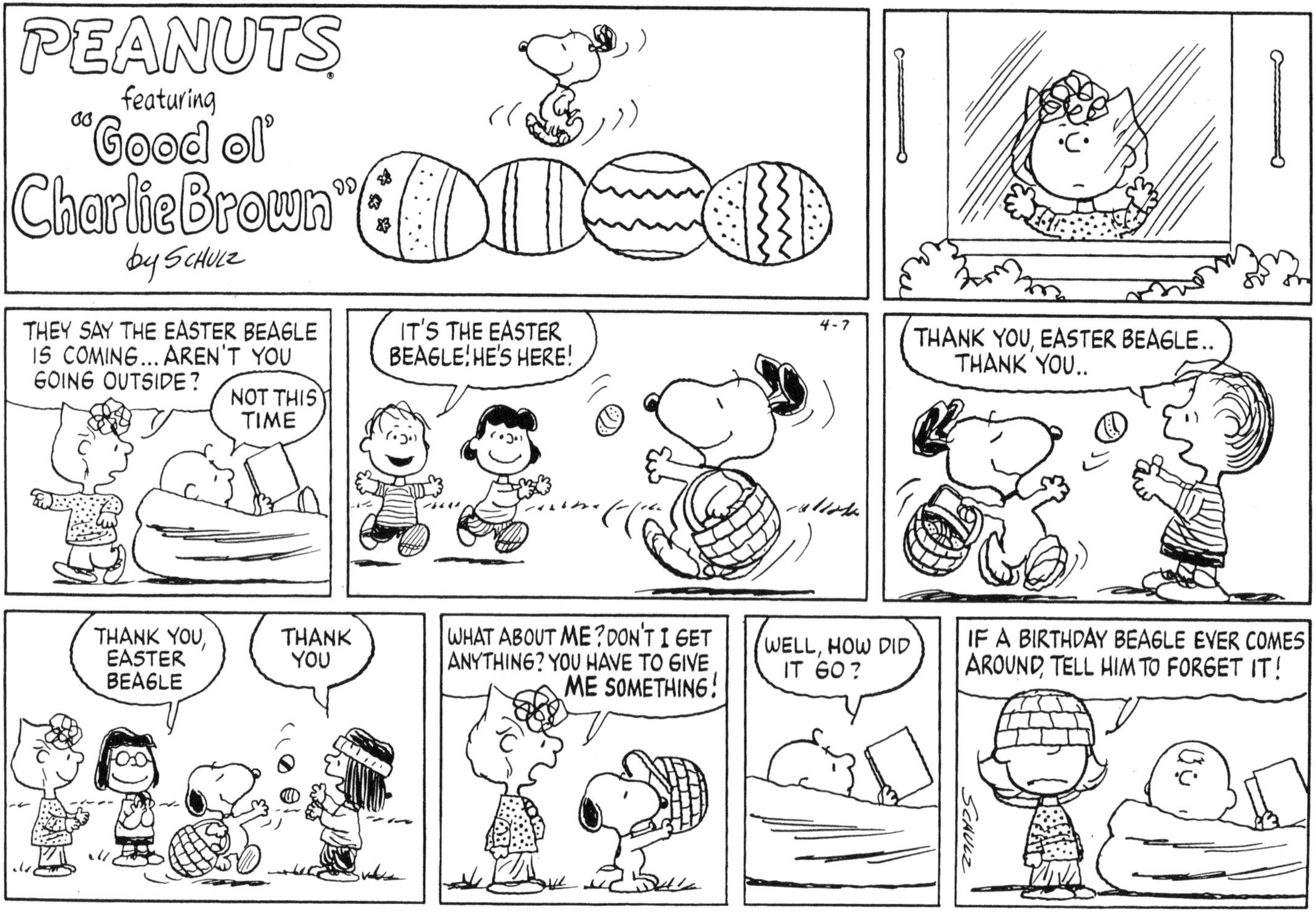
PEANUTS
featuring
"Good ol' Charlie Brown"
by SCHULZ
4-7
THEY SAY THE EASTER BEAGLE IS COMING... AREN'T YOU GOING OUTSIDE?
NOT THIS TIME
IT'S THE EASTER BEAGLE! HE'S HERE!
THANK YOU, EASTER BEAGLE.. THANK YOU..
THANK YOU, EASTER BEAGLE
THANK YOU
WHAT ABOUT ME? DON'T I GET ANYTHING? YOU HAVE TO GIVE ME SOMETHING!
WELL, HOW DID IT GO?
SCHULZ
IF A BIRTHDAY BEAGLE EVER COMES AROUND, TELL HIM TO FORGET IT!

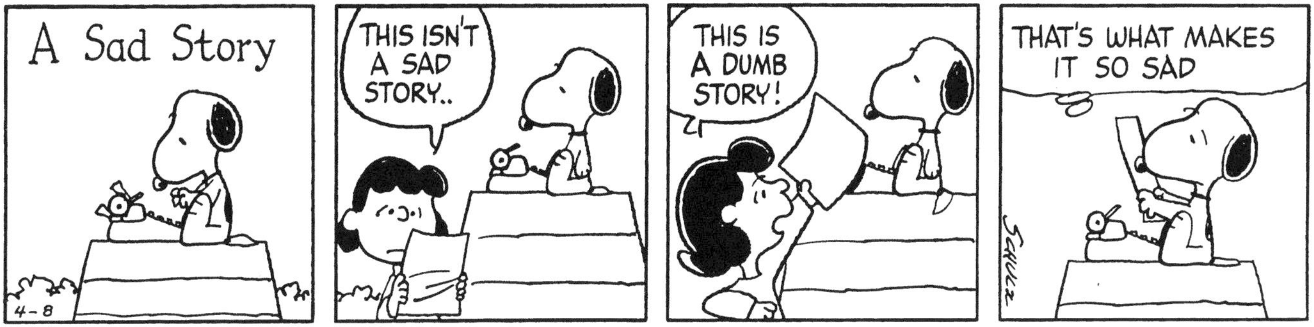
A Sad Story
4-8
THIS ISN'T A SAD STORY..
THIS IS A DUMB STORY!
THAT'S WHAT MAKES IT SO SAD
SCHULZ

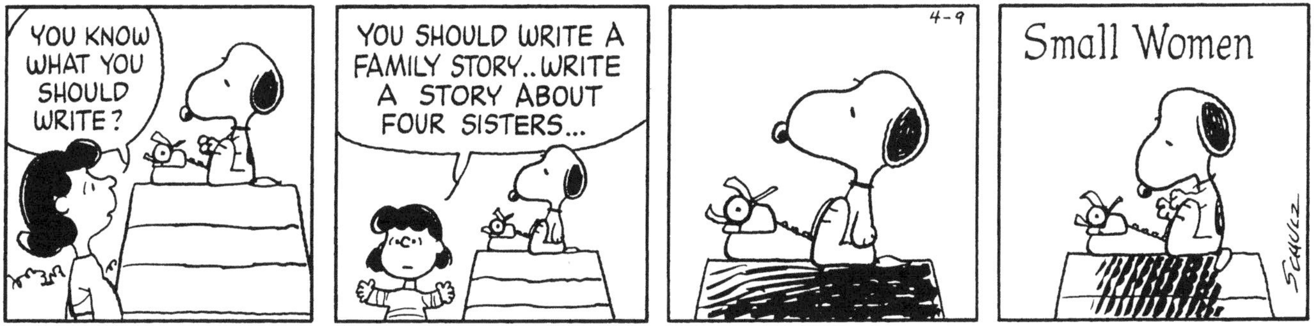
YOU KNOW WHAT YOU SHOULD WRITE?
YOU SHOULD WRITE A FAMILY STORY..WRITE A STORY ABOUT FOUR SISTERS...
4-9
Small Women
SCHULZ

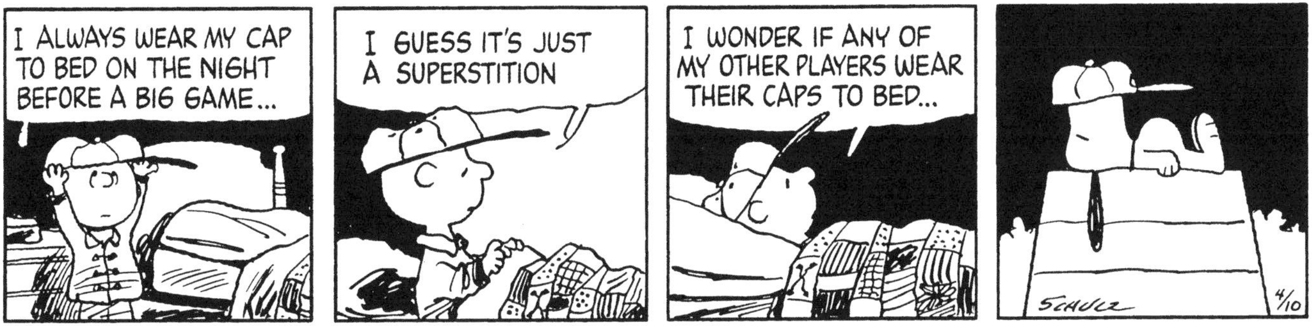
I ALWAYS WEAR MY CAP TO BED ON THE NIGHT BEFORE A BIG GAME...
I GUESS IT'S JUST A SUPERSTITION
I WONDER IF ANY OF MY OTHER PLAYERS WEAR THEIR CAPS TO BED...
SCHULZ
4/10

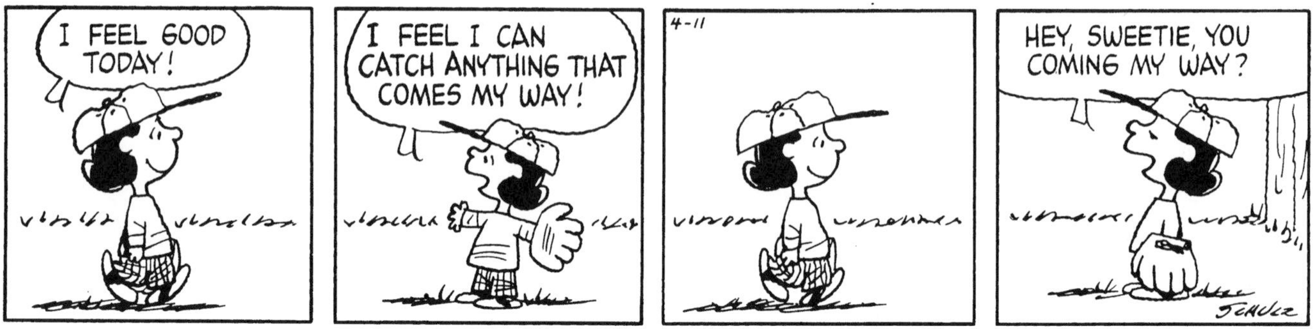
I FEEL GOOD TODAY!
I FEEL I CAN CATCH ANYTHING THAT COMES MY WAY!
4-11
HEY, SWEETIE, YOU COMING MY WAY?
SCHULZ

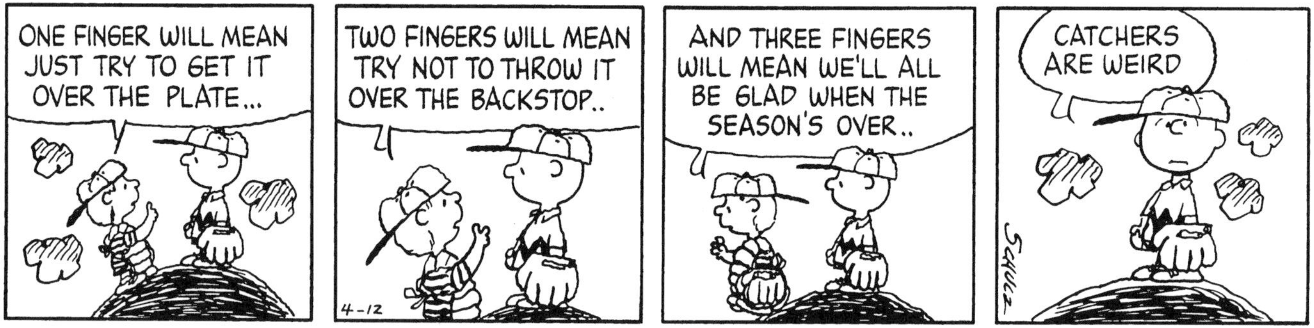
ONE FINGER WILL MEAN JUST TRY TO GET IT OVER THE PLATE...
TWO FINGERS WILL MEAN TRY NOT TO THROW IT OVER THE BACKSTOP..
4-12
AND THREE FINGERS WILL MEAN WE'LL ALL BE GLAD WHEN THE SEASON'S OVER..
CATCHERS ARE WEIRD
SCHULZ

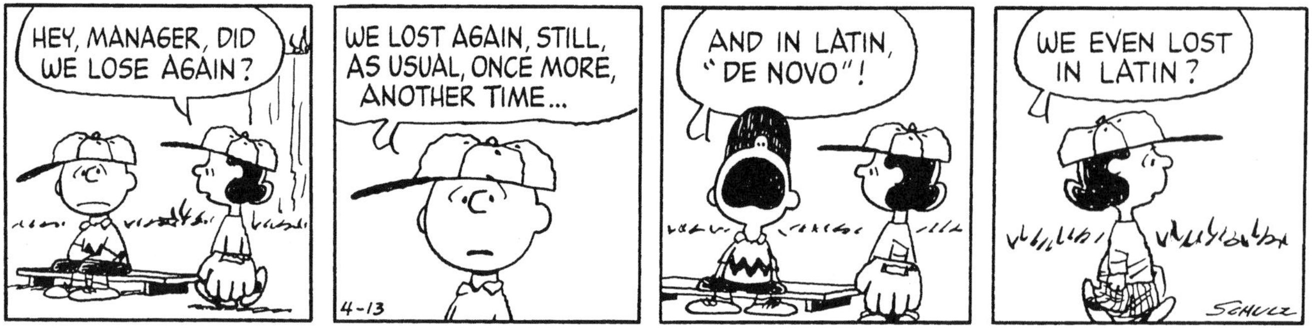
HEY, MANAGER, DID WE LOSE AGAIN?
WE LOST AGAIN, STILL, AS USUAL, ONCE MORE, ANOTHER TIME...
4-13
AND IN LATIN, "DE NOVO"!
WE EVEN LOST IN LATIN?
SCHULZ

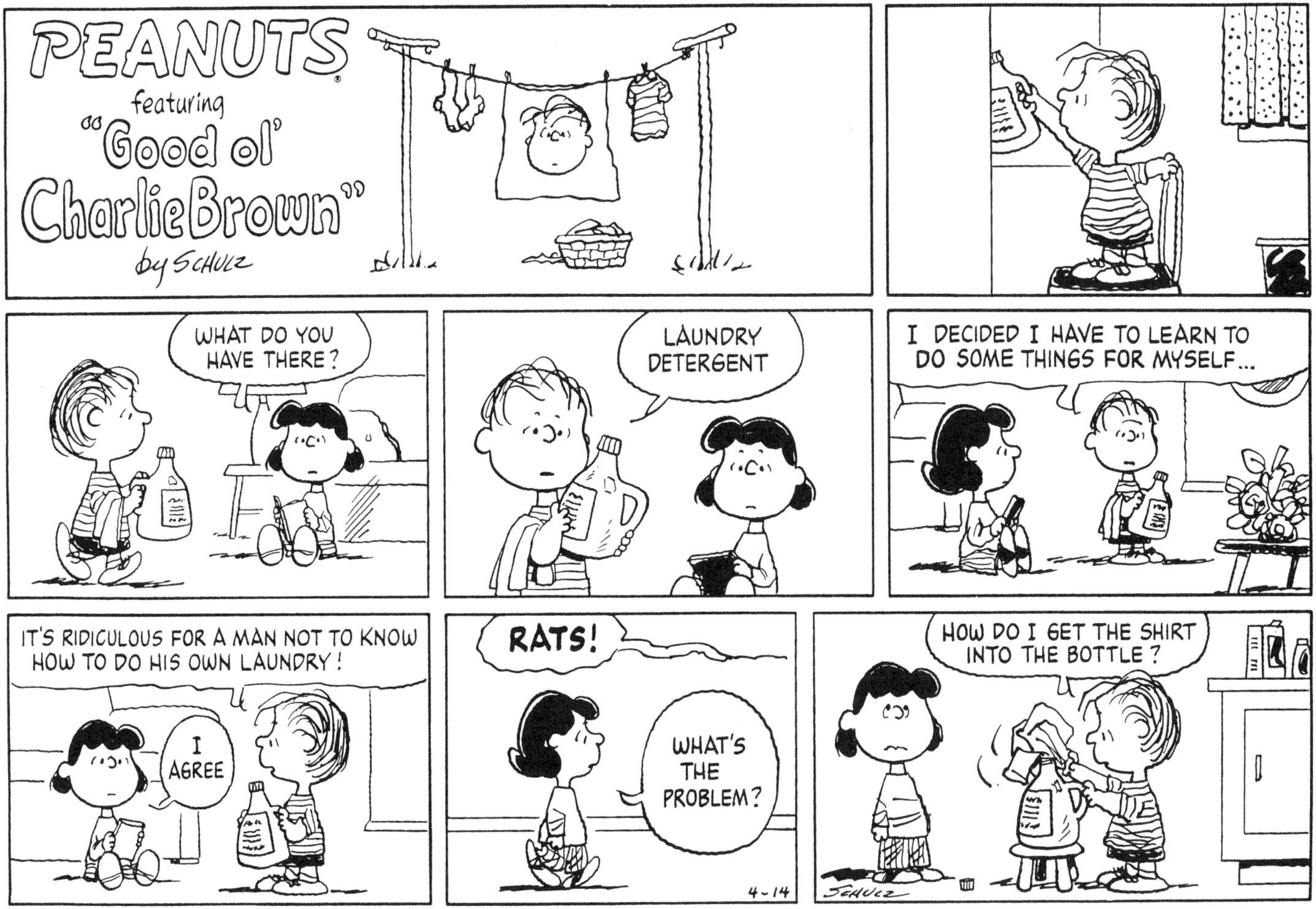
PEANUTS
featuring
"Good ol' Charlie Brown"
by SCHULZ
WHAT DO YOU HAVE THERE?
LAUNDRY DETERGENT
I DECIDED I HAVE TO LEARN TO DO SOME THINGS FOR MYSELF...
IT'S RIDICULOUS FOR A MAN NOT TO KNOW HOW TO DO HIS OWN LAUNDRY!
I AGREE
RATS!
WHAT'S THE PROBLEM?
4-14
HOW DO I GET THE SHIRT INTO THE BOTTLE?
SCHULZ

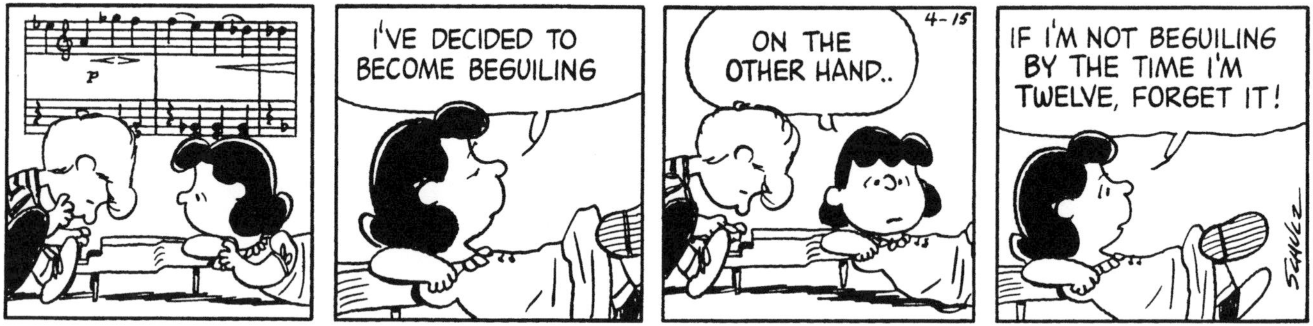
I'VE DECIDED TO BECOME BEGUILING
ON THE OTHER HAND..
4-15
IF I'M NOT BEGUILING BY THE TIME I'M TWELVE, FORGET IT!
SCHULZ

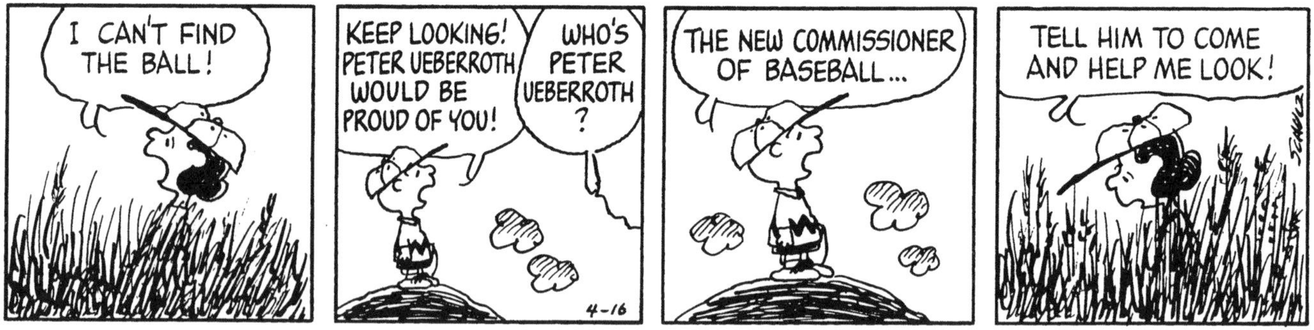
I CAN'T FIND THE BALL!
KEEP LOOKING! PETER UEBERROTH WOULD BE PROUD OF YOU!
WHO'S PETER UEBERROTH?
4-16
THE NEW COMMISSIONER OF BASEBALL...
TELL HIM TO COME AND HELP ME LOOK!
SCHULZ

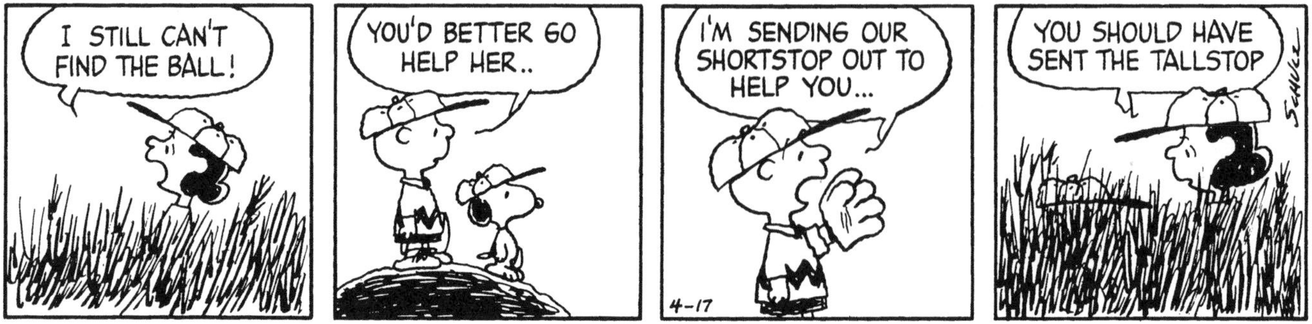
I STILL CAN'T FIND THE BALL!
YOU'D BETTER GO HELP HER..
I'M SENDING OUR SHORTSTOP OUT TO HELP YOU...
4-17
YOU SHOULD HAVE SENT THE TALLSTOP
SCHULZ

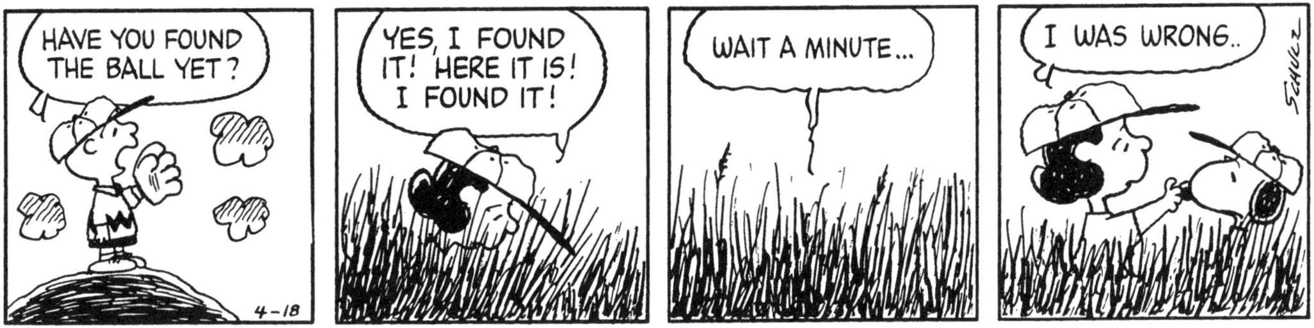
HAVE YOU FOUND THE BALL YET?
4-18
YES, I FOUND IT! HERE IT IS! I FOUND IT!
WAIT A MINUTE...
I WAS WRONG..
SCHULZ

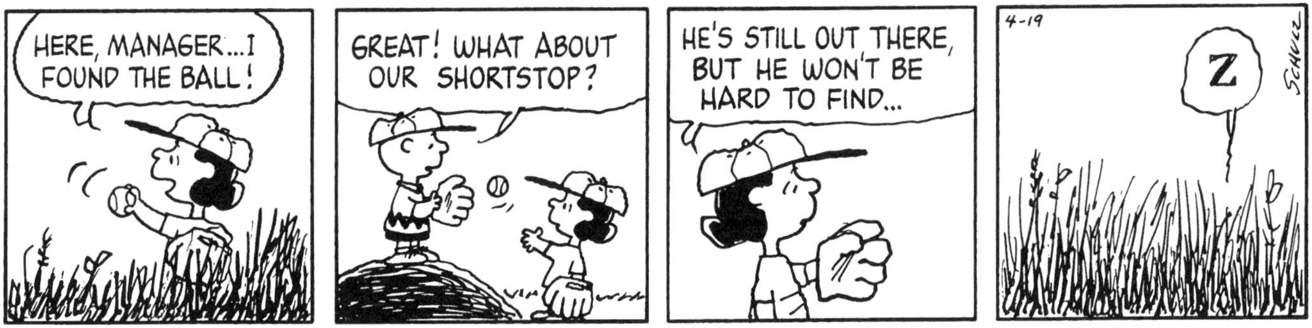
HERE, MANAGER...I FOUND THE BALL!
GREAT! WHAT ABOUT OUR SHORTSTOP?
HE'S STILL OUT THERE, BUT HE WON'T BE HARD TO FIND...
4-19
Z
SCHULZ

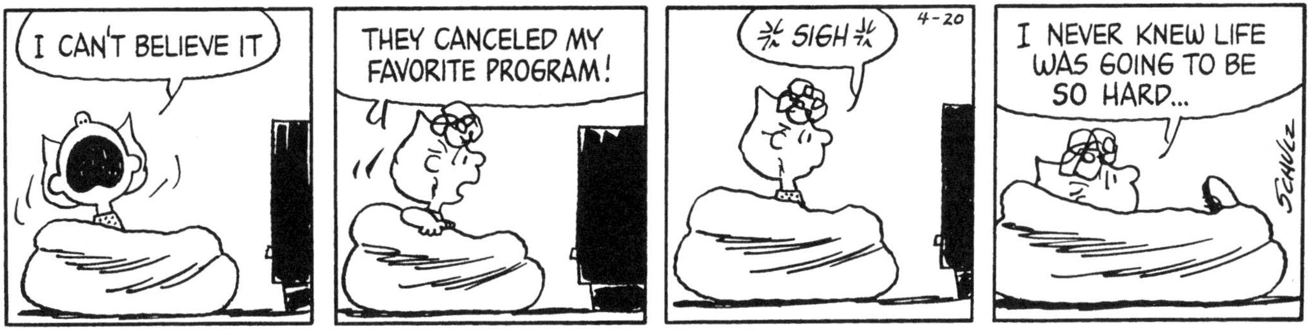
I CAN'T BELIEVE IT
THEY CANCELED MY FAVORITE PROGRAM!
SIGH
4-20
I NEVER KNEW LIFE WAS GOING TO BE SO HARD...
SCHULZ

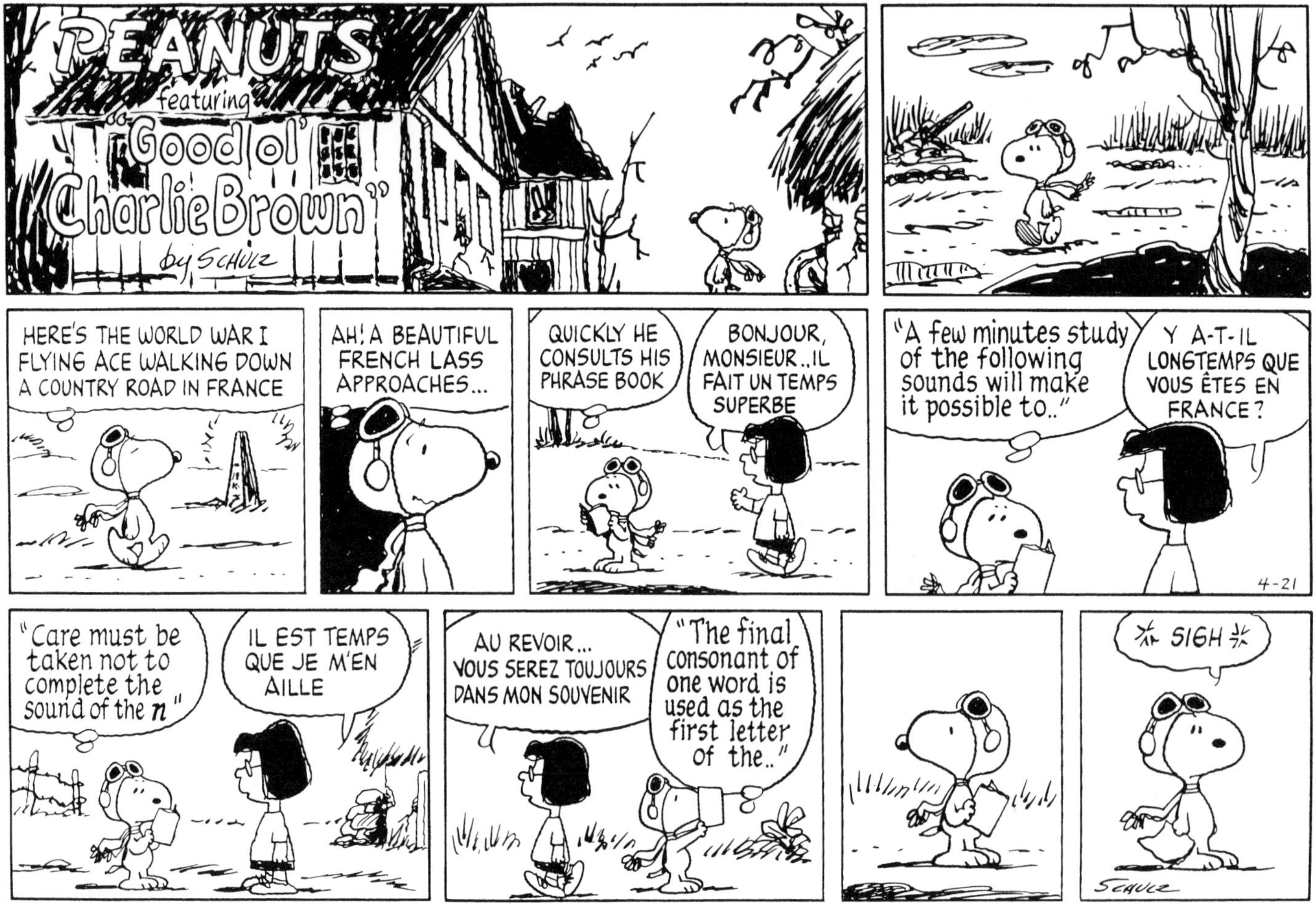
PEANUTS
featuring
"Good ol' Charlie Brown"
by SCHULZ
HERE'S THE WORLD WAR I FLYING ACE WALKING DOWN A COUNTRY ROAD IN FRANCE
AH! A BEAUTIFUL FRENCH LASS APPROACHES...
QUICKLY HE CONSULTS HIS PHRASE BOOK
BONJOUR, MONSIEUR..IL FAIT UN TEMPS SUPERBE
"A few minutes study of the following sounds will make it possible to.."
Y A-T-IL LONGTEMPS QUE VOUS ÊTES EN FRANCE?
4-21
"Care must be taken not to complete the sound of the n"
IL EST TEMPS QUE JE M'EN AILLE
AU REVOIR... VOUS SEREZ TOUJOURS DANS MON SOUVENIR
"The final consonant of one word is used as the first letter of the.."
SIGH
SCHULZ

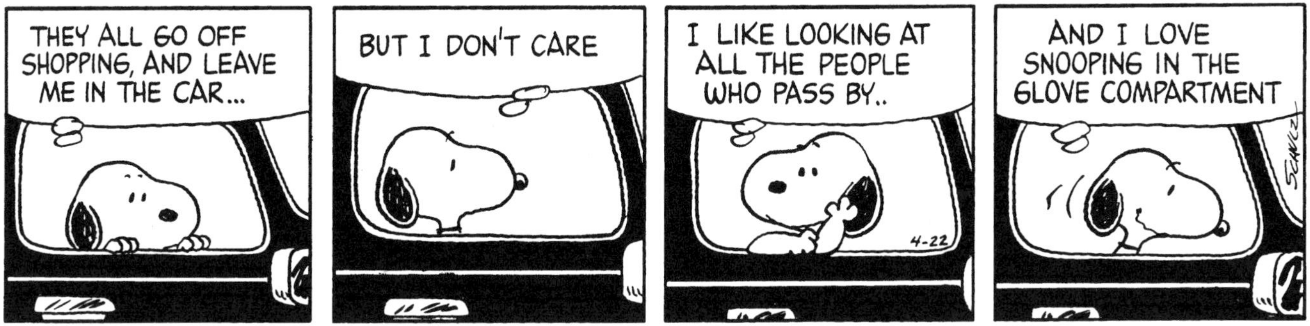
THEY ALL GO OFF SHOPPING, AND LEAVE ME IN THE CAR...
BUT I DON'T CARE
I LIKE LOOKING AT ALL THE PEOPLE WHO PASS BY..
4-22
AND I LOVE SNOOPING IN THE GLOVE COMPARTMENT

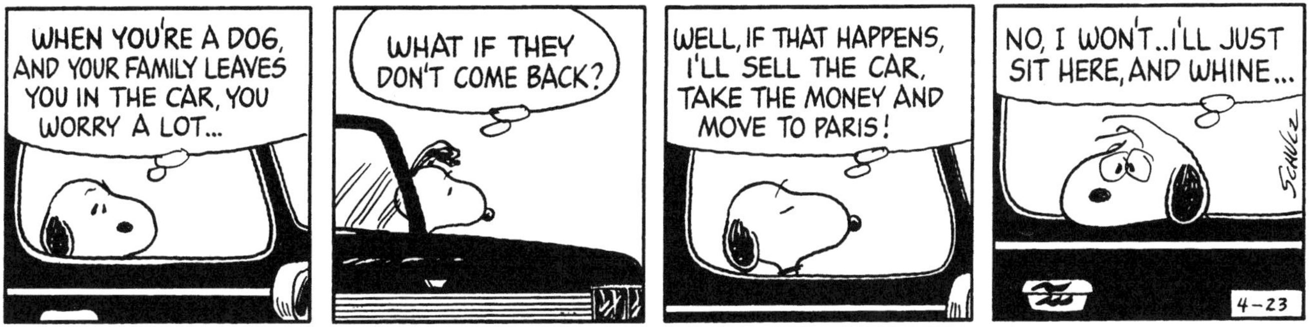
WHEN YOU'RE A DOG, AND YOUR FAMILY LEAVES YOU IN THE CAR, YOU WORRY A LOT...
WHAT IF THEY DON'T COME BACK?
WELL, IF THAT HAPPENS, I'LL SELL THE CAR, TAKE THE MONEY AND MOVE TO PARIS!
NO, I WON'T..I'LL JUST SIT HERE, AND WHINE...
4-23

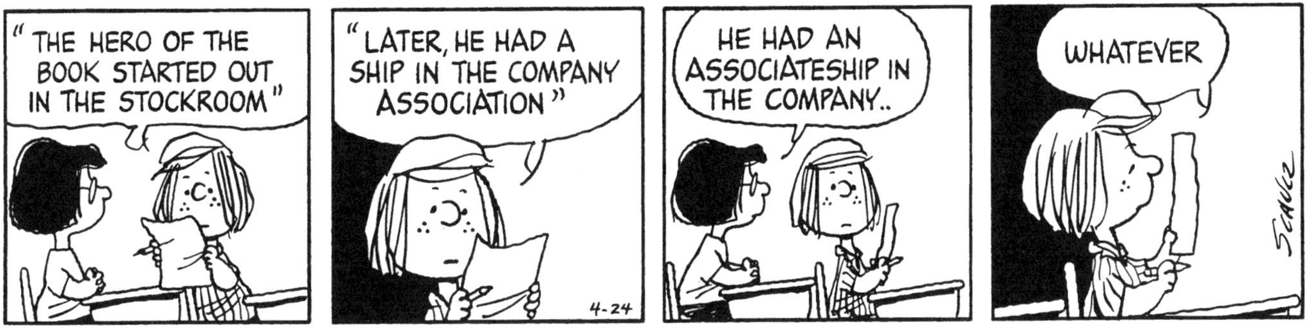
"THE HERO OF THE BOOK STARTED OUT IN THE STOCKROOM"
"LATER, HE HAD A SHIP IN THE COMPANY ASSOCIATION"
4-24
HE HAD AN ASSOCIATESHIP IN THE COMPANY..
WHATEVER

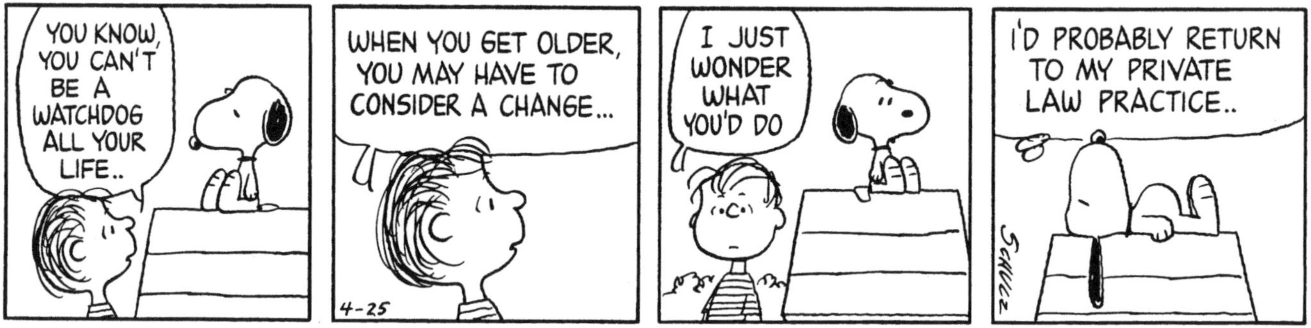
YOU KNOW, YOU CAN'T BE A WATCHDOG ALL YOUR LIFE..
WHEN YOU GET OLDER, YOU MAY HAVE TO CONSIDER A CHANGE...
I JUST WONDER WHAT YOU'D DO
I'D PROBABLY RETURN TO MY PRIVATE LAW PRACTICE..

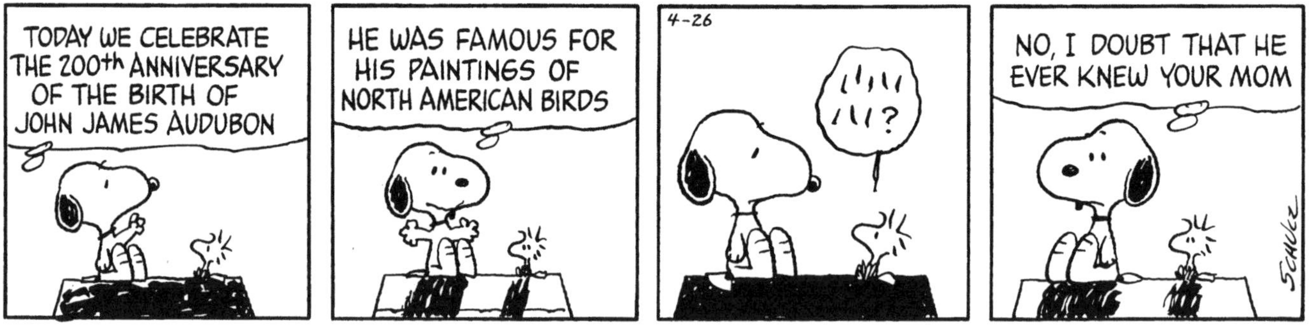
TODAY WE CELEBRATE THE 200th ANNIVERSARY OF THE BIRTH OF JOHN JAMES AUDUBON
HE WAS FAMOUS FOR HIS PAINTINGS OF NORTH AMERICAN BIRDS
NO, I DOUBT THAT HE EVER KNEW YOUR MOM

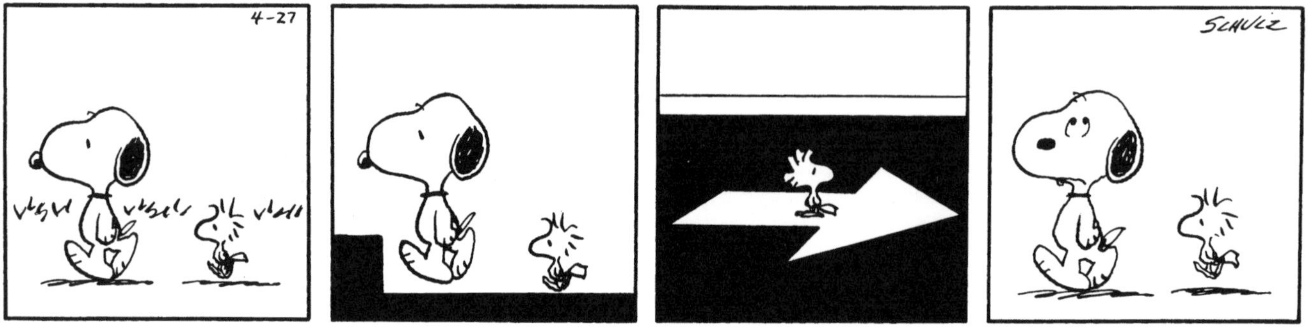

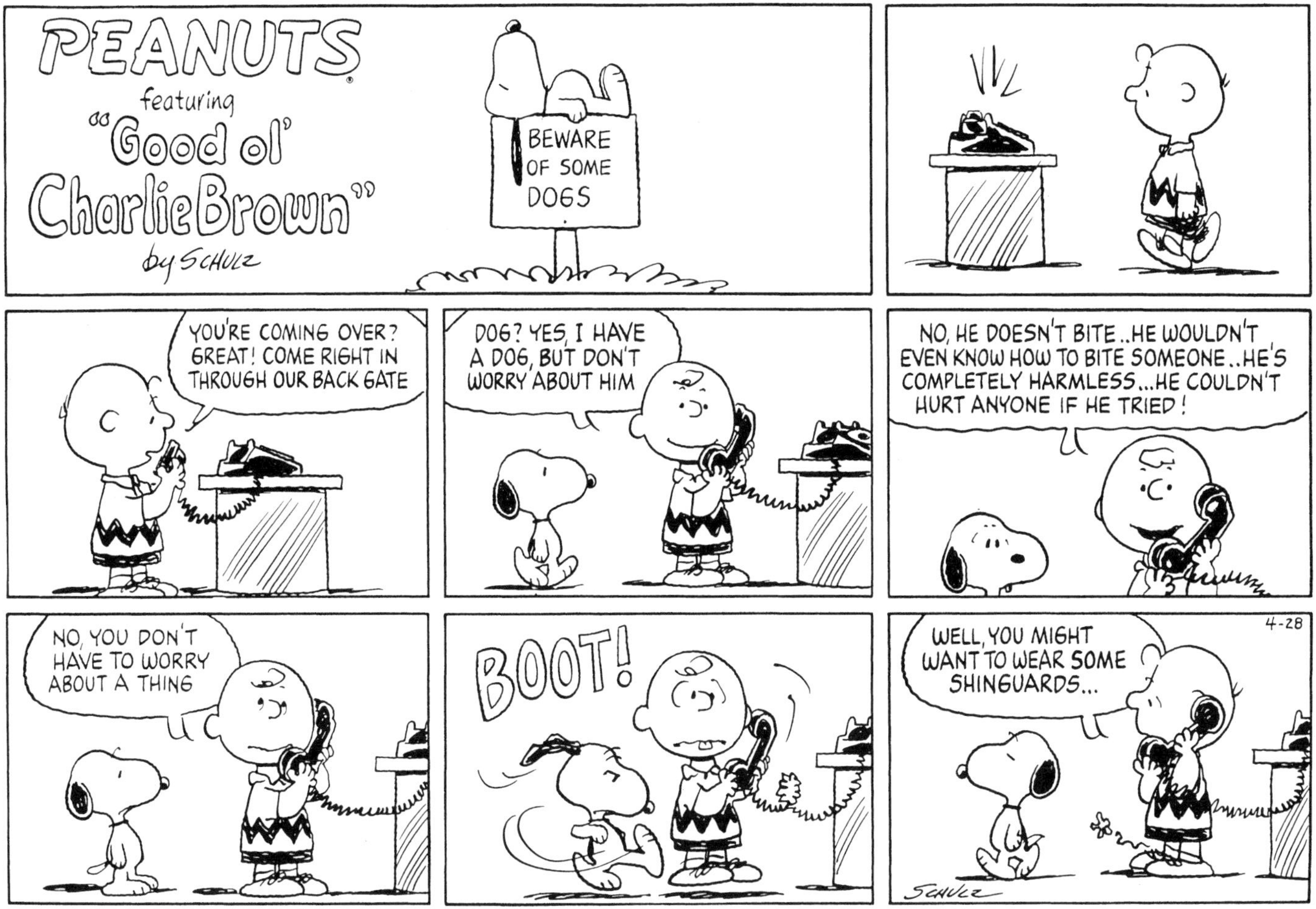

PEANUTS
featuring "Good ol' Charlie Brown" by SCHULZ
BEWARE OF SOME DOGS
YOU'RE COMING OVER? GREAT! COME RIGHT IN THROUGH OUR BACK GATE
DOG? YES, I HAVE A DOG, BUT DON'T WORRY ABOUT HIM
NO, HE DOESN'T BITE..HE WOULDN'T EVEN KNOW HOW TO BITE SOMEONE..HE'S COMPLETELY HARMLESS...HE COULDN'T HURT ANYONE IF HE TRIED!
NO, YOU DON'T HAVE TO WORRY ABOUT A THING
BOOT!
4-28
WELL, YOU MIGHT WANT TO WEAR SOME SHINGUARDS...
SCHULZ

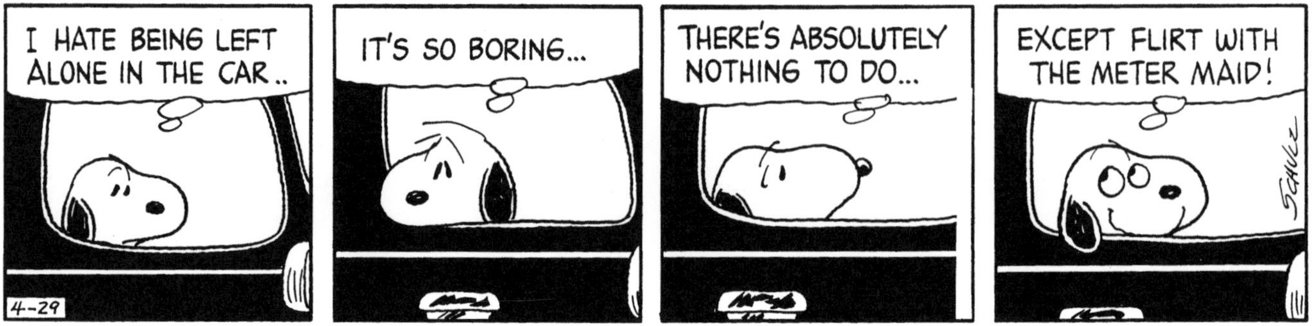
4-29
I HATE BEING LEFT ALONE IN THE CAR..
IT'S SO BORING...
THERE'S ABSOLUTELY NOTHING TO DO...
EXCEPT FLIRT WITH THE METER MAID!

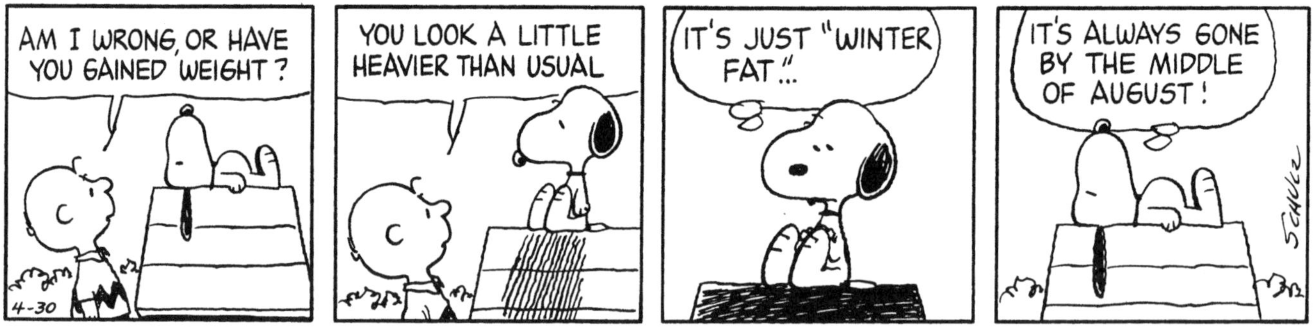
4-30
AM I WRONG, OR HAVE YOU GAINED WEIGHT?
YOU LOOK A LITTLE HEAVIER THAN USUAL
IT'S JUST "WINTER FAT."...
IT'S ALWAYS GONE BY THE MIDDLE OF AUGUST!

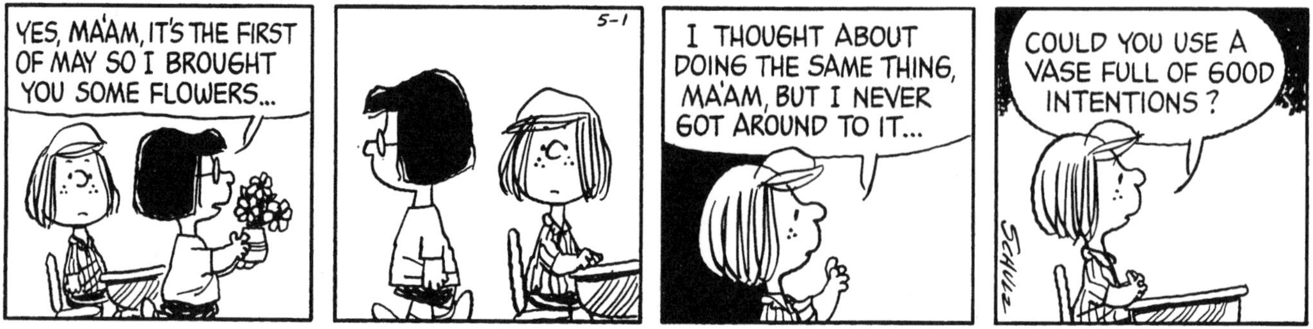
YES, MA'AM, IT'S THE FIRST OF MAY SO I BROUGHT YOU SOME FLOWERS...
5-1
I THOUGHT ABOUT DOING THE SAME THING, MA'AM, BUT I NEVER GOT AROUND TO IT...
COULD YOU USE A VASE FULL OF GOOD INTENTIONS?

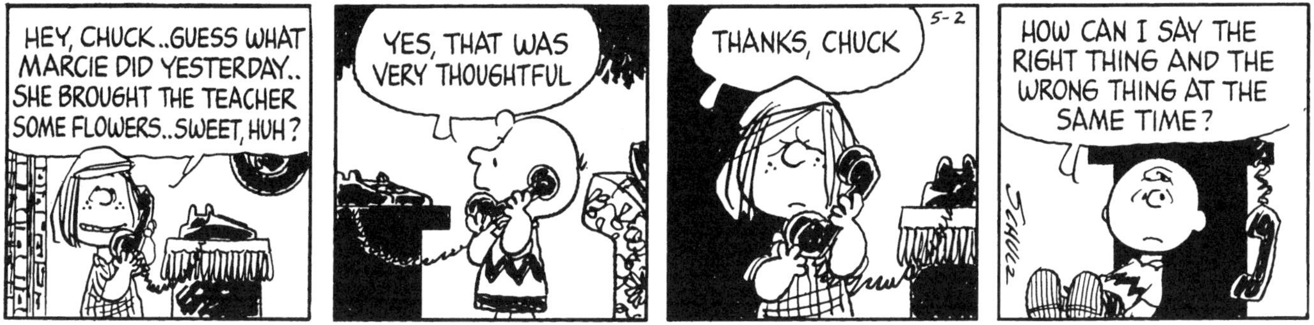
HEY, CHUCK..GUESS WHAT MARCIE DID YESTERDAY.. SHE BROUGHT THE TEACHER SOME FLOWERS..SWEET, HUH?
YES, THAT WAS VERY THOUGHTFUL
THANKS, CHUCK
5-2
HOW CAN I SAY THE RIGHT THING AND THE WRONG THING AT THE SAME TIME?
SCHULZ

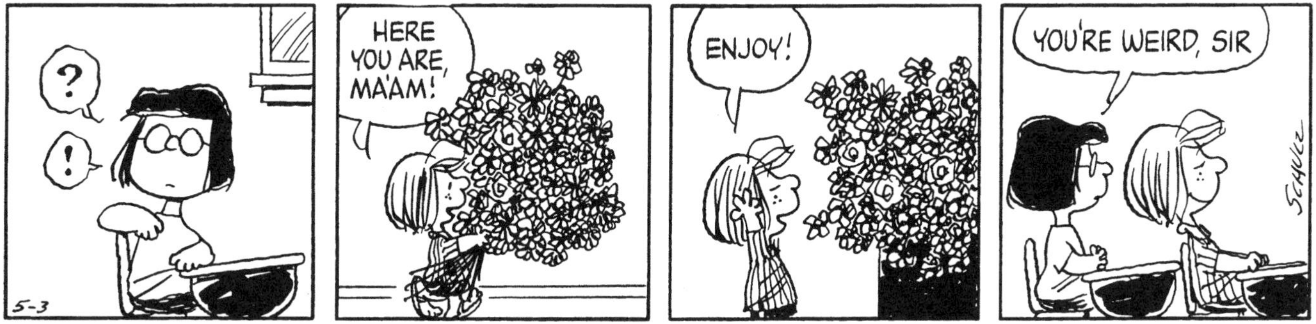
?
!
5-3
HERE YOU ARE, MA'AM!
ENJOY!
YOU'RE WEIRD, SIR
SCHULZ

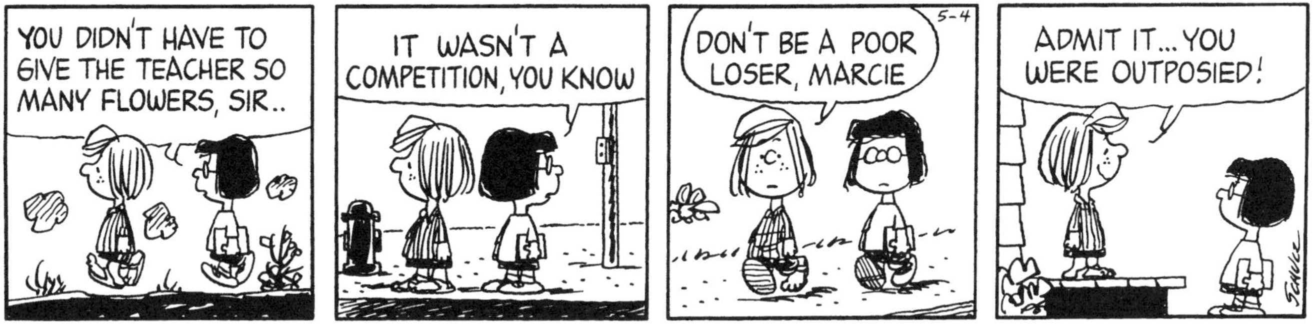
YOU DIDN'T HAVE TO GIVE THE TEACHER SO MANY FLOWERS, SIR..
IT WASN'T A COMPETITION, YOU KNOW
5-4
DON'T BE A POOR LOSER, MARCIE
ADMIT IT... YOU WERE OUTPOSIED!
SCHULZ

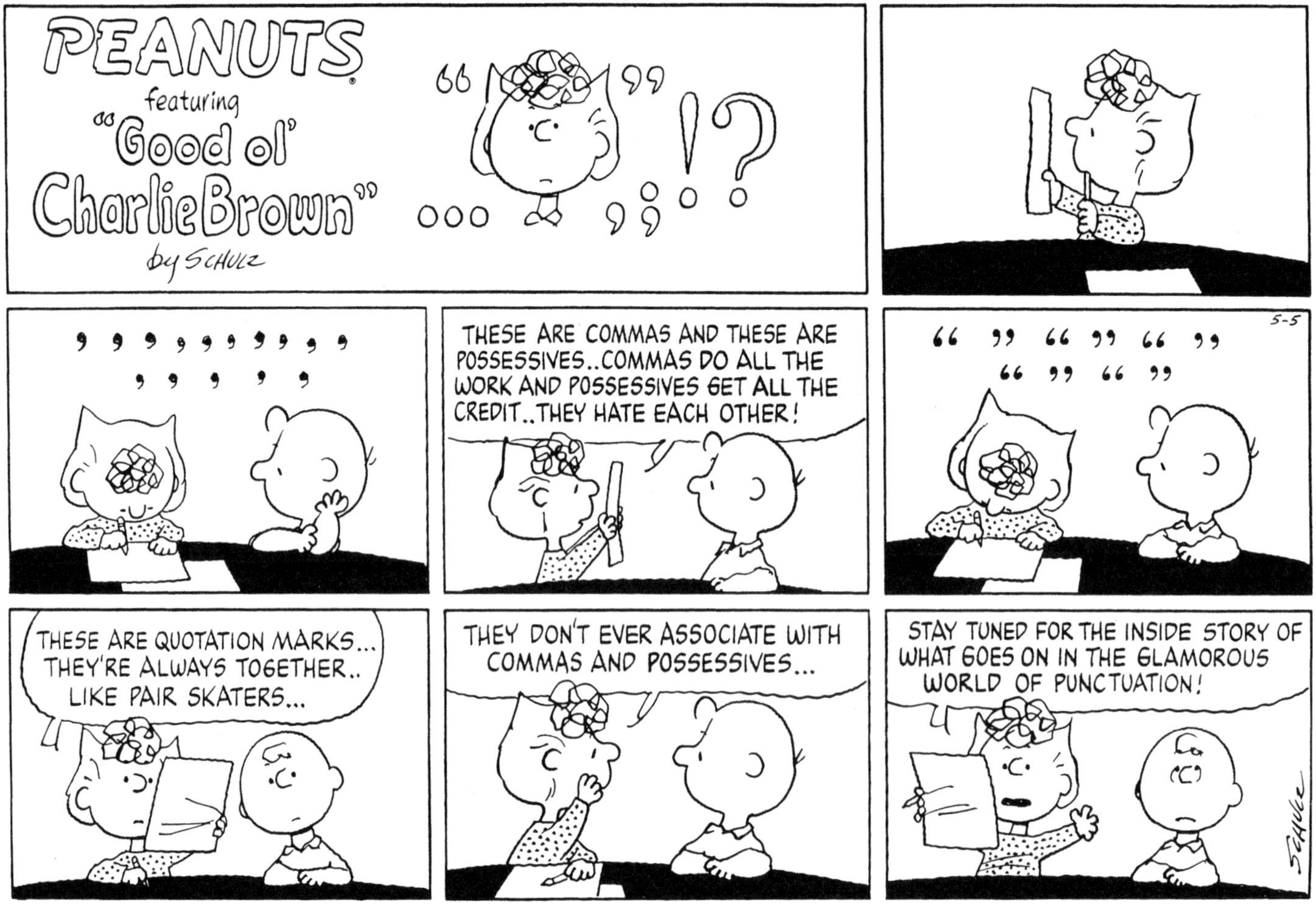
PEANUTS
featuring
"Good ol' Charlie Brown"
by SCHULZ
5-5
THESE ARE COMMAS AND THESE ARE POSSESSIVES..COMMAS DO ALL THE WORK AND POSSESSIVES GET ALL THE CREDIT..THEY HATE EACH OTHER!
THESE ARE QUOTATION MARKS... THEY'RE ALWAYS TOGETHER.. LIKE PAIR SKATERS...
THEY DON'T EVER ASSOCIATE WITH COMMAS AND POSSESSIVES...
STAY TUNED FOR THE INSIDE STORY OF WHAT GOES ON IN THE GLAMOROUS WORLD OF PUNCTUATION!
SCHULZ

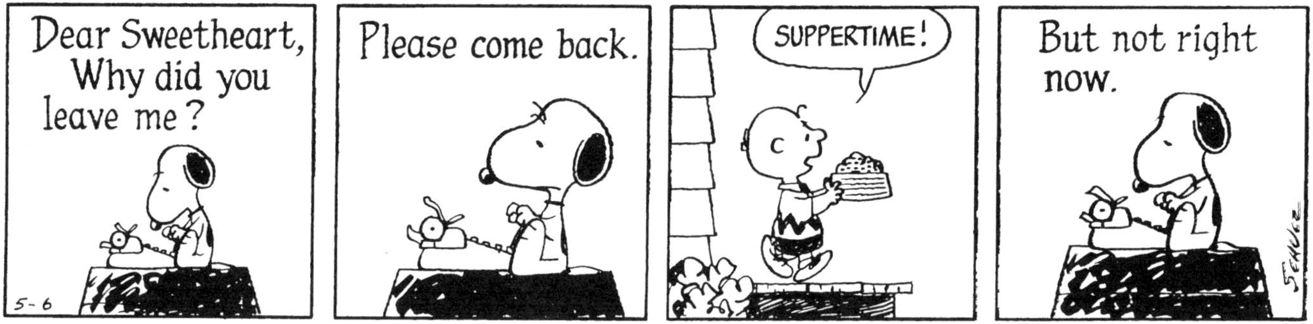
Dear Sweetheart, Why did you leave me?
5-6
Please come back.
SUPPERTIME!
But not right now.

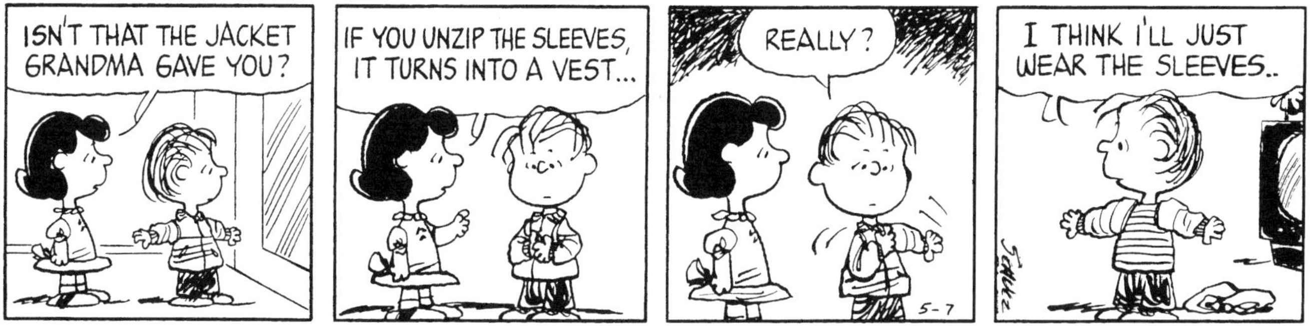
ISN'T THAT THE JACKET GRANDMA GAVE YOU?
IF YOU UNZIP THE SLEEVES, IT TURNS INTO A VEST...
REALLY?
5-7
I THINK I'LL JUST WEAR THE SLEEVES..

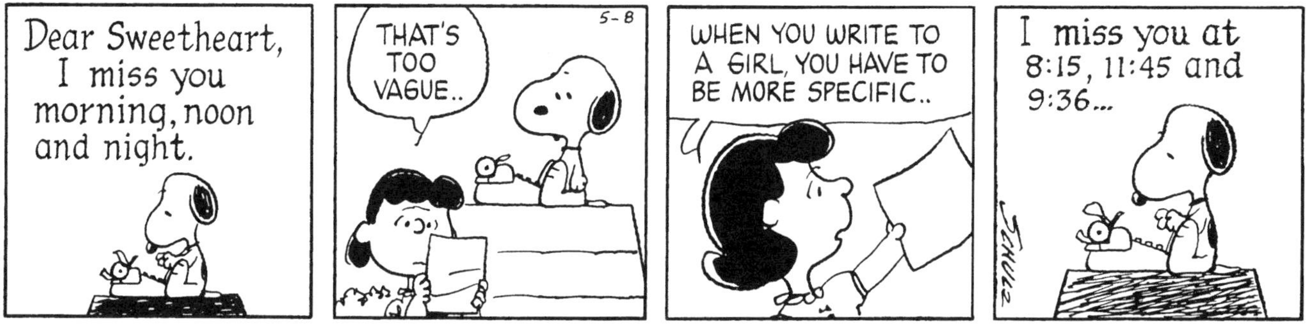
Dear Sweetheart, I miss you morning, noon and night.
5-8
THAT'S TOO VAGUE..
WHEN YOU WRITE TO A GIRL, YOU HAVE TO BE MORE SPECIFIC..
I miss you at 8:15, 11:45 and 9:36...

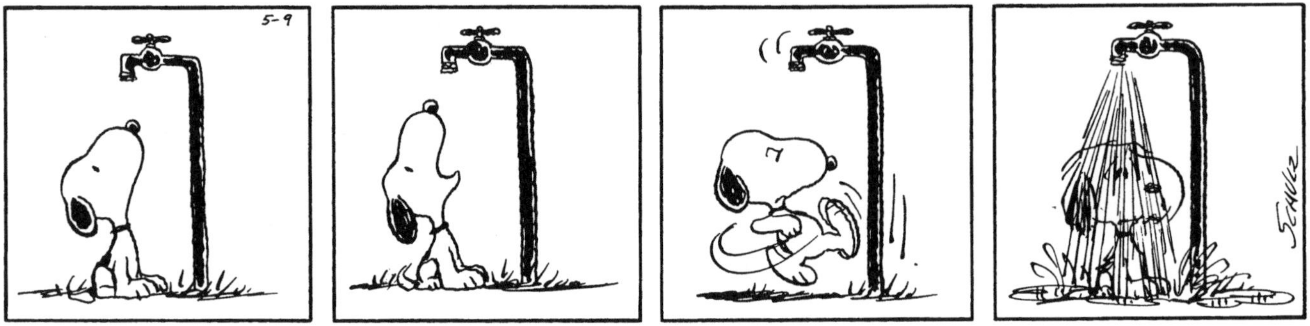
5-9

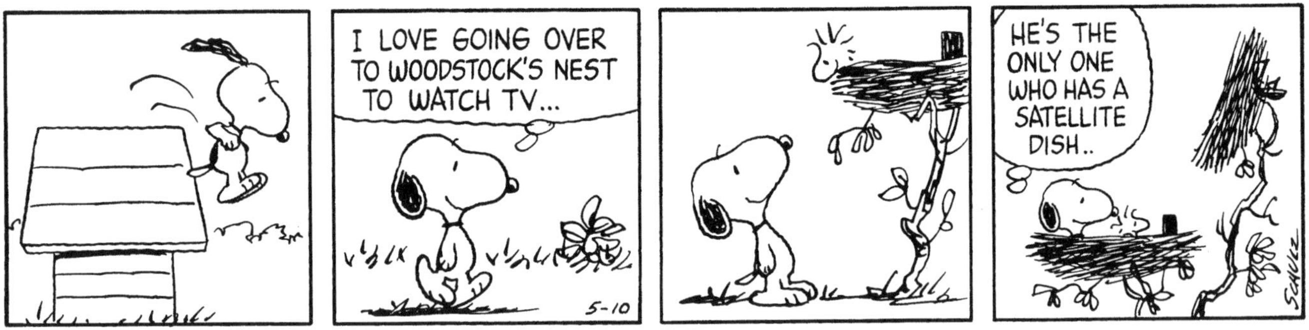
I LOVE GOING OVER TO WOODSTOCK'S NEST TO WATCH TV...
5-10
HE'S THE ONLY ONE WHO HAS A SATELLITE DISH..

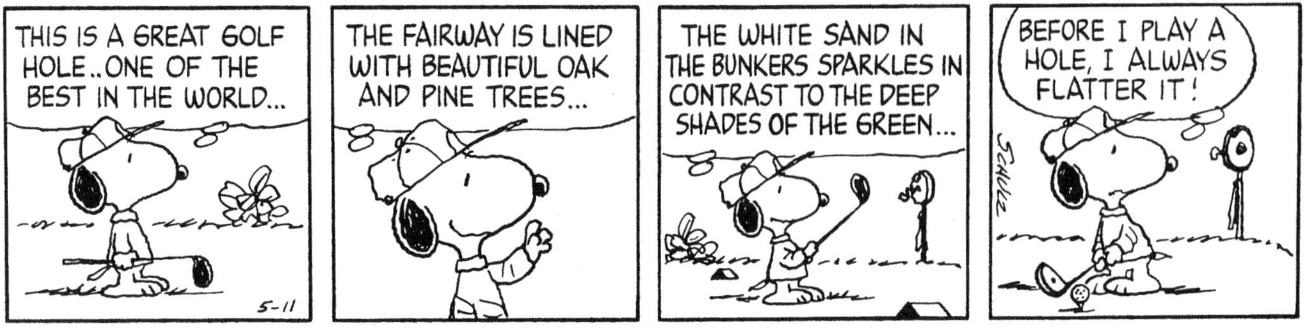
THIS IS A GREAT GOLF HOLE..ONE OF THE BEST IN THE WORLD...
5-11
THE FAIRWAY IS LINED WITH BEAUTIFUL OAK AND PINE TREES...
THE WHITE SAND IN THE BUNKERS SPARKLES IN CONTRAST TO THE DEEP SHADES OF THE GREEN...
BEFORE I PLAY A HOLE, I ALWAYS FLATTER IT!

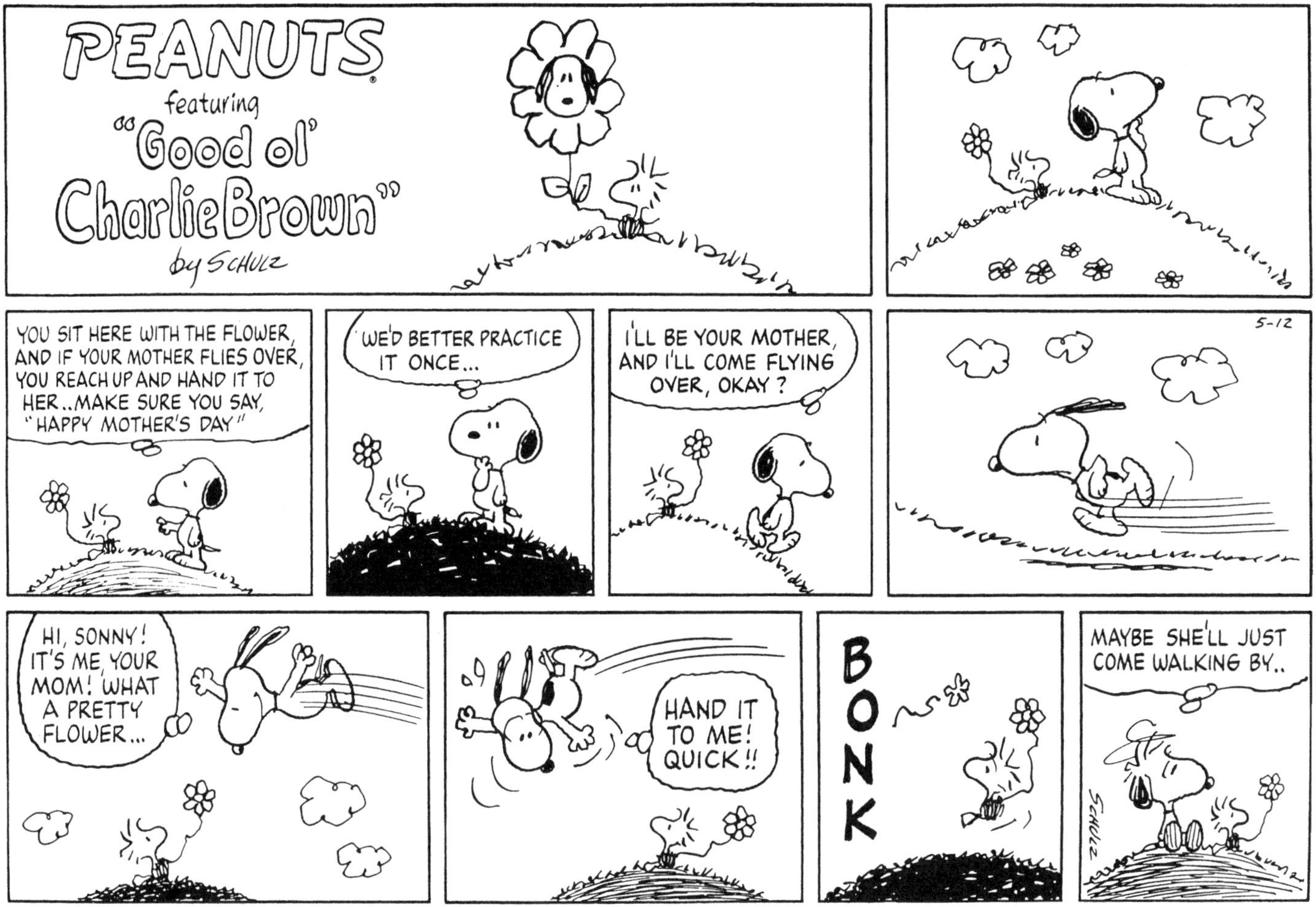
PEANUTS
featuring
"Good ol' CharlieBrown"
by SCHULZ
YOU SIT HERE WITH THE FLOWER, AND IF YOUR MOTHER FLIES OVER, YOU REACH UP AND HAND IT TO HER..MAKE SURE YOU SAY, "HAPPY MOTHER'S DAY"
WE'D BETTER PRACTICE IT ONCE...
I'LL BE YOUR MOTHER, AND I'LL COME FLYING OVER, OKAY ?
5-12
HI, SONNY! IT'S ME, YOUR MOM! WHAT A PRETTY FLOWER...
HAND IT TO ME! QUICK!!
BONK
MAYBE SHE'LL JUST COME WALKING BY..
SCHULZ

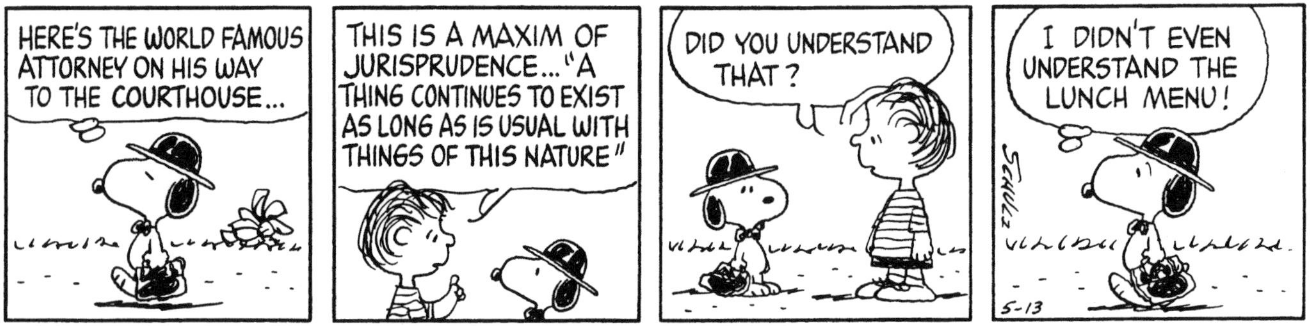
HERE'S THE WORLD FAMOUS ATTORNEY ON HIS WAY TO THE COURTHOUSE...
THIS IS A MAXIM OF JURISPRUDENCE..."A THING CONTINUES TO EXIST AS LONG AS IS USUAL WITH THINGS OF THIS NATURE"
DID YOU UNDERSTAND THAT?
I DIDN'T EVEN UNDERSTAND THE LUNCH MENU!
5-13

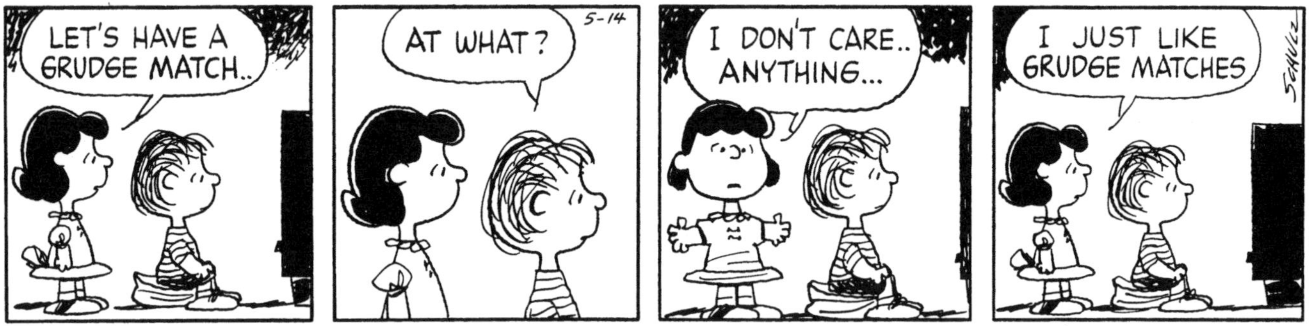
LET'S HAVE A GRUDGE MATCH..
AT WHAT?
5-14
I DON'T CARE.. ANYTHING...
I JUST LIKE GRUDGE MATCHES

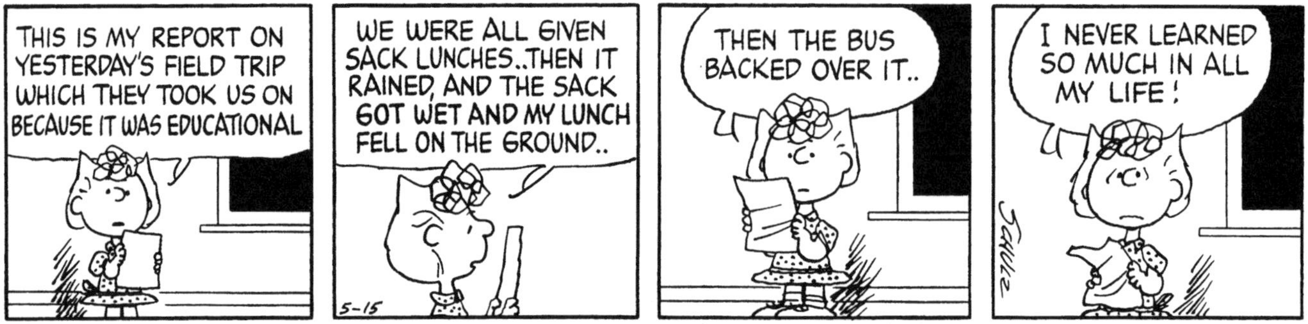
THIS IS MY REPORT ON YESTERDAY'S FIELD TRIP WHICH THEY TOOK US ON BECAUSE IT WAS EDUCATIONAL
WE WERE ALL GIVEN SACK LUNCHES..THEN IT RAINED, AND THE SACK GOT WET AND MY LUNCH FELL ON THE GROUND..
5-15
THEN THE BUS BACKED OVER IT..
I NEVER LEARNED SO MUCH IN ALL MY LIFE!

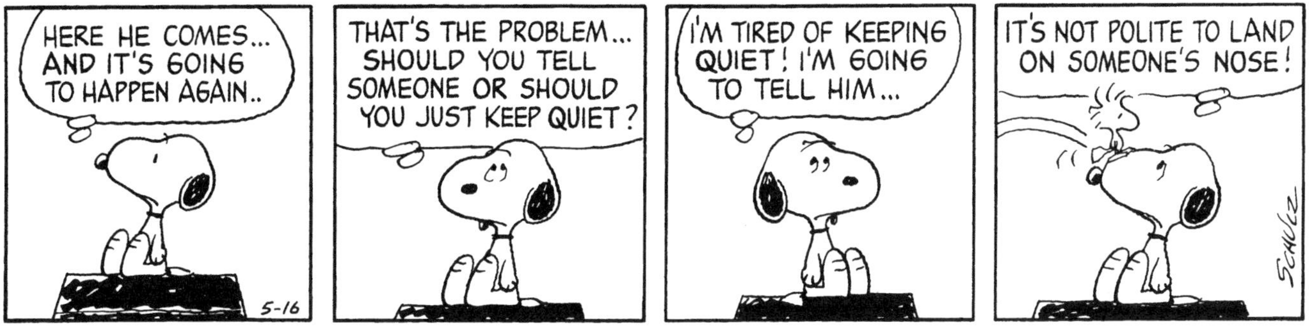
HERE HE COMES... AND IT'S GOING TO HAPPEN AGAIN..
5-16
THAT'S THE PROBLEM... SHOULD YOU TELL SOMEONE OR SHOULD YOU JUST KEEP QUIET?
I'M TIRED OF KEEPING QUIET! I'M GOING TO TELL HIM...
IT'S NOT POLITE TO LAND ON SOMEONE'S NOSE!
SCHULZ

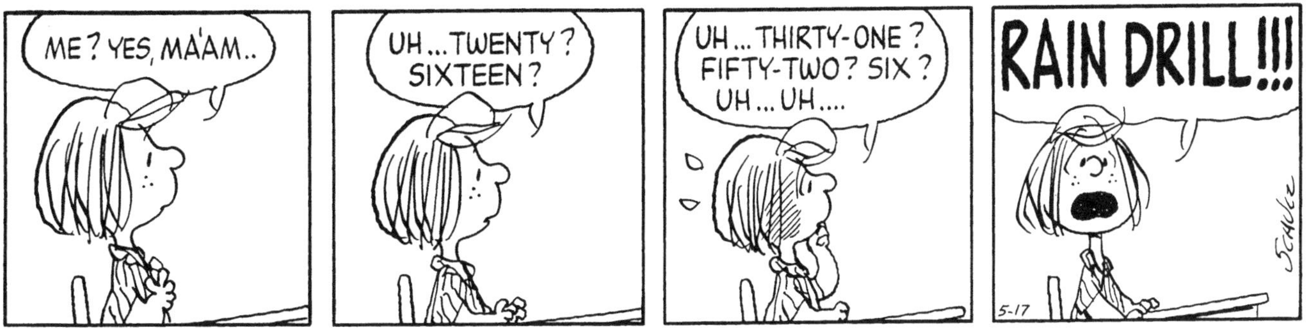
ME? YES, MA'AM..
UH... TWENTY? SIXTEEN?
UH... THIRTY-ONE? FIFTY-TWO? SIX? UH... UH....
RAIN DRILL!!!
5-17
SCHULZ

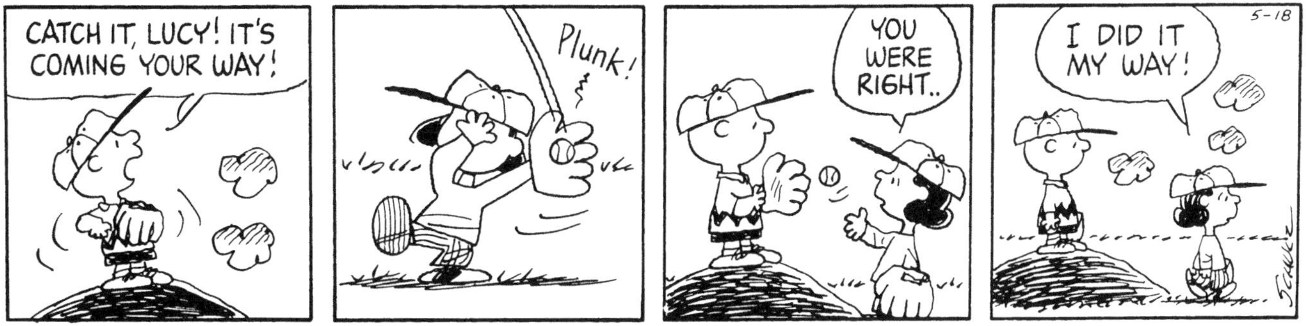
CATCH IT, LUCY! IT'S COMING YOUR WAY!
Plunk!
YOU WERE RIGHT..
5-18
I DID IT MY WAY!
SCHULZ

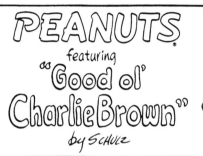

PEANUTS
featuring
"Good ol' Charlie Brown"
by Schulz

YOU'RE KIDDING

NO, I'M SERIOUS

YOU DON'T CARE ANYTHING ABOUT ANYBODY...

YOU NEVER SHOW ANY INTEREST IN WHAT ANYONE ELSE IS DOING..YOU NEVER ASK QUESTIONS...

YOU NEVER ASK ME WHAT I'M READING, HOW I'M DOING IN SCHOOL, WHERE I GOT MY NEW SHOES...

YOU NEVER ASK ME WHAT I THINK ABOUT SOMETHING, OR WHAT I BELIEVE, OR WHAT I KNOW, OR WHERE I'M GOING, OR WHERE I'VE BEEN OR ANYTHING!

5-19

IF YOU'RE GOING TO SHOW INTEREST IN OTHER PEOPLE, YOU HAVE TO ASK QUESTIONS...

HOW HAVE YOU BEEN?

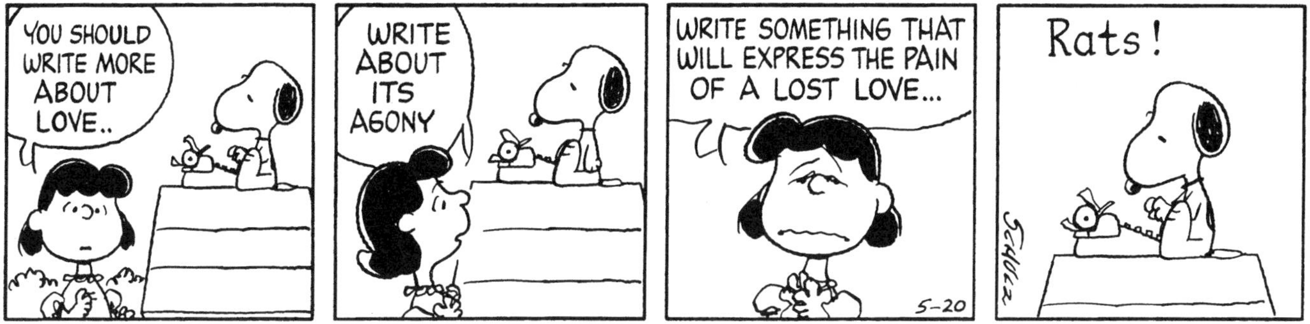
YOU SHOULD WRITE MORE ABOUT LOVE..
WRITE ABOUT ITS AGONY
WRITE SOMETHING THAT WILL EXPRESS THE PAIN OF A LOST LOVE...
5-20
Rats!
SCHULZ

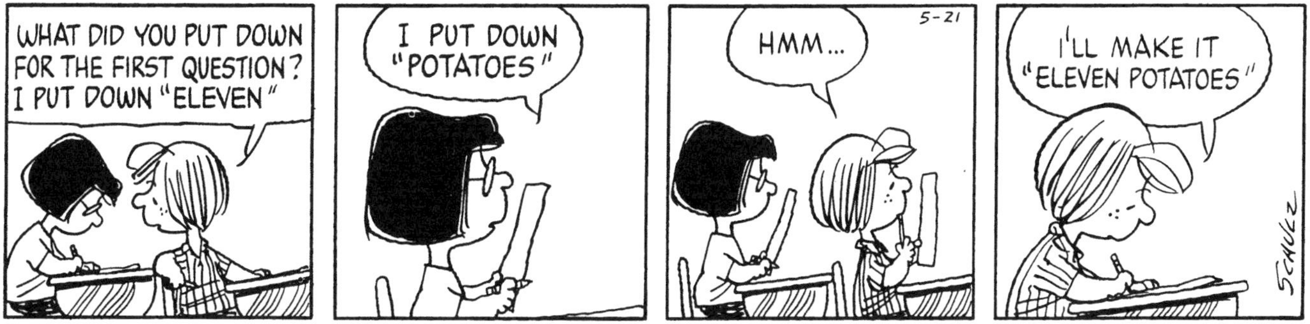
WHAT DID YOU PUT DOWN FOR THE FIRST QUESTION? I PUT DOWN "ELEVEN"
I PUT DOWN "POTATOES"
5-21
HMM...
I'LL MAKE IT "ELEVEN POTATOES"
SCHULZ

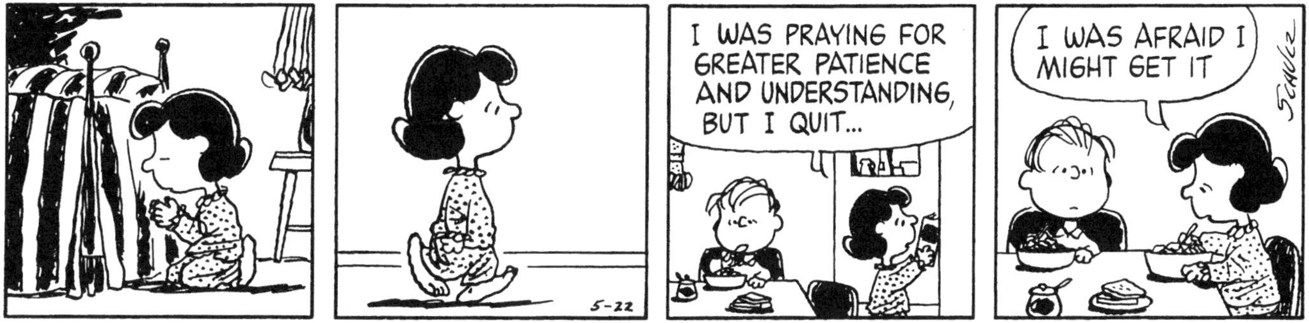
5-22
I WAS PRAYING FOR GREATER PATIENCE AND UNDERSTANDING, BUT I QUIT...
I WAS AFRAID I MIGHT GET IT
SCHULZ

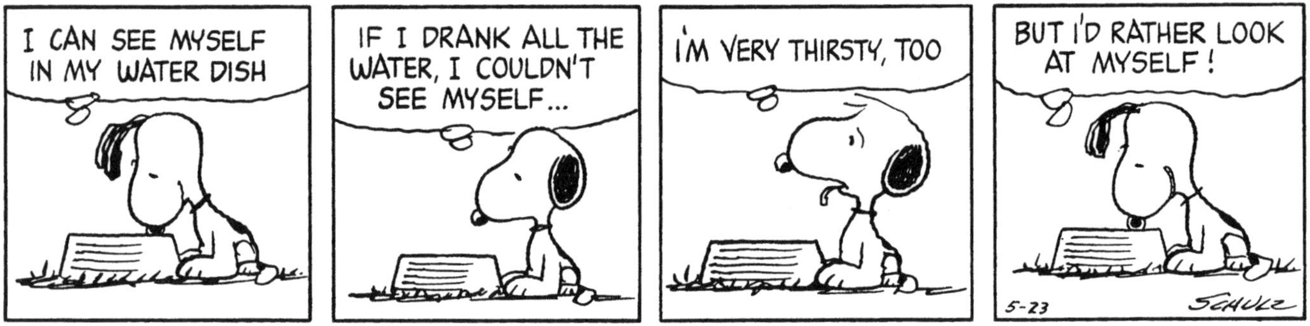
I CAN SEE MYSELF IN MY WATER DISH
IF I DRANK ALL THE WATER, I COULDN'T SEE MYSELF...
I'M VERY THIRSTY, TOO
BUT I'D RATHER LOOK AT MYSELF!
5-23
SCHULZ

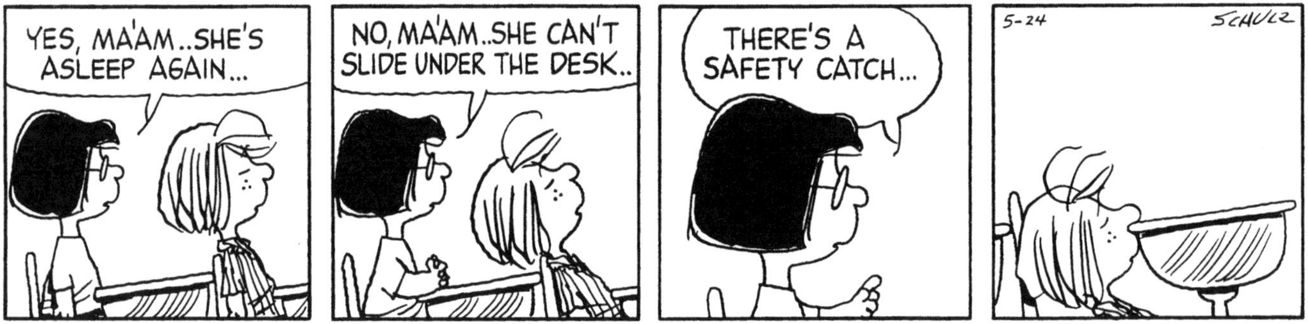
YES, MA'AM..SHE'S ASLEEP AGAIN...
NO, MA'AM..SHE CAN'T SLIDE UNDER THE DESK..
THERE'S A SAFETY CATCH...
5-24
SCHULZ

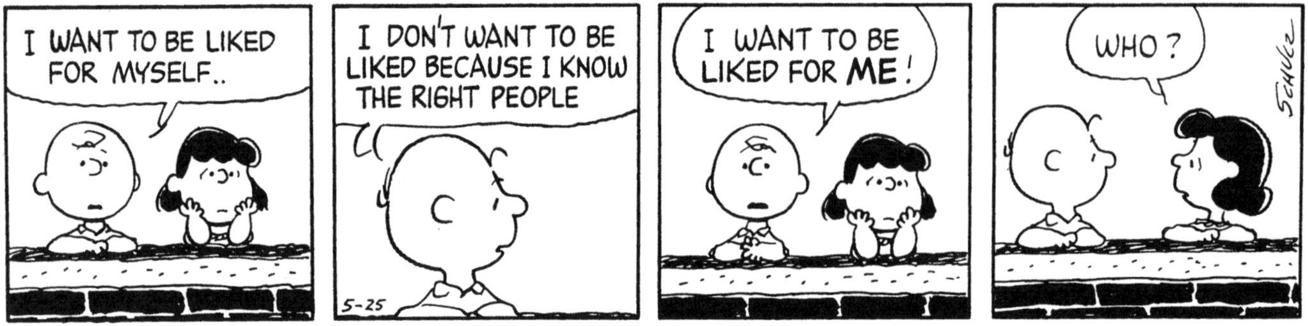
I WANT TO BE LIKED FOR MYSELF..
I DON'T WANT TO BE LIKED BECAUSE I KNOW THE RIGHT PEOPLE
5-25
I WANT TO BE LIKED FOR ME!
WHO?
SCHULZ

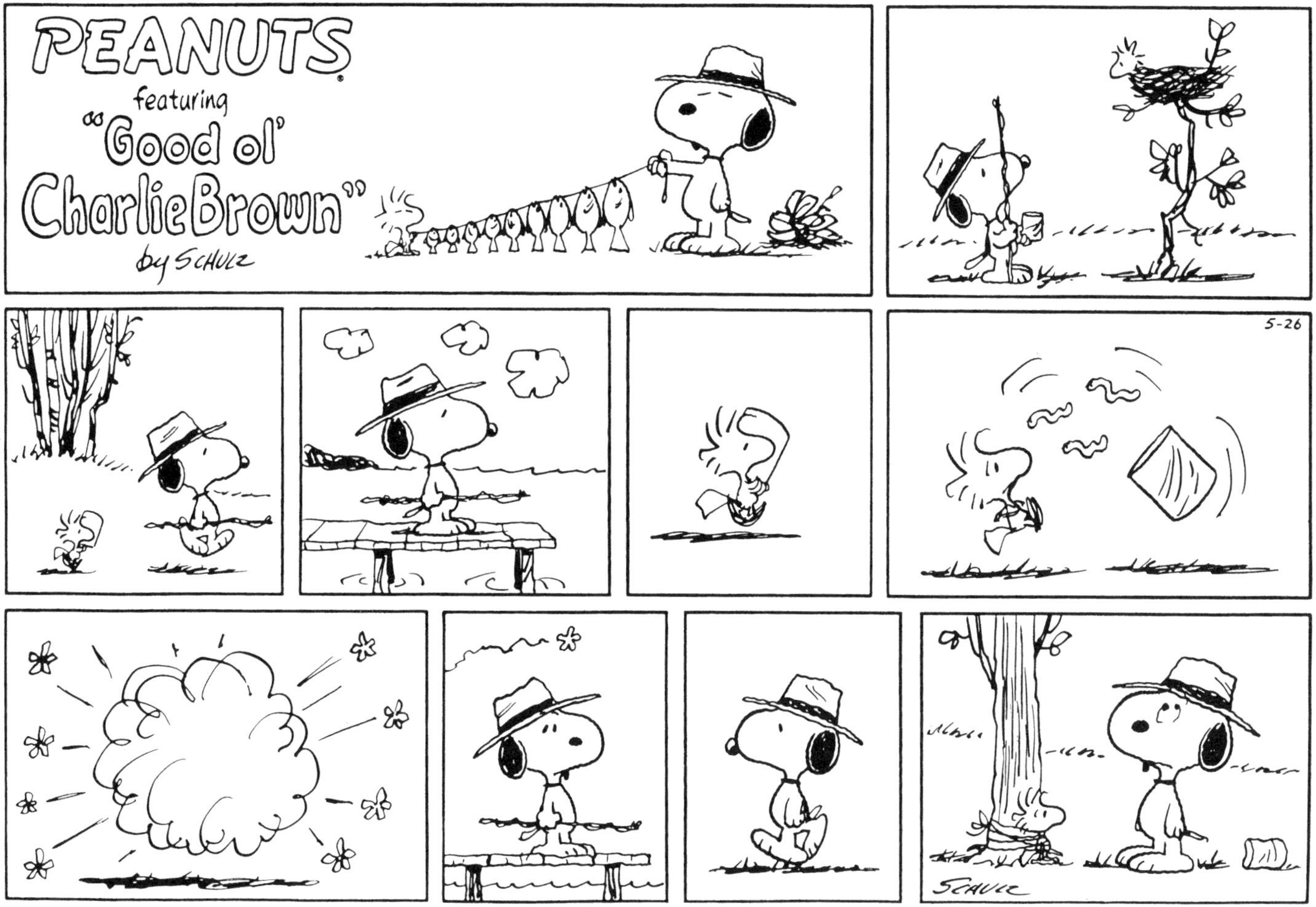
PEANUTS
featuring
"Good ol' Charlie Brown"
by SCHULZ
5-26
SCHULZ

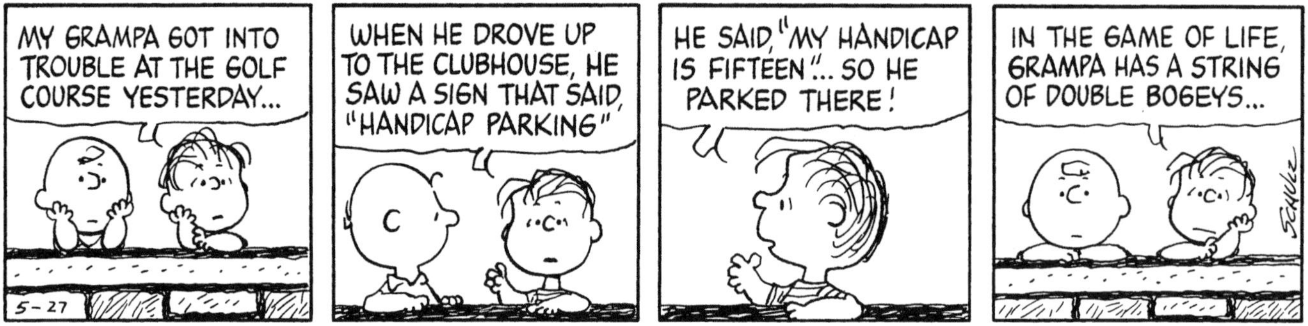
5-27
MY GRAMPA GOT INTO TROUBLE AT THE GOLF COURSE YESTERDAY...
WHEN HE DROVE UP TO THE CLUBHOUSE, HE SAW A SIGN THAT SAID, "HANDICAP PARKING"
HE SAID, "MY HANDICAP IS FIFTEEN"... SO HE PARKED THERE!
IN THE GAME OF LIFE, GRAMPA HAS A STRING OF DOUBLE BOGEYS...
SCHULZ

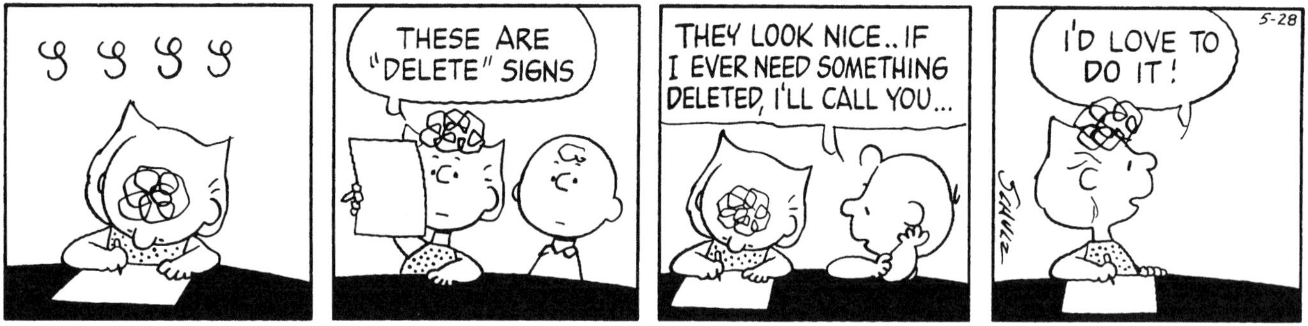
THESE ARE "DELETE" SIGNS
THEY LOOK NICE.. IF I EVER NEED SOMETHING DELETED, I'LL CALL YOU...
SCHULZ
5-28
I'D LOVE TO DO IT!

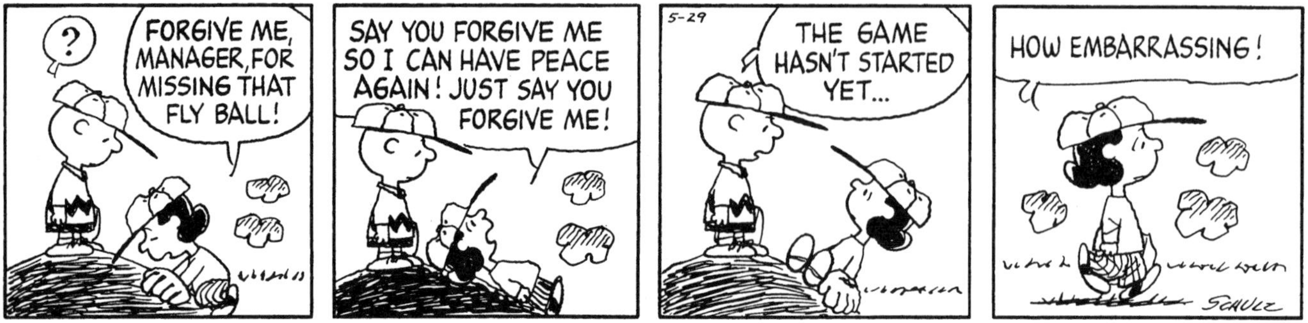
?
FORGIVE ME, MANAGER, FOR MISSING THAT FLY BALL!
SAY YOU FORGIVE ME SO I CAN HAVE PEACE AGAIN! JUST SAY YOU FORGIVE ME!
5-29
THE GAME HASN'T STARTED YET...
HOW EMBARRASSING!
SCHULZ

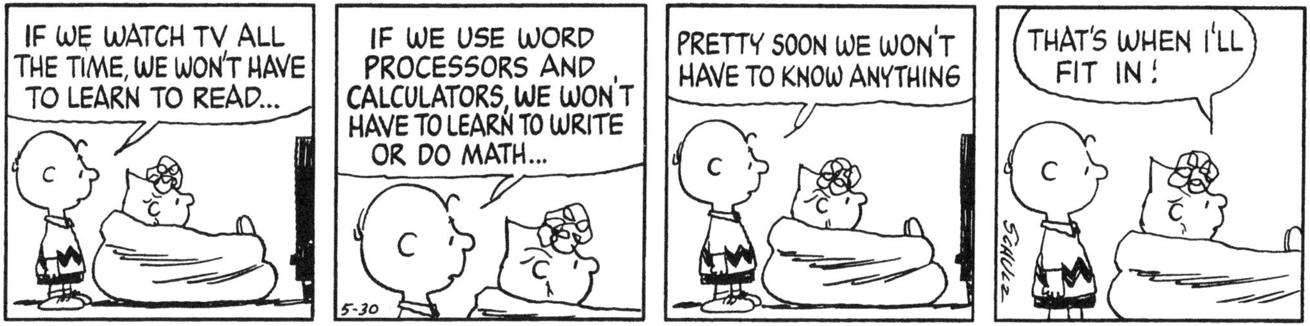
IF WE WATCH TV ALL THE TIME, WE WON'T HAVE TO LEARN TO READ...
IF WE USE WORD PROCESSORS AND CALCULATORS, WE WON'T HAVE TO LEARN TO WRITE OR DO MATH...
5-30
PRETTY SOON WE WON'T HAVE TO KNOW ANYTHING
THAT'S WHEN I'LL FIT IN!

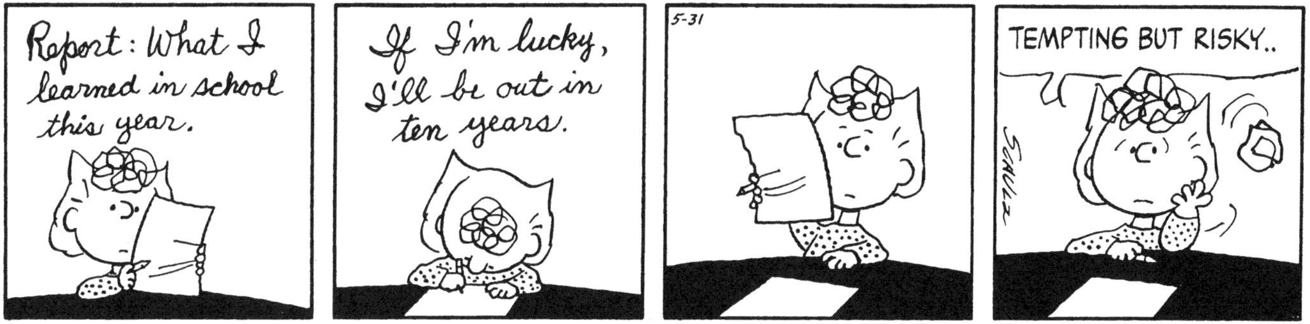
Report: What I learned in school this year.
If I'm lucky, I'll be out in ten years.
5-31
TEMPTING BUT RISKY..

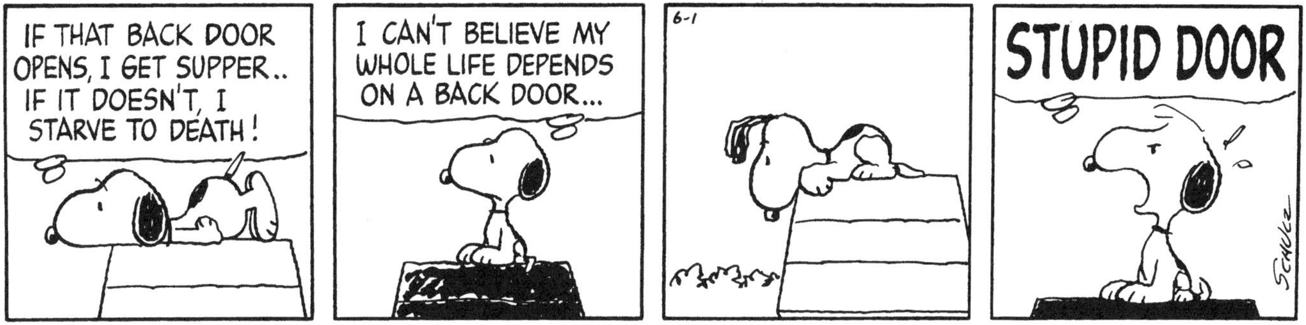
IF THAT BACK DOOR OPENS, I GET SUPPER.. IF IT DOESN'T, I STARVE TO DEATH!
I CAN'T BELIEVE MY WHOLE LIFE DEPENDS ON A BACK DOOR...
6-1
STUPID DOOR

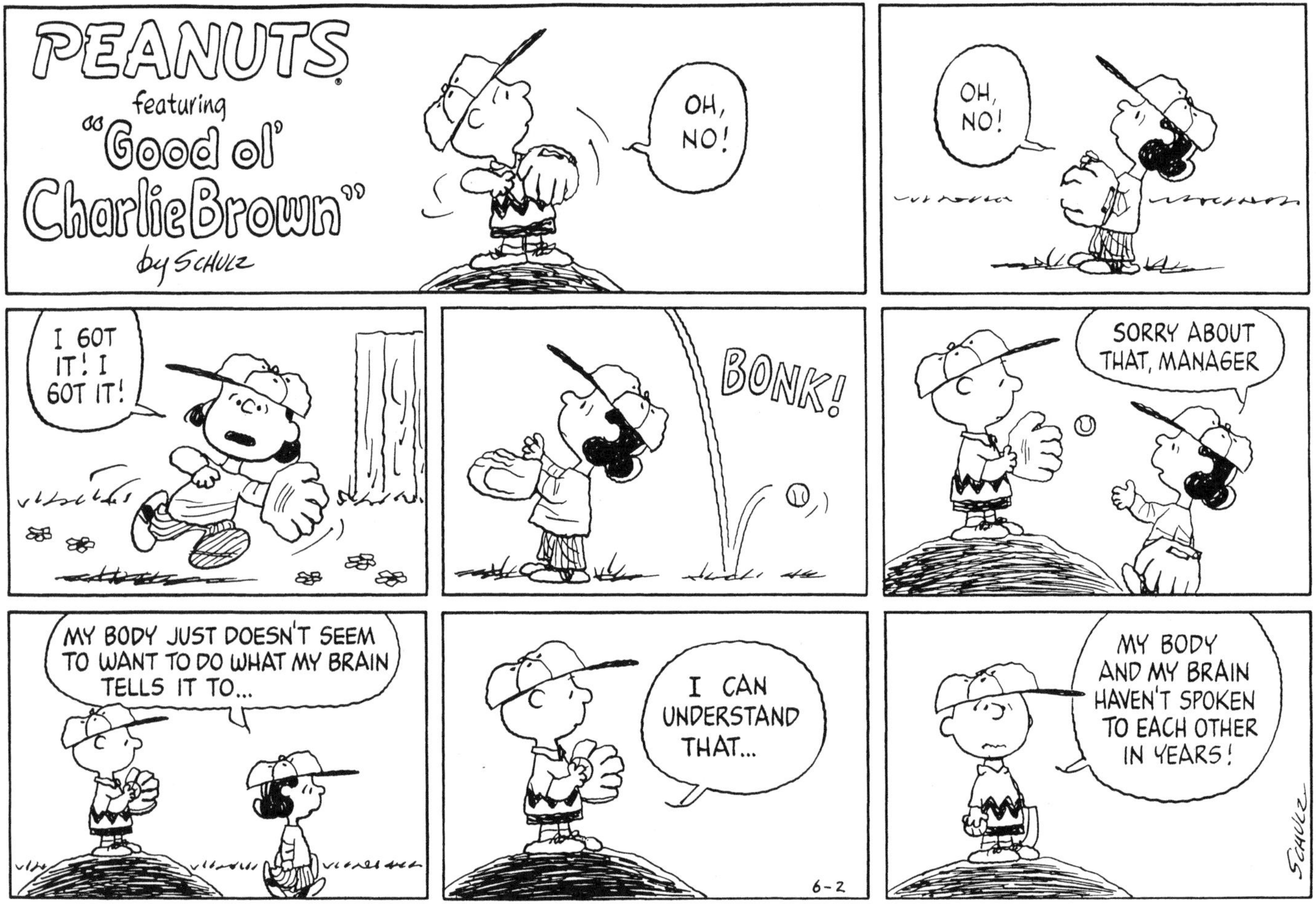
PEANUTS
featuring "Good ol' Charlie Brown"
by SCHULZ
OH, NO!
OH, NO!
I GOT IT! I GOT IT!
BONK!
SORRY ABOUT THAT, MANAGER
MY BODY JUST DOESN'T SEEM TO WANT TO DO WHAT MY BRAIN TELLS IT TO...
I CAN UNDERSTAND THAT...
6-2
MY BODY AND MY BRAIN HAVEN'T SPOKEN TO EACH OTHER IN YEARS!
SCHULZ

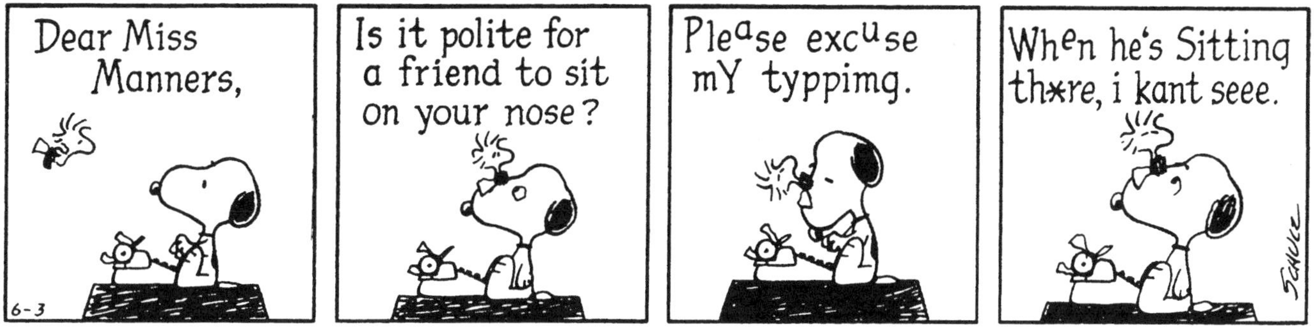
Dear Miss Manners,
Is it polite for a friend to sit on your nose?
Please excuse mY typpimg.
When he's Sitting th*re, i kant seee.
6-3
SCHULZ

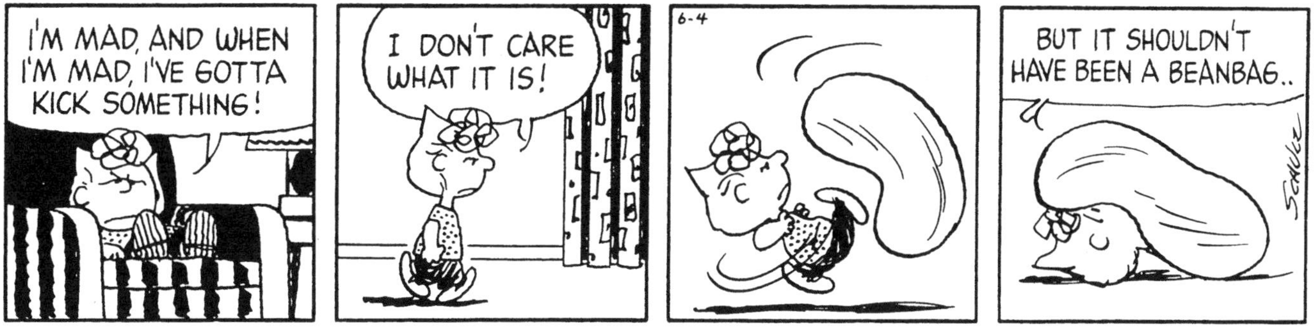
I'M MAD, AND WHEN I'M MAD, I'VE GOTTA KICK SOMETHING!
I DON'T CARE WHAT IT IS!
6-4
BUT IT SHOULDN'T HAVE BEEN A BEANBAG..
SCHULZ

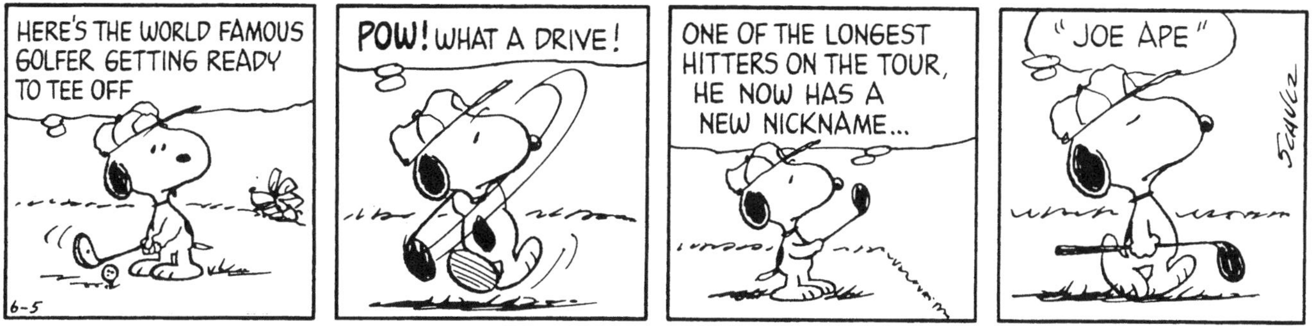
HERE'S THE WORLD FAMOUS GOLFER GETTING READY TO TEE OFF
6-5
POW! WHAT A DRIVE!
ONE OF THE LONGEST HITTERS ON THE TOUR, HE NOW HAS A NEW NICKNAME...
"JOE APE"
SCHULZ

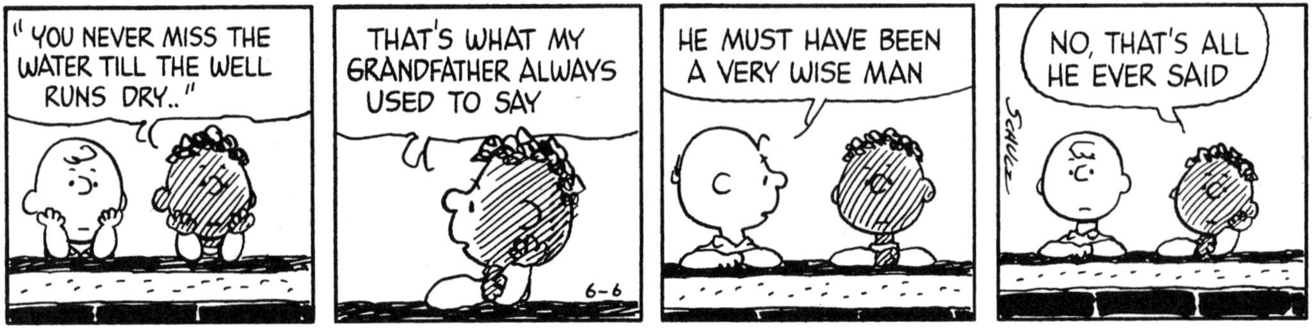
"YOU NEVER MISS THE WATER TILL THE WELL RUNS DRY.."
THAT'S WHAT MY GRANDFATHER ALWAYS USED TO SAY
6-6
HE MUST HAVE BEEN A VERY WISE MAN
NO, THAT'S ALL HE EVER SAID
SCHULZ

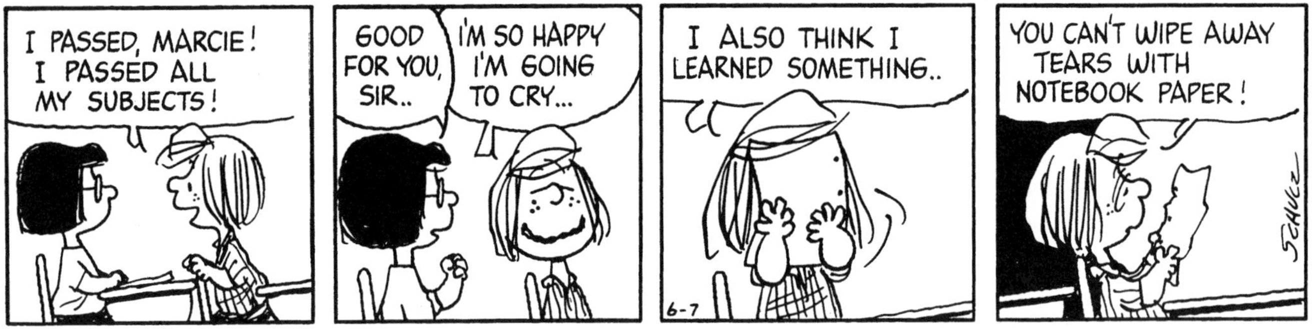
I PASSED, MARCIE! I PASSED ALL MY SUBJECTS!
GOOD FOR YOU, SIR..
I'M SO HAPPY I'M GOING TO CRY...
I ALSO THINK I LEARNED SOMETHING..
6-7
YOU CAN'T WIPE AWAY TEARS WITH NOTEBOOK PAPER!
SCHULZ

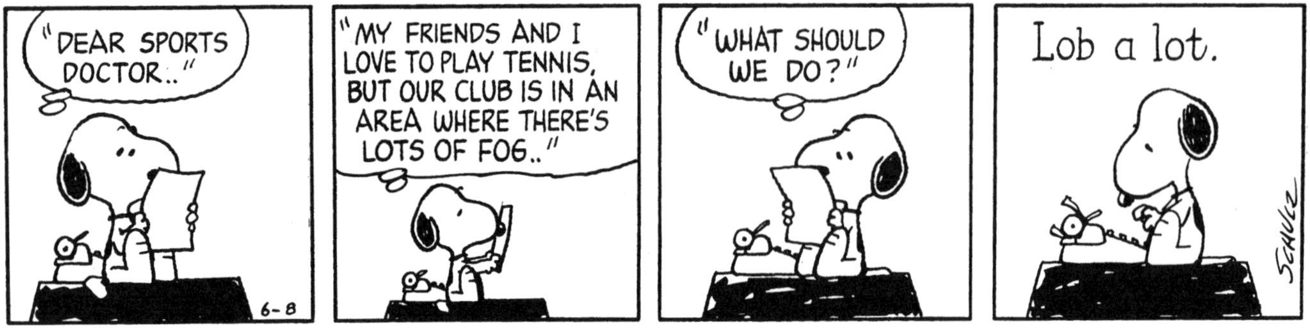
"DEAR SPORTS DOCTOR.."
6-8
"MY FRIENDS AND I LOVE TO PLAY TENNIS, BUT OUR CLUB IS IN AN AREA WHERE THERE'S LOTS OF FOG.."
"WHAT SHOULD WE DO?"
Lob a lot.
SCHULZ

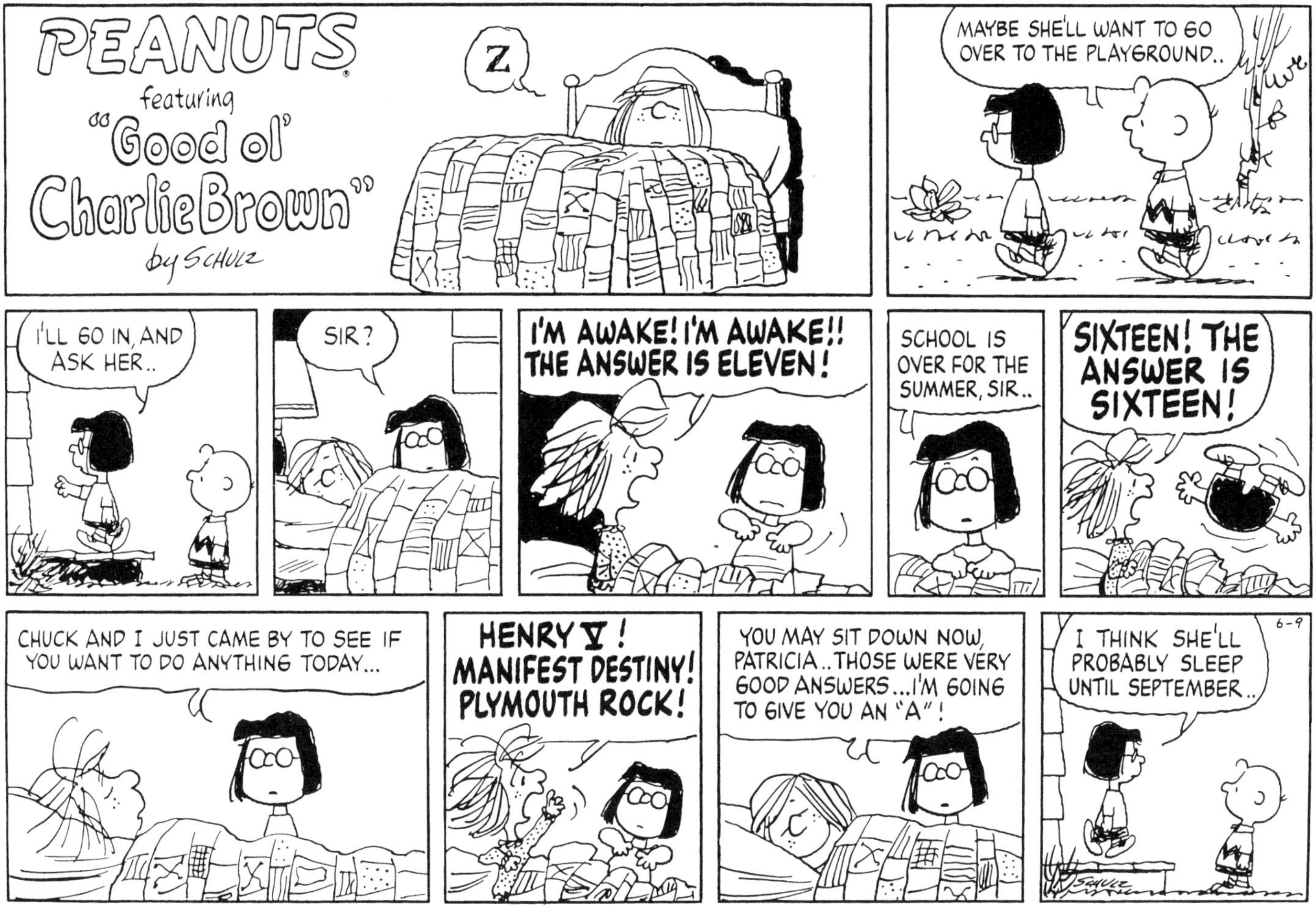
PEANUTS
featuring "Good ol' Charlie Brown"
by SCHULZ
Z
MAYBE SHE'LL WANT TO GO OVER TO THE PLAYGROUND..
I'LL GO IN, AND ASK HER..
SIR?
I'M AWAKE! I'M AWAKE!! THE ANSWER IS ELEVEN!
SCHOOL IS OVER FOR THE SUMMER, SIR..
SIXTEEN! THE ANSWER IS SIXTEEN!
CHUCK AND I JUST CAME BY TO SEE IF YOU WANT TO DO ANYTHING TODAY...
HENRY V! MANIFEST DESTINY! PLYMOUTH ROCK!
YOU MAY SIT DOWN NOW, PATRICIA..THOSE WERE VERY GOOD ANSWERS...I'M GOING TO GIVE YOU AN "A"!
6-9
I THINK SHE'LL PROBABLY SLEEP UNTIL SEPTEMBER..
SCHULZ

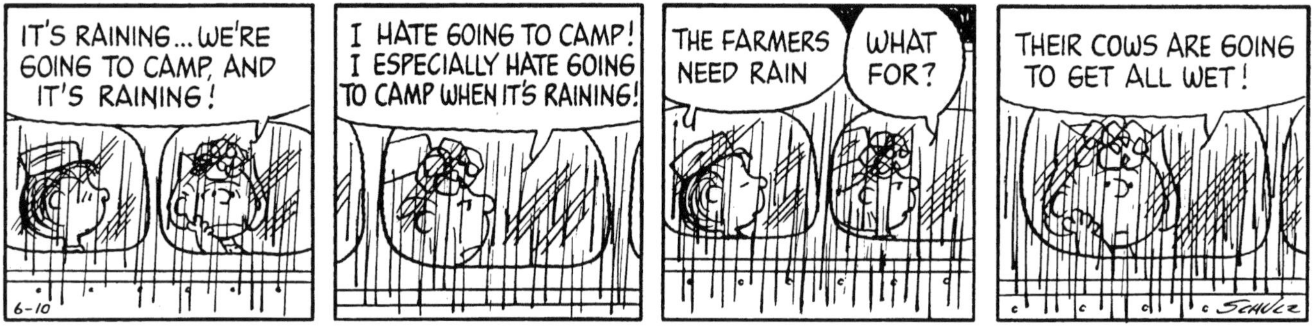
IT'S RAINING... WE'RE GOING TO CAMP, AND IT'S RAINING!
I HATE GOING TO CAMP! I ESPECIALLY HATE GOING TO CAMP WHEN IT'S RAINING!
THE FARMERS NEED RAIN
WHAT FOR?
THEIR COWS ARE GOING TO GET ALL WET!

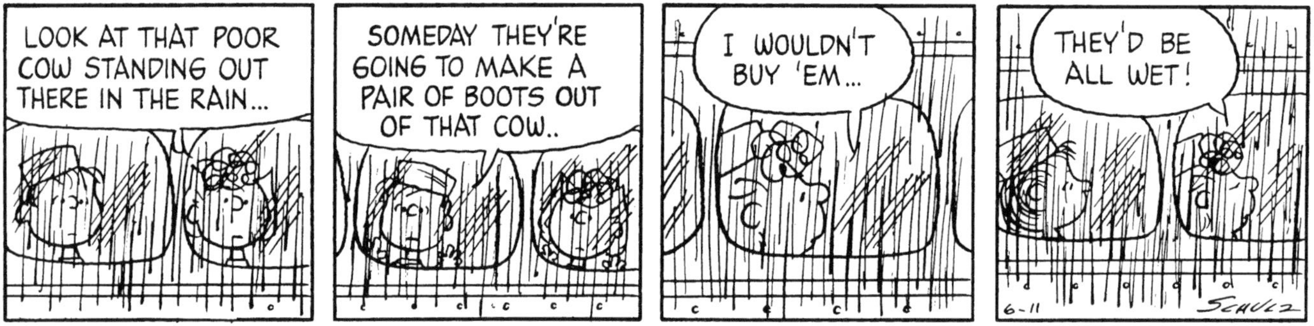
LOOK AT THAT POOR COW STANDING OUT THERE IN THE RAIN...
SOMEDAY THEY'RE GOING TO MAKE A PAIR OF BOOTS OUT OF THAT COW..
I WOULDN'T BUY 'EM...
THEY'D BE ALL WET!

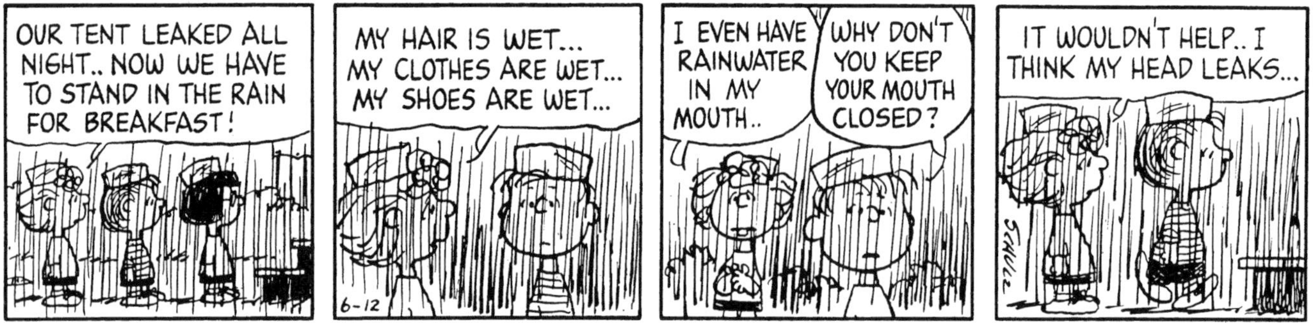
OUR TENT LEAKED ALL NIGHT.. NOW WE HAVE TO STAND IN THE RAIN FOR BREAKFAST!
MY HAIR IS WET... MY CLOTHES ARE WET... MY SHOES ARE WET...
I EVEN HAVE RAINWATER IN MY MOUTH..
WHY DON'T YOU KEEP YOUR MOUTH CLOSED?
IT WOULDN'T HELP.. I THINK MY HEAD LEAKS...

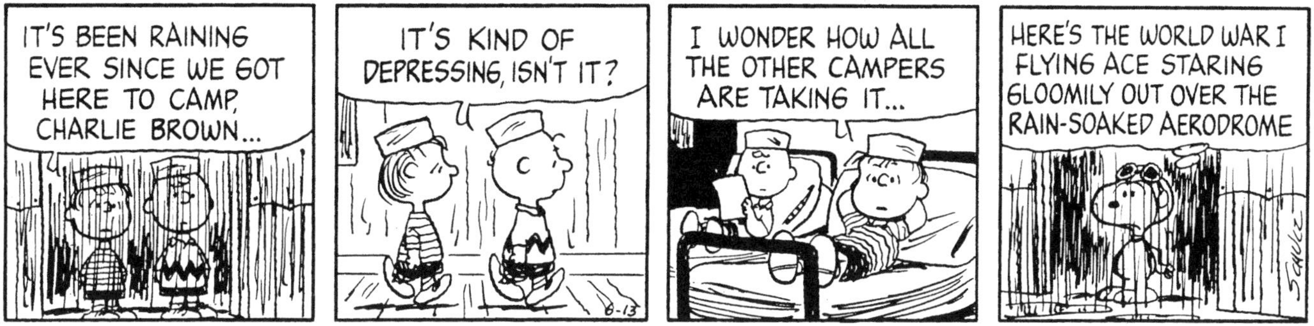
IT'S BEEN RAINING EVER SINCE WE GOT HERE TO CAMP, CHARLIE BROWN...
IT'S KIND OF DEPRESSING, ISN'T IT?
6-13
I WONDER HOW ALL THE OTHER CAMPERS ARE TAKING IT...
HERE'S THE WORLD WAR I FLYING ACE STARING GLOOMILY OUT OVER THE RAIN-SOAKED AERODROME

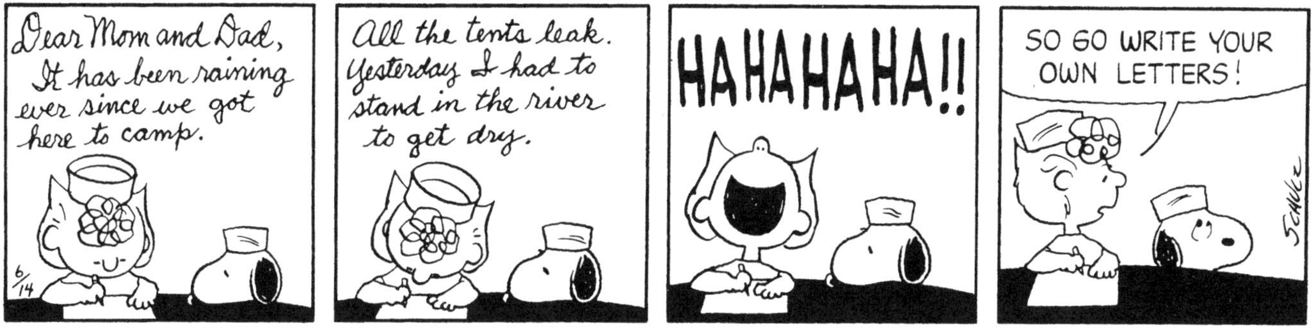
Dear Mom and Dad,
It has been raining ever since we got here to camp.
6/14
All the tents leak. Yesterday I had to stand in the river to get dry.
HAHAHAHA!!
SO GO WRITE YOUR OWN LETTERS!

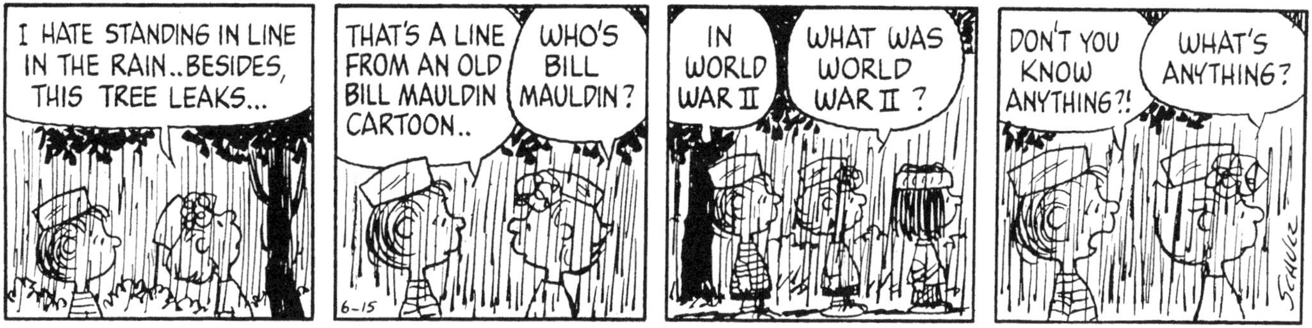
I HATE STANDING IN LINE IN THE RAIN..BESIDES, THIS TREE LEAKS...
THAT'S A LINE FROM AN OLD BILL MAULDIN CARTOON..
WHO'S BILL MAULDIN?
6-15
IN WORLD WAR II
WHAT WAS WORLD WAR II ?
DON'T YOU KNOW ANYTHING?!
WHAT'S ANYTHING?

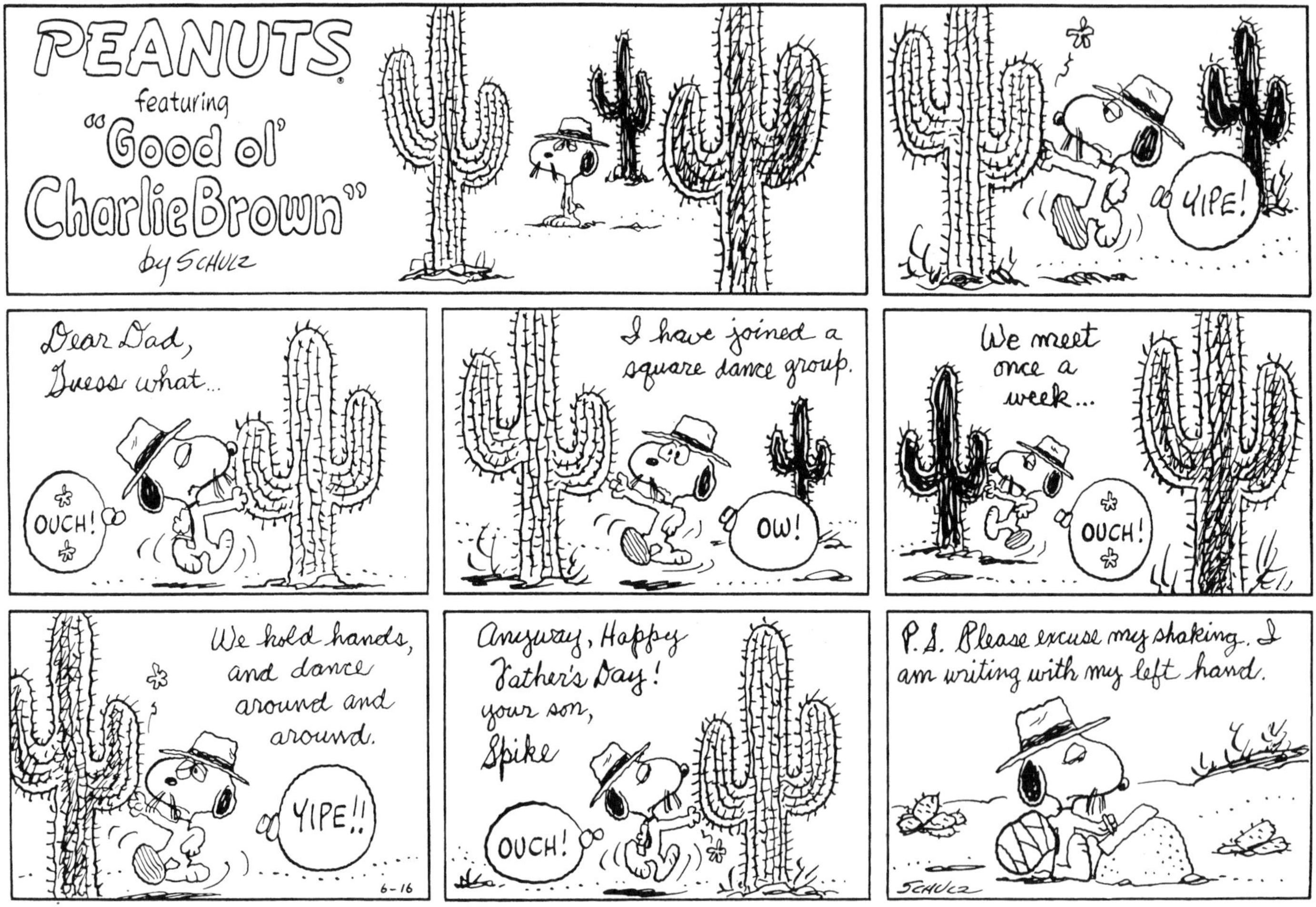
PEANUTS
featuring
"Good ol' Charlie Brown"
by SCHULZ
YIPE!
Dear Dad,
Guess what...
OUCH!
I have joined a square dance group.
OW!
We meet once a week...
OUCH!
We hold hands, and dance around and around.
YIPE!!
6-16
Anyway, Happy Father's Day!
your son,
Spike
OUCH!
P.S. Please excuse my shaking. I am writing with my left hand.
SCHULZ

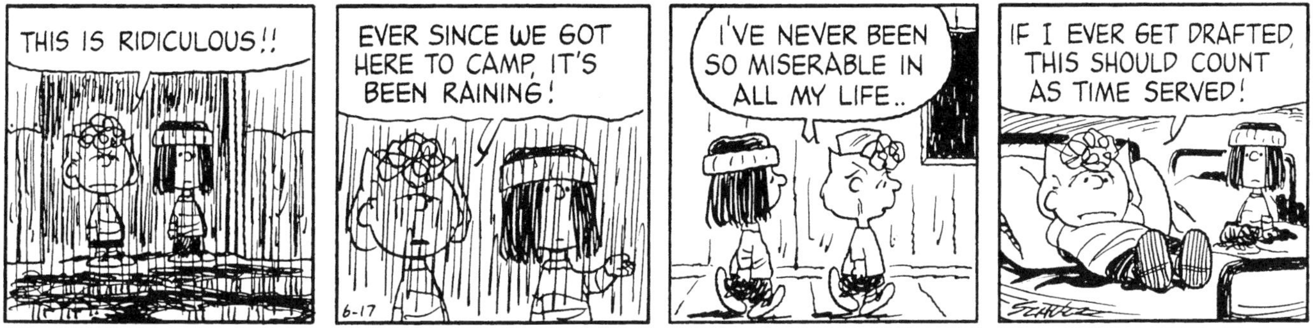
THIS IS RIDICULOUS!!
EVER SINCE WE GOT HERE TO CAMP, IT'S BEEN RAINING!
I'VE NEVER BEEN SO MISERABLE IN ALL MY LIFE..
IF I EVER GET DRAFTED, THIS SHOULD COUNT AS TIME SERVED!

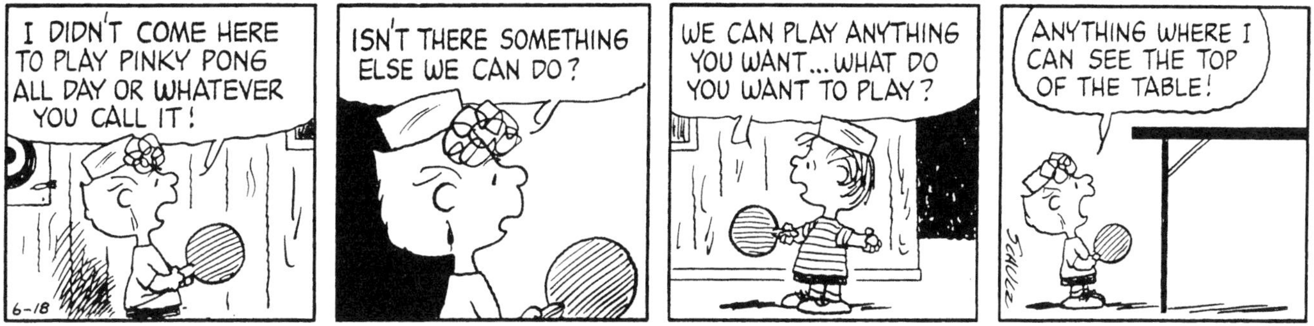
I DIDN'T COME HERE TO PLAY PINKY PONG ALL DAY OR WHATEVER YOU CALL IT!
ISN'T THERE SOMETHING ELSE WE CAN DO?
WE CAN PLAY ANYTHING YOU WANT... WHAT DO YOU WANT TO PLAY?
ANYTHING WHERE I CAN SEE THE TOP OF THE TABLE!

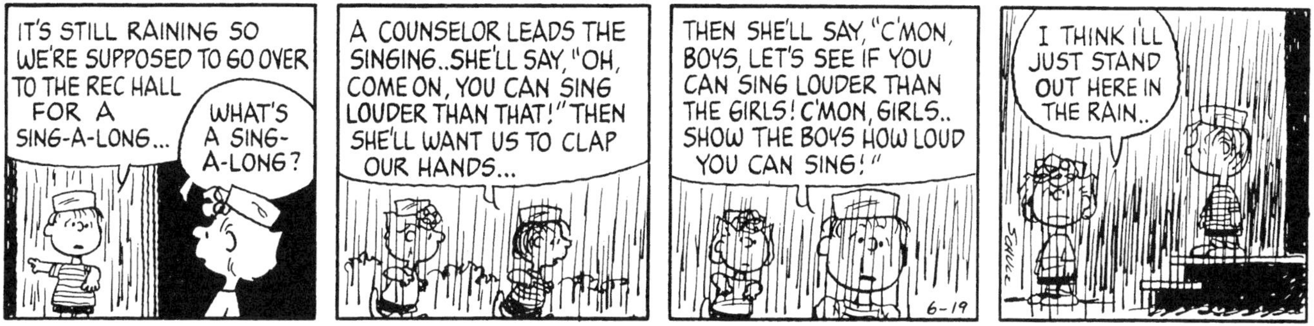
IT'S STILL RAINING SO WE'RE SUPPOSED TO GO OVER TO THE REC HALL FOR A SING-A-LONG...
WHAT'S A SING-A-LONG?
A COUNSELOR LEADS THE SINGING..SHE'LL SAY, "OH, COME ON, YOU CAN SING LOUDER THAN THAT!" THEN SHE'LL WANT US TO CLAP OUR HANDS...
THEN SHE'LL SAY, "C'MON, BOYS, LET'S SEE IF YOU CAN SING LOUDER THAN THE GIRLS! C'MON, GIRLS.. SHOW THE BOYS HOW LOUD YOU CAN SING!"
I THINK I'LL JUST STAND OUT HERE IN THE RAIN..

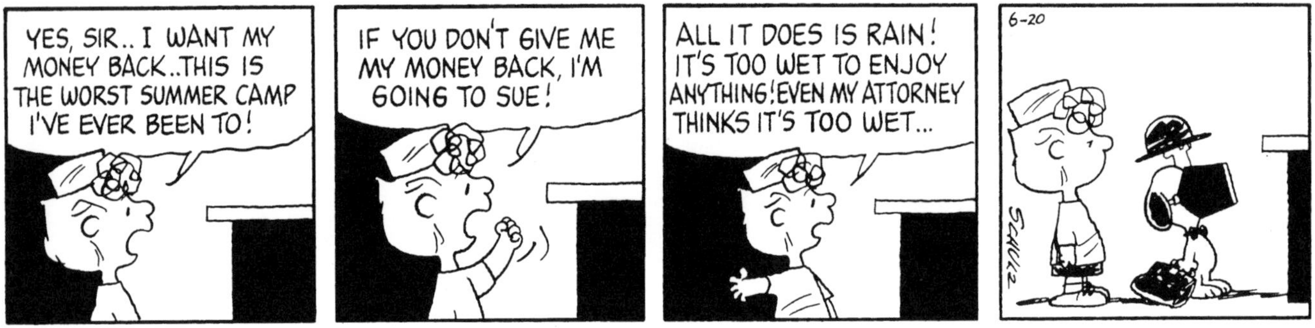
YES, SIR.. I WANT MY MONEY BACK..THIS IS THE WORST SUMMER CAMP I'VE EVER BEEN TO!
IF YOU DON'T GIVE ME MY MONEY BACK, I'M GOING TO SUE!
ALL IT DOES IS RAIN! IT'S TOO WET TO ENJOY ANYTHING! EVEN MY ATTORNEY THINKS IT'S TOO WET...
6-20
SCHULZ

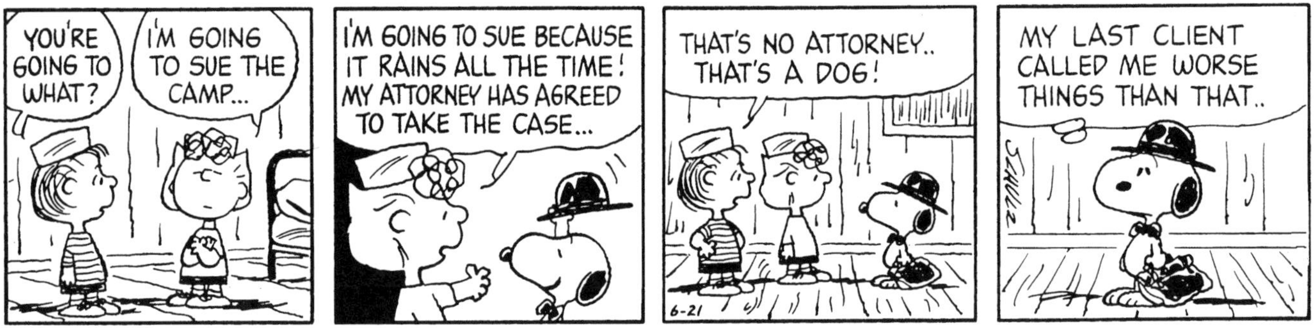
YOU'RE GOING TO WHAT?
I'M GOING TO SUE THE CAMP...
I'M GOING TO SUE BECAUSE IT RAINS ALL THE TIME! MY ATTORNEY HAS AGREED TO TAKE THE CASE...
THAT'S NO ATTORNEY.. THAT'S A DOG!
6-21
MY LAST CLIENT CALLED ME WORSE THINGS THAN THAT..
SCHULZ

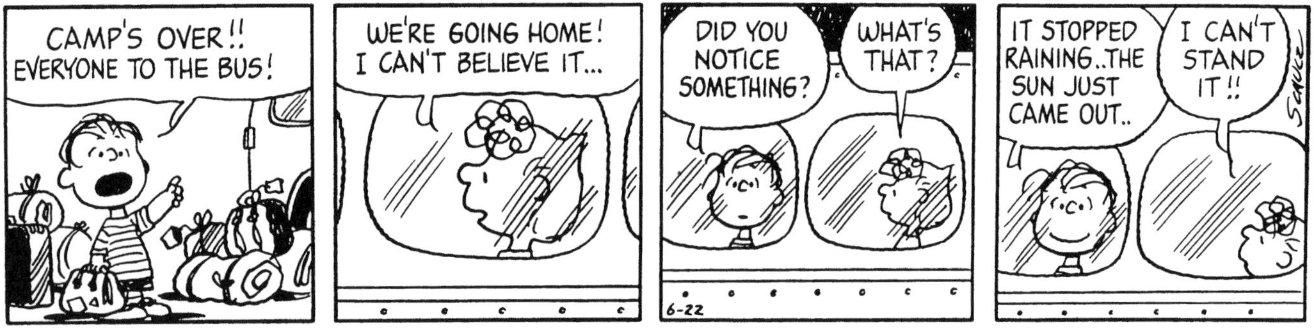
CAMP'S OVER!! EVERYONE TO THE BUS!
WE'RE GOING HOME! I CAN'T BELIEVE IT...
DID YOU NOTICE SOMETHING?
WHAT'S THAT?
6-22
IT STOPPED RAINING..THE SUN JUST CAME OUT..
I CAN'T STAND IT!!
SCHULZ

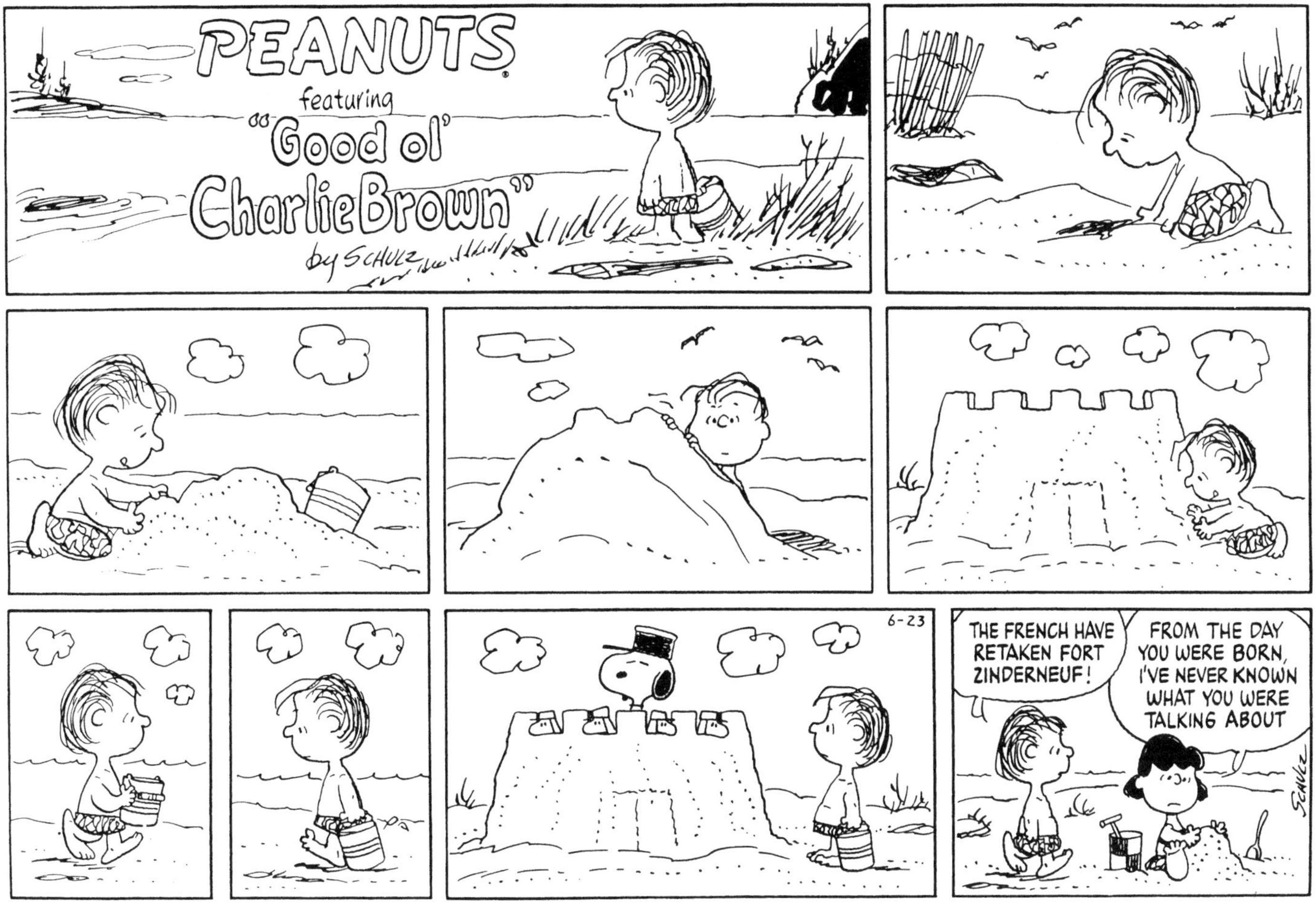
PEANUTS
featuring
"Good ol' CharlieBrown"
by SCHULZ
6-23
THE FRENCH HAVE RETAKEN FORT ZINDERNEUF!
FROM THE DAY YOU WERE BORN, I'VE NEVER KNOWN WHAT YOU WERE TALKING ABOUT
SCHULZ

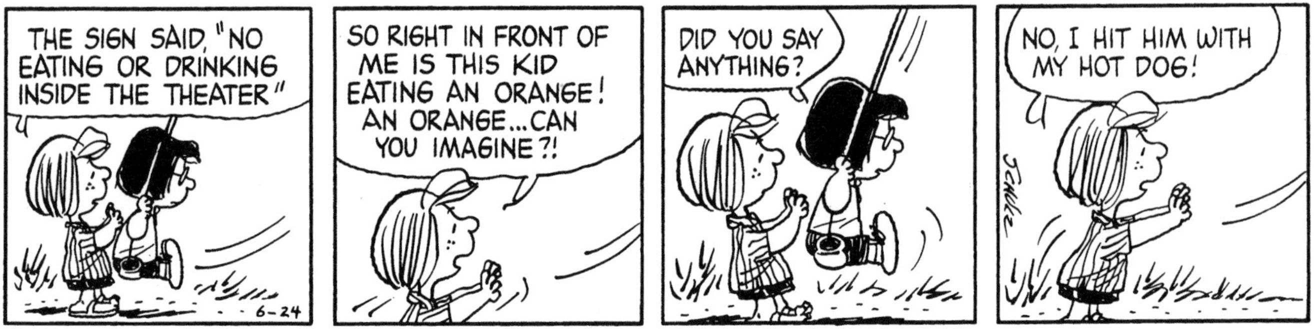
THE SIGN SAID, "NO EATING OR DRINKING INSIDE THE THEATER"
6-24
SO RIGHT IN FRONT OF ME IS THIS KID EATING AN ORANGE! AN ORANGE...CAN YOU IMAGINE?!
DID YOU SAY ANYTHING?
NO, I HIT HIM WITH MY HOT DOG!
SCHULZ

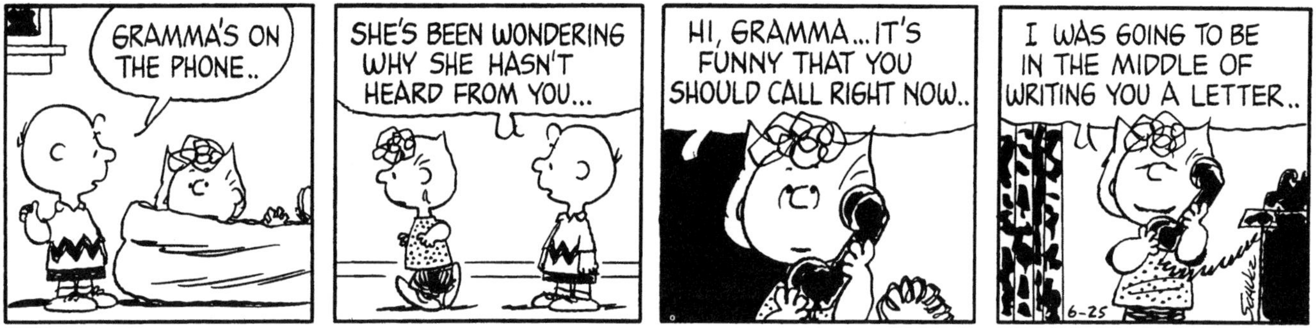
GRAMMA'S ON THE PHONE..
SHE'S BEEN WONDERING WHY SHE HASN'T HEARD FROM YOU...
HI, GRAMMA...IT'S FUNNY THAT YOU SHOULD CALL RIGHT NOW..
I WAS GOING TO BE IN THE MIDDLE OF WRITING YOU A LETTER..
6-25
SCHULZ

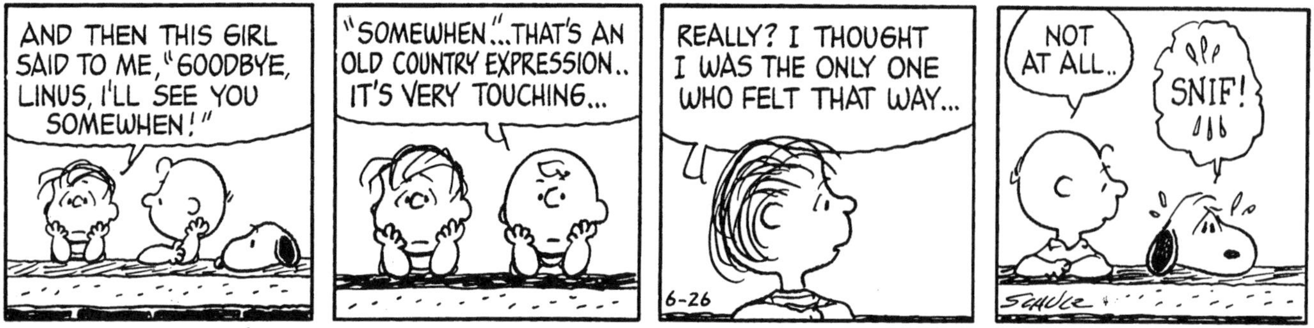
AND THEN THIS GIRL SAID TO ME, "GOODBYE, LINUS, I'LL SEE YOU SOMEWHEN!"
"SOMEWHEN"...THAT'S AN OLD COUNTRY EXPRESSION.. IT'S VERY TOUCHING...
REALLY? I THOUGHT I WAS THE ONLY ONE WHO FELT THAT WAY...
6-26
NOT AT ALL..
SNIF!
SCHULZ

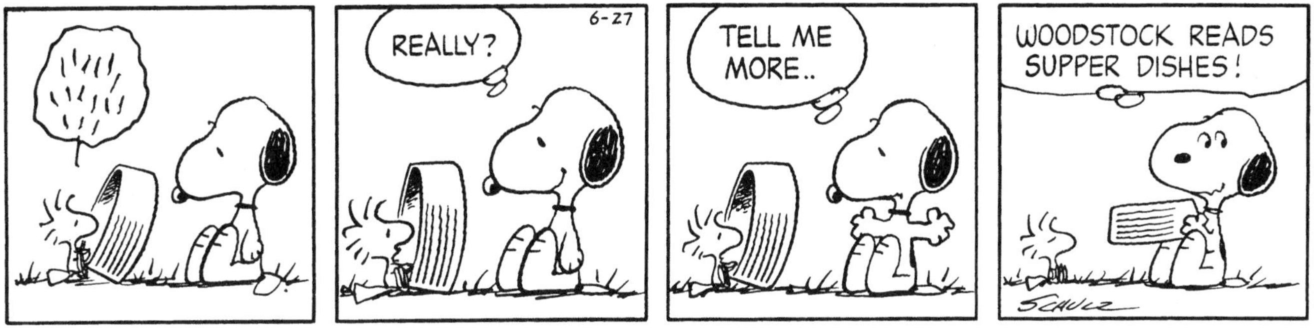
6-27
REALLY?
TELL ME MORE..
WOODSTOCK READS SUPPER DISHES!

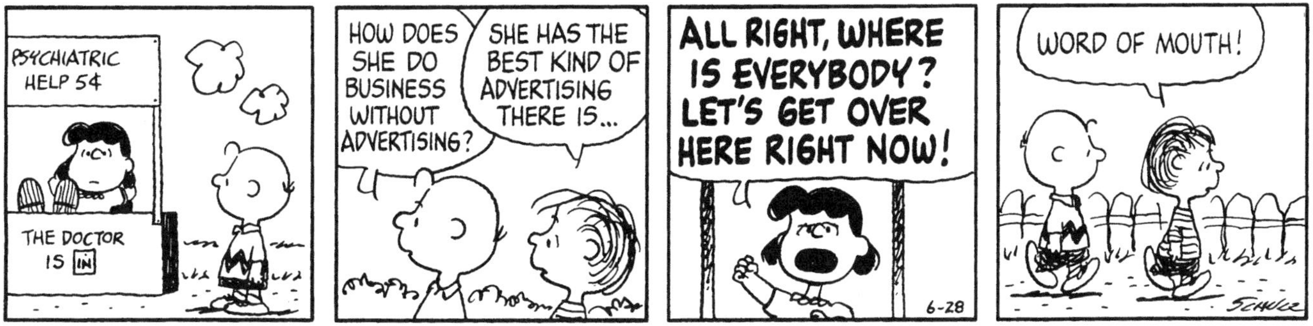
PSYCHIATRIC HELP 5¢
THE DOCTOR IS IN
HOW DOES SHE DO BUSINESS WITHOUT ADVERTISING?
SHE HAS THE BEST KIND OF ADVERTISING THERE IS...
ALL RIGHT, WHERE IS EVERYBODY? LET'S GET OVER HERE RIGHT NOW!
6-28
WORD OF MOUTH!

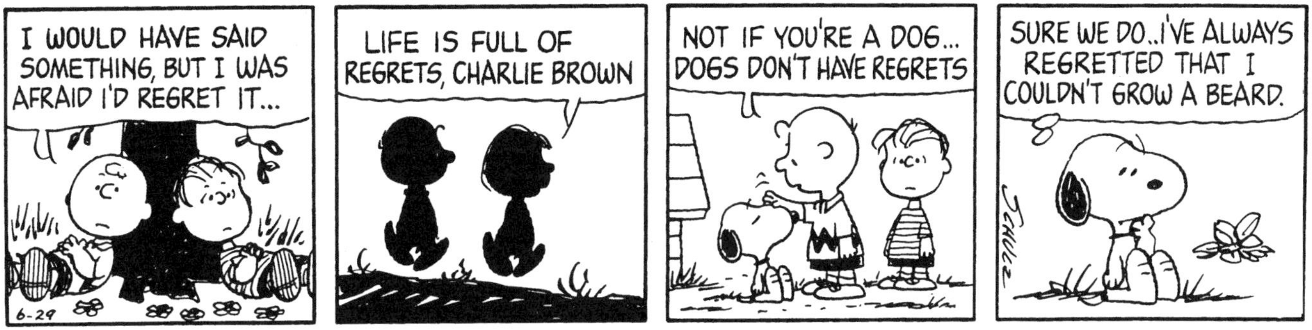
I WOULD HAVE SAID SOMETHING, BUT I WAS AFRAID I'D REGRET IT...
6-29
LIFE IS FULL OF REGRETS, CHARLIE BROWN
NOT IF YOU'RE A DOG... DOGS DON'T HAVE REGRETS
SURE WE DO..I'VE ALWAYS REGRETTED THAT I COULDN'T GROW A BEARD.

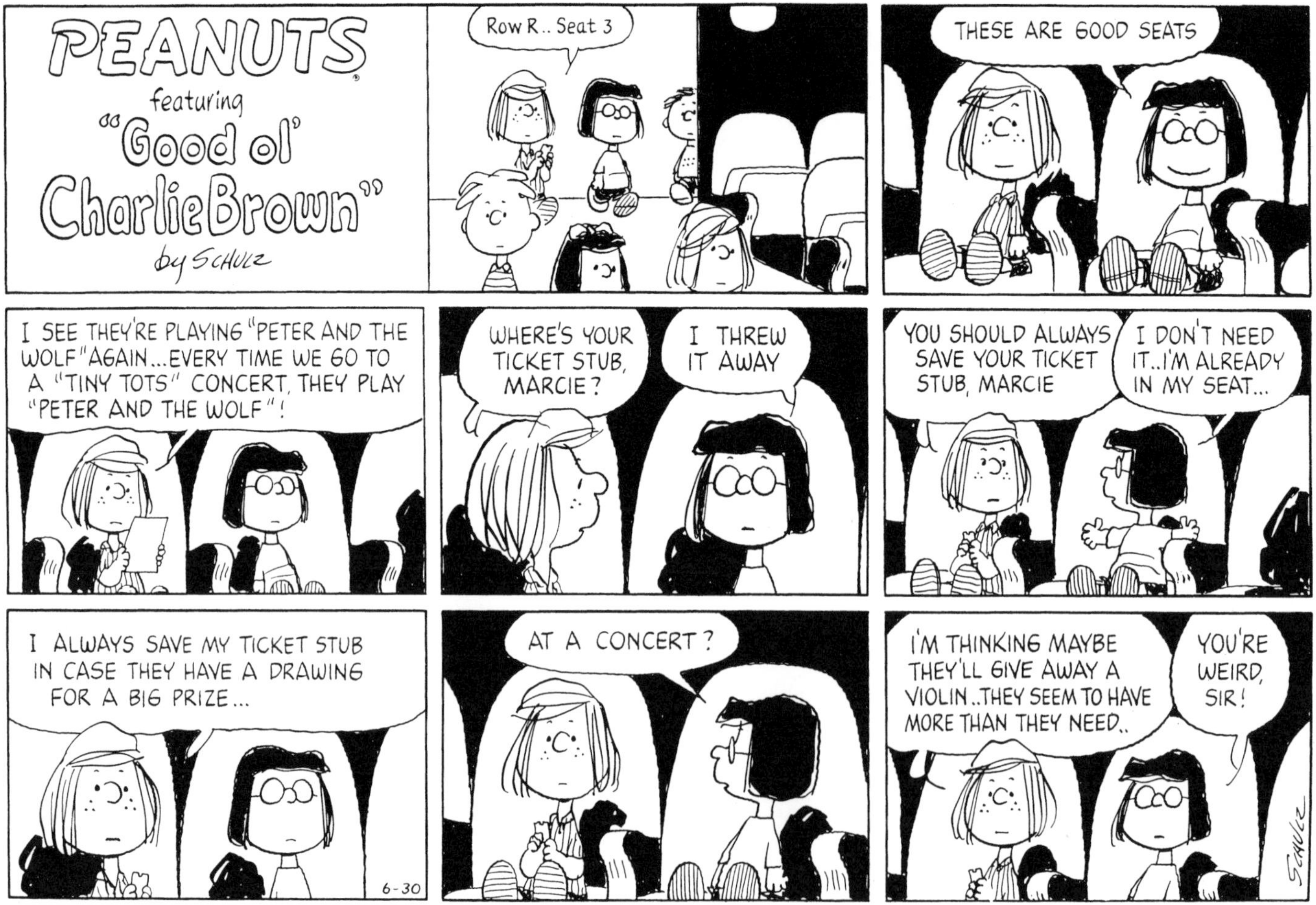
PEANUTS
featuring
"Good ol' CharlieBrown"
by SCHULZ
Row R.. Seat 3
THESE ARE GOOD SEATS
I SEE THEY'RE PLAYING "PETER AND THE WOLF" AGAIN...EVERY TIME WE GO TO A "TINY TOTS" CONCERT, THEY PLAY "PETER AND THE WOLF"!
WHERE'S YOUR TICKET STUB, MARCIE?
I THREW IT AWAY
YOU SHOULD ALWAYS SAVE YOUR TICKET STUB, MARCIE
I DON'T NEED IT..I'M ALREADY IN MY SEAT...
I ALWAYS SAVE MY TICKET STUB IN CASE THEY HAVE A DRAWING FOR A BIG PRIZE...
6-30
AT A CONCERT?
I'M THINKING MAYBE THEY'LL GIVE AWAY A VIOLIN..THEY SEEM TO HAVE MORE THAN THEY NEED..
YOU'RE WEIRD, SIR!
SCHULZ

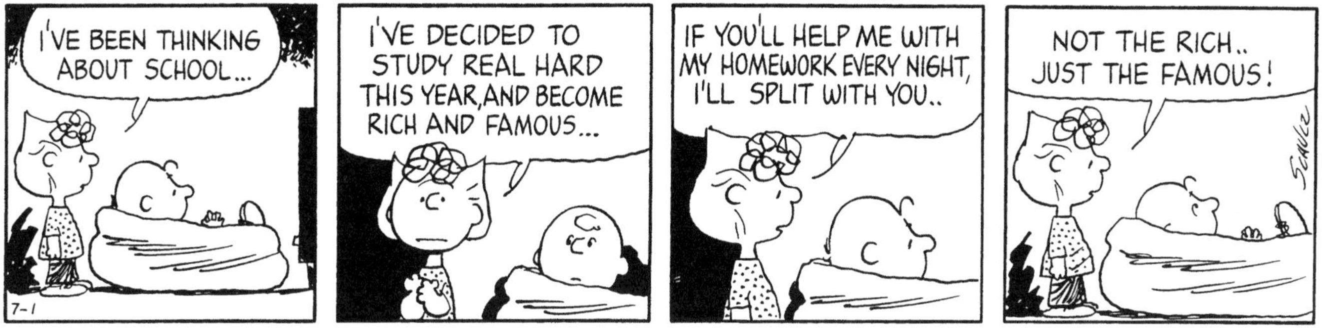
I'VE BEEN THINKING ABOUT SCHOOL...
I'VE DECIDED TO STUDY REAL HARD THIS YEAR, AND BECOME RICH AND FAMOUS...
IF YOU'LL HELP ME WITH MY HOMEWORK EVERY NIGHT, I'LL SPLIT WITH YOU..
NOT THE RICH.. JUST THE FAMOUS!

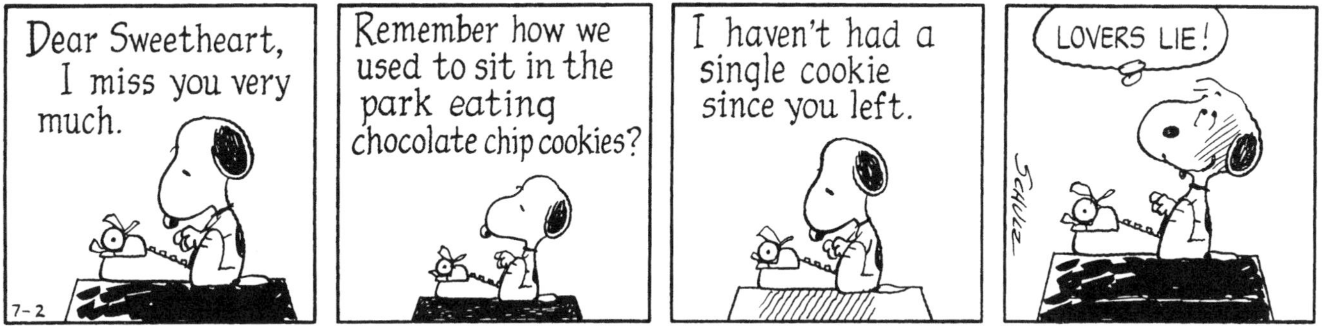
Dear Sweetheart,
I miss you very much.
Remember how we used to sit in the park eating chocolate chip cookies?
I haven't had a single cookie since you left.
LOVERS LIE!

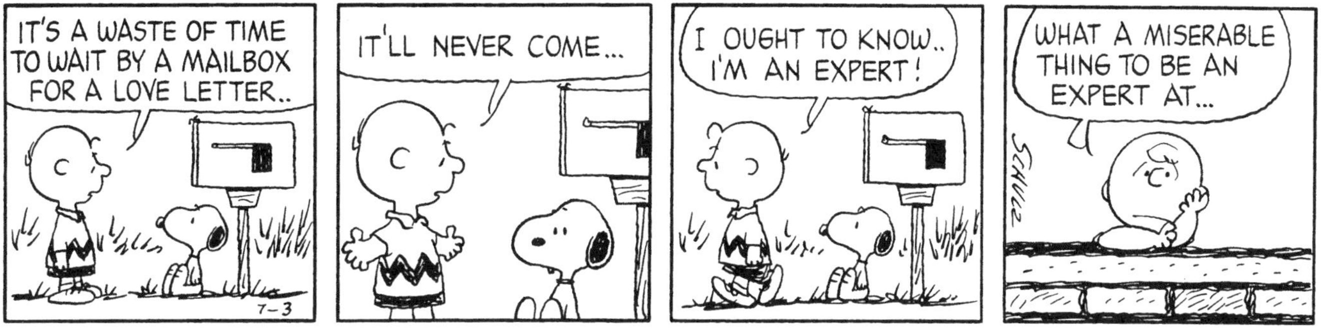
IT'S A WASTE OF TIME TO WAIT BY A MAILBOX FOR A LOVE LETTER..
IT'LL NEVER COME...
I OUGHT TO KNOW.. I'M AN EXPERT!
WHAT A MISERABLE THING TO BE AN EXPERT AT...

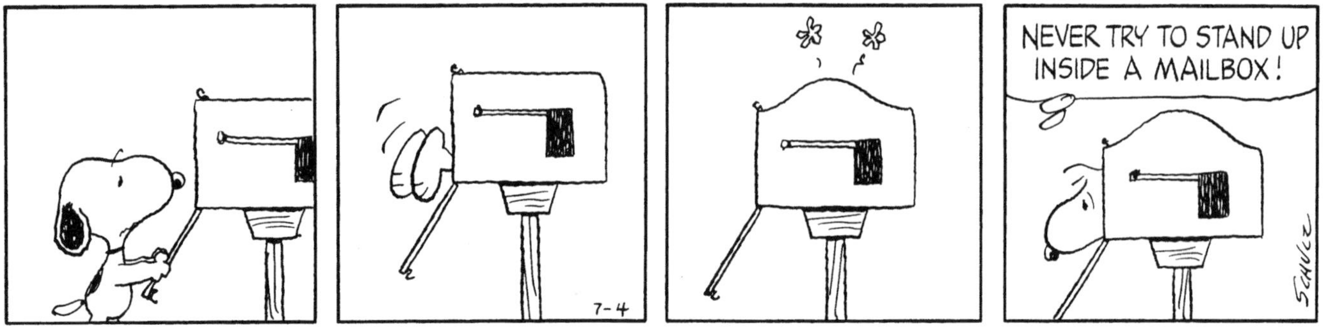
7-4
NEVER TRY TO STAND UP INSIDE A MAILBOX!
SCHULZ

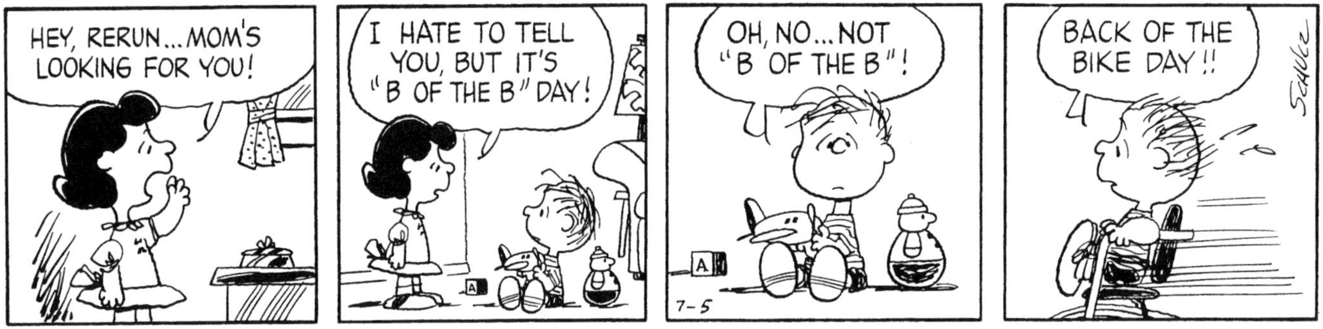
HEY, RERUN...MOM'S LOOKING FOR YOU!
I HATE TO TELL YOU, BUT IT'S "B OF THE B" DAY!
OH, NO...NOT "B OF THE B"!
7-5
BACK OF THE BIKE DAY!!
SCHULZ

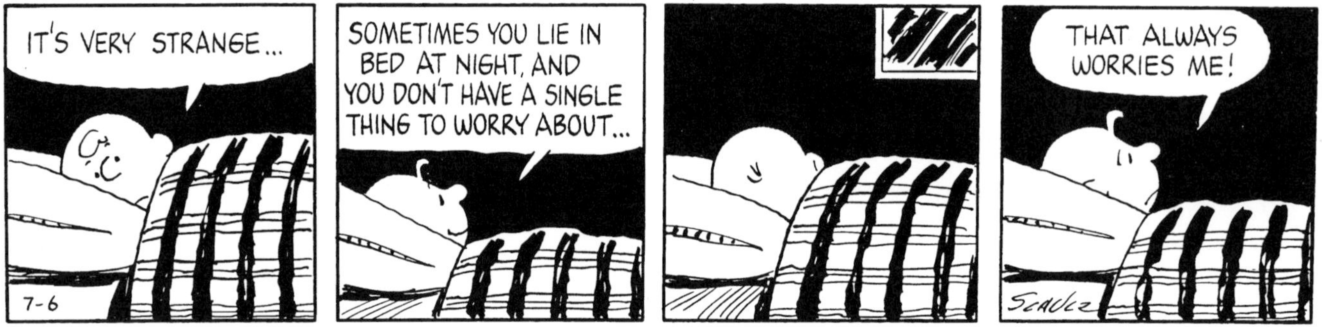
IT'S VERY STRANGE...
7-6
SOMETIMES YOU LIE IN BED AT NIGHT, AND YOU DON'T HAVE A SINGLE THING TO WORRY ABOUT...
THAT ALWAYS WORRIES ME!
SCHULZ

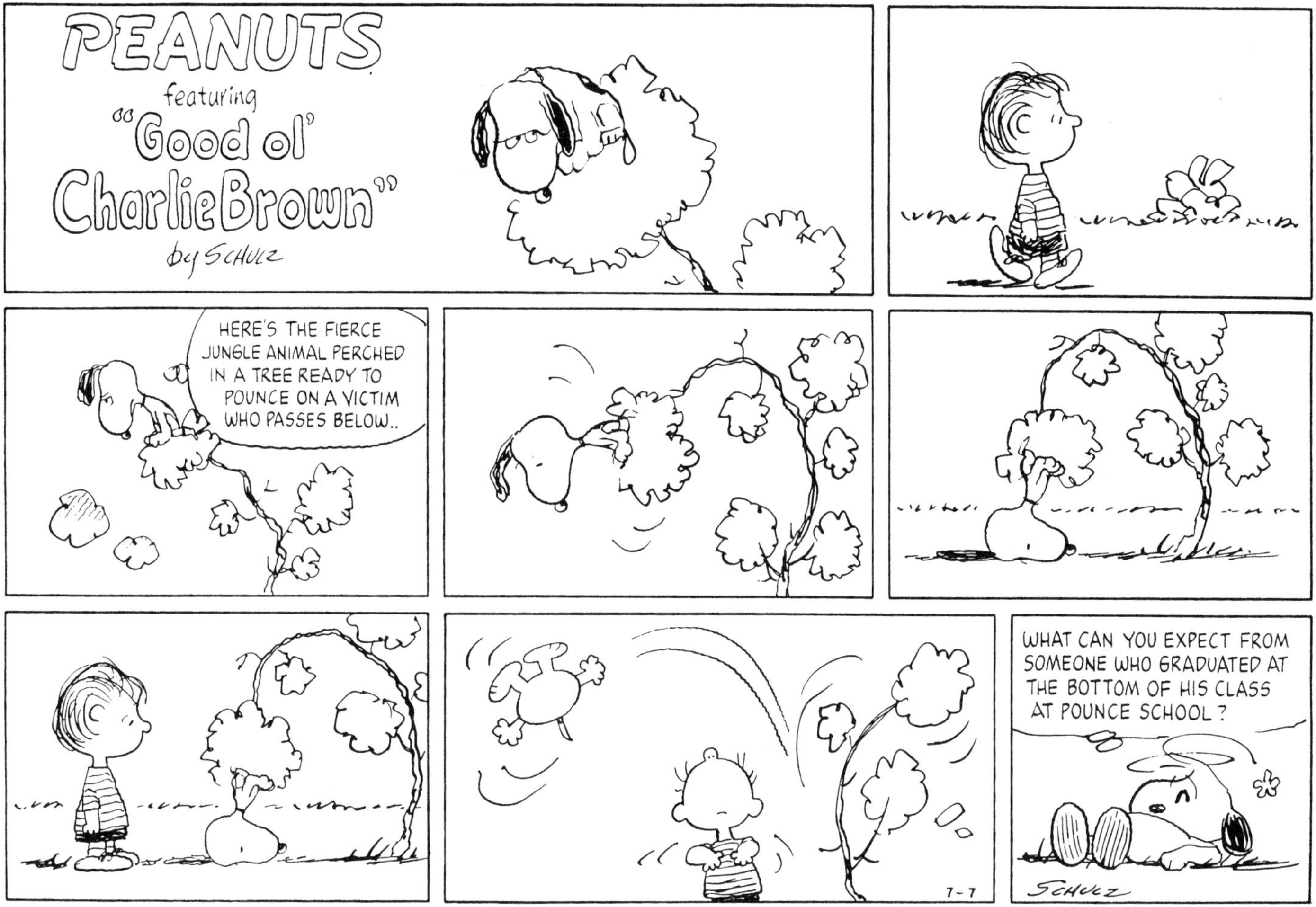
PEANUTS
featuring
"Good ol' CharlieBrown"
by SCHULZ
HERE'S THE FIERCE JUNGLE ANIMAL PERCHED IN A TREE READY TO POUNCE ON A VICTIM WHO PASSES BELOW..
7-7
WHAT CAN YOU EXPECT FROM SOMEONE WHO GRADUATED AT THE BOTTOM OF HIS CLASS AT POUNCE SCHOOL ?
SCHULZ

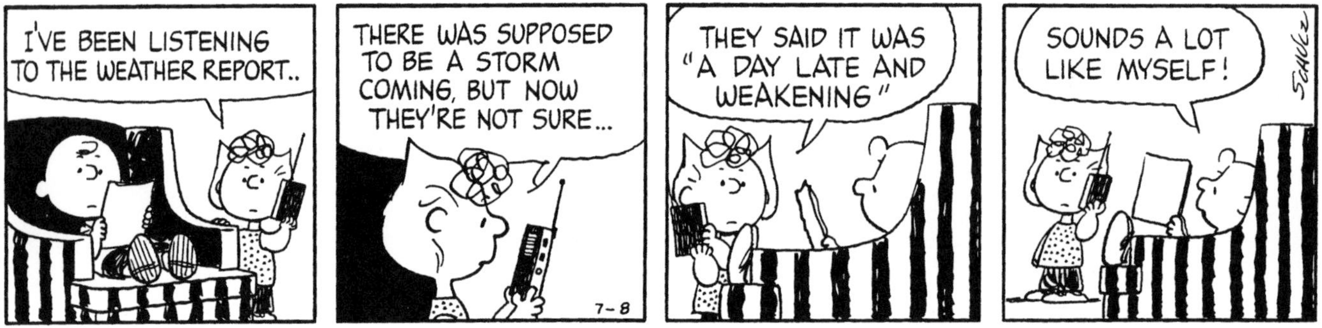
I'VE BEEN LISTENING TO THE WEATHER REPORT..
THERE WAS SUPPOSED TO BE A STORM COMING, BUT NOW THEY'RE NOT SURE...
7-8
THEY SAID IT WAS "A DAY LATE AND WEAKENING"
SOUNDS A LOT LIKE MYSELF!

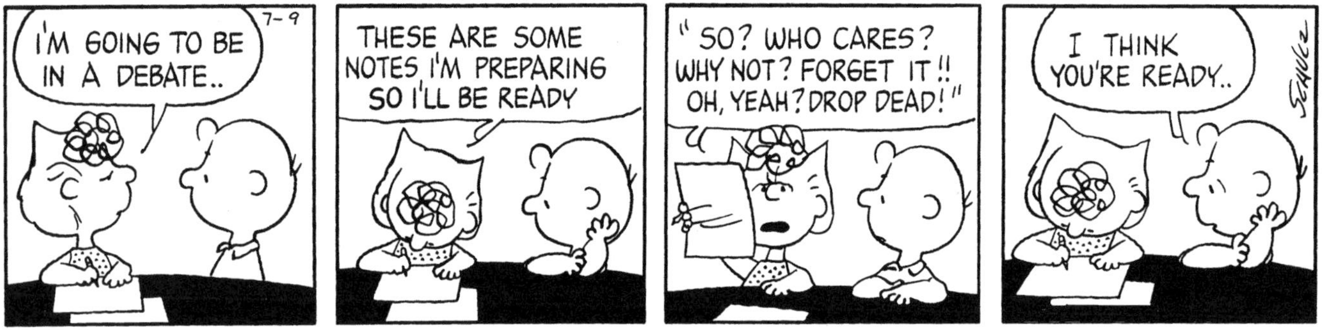
7-9
I'M GOING TO BE IN A DEBATE..
THESE ARE SOME NOTES I'M PREPARING SO I'LL BE READY
"SO? WHO CARES? WHY NOT? FORGET IT!! OH, YEAH? DROP DEAD!"
I THINK YOU'RE READY..

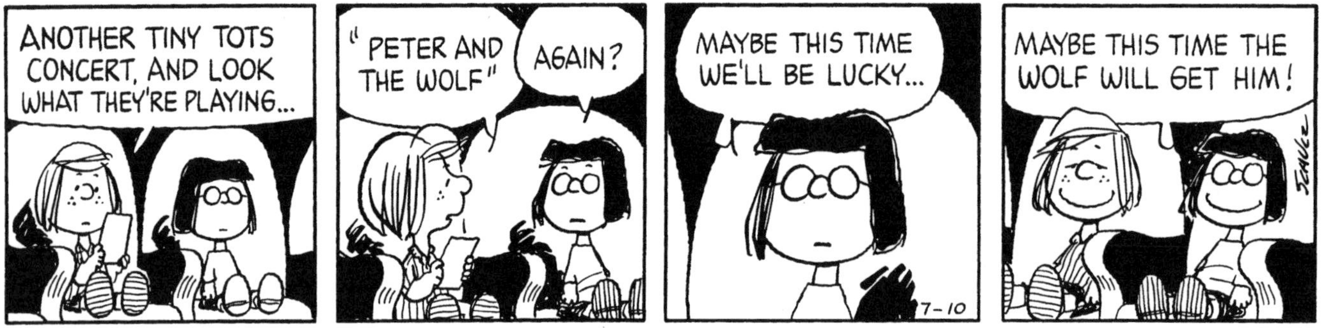
ANOTHER TINY TOTS CONCERT, AND LOOK WHAT THEY'RE PLAYING...
"PETER AND THE WOLF"
AGAIN?
MAYBE THIS TIME WE'LL BE LUCKY...
7-10
MAYBE THIS TIME THE WOLF WILL GET HIM!

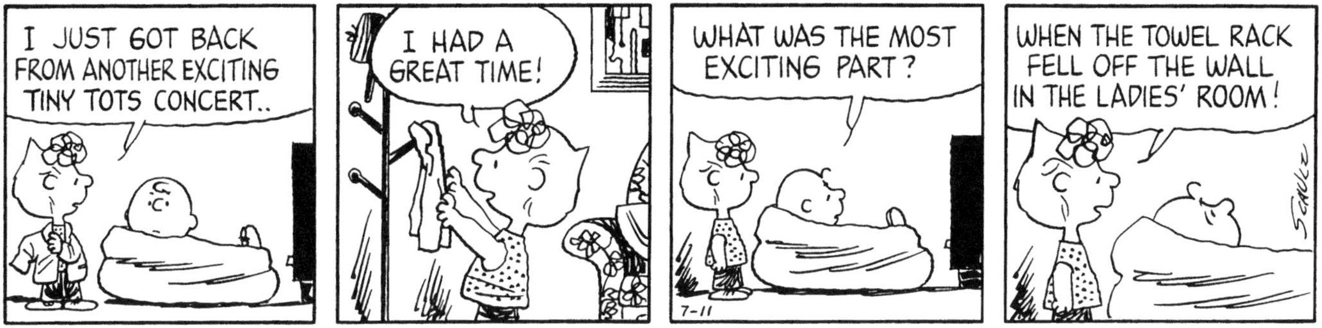
I JUST GOT BACK FROM ANOTHER EXCITING TINY TOTS CONCERT..
I HAD A GREAT TIME!
WHAT WAS THE MOST EXCITING PART?
7-11
WHEN THE TOWEL RACK FELL OFF THE WALL IN THE LADIES' ROOM!
SCHULZ

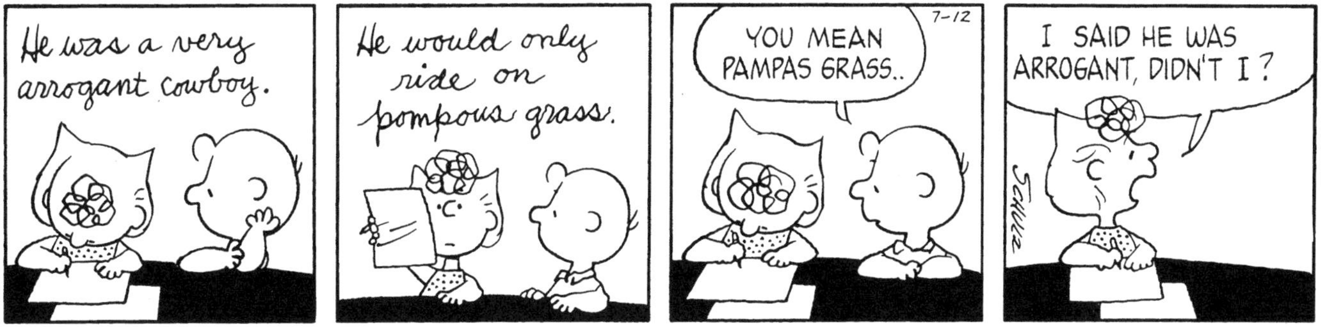
He was a very arrogant cowboy.
He would only ride on pompous grass.
YOU MEAN PAMPAS GRASS..
7-12
I SAID HE WAS ARROGANT, DIDN'T I?
SCHULZ

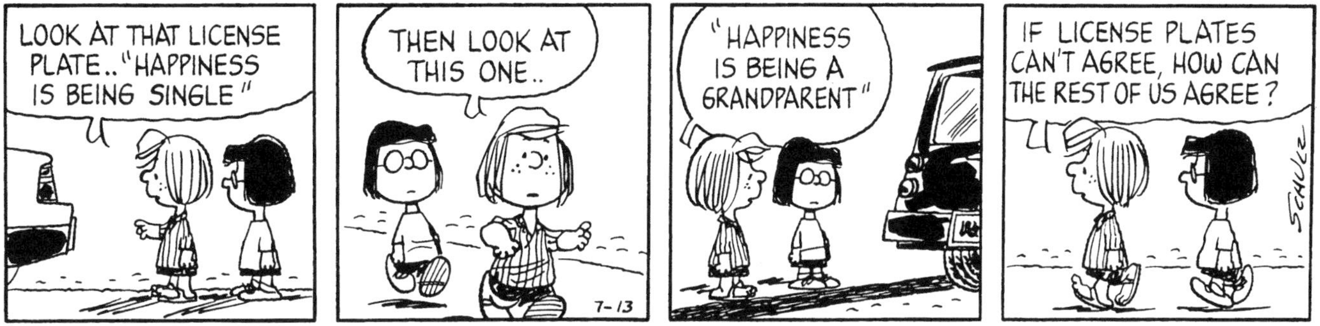
LOOK AT THAT LICENSE PLATE.."HAPPINESS IS BEING SINGLE"
THEN LOOK AT THIS ONE..
7-13
"HAPPINESS IS BEING A GRANDPARENT"
IF LICENSE PLATES CAN'T AGREE, HOW CAN THE REST OF US AGREE?
SCHULZ

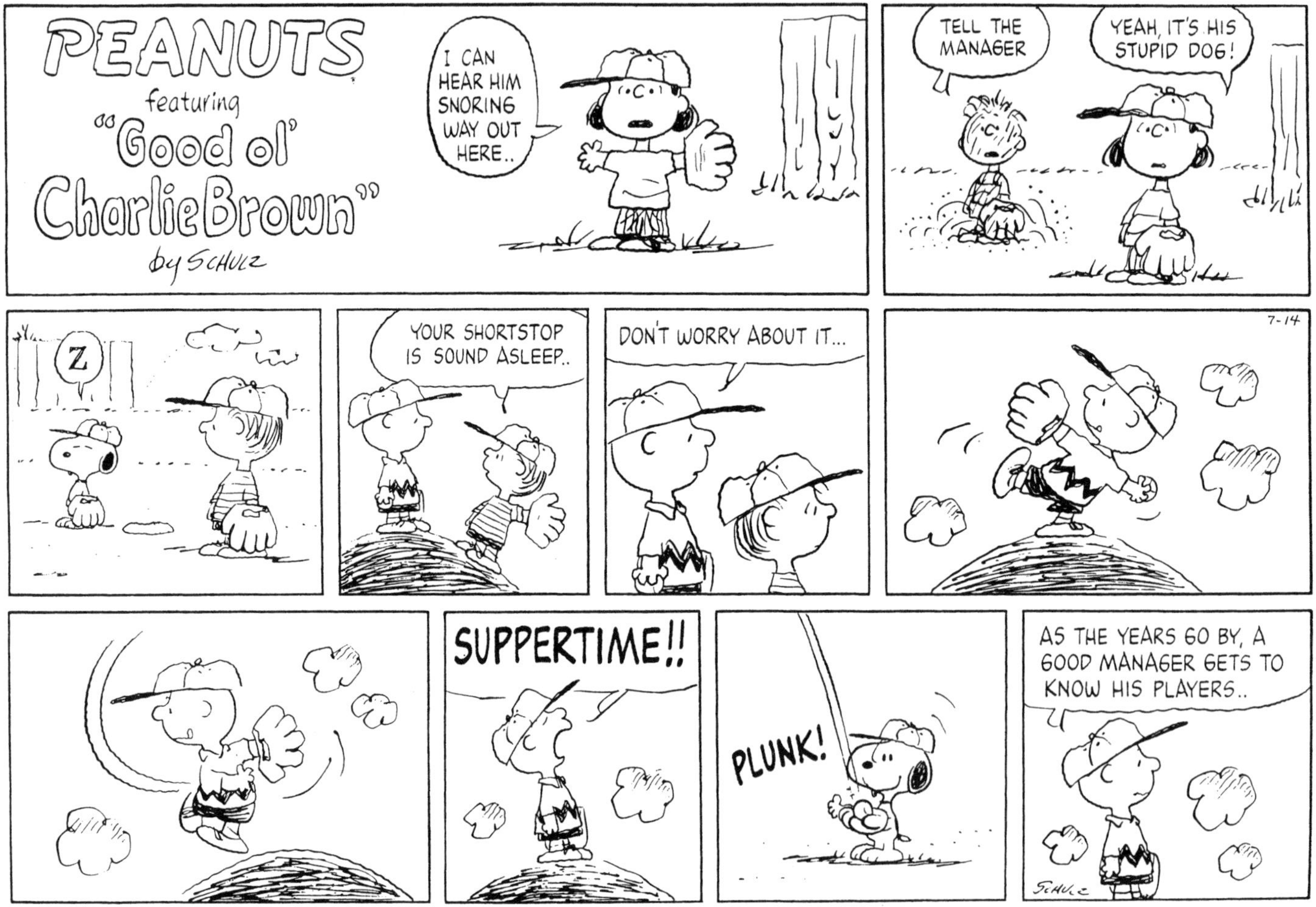
PEANUTS
featuring
"Good ol' Charlie Brown"
by SCHULZ
I CAN HEAR HIM SNORING WAY OUT HERE..
TELL THE MANAGER
YEAH, IT'S HIS STUPID DOG!
Z
YOUR SHORTSTOP IS SOUND ASLEEP..
DON'T WORRY ABOUT IT...
7-14
SUPPERTIME!!
PLUNK!
AS THE YEARS GO BY, A GOOD MANAGER GETS TO KNOW HIS PLAYERS..
SCHULZ

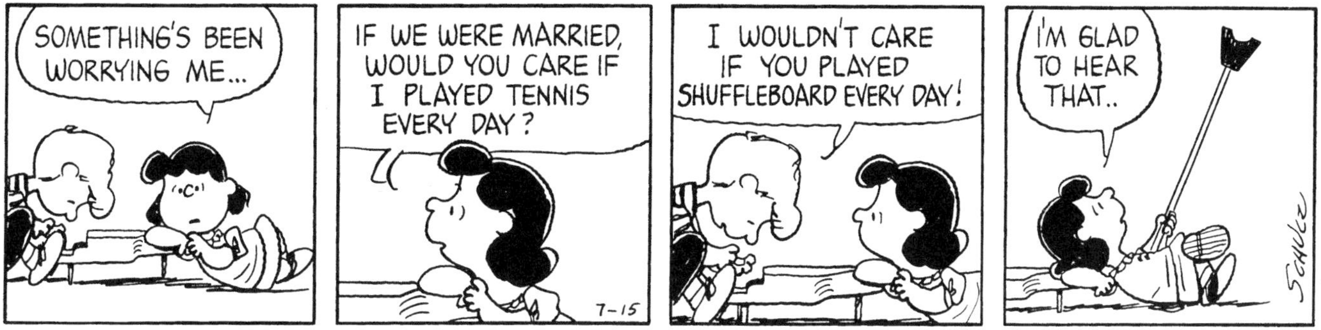
SOMETHING'S BEEN WORRYING ME...
IF WE WERE MARRIED, WOULD YOU CARE IF I PLAYED TENNIS EVERY DAY?
7-15
I WOULDN'T CARE IF YOU PLAYED SHUFFLEBOARD EVERY DAY!
I'M GLAD TO HEAR THAT..
SCHULZ

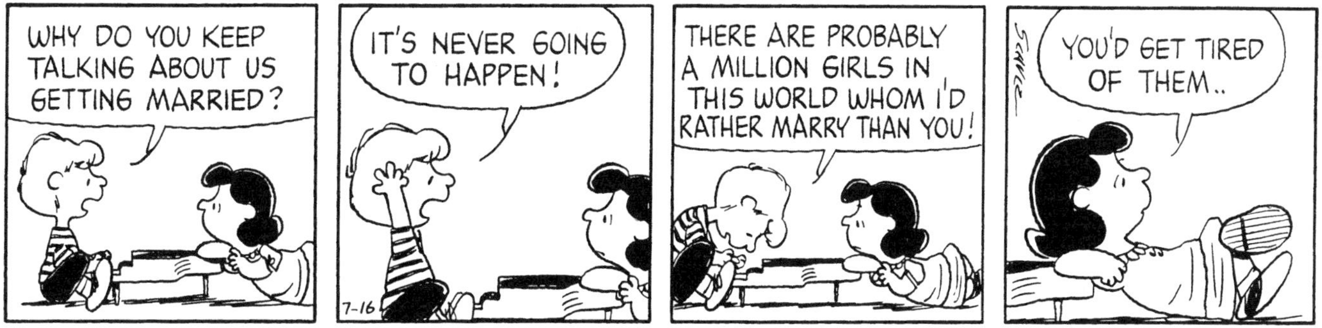
WHY DO YOU KEEP TALKING ABOUT US GETTING MARRIED?
IT'S NEVER GOING TO HAPPEN!
7-16
THERE ARE PROBABLY A MILLION GIRLS IN THIS WORLD WHOM I'D RATHER MARRY THAN YOU!
SCHULZ
YOU'D GET TIRED OF THEM..

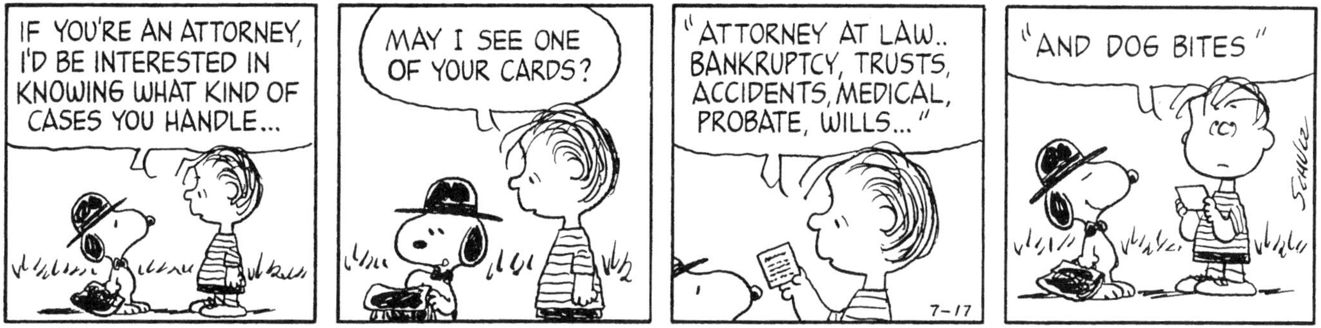
IF YOU'RE AN ATTORNEY, I'D BE INTERESTED IN KNOWING WHAT KIND OF CASES YOU HANDLE...
MAY I SEE ONE OF YOUR CARDS?
"ATTORNEY AT LAW.. BANKRUPTCY, TRUSTS, ACCIDENTS, MEDICAL, PROBATE, WILLS..."
7-17
"AND DOG BITES"
SCHULZ

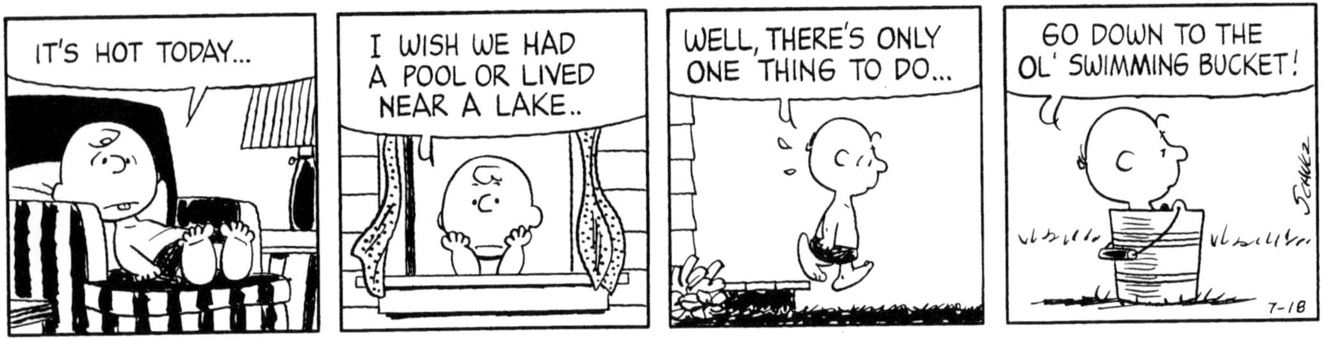
IT'S HOT TODAY...
I WISH WE HAD A POOL OR LIVED NEAR A LAKE..
WELL, THERE'S ONLY ONE THING TO DO...
GO DOWN TO THE OL' SWIMMING BUCKET!
7-18

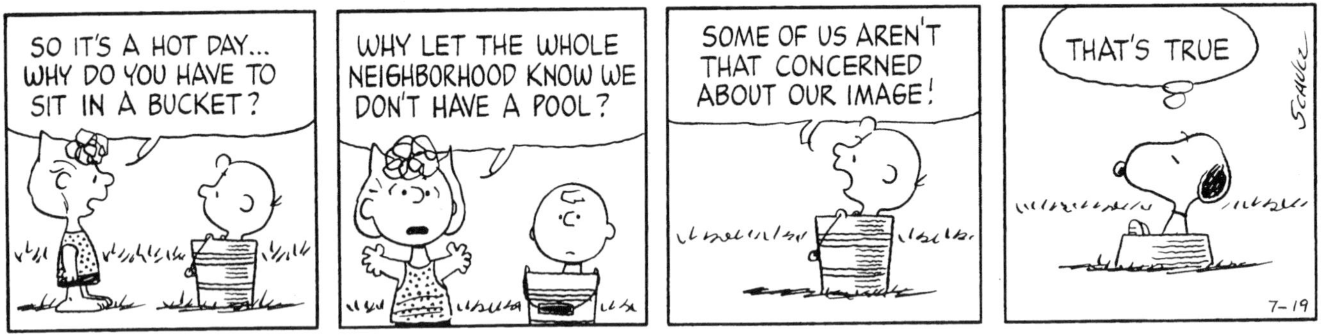
SO IT'S A HOT DAY... WHY DO YOU HAVE TO SIT IN A BUCKET?
WHY LET THE WHOLE NEIGHBORHOOD KNOW WE DON'T HAVE A POOL?
SOME OF US AREN'T THAT CONCERNED ABOUT OUR IMAGE!
THAT'S TRUE
7-19

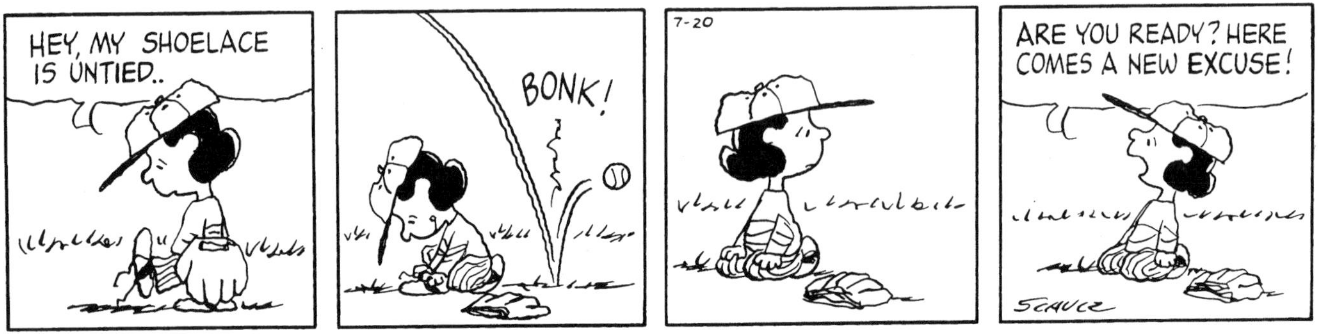
HEY, MY SHOELACE IS UNTIED..
BONK!
7-20
ARE YOU READY? HERE COMES A NEW EXCUSE!

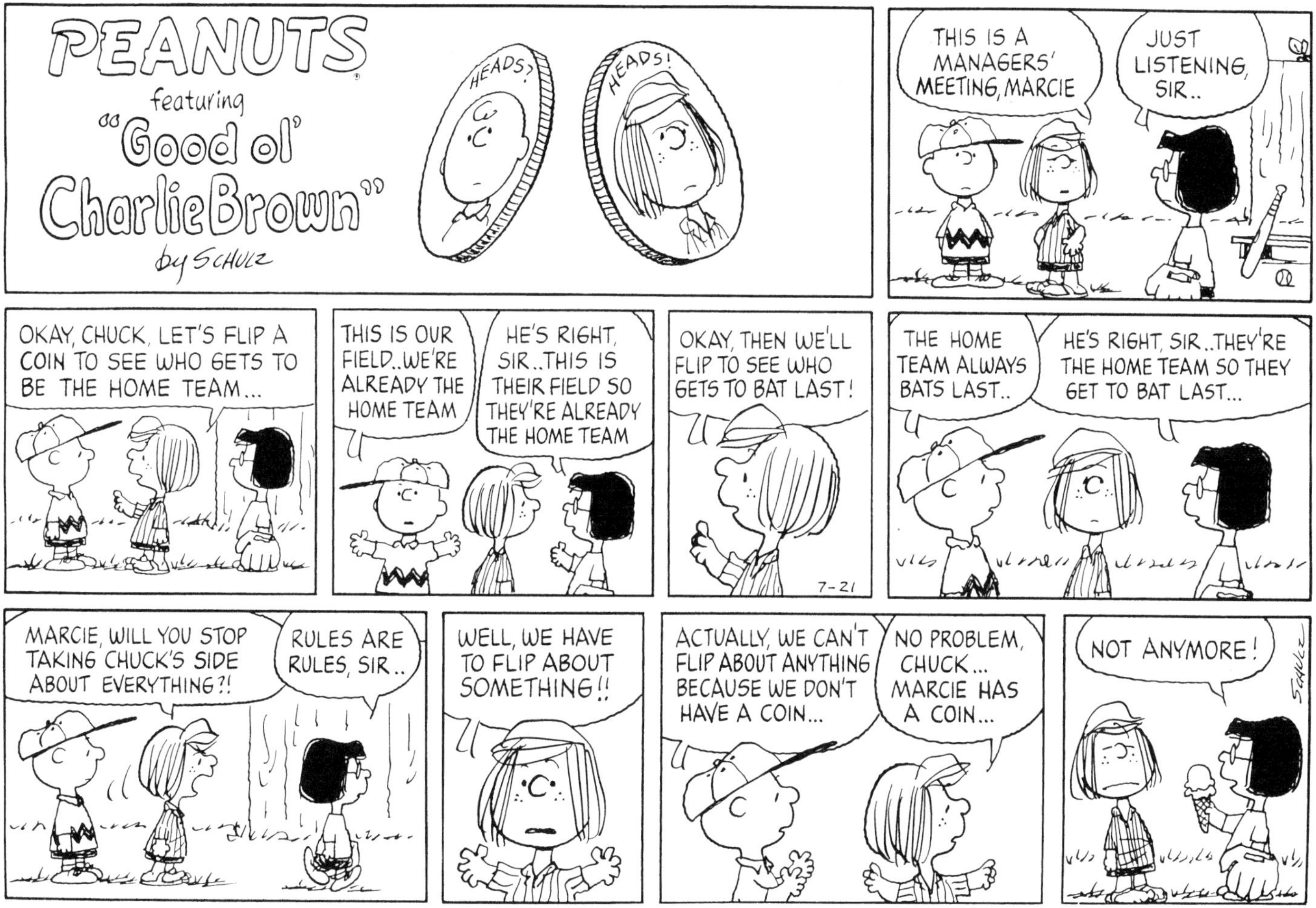
PEANUTS
featuring "Good ol' Charlie Brown"
by SCHULZ
HEADS?
HEADS!
THIS IS A MANAGERS' MEETING, MARCIE
JUST LISTENING, SIR..
OKAY, CHUCK, LET'S FLIP A COIN TO SEE WHO GETS TO BE THE HOME TEAM...
THIS IS OUR FIELD..WE'RE ALREADY THE HOME TEAM
HE'S RIGHT, SIR..THIS IS THEIR FIELD SO THEY'RE ALREADY THE HOME TEAM
OKAY, THEN WE'LL FLIP TO SEE WHO GETS TO BAT LAST!
7-21
THE HOME TEAM ALWAYS BATS LAST..
HE'S RIGHT, SIR..THEY'RE THE HOME TEAM SO THEY GET TO BAT LAST...
MARCIE, WILL YOU STOP TAKING CHUCK'S SIDE ABOUT EVERYTHING?!
RULES ARE RULES, SIR..
WELL, WE HAVE TO FLIP ABOUT SOMETHING!!
ACTUALLY, WE CAN'T FLIP ABOUT ANYTHING BECAUSE WE DON'T HAVE A COIN...
NO PROBLEM, CHUCK... MARCIE HAS A COIN...
NOT ANYMORE!
SCHULZ

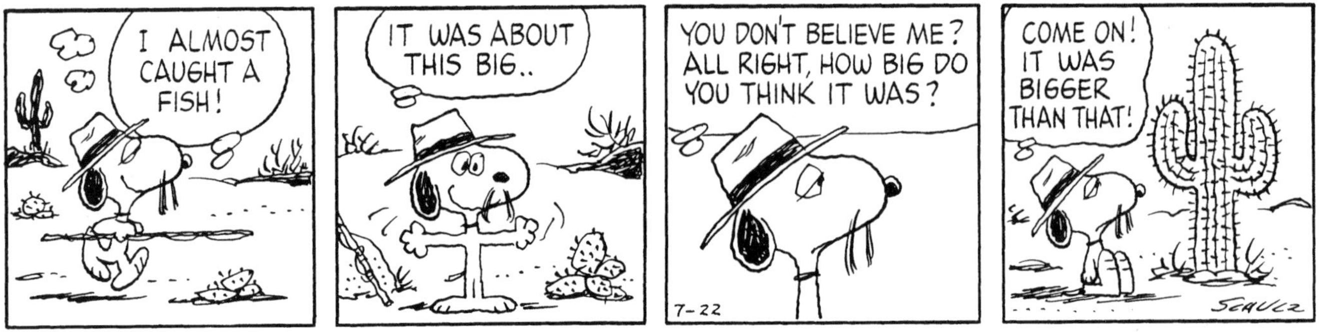
I ALMOST CAUGHT A FISH!
IT WAS ABOUT THIS BIG..
YOU DON'T BELIEVE ME? ALL RIGHT, HOW BIG DO YOU THINK IT WAS?
COME ON! IT WAS BIGGER THAN THAT!
7-22

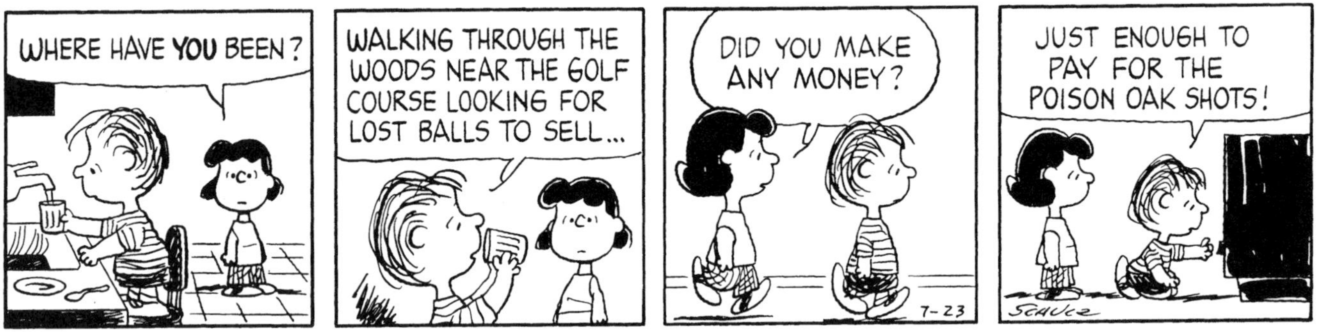
WHERE HAVE YOU BEEN?
WALKING THROUGH THE WOODS NEAR THE GOLF COURSE LOOKING FOR LOST BALLS TO SELL...
DID YOU MAKE ANY MONEY?
JUST ENOUGH TO PAY FOR THE POISON OAK SHOTS!
7-23

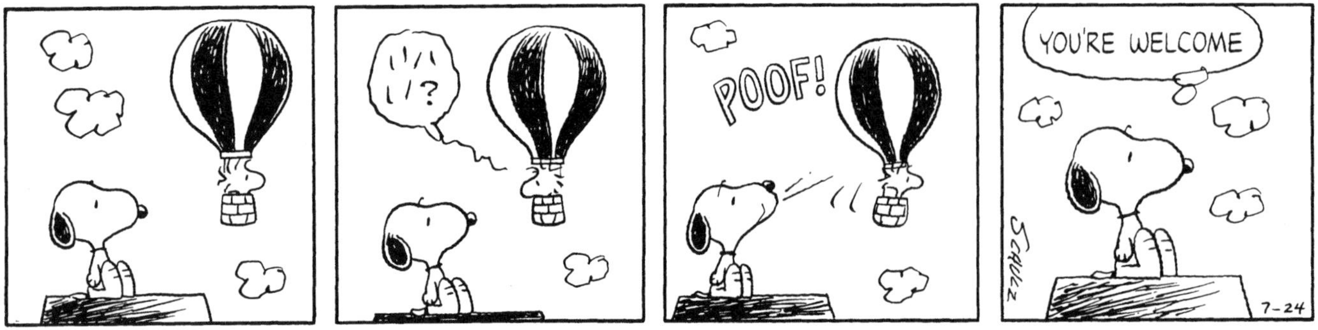
POOF!
YOU'RE WELCOME
7-24

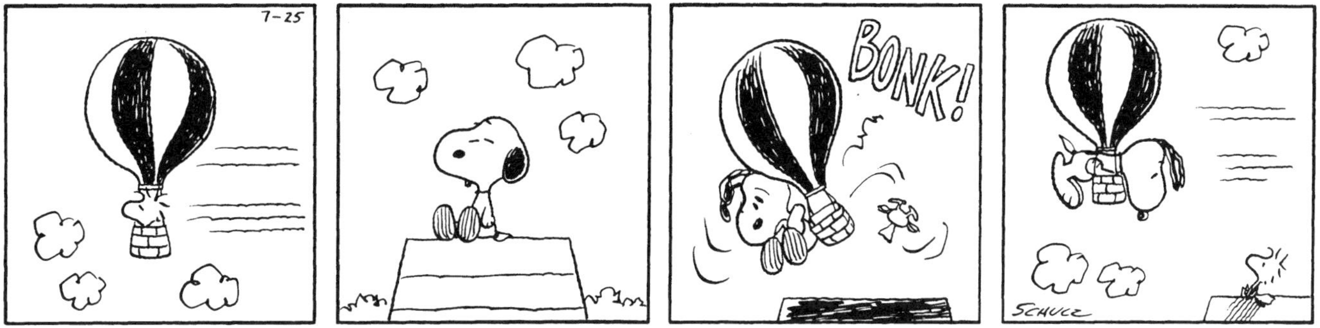
7-25
BONK!
SCHULZ

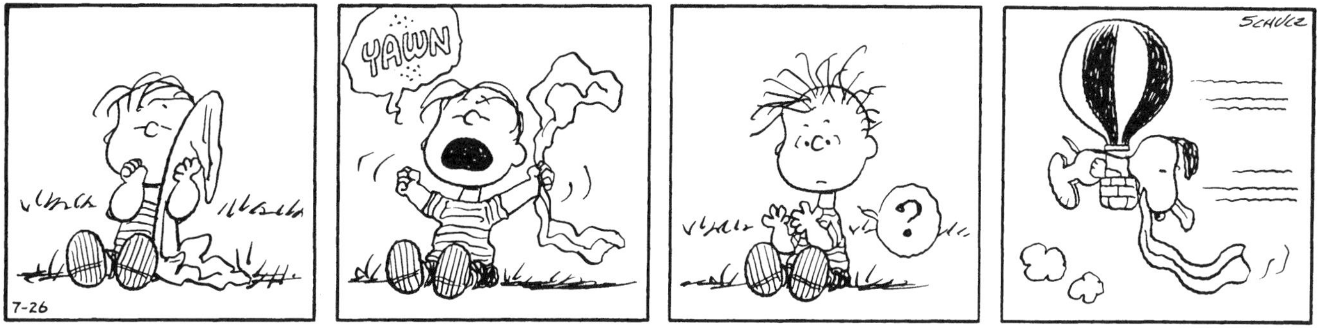
7-26
YAWN
?
SCHULZ

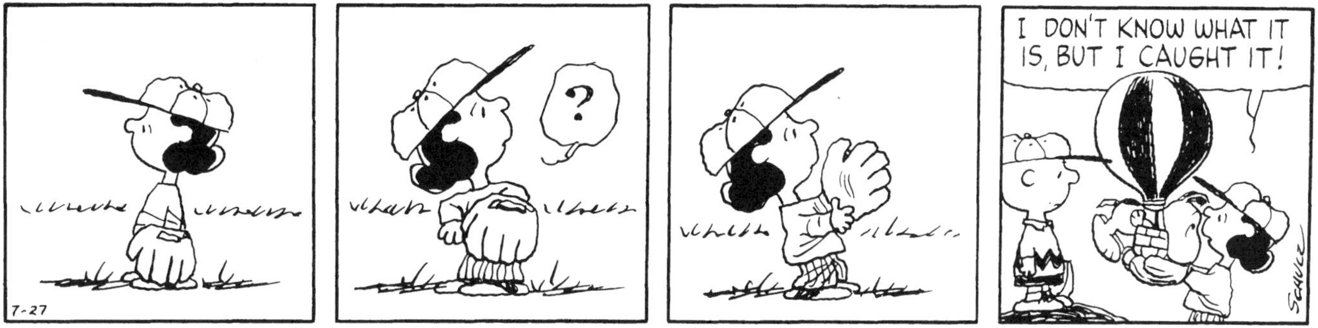
7-27
?
I DON'T KNOW WHAT IT IS, BUT I CAUGHT IT!
SCHULZ

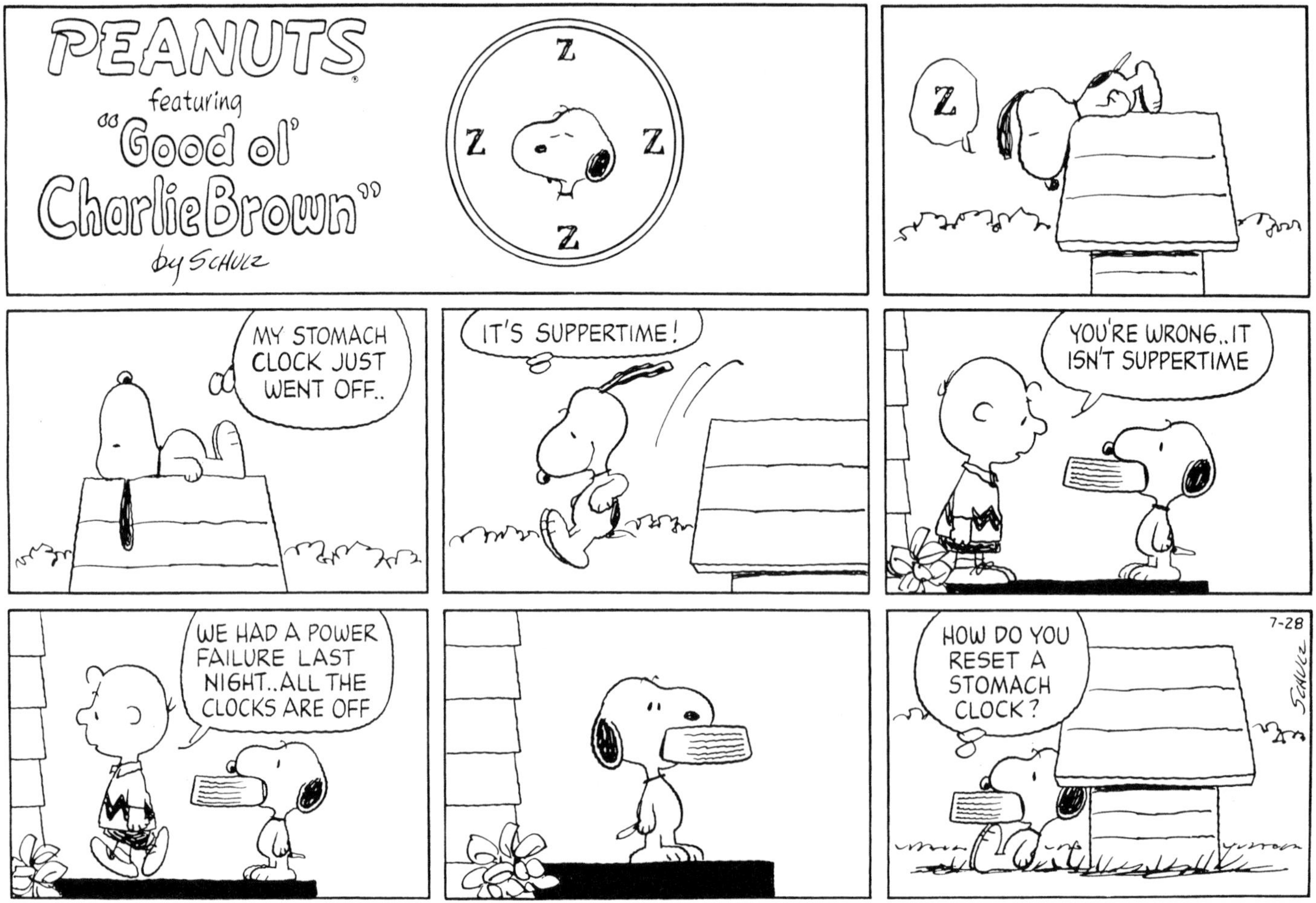
PEANUTS
featuring
"Good ol' CharlieBrown"
by SCHULZ
Z
Z
Z
Z
Z
MY STOMACH CLOCK JUST WENT OFF..
IT'S SUPPERTIME!
YOU'RE WRONG..IT ISN'T SUPPERTIME
WE HAD A POWER FAILURE LAST NIGHT..ALL THE CLOCKS ARE OFF
HOW DO YOU RESET A STOMACH CLOCK?
7-28
SCHULZ

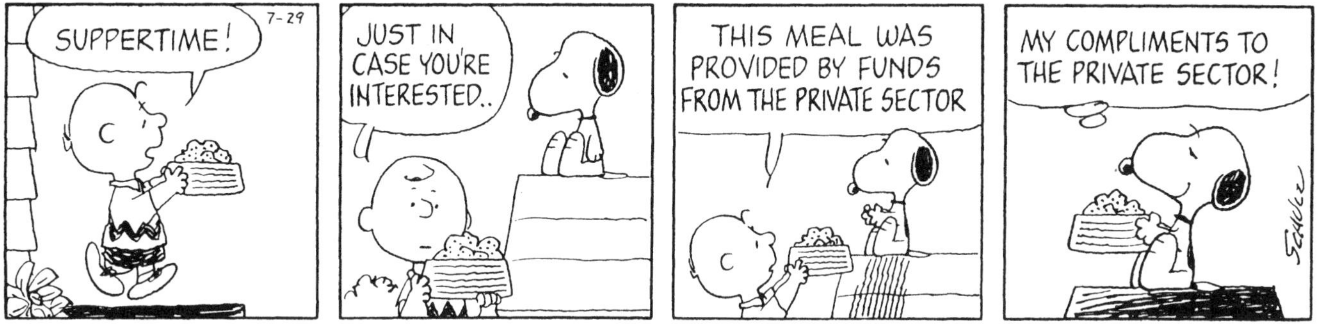
7-29
SUPPERTIME!
JUST IN CASE YOU'RE INTERESTED..
THIS MEAL WAS PROVIDED BY FUNDS FROM THE PRIVATE SECTOR
MY COMPLIMENTS TO THE PRIVATE SECTOR!
SCHULZ

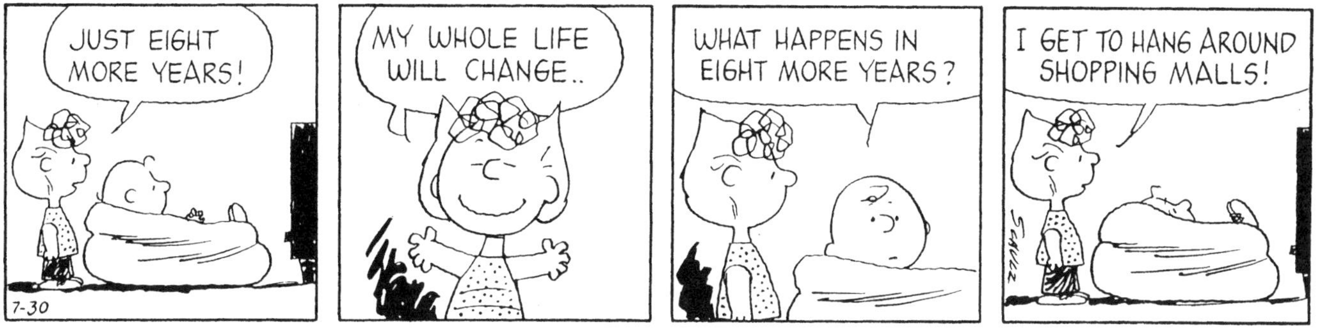
JUST EIGHT MORE YEARS!
7-30
MY WHOLE LIFE WILL CHANGE..
WHAT HAPPENS IN EIGHT MORE YEARS?
I GET TO HANG AROUND SHOPPING MALLS!
SCHULZ

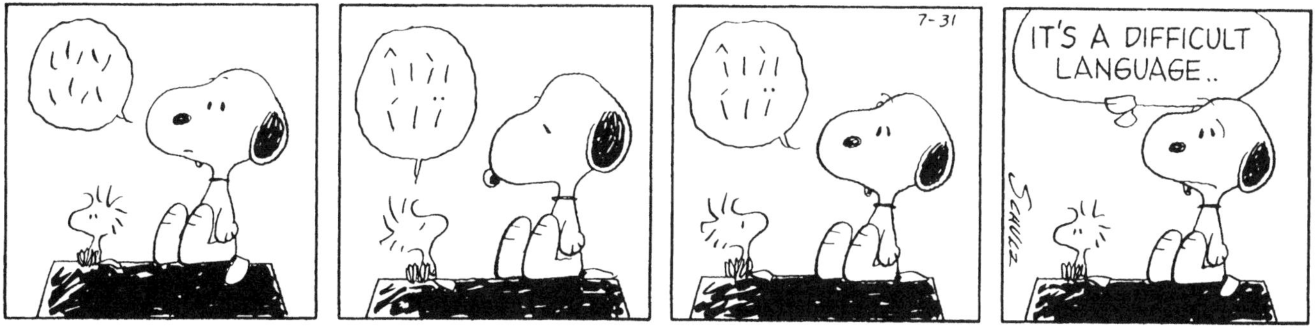
7-31
SCHULZ
IT'S A DIFFICULT LANGUAGE..

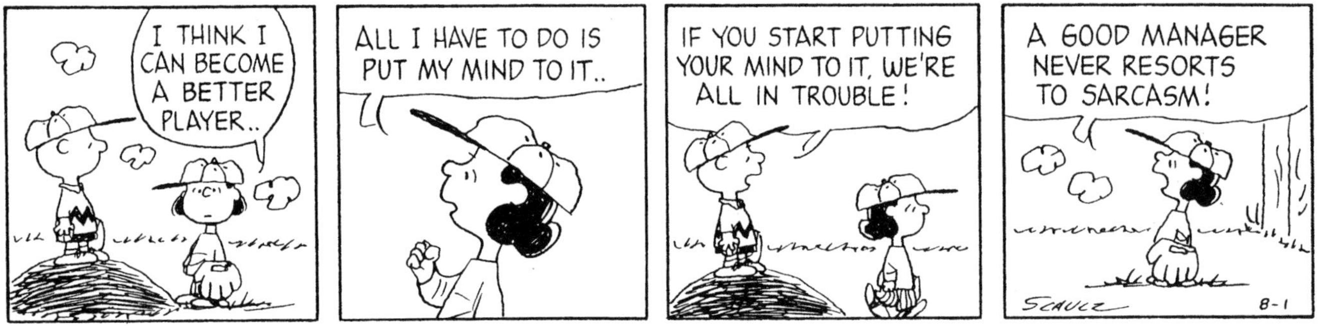
I THINK I CAN BECOME A BETTER PLAYER..
ALL I HAVE TO DO IS PUT MY MIND TO IT..
IF YOU START PUTTING YOUR MIND TO IT, WE'RE ALL IN TROUBLE!
A GOOD MANAGER NEVER RESORTS TO SARCASM!
SCHULZ
8-1

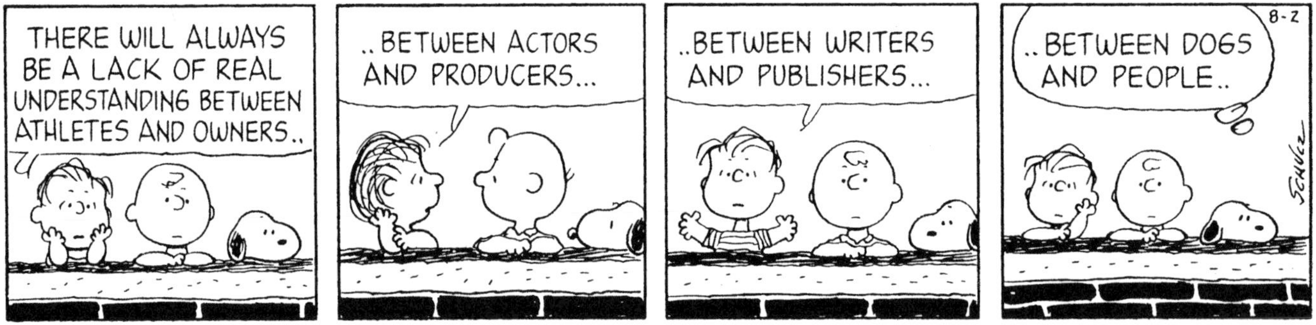
THERE WILL ALWAYS BE A LACK OF REAL UNDERSTANDING BETWEEN ATHLETES AND OWNERS..
..BETWEEN ACTORS AND PRODUCERS...
..BETWEEN WRITERS AND PUBLISHERS...
8-2
..BETWEEN DOGS AND PEOPLE..
SCHULZ

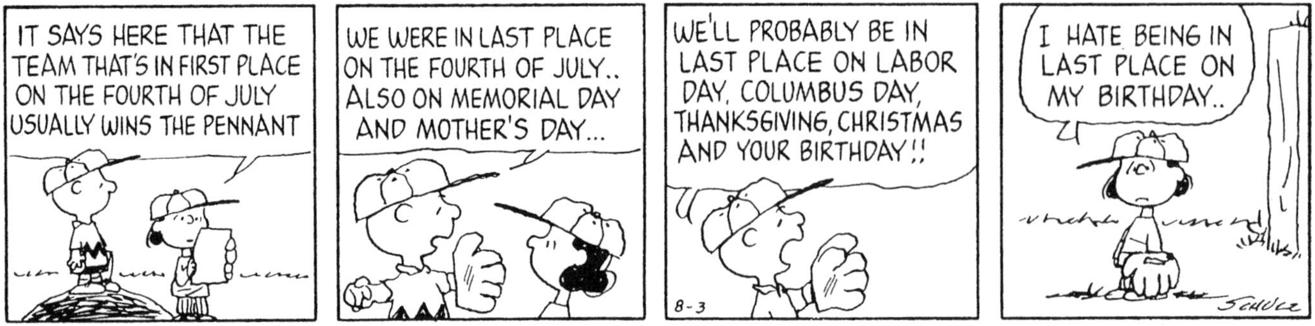
IT SAYS HERE THAT THE TEAM THAT'S IN FIRST PLACE ON THE FOURTH OF JULY USUALLY WINS THE PENNANT
WE WERE IN LAST PLACE ON THE FOURTH OF JULY.. ALSO ON MEMORIAL DAY AND MOTHER'S DAY...
WE'LL PROBABLY BE IN LAST PLACE ON LABOR DAY, COLUMBUS DAY, THANKSGIVING, CHRISTMAS AND YOUR BIRTHDAY!!
8-3
I HATE BEING IN LAST PLACE ON MY BIRTHDAY..
SCHULZ

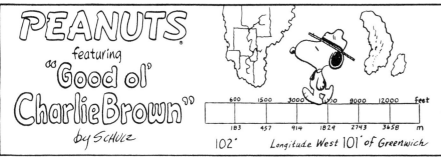

PEANUTS
featuring
"Good ol' Charlie Brown"
by SCHULZ

102° Longitude West 101° of Greenwich

600	1500	3000		9000	12000	feet
183	457	914	1829	2743	3658	m

EVERYONE READY?

OKAY, TROOPS, TODAY WE'RE GOING TO LEARN ABOUT DIRECTIONS AND MAP READING..

8-4

REMEMBER WHAT I TOLD YOU ABOUT THE MOON? YOU CAN ALWAYS TELL WHICH WAY IS WEST BECAUSE THE MOON IS ALWAYS OVER HOLLYWOOD...

IF YOU CAN'T SEE THE MOON, OF COURSE, YOU HAVE TO USE A MAP...

NOW, I WANT YOU TO TAKE THIS MAP, AND SHOW ME WHERE WE ARE RIGHT NOW..

PUT THE MAP SOMEPLACE WHERE YOU CAN ALL SEE IT...

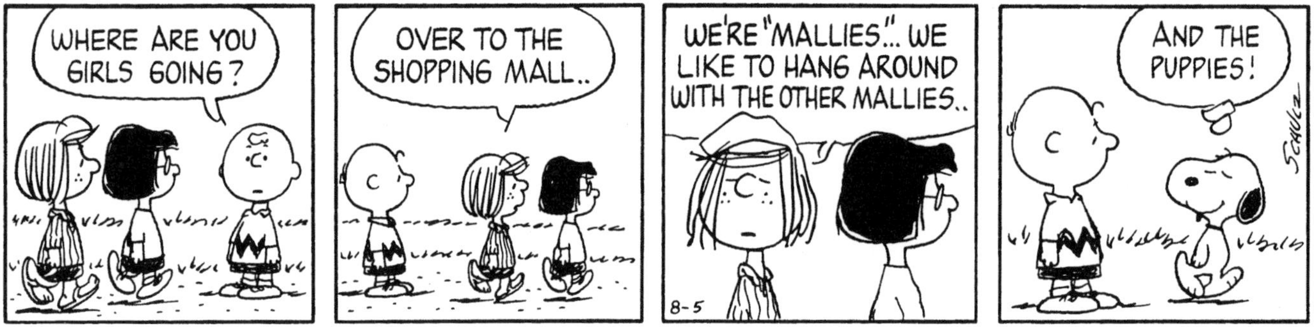
WHERE ARE YOU GIRLS GOING?
OVER TO THE SHOPPING MALL..
WE'RE "MALLIES"... WE LIKE TO HANG AROUND WITH THE OTHER MALLIES..
AND THE PUPPIES!
8-5

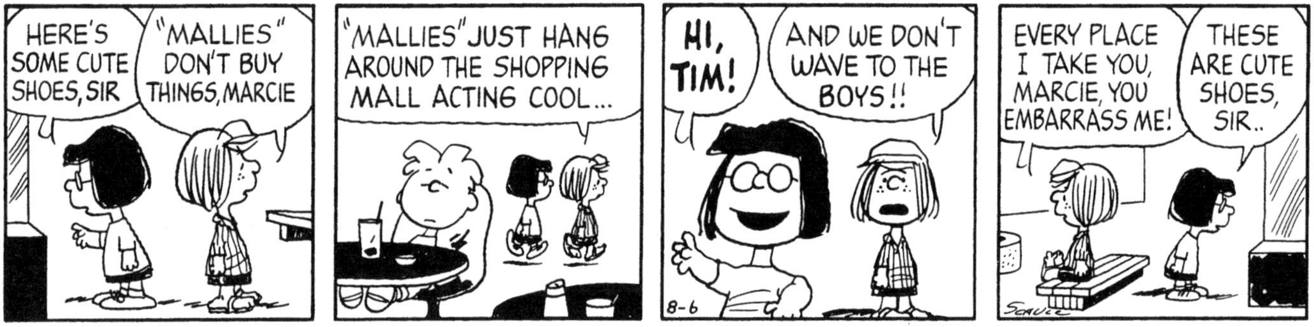
HERE'S SOME CUTE SHOES, SIR
"MALLIES" DON'T BUY THINGS, MARCIE
"MALLIES" JUST HANG AROUND THE SHOPPING MALL ACTING COOL...
HI, TIM!
AND WE DON'T WAVE TO THE BOYS!!
8-6
EVERY PLACE I TAKE YOU, MARCIE, YOU EMBARRASS ME!
THESE ARE CUTE SHOES, SIR..

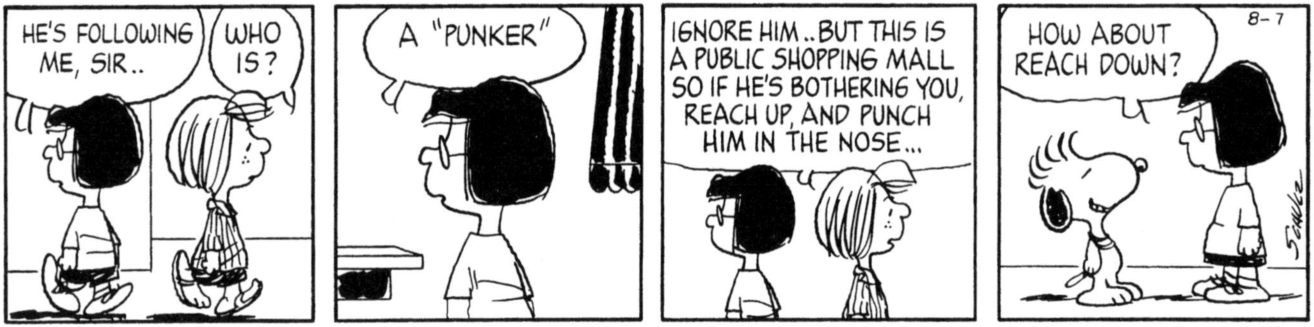
HE'S FOLLOWING ME, SIR..
WHO IS?
A "PUNKER"
IGNORE HIM..BUT THIS IS A PUBLIC SHOPPING MALL SO IF HE'S BOTHERING YOU, REACH UP, AND PUNCH HIM IN THE NOSE...
8-7
HOW ABOUT REACH DOWN?

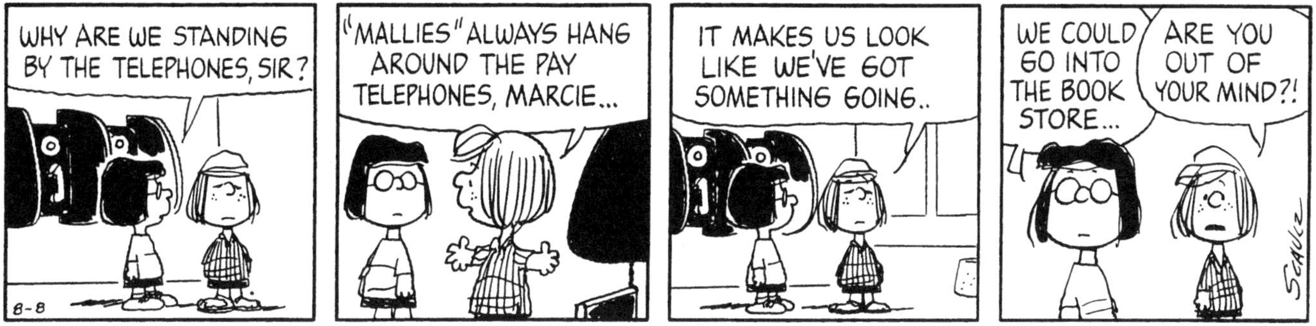
WHY ARE WE STANDING BY THE TELEPHONES, SIR?
8-8
"MALLIES" ALWAYS HANG AROUND THE PAY TELEPHONES, MARCIE...
IT MAKES US LOOK LIKE WE'VE GOT SOMETHING GOING..
WE COULD GO INTO THE BOOK STORE...
ARE YOU OUT OF YOUR MIND?!
SCHULZ

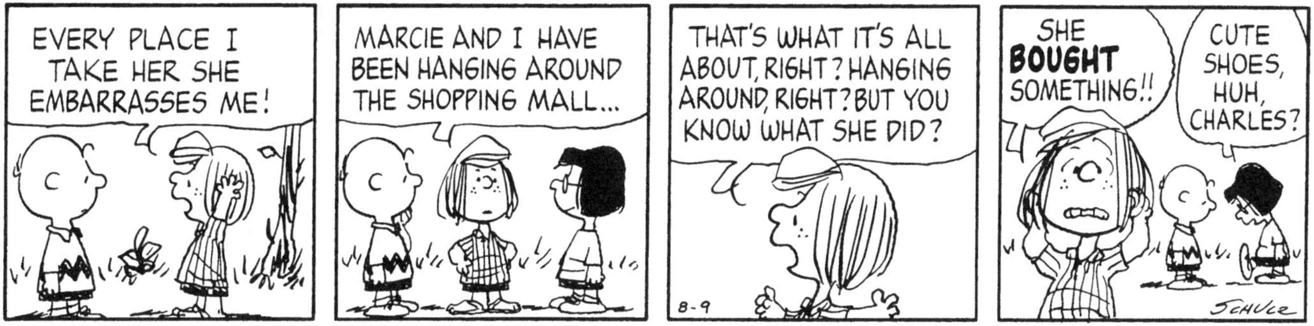
EVERY PLACE I TAKE HER SHE EMBARRASSES ME!
MARCIE AND I HAVE BEEN HANGING AROUND THE SHOPPING MALL...
THAT'S WHAT IT'S ALL ABOUT, RIGHT? HANGING AROUND, RIGHT? BUT YOU KNOW WHAT SHE DID?
8-9
SHE **BOUGHT** SOMETHING!!
CUTE SHOES, HUH, CHARLES?
SCHULZ

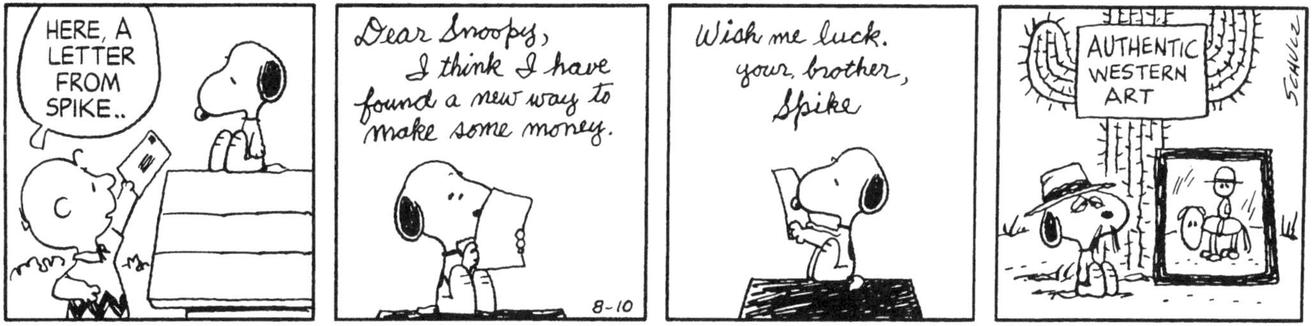
HERE, A LETTER FROM SPIKE..
Dear Snoopy,
I think I have found a new way to make some money.
8-10
Wish me luck.
your brother,
Spike
AUTHENTIC WESTERN ART
SCHULZ

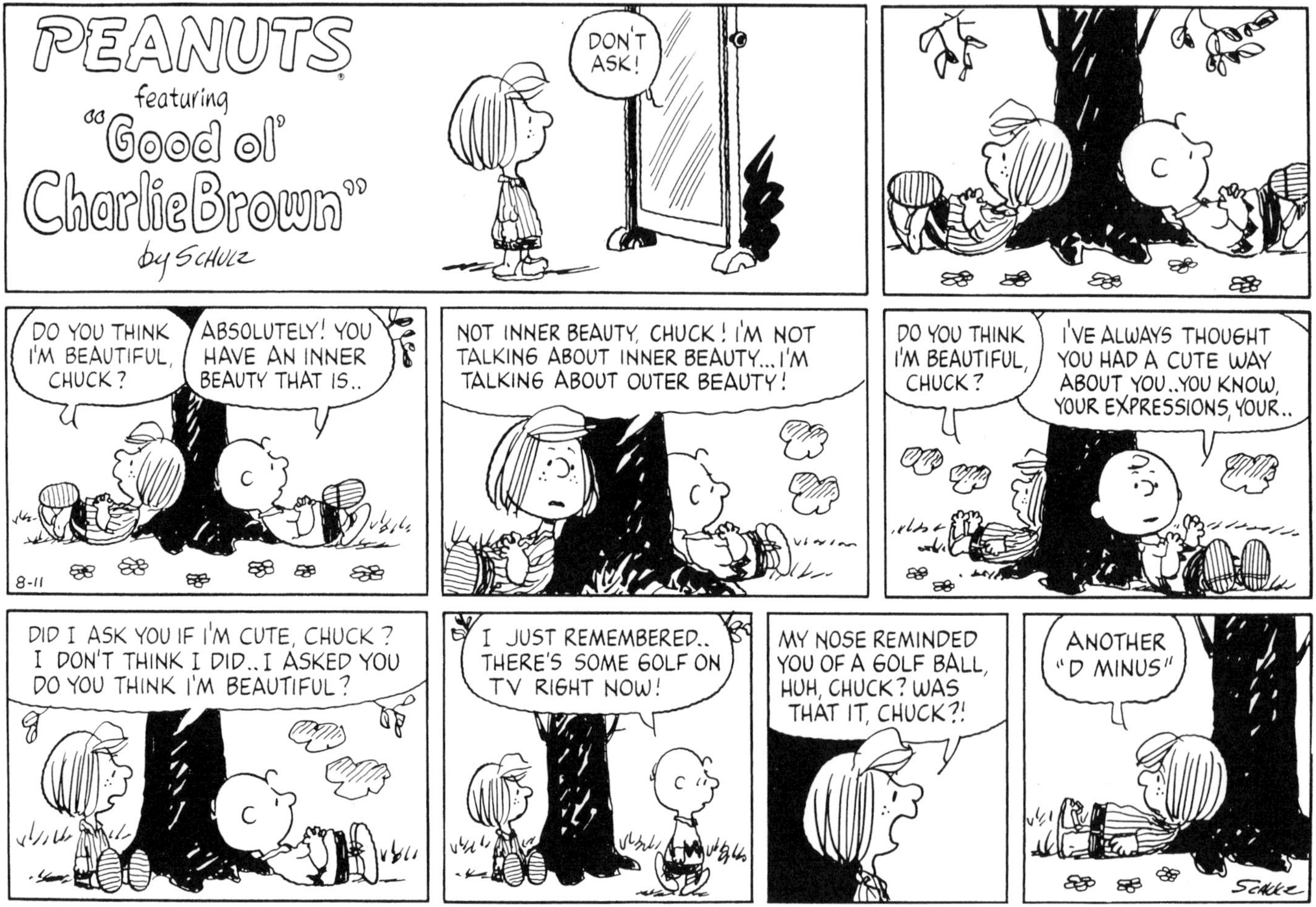
PEANUTS
featuring "Good ol' Charlie Brown"
by SCHULZ
DON'T ASK!
DO YOU THINK I'M BEAUTIFUL, CHUCK?
ABSOLUTELY! YOU HAVE AN INNER BEAUTY THAT IS..
8-11
NOT INNER BEAUTY, CHUCK! I'M NOT TALKING ABOUT INNER BEAUTY... I'M TALKING ABOUT OUTER BEAUTY!
DO YOU THINK I'M BEAUTIFUL, CHUCK?
I'VE ALWAYS THOUGHT YOU HAD A CUTE WAY ABOUT YOU..YOU KNOW, YOUR EXPRESSIONS, YOUR..
DID I ASK YOU IF I'M CUTE, CHUCK? I DON'T THINK I DID..I ASKED YOU DO YOU THINK I'M BEAUTIFUL?
I JUST REMEMBERED.. THERE'S SOME GOLF ON TV RIGHT NOW!
MY NOSE REMINDED YOU OF A GOLF BALL, HUH, CHUCK? WAS THAT IT, CHUCK?!
ANOTHER "D MINUS"
SCHULZ

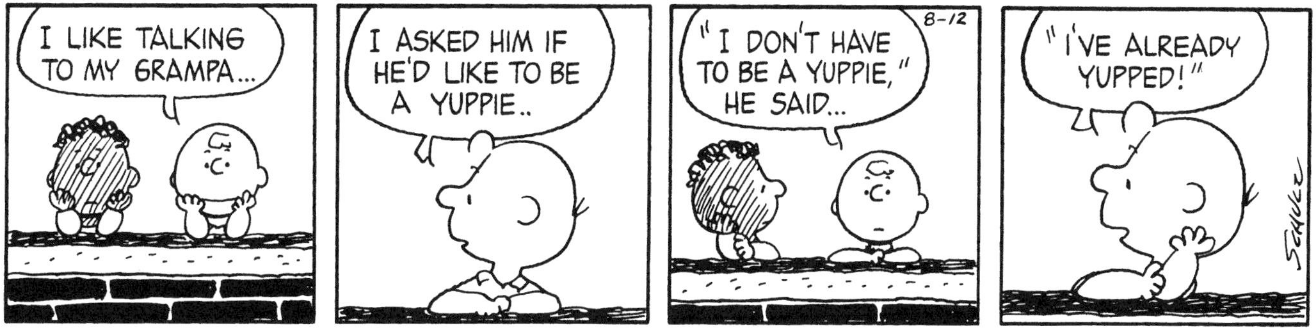
I LIKE TALKING TO MY GRAMPA...
I ASKED HIM IF HE'D LIKE TO BE A YUPPIE..
8-12
"I DON'T HAVE TO BE A YUPPIE," HE SAID...
"I'VE ALREADY YUPPED!"
SCHULZ

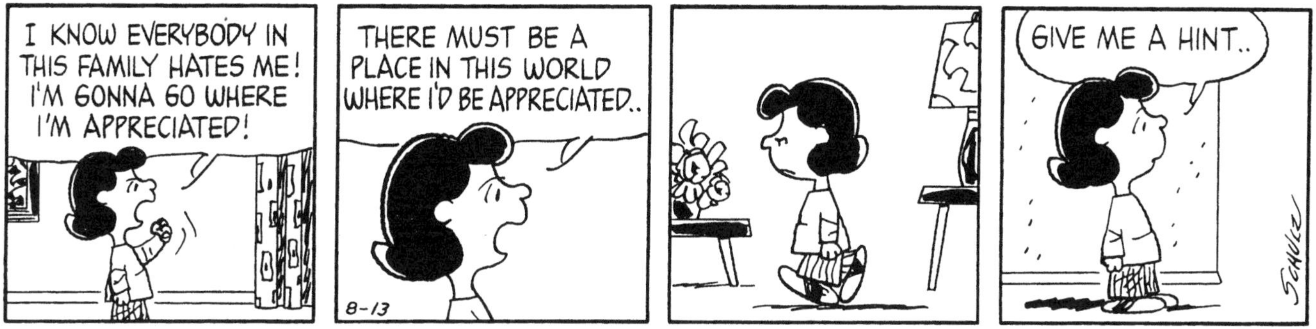
I KNOW EVERYBODY IN THIS FAMILY HATES ME! I'M GONNA GO WHERE I'M APPRECIATED!
THERE MUST BE A PLACE IN THIS WORLD WHERE I'D BE APPRECIATED..
8-13
GIVE ME A HINT..
SCHULZ

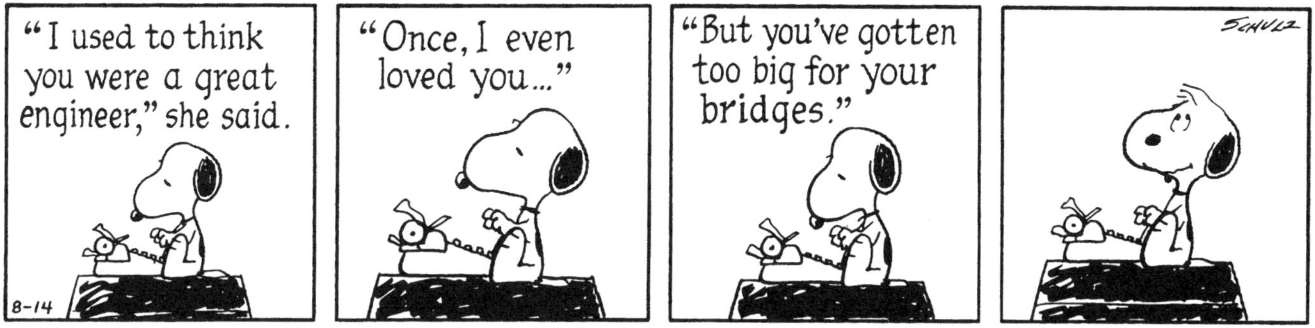
"I used to think you were a great engineer," she said.
8-14
"Once, I even loved you..."
"But you've gotten too big for your bridges."
SCHULZ

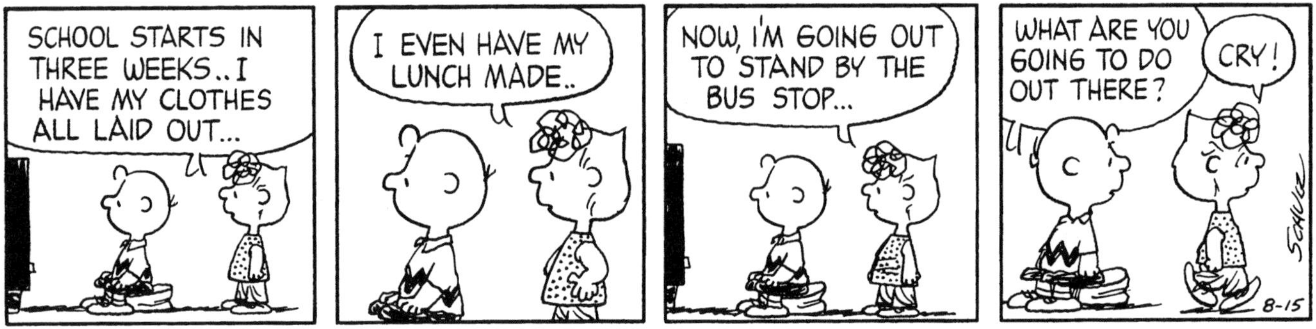
SCHOOL STARTS IN THREE WEEKS..I HAVE MY CLOTHES ALL LAID OUT...
I EVEN HAVE MY LUNCH MADE..
NOW, I'M GOING OUT TO STAND BY THE BUS STOP...
WHAT ARE YOU GOING TO DO OUT THERE?
CRY!
8-15

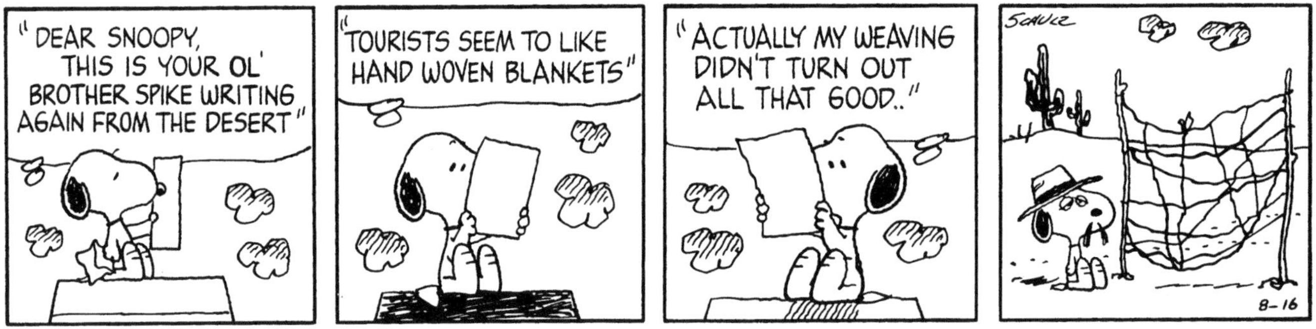
"DEAR SNOOPY, THIS IS YOUR OL' BROTHER SPIKE WRITING AGAIN FROM THE DESERT"
"TOURISTS SEEM TO LIKE HAND WOVEN BLANKETS"
"ACTUALLY MY WEAVING DIDN'T TURN OUT ALL THAT GOOD.."
8-16

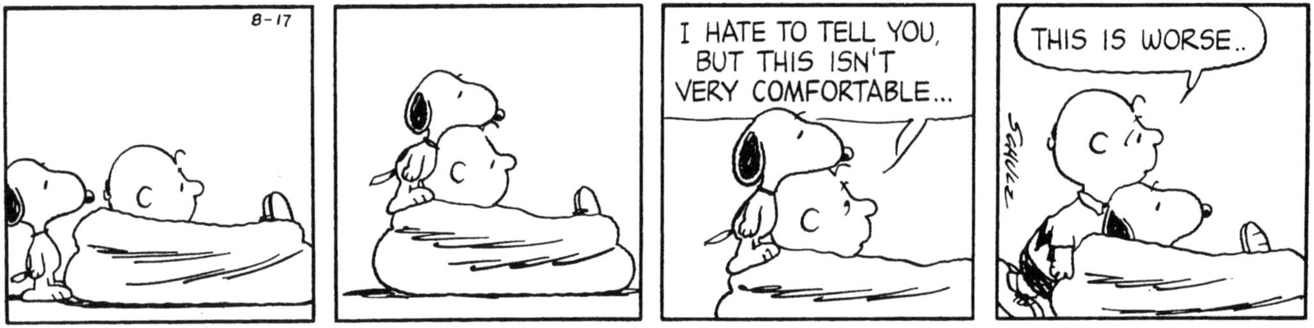
8-17
I HATE TO TELL YOU, BUT THIS ISN'T VERY COMFORTABLE...
THIS IS WORSE..

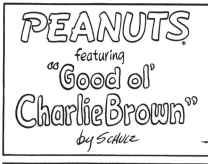

PEANUTS
featuring
"Good ol' Charlie Brown"
by SCHULZ

PREPARE TO DON MASKS.. DON MASKS!

HERE'S THE WORLD FAMOUS EXPLORER LEADING HIS TEAM OF DIVERS TO AN UNDERWATER EXPEDITION...

STAY RIGHT WHERE YOU ARE!! FORGET IT!

Hey!! WHAT ARE YOU DOING?

8-18

AAUGH!

SSSSSS

JACQUES COUSTEAU WOULD NEVER HIDE IN A TREE!

JACQUES COUSTEAU ONLY WORRIES ABOUT SHARKS..

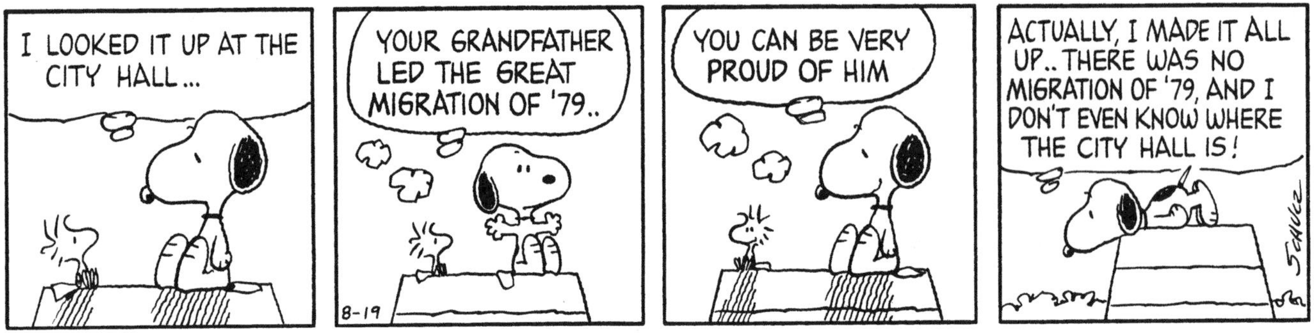
I LOOKED IT UP AT THE CITY HALL...
YOUR GRANDFATHER LED THE GREAT MIGRATION OF '79..
8-19
YOU CAN BE VERY PROUD OF HIM
ACTUALLY, I MADE IT ALL UP.. THERE WAS NO MIGRATION OF '79, AND I DON'T EVEN KNOW WHERE THE CITY HALL IS!
SCHULZ

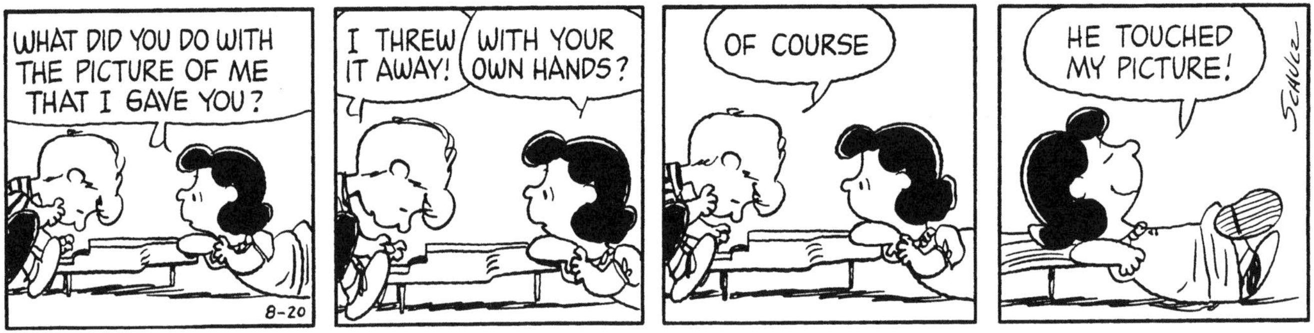
WHAT DID YOU DO WITH THE PICTURE OF ME THAT I GAVE YOU?
8-20
I THREW IT AWAY!
WITH YOUR OWN HANDS?
OF COURSE
HE TOUCHED MY PICTURE!
SCHULZ

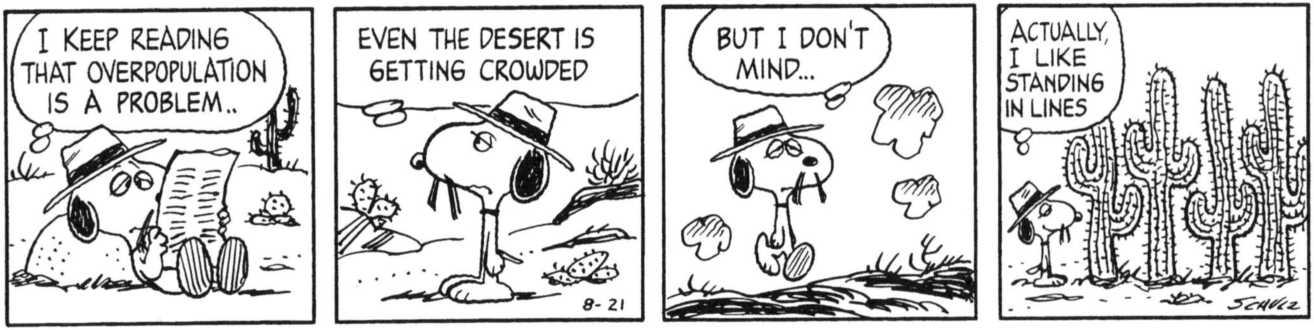
I KEEP READING THAT OVERPOPULATION IS A PROBLEM..
EVEN THE DESERT IS GETTING CROWDED
8-21
BUT I DON'T MIND...
ACTUALLY, I LIKE STANDING IN LINES
SCHULZ

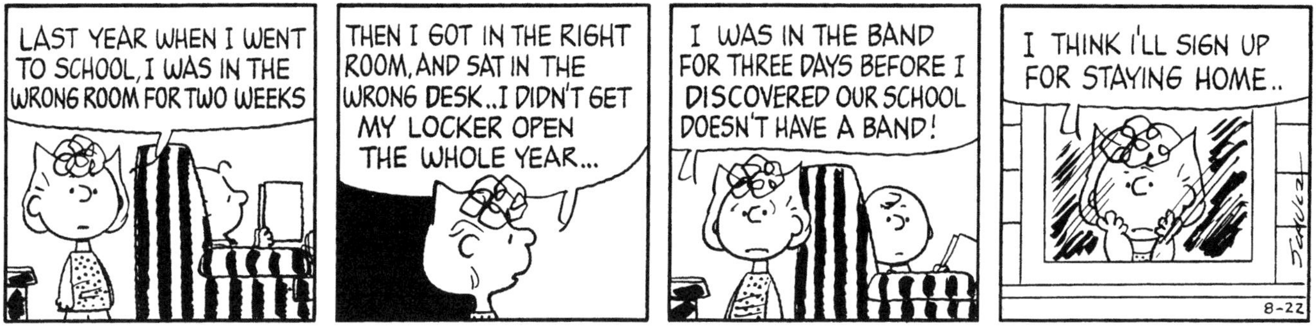
LAST YEAR WHEN I WENT TO SCHOOL, I WAS IN THE WRONG ROOM FOR TWO WEEKS
THEN I GOT IN THE RIGHT ROOM, AND SAT IN THE WRONG DESK.. I DIDN'T GET MY LOCKER OPEN THE WHOLE YEAR...
I WAS IN THE BAND FOR THREE DAYS BEFORE I DISCOVERED OUR SCHOOL DOESN'T HAVE A BAND!
I THINK I'LL SIGN UP FOR STAYING HOME..
SCHULZ
8-22

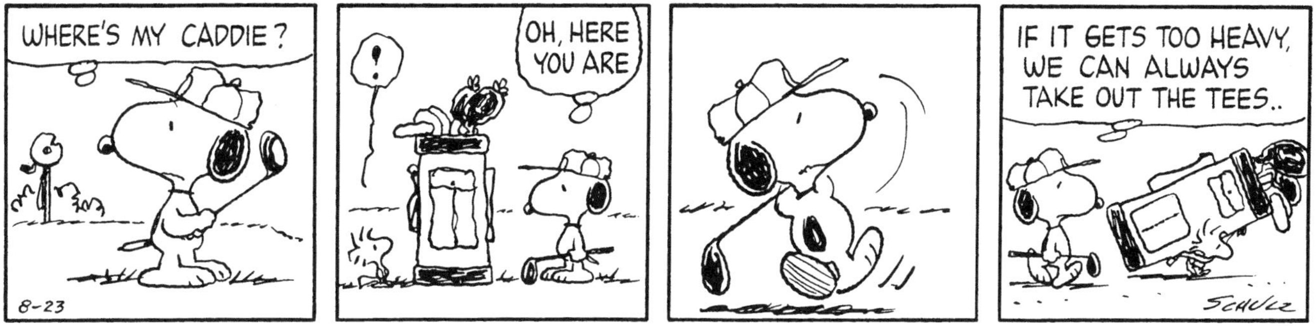
WHERE'S MY CADDIE?
8-23
!
OH, HERE YOU ARE
IF IT GETS TOO HEAVY, WE CAN ALWAYS TAKE OUT THE TEES..
SCHULZ

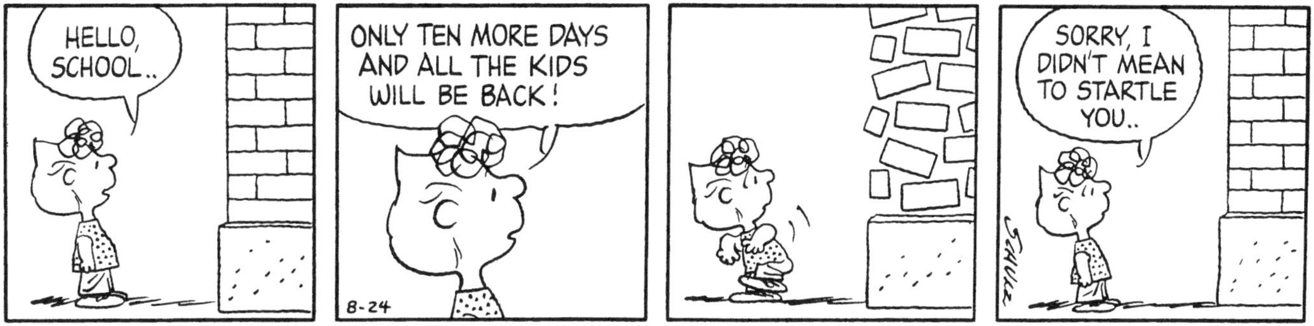
HELLO, SCHOOL..
ONLY TEN MORE DAYS AND ALL THE KIDS WILL BE BACK!
8-24
SORRY, I DIDN'T MEAN TO STARTLE YOU..
SCHULZ

PEANUTS
featuring
"Good ol'
Charlie Brown"
by SCHULZ

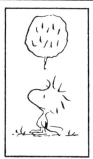

8-25

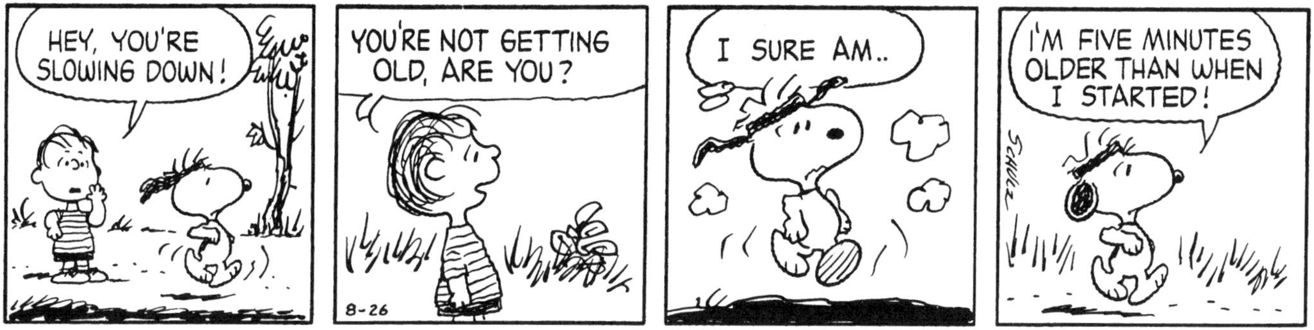
HEY, YOU'RE SLOWING DOWN!
YOU'RE NOT GETTING OLD, ARE YOU?
8-26
I SURE AM..
I'M FIVE MINUTES OLDER THAN WHEN I STARTED!
SCHULZ

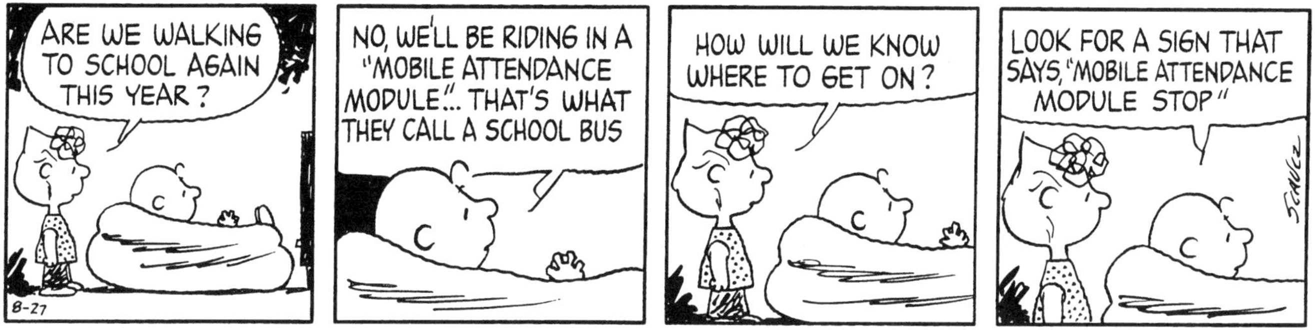
ARE WE WALKING TO SCHOOL AGAIN THIS YEAR?
8-27
NO, WE'LL BE RIDING IN A "MOBILE ATTENDANCE MODULE"... THAT'S WHAT THEY CALL A SCHOOL BUS
HOW WILL WE KNOW WHERE TO GET ON?
LOOK FOR A SIGN THAT SAYS, "MOBILE ATTENDANCE MODULE STOP"
SCHULZ

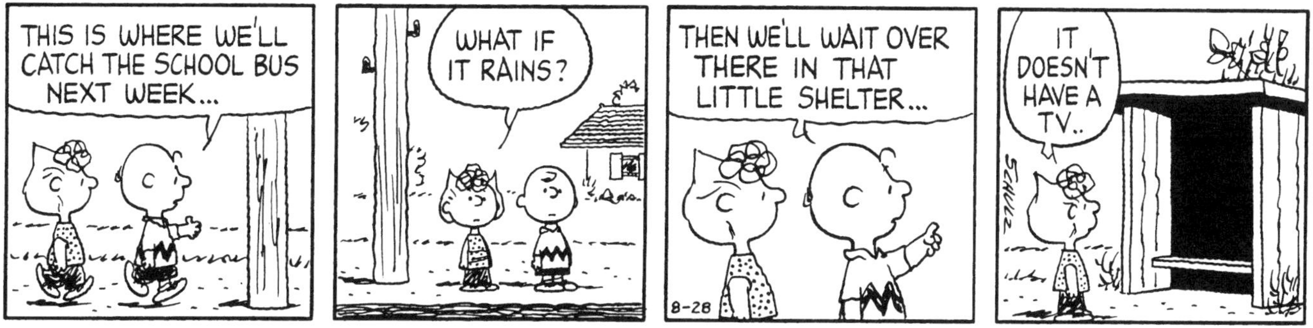
THIS IS WHERE WE'LL CATCH THE SCHOOL BUS NEXT WEEK...
WHAT IF IT RAINS?
THEN WE'LL WAIT OVER THERE IN THAT LITTLE SHELTER...
8-28
IT DOESN'T HAVE A TV..
SCHULZ

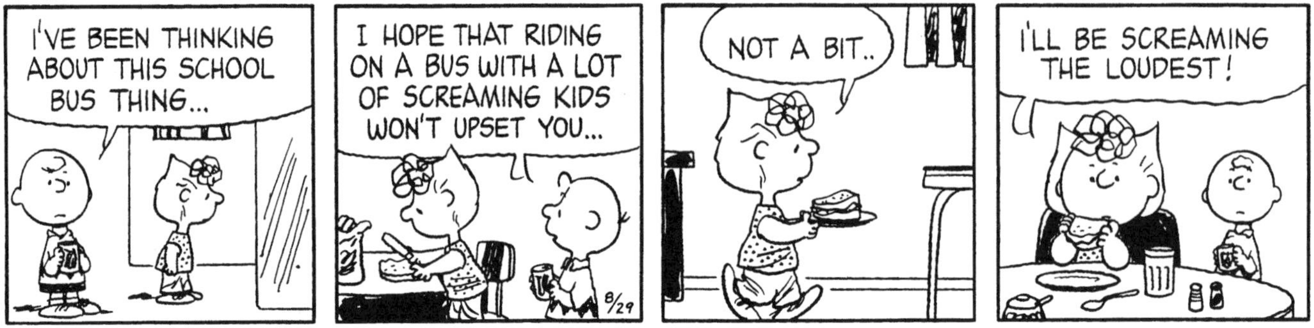
I'VE BEEN THINKING ABOUT THIS SCHOOL BUS THING...
I HOPE THAT RIDING ON A BUS WITH A LOT OF SCREAMING KIDS WON'T UPSET YOU...
8/29
NOT A BIT..
I'LL BE SCREAMING THE LOUDEST!

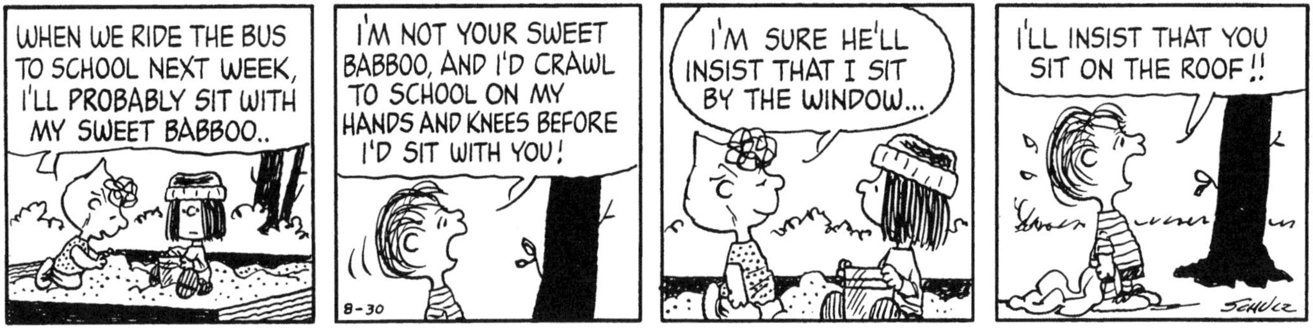
WHEN WE RIDE THE BUS TO SCHOOL NEXT WEEK, I'LL PROBABLY SIT WITH MY SWEET BABBOO..
I'M NOT YOUR SWEET BABBOO, AND I'D CRAWL TO SCHOOL ON MY HANDS AND KNEES BEFORE I'D SIT WITH YOU!
8-30
I'M SURE HE'LL INSIST THAT I SIT BY THE WINDOW...
I'LL INSIST THAT YOU SIT ON THE ROOF!!
SCHULZ

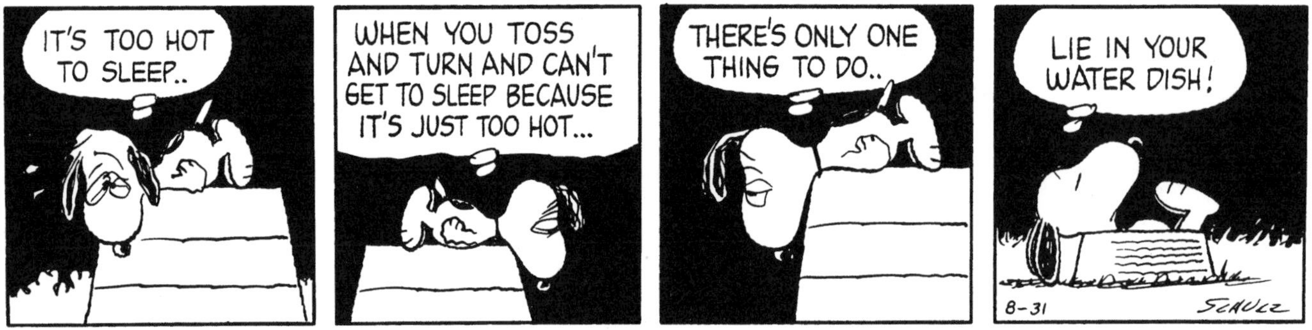
IT'S TOO HOT TO SLEEP..
WHEN YOU TOSS AND TURN AND CAN'T GET TO SLEEP BECAUSE IT'S JUST TOO HOT...
THERE'S ONLY ONE THING TO DO..
LIE IN YOUR WATER DISH!
8-31
SCHULZ

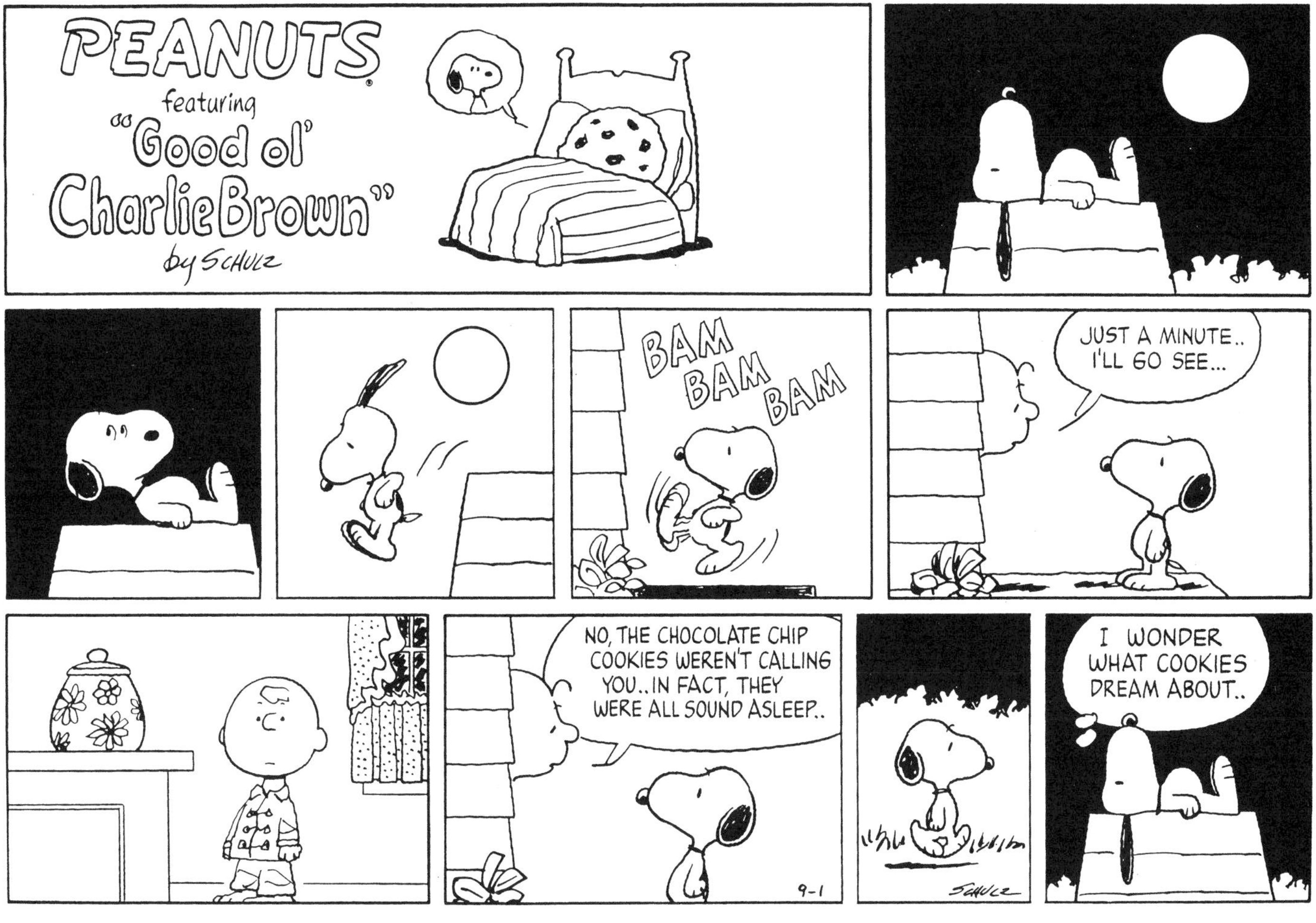
PEANUTS
featuring
"Good ol' Charlie Brown"
by SCHULZ
BAM
BAM
BAM
JUST A MINUTE.. I'LL GO SEE...
NO, THE CHOCOLATE CHIP COOKIES WEREN'T CALLING YOU..IN FACT, THEY WERE ALL SOUND ASLEEP..
9-1
SCHULZ
I WONDER WHAT COOKIES DREAM ABOUT..

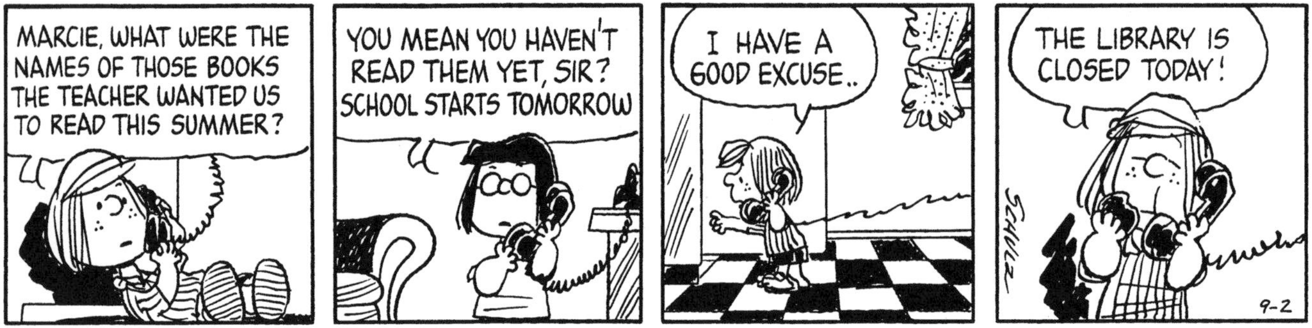
MARCIE, WHAT WERE THE NAMES OF THOSE BOOKS THE TEACHER WANTED US TO READ THIS SUMMER?
YOU MEAN YOU HAVEN'T READ THEM YET, SIR? SCHOOL STARTS TOMORROW
I HAVE A GOOD EXCUSE..
THE LIBRARY IS CLOSED TODAY!
9-2

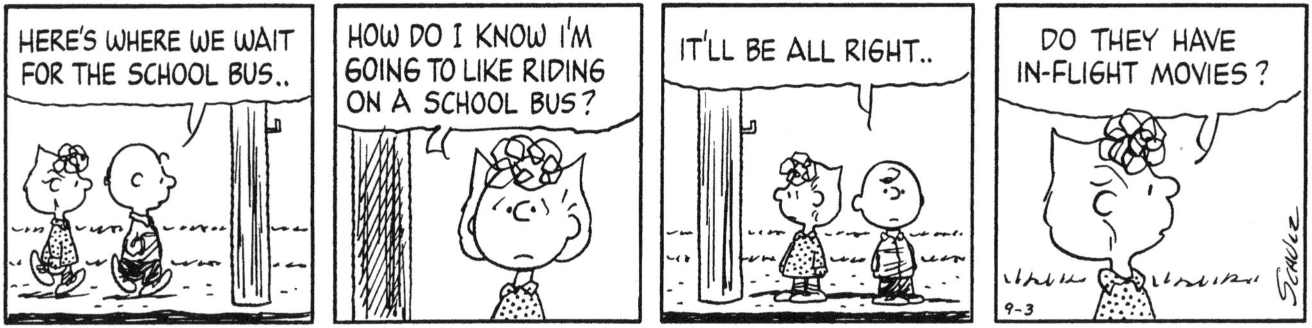
HERE'S WHERE WE WAIT FOR THE SCHOOL BUS..
HOW DO I KNOW I'M GOING TO LIKE RIDING ON A SCHOOL BUS?
IT'LL BE ALL RIGHT..
DO THEY HAVE IN-FLIGHT MOVIES?
9-3

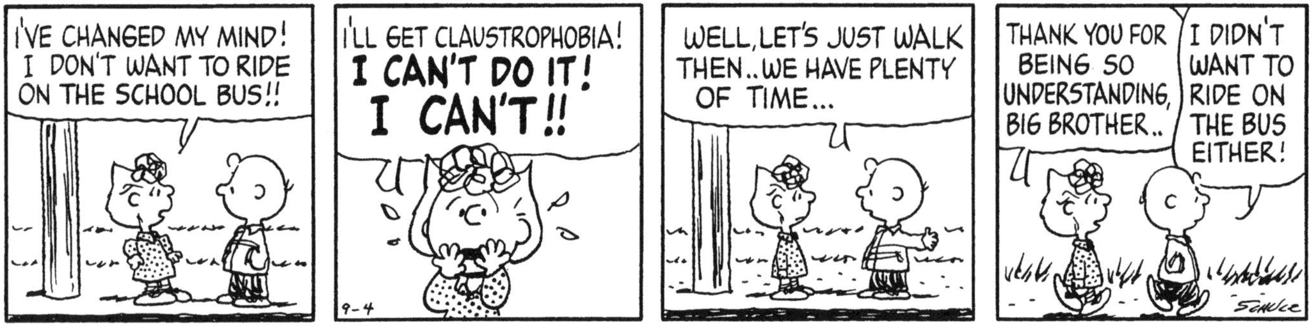
I'VE CHANGED MY MIND! I DON'T WANT TO RIDE ON THE SCHOOL BUS!!
I'LL GET CLAUSTROPHOBIA! I CAN'T DO IT! I CAN'T!!
9-4
WELL, LET'S JUST WALK THEN..WE HAVE PLENTY OF TIME...
THANK YOU FOR BEING SO UNDERSTANDING, BIG BROTHER..
I DIDN'T WANT TO RIDE ON THE BUS EITHER!

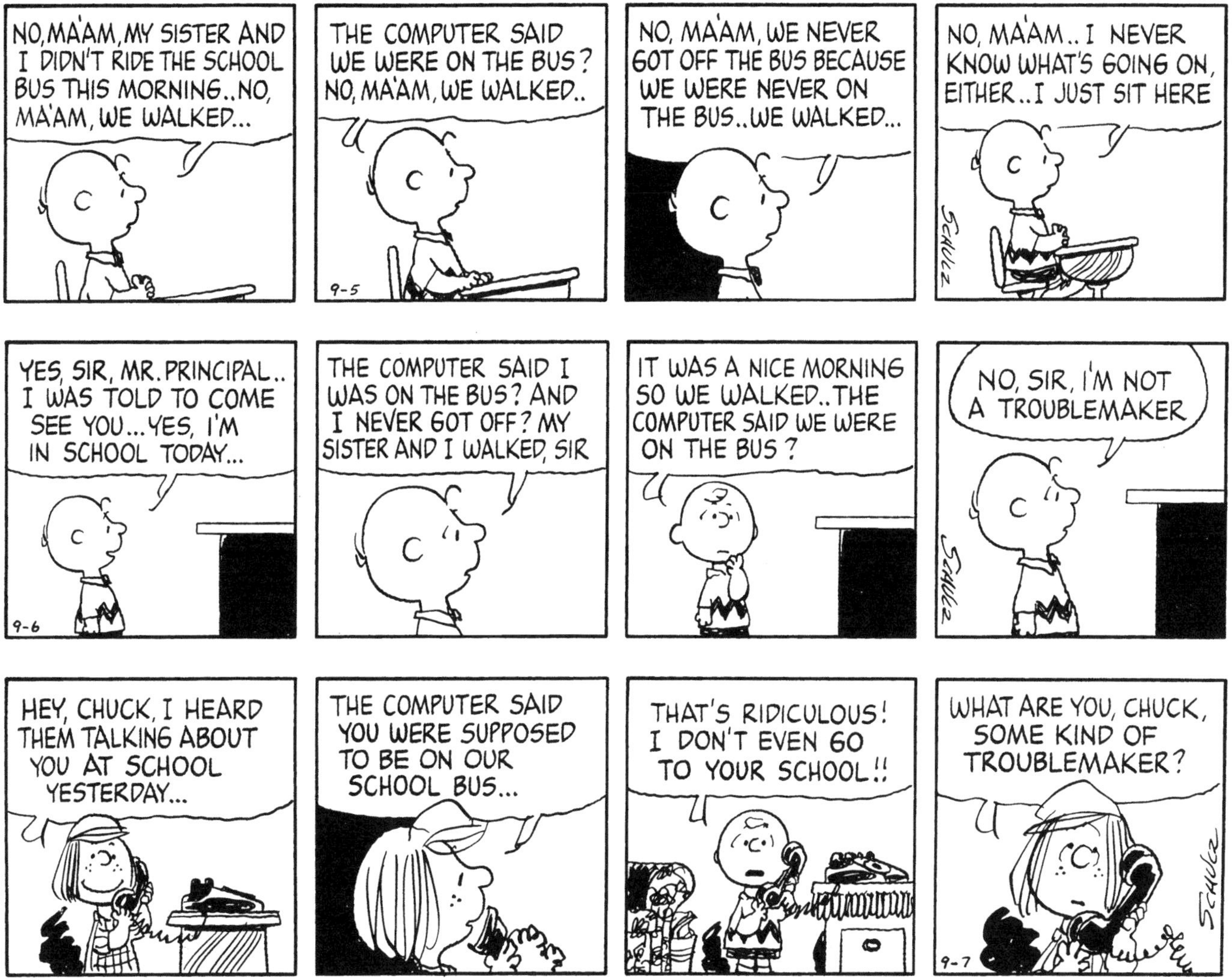
NO, MA'AM, MY SISTER AND I DIDN'T RIDE THE SCHOOL BUS THIS MORNING..NO, MA'AM, WE WALKED...
THE COMPUTER SAID WE WERE ON THE BUS? NO, MA'AM, WE WALKED..
9-5
NO, MA'AM, WE NEVER GOT OFF THE BUS BECAUSE WE WERE NEVER ON THE BUS..WE WALKED...
NO, MA'AM.. I NEVER KNOW WHAT'S GOING ON, EITHER..I JUST SIT HERE
SCHULZ
YES, SIR, MR. PRINCIPAL.. I WAS TOLD TO COME SEE YOU...YES, I'M IN SCHOOL TODAY...
9-6
THE COMPUTER SAID I WAS ON THE BUS? AND I NEVER GOT OFF? MY SISTER AND I WALKED, SIR
IT WAS A NICE MORNING SO WE WALKED..THE COMPUTER SAID WE WERE ON THE BUS?
NO, SIR, I'M NOT A TROUBLEMAKER
SCHULZ
HEY, CHUCK, I HEARD THEM TALKING ABOUT YOU AT SCHOOL YESTERDAY...
THE COMPUTER SAID YOU WERE SUPPOSED TO BE ON OUR SCHOOL BUS...
THAT'S RIDICULOUS! I DON'T EVEN GO TO YOUR SCHOOL!!
WHAT ARE YOU, CHUCK, SOME KIND OF TROUBLEMAKER?
SCHULZ
9-7

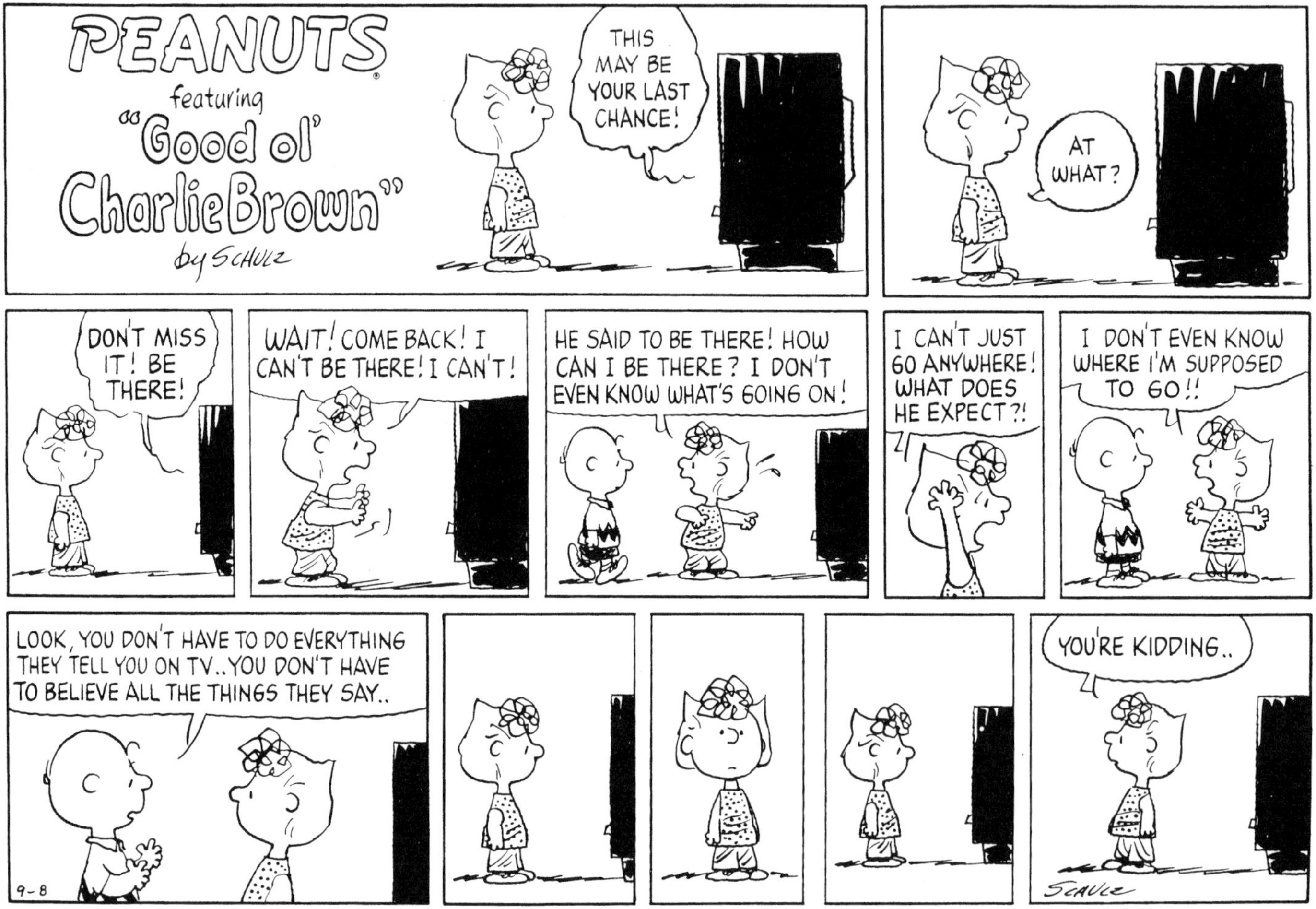
PEANUTS
featuring
"Good ol' Charlie Brown"
by SCHULZ
THIS MAY BE YOUR LAST CHANCE!
AT WHAT?
DON'T MISS IT! BE THERE!
WAIT! COME BACK! I CAN'T BE THERE! I CAN'T!
HE SAID TO BE THERE! HOW CAN I BE THERE? I DON'T EVEN KNOW WHAT'S GOING ON!
I CAN'T JUST GO ANYWHERE! WHAT DOES HE EXPECT?!
I DON'T EVEN KNOW WHERE I'M SUPPOSED TO GO!!
LOOK, YOU DON'T HAVE TO DO EVERYTHING THEY TELL YOU ON TV..YOU DON'T HAVE TO BELIEVE ALL THE THINGS THEY SAY..
9-8
YOU'RE KIDDING..
SCHULZ

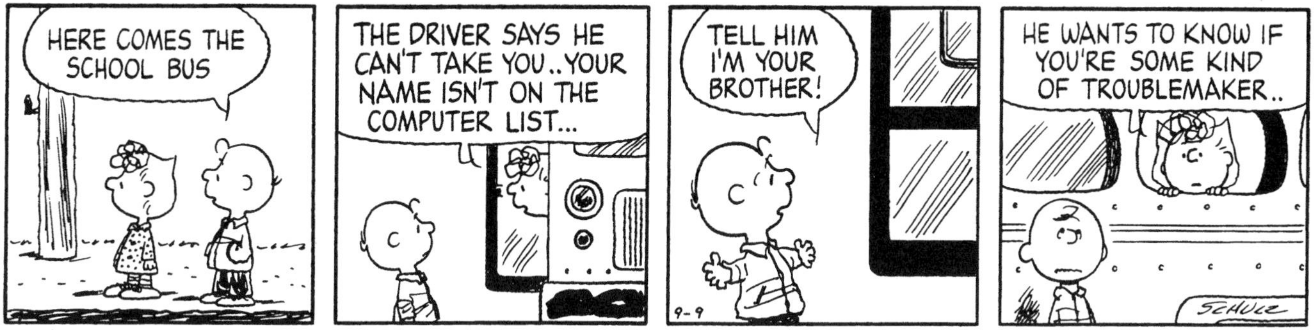
HERE COMES THE SCHOOL BUS
THE DRIVER SAYS HE CAN'T TAKE YOU..YOUR NAME ISN'T ON THE COMPUTER LIST...
TELL HIM I'M YOUR BROTHER!
9-9
HE WANTS TO KNOW IF YOU'RE SOME KIND OF TROUBLEMAKER..
SCHULZ

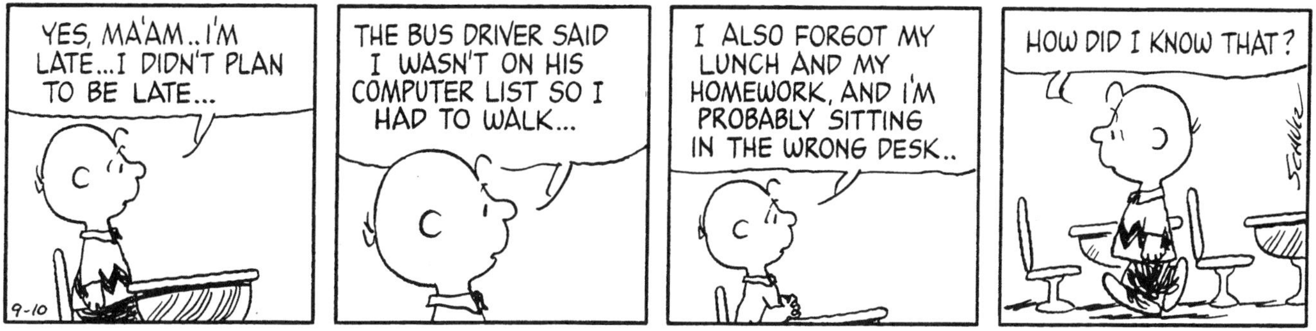
YES, MA'AM..I'M LATE...I DIDN'T PLAN TO BE LATE...
9-10
THE BUS DRIVER SAID I WASN'T ON HIS COMPUTER LIST SO I HAD TO WALK...
I ALSO FORGOT MY LUNCH AND MY HOMEWORK, AND I'M PROBABLY SITTING IN THE WRONG DESK..
HOW DID I KNOW THAT?
SCHULZ

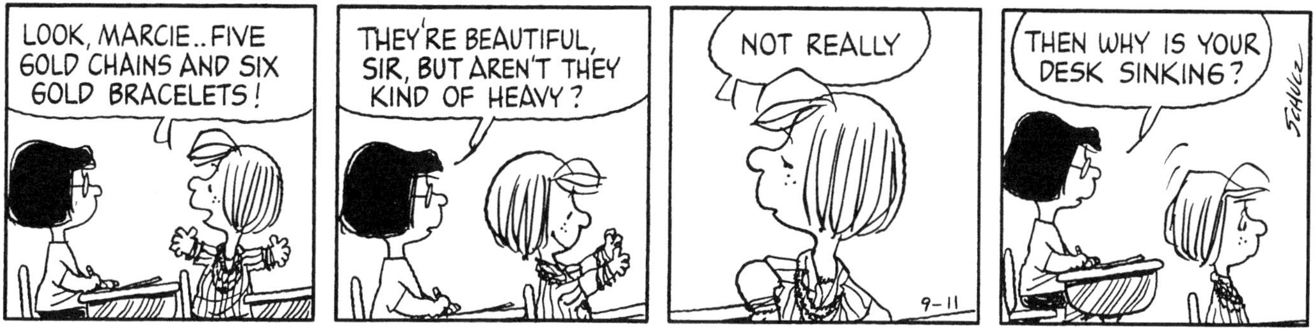
LOOK, MARCIE..FIVE GOLD CHAINS AND SIX GOLD BRACELETS!
THEY'RE BEAUTIFUL, SIR, BUT AREN'T THEY KIND OF HEAVY?
NOT REALLY
9-11
THEN WHY IS YOUR DESK SINKING?
SCHULZ

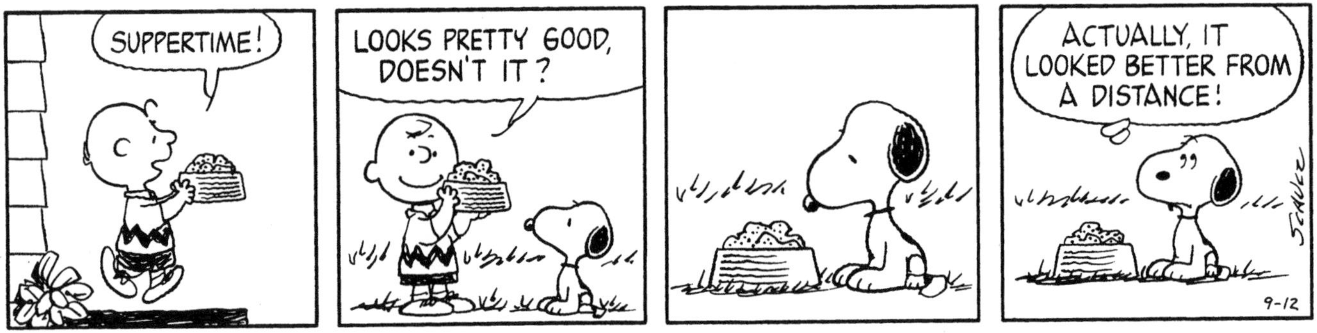
SUPPERTIME!
LOOKS PRETTY GOOD, DOESN'T IT?
ACTUALLY, IT LOOKED BETTER FROM A DISTANCE!
9-12

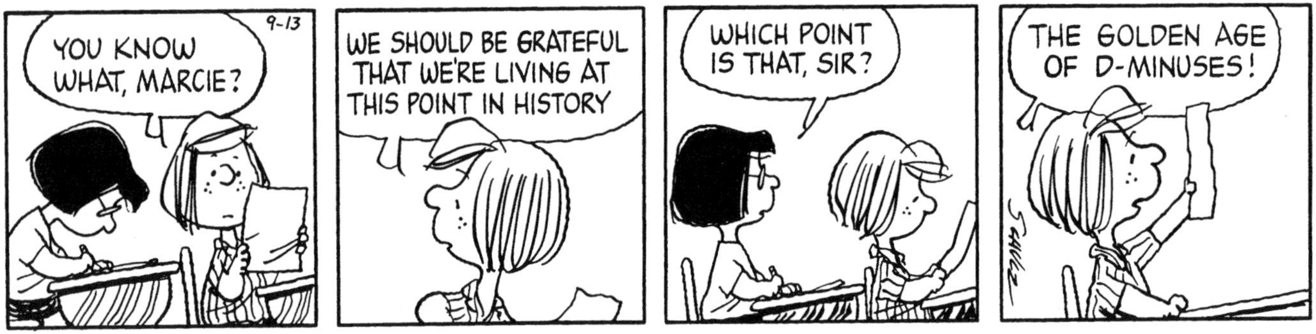
9-13
YOU KNOW WHAT, MARCIE?
WE SHOULD BE GRATEFUL THAT WE'RE LIVING AT THIS POINT IN HISTORY
WHICH POINT IS THAT, SIR?
THE GOLDEN AGE OF D-MINUSES!

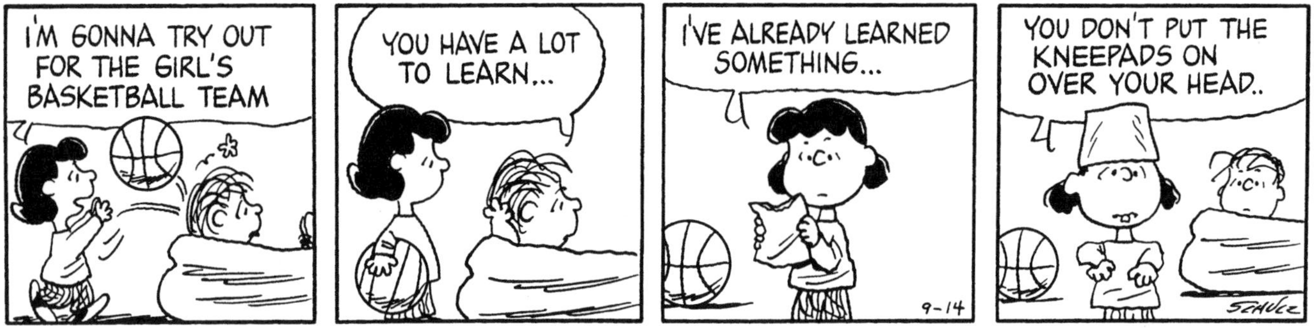
I'M GONNA TRY OUT FOR THE GIRL'S BASKETBALL TEAM
YOU HAVE A LOT TO LEARN...
I'VE ALREADY LEARNED SOMETHING...
9-14
YOU DON'T PUT THE KNEEPADS ON OVER YOUR HEAD..

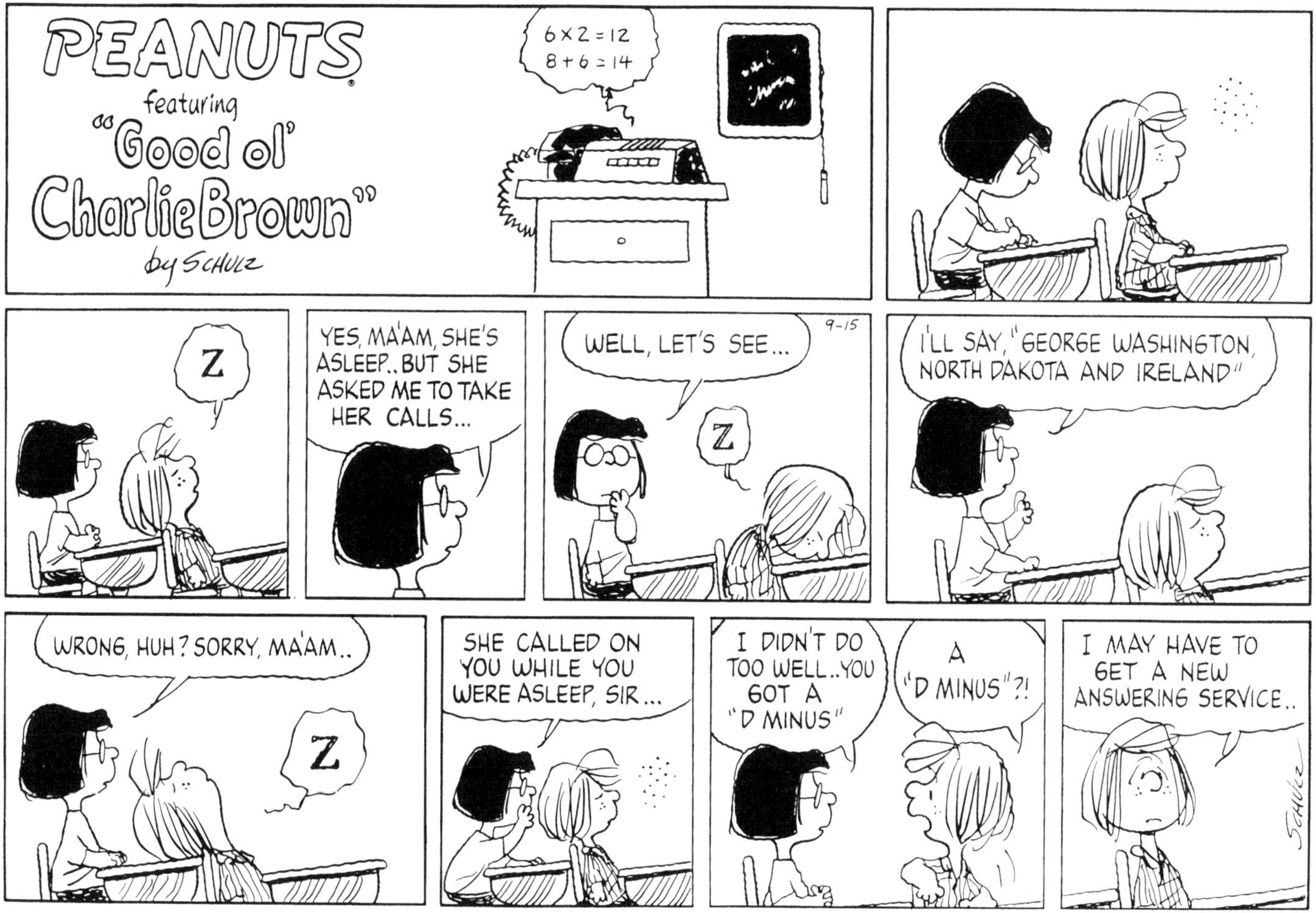
PEANUTS
featuring
"Good ol' Charlie Brown"
by SCHULZ
6×2=12
8+6=14
Z
YES, MA'AM, SHE'S ASLEEP.. BUT SHE ASKED ME TO TAKE HER CALLS...
WELL, LET'S SEE...
9-15
Z
I'LL SAY, "GEORGE WASHINGTON, NORTH DAKOTA AND IRELAND"
WRONG, HUH? SORRY, MA'AM..
Z
SHE CALLED ON YOU WHILE YOU WERE ASLEEP, SIR...
I DIDN'T DO TOO WELL.. YOU GOT A "D MINUS"
A "D MINUS"?!
I MAY HAVE TO GET A NEW ANSWERING SERVICE..
SCHULZ

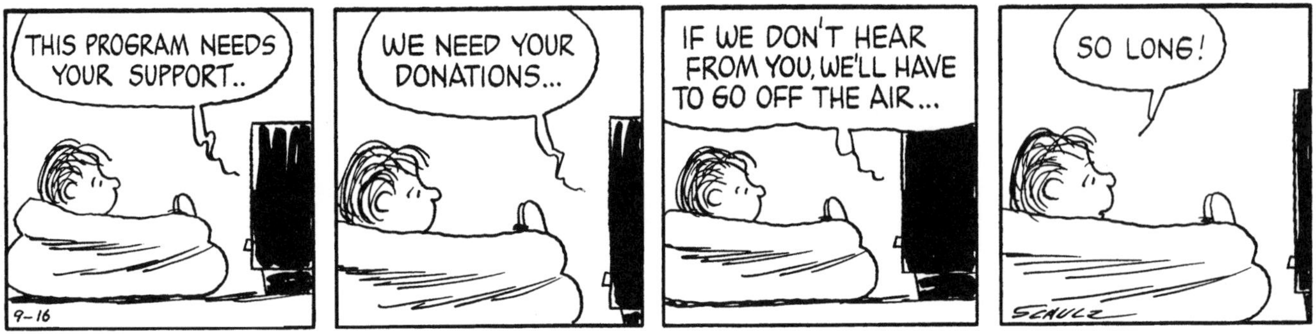
THIS PROGRAM NEEDS YOUR SUPPORT..
WE NEED YOUR DONATIONS...
IF WE DON'T HEAR FROM YOU, WE'LL HAVE TO GO OFF THE AIR...
SO LONG!
9-16
SCHULZ

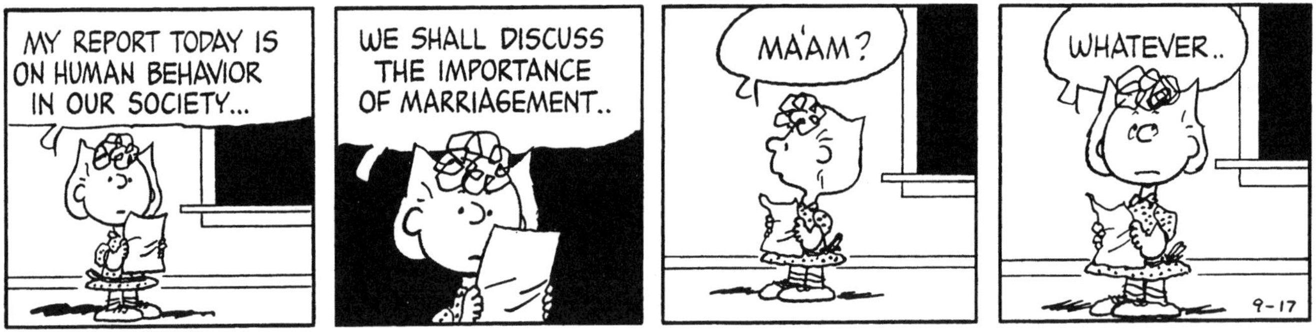
MY REPORT TODAY IS ON HUMAN BEHAVIOR IN OUR SOCIETY...
WE SHALL DISCUSS THE IMPORTANCE OF MARRIAGEMENT..
MA'AM?
WHATEVER..
9-17

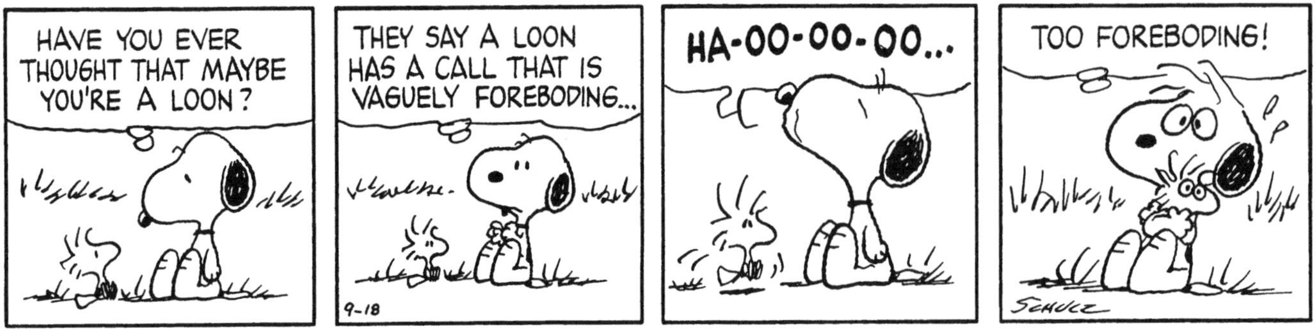
HAVE YOU EVER THOUGHT THAT MAYBE YOU'RE A LOON?
THEY SAY A LOON HAS A CALL THAT IS VAGUELY FOREBODING...
HA-OO-OO-OO...
TOO FOREBODING!
9-18
SCHULZ

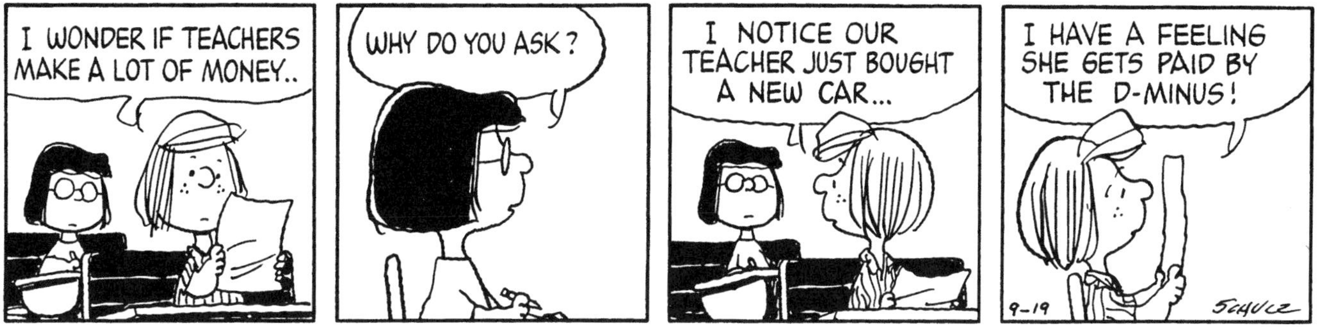
I WONDER IF TEACHERS MAKE A LOT OF MONEY..
WHY DO YOU ASK?
I NOTICE OUR TEACHER JUST BOUGHT A NEW CAR...
I HAVE A FEELING SHE GETS PAID BY THE D-MINUS!
9-19
SCHULZ

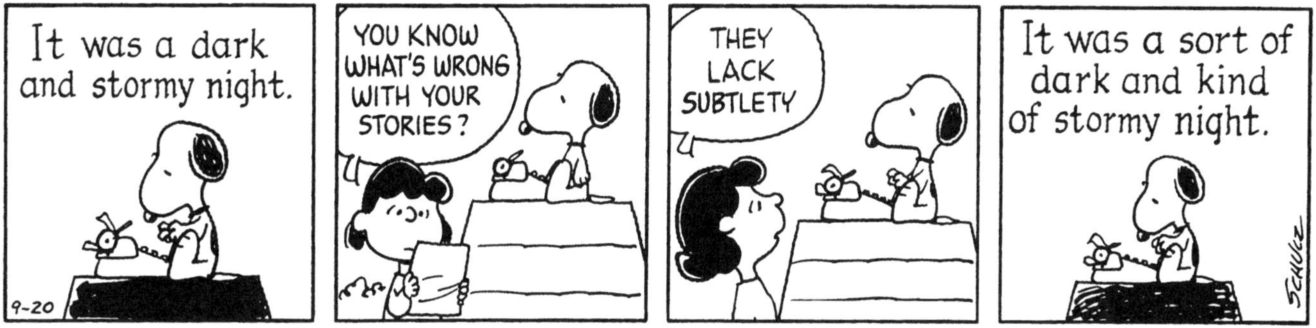
It was a dark and stormy night.
9-20
YOU KNOW WHAT'S WRONG WITH YOUR STORIES?
THEY LACK SUBTLETY
It was a sort of dark and kind of stormy night.
SCHULZ

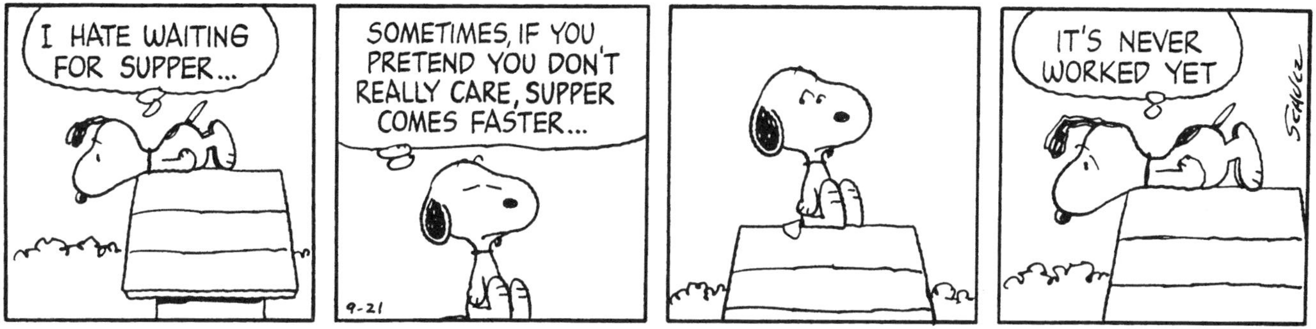
I HATE WAITING FOR SUPPER...
SOMETIMES, IF YOU PRETEND YOU DON'T REALLY CARE, SUPPER COMES FASTER...
9-21
IT'S NEVER WORKED YET
SCHULZ

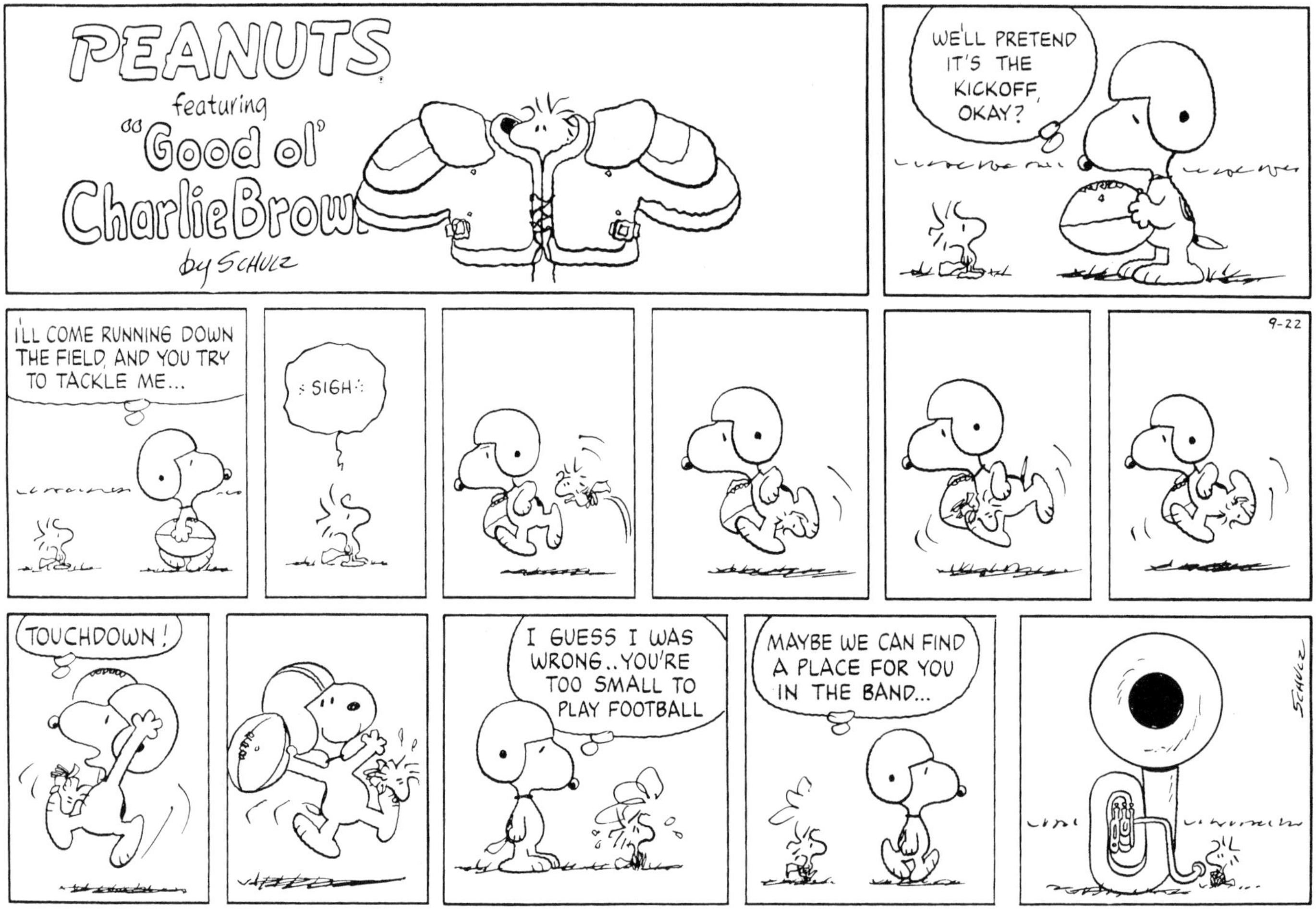
PEANUTS
featuring
"Good ol' Charlie Brown"
by SCHULZ
WE'LL PRETEND IT'S THE KICKOFF, OKAY?
I'LL COME RUNNING DOWN THE FIELD, AND YOU TRY TO TACKLE ME...
SIGH
9-22
TOUCHDOWN!
I GUESS I WAS WRONG..YOU'RE TOO SMALL TO PLAY FOOTBALL
MAYBE WE CAN FIND A PLACE FOR YOU IN THE BAND...
SCHULZ

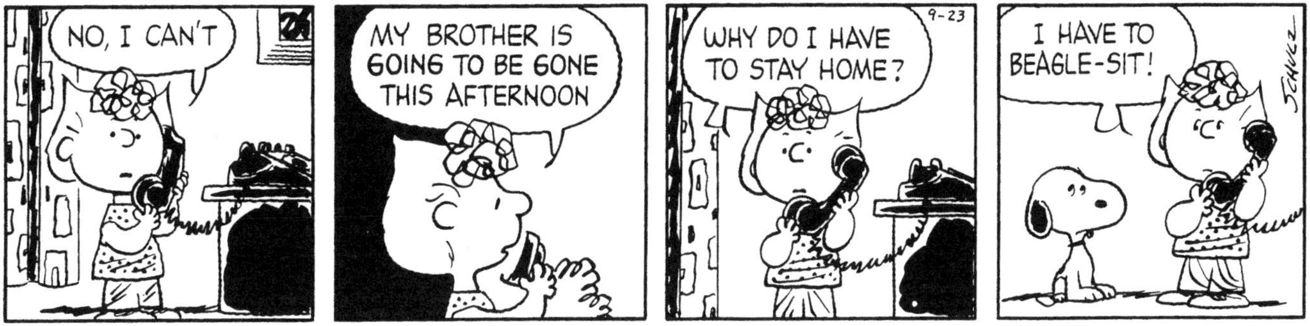
NO, I CAN'T
MY BROTHER IS GOING TO BE GONE THIS AFTERNOON
9-23
WHY DO I HAVE TO STAY HOME?
I HAVE TO BEAGLE-SIT!
SCHULZ

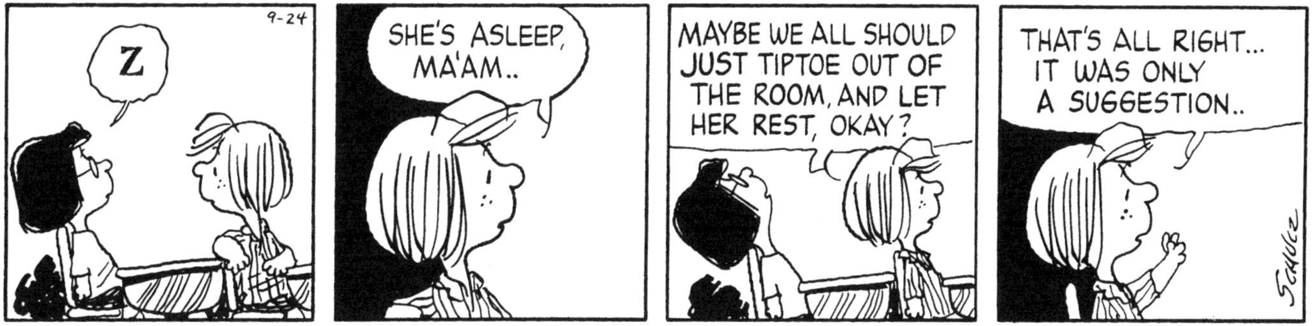
9-24
Z
SHE'S ASLEEP, MA'AM..
MAYBE WE ALL SHOULD JUST TIPTOE OUT OF THE ROOM, AND LET HER REST, OKAY?
THAT'S ALL RIGHT... IT WAS ONLY A SUGGESTION..
SCHULZ

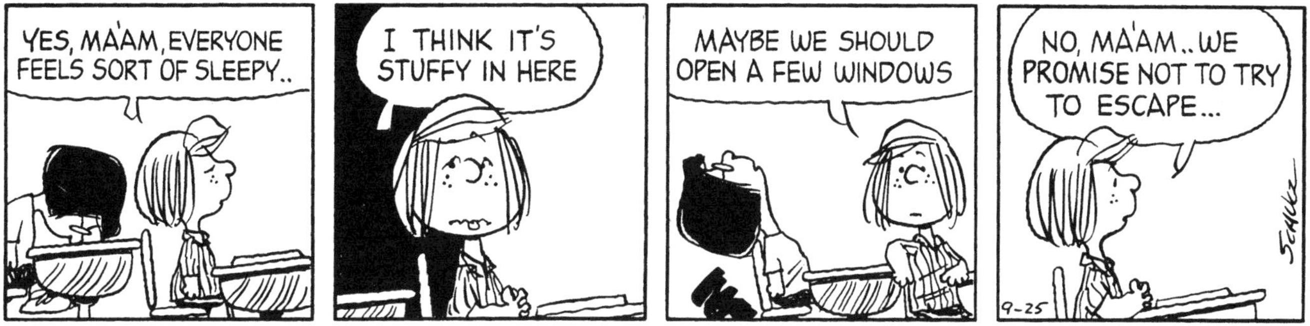
YES, MA'AM, EVERYONE FEELS SORT OF SLEEPY..
I THINK IT'S STUFFY IN HERE
MAYBE WE SHOULD OPEN A FEW WINDOWS
NO, MA'AM.. WE PROMISE NOT TO TRY TO ESCAPE...
SCHULZ
9-25

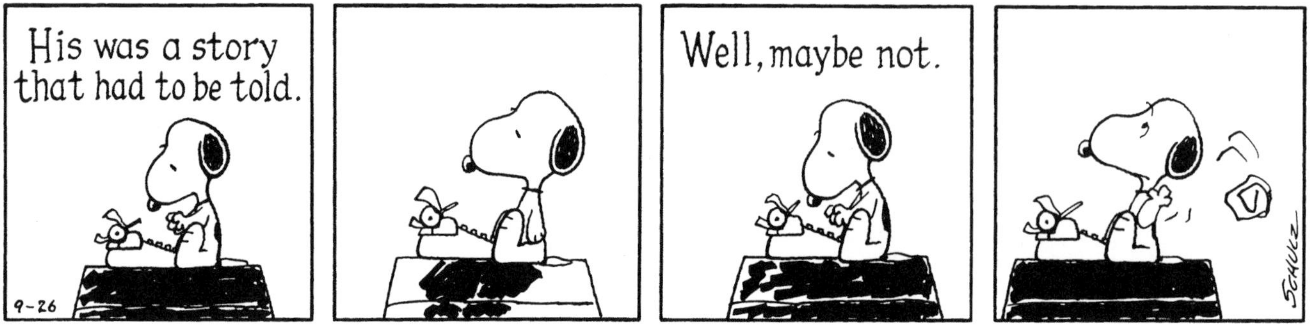
His was a story that had to be told.
Well, maybe not.
9-26
SCHULZ

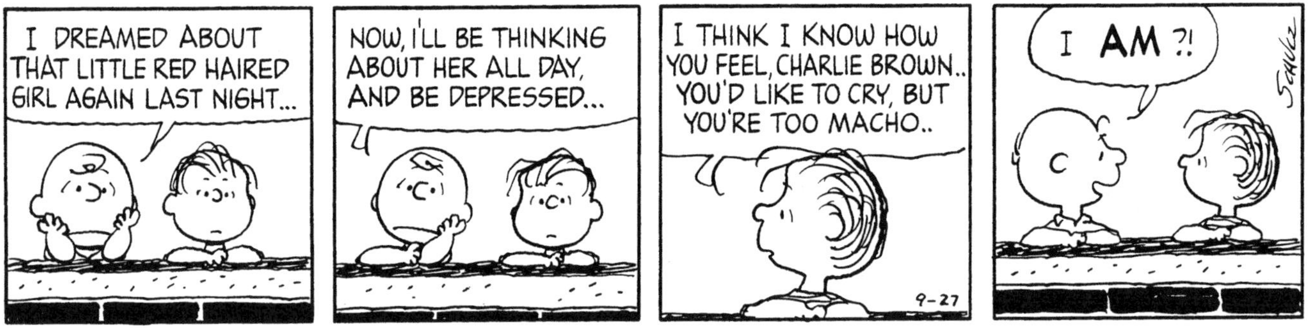
I DREAMED ABOUT THAT LITTLE RED HAIRED GIRL AGAIN LAST NIGHT...
NOW, I'LL BE THINKING ABOUT HER ALL DAY, AND BE DEPRESSED...
I THINK I KNOW HOW YOU FEEL, CHARLIE BROWN.. YOU'D LIKE TO CRY, BUT YOU'RE TOO MACHO..
I AM ?!
9-27
SCHULZ

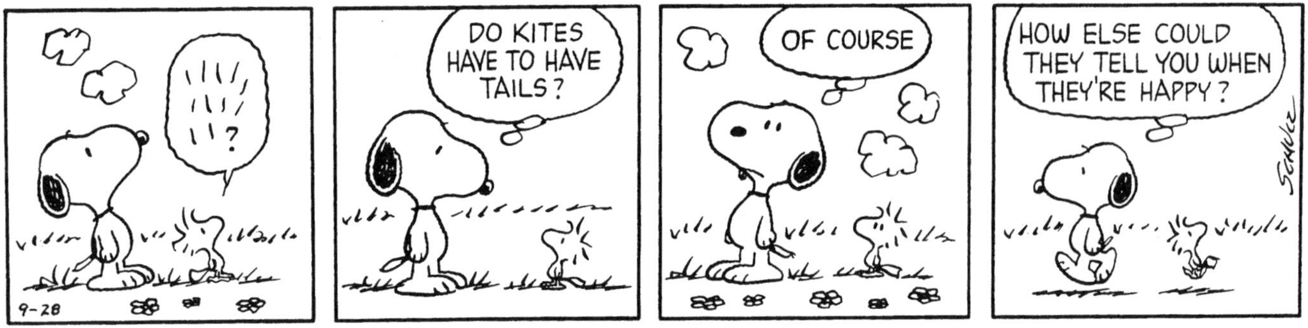
?
DO KITES HAVE TO HAVE TAILS?
OF COURSE
HOW ELSE COULD THEY TELL YOU WHEN THEY'RE HAPPY?
9-28
SCHULZ

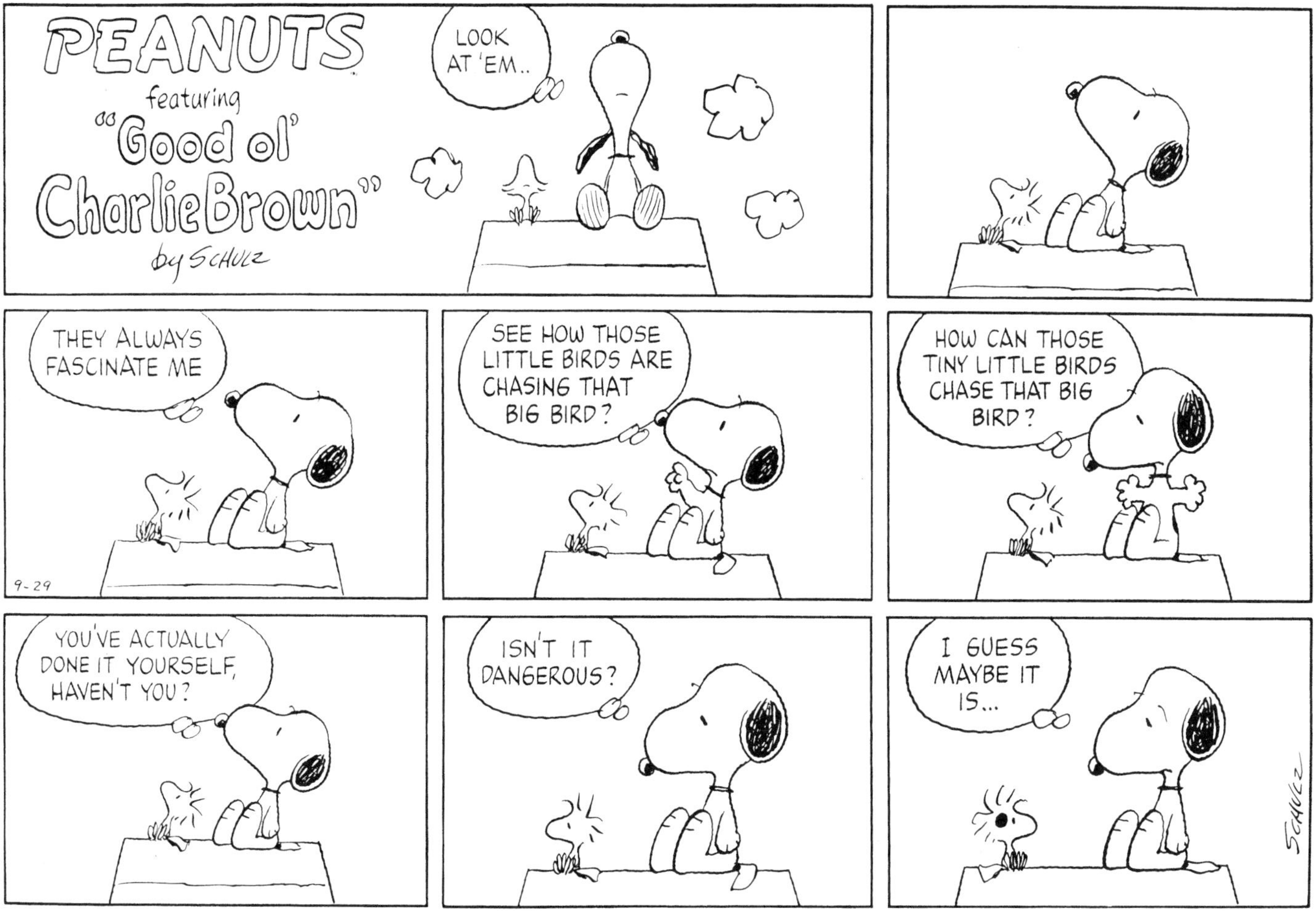
PEANUTS
featuring
"Good ol' CharlieBrown"
by SCHULZ
LOOK AT 'EM..
THEY ALWAYS FASCINATE ME
9-29
SEE HOW THOSE LITTLE BIRDS ARE CHASING THAT BIG BIRD?
HOW CAN THOSE TINY LITTLE BIRDS CHASE THAT BIG BIRD?
YOU'VE ACTUALLY DONE IT YOURSELF, HAVEN'T YOU?
ISN'T IT DANGEROUS?
I GUESS MAYBE IT IS...
SCHULZ

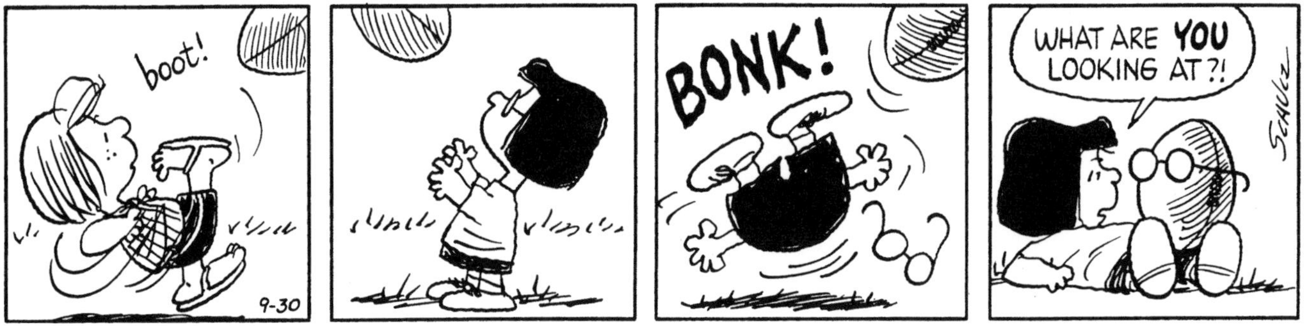
boot!
9-30
BONK!
WHAT ARE **YOU** LOOKING AT?!
SCHULZ

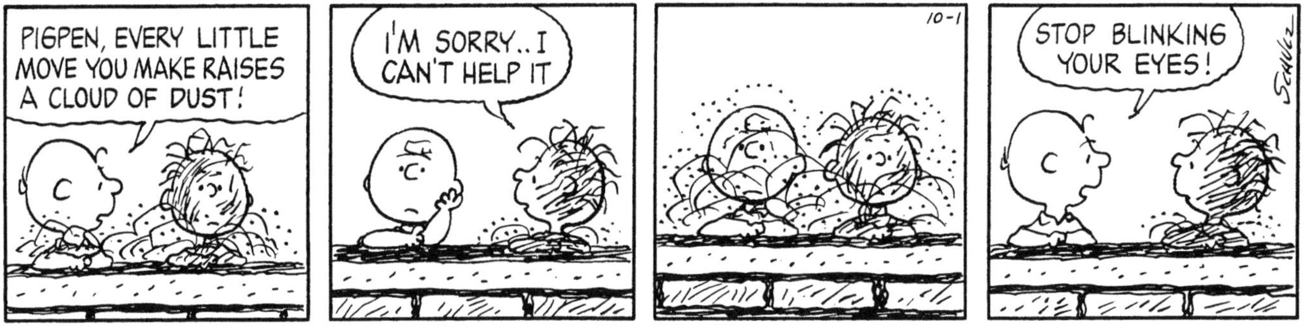
PIGPEN, EVERY LITTLE MOVE YOU MAKE RAISES A CLOUD OF DUST!
I'M SORRY.. I CAN'T HELP IT
10-1
STOP BLINKING YOUR EYES!
SCHULZ

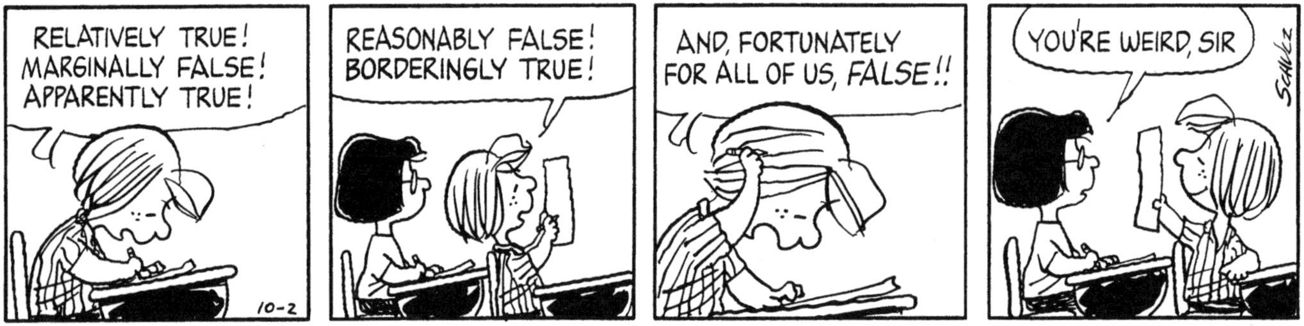
RELATIVELY TRUE! MARGINALLY FALSE! APPARENTLY TRUE!
10-2
REASONABLY FALSE! BORDERINGLY TRUE!
AND, FORTUNATELY FOR ALL OF US, *FALSE*!!
YOU'RE WEIRD, SIR
SCHULZ

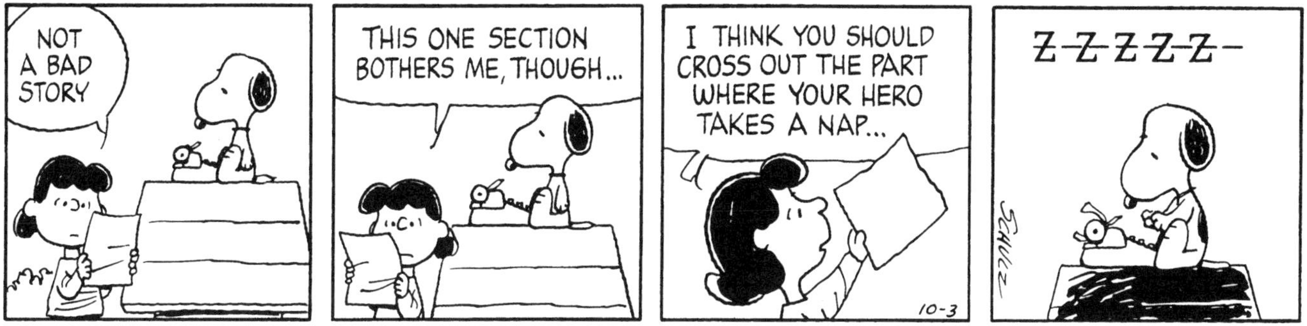
NOT A BAD STORY
THIS ONE SECTION BOTHERS ME, THOUGH...
I THINK YOU SHOULD CROSS OUT THE PART WHERE YOUR HERO TAKES A NAP...
10-3
Z-Z-Z-Z-Z-
SCHULZ

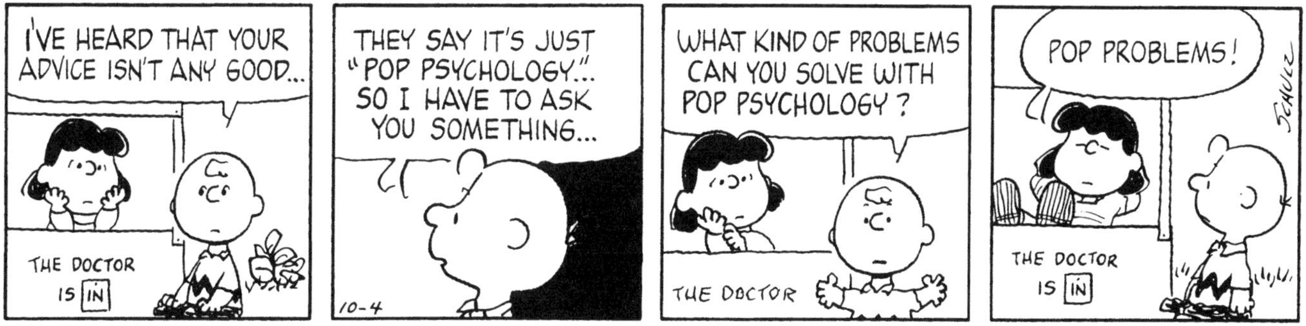
I'VE HEARD THAT YOUR ADVICE ISN'T ANY GOOD...
THE DOCTOR IS IN
THEY SAY IT'S JUST "POP PSYCHOLOGY"... SO I HAVE TO ASK YOU SOMETHING...
10-4
WHAT KIND OF PROBLEMS CAN YOU SOLVE WITH POP PSYCHOLOGY?
THE DOCTOR
POP PROBLEMS!
SCHULZ
THE DOCTOR IS IN

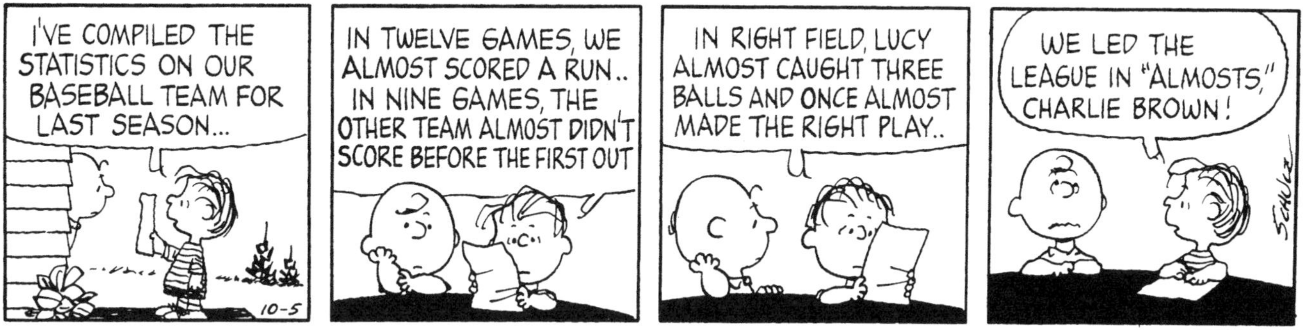
I'VE COMPILED THE STATISTICS ON OUR BASEBALL TEAM FOR LAST SEASON...
10-5
IN TWELVE GAMES, WE ALMOST SCORED A RUN.. IN NINE GAMES, THE OTHER TEAM ALMOST DIDN'T SCORE BEFORE THE FIRST OUT
IN RIGHT FIELD, LUCY ALMOST CAUGHT THREE BALLS AND ONCE ALMOST MADE THE RIGHT PLAY..
WE LED THE LEAGUE IN "ALMOSTS," CHARLIE BROWN!
SCHULZ

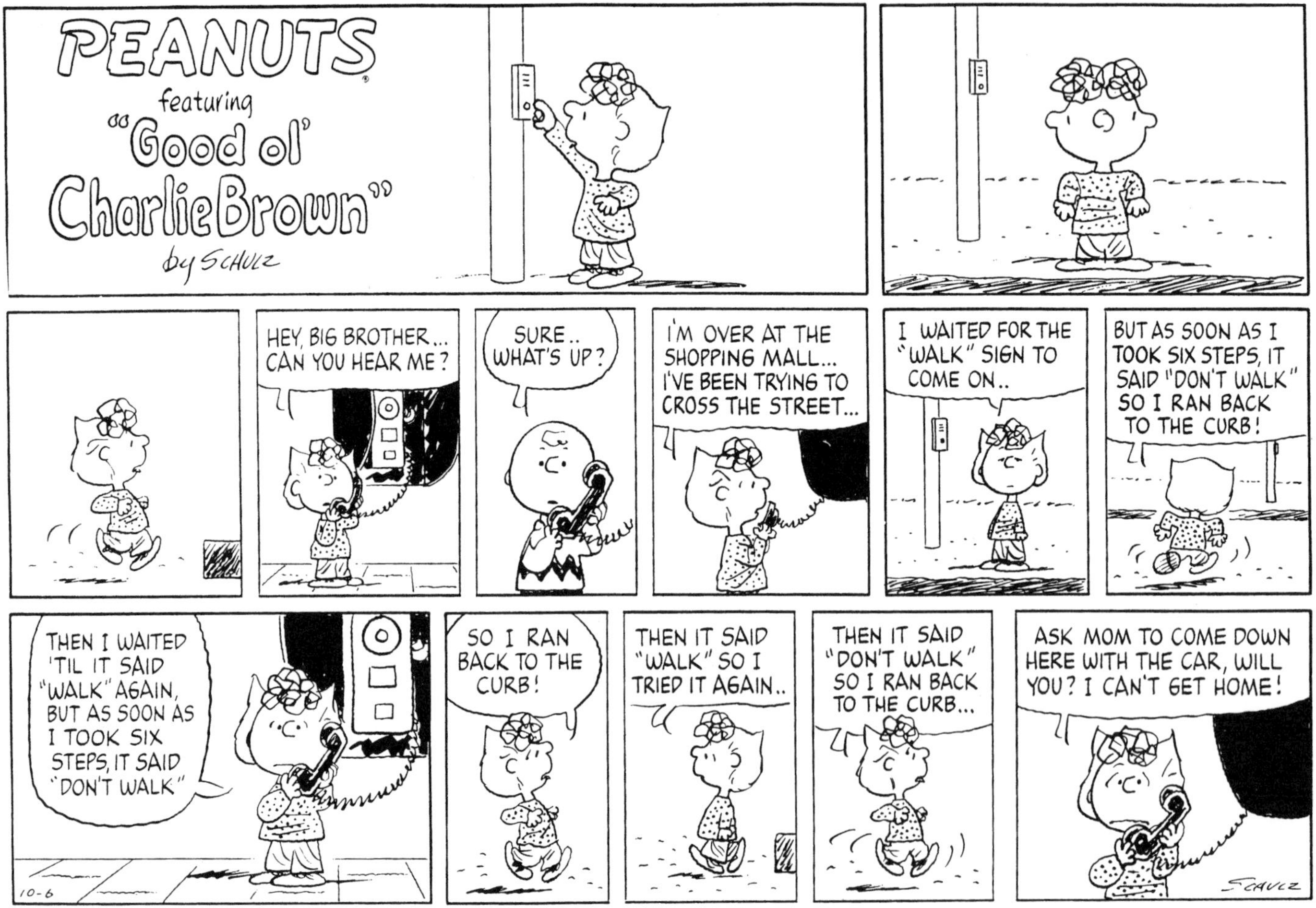
PEANUTS
featuring "Good ol' Charlie Brown"
by SCHULZ
HEY, BIG BROTHER... CAN YOU HEAR ME?
SURE.. WHAT'S UP?
I'M OVER AT THE SHOPPING MALL... I'VE BEEN TRYING TO CROSS THE STREET...
I WAITED FOR THE "WALK" SIGN TO COME ON..
BUT AS SOON AS I TOOK SIX STEPS, IT SAID "DON'T WALK" SO I RAN BACK TO THE CURB!
THEN I WAITED 'TIL IT SAID "WALK" AGAIN, BUT AS SOON AS I TOOK SIX STEPS, IT SAID "DON'T WALK"
10-6
SO I RAN BACK TO THE CURB!
THEN IT SAID "WALK" SO I TRIED IT AGAIN..
THEN IT SAID "DON'T WALK" SO I RAN BACK TO THE CURB...
ASK MOM TO COME DOWN HERE WITH THE CAR, WILL YOU? I CAN'T GET HOME!
SCHULZ

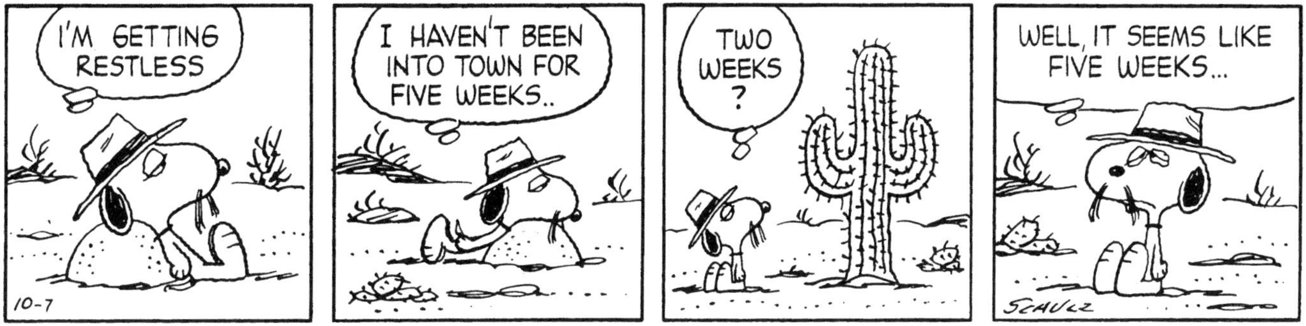
I'M GETTING RESTLESS
I HAVEN'T BEEN INTO TOWN FOR FIVE WEEKS..
TWO WEEKS ?
WELL, IT SEEMS LIKE FIVE WEEKS...
10-7
SCHULZ

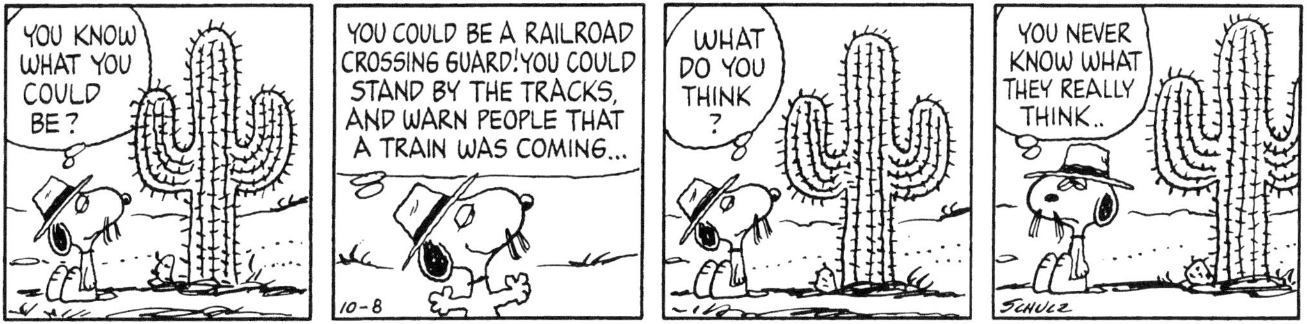
YOU KNOW WHAT YOU COULD BE ?
YOU COULD BE A RAILROAD CROSSING GUARD! YOU COULD STAND BY THE TRACKS, AND WARN PEOPLE THAT A TRAIN WAS COMING...
WHAT DO YOU THINK ?
YOU NEVER KNOW WHAT THEY REALLY THINK..
10-8
SCHULZ

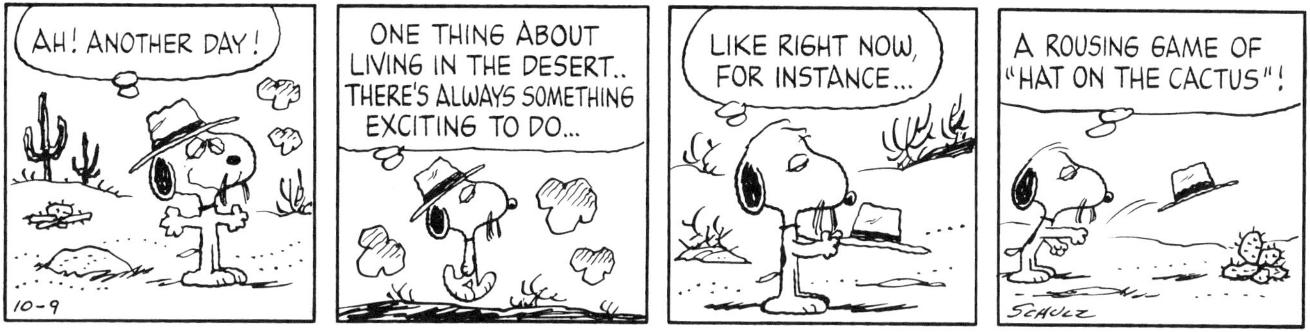
AH! ANOTHER DAY!
ONE THING ABOUT LIVING IN THE DESERT.. THERE'S ALWAYS SOMETHING EXCITING TO DO...
LIKE RIGHT NOW, FOR INSTANCE...
A ROUSING GAME OF "HAT ON THE CACTUS"!
10-9
SCHULZ

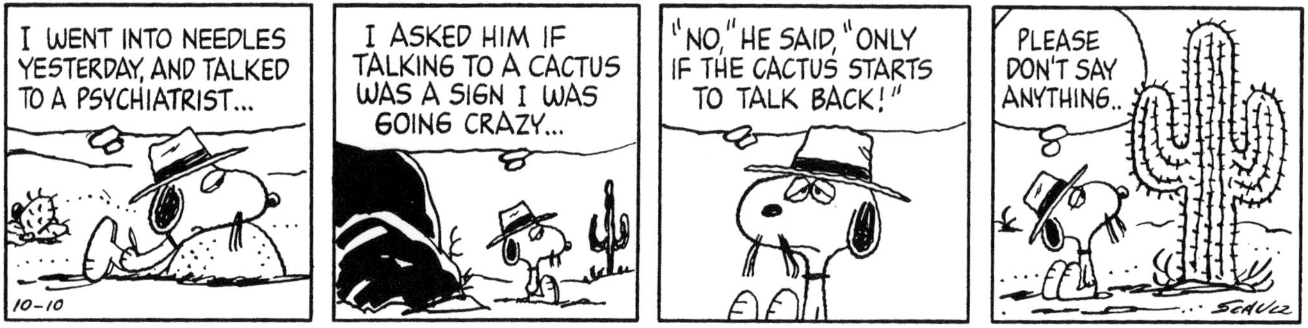
I WENT INTO NEEDLES YESTERDAY, AND TALKED TO A PSYCHIATRIST...
10-10
I ASKED HIM IF TALKING TO A CACTUS WAS A SIGN I WAS GOING CRAZY...
"NO," HE SAID, "ONLY IF THE CACTUS STARTS TO TALK BACK!"
PLEASE DON'T SAY ANYTHING..
SCHULZ

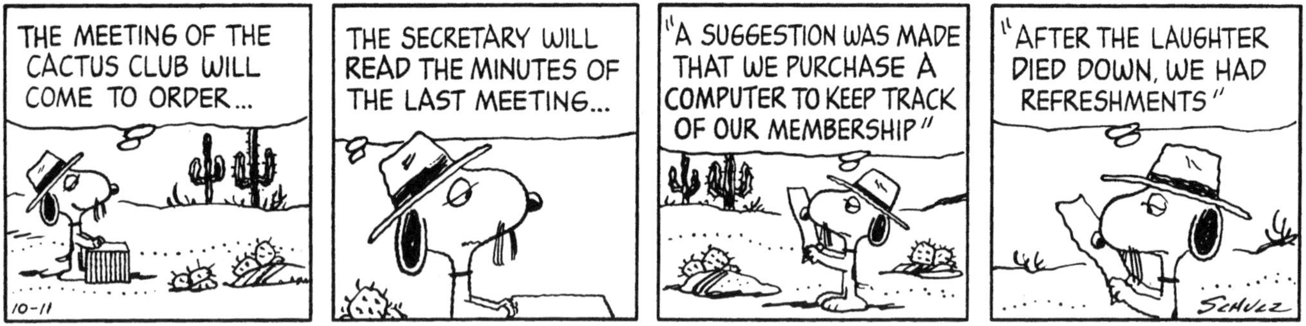
THE MEETING OF THE CACTUS CLUB WILL COME TO ORDER...
10-11
THE SECRETARY WILL READ THE MINUTES OF THE LAST MEETING...
"A SUGGESTION WAS MADE THAT WE PURCHASE A COMPUTER TO KEEP TRACK OF OUR MEMBERSHIP"
"AFTER THE LAUGHTER DIED DOWN, WE HAD REFRESHMENTS"
SCHULZ

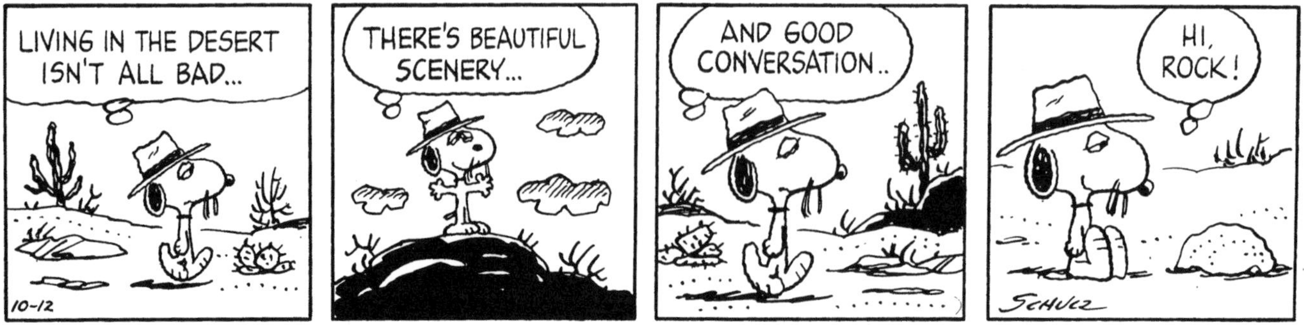
LIVING IN THE DESERT ISN'T ALL BAD...
10-12
THERE'S BEAUTIFUL SCENERY...
AND GOOD CONVERSATION..
HI, ROCK!
SCHULZ

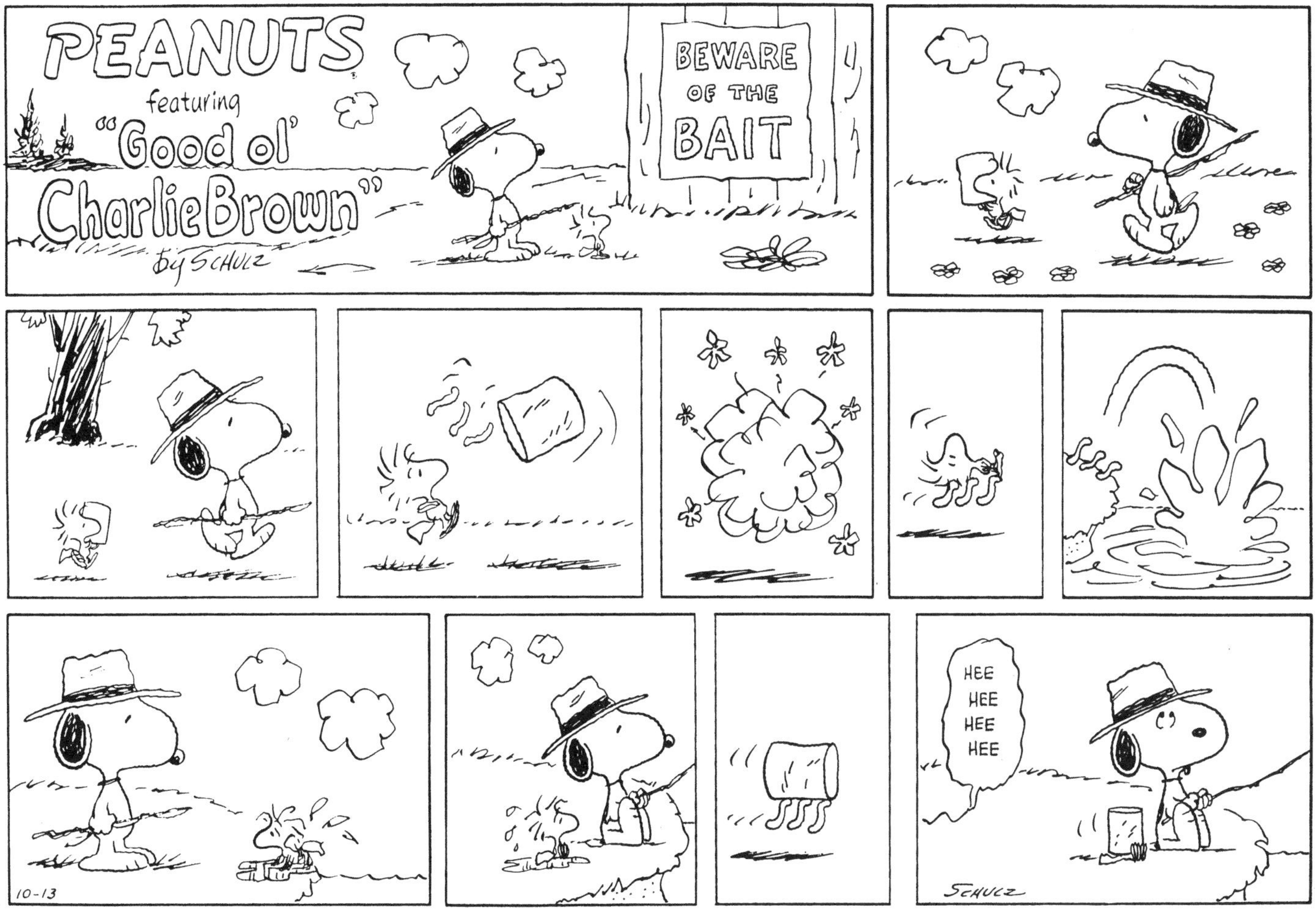
PEANUTS
featuring
"Good ol' Charlie Brown"
by SCHULZ
BEWARE OF THE BAIT
10-13
HEE HEE HEE HEE
SCHULZ

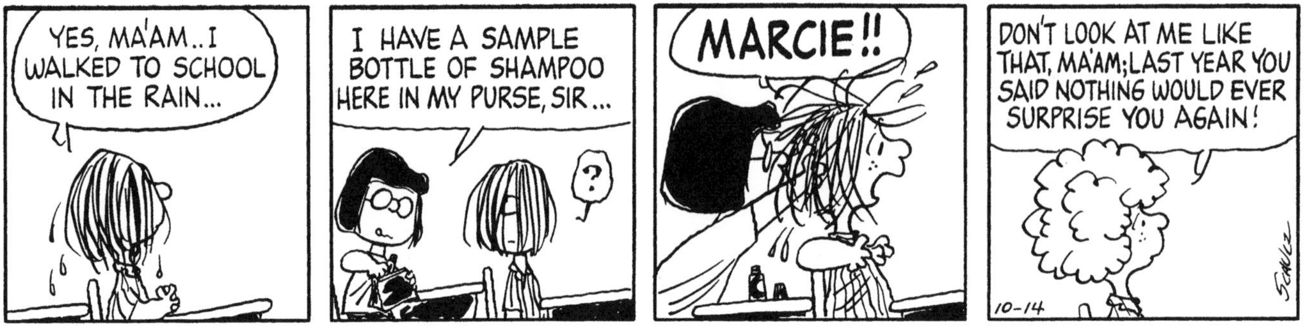
YES, MA'AM..I WALKED TO SCHOOL IN THE RAIN...
I HAVE A SAMPLE BOTTLE OF SHAMPOO HERE IN MY PURSE, SIR...
?
MARCIE!!
DON'T LOOK AT ME LIKE THAT, MA'AM; LAST YEAR YOU SAID NOTHING WOULD EVER SURPRISE YOU AGAIN!
SCHULZ
10-14

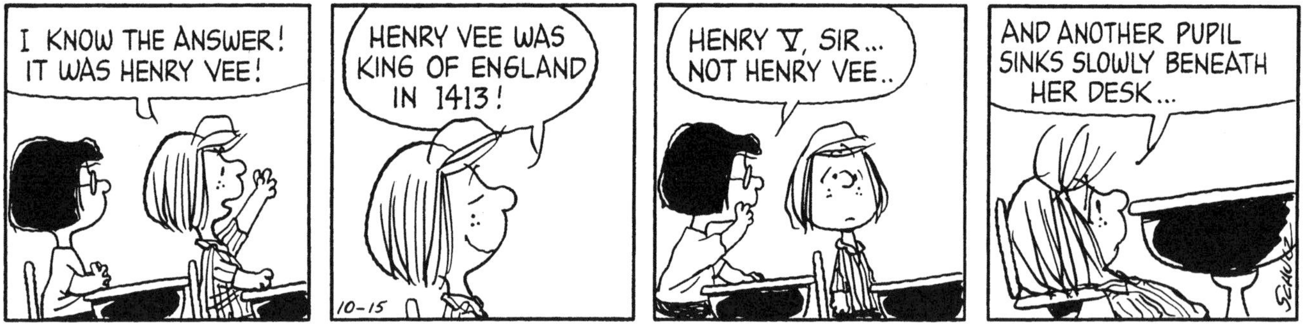
I KNOW THE ANSWER! IT WAS HENRY VEE!
HENRY VEE WAS KING OF ENGLAND IN 1413!
10-15
HENRY V, SIR... NOT HENRY VEE..
AND ANOTHER PUPIL SINKS SLOWLY BENEATH HER DESK...
SCHULZ

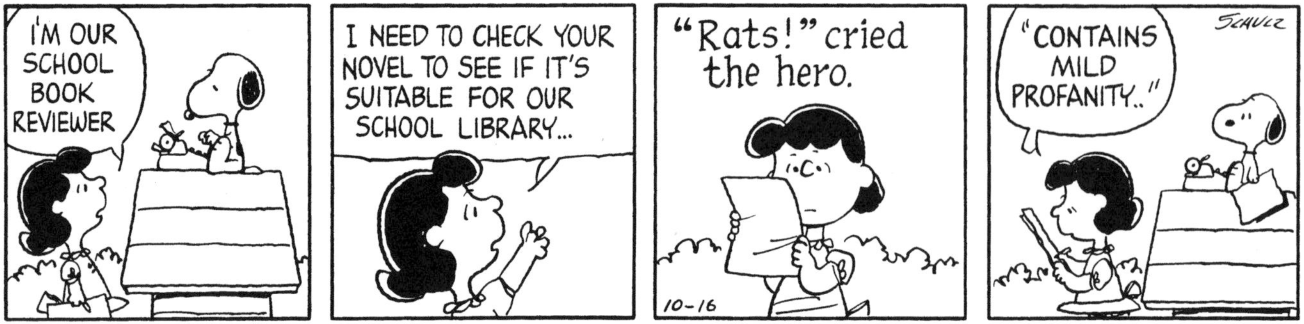
I'M OUR SCHOOL BOOK REVIEWER
I NEED TO CHECK YOUR NOVEL TO SEE IF IT'S SUITABLE FOR OUR SCHOOL LIBRARY...
"Rats!" cried the hero.
10-16
"CONTAINS MILD PROFANITY.."
SCHULZ

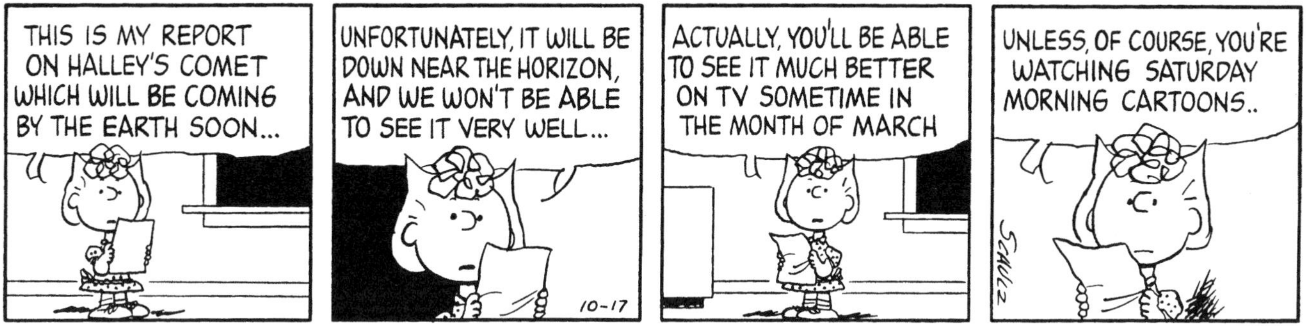
THIS IS MY REPORT ON HALLEY'S COMET WHICH WILL BE COMING BY THE EARTH SOON...
UNFORTUNATELY, IT WILL BE DOWN NEAR THE HORIZON, AND WE WON'T BE ABLE TO SEE IT VERY WELL...
10-17
ACTUALLY, YOU'LL BE ABLE TO SEE IT MUCH BETTER ON TV SOMETIME IN THE MONTH OF MARCH
UNLESS, OF COURSE, YOU'RE WATCHING SATURDAY MORNING CARTOONS..
SCHULZ

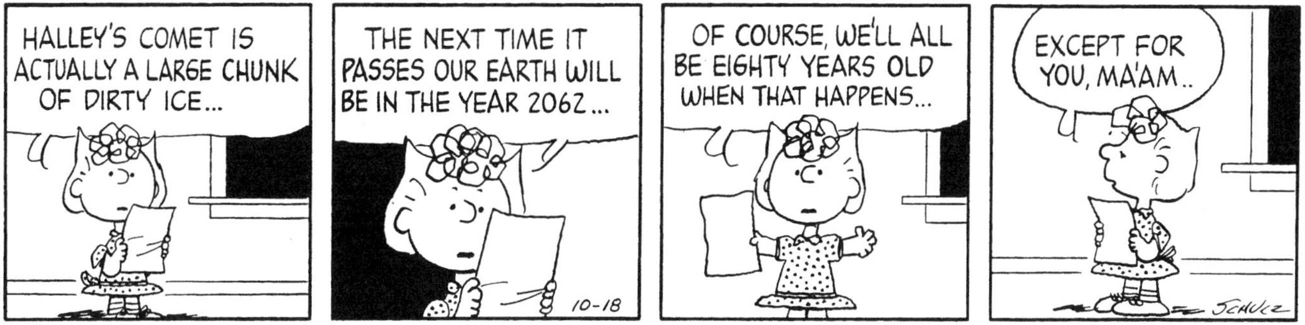
HALLEY'S COMET IS ACTUALLY A LARGE CHUNK OF DIRTY ICE...
THE NEXT TIME IT PASSES OUR EARTH WILL BE IN THE YEAR 2062...
10-18
OF COURSE, WE'LL ALL BE EIGHTY YEARS OLD WHEN THAT HAPPENS...
EXCEPT FOR YOU, MA'AM..
SCHULZ

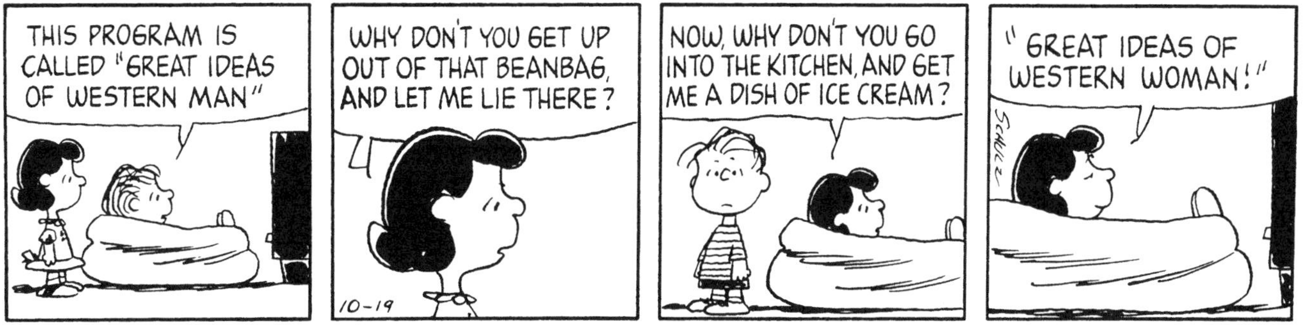
THIS PROGRAM IS CALLED "GREAT IDEAS OF WESTERN MAN"
WHY DON'T YOU GET UP OUT OF THAT BEANBAG, AND LET ME LIE THERE?
10-19
NOW, WHY DON'T YOU GO INTO THE KITCHEN, AND GET ME A DISH OF ICE CREAM?
"GREAT IDEAS OF WESTERN WOMAN!"
SCHULZ

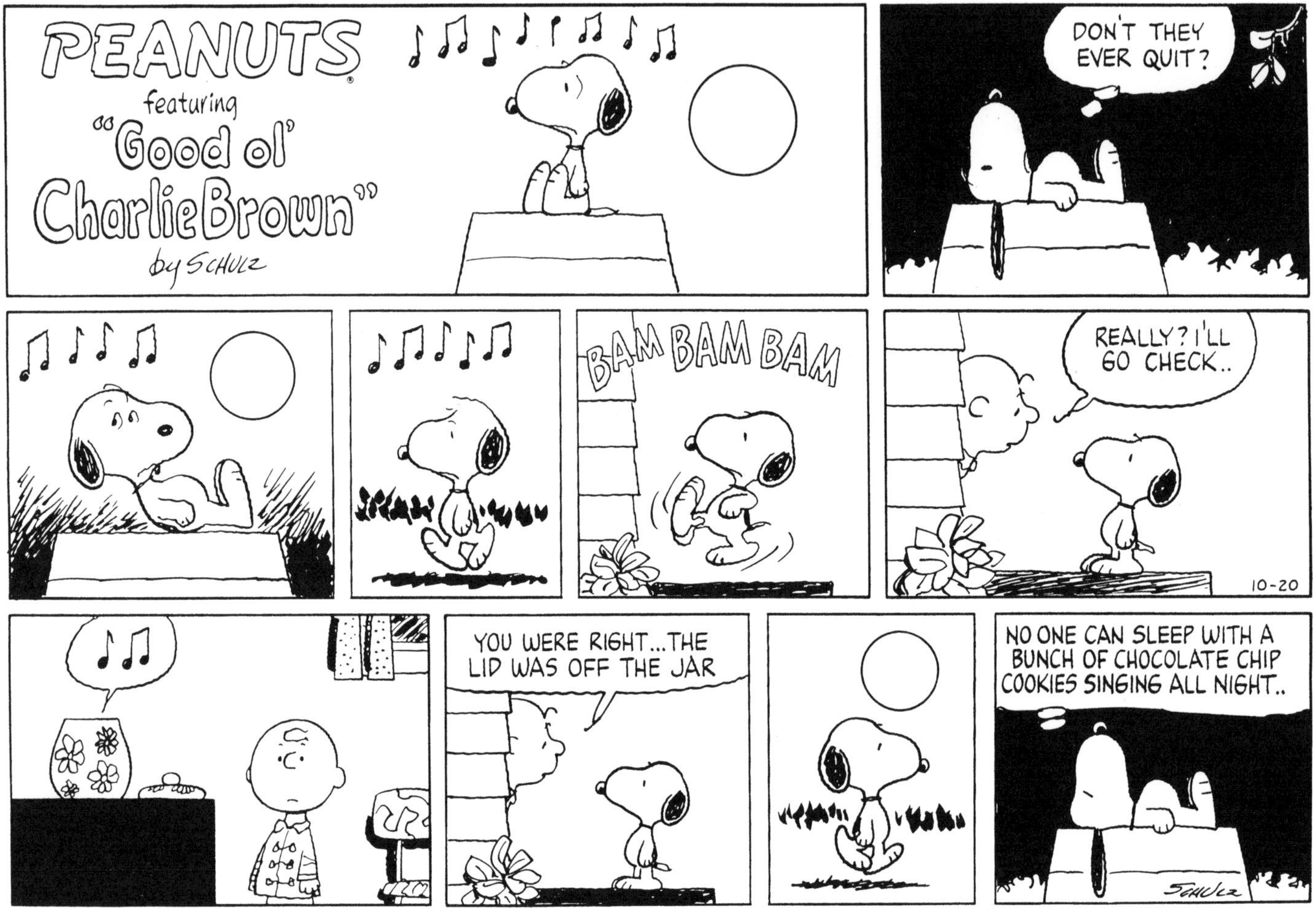
PEANUTS
featuring
"Good ol' Charlie Brown"
by SCHULZ
DON'T THEY EVER QUIT?
BAM BAM BAM
REALLY? I'LL GO CHECK..
10-20
YOU WERE RIGHT...THE LID WAS OFF THE JAR
NO ONE CAN SLEEP WITH A BUNCH OF CHOCOLATE CHIP COOKIES SINGING ALL NIGHT..
SCHULZ

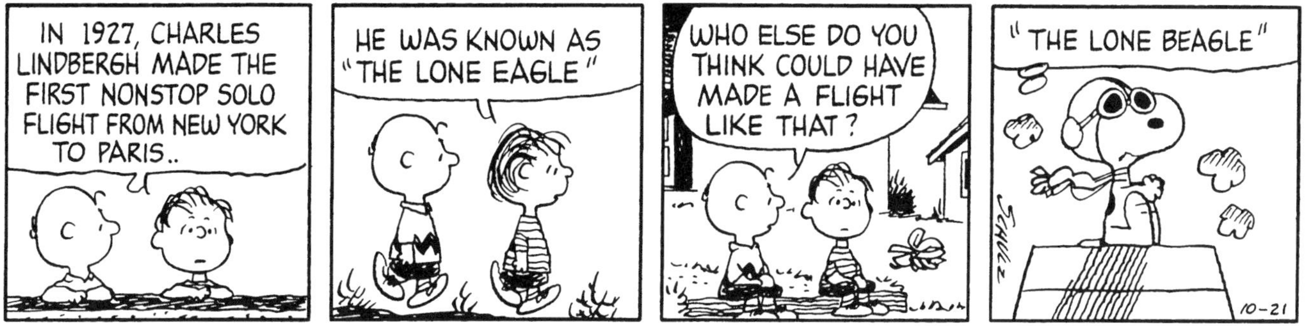
IN 1927, CHARLES LINDBERGH MADE THE FIRST NONSTOP SOLO FLIGHT FROM NEW YORK TO PARIS..
HE WAS KNOWN AS "THE LONE EAGLE"
WHO ELSE DO YOU THINK COULD HAVE MADE A FLIGHT LIKE THAT?
"THE LONE BEAGLE"

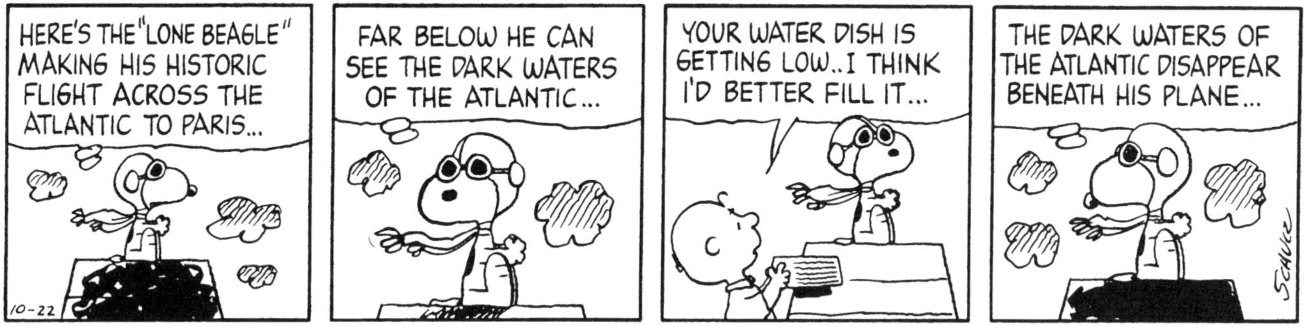
HERE'S THE "LONE BEAGLE" MAKING HIS HISTORIC FLIGHT ACROSS THE ATLANTIC TO PARIS...
FAR BELOW HE CAN SEE THE DARK WATERS OF THE ATLANTIC...
YOUR WATER DISH IS GETTING LOW..I THINK I'D BETTER FILL IT...
THE DARK WATERS OF THE ATLANTIC DISAPPEAR BENEATH HIS PLANE...

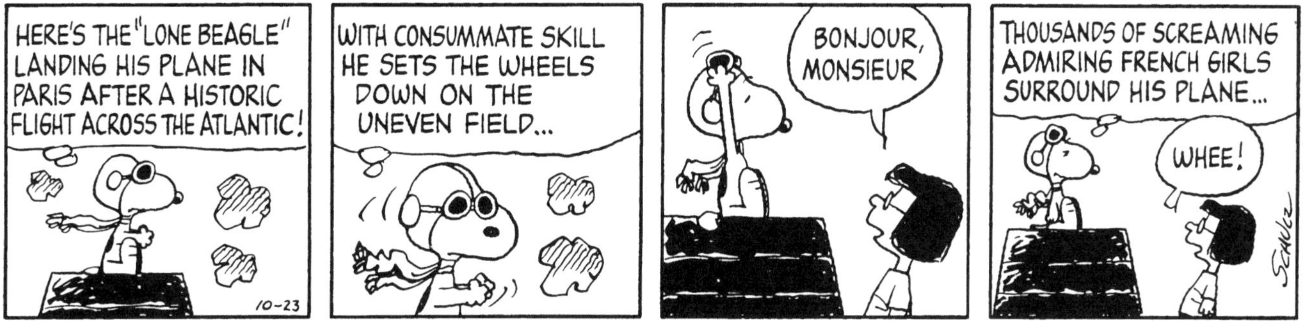
HERE'S THE "LONE BEAGLE" LANDING HIS PLANE IN PARIS AFTER A HISTORIC FLIGHT ACROSS THE ATLANTIC!
WITH CONSUMMATE SKILL HE SETS THE WHEELS DOWN ON THE UNEVEN FIELD...
BONJOUR, MONSIEUR
THOUSANDS OF SCREAMING ADMIRING FRENCH GIRLS SURROUND HIS PLANE...
WHEE!

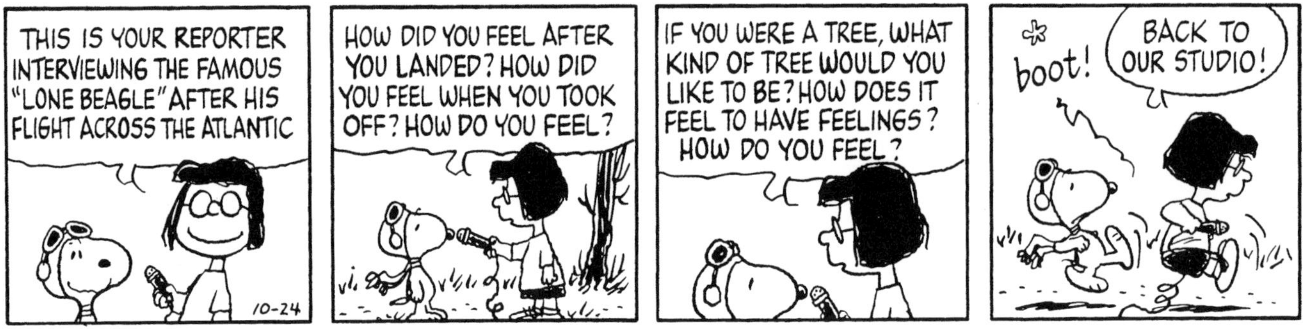
THIS IS YOUR REPORTER INTERVIEWING THE FAMOUS "LONE BEAGLE" AFTER HIS FLIGHT ACROSS THE ATLANTIC
10-24
HOW DID YOU FEEL AFTER YOU LANDED? HOW DID YOU FEEL WHEN YOU TOOK OFF? HOW DO YOU FEEL?
IF YOU WERE A TREE, WHAT KIND OF TREE WOULD YOU LIKE TO BE? HOW DOES IT FEEL TO HAVE FEELINGS? HOW DO YOU FEEL?
boot!
BACK TO OUR STUDIO!

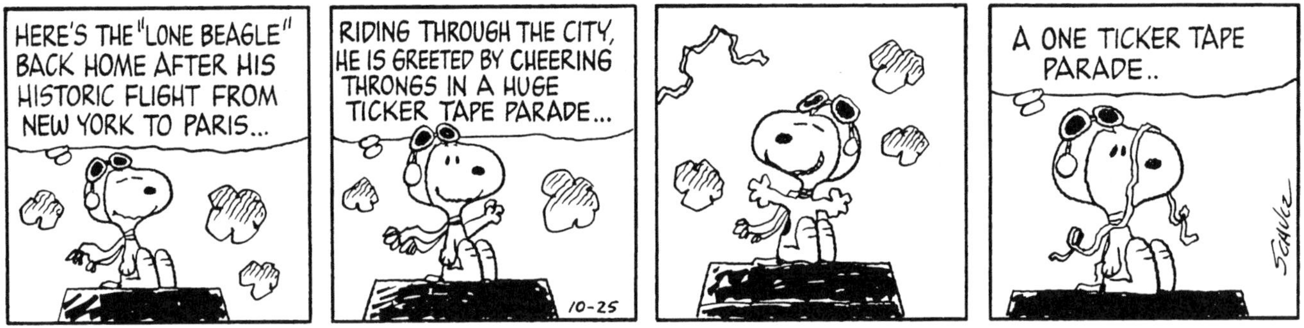
HERE'S THE "LONE BEAGLE" BACK HOME AFTER HIS HISTORIC FLIGHT FROM NEW YORK TO PARIS...
RIDING THROUGH THE CITY, HE IS GREETED BY CHEERING THRONGS IN A HUGE TICKER TAPE PARADE...
10-25
A ONE TICKER TAPE PARADE..
SCHULZ

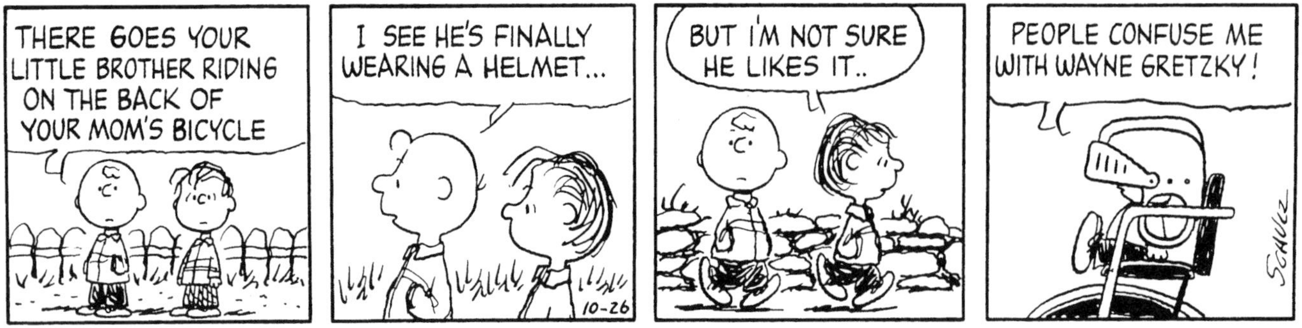
THERE GOES YOUR LITTLE BROTHER RIDING ON THE BACK OF YOUR MOM'S BICYCLE
I SEE HE'S FINALLY WEARING A HELMET...
10-26
BUT I'M NOT SURE HE LIKES IT..
PEOPLE CONFUSE ME WITH WAYNE GRETZKY!
SCHULZ

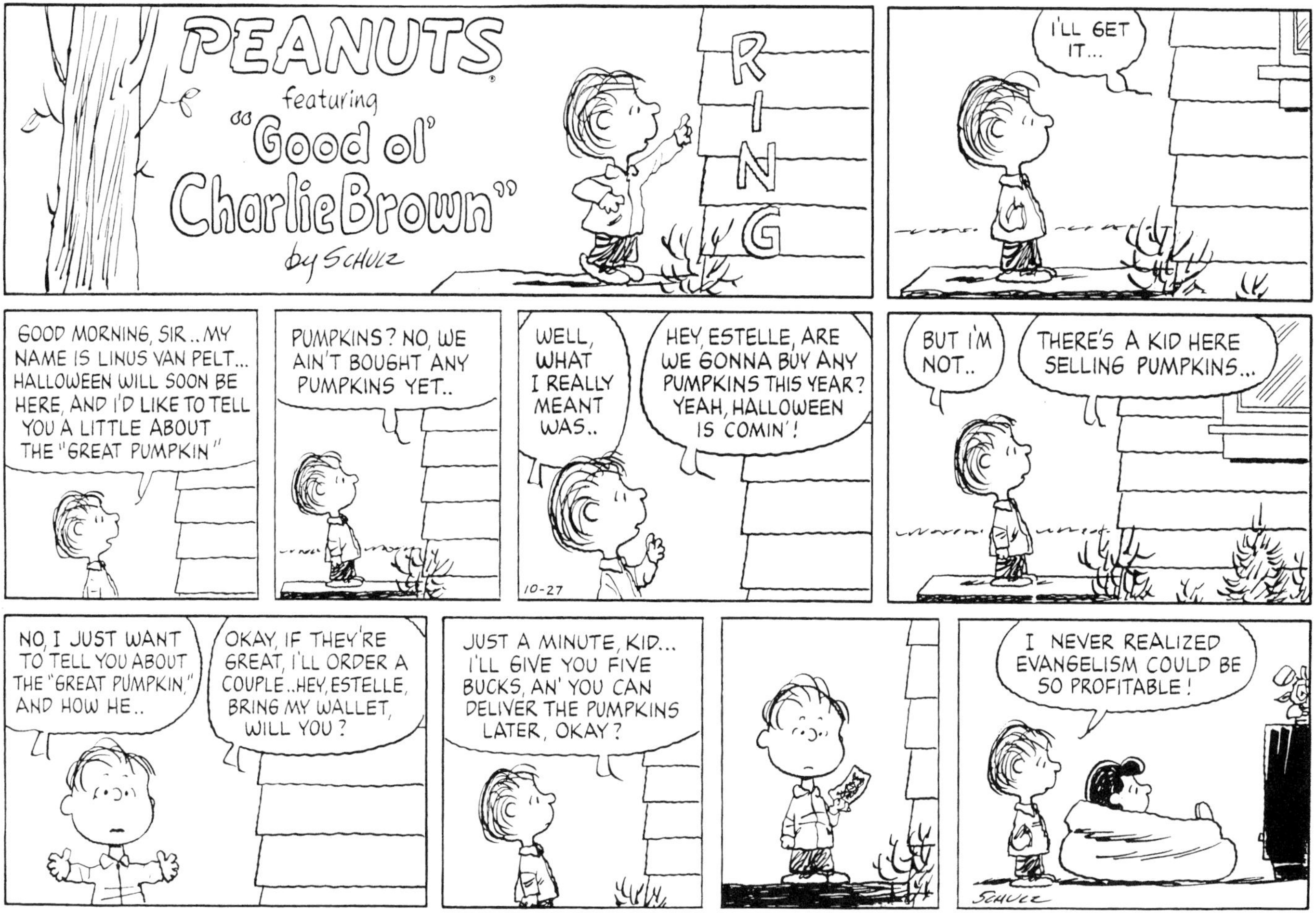

PEANUTS
featuring "Good ol' CharlieBrown"
by SCHULZ
RING
I'LL GET IT...
GOOD MORNING, SIR.. MY NAME IS LINUS VAN PELT... HALLOWEEN WILL SOON BE HERE, AND I'D LIKE TO TELL YOU A LITTLE ABOUT THE "GREAT PUMPKIN"
PUMPKINS? NO, WE AIN'T BOUGHT ANY PUMPKINS YET..
WELL, WHAT I REALLY MEANT WAS..
HEY, ESTELLE, ARE WE GONNA BUY ANY PUMPKINS THIS YEAR? YEAH, HALLOWEEN IS COMIN'!
10-27
BUT I'M NOT..
THERE'S A KID HERE SELLING PUMPKINS...
NO, I JUST WANT TO TELL YOU ABOUT THE "GREAT PUMPKIN," AND HOW HE..
OKAY, IF THEY'RE GREAT, I'LL ORDER A COUPLE..HEY, ESTELLE, BRING MY WALLET, WILL YOU?
JUST A MINUTE, KID... I'LL GIVE YOU FIVE BUCKS, AN' YOU CAN DELIVER THE PUMPKINS LATER, OKAY?
I NEVER REALIZED EVANGELISM COULD BE SO PROFITABLE!
SCHULZ

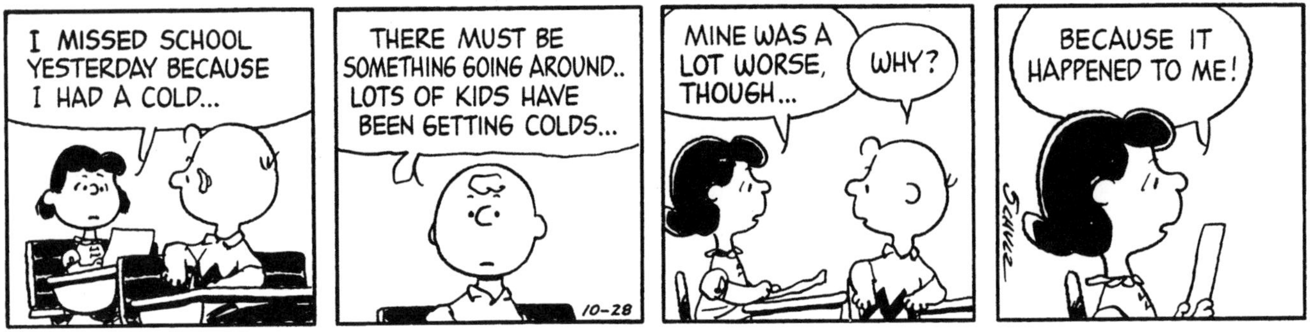

I MISSED SCHOOL YESTERDAY BECAUSE I HAD A COLD...
THERE MUST BE SOMETHING GOING AROUND.. LOTS OF KIDS HAVE BEEN GETTING COLDS...
10-28
MINE WAS A LOT WORSE, THOUGH...
WHY?
BECAUSE IT HAPPENED TO ME!

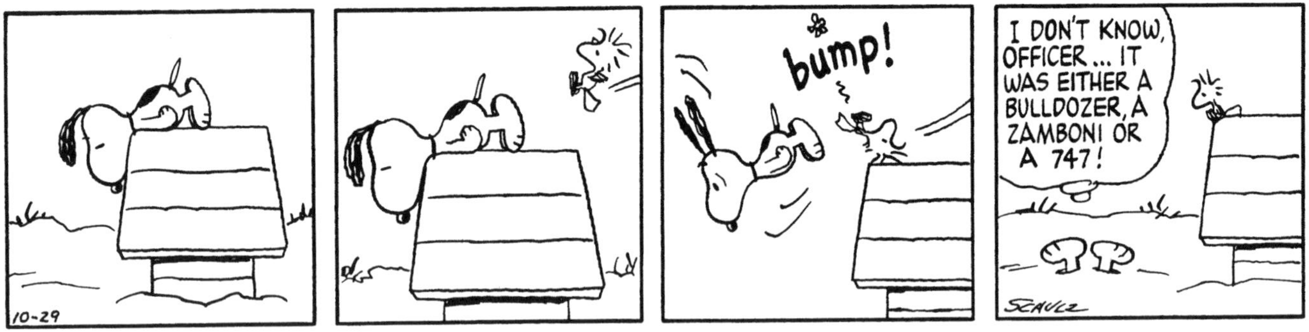

10-29
bump!
I DON'T KNOW, OFFICER... IT WAS EITHER A BULLDOZER, A ZAMBONI OR A 747!

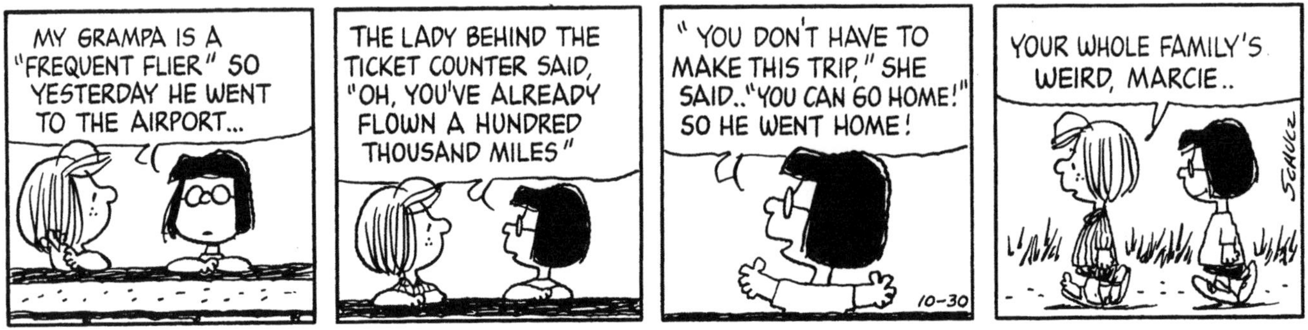

MY GRAMPA IS A "FREQUENT FLIER" SO YESTERDAY HE WENT TO THE AIRPORT...
THE LADY BEHIND THE TICKET COUNTER SAID, "OH, YOU'VE ALREADY FLOWN A HUNDRED THOUSAND MILES"
"YOU DON'T HAVE TO MAKE THIS TRIP," SHE SAID.."YOU CAN GO HOME!" SO HE WENT HOME!
10-30
YOUR WHOLE FAMILY'S WEIRD, MARCIE..

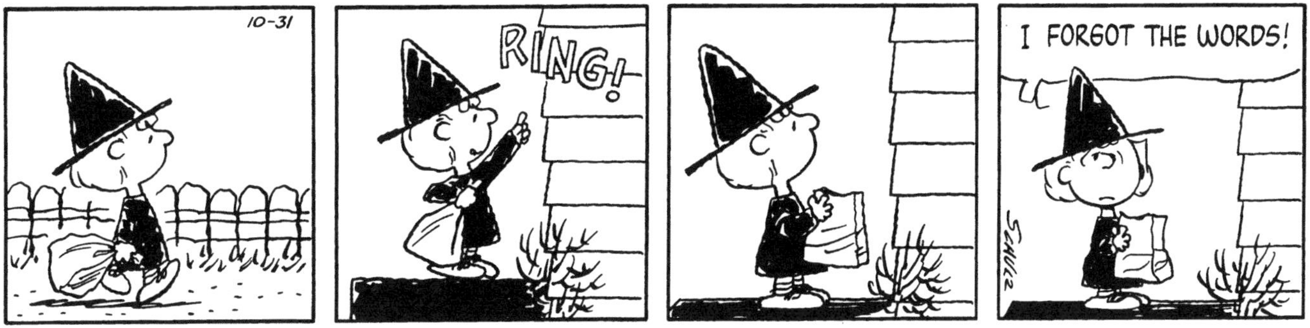
10-31
RING!
I FORGOT THE WORDS!

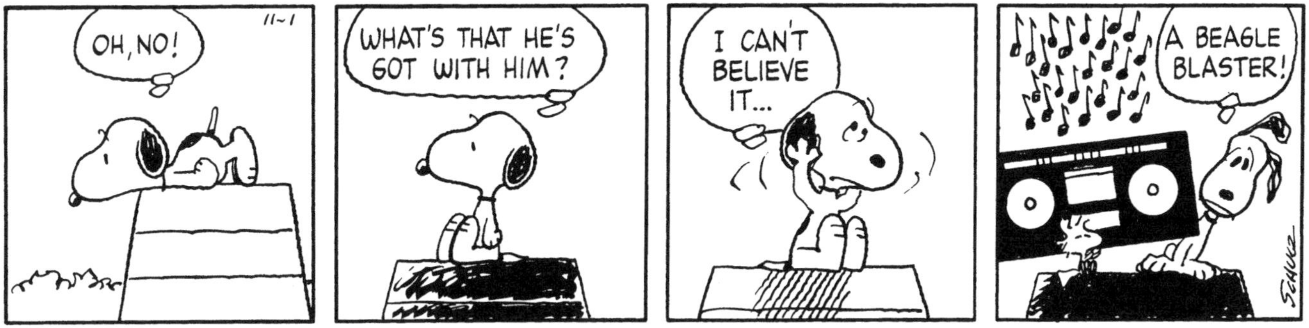
11-1
OH, NO!
WHAT'S THAT HE'S GOT WITH HIM?
I CAN'T BELIEVE IT...
A BEAGLE BLASTER!

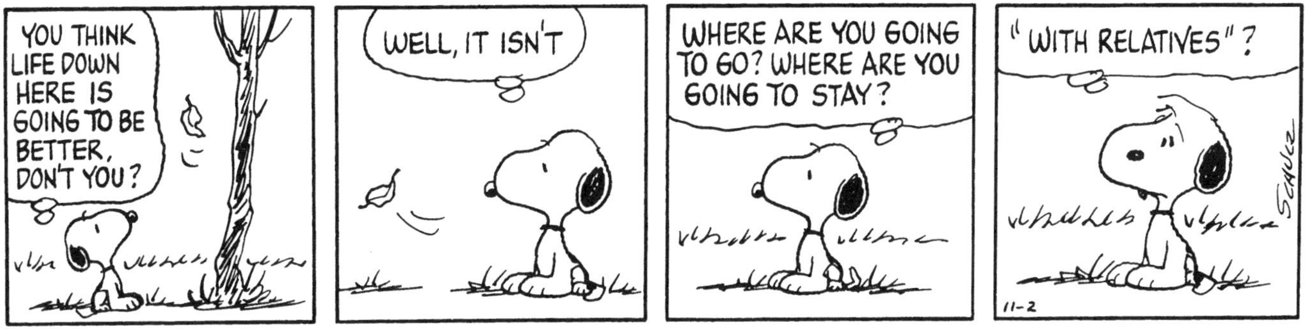
YOU THINK LIFE DOWN HERE IS GOING TO BE BETTER, DON'T YOU?
WELL, IT ISN'T
WHERE ARE YOU GOING TO GO? WHERE ARE YOU GOING TO STAY?
"WITH RELATIVES"?
11-2

PEANUTS
featuring
"Good ol' Charlie Brown"
by SCHULZ
IT'S A LETTER FROM YOUR BROTHER SPIKE..
"DEAR SNOOPY, SOMETHING WONDERFUL JUST HAPPENED..."
"A MAN CAME BY HERE, AND OFFERED TO SELL ME A MAGIC CAPE.."
"HE TOLD ME IF I WORE THIS MAGIC CAPE, I'D BE TRANSPORTED TO A LAND OF PARADISE!"
"HE SAID THE CAPE WAS ON SALE... NOT WANTING TO MISS SUCH A BARGAIN, I GAVE HIM MY ONLY DOLLAR..."
"SO BY THE TIME YOU GET THIS LETTER, I'LL BE LIVING IN PARADISE"
11-3
THEN AGAIN, MAYBE I'VE BEEN HAD...
SCHULZ

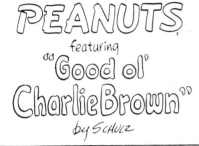

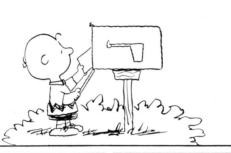

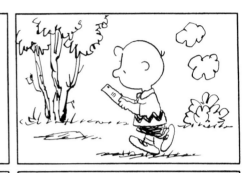

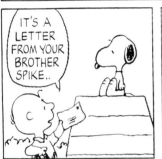

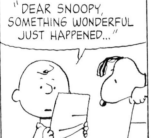

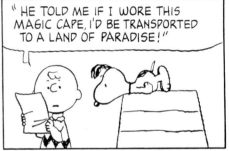

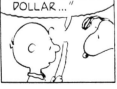

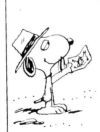

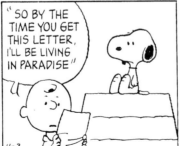

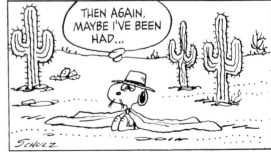

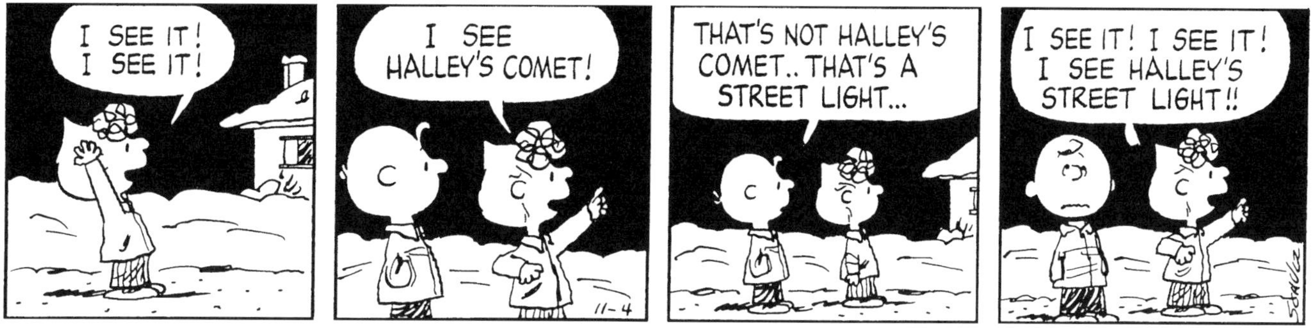
I SEE IT! I SEE IT!
I SEE HALLEY'S COMET!
11-4
THAT'S NOT HALLEY'S COMET.. THAT'S A STREET LIGHT...
I SEE IT! I SEE IT! I SEE HALLEY'S STREET LIGHT!!
SCHULZ

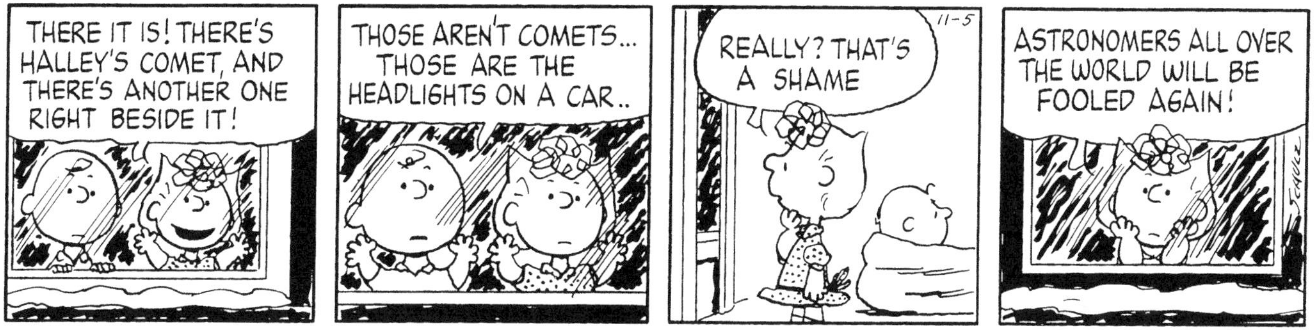
THERE IT IS! THERE'S HALLEY'S COMET, AND THERE'S ANOTHER ONE RIGHT BESIDE IT!
THOSE AREN'T COMETS... THOSE ARE THE HEADLIGHTS ON A CAR..
11-5
REALLY? THAT'S A SHAME
ASTRONOMERS ALL OVER THE WORLD WILL BE FOOLED AGAIN!
SCHULZ

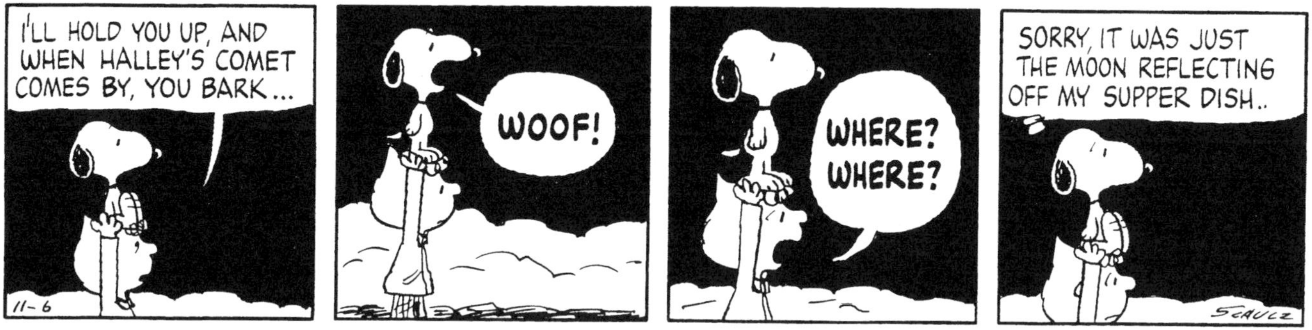
I'LL HOLD YOU UP, AND WHEN HALLEY'S COMET COMES BY, YOU BARK...
11-6
WOOF!
WHERE? WHERE?
SORRY, IT WAS JUST THE MOON REFLECTING OFF MY SUPPER DISH..
SCHULZ

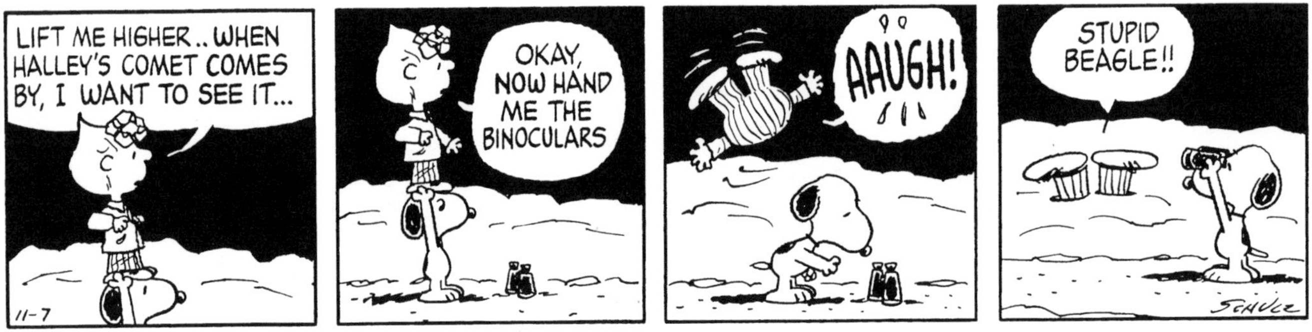
LIFT ME HIGHER.. WHEN HALLEY'S COMET COMES BY, I WANT TO SEE IT...
11-7
OKAY, NOW HAND ME THE BINOCULARS
AAUGH!
STUPID BEAGLE!!
SCHULZ

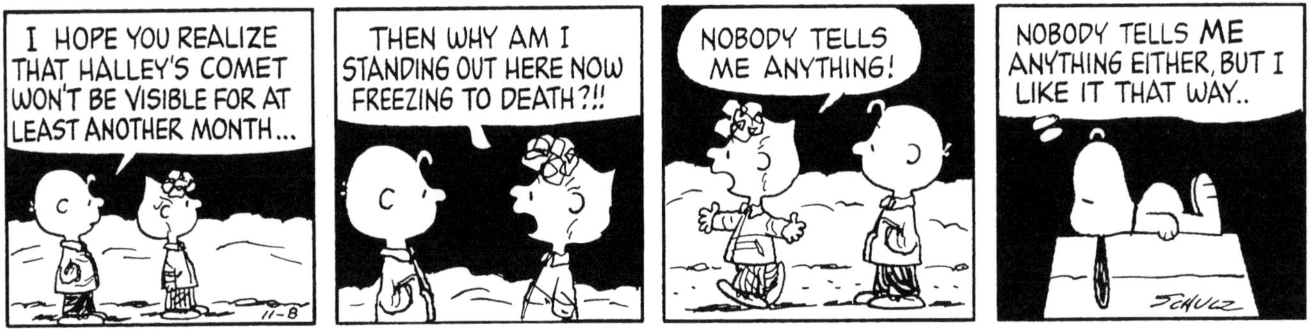
I HOPE YOU REALIZE THAT HALLEY'S COMET WON'T BE VISIBLE FOR AT LEAST ANOTHER MONTH...
11-8
THEN WHY AM I STANDING OUT HERE NOW FREEZING TO DEATH?!!
NOBODY TELLS ME ANYTHING!
NOBODY TELLS ME ANYTHING EITHER, BUT I LIKE IT THAT WAY..
SCHULZ

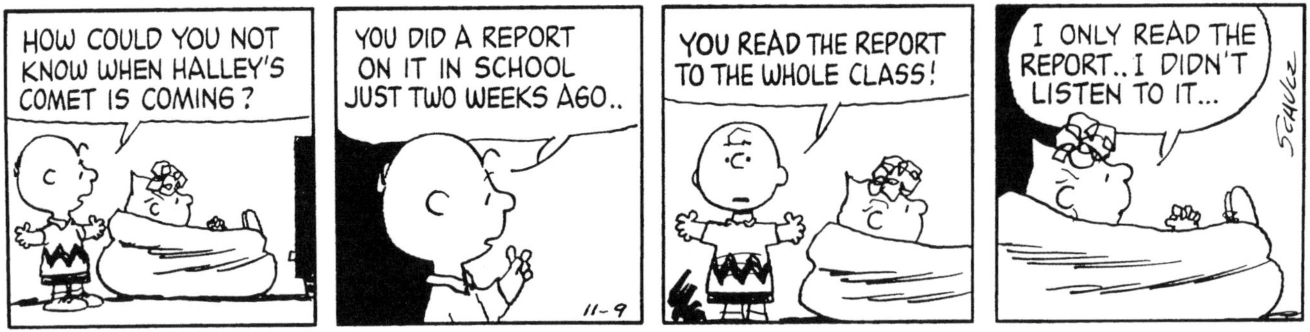
HOW COULD YOU NOT KNOW WHEN HALLEY'S COMET IS COMING?
YOU DID A REPORT ON IT IN SCHOOL JUST TWO WEEKS AGO..
11-9
YOU READ THE REPORT TO THE WHOLE CLASS!
I ONLY READ THE REPORT.. I DIDN'T LISTEN TO IT...
SCHULZ

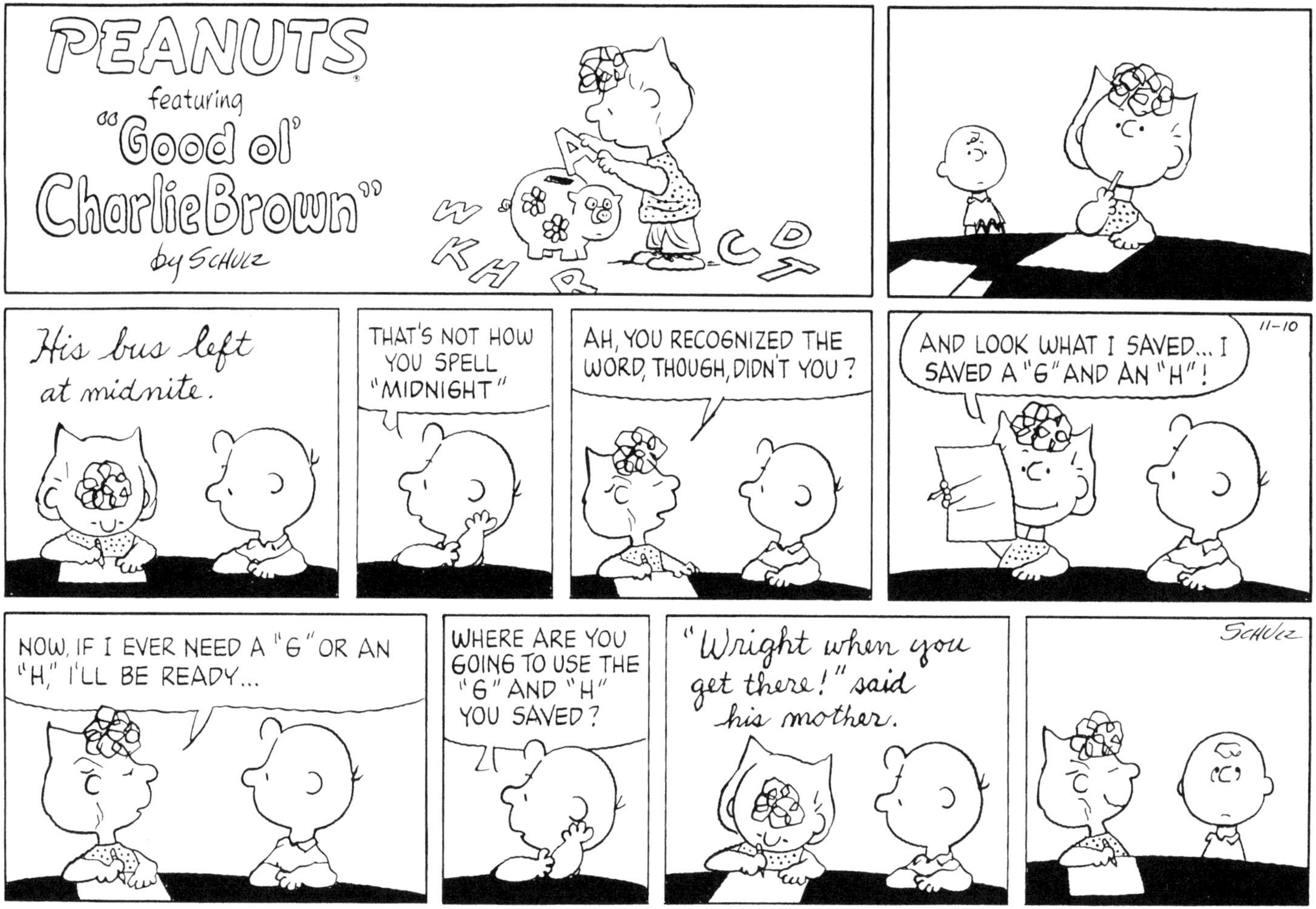
PEANUTS
featuring "Good ol' Charlie Brown"
by SCHULZ
His bus left at midnite.
THAT'S NOT HOW YOU SPELL "MIDNIGHT"
AH, YOU RECOGNIZED THE WORD, THOUGH, DIDN'T YOU?
11-10
AND LOOK WHAT I SAVED... I SAVED A "G" AND AN "H"!
NOW, IF I EVER NEED A "G" OR AN "H," I'LL BE READY...
WHERE ARE YOU GOING TO USE THE "G" AND "H" YOU SAVED?
"Wright when you get there!" said his mother.
SCHULZ

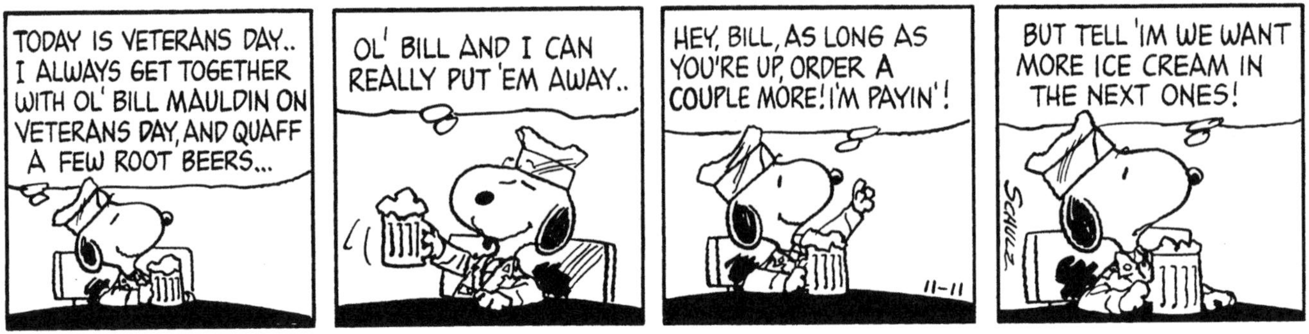
TODAY IS VETERANS DAY.. I ALWAYS GET TOGETHER WITH OL' BILL MAULDIN ON VETERANS DAY, AND QUAFF A FEW ROOT BEERS...
OL' BILL AND I CAN REALLY PUT 'EM AWAY..
HEY, BILL, AS LONG AS YOU'RE UP, ORDER A COUPLE MORE! I'M PAYIN'!
11-11
BUT TELL 'IM WE WANT MORE ICE CREAM IN THE NEXT ONES!
SCHULZ

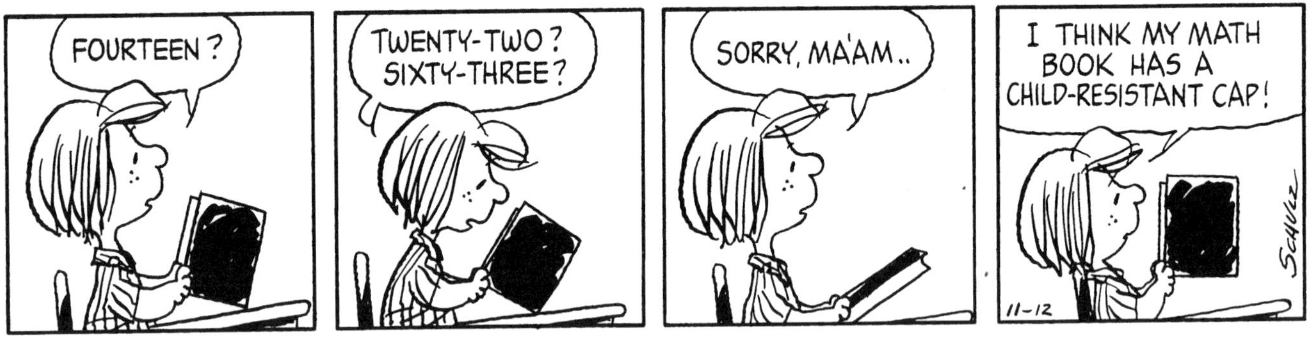
FOURTEEN?
TWENTY-TWO? SIXTY-THREE?
SORRY, MA'AM..
I THINK MY MATH BOOK HAS A CHILD-RESISTANT CAP!
SCHULZ
11-12

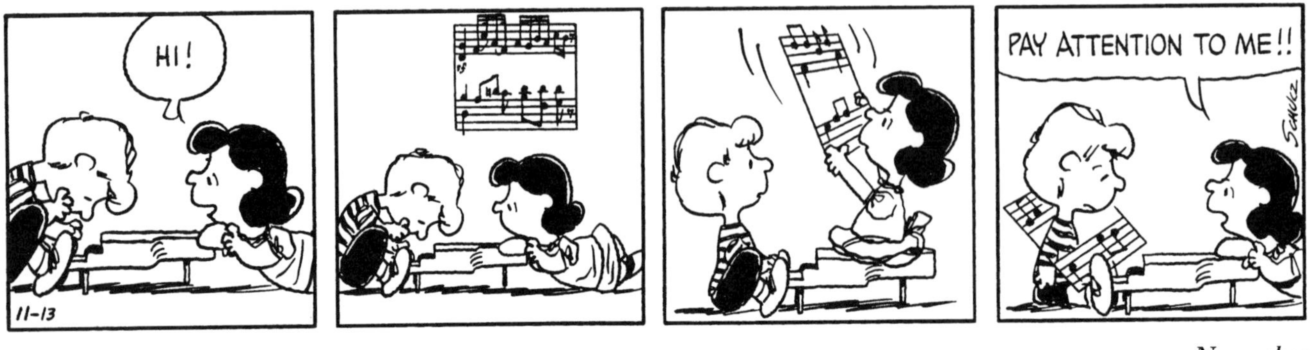
HI!
11-13
PAY ATTENTION TO ME!!
SCHULZ

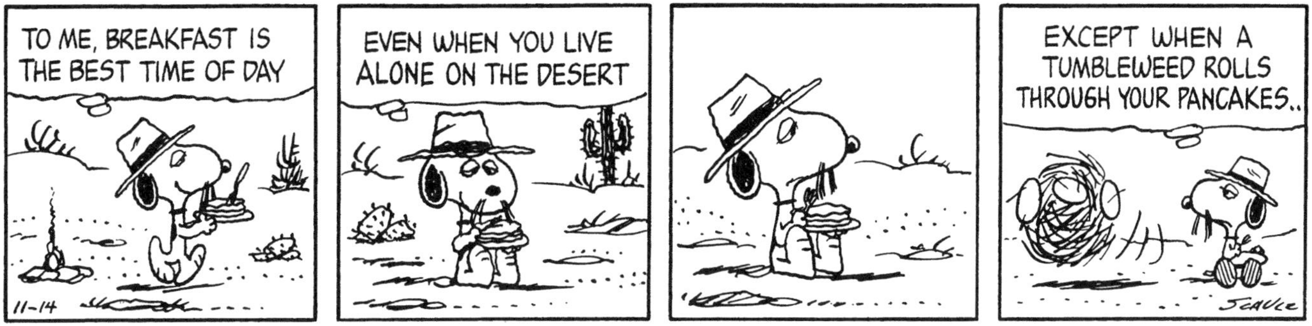
TO ME, BREAKFAST IS THE BEST TIME OF DAY
11-14
EVEN WHEN YOU LIVE ALONE ON THE DESERT
EXCEPT WHEN A TUMBLEWEED ROLLS THROUGH YOUR PANCAKES..

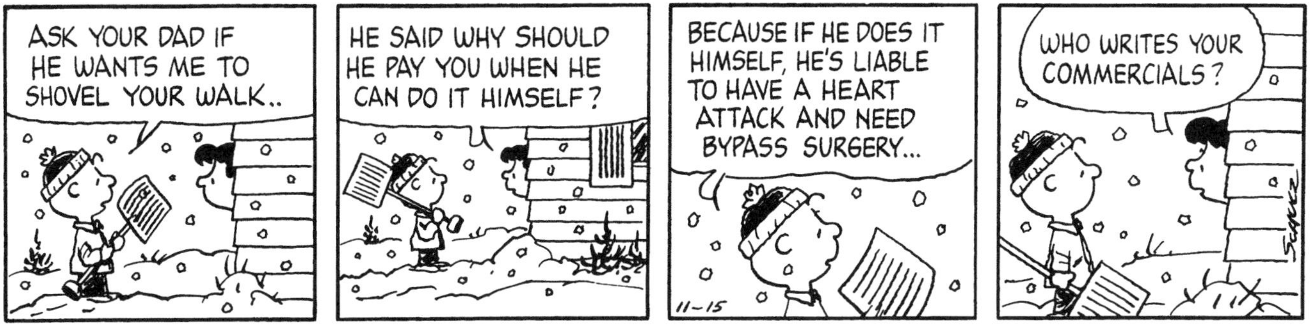
ASK YOUR DAD IF HE WANTS ME TO SHOVEL YOUR WALK..
HE SAID WHY SHOULD HE PAY YOU WHEN HE CAN DO IT HIMSELF?
BECAUSE IF HE DOES IT HIMSELF, HE'S LIABLE TO HAVE A HEART ATTACK AND NEED BYPASS SURGERY...
11-15
WHO WRITES YOUR COMMERCIALS?

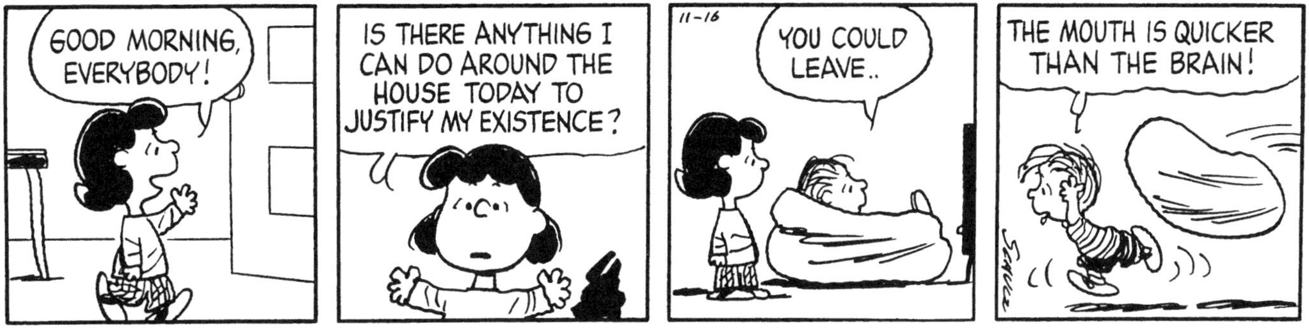
GOOD MORNING, EVERYBODY!
IS THERE ANYTHING I CAN DO AROUND THE HOUSE TODAY TO JUSTIFY MY EXISTENCE?
11-16
YOU COULD LEAVE..
THE MOUTH IS QUICKER THAN THE BRAIN!

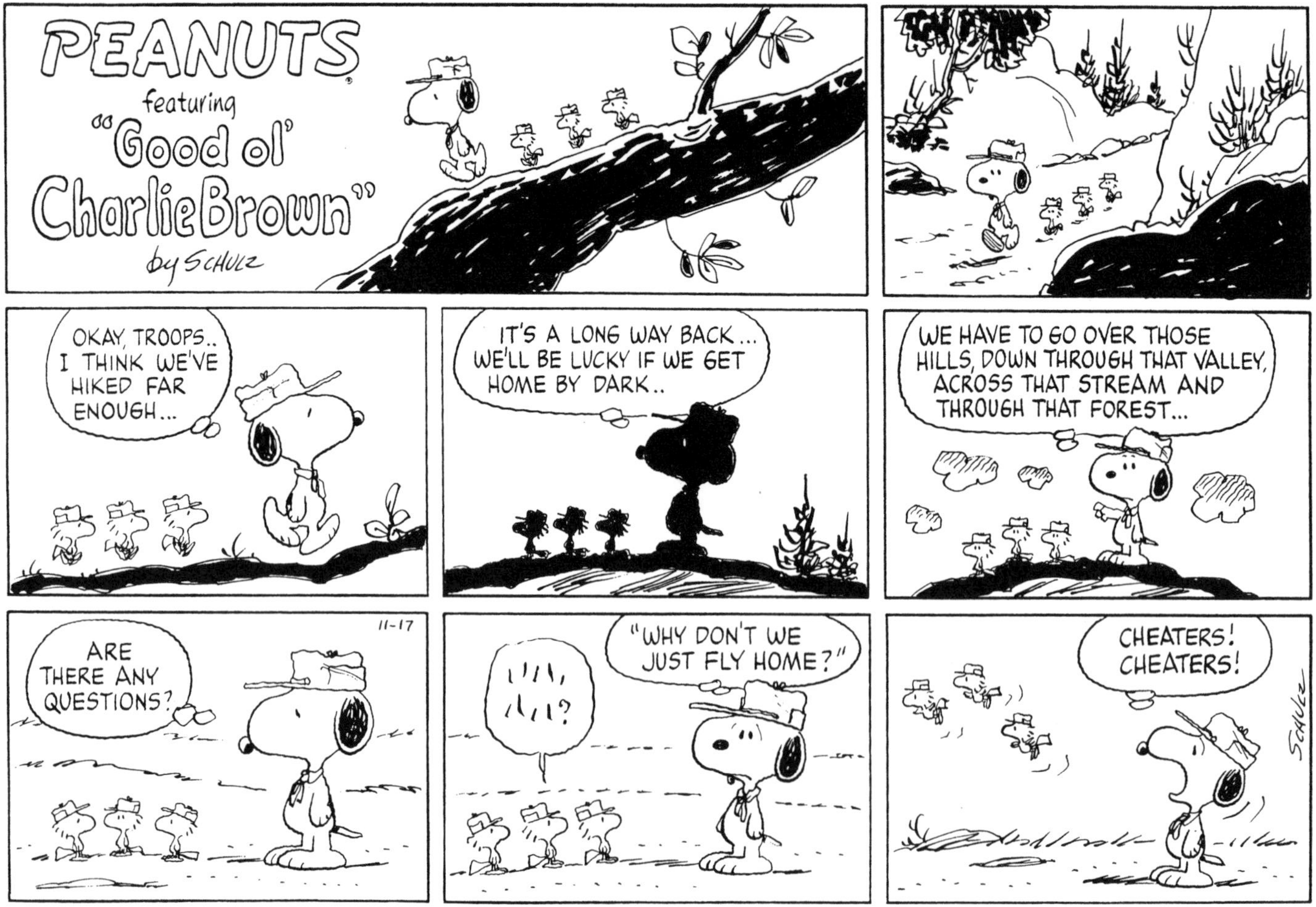
PEANUTS
featuring
"Good ol' CharlieBrown"
by SCHULZ
OKAY, TROOPS.. I THINK WE'VE HIKED FAR ENOUGH...
IT'S A LONG WAY BACK... WE'LL BE LUCKY IF WE GET HOME BY DARK..
WE HAVE TO GO OVER THOSE HILLS, DOWN THROUGH THAT VALLEY, ACROSS THAT STREAM AND THROUGH THAT FOREST...
11-17
ARE THERE ANY QUESTIONS?
"WHY DON'T WE JUST FLY HOME?"
CHEATERS! CHEATERS!
SCHULZ

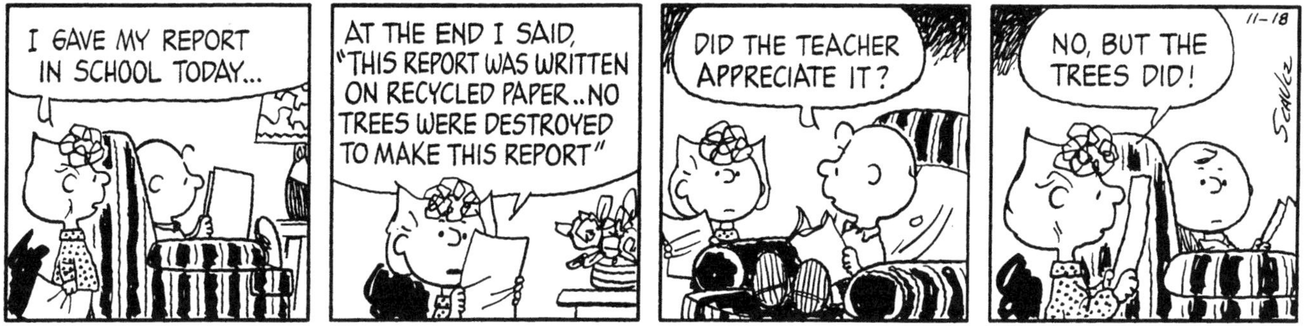
I GAVE MY REPORT IN SCHOOL TODAY...
AT THE END I SAID, "THIS REPORT WAS WRITTEN ON RECYCLED PAPER..NO TREES WERE DESTROYED TO MAKE THIS REPORT"
DID THE TEACHER APPRECIATE IT?
11-18
NO, BUT THE TREES DID!

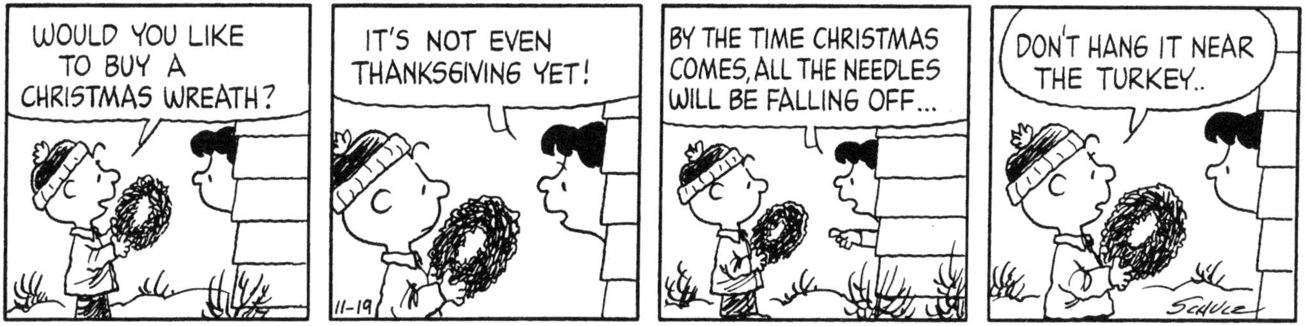
WOULD YOU LIKE TO BUY A CHRISTMAS WREATH?
IT'S NOT EVEN THANKSGIVING YET!
11-19
BY THE TIME CHRISTMAS COMES, ALL THE NEEDLES WILL BE FALLING OFF...
DON'T HANG IT NEAR THE TURKEY..

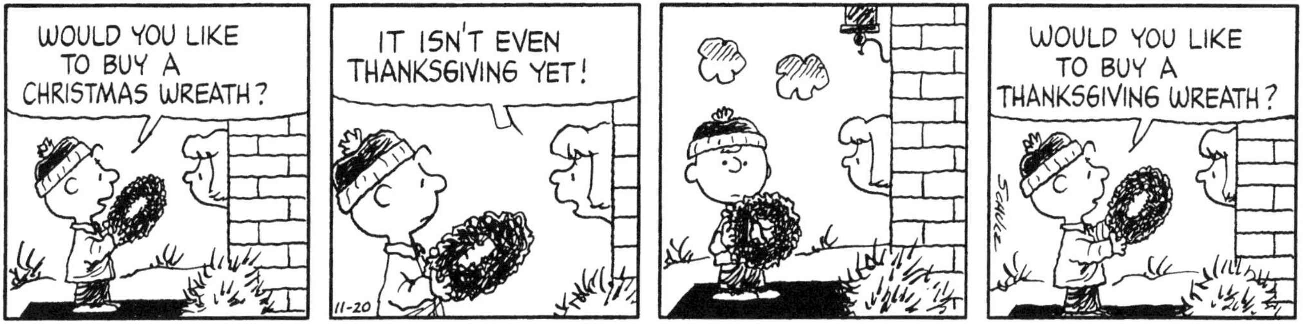
WOULD YOU LIKE TO BUY A CHRISTMAS WREATH?
IT ISN'T EVEN THANKSGIVING YET!
11-20
WOULD YOU LIKE TO BUY A THANKSGIVING WREATH?

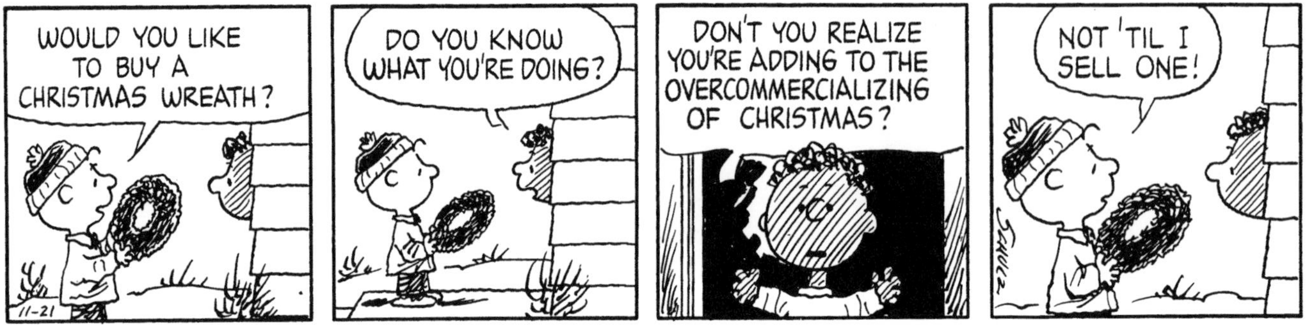

11-21
WOULD YOU LIKE TO BUY A CHRISTMAS WREATH?
DO YOU KNOW WHAT YOU'RE DOING?
DON'T YOU REALIZE YOU'RE ADDING TO THE OVERCOMMERCIALIZING OF CHRISTMAS?
NOT 'TIL I SELL ONE!

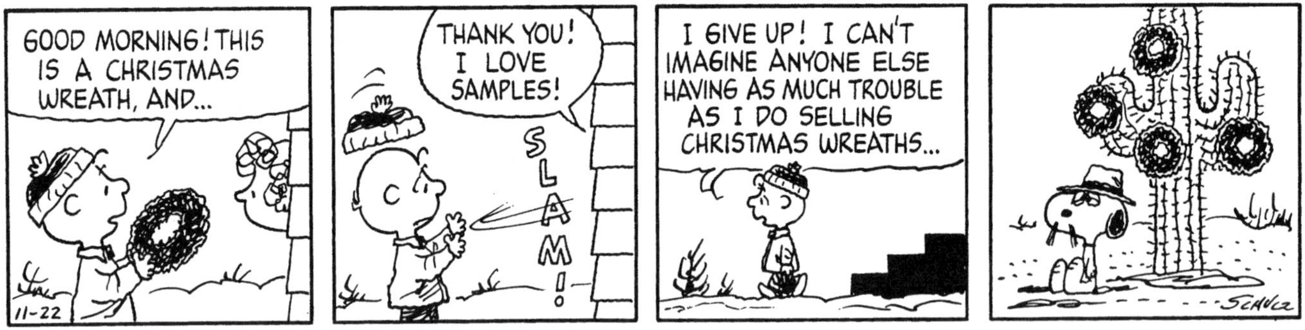

11-22
GOOD MORNING! THIS IS A CHRISTMAS WREATH, AND...
THANK YOU! I LOVE SAMPLES!
SLAM!
I GIVE UP! I CAN'T IMAGINE ANYONE ELSE HAVING AS MUCH TROUBLE AS I DO SELLING CHRISTMAS WREATHS...

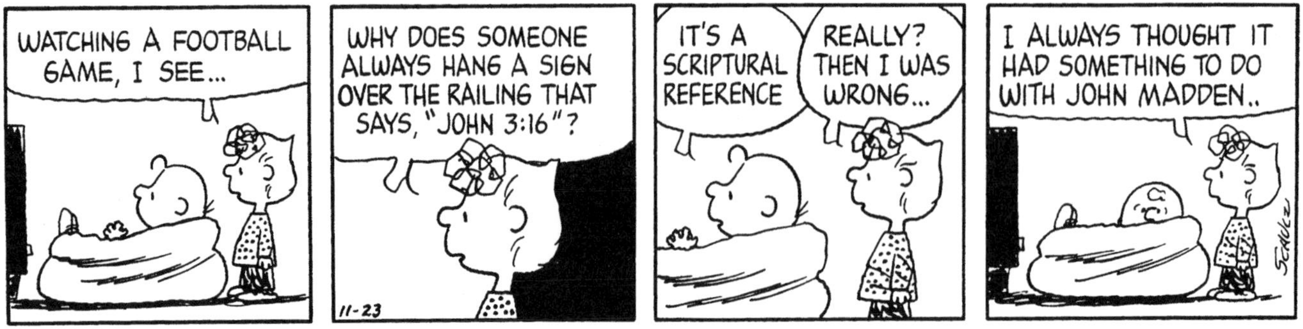

WATCHING A FOOTBALL GAME, I SEE...
WHY DOES SOMEONE ALWAYS HANG A SIGN OVER THE RAILING THAT SAYS, "JOHN 3:16"?
11-23
IT'S A SCRIPTURAL REFERENCE
REALLY? THEN I WAS WRONG...
I ALWAYS THOUGHT IT HAD SOMETHING TO DO WITH JOHN MADDEN..

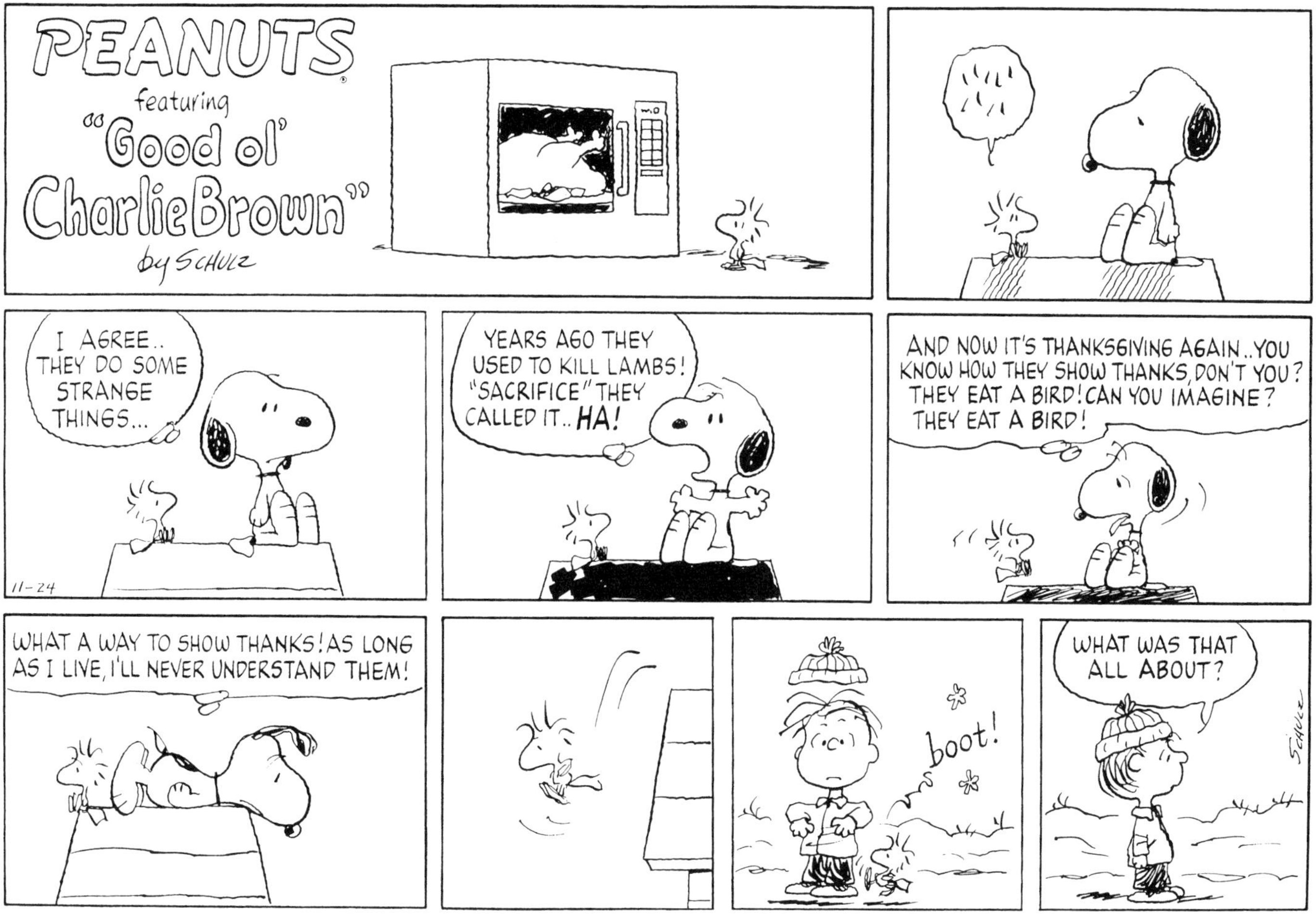
PEANUTS
featuring
"Good ol' Charlie Brown"
by SCHULZ
I AGREE.. THEY DO SOME STRANGE THINGS...
11-24
YEARS AGO THEY USED TO KILL LAMBS! "SACRIFICE" THEY CALLED IT.. HA!
AND NOW IT'S THANKSGIVING AGAIN.. YOU KNOW HOW THEY SHOW THANKS, DON'T YOU? THEY EAT A BIRD! CAN YOU IMAGINE? THEY EAT A BIRD!
WHAT A WAY TO SHOW THANKS! AS LONG AS I LIVE, I'LL NEVER UNDERSTAND THEM!
boot!
WHAT WAS THAT ALL ABOUT?
SCHULZ

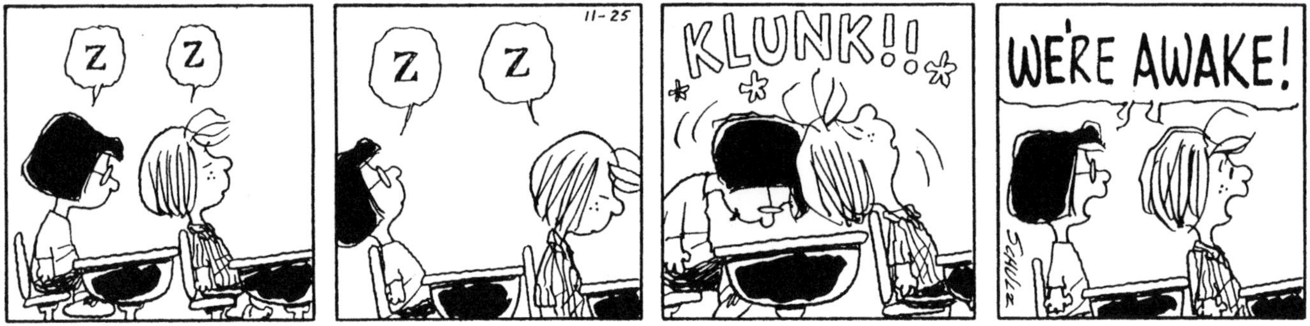
Z
Z
11-25
Z
Z
KLUNK!!
WE'RE AWAKE!
SCHULZ

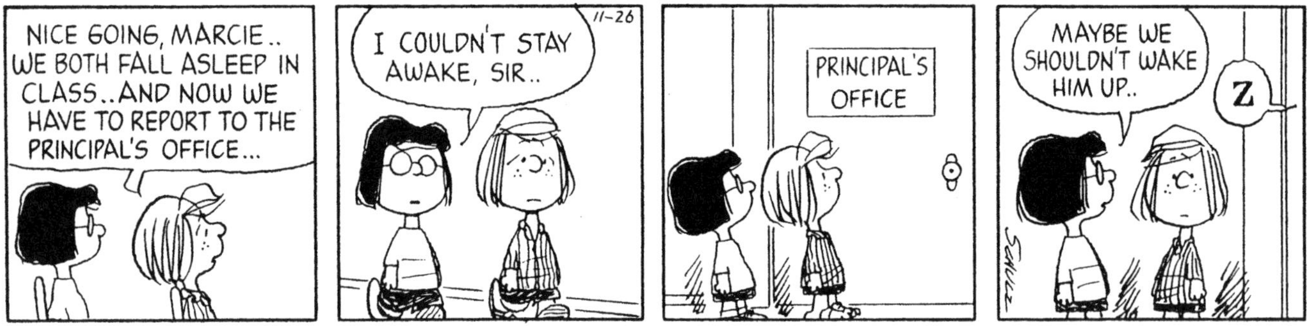
NICE GOING, MARCIE.. WE BOTH FALL ASLEEP IN CLASS..AND NOW WE HAVE TO REPORT TO THE PRINCIPAL'S OFFICE...
11-26
I COULDN'T STAY AWAKE, SIR..
PRINCIPAL'S OFFICE
MAYBE WE SHOULDN'T WAKE HIM UP..
Z
SCHULZ

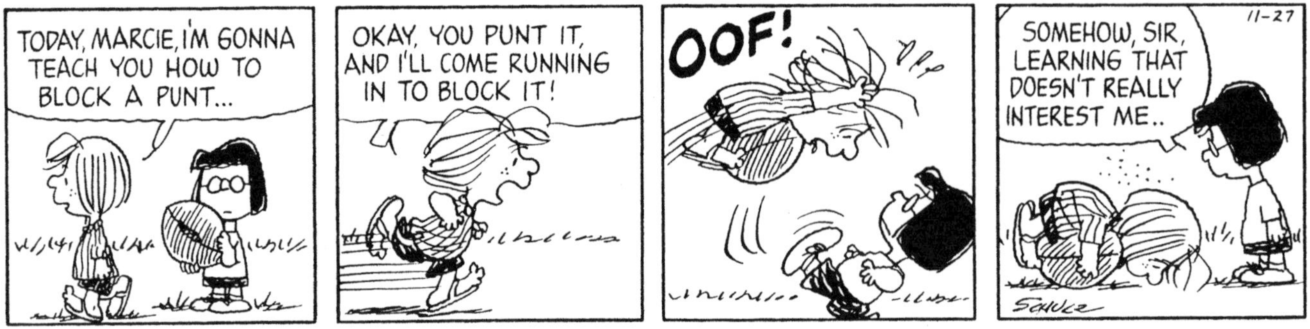
TODAY, MARCIE, I'M GONNA TEACH YOU HOW TO BLOCK A PUNT...
OKAY, YOU PUNT IT, AND I'LL COME RUNNING IN TO BLOCK IT!
OOF!
11-27
SOMEHOW, SIR, LEARNING THAT DOESN'T REALLY INTEREST ME..
SCHULZ

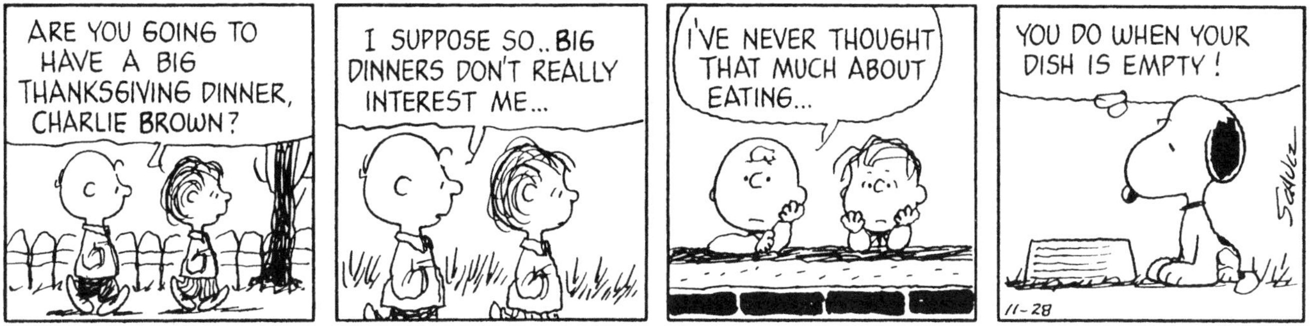
ARE YOU GOING TO HAVE A BIG THANKSGIVING DINNER, CHARLIE BROWN?
I SUPPOSE SO.. BIG DINNERS DON'T REALLY INTEREST ME...
I'VE NEVER THOUGHT THAT MUCH ABOUT EATING...
YOU DO WHEN YOUR DISH IS EMPTY !
11-28

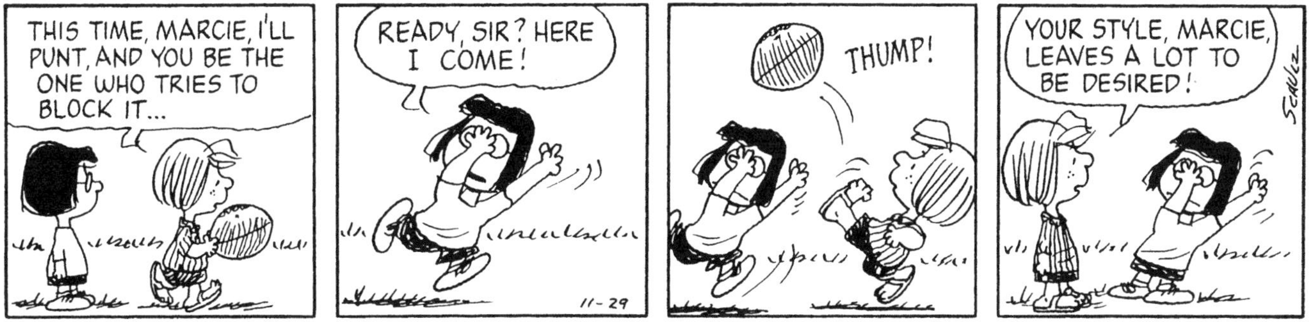
THIS TIME, MARCIE, I'LL PUNT, AND YOU BE THE ONE WHO TRIES TO BLOCK IT...
READY, SIR? HERE I COME!
11-29
THUMP!
YOUR STYLE, MARCIE, LEAVES A LOT TO BE DESIRED!

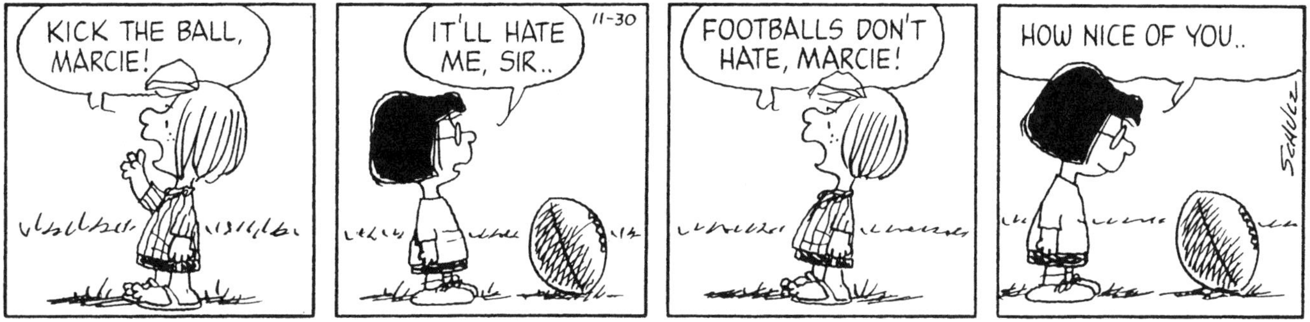
KICK THE BALL, MARCIE!
IT'LL HATE ME, SIR..
11-30
FOOTBALLS DON'T HATE, MARCIE!
HOW NICE OF YOU..

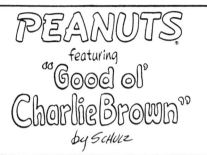

Peanuts
featuring
"Good ol'
Charlie Brown"
by Schulz

·SIGH·

THERE'S THE TELEPHONE..I'D GIVE ANYTHING TO HAVE THE NERVE TO CALL THAT LITTLE RED HAIRED GIRL...

WHY DON'T YOU JUST DO IT?

BECAUSE I KNOW SHE WOULDN'T WANT TO TALK TO ME...

THAT'S RIDICULOUS, CHARLIE BROWN.. WE SEE HER IN SCHOOL EVERY DAY... SHE'S A VERY NICE PERSON!

SHE'LL TALK TO YOU..I KNOW SHE WILL...

I DOUBT IT..I'D JUST BE MAKING A FOOL OF MYSELF

12-1

GO AHEAD.. DO IT! CALL HER!

ALL RIGHT, BUT I'LL BET SHE WON'T EVEN GIVE ME THE TIME OF DAY...

WELL, WHAT HAPPENED?

SHE SAID IT WAS FOUR O'CLOCK!

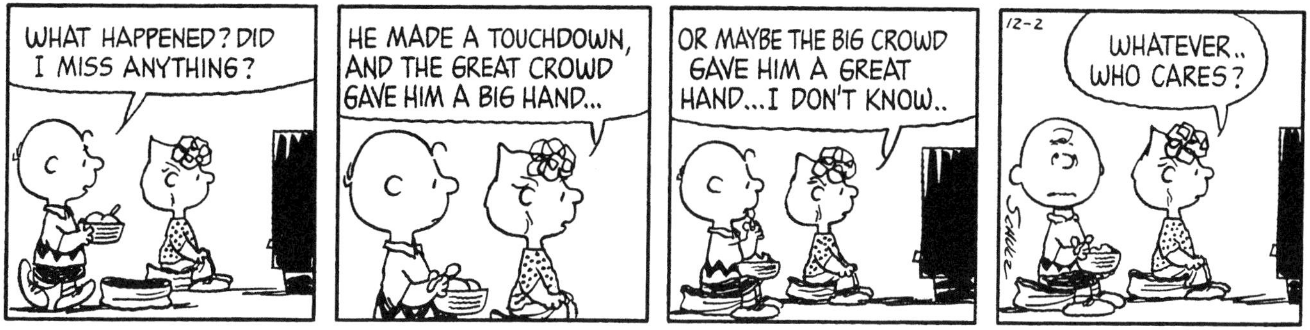
WHAT HAPPENED? DID I MISS ANYTHING?
HE MADE A TOUCHDOWN, AND THE GREAT CROWD GAVE HIM A BIG HAND...
OR MAYBE THE BIG CROWD GAVE HIM A GREAT HAND...I DON'T KNOW..
12-2
WHATEVER.. WHO CARES?

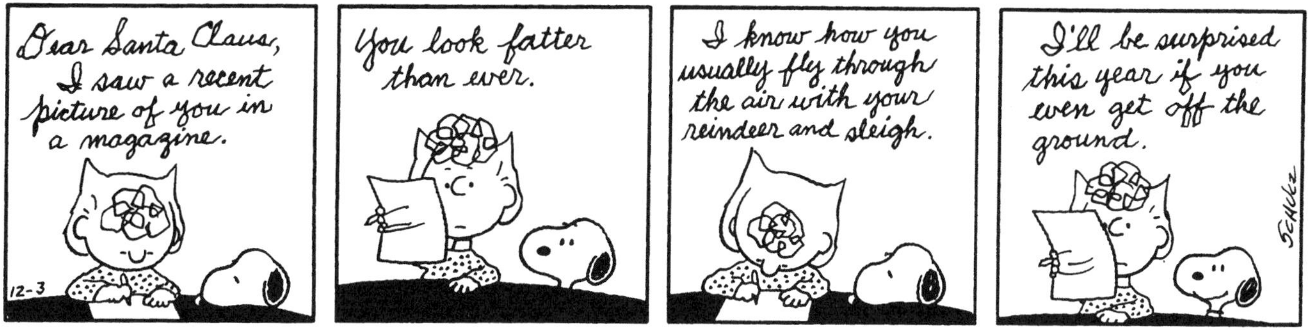
Dear Santa Claus,
I saw a recent picture of you in a magazine.
12-3
You look fatter than ever.
I know how you usually fly through the air with your reindeer and sleigh.
I'll be surprised this year if you even get off the ground.

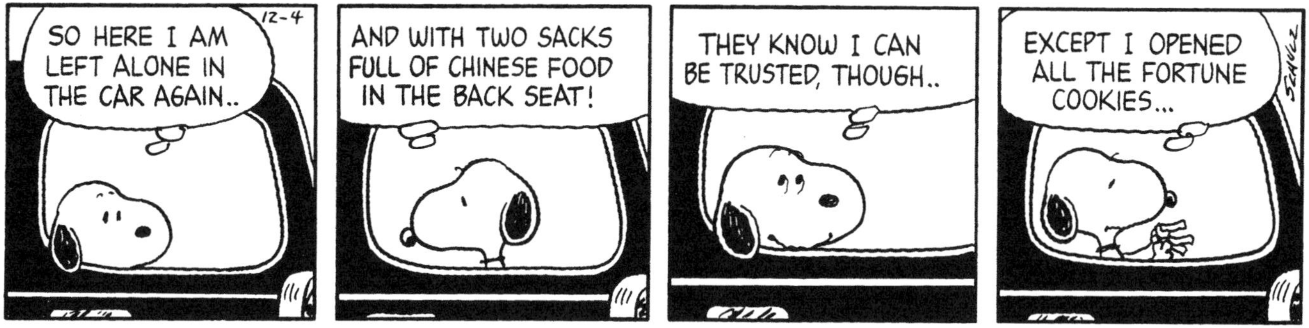
12-4
SO HERE I AM LEFT ALONE IN THE CAR AGAIN..
AND WITH TWO SACKS FULL OF CHINESE FOOD IN THE BACK SEAT!
THEY KNOW I CAN BE TRUSTED, THOUGH..
EXCEPT I OPENED ALL THE FORTUNE COOKIES...

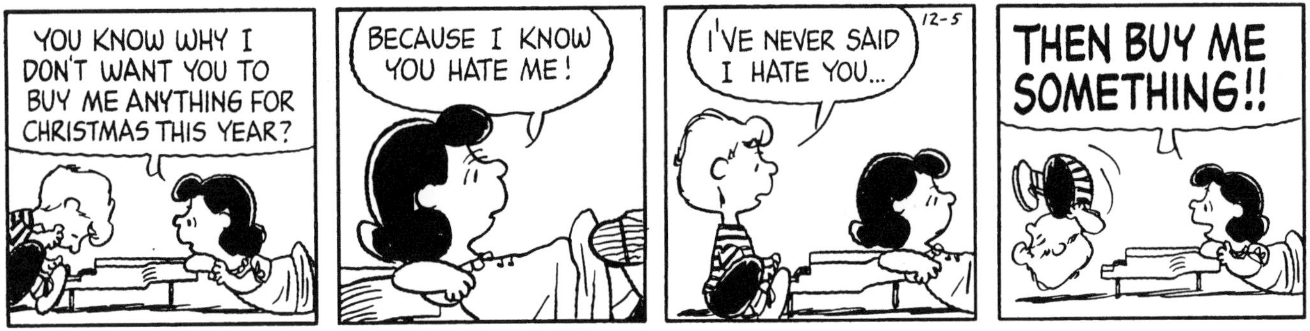
YOU KNOW WHY I DON'T WANT YOU TO BUY ME ANYTHING FOR CHRISTMAS THIS YEAR?
BECAUSE I KNOW YOU HATE ME!
12-5
I'VE NEVER SAID I HATE YOU...
THEN BUY ME SOMETHING!!

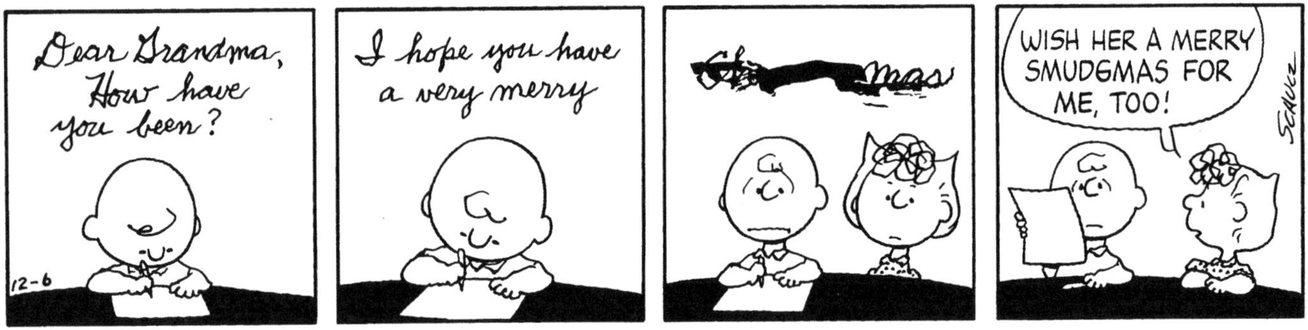
Dear Grandma, How have you been?
12-6
I hope you have a very merry
WISH HER A MERRY SMUDGMAS FOR ME, TOO!
SCHULZ

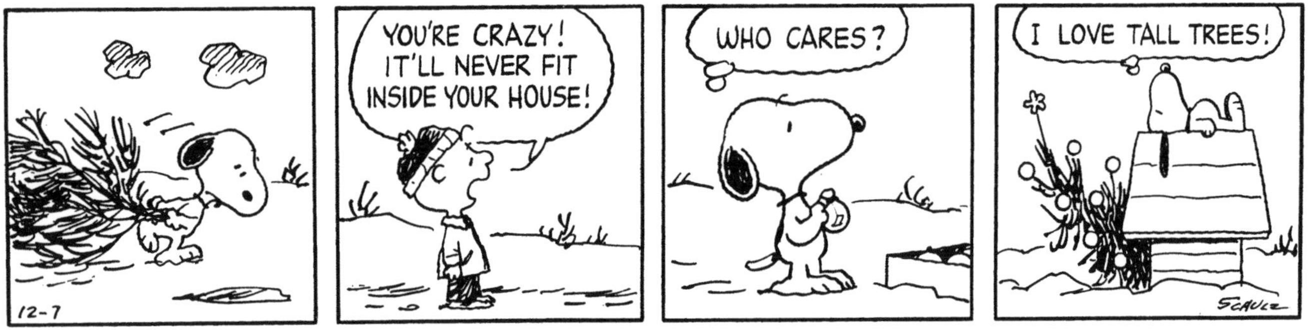
12-7
YOU'RE CRAZY! IT'LL NEVER FIT INSIDE YOUR HOUSE!
WHO CARES?
I LOVE TALL TREES!
SCHULZ

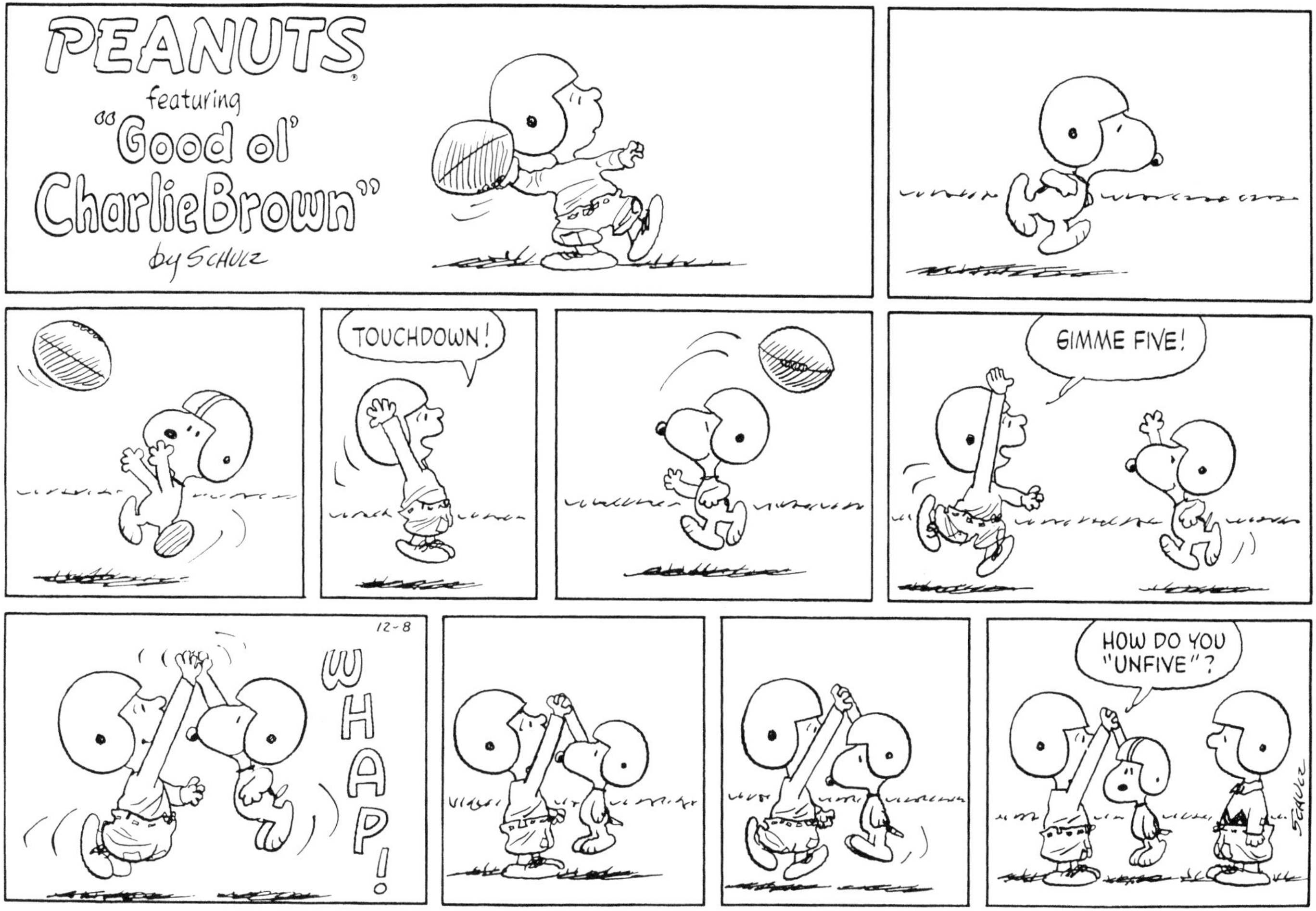
PEANUTS
featuring
"Good ol' Charlie Brown"
by SCHULZ
TOUCHDOWN!
GIMME FIVE!
12-8
WHAP!
HOW DO YOU "UNFIVE"?
SCHULZ

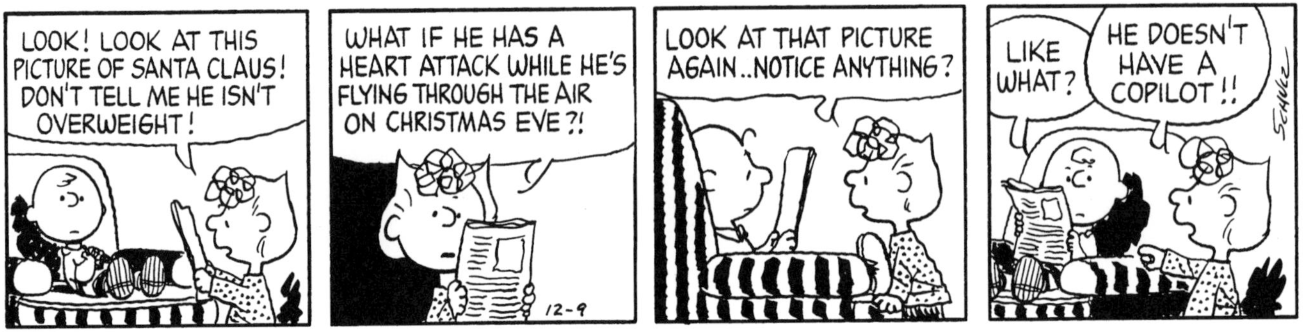
LOOK! LOOK AT THIS PICTURE OF SANTA CLAUS! DON'T TELL ME HE ISN'T OVERWEIGHT!
WHAT IF HE HAS A HEART ATTACK WHILE HE'S FLYING THROUGH THE AIR ON CHRISTMAS EVE?!
12-9
LOOK AT THAT PICTURE AGAIN..NOTICE ANYTHING?
LIKE WHAT?
HE DOESN'T HAVE A COPILOT!!
SCHULZ

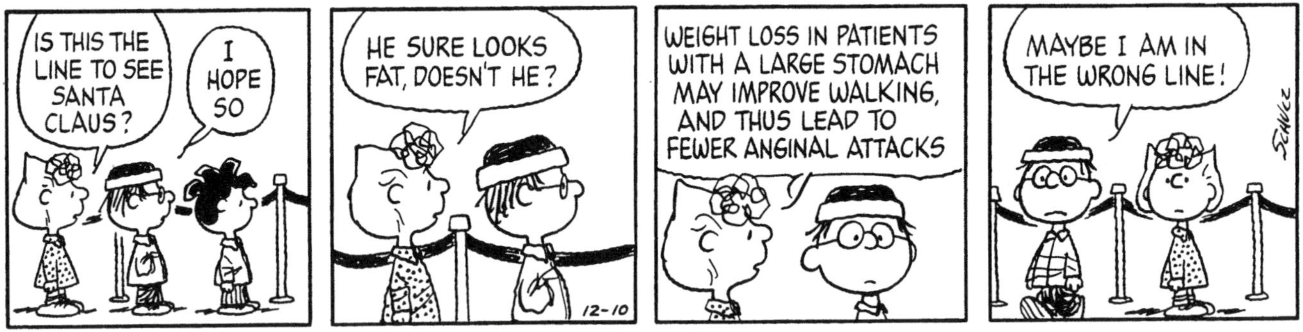
IS THIS THE LINE TO SEE SANTA CLAUS?
I HOPE SO
HE SURE LOOKS FAT, DOESN'T HE?
12-10
WEIGHT LOSS IN PATIENTS WITH A LARGE STOMACH MAY IMPROVE WALKING, AND THUS LEAD TO FEWER ANGINAL ATTACKS
MAYBE I AM IN THE WRONG LINE!
SCHULZ

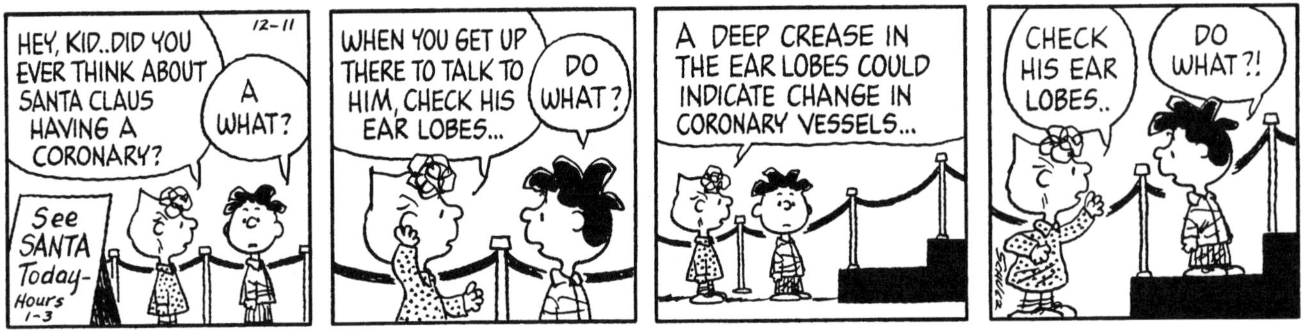
12-11
HEY, KID..DID YOU EVER THINK ABOUT SANTA CLAUS HAVING A CORONARY?
A WHAT?
See SANTA Today-
Hours 1-3
WHEN YOU GET UP THERE TO TALK TO HIM, CHECK HIS EAR LOBES...
DO WHAT?
A DEEP CREASE IN THE EAR LOBES COULD INDICATE CHANGE IN CORONARY VESSELS...
CHECK HIS EAR LOBES..
DO WHAT?!
SCHULZ

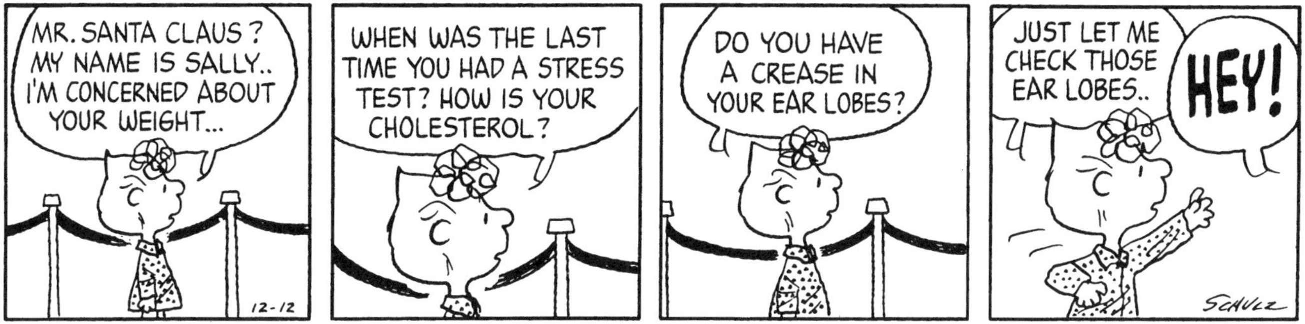
MR. SANTA CLAUS? MY NAME IS SALLY.. I'M CONCERNED ABOUT YOUR WEIGHT...
12-12
WHEN WAS THE LAST TIME YOU HAD A STRESS TEST? HOW IS YOUR CHOLESTEROL?
DO YOU HAVE A CREASE IN YOUR EAR LOBES?
JUST LET ME CHECK THOSE EAR LOBES..
HEY!
SCHULZ

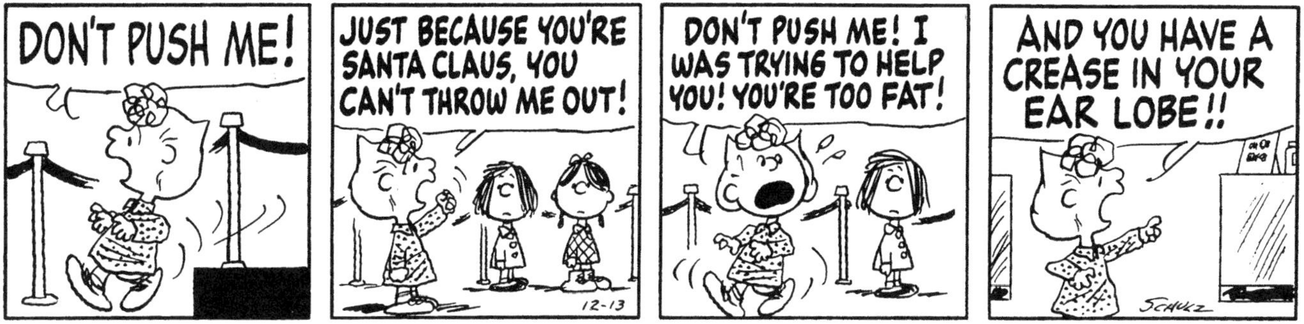
DON'T PUSH ME!
JUST BECAUSE YOU'RE SANTA CLAUS, YOU CAN'T THROW ME OUT!
12-13
DON'T PUSH ME! I WAS TRYING TO HELP YOU! YOU'RE TOO FAT!
AND YOU HAVE A CREASE IN YOUR EAR LOBE!!
SCHULZ

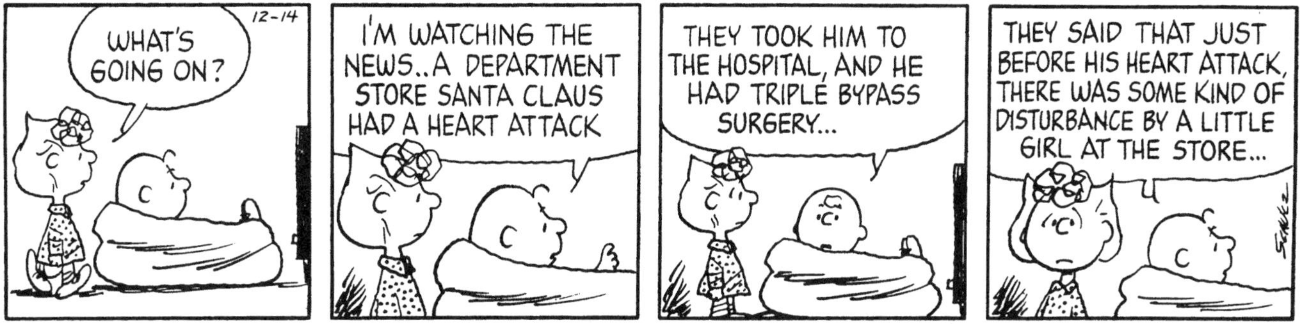
12-14
WHAT'S GOING ON?
I'M WATCHING THE NEWS..A DEPARTMENT STORE SANTA CLAUS HAD A HEART ATTACK
THEY TOOK HIM TO THE HOSPITAL, AND HE HAD TRIPLE BYPASS SURGERY...
THEY SAID THAT JUST BEFORE HIS HEART ATTACK, THERE WAS SOME KIND OF DISTURBANCE BY A LITTLE GIRL AT THE STORE...
SCHULZ

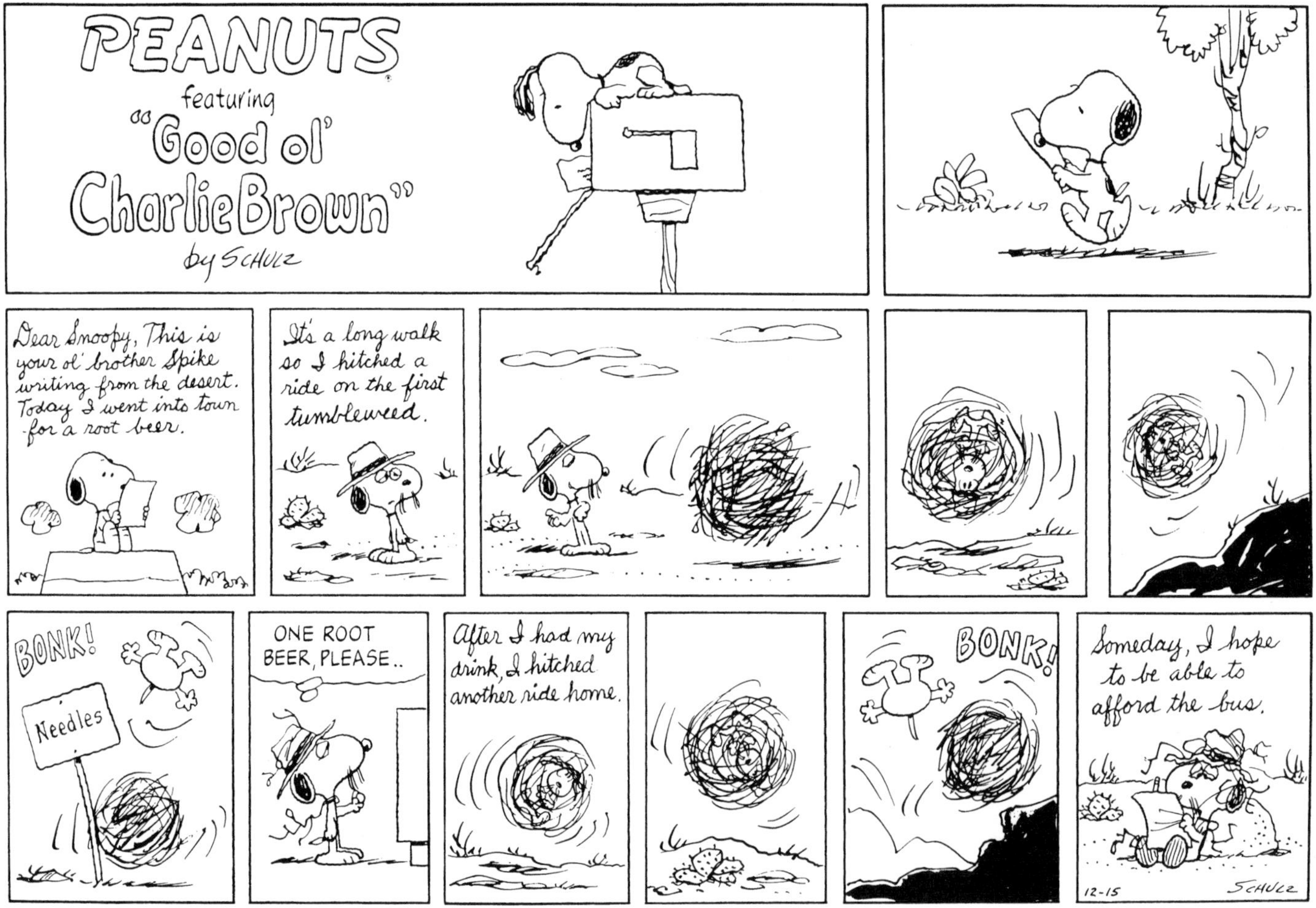
PEANUTS
featuring
"Good ol' CharlieBrown"
by SCHULZ
Dear Snoopy, This is your ol' brother Spike writing from the desert. Today I went into town for a root beer.
It's a long walk so I hitched a ride on the first tumbleweed.
BONK!
Needles
ONE ROOT BEER, PLEASE..
After I had my drink, I hitched another ride home.
BONK!
Someday, I hope to be able to afford the bus.
12-15
SCHULZ

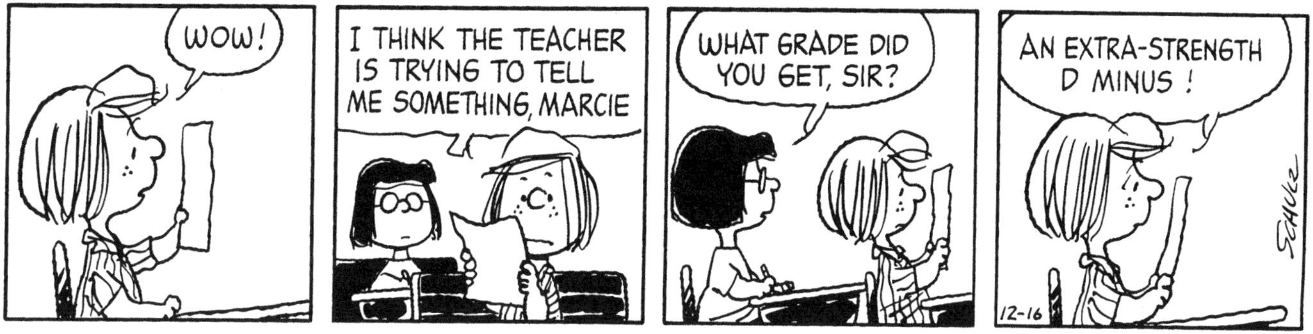
WOW!
I THINK THE TEACHER IS TRYING TO TELL ME SOMETHING, MARCIE
WHAT GRADE DID YOU GET, SIR?
AN EXTRA-STRENGTH D MINUS!
12-16

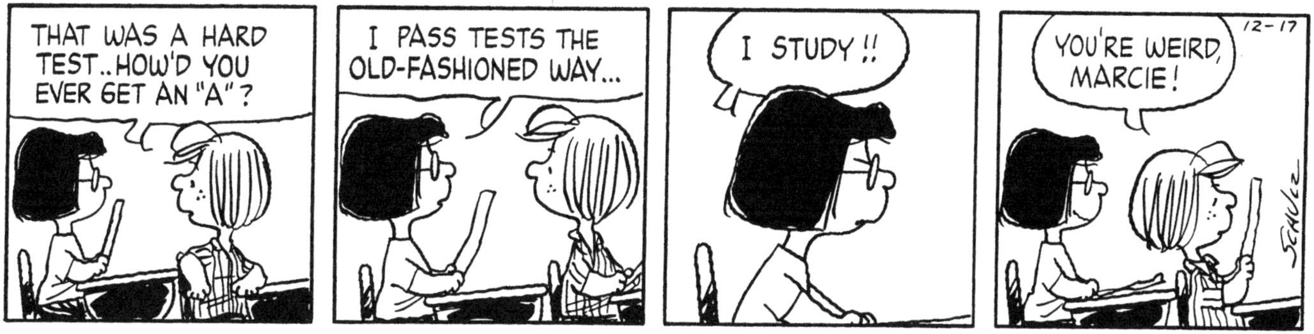
THAT WAS A HARD TEST.. HOW'D YOU EVER GET AN "A"?
I PASS TESTS THE OLD-FASHIONED WAY...
I STUDY!!
YOU'RE WEIRD, MARCIE!
12-17

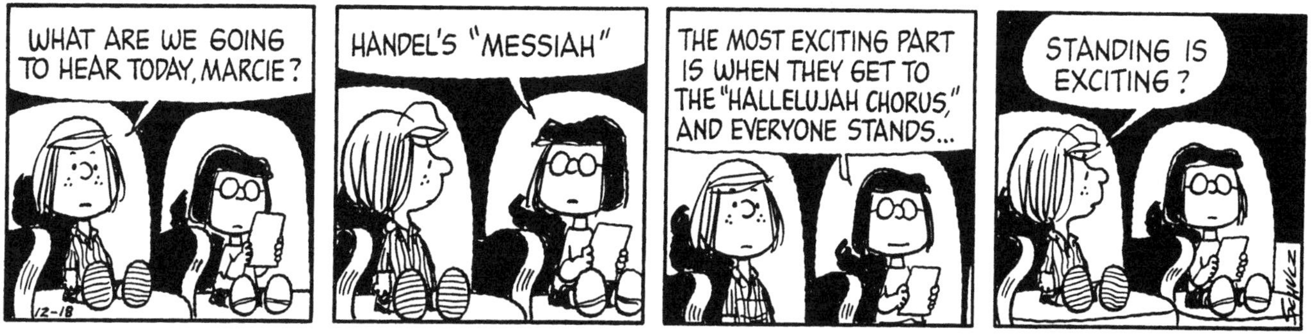
WHAT ARE WE GOING TO HEAR TODAY, MARCIE?
HANDEL'S "MESSIAH"
THE MOST EXCITING PART IS WHEN THEY GET TO THE "HALLELUJAH CHORUS," AND EVERYONE STANDS...
STANDING IS EXCITING?
12-18

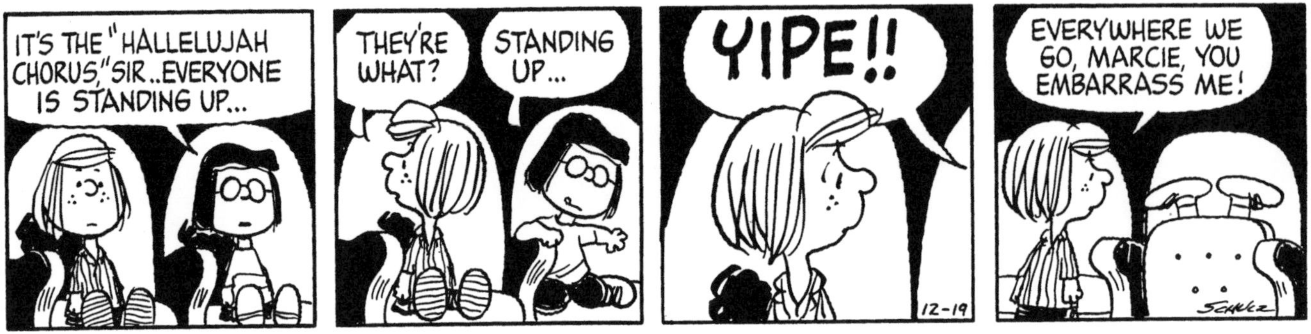
IT'S THE "HALLELUJAH CHORUS," SIR.. EVERYONE IS STANDING UP...
THEY'RE WHAT?
STANDING UP...
YIPE!!
12-19
EVERYWHERE WE GO, MARCIE, YOU EMBARRASS ME!
SCHULZ

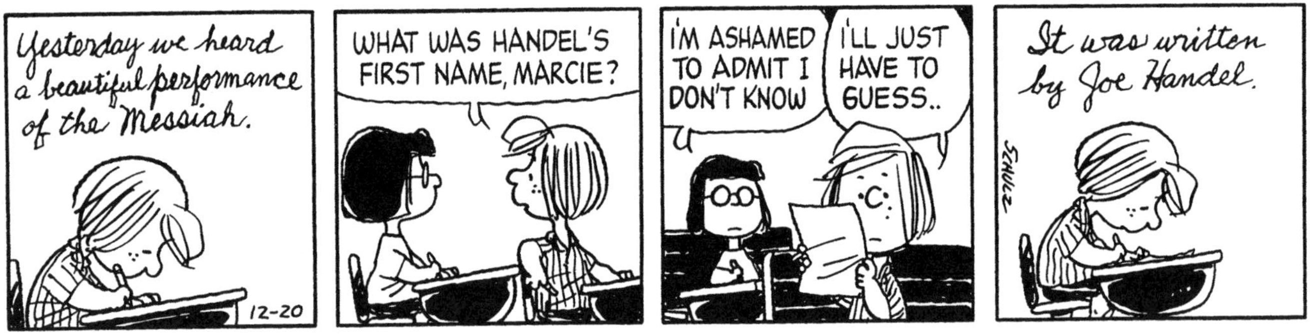
Yesterday we heard a beautiful performance of the Messiah.
12-20
WHAT WAS HANDEL'S FIRST NAME, MARCIE?
I'M ASHAMED TO ADMIT I DON'T KNOW
I'LL JUST HAVE TO GUESS..
It was written by Joe Handel.
SCHULZ

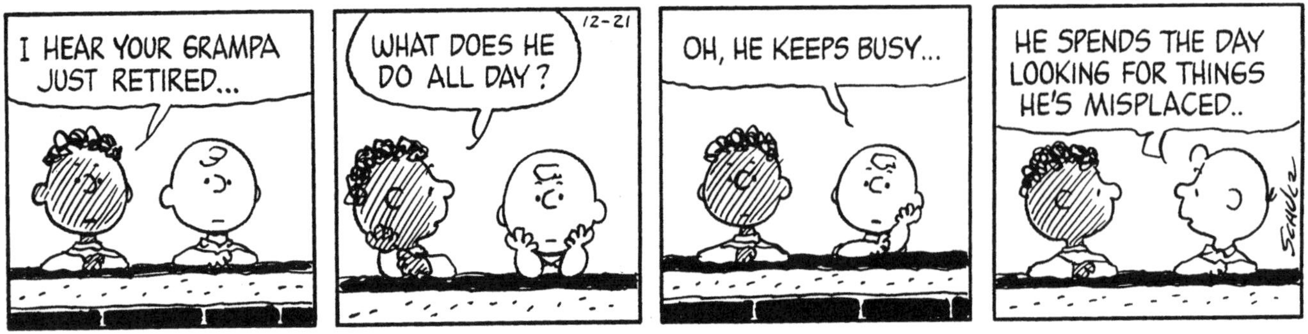
I HEAR YOUR GRAMPA JUST RETIRED...
12-21
WHAT DOES HE DO ALL DAY?
OH, HE KEEPS BUSY...
HE SPENDS THE DAY LOOKING FOR THINGS HE'S MISPLACED..
SCHULZ

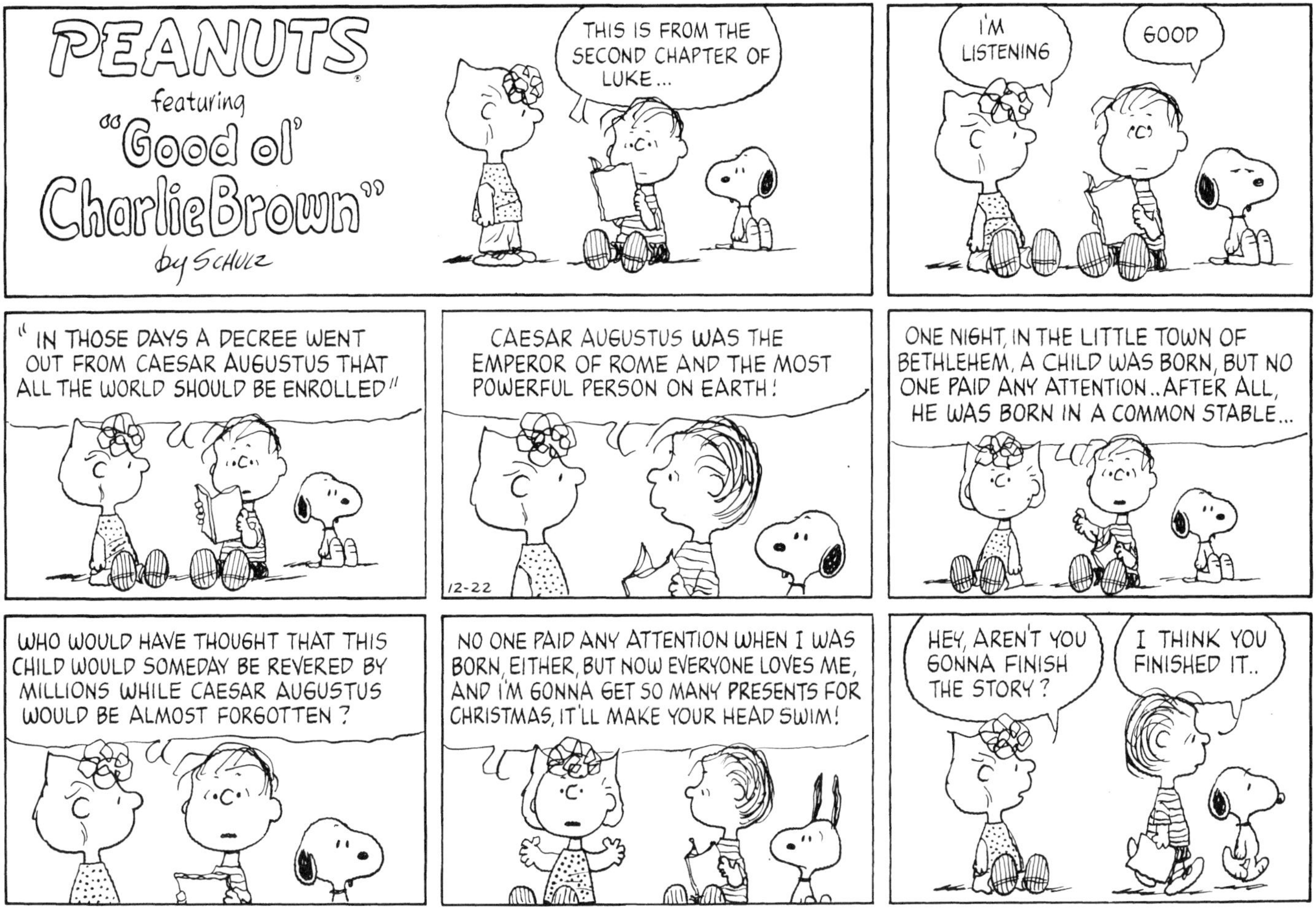
PEANUTS
featuring "Good ol' Charlie Brown"
by SCHULZ
THIS IS FROM THE SECOND CHAPTER OF LUKE...
I'M LISTENING
GOOD
" IN THOSE DAYS A DECREE WENT OUT FROM CAESAR AUGUSTUS THAT ALL THE WORLD SHOULD BE ENROLLED"
CAESAR AUGUSTUS WAS THE EMPEROR OF ROME AND THE MOST POWERFUL PERSON ON EARTH!
12-22
ONE NIGHT, IN THE LITTLE TOWN OF BETHLEHEM, A CHILD WAS BORN, BUT NO ONE PAID ANY ATTENTION.. AFTER ALL, HE WAS BORN IN A COMMON STABLE...
WHO WOULD HAVE THOUGHT THAT THIS CHILD WOULD SOMEDAY BE REVERED BY MILLIONS WHILE CAESAR AUGUSTUS WOULD BE ALMOST FORGOTTEN?
NO ONE PAID ANY ATTENTION WHEN I WAS BORN, EITHER, BUT NOW EVERYONE LOVES ME, AND I'M GONNA GET SO MANY PRESENTS FOR CHRISTMAS, IT'LL MAKE YOUR HEAD SWIM!
HEY, AREN'T YOU GONNA FINISH THE STORY?
I THINK YOU FINISHED IT..

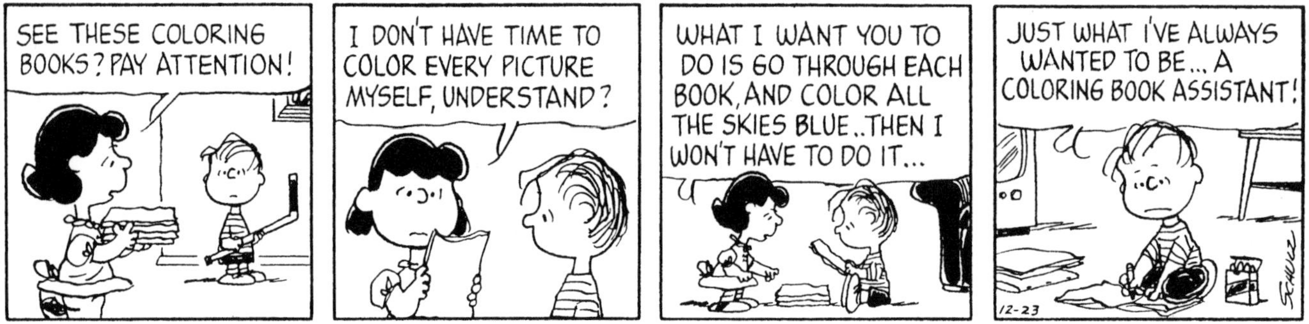
SEE THESE COLORING BOOKS? PAY ATTENTION!
I DON'T HAVE TIME TO COLOR EVERY PICTURE MYSELF, UNDERSTAND?
WHAT I WANT YOU TO DO IS GO THROUGH EACH BOOK, AND COLOR ALL THE SKIES BLUE..THEN I WON'T HAVE TO DO IT...
JUST WHAT I'VE ALWAYS WANTED TO BE... A COLORING BOOK ASSISTANT!
12-23
SCHULZ

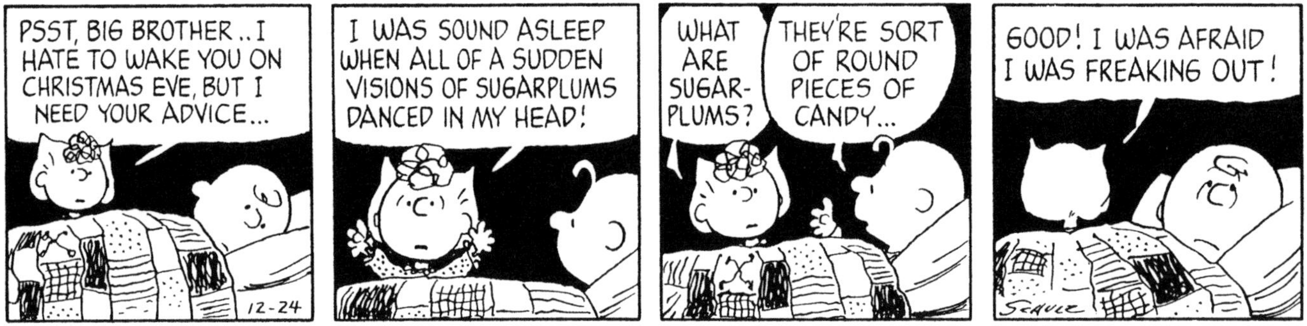
PSST, BIG BROTHER..I HATE TO WAKE YOU ON CHRISTMAS EVE, BUT I NEED YOUR ADVICE...
12-24
I WAS SOUND ASLEEP WHEN ALL OF A SUDDEN VISIONS OF SUGARPLUMS DANCED IN MY HEAD!
WHAT ARE SUGAR-PLUMS?
THEY'RE SORT OF ROUND PIECES OF CANDY...
GOOD! I WAS AFRAID I WAS FREAKING OUT!
SCHULZ

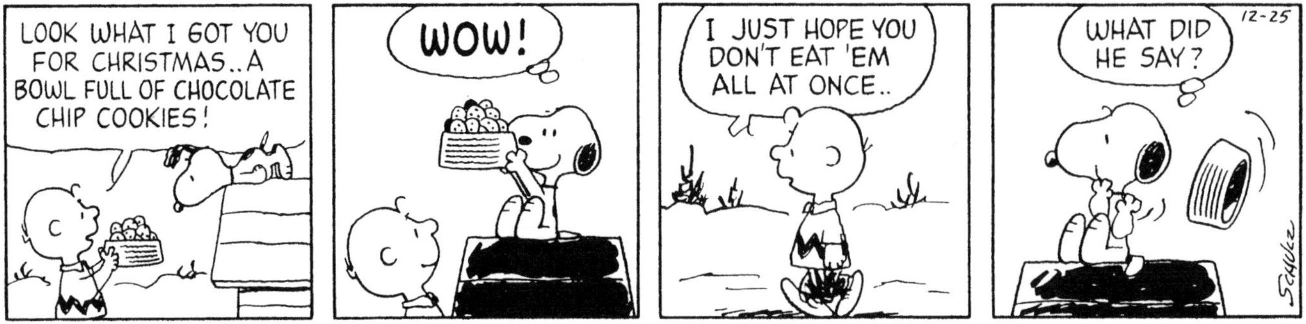
LOOK WHAT I GOT YOU FOR CHRISTMAS..A BOWL FULL OF CHOCOLATE CHIP COOKIES!
WOW!
I JUST HOPE YOU DON'T EAT 'EM ALL AT ONCE..
12-25
WHAT DID HE SAY?
SCHULZ

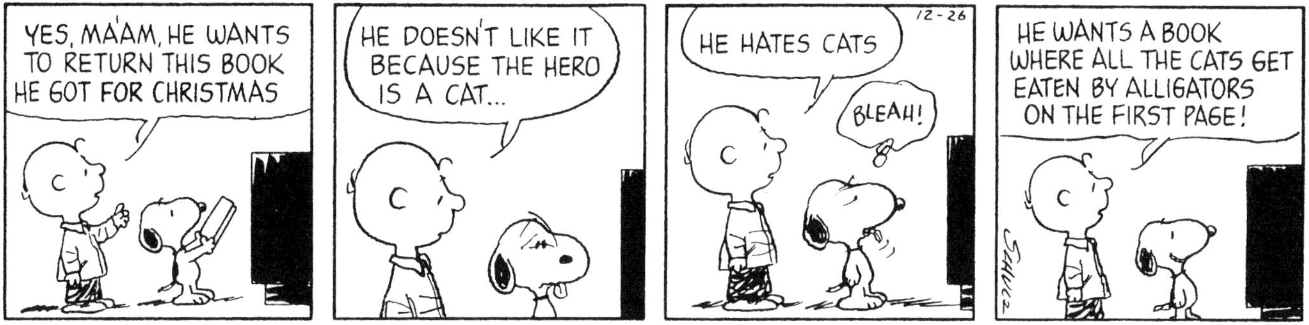
YES, MA'AM, HE WANTS TO RETURN THIS BOOK HE GOT FOR CHRISTMAS
HE DOESN'T LIKE IT BECAUSE THE HERO IS A CAT...
12-26
HE HATES CATS
BLEAH!
HE WANTS A BOOK WHERE ALL THE CATS GET EATEN BY ALLIGATORS ON THE FIRST PAGE!

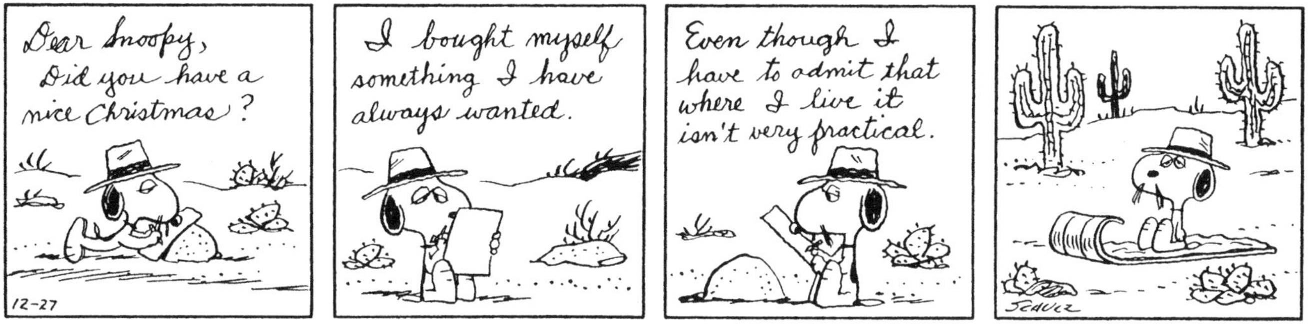
Dear Snoopy, Did you have a nice Christmas?
12-27
I bought myself something I have always wanted.
Even though I have to admit that where I live it isn't very practical.

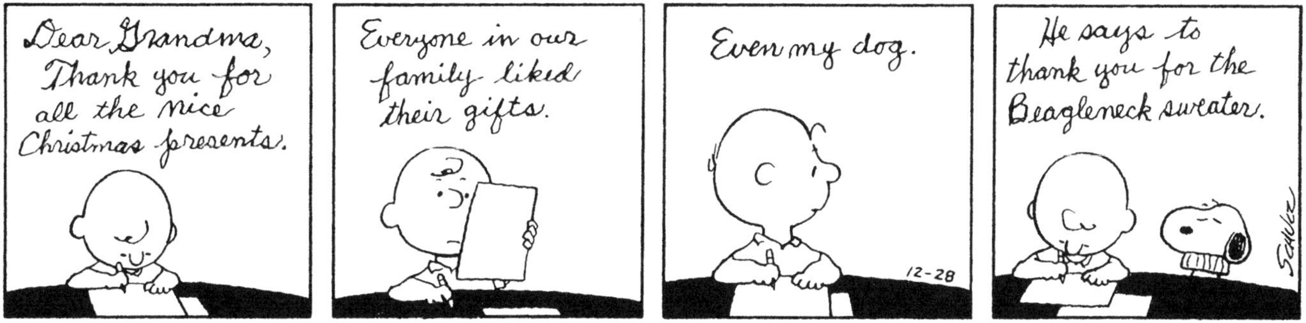
Dear Grandma, Thank you for all the nice Christmas presents.
Everyone in our family liked their gifts.
Even my dog.
12-28
He says to thank you for the Beagleneck sweater.

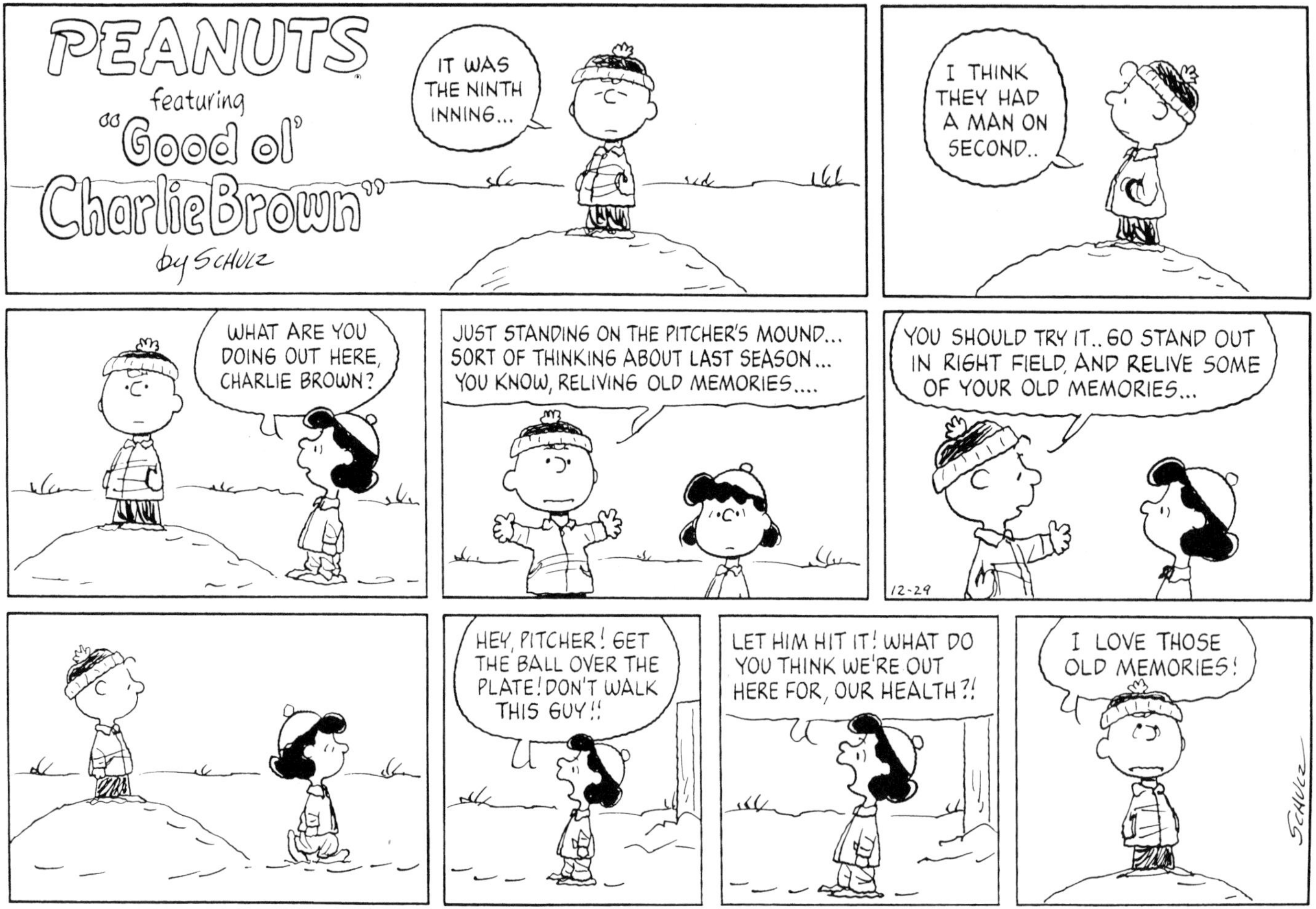
PEANUTS
featuring "Good ol' CharlieBrown"
by SCHULZ
IT WAS THE NINTH INNING...
I THINK THEY HAD A MAN ON SECOND..
WHAT ARE YOU DOING OUT HERE, CHARLIE BROWN?
JUST STANDING ON THE PITCHER'S MOUND... SORT OF THINKING ABOUT LAST SEASON... YOU KNOW, RELIVING OLD MEMORIES....
YOU SHOULD TRY IT.. GO STAND OUT IN RIGHT FIELD, AND RELIVE SOME OF YOUR OLD MEMORIES...
12-29
HEY, PITCHER! GET THE BALL OVER THE PLATE! DON'T WALK THIS GUY!!
LET HIM HIT IT! WHAT DO YOU THINK WE'RE OUT HERE FOR, OUR HEALTH?!
I LOVE THOSE OLD MEMORIES!
SCHULZ

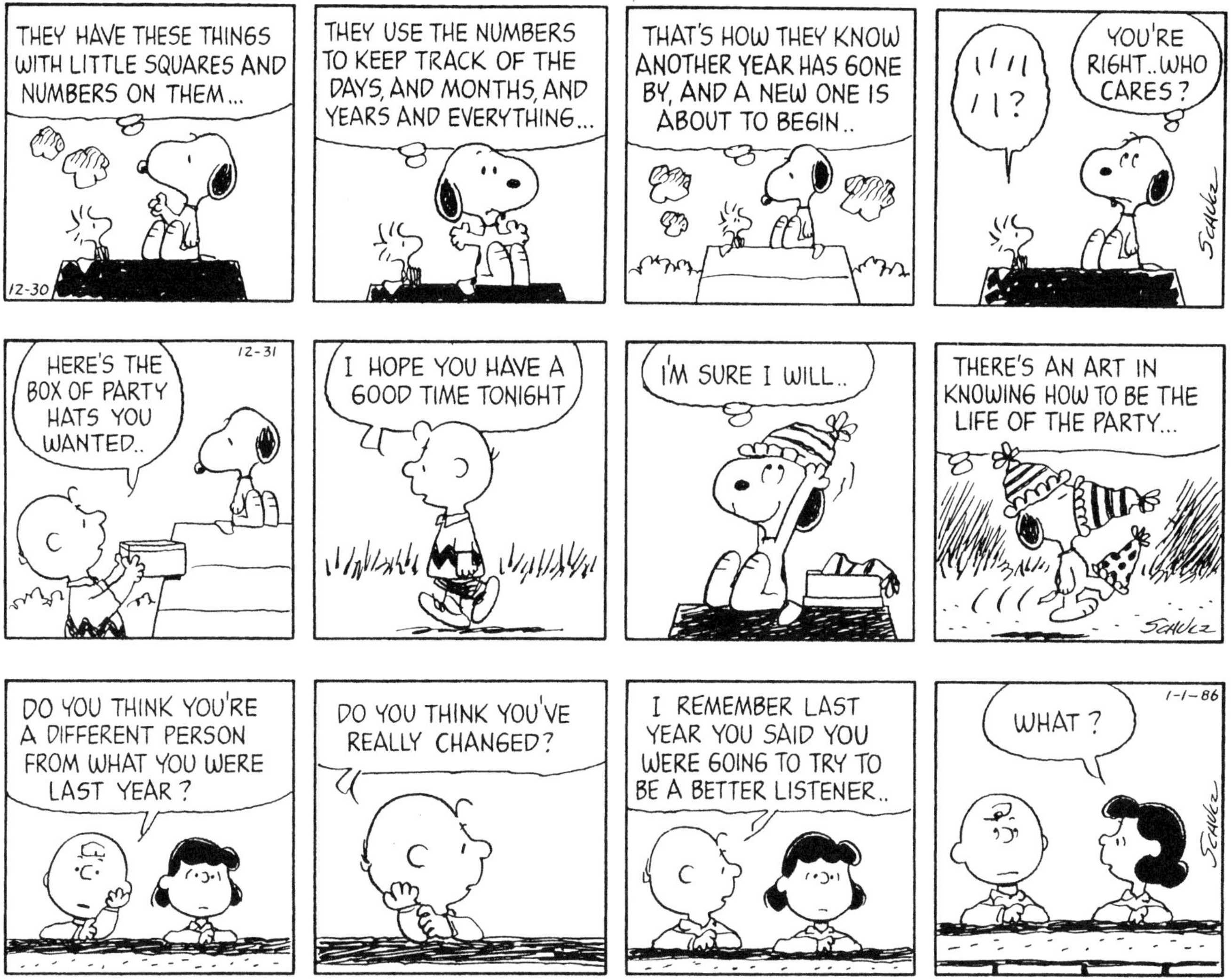
THEY HAVE THESE THINGS WITH LITTLE SQUARES AND NUMBERS ON THEM...
12-30
THEY USE THE NUMBERS TO KEEP TRACK OF THE DAYS, AND MONTHS, AND YEARS AND EVERYTHING...
THAT'S HOW THEY KNOW ANOTHER YEAR HAS GONE BY, AND A NEW ONE IS ABOUT TO BEGIN..
YOU'RE RIGHT..WHO CARES?
SCHULZ
12-31
HERE'S THE BOX OF PARTY HATS YOU WANTED..
I HOPE YOU HAVE A GOOD TIME TONIGHT
I'M SURE I WILL..
THERE'S AN ART IN KNOWING HOW TO BE THE LIFE OF THE PARTY...
SCHULZ
DO YOU THINK YOU'RE A DIFFERENT PERSON FROM WHAT YOU WERE LAST YEAR?
DO YOU THINK YOU'VE REALLY CHANGED?
I REMEMBER LAST YEAR YOU SAID YOU WERE GOING TO TRY TO BE A BETTER LISTENER..
1-1-86
WHAT?
SCHULZ

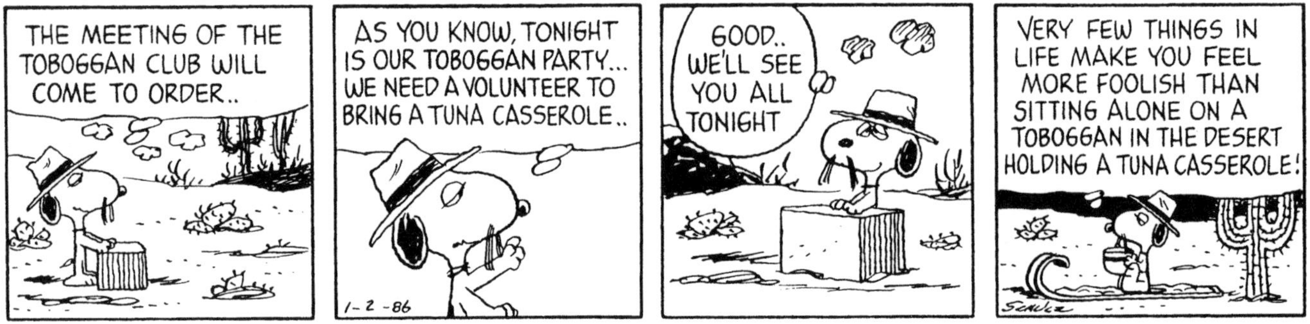
THE MEETING OF THE TOBOGGAN CLUB WILL COME TO ORDER..
AS YOU KNOW, TONIGHT IS OUR TOBOGGAN PARTY... WE NEED A VOLUNTEER TO BRING A TUNA CASSEROLE..
1-2-86
GOOD.. WE'LL SEE YOU ALL TONIGHT
VERY FEW THINGS IN LIFE MAKE YOU FEEL MORE FOOLISH THAN SITTING ALONE ON A TOBOGGAN IN THE DESERT HOLDING A TUNA CASSEROLE!

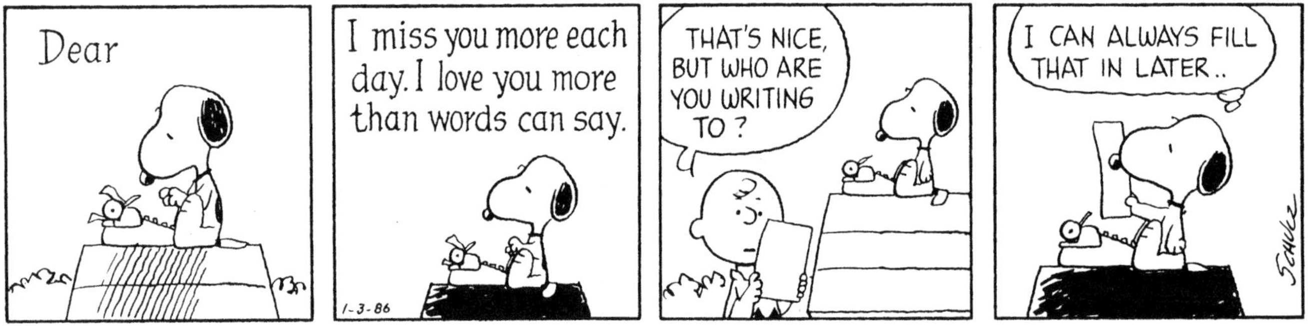
Dear
I miss you more each day. I love you more than words can say.
1-3-86
THAT'S NICE, BUT WHO ARE YOU WRITING TO?
I CAN ALWAYS FILL THAT IN LATER..

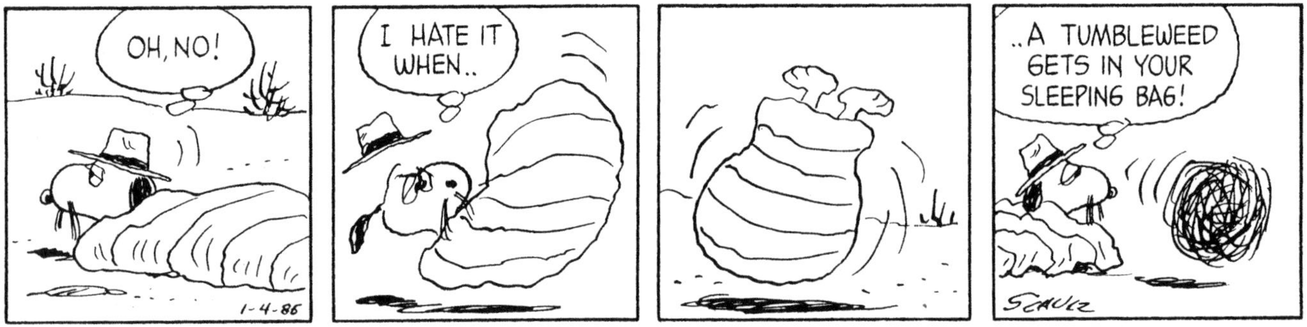
OH, NO!
1-4-86
I HATE IT WHEN..
..A TUMBLEWEED GETS IN YOUR SLEEPING BAG!

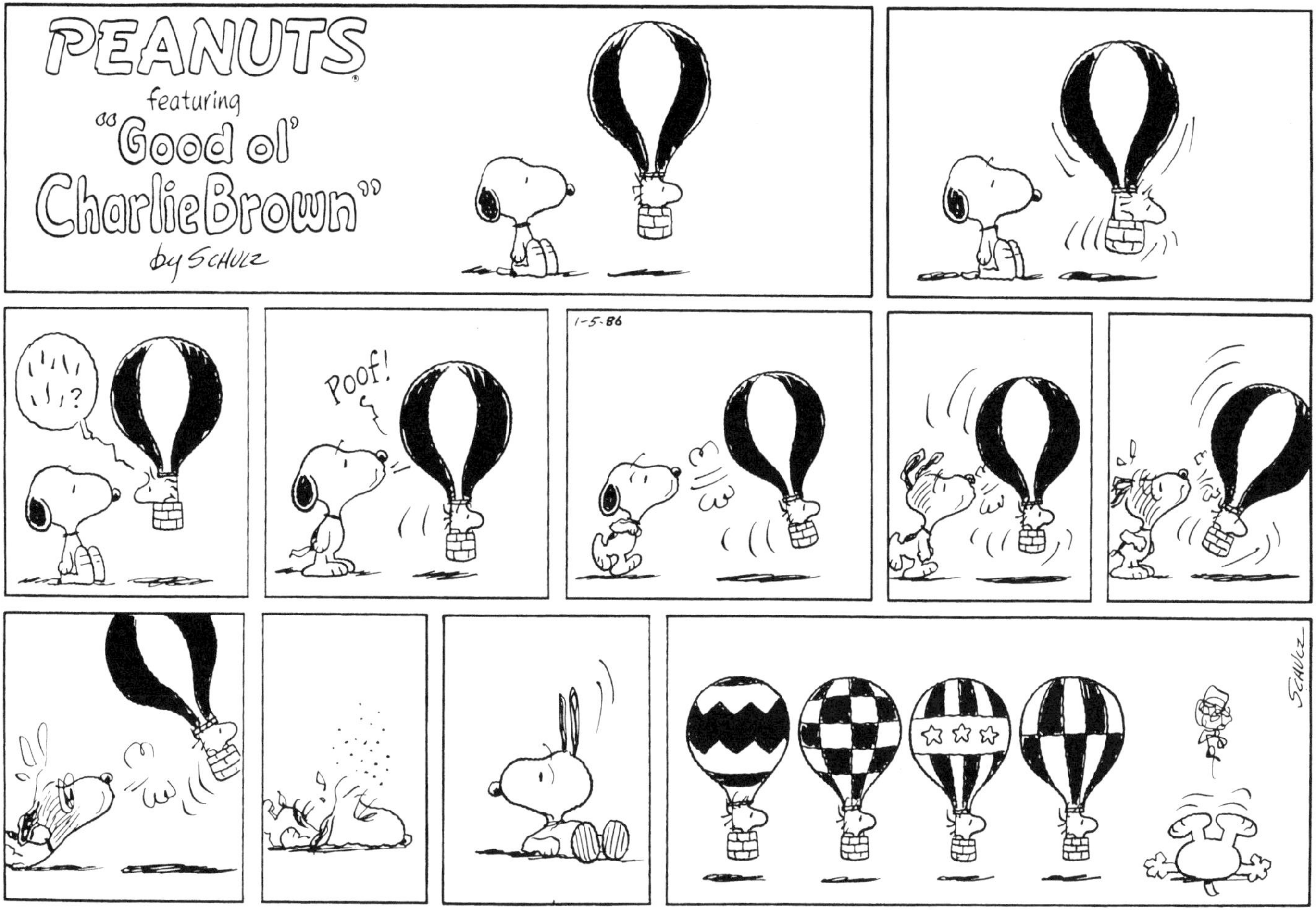
PEANUTS
featuring
"Good ol' Charlie Brown"
by SCHULZ
Poof!
1-5-86
SCHULZ

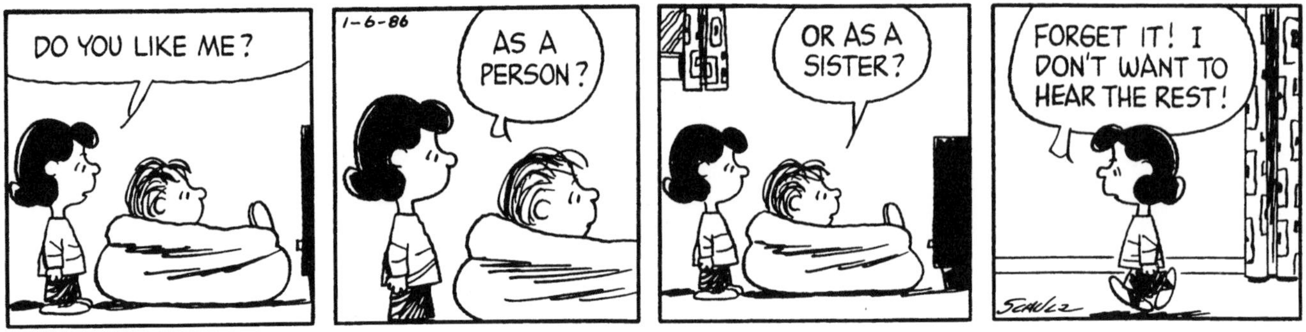
DO YOU LIKE ME?
1-6-86
AS A PERSON?
OR AS A SISTER?
FORGET IT! I DON'T WANT TO HEAR THE REST!

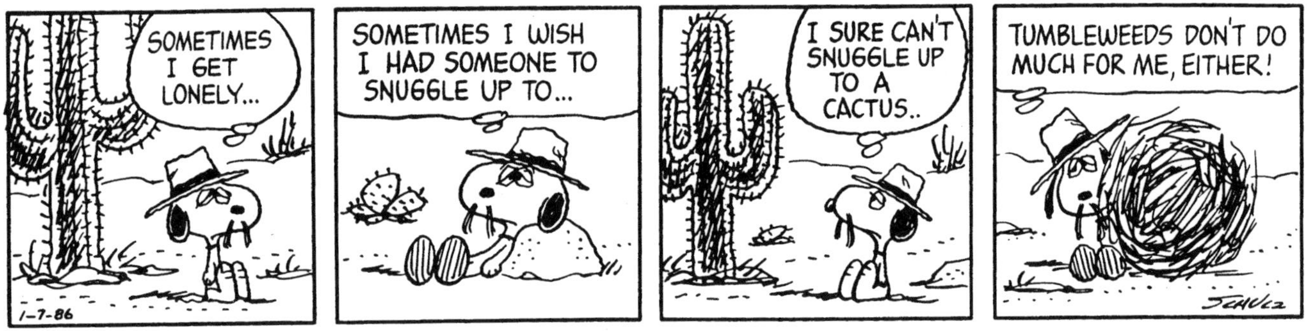
SOMETIMES I GET LONELY...
1-7-86
SOMETIMES I WISH I HAD SOMEONE TO SNUGGLE UP TO...
I SURE CAN'T SNUGGLE UP TO A CACTUS..
TUMBLEWEEDS DON'T DO MUCH FOR ME, EITHER!

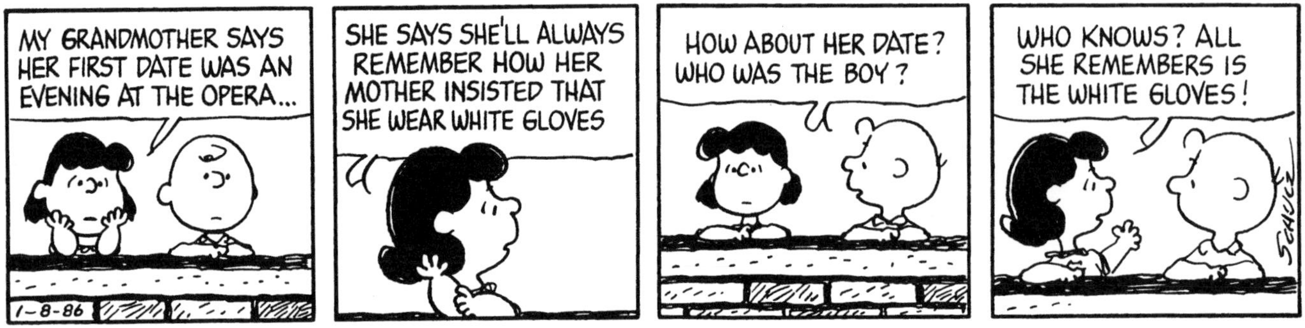
MY GRANDMOTHER SAYS HER FIRST DATE WAS AN EVENING AT THE OPERA...
1-8-86
SHE SAYS SHE'LL ALWAYS REMEMBER HOW HER MOTHER INSISTED THAT SHE WEAR WHITE GLOVES
HOW ABOUT HER DATE? WHO WAS THE BOY?
WHO KNOWS? ALL SHE REMEMBERS IS THE WHITE GLOVES!

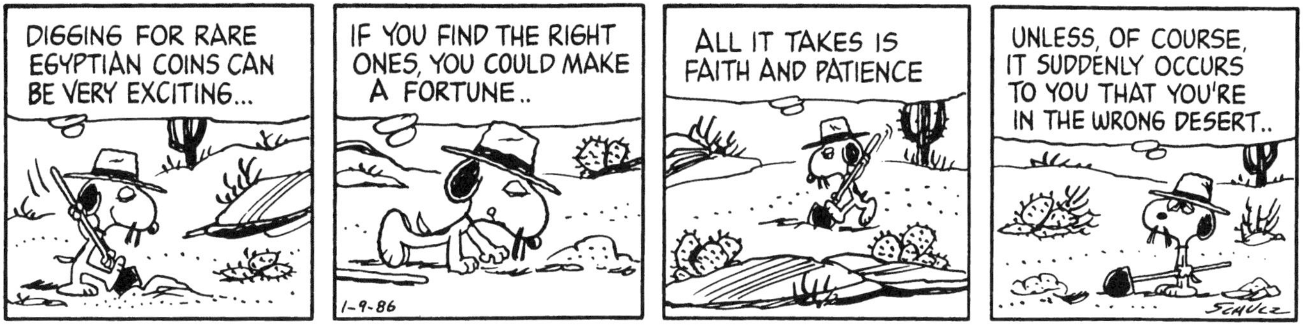
DIGGING FOR RARE EGYPTIAN COINS CAN BE VERY EXCITING...
IF YOU FIND THE RIGHT ONES, YOU COULD MAKE A FORTUNE..
1-9-86
ALL IT TAKES IS FAITH AND PATIENCE
UNLESS, OF COURSE, IT SUDDENLY OCCURS TO YOU THAT YOU'RE IN THE WRONG DESERT..
SCHULZ

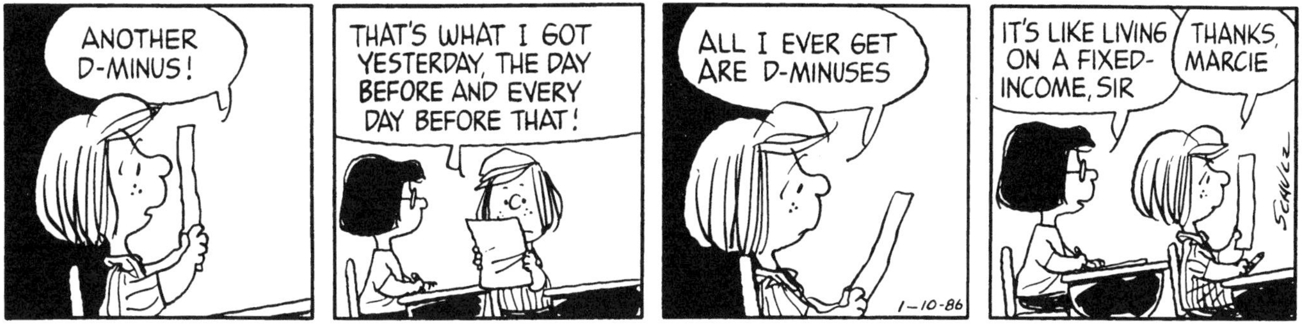
ANOTHER D-MINUS!
THAT'S WHAT I GOT YESTERDAY, THE DAY BEFORE AND EVERY DAY BEFORE THAT!
ALL I EVER GET ARE D-MINUSES
1-10-86
IT'S LIKE LIVING ON A FIXED-INCOME, SIR
THANKS, MARCIE
SCHULZ

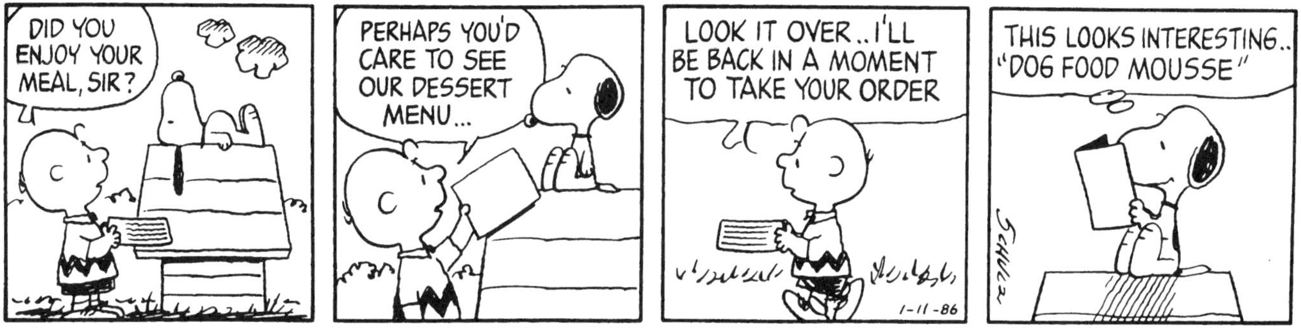
DID YOU ENJOY YOUR MEAL, SIR?
PERHAPS YOU'D CARE TO SEE OUR DESSERT MENU...
LOOK IT OVER..I'LL BE BACK IN A MOMENT TO TAKE YOUR ORDER
1-11-86
THIS LOOKS INTERESTING.. "DOG FOOD MOUSSE"
SCHULZ

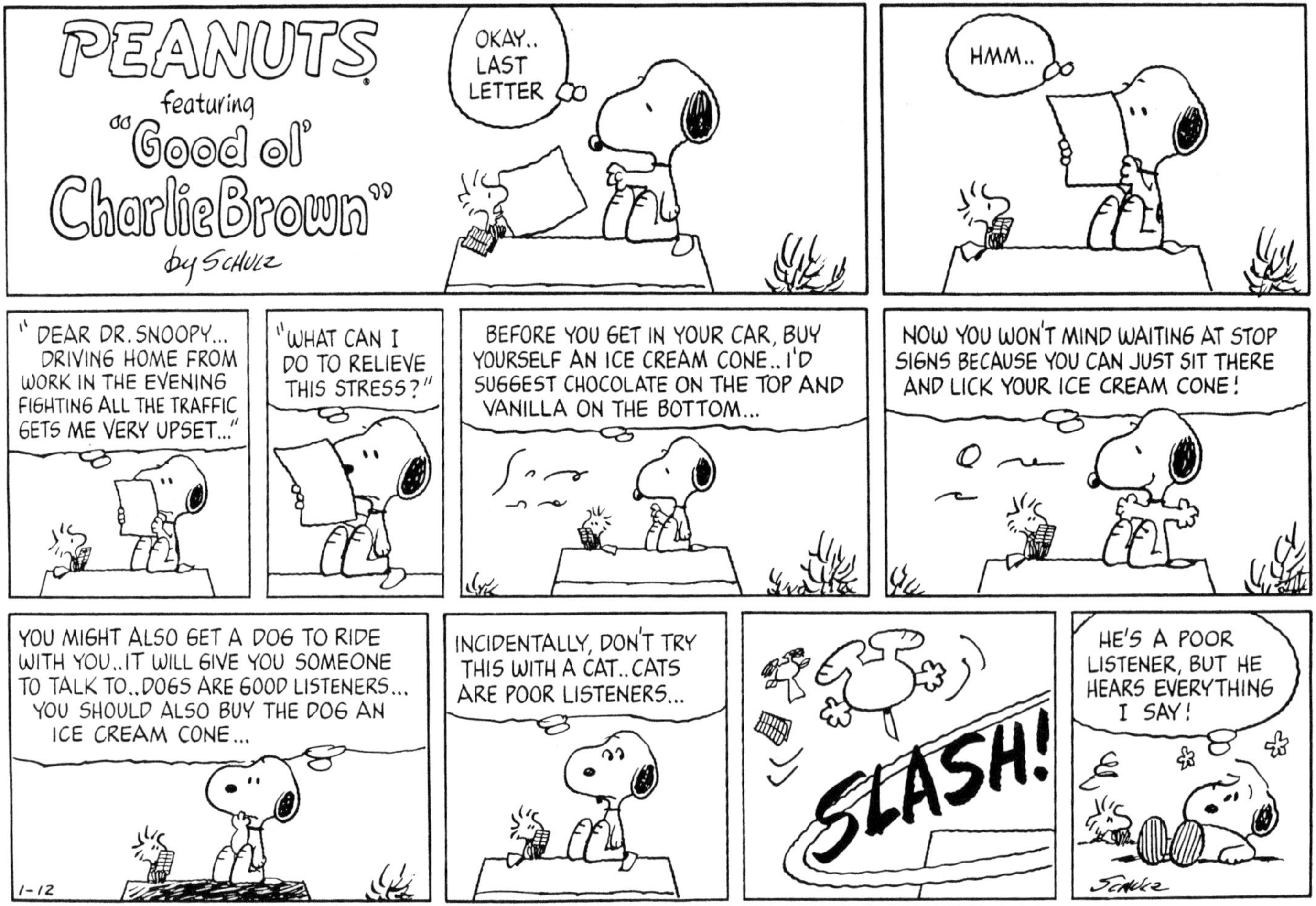
PEANUTS
featuring
"Good ol' Charlie Brown"
by SCHULZ
OKAY.. LAST LETTER
HMM..
" DEAR DR. SNOOPY... DRIVING HOME FROM WORK IN THE EVENING FIGHTING ALL THE TRAFFIC GETS ME VERY UPSET..."
"WHAT CAN I DO TO RELIEVE THIS STRESS?"
BEFORE YOU GET IN YOUR CAR, BUY YOURSELF AN ICE CREAM CONE.. I'D SUGGEST CHOCOLATE ON THE TOP AND VANILLA ON THE BOTTOM...
NOW YOU WON'T MIND WAITING AT STOP SIGNS BECAUSE YOU CAN JUST SIT THERE AND LICK YOUR ICE CREAM CONE!
YOU MIGHT ALSO GET A DOG TO RIDE WITH YOU..IT WILL GIVE YOU SOMEONE TO TALK TO..DOGS ARE GOOD LISTENERS... YOU SHOULD ALSO BUY THE DOG AN ICE CREAM CONE...
1-12
INCIDENTALLY, DON'T TRY THIS WITH A CAT..CATS ARE POOR LISTENERS...
SLASH!
HE'S A POOR LISTENER, BUT HE HEARS EVERYTHING I SAY!
SCHULZ

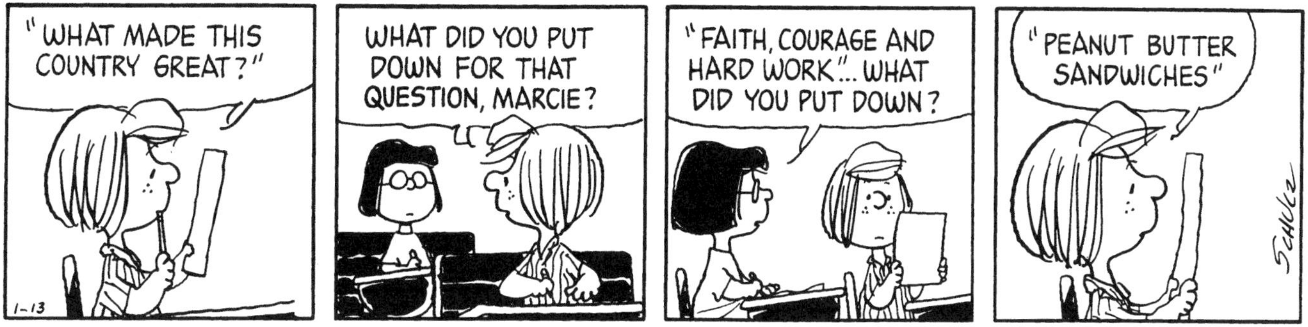
"WHAT MADE THIS COUNTRY GREAT?"
1-13
WHAT DID YOU PUT DOWN FOR THAT QUESTION, MARCIE?
"FAITH, COURAGE AND HARD WORK"... WHAT DID YOU PUT DOWN?
"PEANUT BUTTER SANDWICHES"
SCHULZ

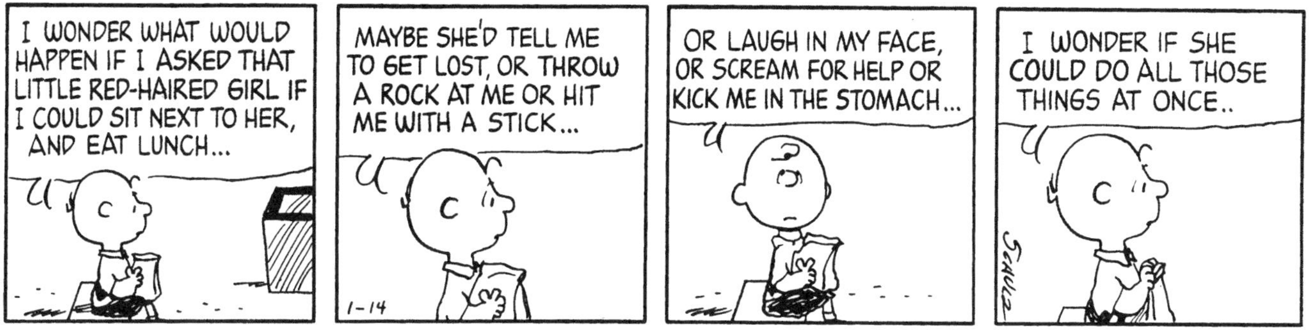
I WONDER WHAT WOULD HAPPEN IF I ASKED THAT LITTLE RED-HAIRED GIRL IF I COULD SIT NEXT TO HER, AND EAT LUNCH...
MAYBE SHE'D TELL ME TO GET LOST, OR THROW A ROCK AT ME OR HIT ME WITH A STICK...
1-14
OR LAUGH IN MY FACE, OR SCREAM FOR HELP OR KICK ME IN THE STOMACH...
I WONDER IF SHE COULD DO ALL THOSE THINGS AT ONCE..
SCHULZ

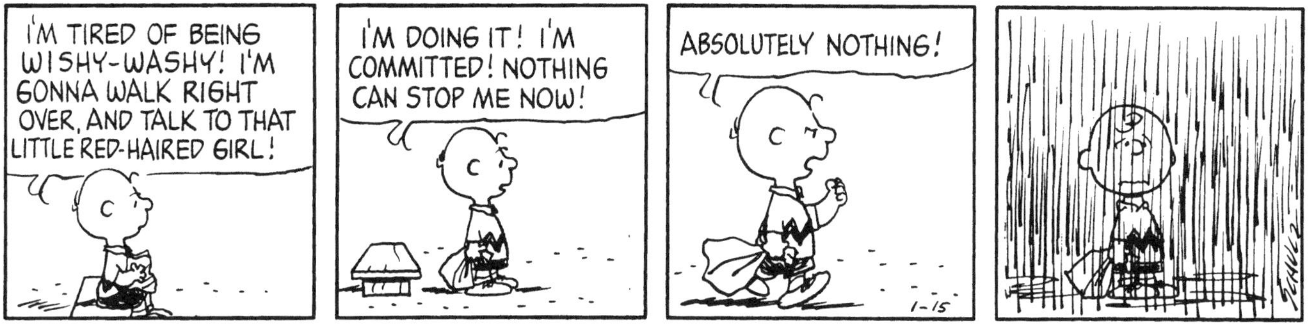
I'M TIRED OF BEING WISHY-WASHY! I'M GONNA WALK RIGHT OVER, AND TALK TO THAT LITTLE RED-HAIRED GIRL!
I'M DOING IT! I'M COMMITTED! NOTHING CAN STOP ME NOW!
ABSOLUTELY NOTHING!
1-15
SCHULZ

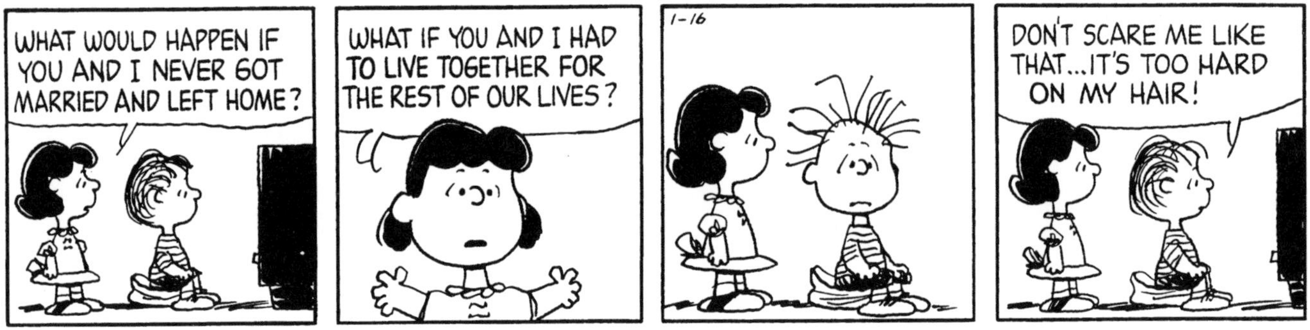
WHAT WOULD HAPPEN IF YOU AND I NEVER GOT MARRIED AND LEFT HOME?
WHAT IF YOU AND I HAD TO LIVE TOGETHER FOR THE REST OF OUR LIVES?
1-16
DON'T SCARE ME LIKE THAT...IT'S TOO HARD ON MY HAIR!

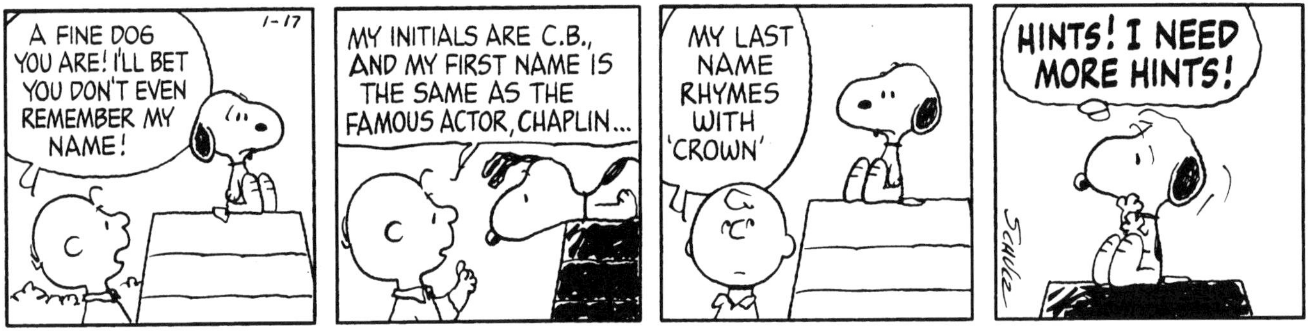
1-17
A FINE DOG YOU ARE! I'LL BET YOU DON'T EVEN REMEMBER MY NAME!
MY INITIALS ARE C.B., AND MY FIRST NAME IS THE SAME AS THE FAMOUS ACTOR, CHAPLIN...
MY LAST NAME RHYMES WITH 'CROWN'
HINTS! I NEED MORE HINTS!
SCHULZ

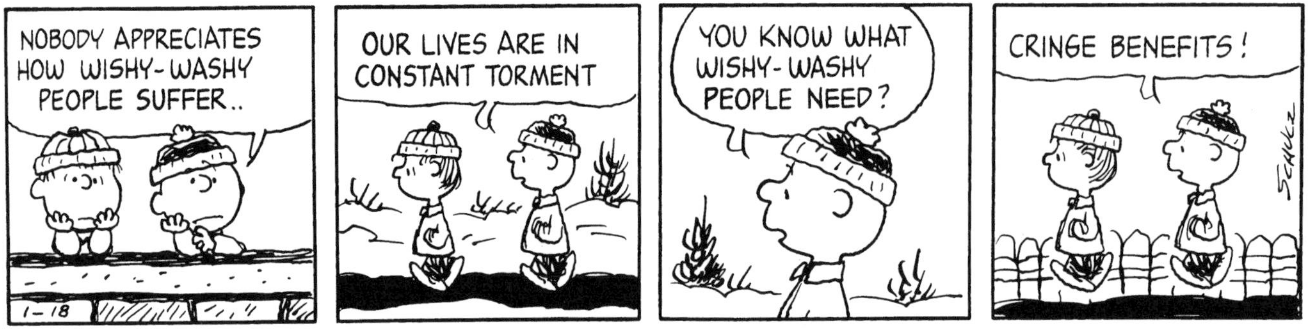
NOBODY APPRECIATES HOW WISHY-WASHY PEOPLE SUFFER..
1-18
OUR LIVES ARE IN CONSTANT TORMENT
YOU KNOW WHAT WISHY-WASHY PEOPLE NEED?
CRINGE BENEFITS!
SCHULZ

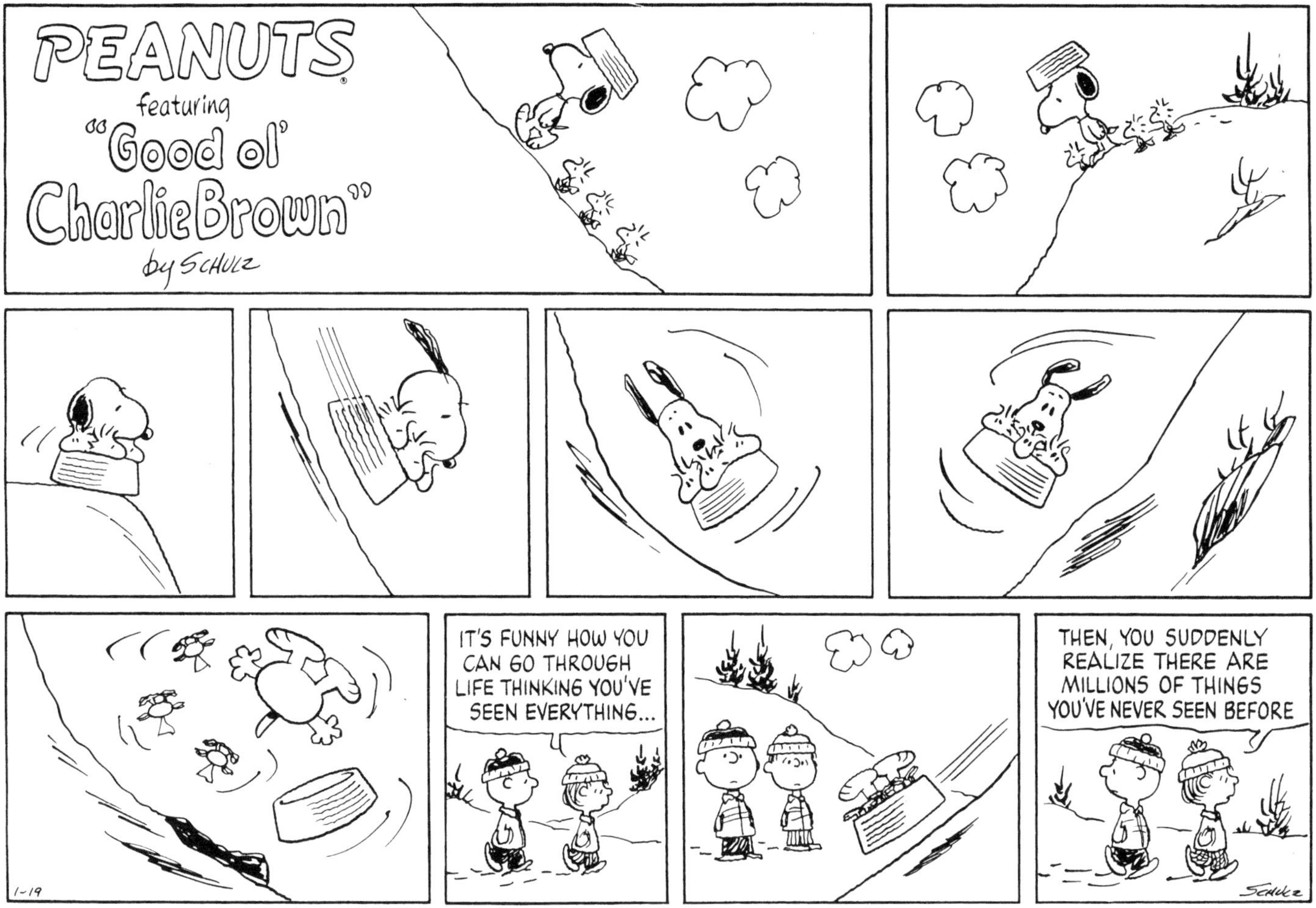
PEANUTS
featuring
"Good ol' Charlie Brown"
by SCHULZ
1-19
IT'S FUNNY HOW YOU CAN GO THROUGH LIFE THINKING YOU'VE SEEN EVERYTHING...
THEN, YOU SUDDENLY REALIZE THERE ARE MILLIONS OF THINGS YOU'VE NEVER SEEN BEFORE
SCHULZ

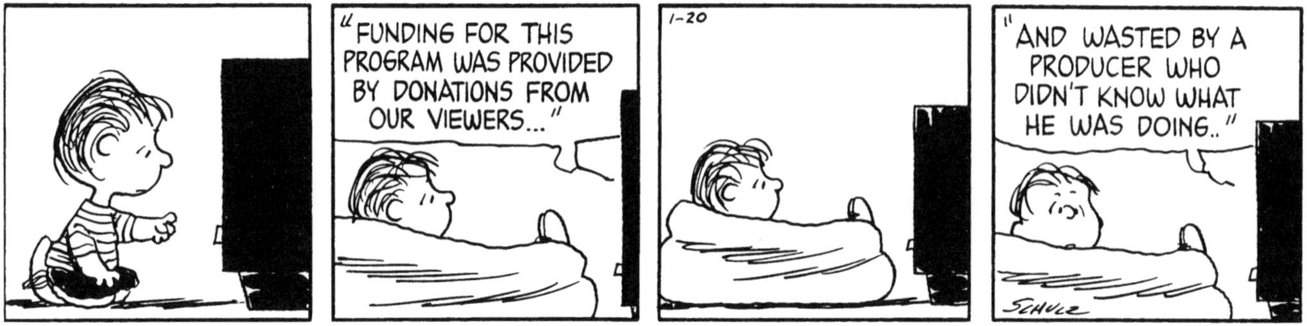
"FUNDING FOR THIS PROGRAM WAS PROVIDED BY DONATIONS FROM OUR VIEWERS..."
"AND WASTED BY A PRODUCER WHO DIDN'T KNOW WHAT HE WAS DOING.."

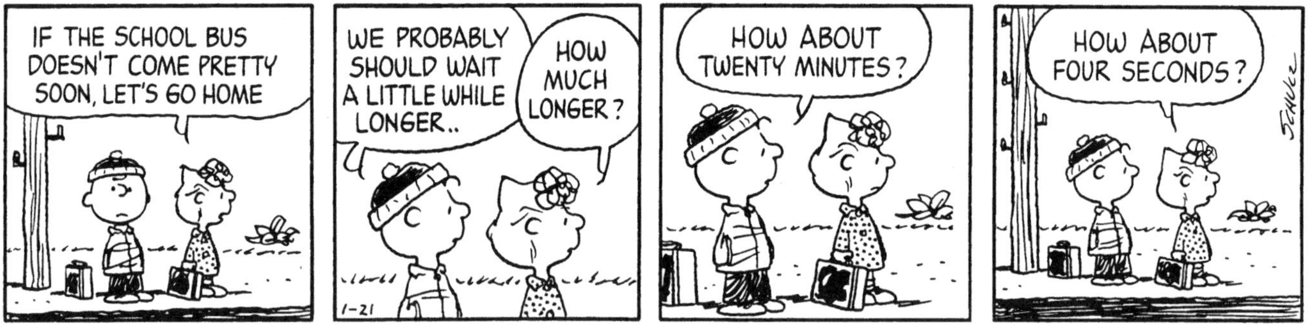
IF THE SCHOOL BUS DOESN'T COME PRETTY SOON, LET'S GO HOME
WE PROBABLY SHOULD WAIT A LITTLE WHILE LONGER..
HOW MUCH LONGER?
HOW ABOUT TWENTY MINUTES?
HOW ABOUT FOUR SECONDS?

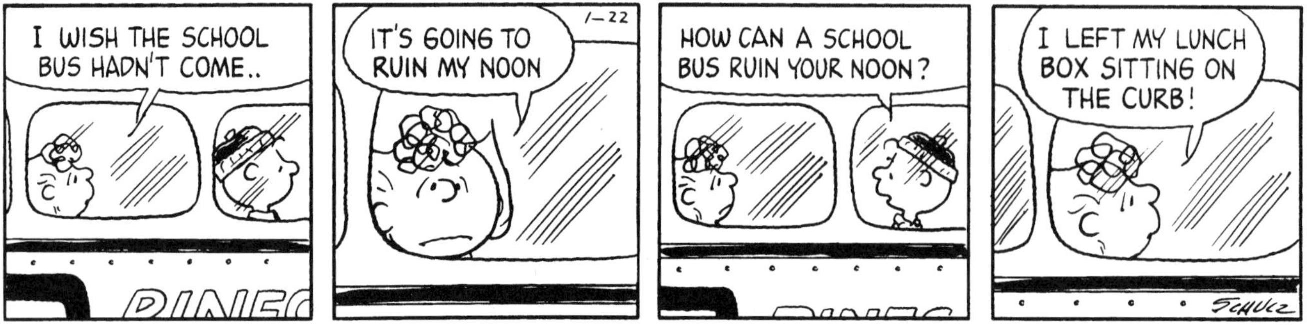
I WISH THE SCHOOL BUS HADN'T COME..
IT'S GOING TO RUIN MY NOON
HOW CAN A SCHOOL BUS RUIN YOUR NOON?
I LEFT MY LUNCH BOX SITTING ON THE CURB!

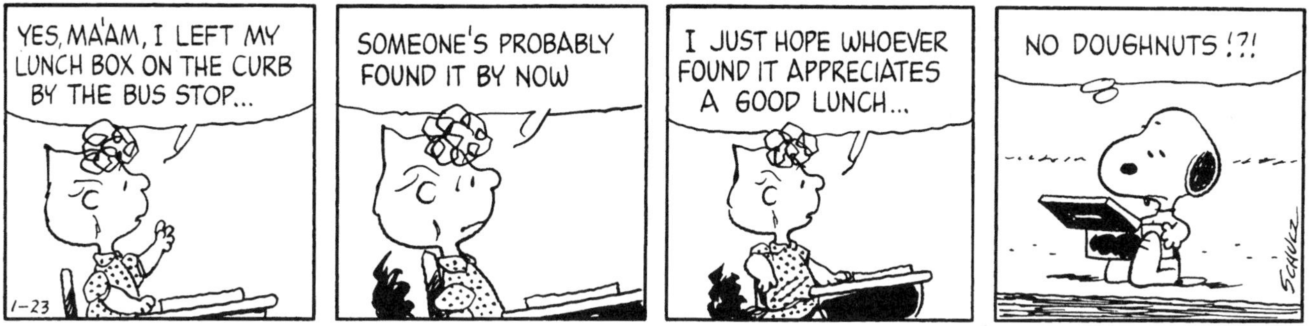
YES, MA'AM, I LEFT MY LUNCH BOX ON THE CURB BY THE BUS STOP...
SOMEONE'S PROBABLY FOUND IT BY NOW
I JUST HOPE WHOEVER FOUND IT APPRECIATES A GOOD LUNCH...
NO DOUGHNUTS !?!

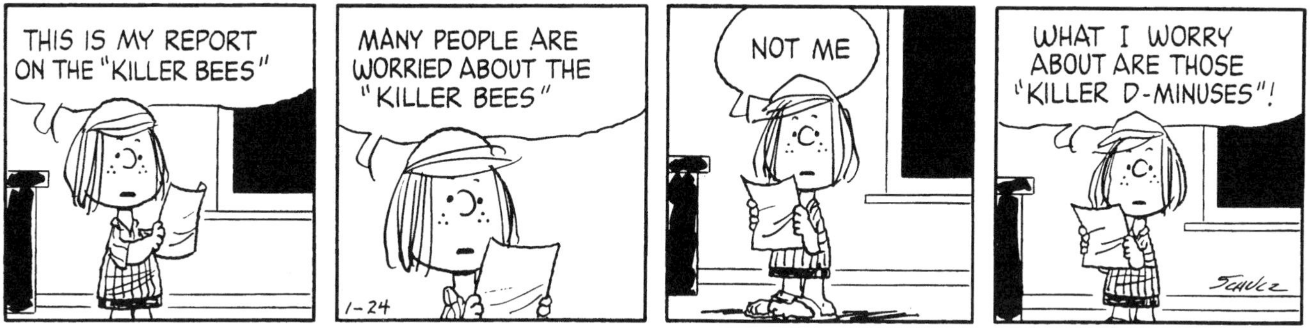
THIS IS MY REPORT ON THE "KILLER BEES"
MANY PEOPLE ARE WORRIED ABOUT THE "KILLER BEES"
NOT ME
WHAT I WORRY ABOUT ARE THOSE "KILLER D-MINUSES"!

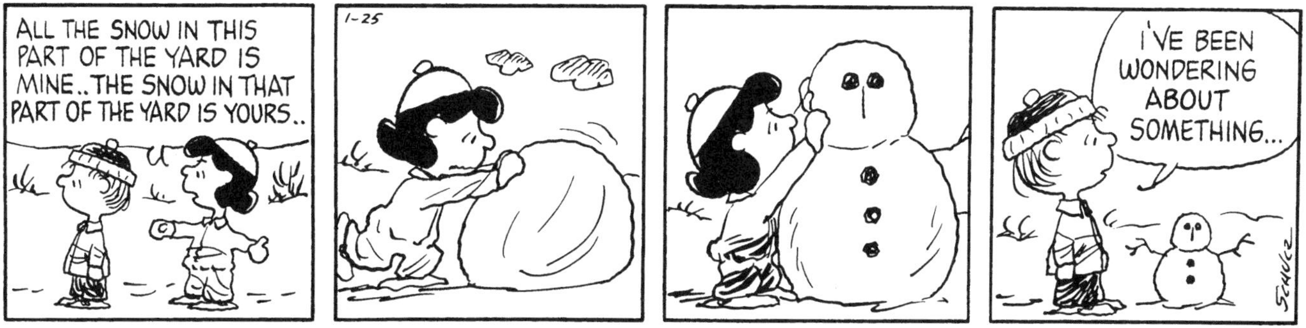
ALL THE SNOW IN THIS PART OF THE YARD IS MINE.. THE SNOW IN THAT PART OF THE YARD IS YOURS..
I'VE BEEN WONDERING ABOUT SOMETHING...

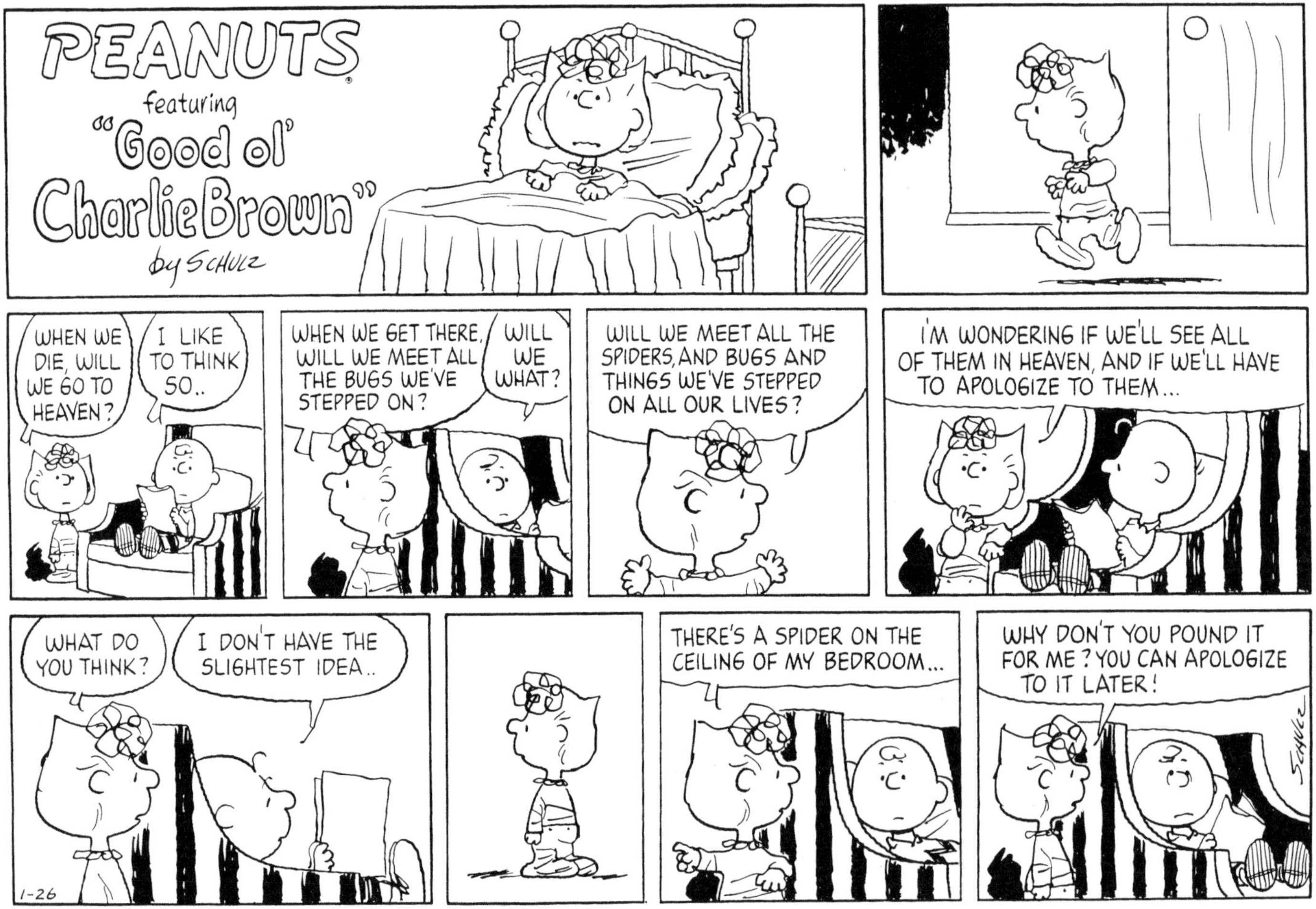
PEANUTS®
featuring "Good ol' Charlie Brown"
by SCHULZ
WHEN WE DIE, WILL WE GO TO HEAVEN?
I LIKE TO THINK SO..
WHEN WE GET THERE, WILL WE MEET ALL THE BUGS WE'VE STEPPED ON?
WILL WE WHAT?
WILL WE MEET ALL THE SPIDERS, AND BUGS AND THINGS WE'VE STEPPED ON ALL OUR LIVES?
I'M WONDERING IF WE'LL SEE ALL OF THEM IN HEAVEN, AND IF WE'LL HAVE TO APOLOGIZE TO THEM...
WHAT DO YOU THINK?
I DON'T HAVE THE SLIGHTEST IDEA..
1-26
THERE'S A SPIDER ON THE CEILING OF MY BEDROOM...
WHY DON'T YOU POUND IT FOR ME? YOU CAN APOLOGIZE TO IT LATER!
SCHULZ

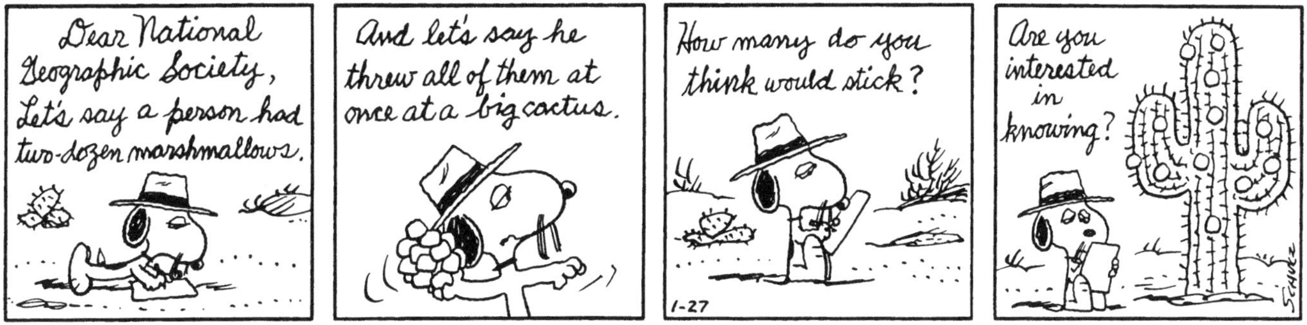
Dear National Geographic Society,
Let's say a person had two-dozen marshmallows.
And let's say he threw all of them at once at a big cactus.
How many do you think would stick?
1-27
Are you interested in knowing?
SCHULZ

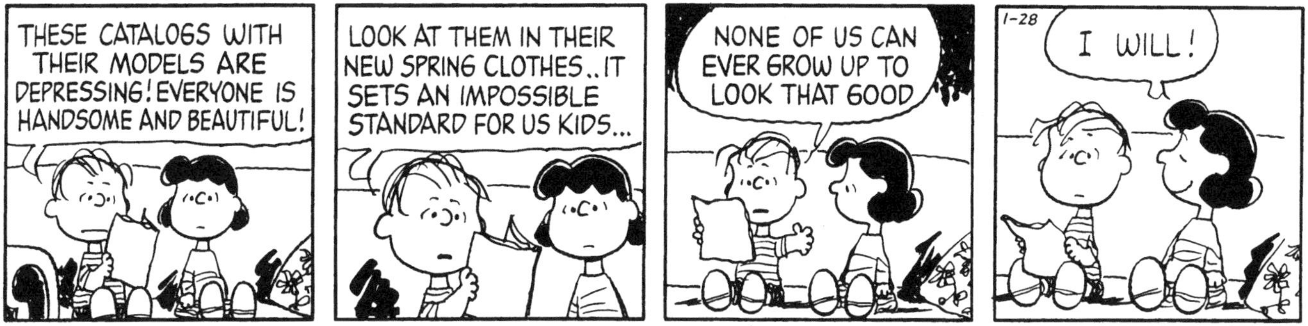
THESE CATALOGS WITH THEIR MODELS ARE DEPRESSING! EVERYONE IS HANDSOME AND BEAUTIFUL!
LOOK AT THEM IN THEIR NEW SPRING CLOTHES.. IT SETS AN IMPOSSIBLE STANDARD FOR US KIDS...
NONE OF US CAN EVER GROW UP TO LOOK THAT GOOD
1-28
I WILL!

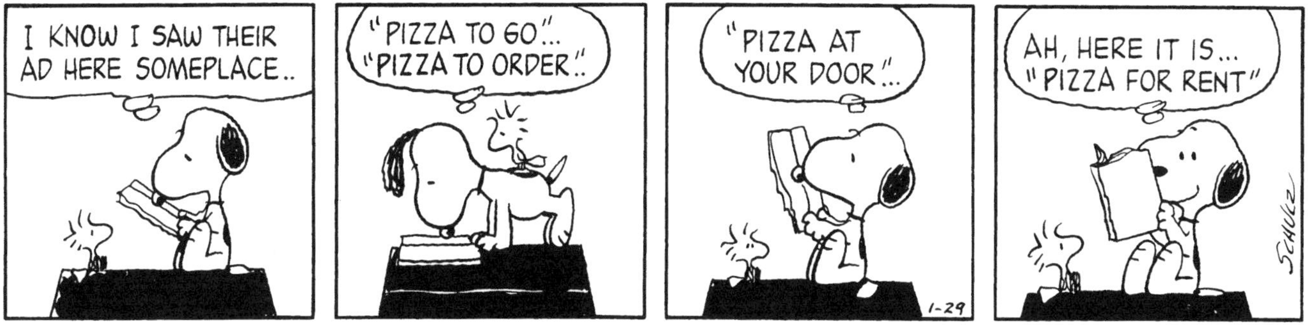
I KNOW I SAW THEIR AD HERE SOMEPLACE..
"PIZZA TO GO"... "PIZZA TO ORDER"...
"PIZZA AT YOUR DOOR"...
1-29
AH, HERE IT IS... "PIZZA FOR RENT"
SCHULZ

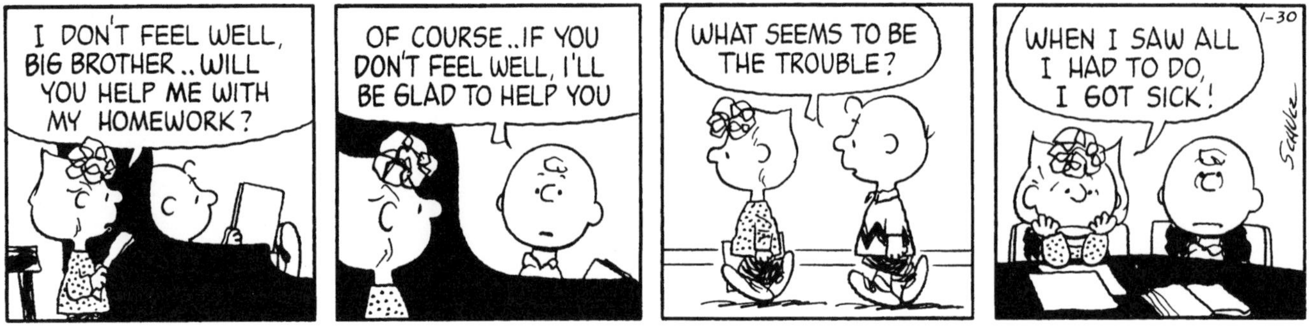
I DON'T FEEL WELL, BIG BROTHER.. WILL YOU HELP ME WITH MY HOMEWORK?
OF COURSE..IF YOU DON'T FEEL WELL, I'LL BE GLAD TO HELP YOU
WHAT SEEMS TO BE THE TROUBLE?
1-30
WHEN I SAW ALL I HAD TO DO, I GOT SICK!

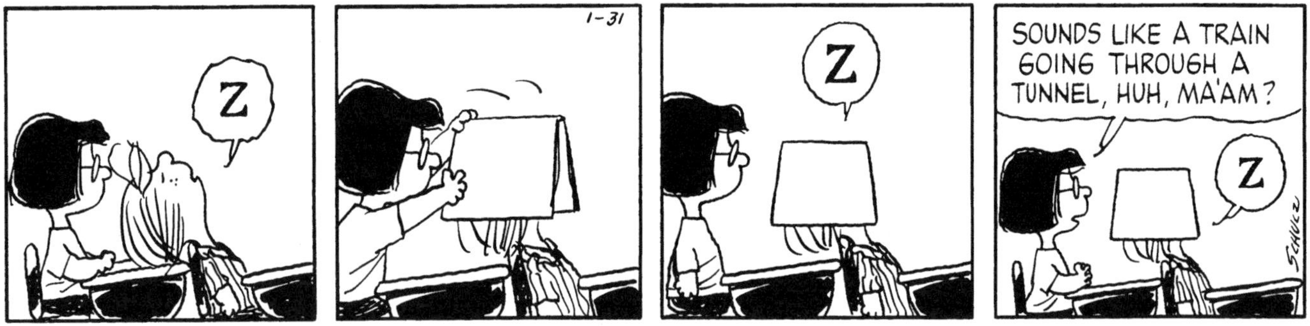
Z
1-31
Z
SOUNDS LIKE A TRAIN GOING THROUGH A TUNNEL, HUH, MA'AM?
Z

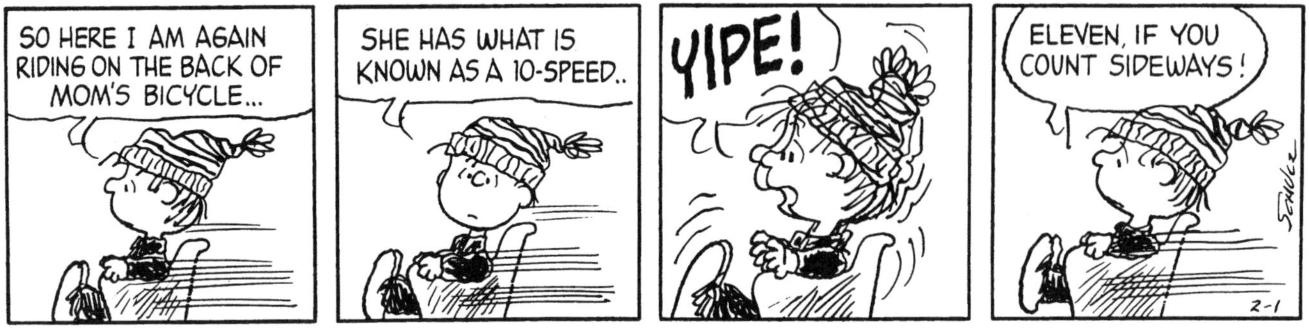
SO HERE I AM AGAIN RIDING ON THE BACK OF MOM'S BICYCLE...
SHE HAS WHAT IS KNOWN AS A 10-SPEED..
YIPE!
ELEVEN, IF YOU COUNT SIDEWAYS!
2-1

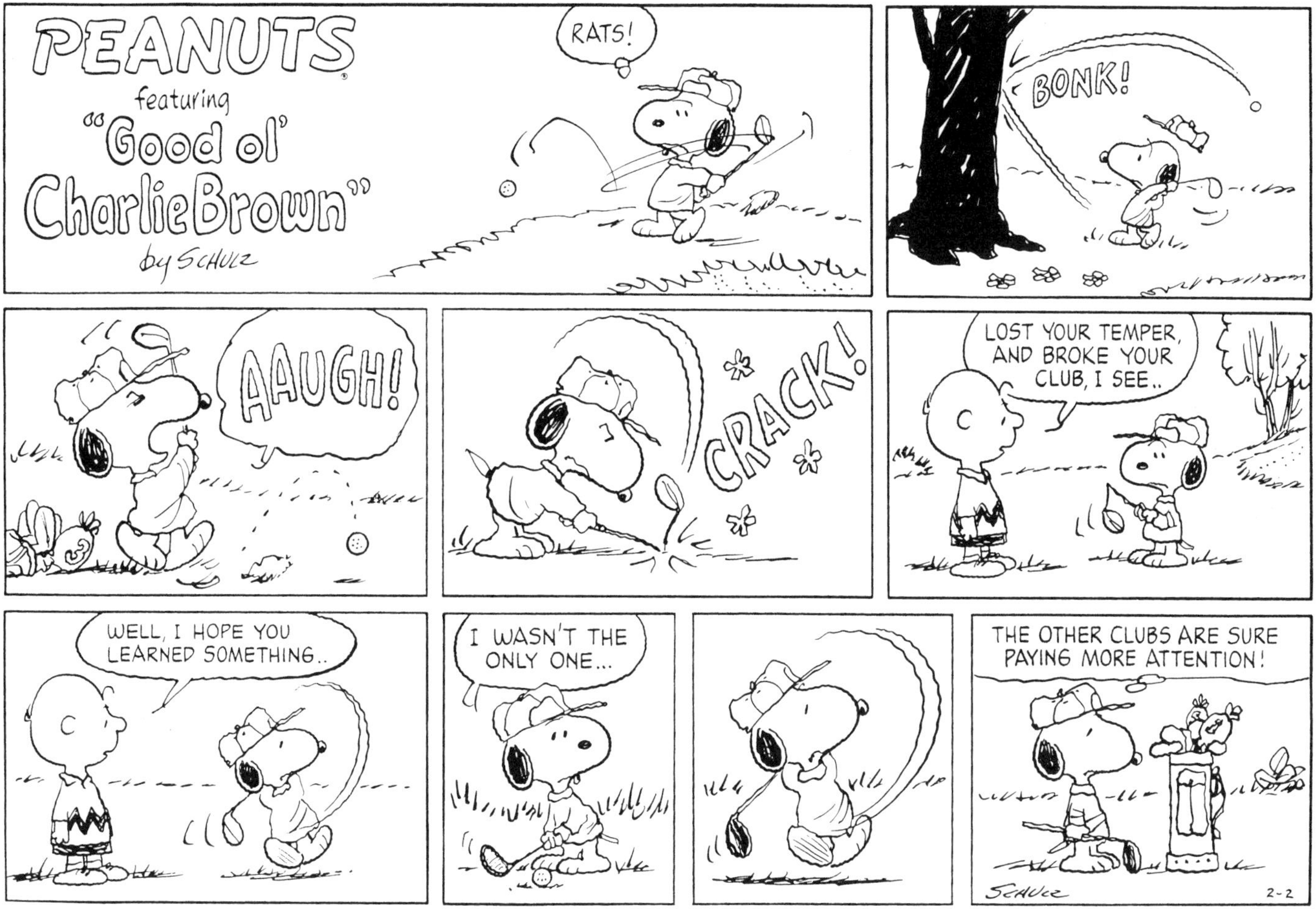
PEANUTS
featuring
"Good ol' Charlie Brown"
by SCHULZ
RATS!
BONK!
AAUGH!
CRACK!
LOST YOUR TEMPER, AND BROKE YOUR CLUB, I SEE..
WELL, I HOPE YOU LEARNED SOMETHING..
I WASN'T THE ONLY ONE...
THE OTHER CLUBS ARE SURE PAYING MORE ATTENTION!
SCHULZ
2-2

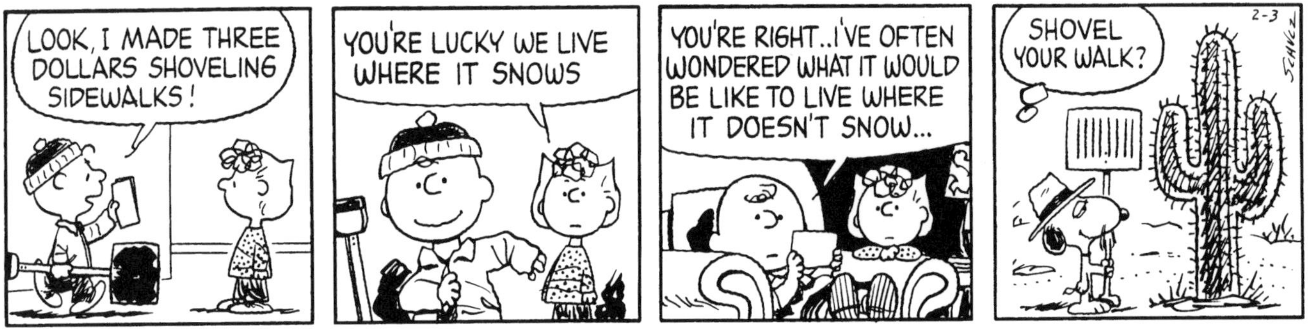
LOOK, I MADE THREE DOLLARS SHOVELING SIDEWALKS!
YOU'RE LUCKY WE LIVE WHERE IT SNOWS
YOU'RE RIGHT..I'VE OFTEN WONDERED WHAT IT WOULD BE LIKE TO LIVE WHERE IT DOESN'T SNOW...
SHOVEL YOUR WALK?
2-3

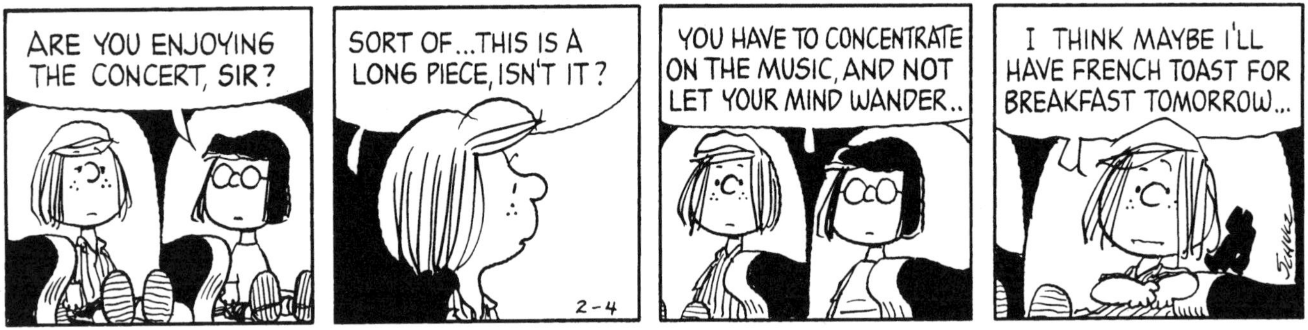
ARE YOU ENJOYING THE CONCERT, SIR?
SORT OF...THIS IS A LONG PIECE, ISN'T IT?
2-4
YOU HAVE TO CONCENTRATE ON THE MUSIC, AND NOT LET YOUR MIND WANDER..
I THINK MAYBE I'LL HAVE FRENCH TOAST FOR BREAKFAST TOMORROW...

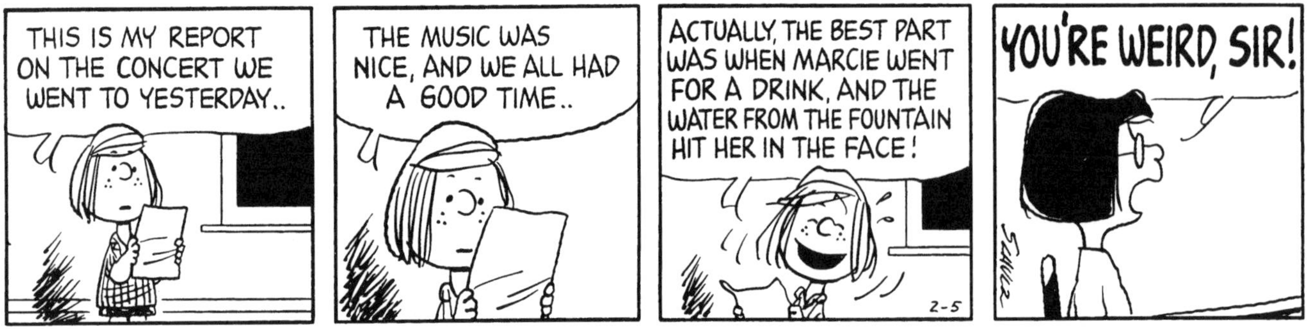
THIS IS MY REPORT ON THE CONCERT WE WENT TO YESTERDAY..
THE MUSIC WAS NICE, AND WE ALL HAD A GOOD TIME..
ACTUALLY, THE BEST PART WAS WHEN MARCIE WENT FOR A DRINK, AND THE WATER FROM THE FOUNTAIN HIT HER IN THE FACE!
2-5
YOU'RE WEIRD, SIR!

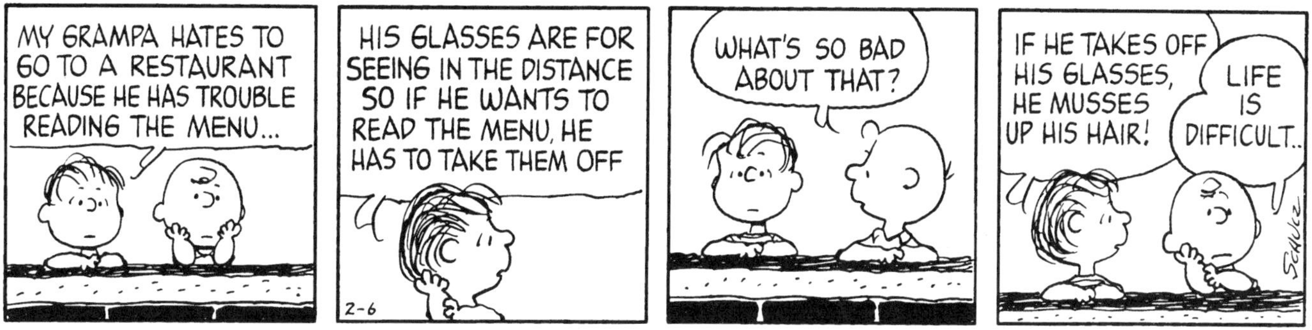
MY GRAMPA HATES TO GO TO A RESTAURANT BECAUSE HE HAS TROUBLE READING THE MENU...
HIS GLASSES ARE FOR SEEING IN THE DISTANCE SO IF HE WANTS TO READ THE MENU, HE HAS TO TAKE THEM OFF
2-6
WHAT'S SO BAD ABOUT THAT?
IF HE TAKES OFF HIS GLASSES, HE MUSSES UP HIS HAIR!
LIFE IS DIFFICULT..
SCHULZ

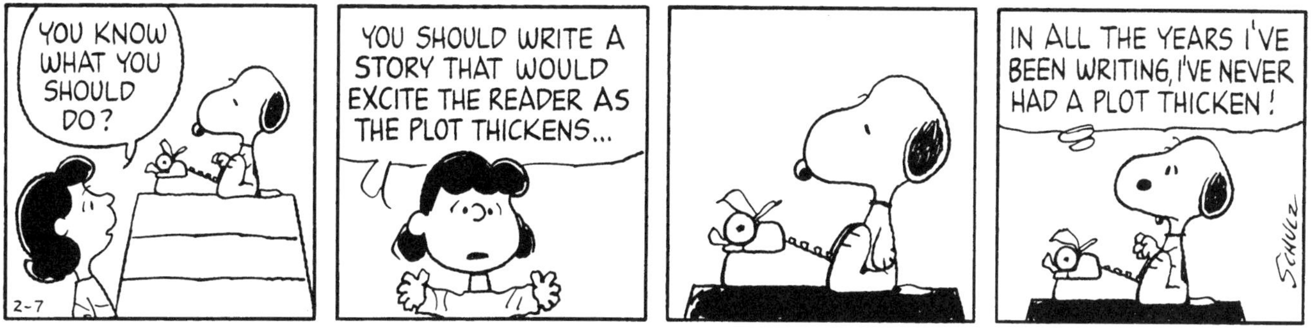
YOU KNOW WHAT YOU SHOULD DO?
2-7
YOU SHOULD WRITE A STORY THAT WOULD EXCITE THE READER AS THE PLOT THICKENS...
IN ALL THE YEARS I'VE BEEN WRITING, I'VE NEVER HAD A PLOT THICKEN!
SCHULZ

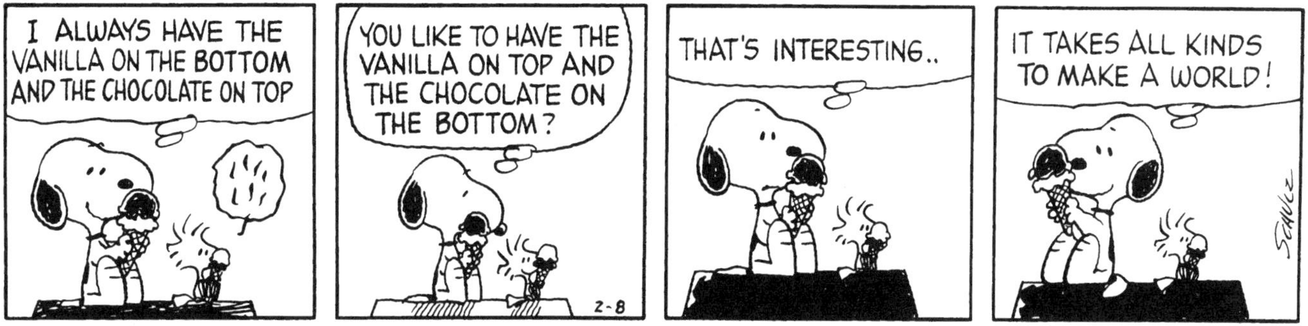
I ALWAYS HAVE THE VANILLA ON THE BOTTOM AND THE CHOCOLATE ON TOP
YOU LIKE TO HAVE THE VANILLA ON TOP AND THE CHOCOLATE ON THE BOTTOM?
2-8
THAT'S INTERESTING..
IT TAKES ALL KINDS TO MAKE A WORLD!
SCHULZ

PEANUTS
featuring
"Good ol' Charlie Brown"
by Schulz

HEY, DOG!

I'M GOING TO MAKE MY OWN VALENTINES THIS YEAR..

I'M GOING TO CUT OUT SOME PRETTY RED HEARTS, AND GLUE LACE AROUND THEM...

WHAT I WANT YOU TO DO IS TYPE OUT A NICE VERSE

Chocolate chip cookies are red. Chocolate chip cookies are blue. Chocolate chip cookies are sweet. So are you.

THIS IS TERRIBLE! I CAN'T MAKE A VALENTINE WITH THAT! WRITE ANOTHER ONE!!

2-9

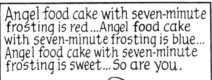

Angel food cake with seven-minute frosting is red...Angel food cake with seven-minute frosting is blue... Angel food cake with seven-minute frosting is sweet... So are you.

THAT'S THE DUMBEST THING I'VE EVER READ!

I GUESS I MISUNDERSTOOD... I THOUGHT SHE WANTED SOMETHING SENTIMENTAL..

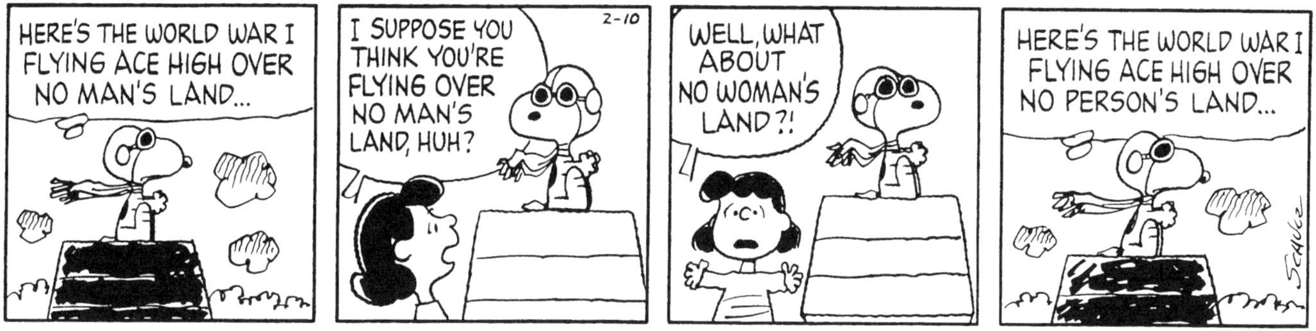
HERE'S THE WORLD WAR I FLYING ACE HIGH OVER NO MAN'S LAND...
2-10
I SUPPOSE YOU THINK YOU'RE FLYING OVER NO MAN'S LAND, HUH?
WELL, WHAT ABOUT NO WOMAN'S LAND?!
HERE'S THE WORLD WAR I FLYING ACE HIGH OVER NO PERSON'S LAND...
SCHULZ

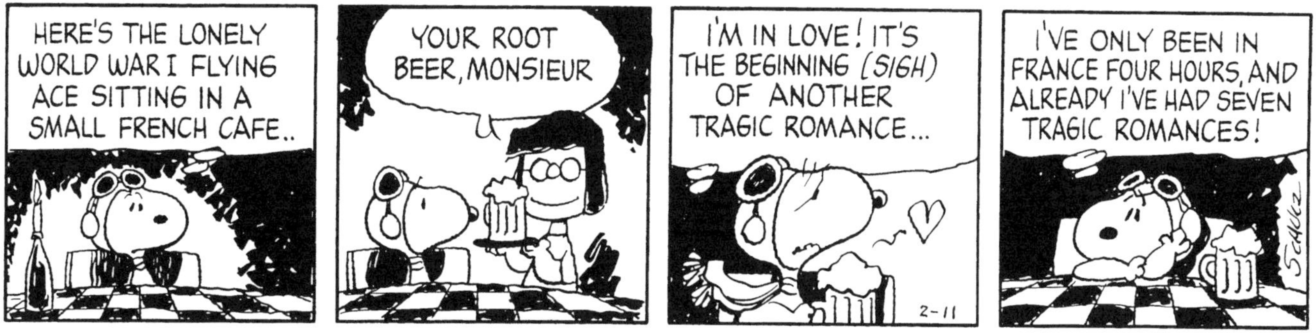
HERE'S THE LONELY WORLD WAR I FLYING ACE SITTING IN A SMALL FRENCH CAFE..
YOUR ROOT BEER, MONSIEUR
I'M IN LOVE! IT'S THE BEGINNING (SIGH) OF ANOTHER TRAGIC ROMANCE...
2-11
I'VE ONLY BEEN IN FRANCE FOUR HOURS, AND ALREADY I'VE HAD SEVEN TRAGIC ROMANCES!
SCHULZ

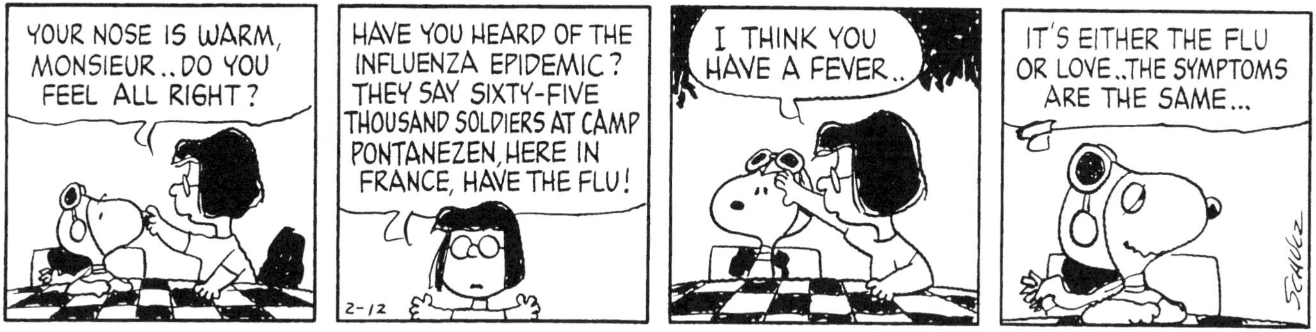
YOUR NOSE IS WARM, MONSIEUR..DO YOU FEEL ALL RIGHT?
HAVE YOU HEARD OF THE INFLUENZA EPIDEMIC? THEY SAY SIXTY-FIVE THOUSAND SOLDIERS AT CAMP PONTANEZEN, HERE IN FRANCE, HAVE THE FLU!
2-12
I THINK YOU HAVE A FEVER..
IT'S EITHER THE FLU OR LOVE..THE SYMPTOMS ARE THE SAME...
SCHULZ

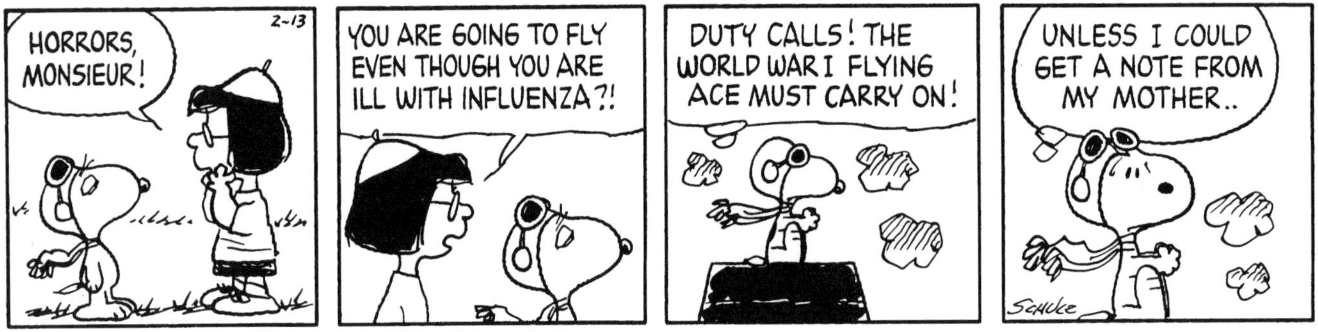
2-13
HORRORS, MONSIEUR!
YOU ARE GOING TO FLY EVEN THOUGH YOU ARE ILL WITH INFLUENZA?!
DUTY CALLS! THE WORLD WAR I FLYING ACE MUST CARRY ON!
UNLESS I COULD GET A NOTE FROM MY MOTHER..

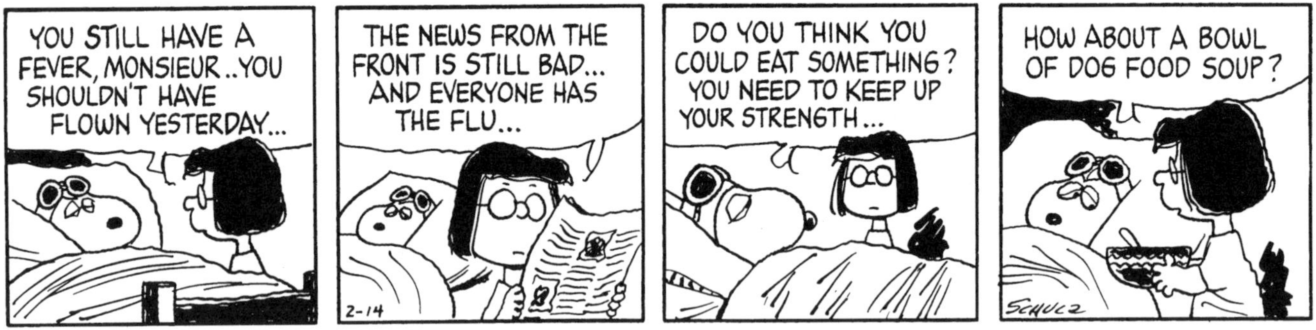
YOU STILL HAVE A FEVER, MONSIEUR..YOU SHOULDN'T HAVE FLOWN YESTERDAY...
THE NEWS FROM THE FRONT IS STILL BAD... AND EVERYONE HAS THE FLU...
2-14
DO YOU THINK YOU COULD EAT SOMETHING? YOU NEED TO KEEP UP YOUR STRENGTH...
HOW ABOUT A BOWL OF DOG FOOD SOUP?

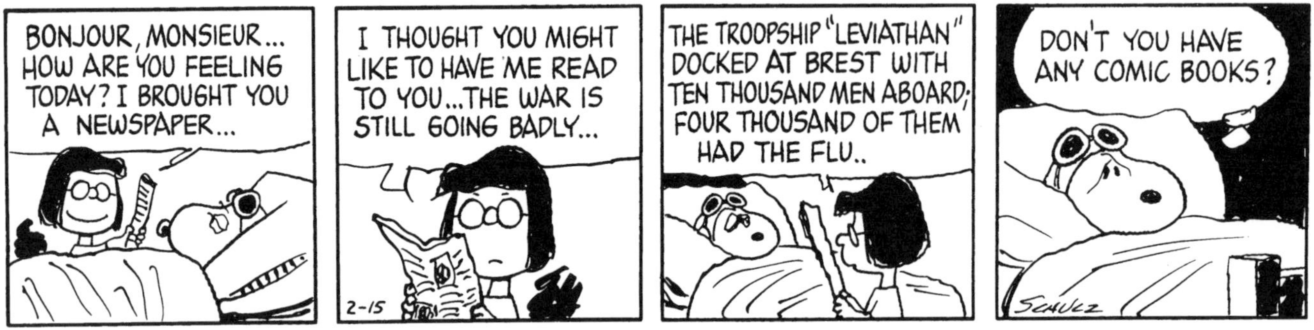
BONJOUR, MONSIEUR... HOW ARE YOU FEELING TODAY? I BROUGHT YOU A NEWSPAPER...
I THOUGHT YOU MIGHT LIKE TO HAVE ME READ TO YOU...THE WAR IS STILL GOING BADLY...
2-15
THE TROOPSHIP "LEVIATHAN" DOCKED AT BREST WITH TEN THOUSAND MEN ABOARD; FOUR THOUSAND OF THEM HAD THE FLU..
DON'T YOU HAVE ANY COMIC BOOKS?

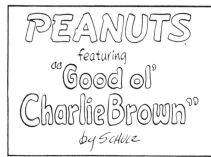

PEANUTS

featuring

"Good ol' Charlie Brown"

by Schulz

HERE WE ARE.. GOING DOWN

Library HOURS

DID YOU SEE THAT? HIS INITIALS WERE ON ONE OF THE BUTTONS IN THE ELEVATOR...

IT SAID, "LL"

2-16

WHAT'S "LL"?

LOUIS L'AMOUR! HE WRITES ALL THOSE WESTERNS..

THAT'S PRETTY NEAT HAVING YOUR INITIALS ON AN ELEVATOR BUTTON!

I DON'T THINK "LL" MEANS LOUIS L'AMOUR.. I THINK IT MEANS "LOWER LOBBY"

REALLY? WHAT DID **HE** WRITE?

Schulz

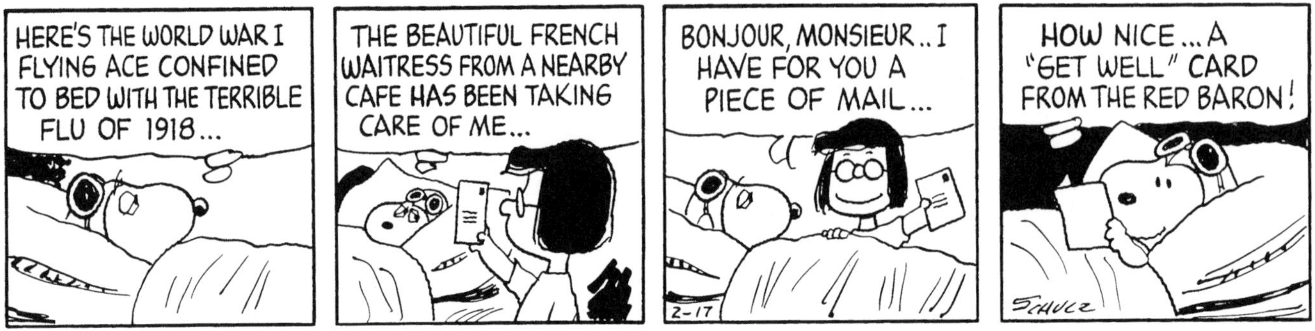
HERE'S THE WORLD WAR I FLYING ACE CONFINED TO BED WITH THE TERRIBLE FLU OF 1918...
THE BEAUTIFUL FRENCH WAITRESS FROM A NEARBY CAFE HAS BEEN TAKING CARE OF ME...
BONJOUR, MONSIEUR.. I HAVE FOR YOU A PIECE OF MAIL...
HOW NICE... A "GET WELL" CARD FROM THE RED BARON!
2-17
SCHULZ

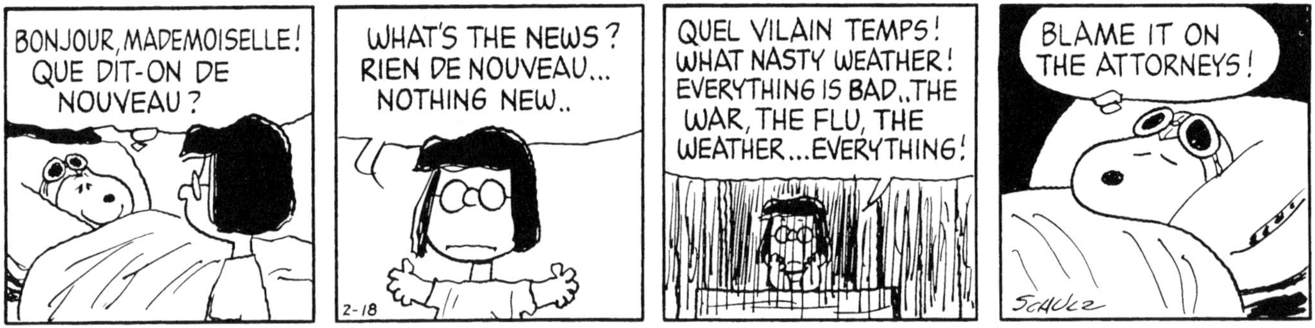
BONJOUR, MADEMOISELLE! QUE DIT-ON DE NOUVEAU?
WHAT'S THE NEWS? RIEN DE NOUVEAU... NOTHING NEW..
QUEL VILAIN TEMPS! WHAT NASTY WEATHER! EVERYTHING IS BAD..THE WAR, THE FLU, THE WEATHER...EVERYTHING!
BLAME IT ON THE ATTORNEYS!
2-18
SCHULZ

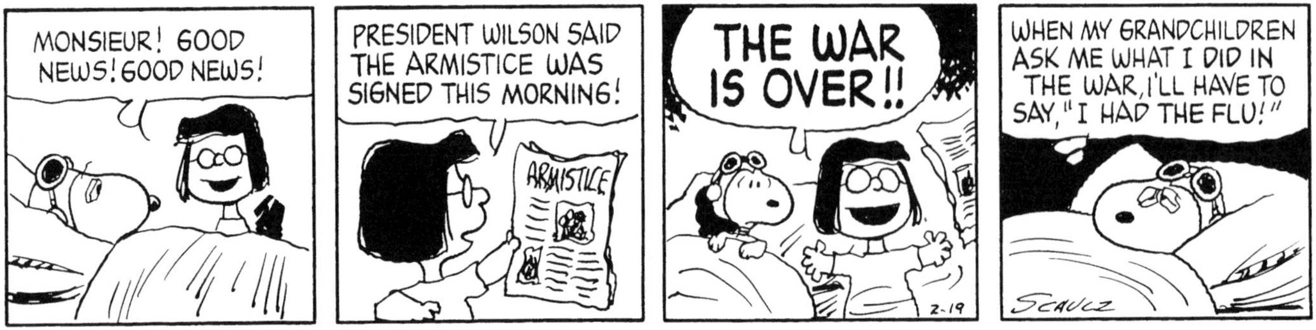
MONSIEUR! GOOD NEWS! GOOD NEWS!
PRESIDENT WILSON SAID THE ARMISTICE WAS SIGNED THIS MORNING!
ARMISTICE
THE WAR IS OVER!!
WHEN MY GRANDCHILDREN ASK ME WHAT I DID IN THE WAR, I'LL HAVE TO SAY, "I HAD THE FLU!"
2-19
SCHULZ

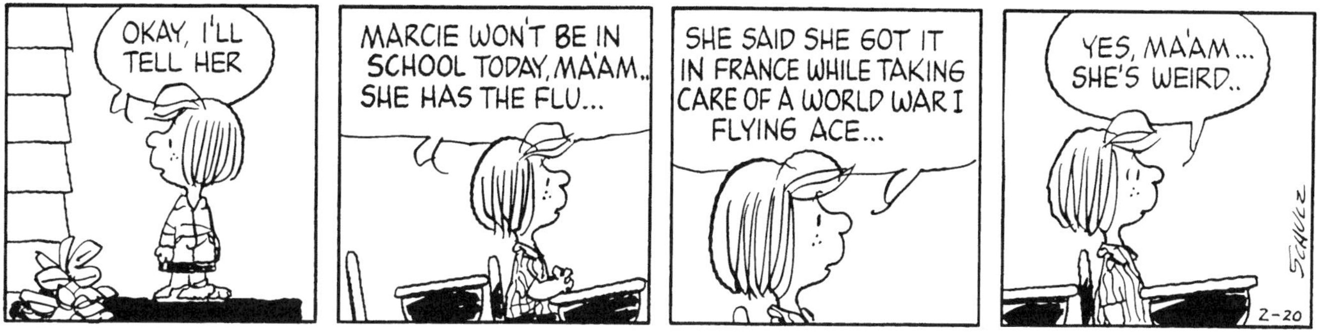
OKAY, I'LL TELL HER
MARCIE WON'T BE IN SCHOOL TODAY, MA'AM.. SHE HAS THE FLU...
SHE SAID SHE GOT IT IN FRANCE WHILE TAKING CARE OF A WORLD WAR I FLYING ACE...
YES, MA'AM... SHE'S WEIRD..
SCHULZ
2-20

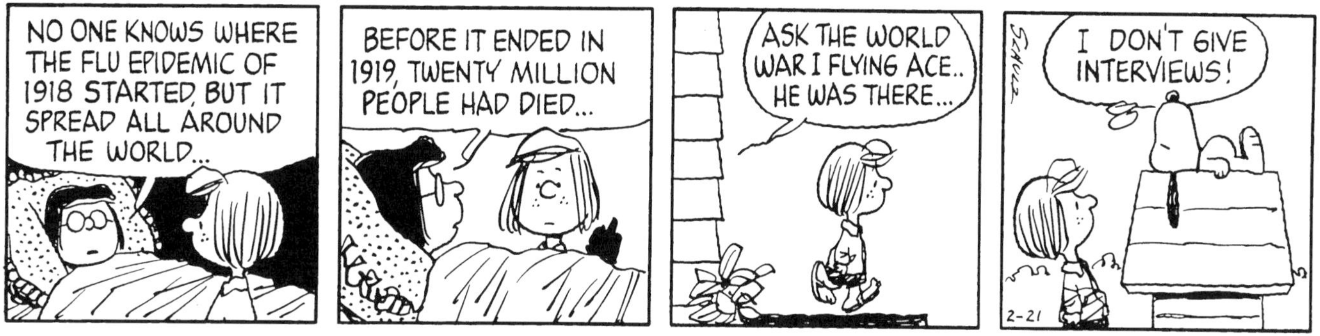
NO ONE KNOWS WHERE THE FLU EPIDEMIC OF 1918 STARTED, BUT IT SPREAD ALL AROUND THE WORLD...
BEFORE IT ENDED IN 1919, TWENTY MILLION PEOPLE HAD DIED...
ASK THE WORLD WAR I FLYING ACE.. HE WAS THERE...
I DON'T GIVE INTERVIEWS!
SCHULZ
2-21

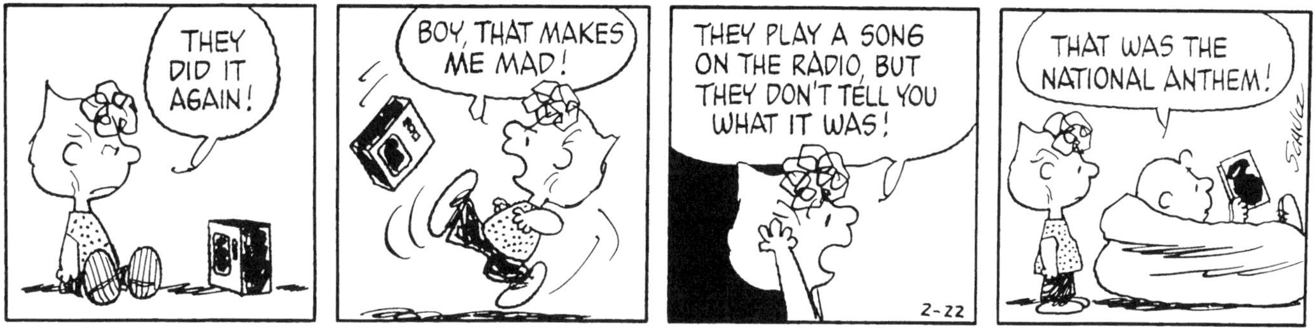
THEY DID IT AGAIN!
BOY, THAT MAKES ME MAD!
THEY PLAY A SONG ON THE RADIO, BUT THEY DON'T TELL YOU WHAT IT WAS!
2-22
THAT WAS THE NATIONAL ANTHEM!
SCHULZ

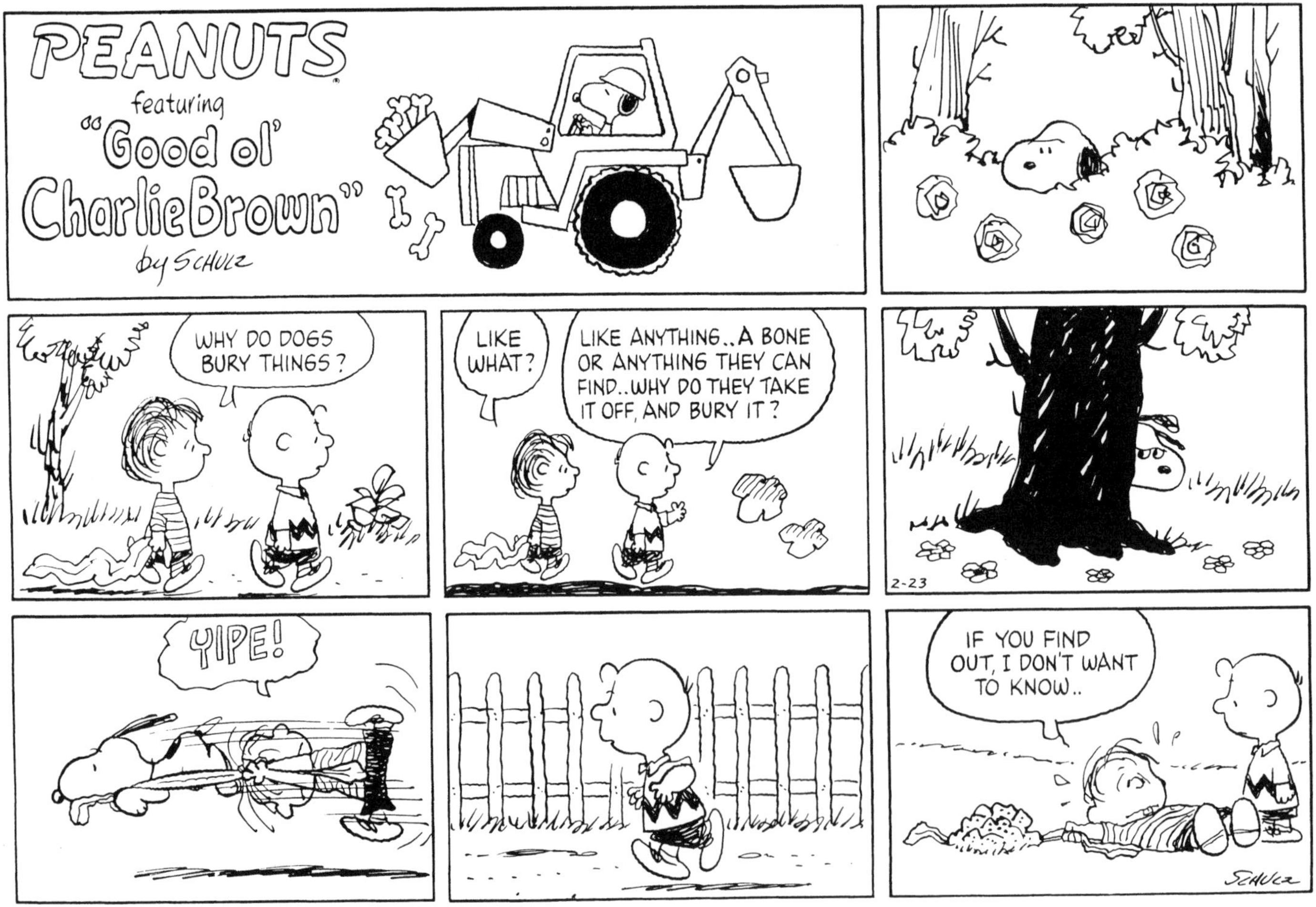
PEANUTS
featuring
"Good ol' CharlieBrown"
by SCHULZ
WHY DO DOGS BURY THINGS?
LIKE WHAT?
LIKE ANYTHING..A BONE OR ANYTHING THEY CAN FIND..WHY DO THEY TAKE IT OFF, AND BURY IT?
2-23
YIPE!
IF YOU FIND OUT, I DON'T WANT TO KNOW..
SCHULZ

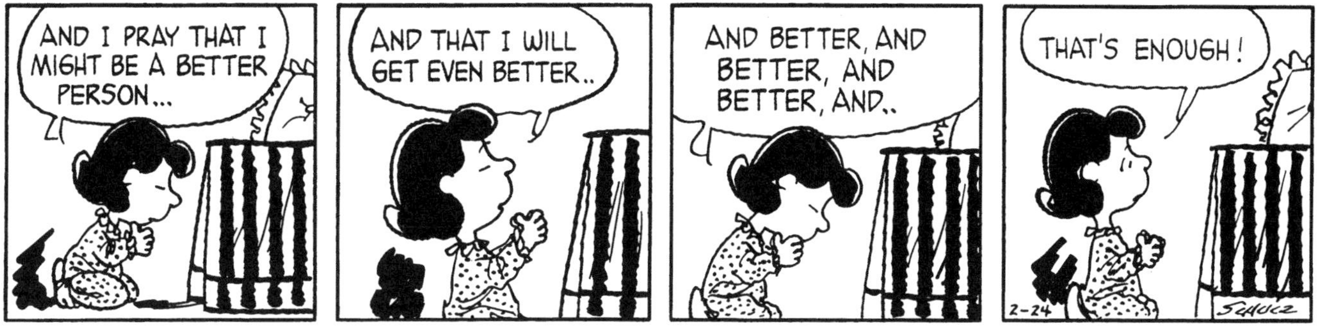
AND I PRAY THAT I MIGHT BE A BETTER PERSON...
AND THAT I WILL GET EVEN BETTER..
AND BETTER, AND BETTER, AND BETTER, AND..
THAT'S ENOUGH!
2-24
SCHULZ

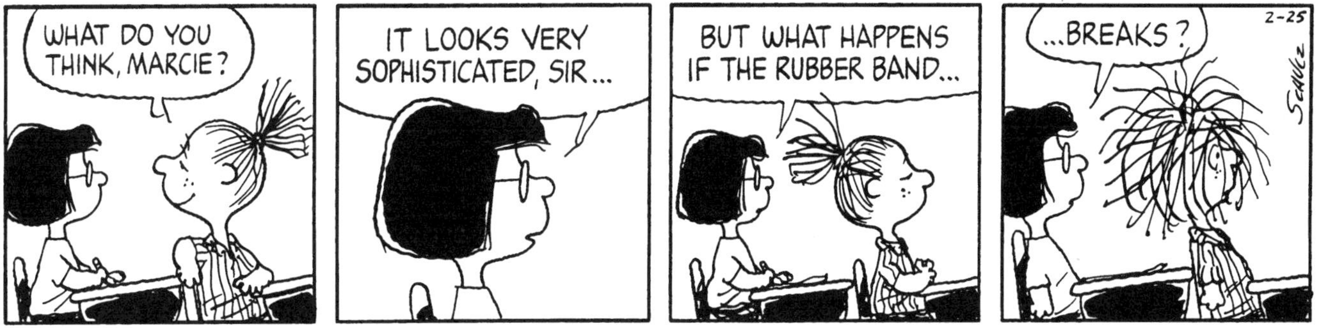
WHAT DO YOU THINK, MARCIE?
IT LOOKS VERY SOPHISTICATED, SIR...
BUT WHAT HAPPENS IF THE RUBBER BAND...
...BREAKS?
2-25
SCHULZ

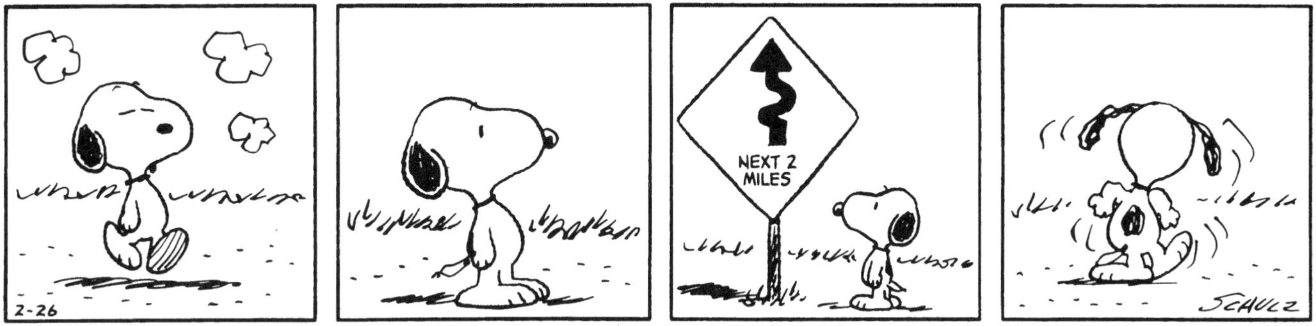
2-26
NEXT 2 MILES
SCHULZ

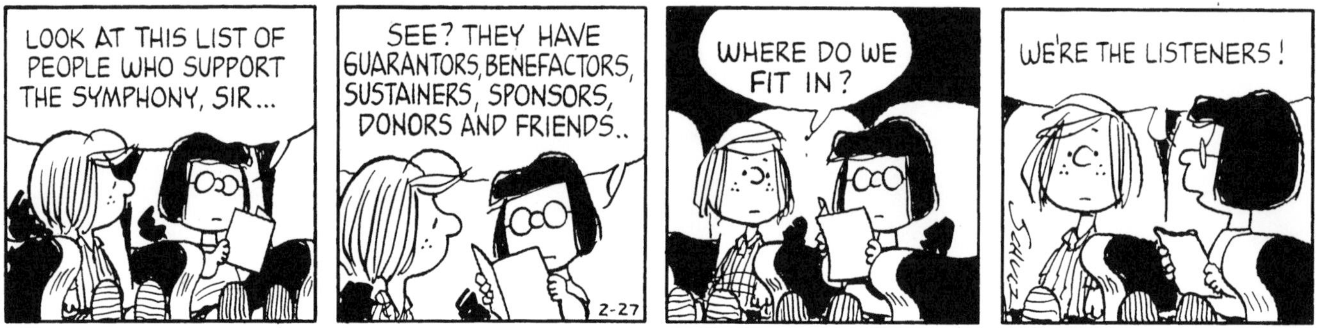
LOOK AT THIS LIST OF PEOPLE WHO SUPPORT THE SYMPHONY, SIR...
SEE? THEY HAVE GUARANTORS, BENEFACTORS, SUSTAINERS, SPONSORS, DONORS AND FRIENDS..
2-27
WHERE DO WE FIT IN?
WE'RE THE LISTENERS!

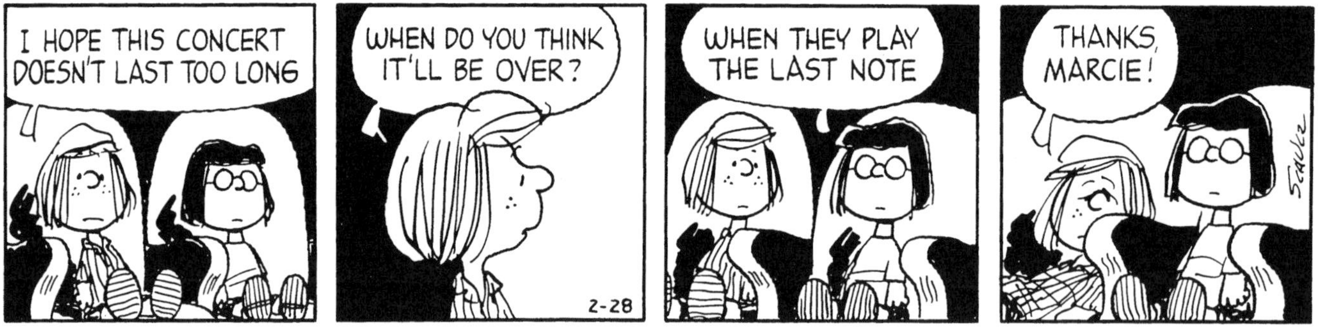
I HOPE THIS CONCERT DOESN'T LAST TOO LONG
WHEN DO YOU THINK IT'LL BE OVER?
2-28
WHEN THEY PLAY THE LAST NOTE
THANKS, MARCIE!

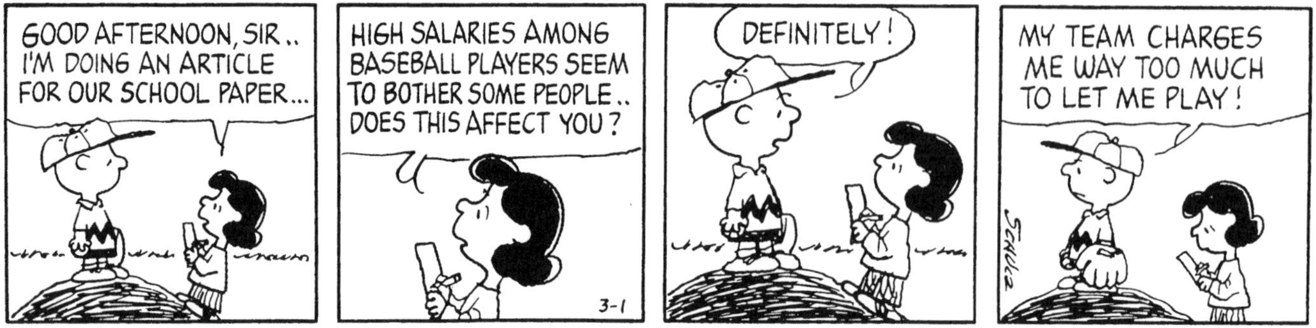
GOOD AFTERNOON, SIR.. I'M DOING AN ARTICLE FOR OUR SCHOOL PAPER...
HIGH SALARIES AMONG BASEBALL PLAYERS SEEM TO BOTHER SOME PEOPLE.. DOES THIS AFFECT YOU?
3-1
DEFINITELY!
MY TEAM CHARGES ME WAY TOO MUCH TO LET ME PLAY!

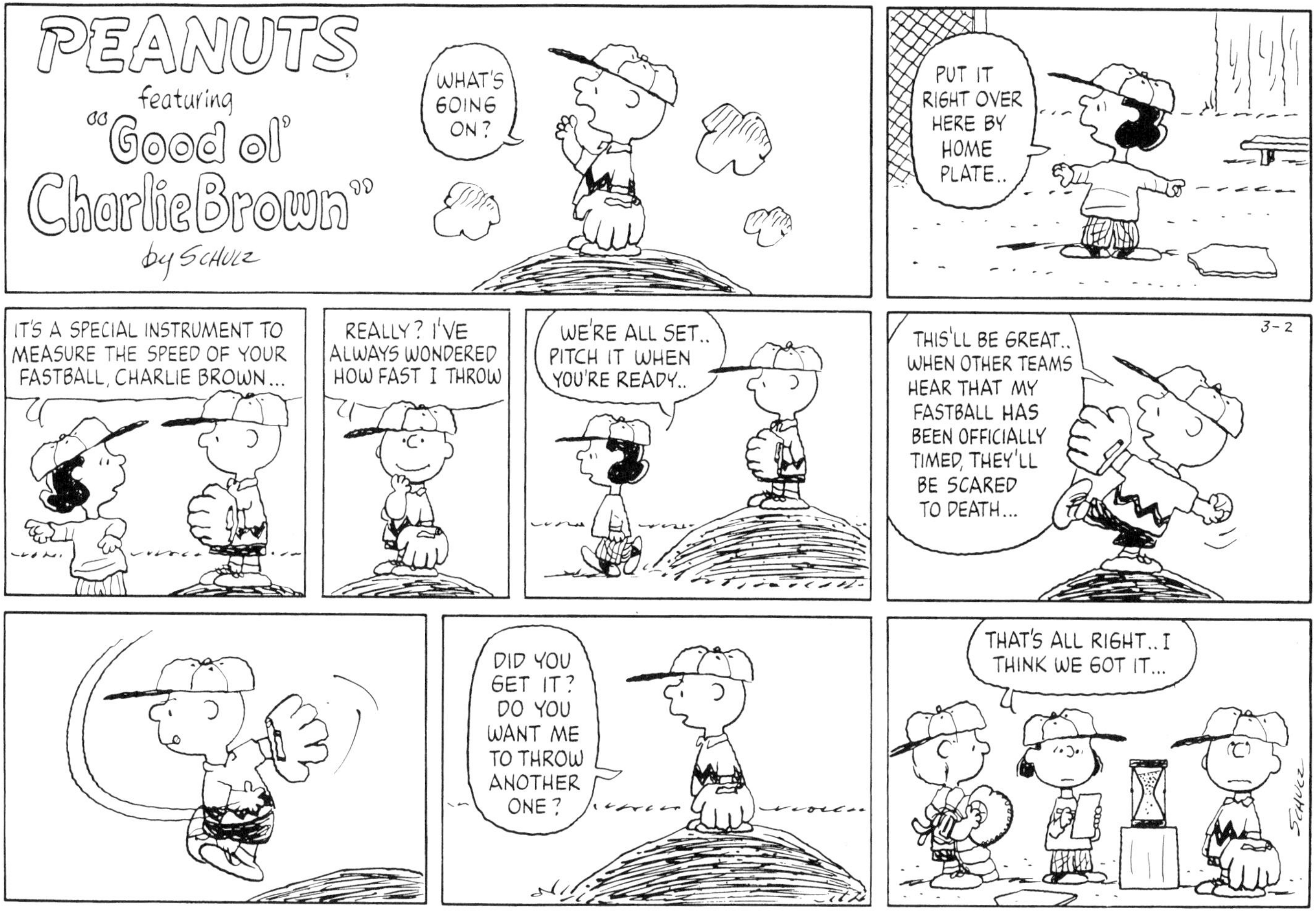
PEANUTS
featuring "Good ol' CharlieBrown"
by SCHULZ
WHAT'S GOING ON?
PUT IT RIGHT OVER HERE BY HOME PLATE..
IT'S A SPECIAL INSTRUMENT TO MEASURE THE SPEED OF YOUR FASTBALL, CHARLIE BROWN...
REALLY? I'VE ALWAYS WONDERED HOW FAST I THROW
WE'RE ALL SET.. PITCH IT WHEN YOU'RE READY..
3-2
THIS'LL BE GREAT.. WHEN OTHER TEAMS HEAR THAT MY FASTBALL HAS BEEN OFFICIALLY TIMED, THEY'LL BE SCARED TO DEATH...
DID YOU GET IT? DO YOU WANT ME TO THROW ANOTHER ONE?
THAT'S ALL RIGHT.. I THINK WE GOT IT...
SCHULZ

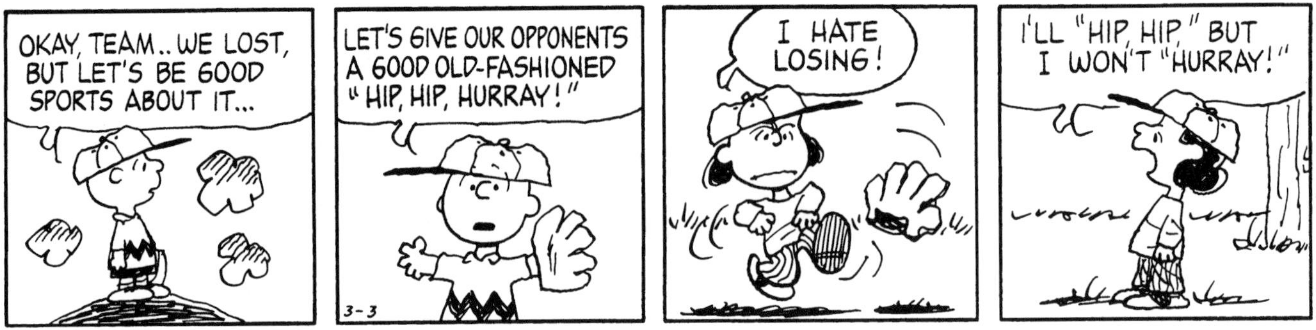
OKAY, TEAM.. WE LOST, BUT LET'S BE GOOD SPORTS ABOUT IT...
LET'S GIVE OUR OPPONENTS A GOOD OLD-FASHIONED "HIP, HIP, HURRAY!"
3-3
I HATE LOSING!
I'LL "HIP, HIP," BUT I WON'T "HURRAY!"

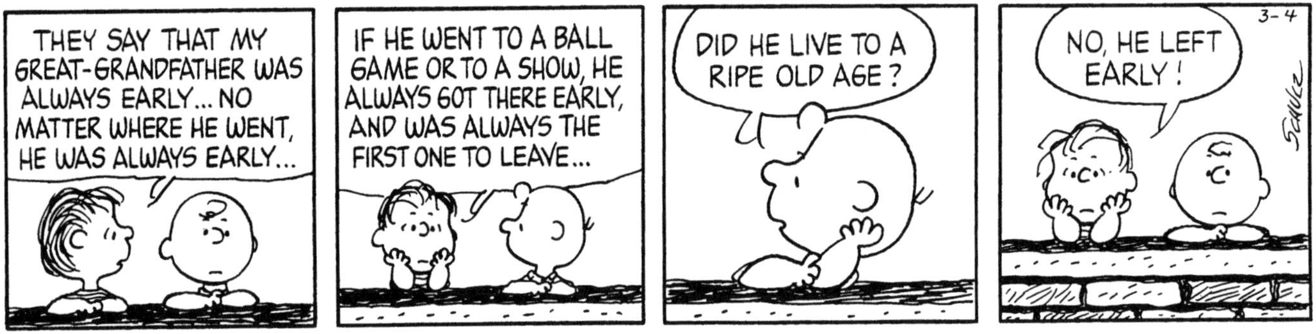
THEY SAY THAT MY GREAT-GRANDFATHER WAS ALWAYS EARLY... NO MATTER WHERE HE WENT, HE WAS ALWAYS EARLY...
IF HE WENT TO A BALL GAME OR TO A SHOW, HE ALWAYS GOT THERE EARLY, AND WAS ALWAYS THE FIRST ONE TO LEAVE...
DID HE LIVE TO A RIPE OLD AGE?
3-4
NO, HE LEFT EARLY!
SCHULZ

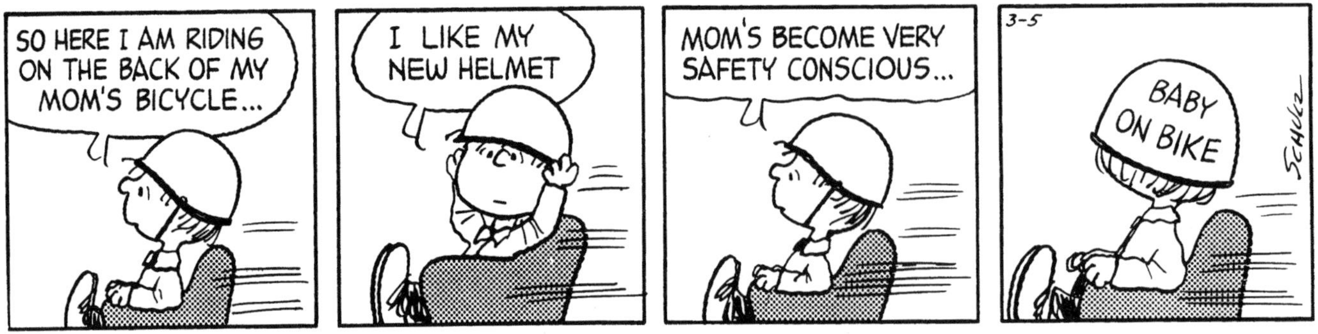
SO HERE I AM RIDING ON THE BACK OF MY MOM'S BICYCLE...
I LIKE MY NEW HELMET
MOM'S BECOME VERY SAFETY CONSCIOUS...
3-5
BABY ON BIKE
SCHULZ

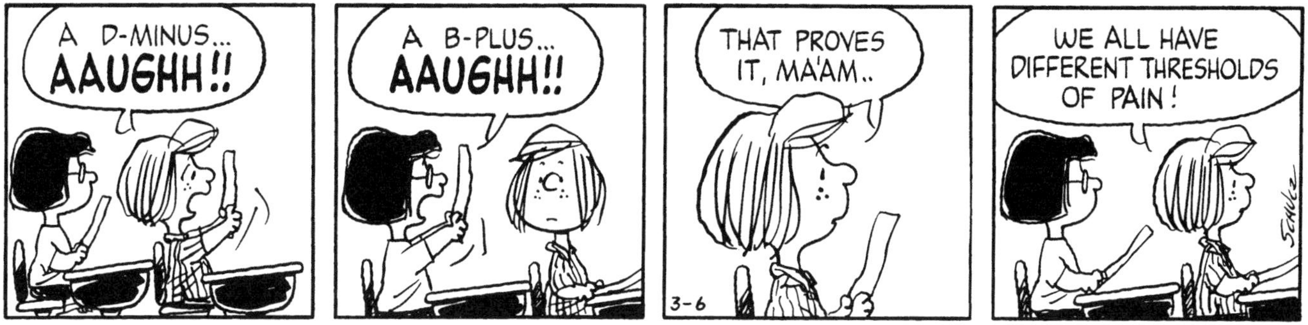
A D-MINUS... AAUGHH!!
A B-PLUS... AAUGHH!!
THAT PROVES IT, MA'AM..
3-6
WE ALL HAVE DIFFERENT THRESHOLDS OF PAIN!

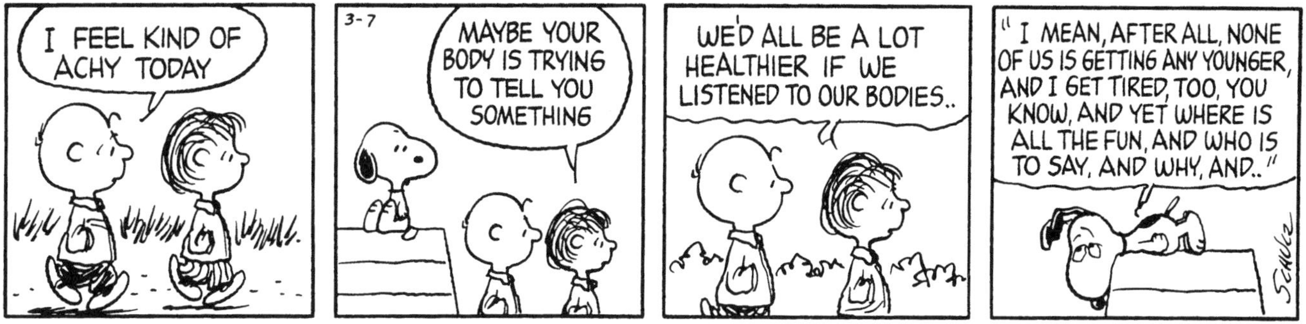
I FEEL KIND OF ACHY TODAY
3-7
MAYBE YOUR BODY IS TRYING TO TELL YOU SOMETHING
WE'D ALL BE A LOT HEALTHIER IF WE LISTENED TO OUR BODIES..
"I MEAN, AFTER ALL, NONE OF US IS GETTING ANY YOUNGER, AND I GET TIRED, TOO, YOU KNOW, AND YET WHERE IS ALL THE FUN, AND WHO IS TO SAY, AND WHY, AND.."

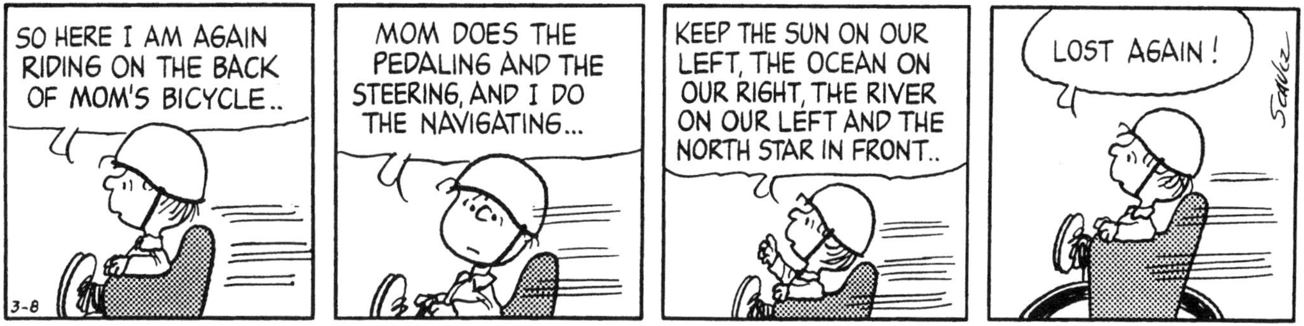
SO HERE I AM AGAIN RIDING ON THE BACK OF MOM'S BICYCLE..
3-8
MOM DOES THE PEDALING AND THE STEERING, AND I DO THE NAVIGATING...
KEEP THE SUN ON OUR LEFT, THE OCEAN ON OUR RIGHT, THE RIVER ON OUR LEFT AND THE NORTH STAR IN FRONT..
LOST AGAIN!

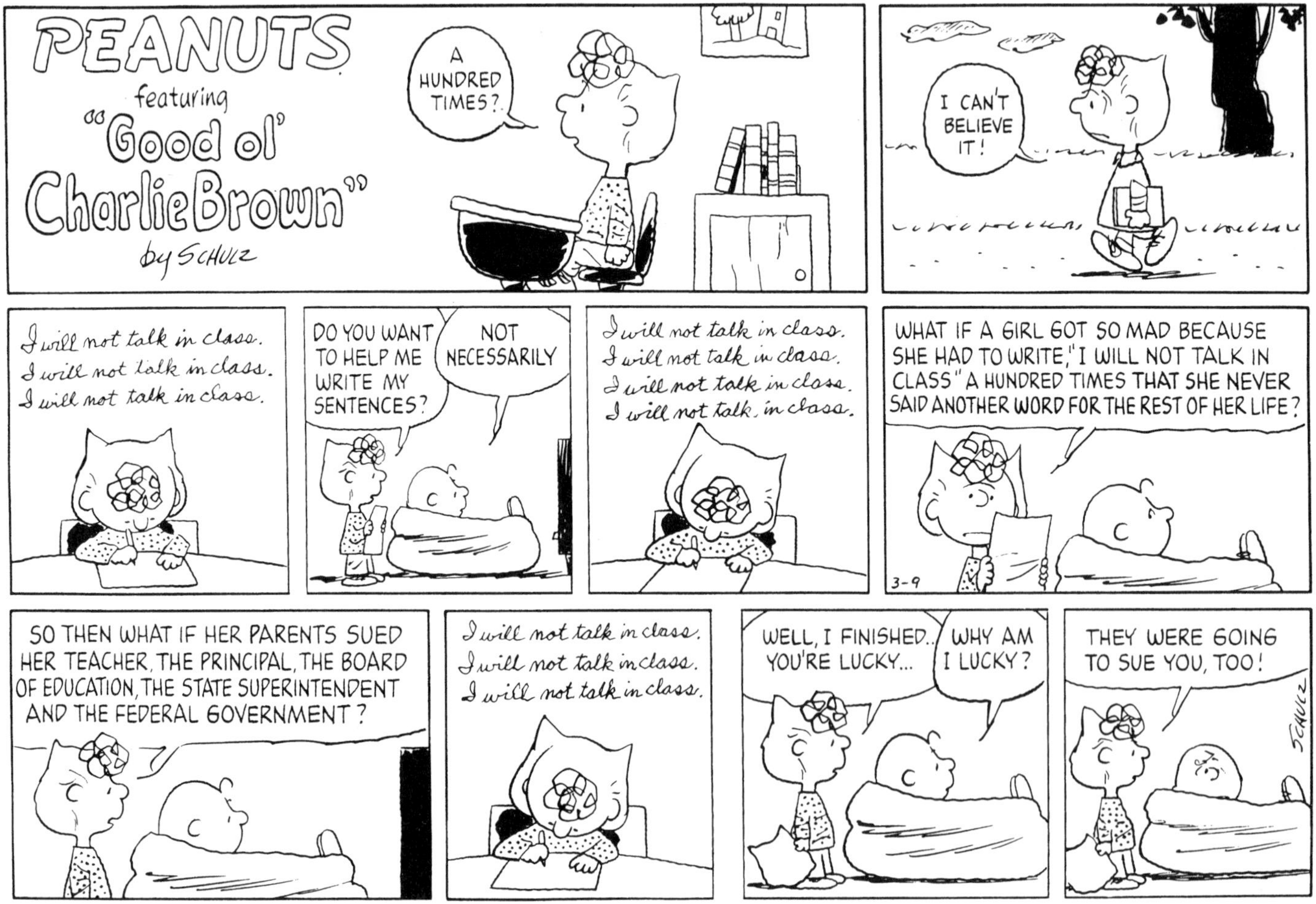

PEANUTS
featuring "Good ol' Charlie Brown"
by SCHULZ
A HUNDRED TIMES?
I CAN'T BELIEVE IT!
I will not talk in class.
I will not talk in class.
I will not talk in class.
DO YOU WANT TO HELP ME WRITE MY SENTENCES?
NOT NECESSARILY
I will not talk in class.
I will not talk in class.
I will not talk in class.
I will not talk in class.
WHAT IF A GIRL GOT SO MAD BECAUSE SHE HAD TO WRITE, "I WILL NOT TALK IN CLASS" A HUNDRED TIMES THAT SHE NEVER SAID ANOTHER WORD FOR THE REST OF HER LIFE?
3-9
SO THEN WHAT IF HER PARENTS SUED HER TEACHER, THE PRINCIPAL, THE BOARD OF EDUCATION, THE STATE SUPERINTENDENT AND THE FEDERAL GOVERNMENT?
I will not talk in class.
I will not talk in class.
I will not talk in class.
WELL, I FINISHED... YOU'RE LUCKY...
WHY AM I LUCKY?
THEY WERE GOING TO SUE YOU, TOO!
SCHULZ

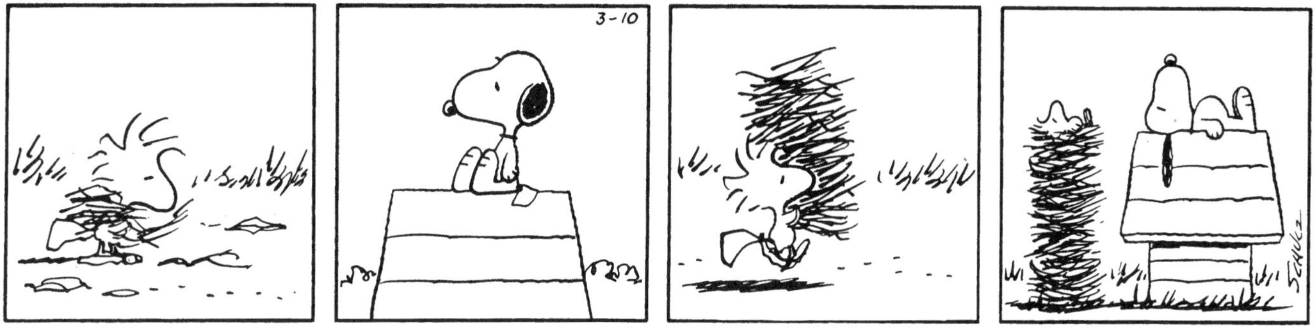
3-10
SCHULZ

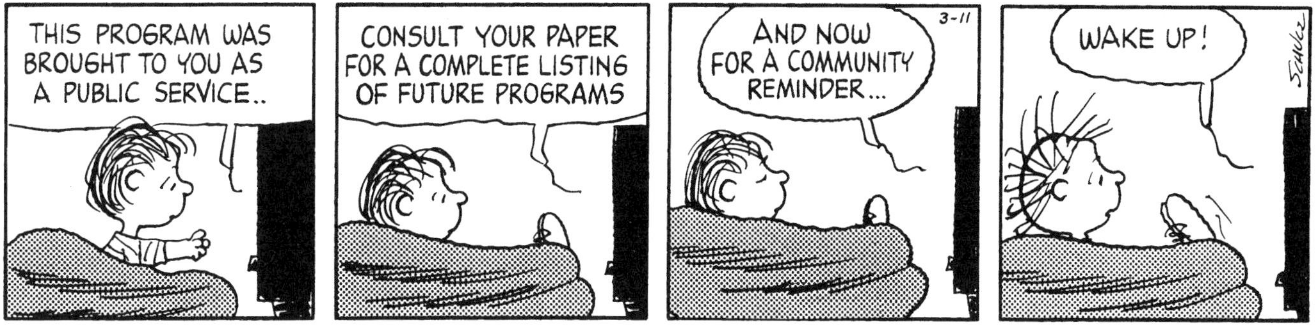
THIS PROGRAM WAS BROUGHT TO YOU AS A PUBLIC SERVICE..
CONSULT YOUR PAPER FOR A COMPLETE LISTING OF FUTURE PROGRAMS
3-11
AND NOW FOR A COMMUNITY REMINDER...
WAKE UP!
SCHULZ

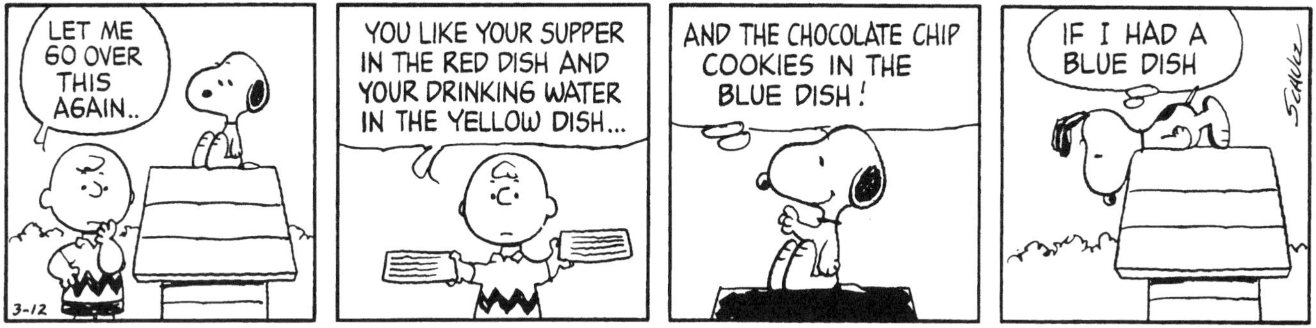
LET ME GO OVER THIS AGAIN..
3-12
YOU LIKE YOUR SUPPER IN THE RED DISH AND YOUR DRINKING WATER IN THE YELLOW DISH...
AND THE CHOCOLATE CHIP COOKIES IN THE BLUE DISH!
IF I HAD A BLUE DISH
SCHULZ

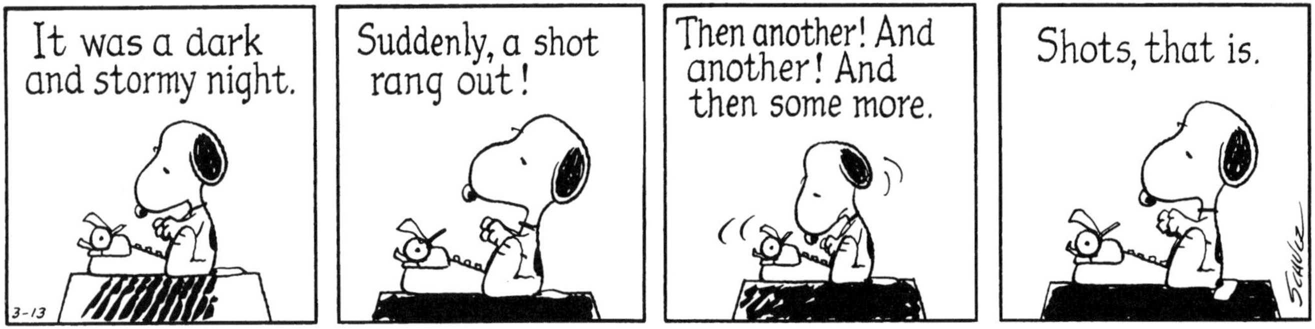
It was a dark and stormy night.
3-13
Suddenly, a shot rang out!
Then another! And another! And then some more.
Shots, that is.
SCHULZ

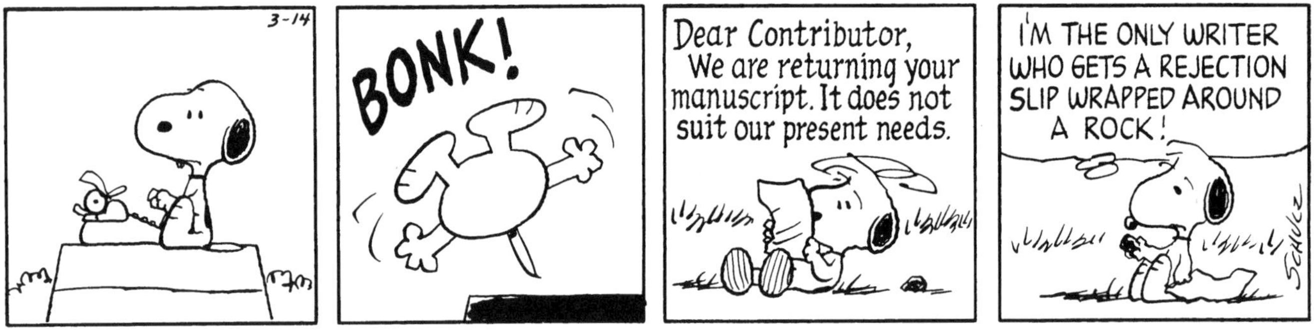
3-14
BONK!
Dear Contributor,
We are returning your manuscript. It does not suit our present needs.
I'M THE ONLY WRITER WHO GETS A REJECTION SLIP WRAPPED AROUND A ROCK!
SCHULZ

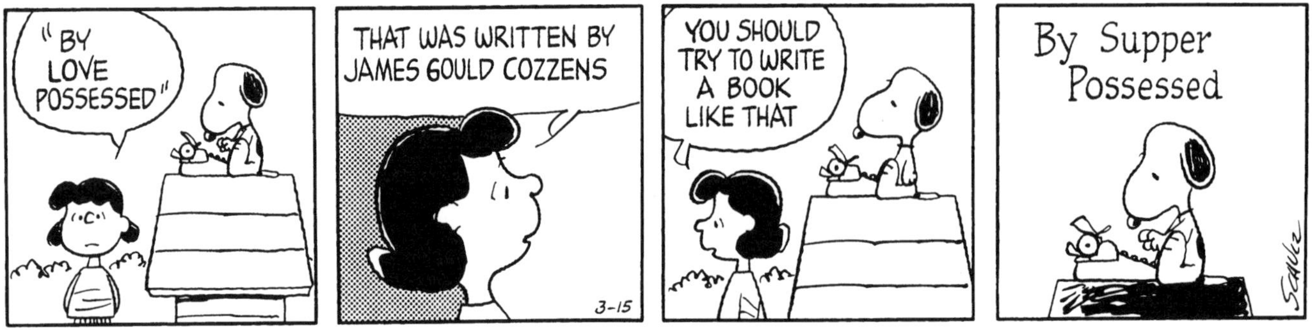
"BY LOVE POSSESSED"
THAT WAS WRITTEN BY JAMES GOULD COZZENS
3-15
YOU SHOULD TRY TO WRITE A BOOK LIKE THAT
By Supper Possessed
SCHULZ

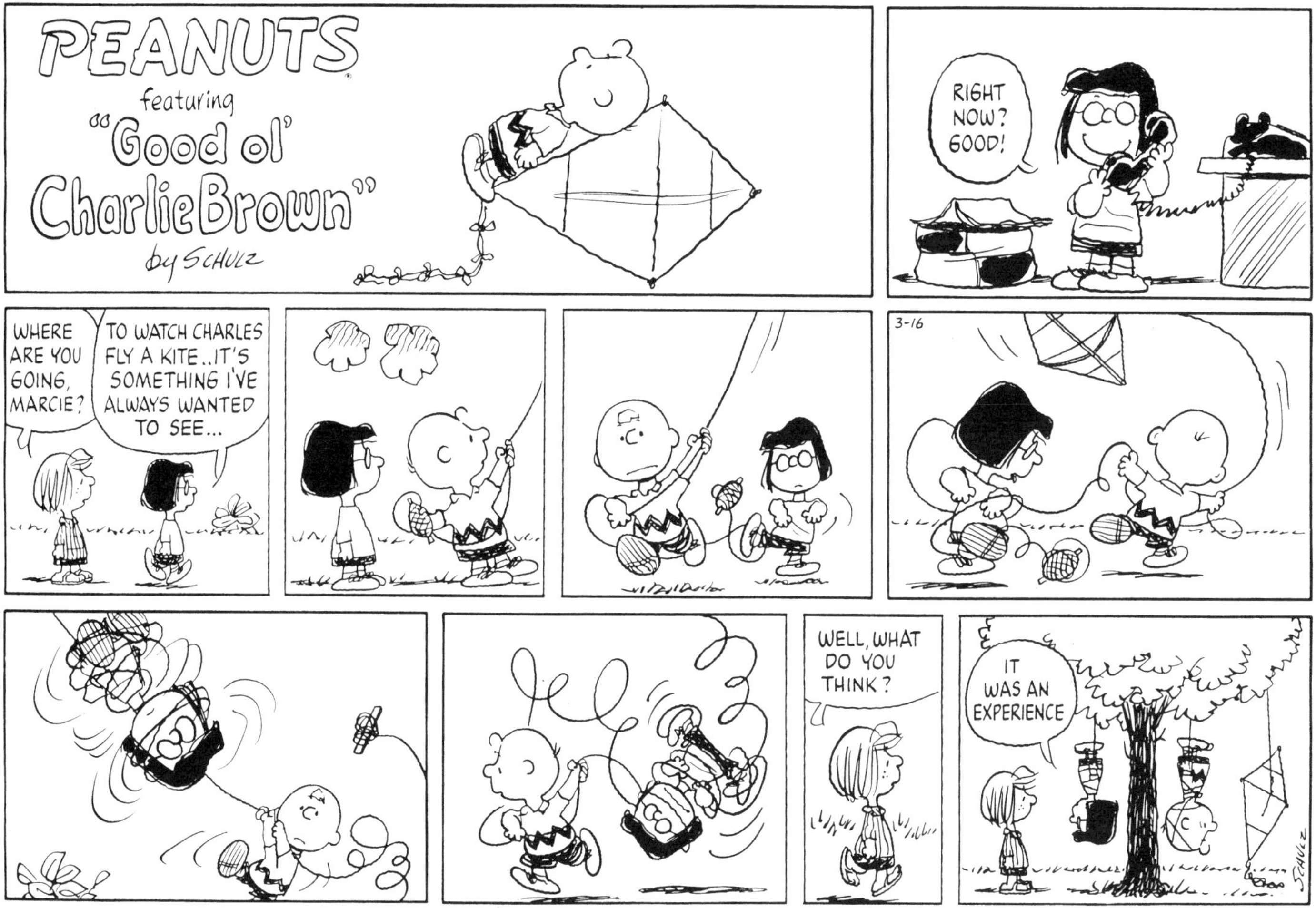
PEANUTS
featuring
"Good ol' CharlieBrown"
by SCHULZ
RIGHT NOW? GOOD!
WHERE ARE YOU GOING, MARCIE?
TO WATCH CHARLES FLY A KITE..IT'S SOMETHING I'VE ALWAYS WANTED TO SEE...
3-16
WELL, WHAT DO YOU THINK?
IT WAS AN EXPERIENCE
SCHULZ

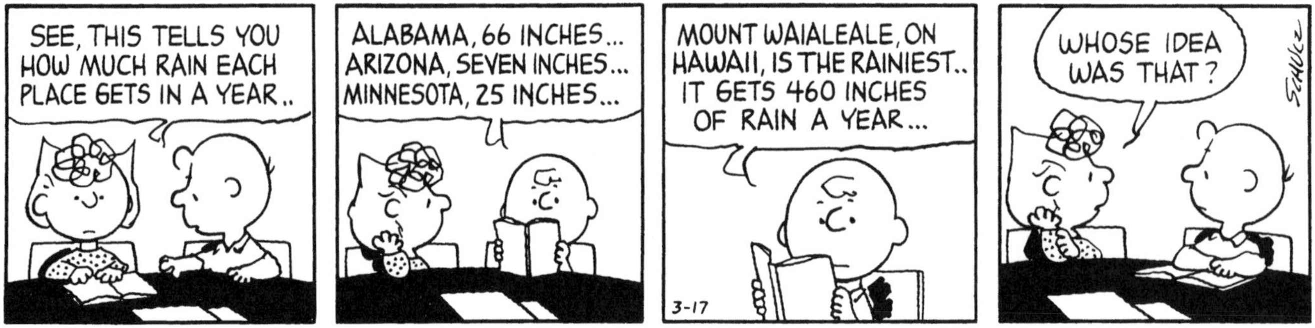
SEE, THIS TELLS YOU HOW MUCH RAIN EACH PLACE GETS IN A YEAR..
ALABAMA, 66 INCHES... ARIZONA, SEVEN INCHES... MINNESOTA, 25 INCHES...
MOUNT WAIALEALE, ON HAWAII, IS THE RAINIEST.. IT GETS 460 INCHES OF RAIN A YEAR...
3-17
WHOSE IDEA WAS THAT?

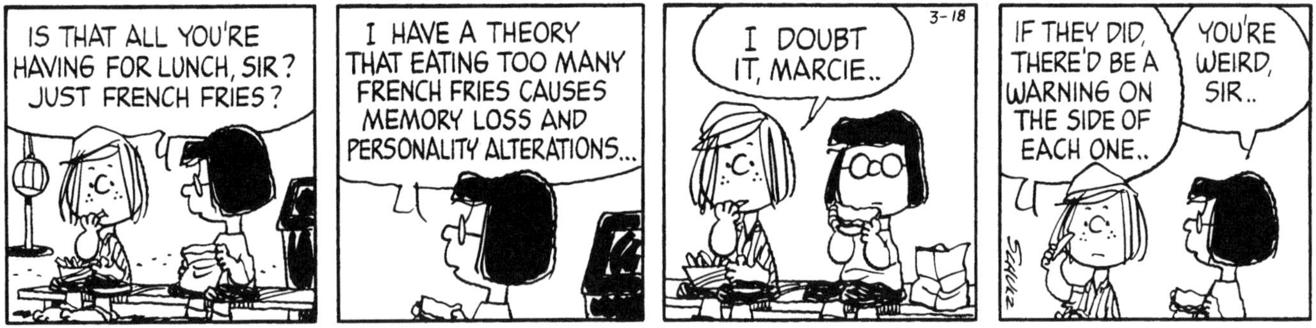
IS THAT ALL YOU'RE HAVING FOR LUNCH, SIR? JUST FRENCH FRIES?
I HAVE A THEORY THAT EATING TOO MANY FRENCH FRIES CAUSES MEMORY LOSS AND PERSONALITY ALTERATIONS...
3-18
I DOUBT IT, MARCIE..
IF THEY DID, THERE'D BE A WARNING ON THE SIDE OF EACH ONE..
YOU'RE WEIRD, SIR..

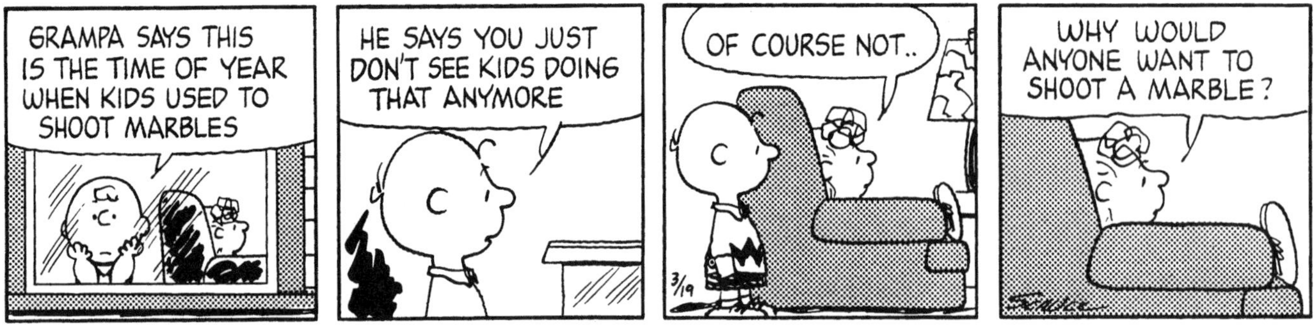
GRAMPA SAYS THIS IS THE TIME OF YEAR WHEN KIDS USED TO SHOOT MARBLES
HE SAYS YOU JUST DON'T SEE KIDS DOING THAT ANYMORE
OF COURSE NOT..
3/19
WHY WOULD ANYONE WANT TO SHOOT A MARBLE?

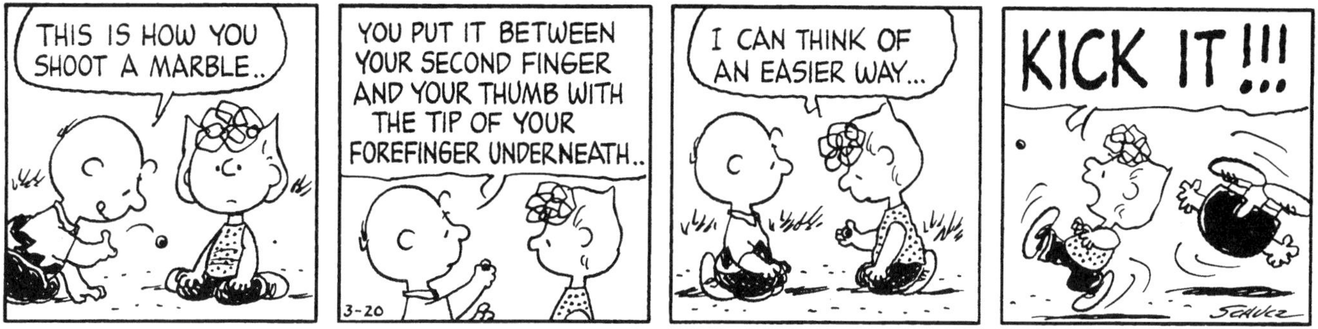
THIS IS HOW YOU SHOOT A MARBLE..
YOU PUT IT BETWEEN YOUR SECOND FINGER AND YOUR THUMB WITH THE TIP OF YOUR FOREFINGER UNDERNEATH..
3-20
I CAN THINK OF AN EASIER WAY...
KICK IT!!!
SCHULZ

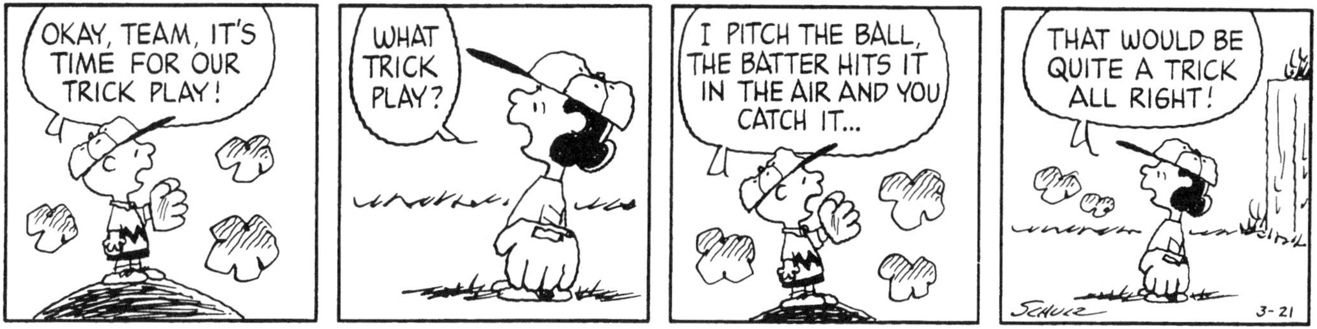
OKAY, TEAM, IT'S TIME FOR OUR TRICK PLAY!
WHAT TRICK PLAY?
I PITCH THE BALL, THE BATTER HITS IT IN THE AIR AND YOU CATCH IT...
THAT WOULD BE QUITE A TRICK ALL RIGHT!
SCHULZ
3-21

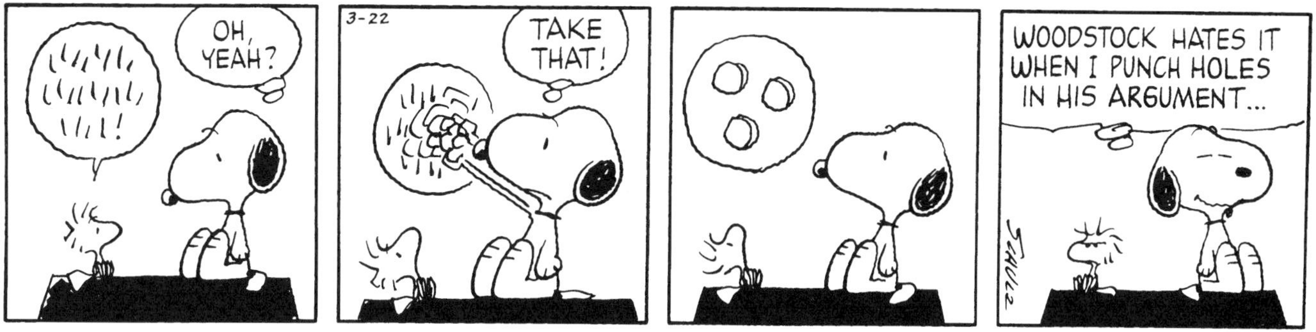
OH, YEAH?
3-22
TAKE THAT!
WOODSTOCK HATES IT WHEN I PUNCH HOLES IN HIS ARGUMENT...
SCHULZ

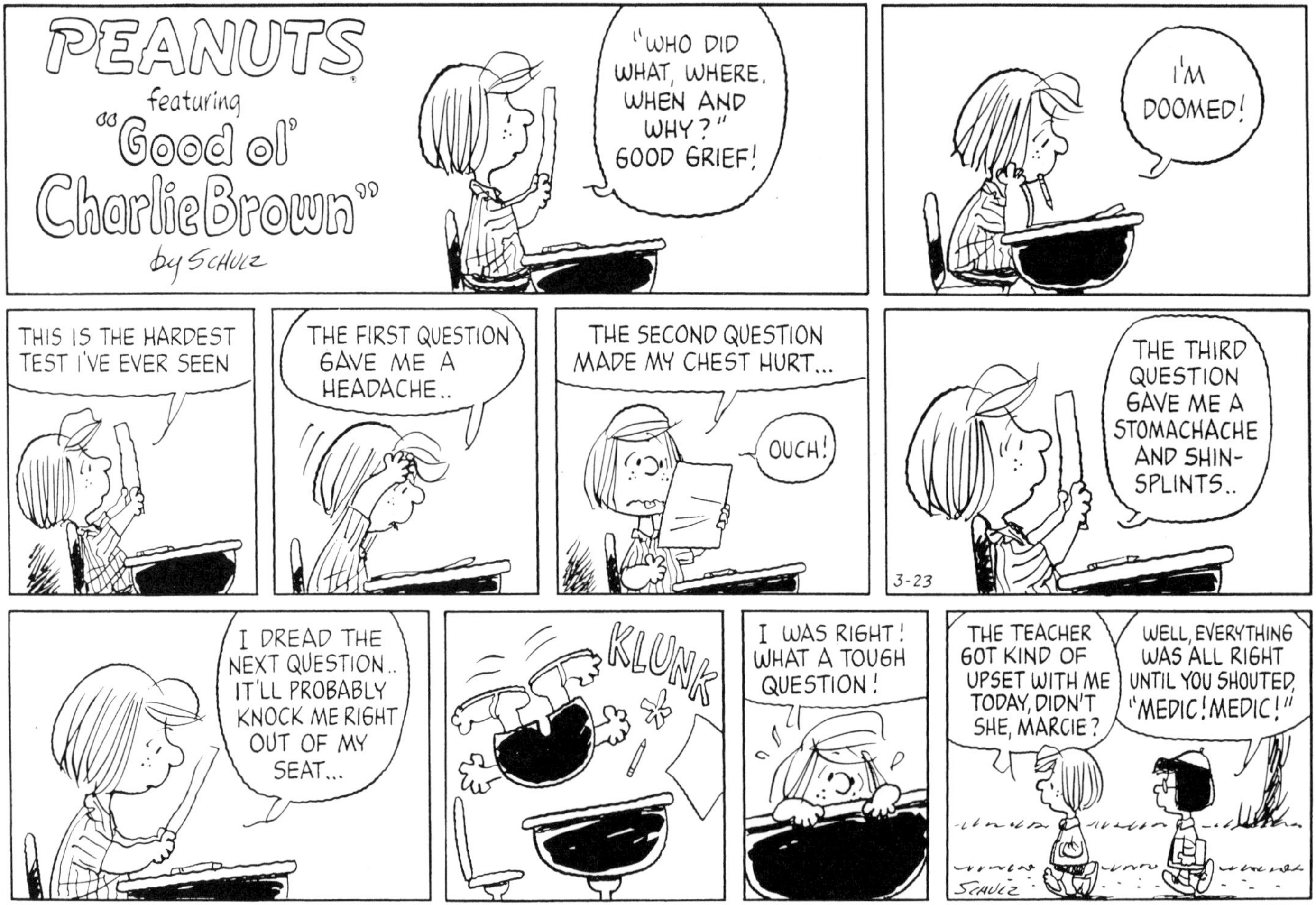
PEANUTS
featuring
"Good ol' Charlie Brown"
by SCHULZ
"WHO DID WHAT, WHERE, WHEN AND WHY?" GOOD GRIEF!
I'M DOOMED!
THIS IS THE HARDEST TEST I'VE EVER SEEN
THE FIRST QUESTION GAVE ME A HEADACHE..
THE SECOND QUESTION MADE MY CHEST HURT...
OUCH!
3-23
THE THIRD QUESTION GAVE ME A STOMACHACHE AND SHIN-SPLINTS..
I DREAD THE NEXT QUESTION.. IT'LL PROBABLY KNOCK ME RIGHT OUT OF MY SEAT...
KLUNK
I WAS RIGHT! WHAT A TOUGH QUESTION!
THE TEACHER GOT KIND OF UPSET WITH ME TODAY, DIDN'T SHE, MARCIE?
WELL, EVERYTHING WAS ALL RIGHT UNTIL YOU SHOUTED, "MEDIC! MEDIC!"
SCHULZ

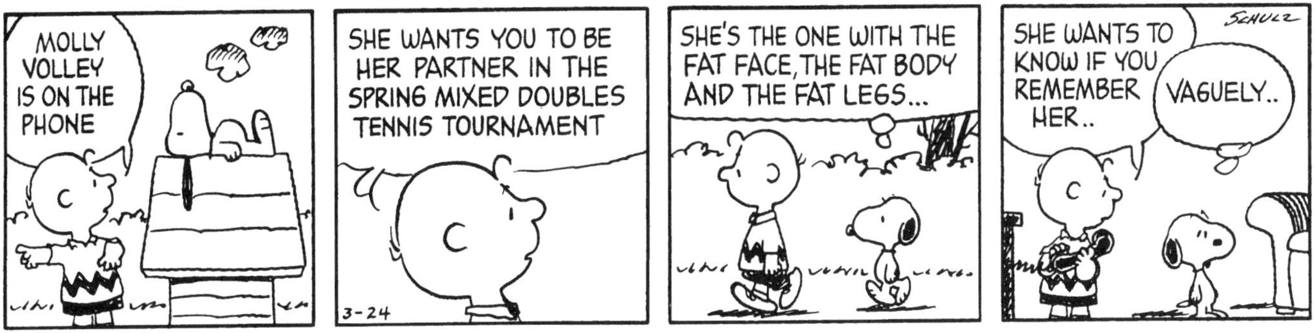
MOLLY VOLLEY IS ON THE PHONE
SHE WANTS YOU TO BE HER PARTNER IN THE SPRING MIXED DOUBLES TENNIS TOURNAMENT
SHE'S THE ONE WITH THE FAT FACE, THE FAT BODY AND THE FAT LEGS...
SHE WANTS TO KNOW IF YOU REMEMBER HER..
VAGUELY..
SCHULZ
3-24

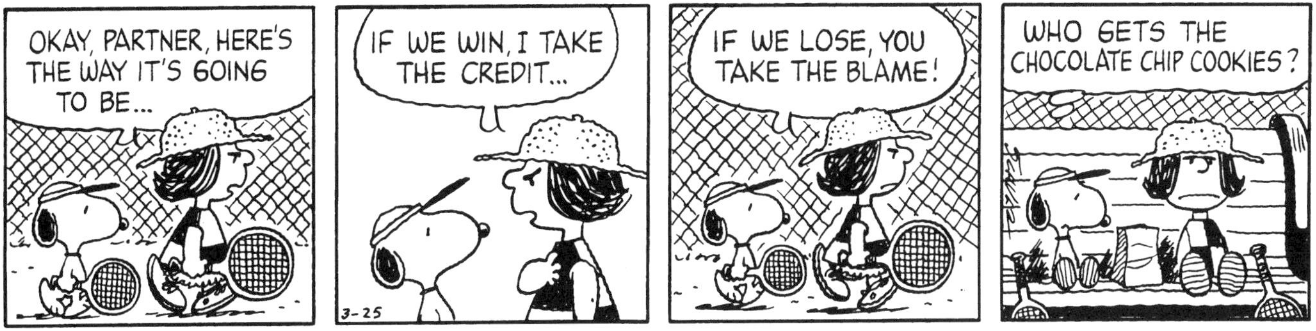
OKAY, PARTNER, HERE'S THE WAY IT'S GOING TO BE...
IF WE WIN, I TAKE THE CREDIT...
IF WE LOSE, YOU TAKE THE BLAME!
WHO GETS THE CHOCOLATE CHIP COOKIES?
SCHULZ
3-25

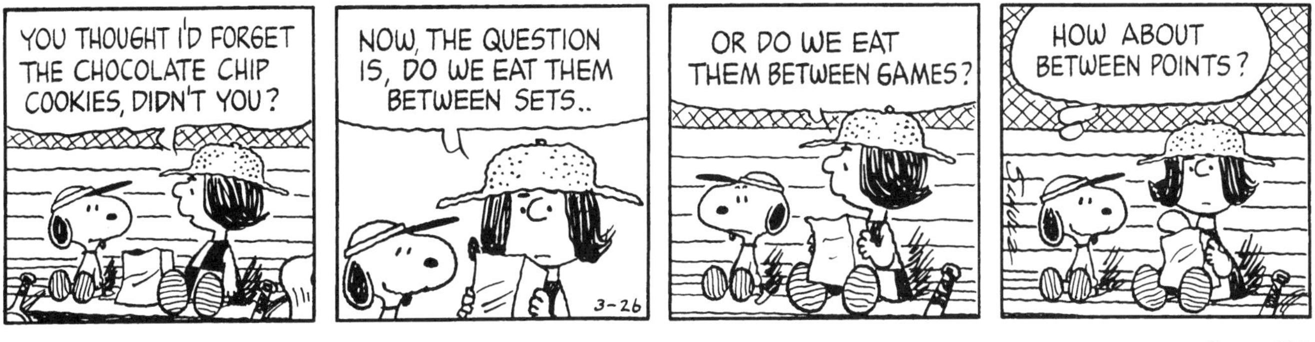
YOU THOUGHT I'D FORGET THE CHOCOLATE CHIP COOKIES, DIDN'T YOU?
NOW, THE QUESTION IS, DO WE EAT THEM BETWEEN SETS..
OR DO WE EAT THEM BETWEEN GAMES?
HOW ABOUT BETWEEN POINTS?
SCHULZ
3-26

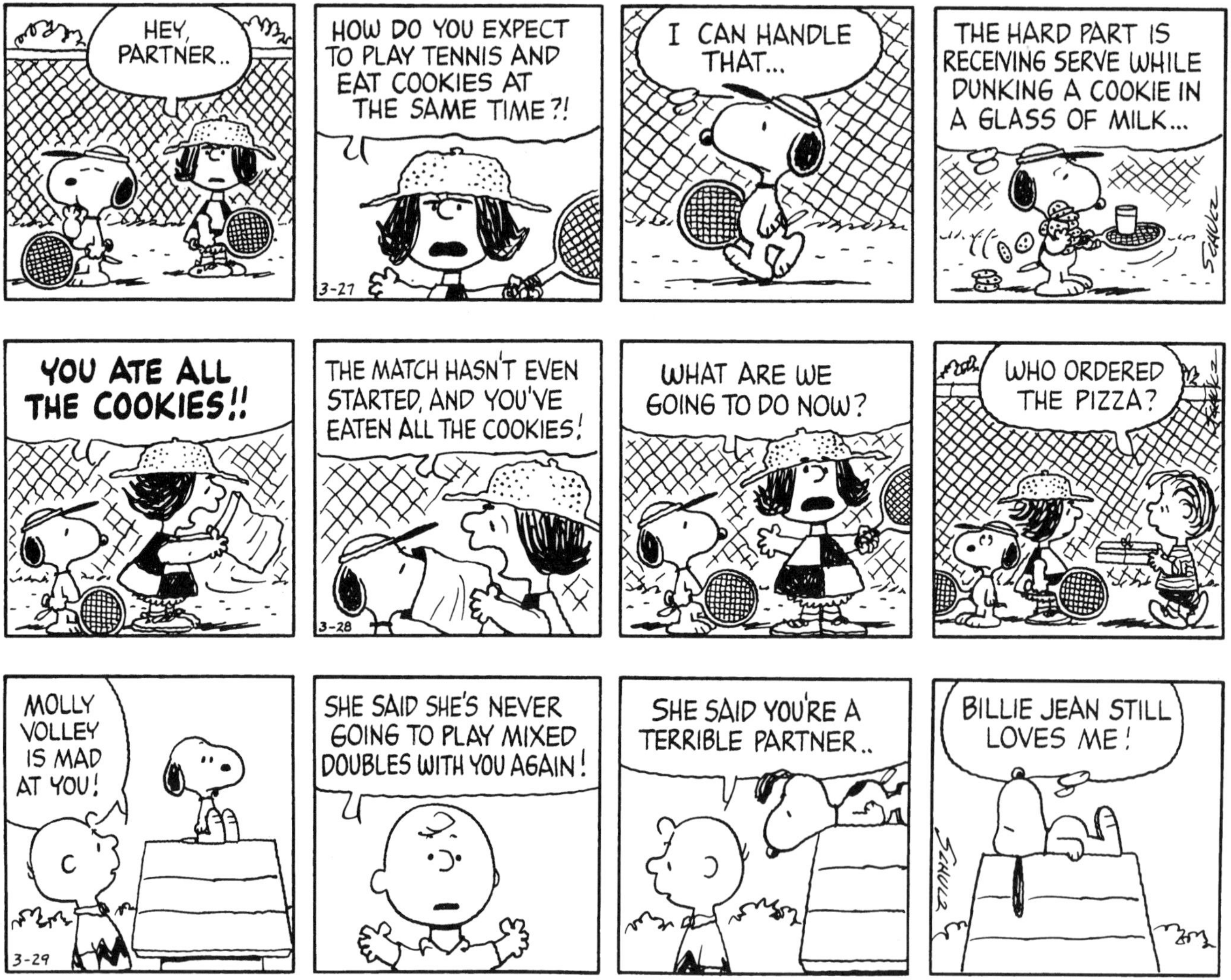
HEY, PARTNER..
HOW DO YOU EXPECT TO PLAY TENNIS AND EAT COOKIES AT THE SAME TIME?!
3-27
I CAN HANDLE THAT...
THE HARD PART IS RECEIVING SERVE WHILE DUNKING A COOKIE IN A GLASS OF MILK...
SCHULZ
YOU ATE ALL THE COOKIES!!
THE MATCH HASN'T EVEN STARTED, AND YOU'VE EATEN ALL THE COOKIES!
3-28
WHAT ARE WE GOING TO DO NOW?
WHO ORDERED THE PIZZA?
SCHULZ
MOLLY VOLLEY IS MAD AT YOU!
3-29
SHE SAID SHE'S NEVER GOING TO PLAY MIXED DOUBLES WITH YOU AGAIN!
SHE SAID YOU'RE A TERRIBLE PARTNER..
SCHULZ
BILLIE JEAN STILL LOVES ME!

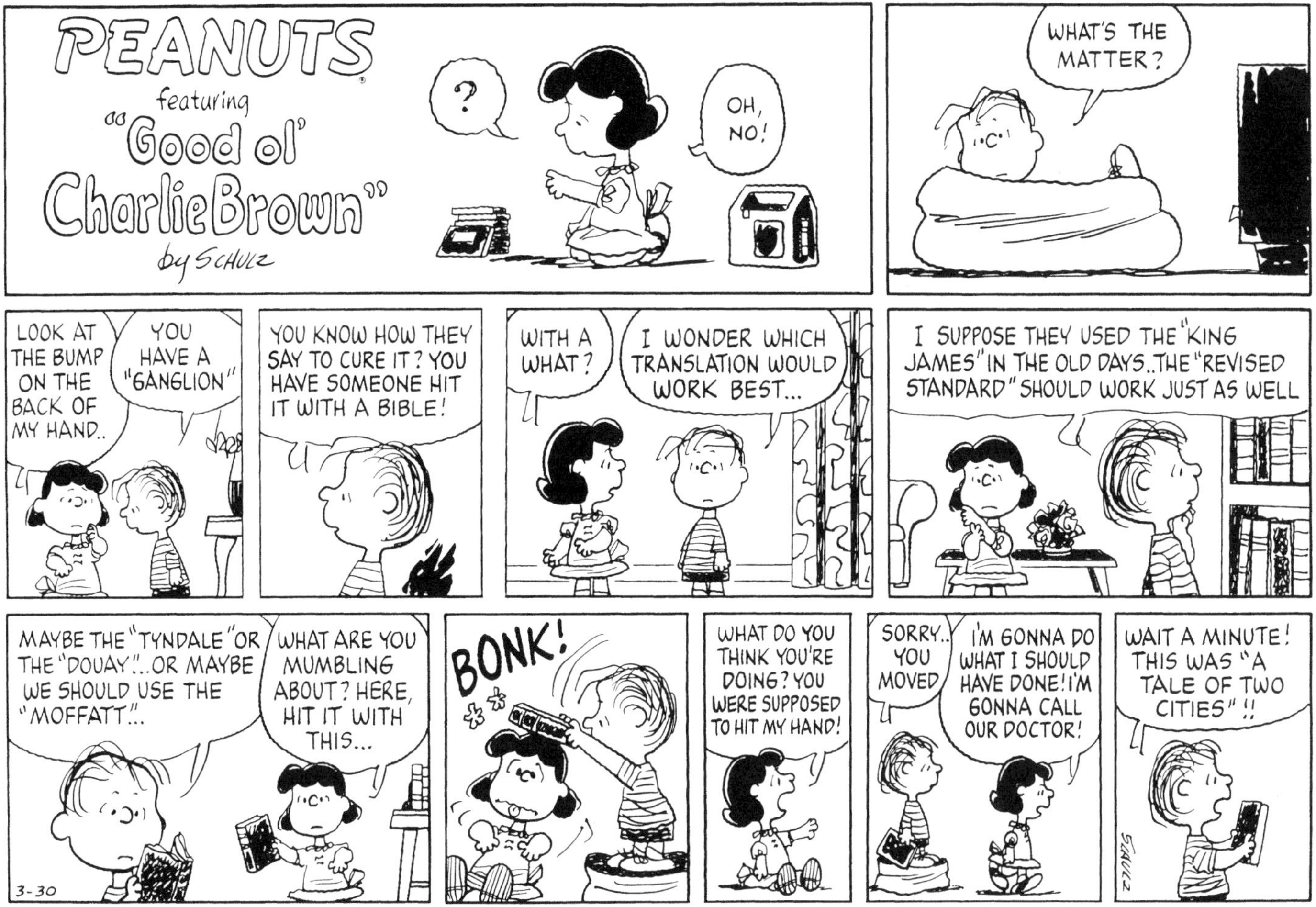
PEANUTS
featuring "Good ol' Charlie Brown"
by SCHULZ
?
OH, NO!
WHAT'S THE MATTER?
LOOK AT THE BUMP ON THE BACK OF MY HAND..
YOU HAVE A "GANGLION"
YOU KNOW HOW THEY SAY TO CURE IT? YOU HAVE SOMEONE HIT IT WITH A BIBLE!
WITH A WHAT?
I WONDER WHICH TRANSLATION WOULD WORK BEST...
I SUPPOSE THEY USED THE "KING JAMES" IN THE OLD DAYS..THE "REVISED STANDARD" SHOULD WORK JUST AS WELL
MAYBE THE "TYNDALE" OR THE "DOUAY"...OR MAYBE WE SHOULD USE THE "MOFFATT"...
WHAT ARE YOU MUMBLING ABOUT? HERE, HIT IT WITH THIS...
3-30
BONK!
WHAT DO YOU THINK YOU'RE DOING? YOU WERE SUPPOSED TO HIT MY HAND!
SORRY.. YOU MOVED
I'M GONNA DO WHAT I SHOULD HAVE DONE! I'M GONNA CALL OUR DOCTOR!
WAIT A MINUTE! THIS WAS "A TALE OF TWO CITIES" !!
SCHULZ

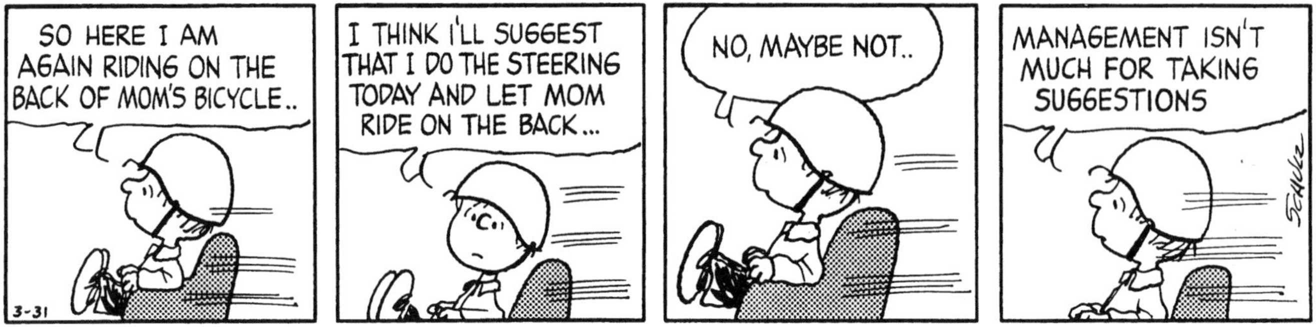
SO HERE I AM AGAIN RIDING ON THE BACK OF MOM'S BICYCLE..
3-31
I THINK I'LL SUGGEST THAT I DO THE STEERING TODAY AND LET MOM RIDE ON THE BACK...
NO, MAYBE NOT..
MANAGEMENT ISN'T MUCH FOR TAKING SUGGESTIONS

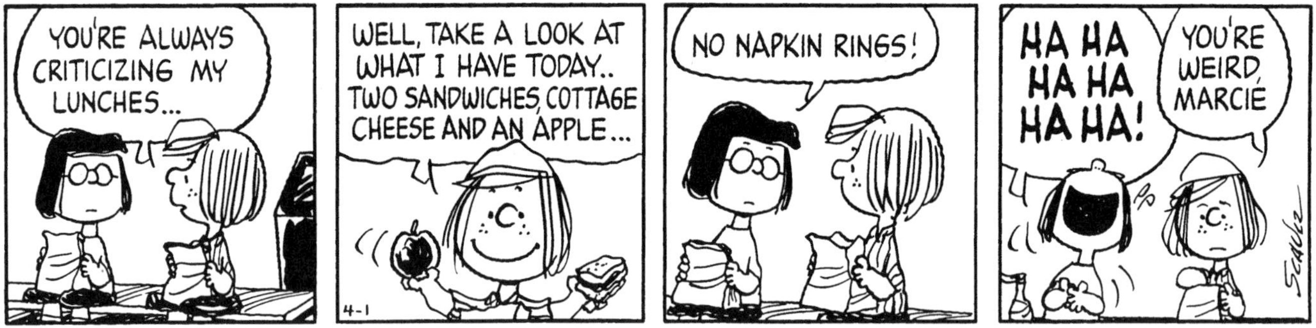
YOU'RE ALWAYS CRITICIZING MY LUNCHES...
WELL, TAKE A LOOK AT WHAT I HAVE TODAY.. TWO SANDWICHES, COTTAGE CHEESE AND AN APPLE...
4-1
NO NAPKIN RINGS!
HA HA HA HA HA HA!
YOU'RE WEIRD, MARCIE

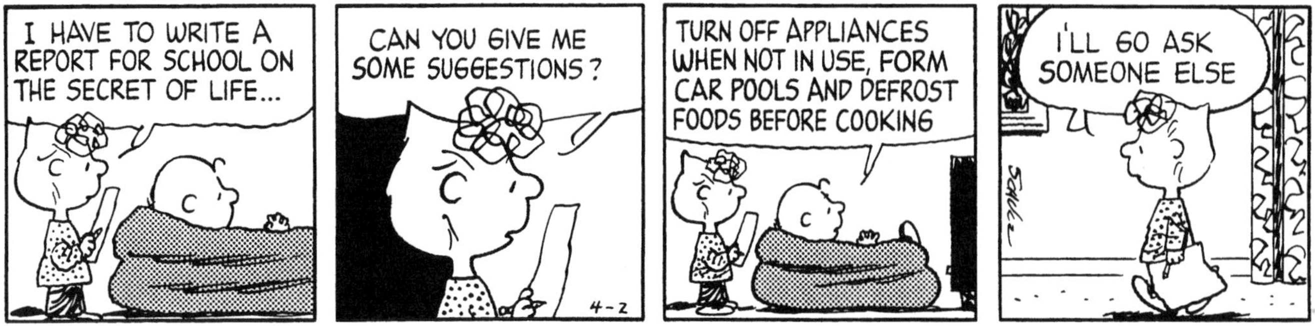
I HAVE TO WRITE A REPORT FOR SCHOOL ON THE SECRET OF LIFE...
CAN YOU GIVE ME SOME SUGGESTIONS?
4-2
TURN OFF APPLIANCES WHEN NOT IN USE, FORM CAR POOLS AND DEFROST FOODS BEFORE COOKING
I'LL GO ASK SOMEONE ELSE

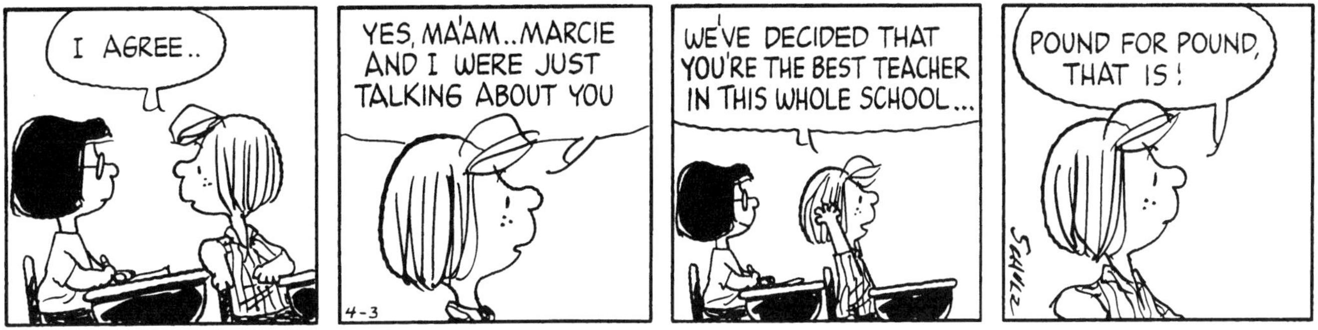
I AGREE..
YES, MA'AM..MARCIE AND I WERE JUST TALKING ABOUT YOU
4-3
WE'VE DECIDED THAT YOU'RE THE BEST TEACHER IN THIS WHOLE SCHOOL...
POUND FOR POUND, THAT IS!
SCHULZ

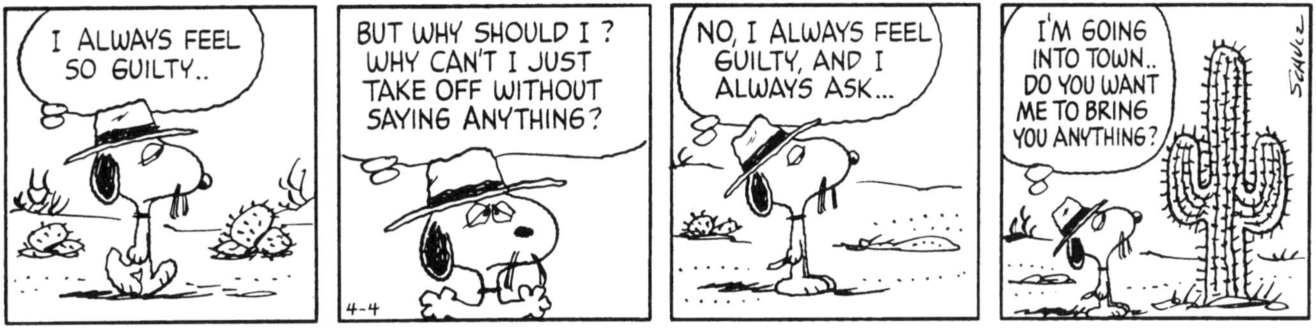
I ALWAYS FEEL SO GUILTY..
BUT WHY SHOULD I ? WHY CAN'T I JUST TAKE OFF WITHOUT SAYING ANYTHING?
4-4
NO, I ALWAYS FEEL GUILTY, AND I ALWAYS ASK...
I'M GOING INTO TOWN.. DO YOU WANT ME TO BRING YOU ANYTHING?
SCHULZ

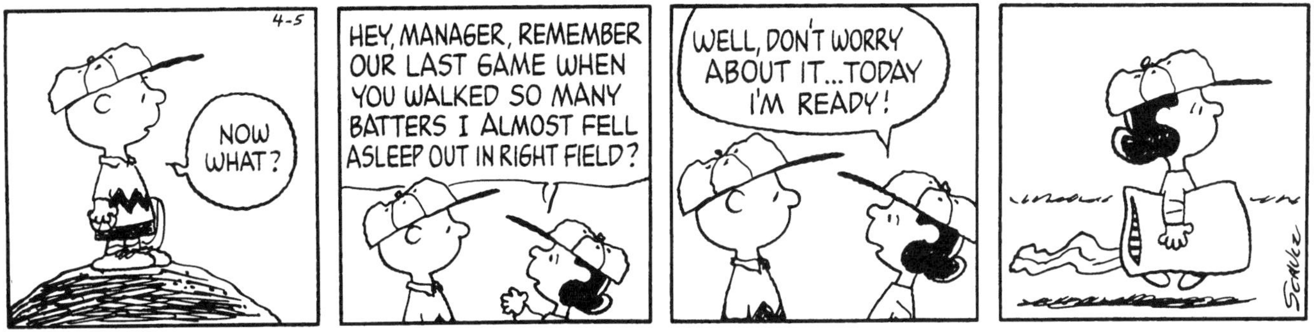
4-5
NOW WHAT?
HEY, MANAGER, REMEMBER OUR LAST GAME WHEN YOU WALKED SO MANY BATTERS I ALMOST FELL ASLEEP OUT IN RIGHT FIELD?
WELL, DON'T WORRY ABOUT IT...TODAY I'M READY!
SCHULZ

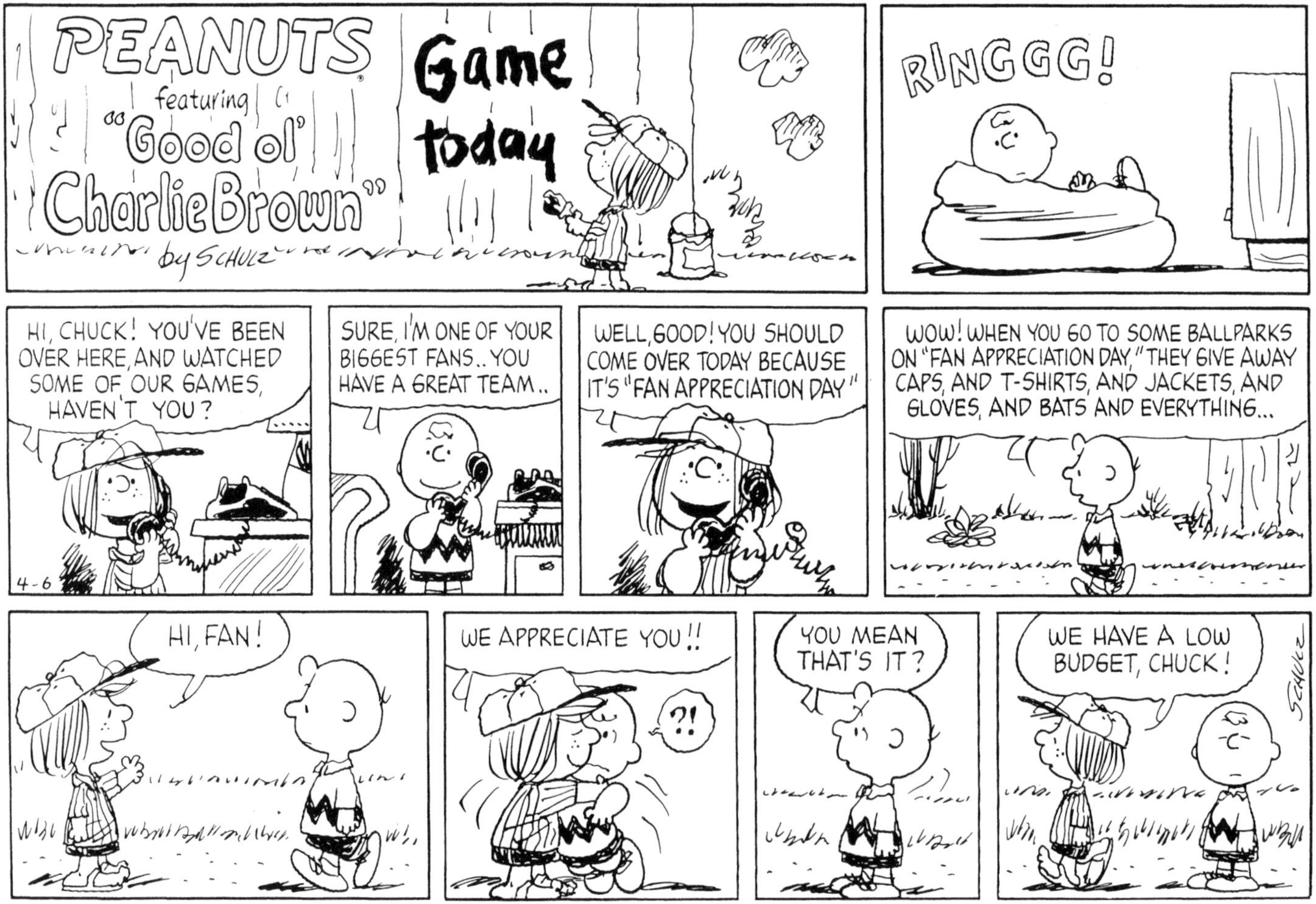
PEANUTS
featuring "Good ol' Charlie Brown"
by SCHULZ
Game today
RINGGG!
HI, CHUCK! YOU'VE BEEN OVER HERE, AND WATCHED SOME OF OUR GAMES, HAVEN'T YOU?
4-6
SURE, I'M ONE OF YOUR BIGGEST FANS.. YOU HAVE A GREAT TEAM..
WELL, GOOD! YOU SHOULD COME OVER TODAY BECAUSE IT'S "FAN APPRECIATION DAY"
WOW! WHEN YOU GO TO SOME BALLPARKS ON "FAN APPRECIATION DAY," THEY GIVE AWAY CAPS, AND T-SHIRTS, AND JACKETS, AND GLOVES, AND BATS AND EVERYTHING...
HI, FAN!
WE APPRECIATE YOU!!
?!
YOU MEAN THAT'S IT?
WE HAVE A LOW BUDGET, CHUCK!
SCHULZ

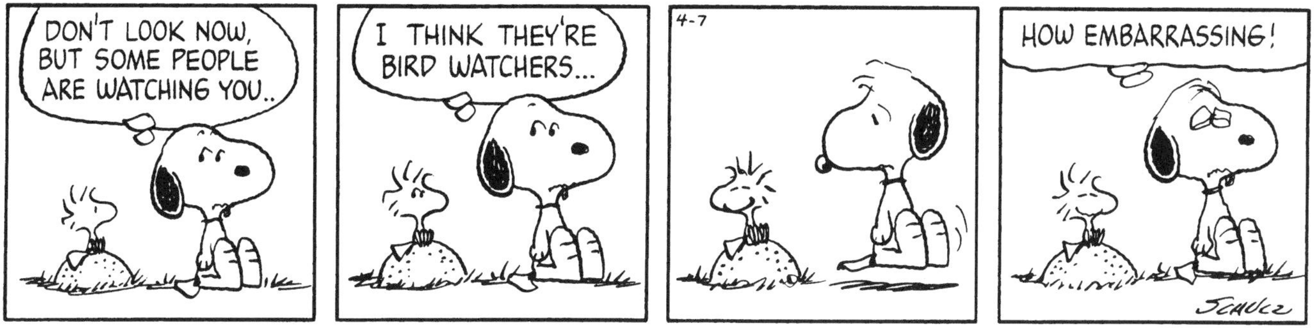
DON'T LOOK NOW, BUT SOME PEOPLE ARE WATCHING YOU..
I THINK THEY'RE BIRD WATCHERS...
4-7
HOW EMBARRASSING!

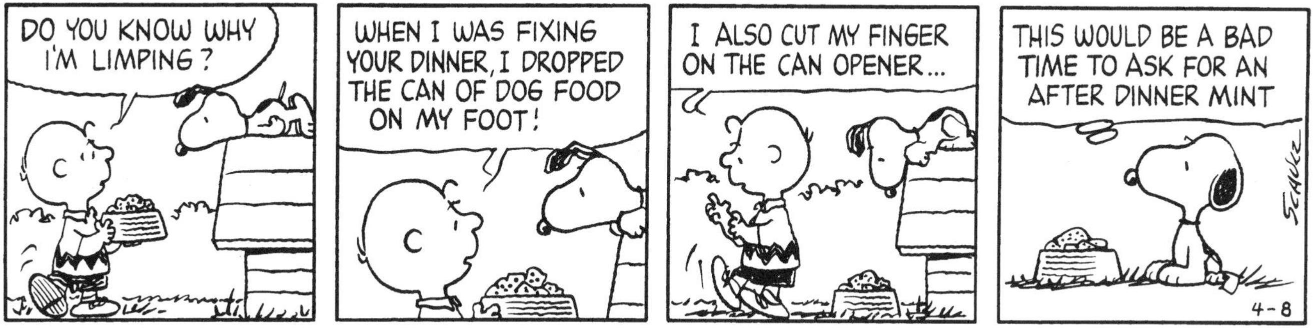
DO YOU KNOW WHY I'M LIMPING?
WHEN I WAS FIXING YOUR DINNER, I DROPPED THE CAN OF DOG FOOD ON MY FOOT!
I ALSO CUT MY FINGER ON THE CAN OPENER...
THIS WOULD BE A BAD TIME TO ASK FOR AN AFTER DINNER MINT
4-8

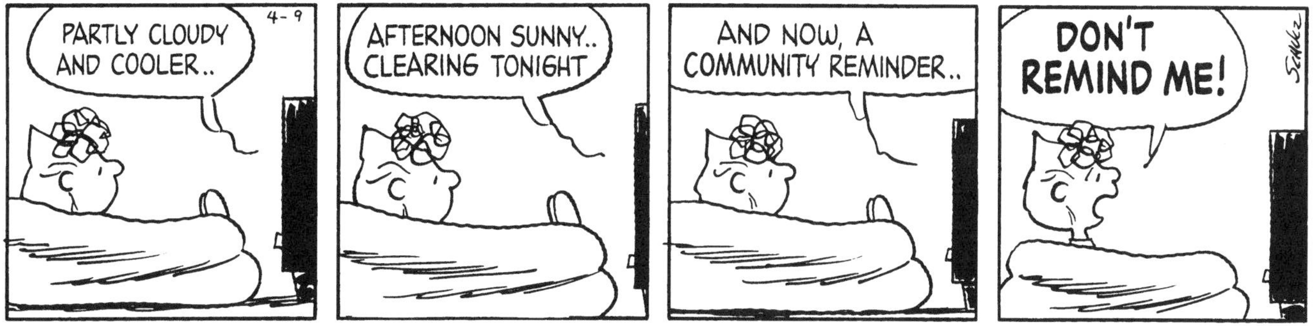
4-9
PARTLY CLOUDY AND COOLER..
AFTERNOON SUNNY.. CLEARING TONIGHT
AND NOW, A COMMUNITY REMINDER..
DON'T REMIND ME!

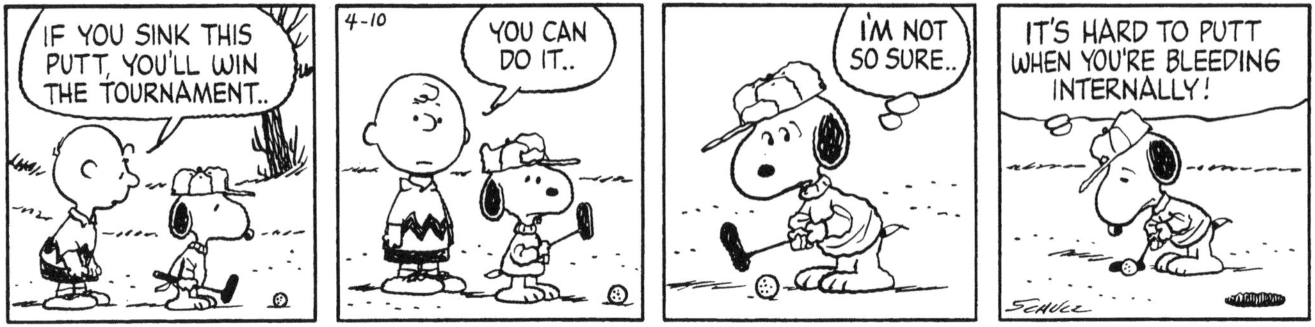
4-10
IF YOU SINK THIS PUTT, YOU'LL WIN THE TOURNAMENT..
YOU CAN DO IT..
I'M NOT SO SURE..
IT'S HARD TO PUTT WHEN YOU'RE BLEEDING INTERNALLY!
SCHULZ

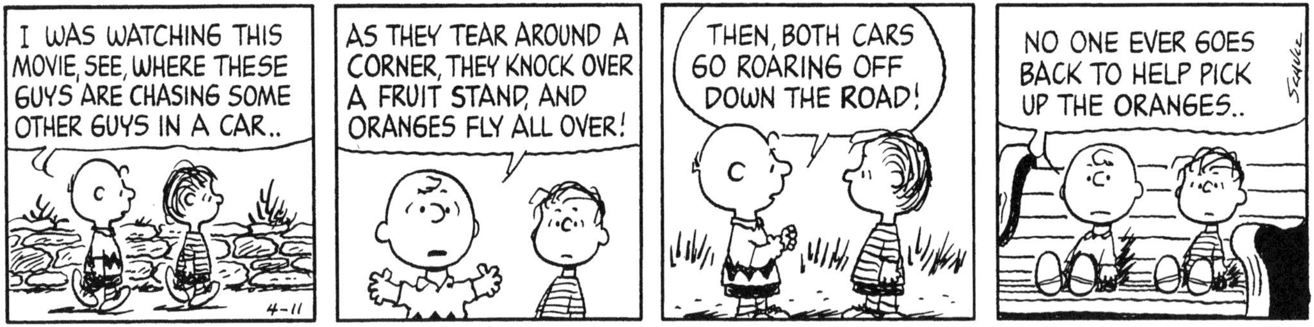
I WAS WATCHING THIS MOVIE, SEE, WHERE THESE GUYS ARE CHASING SOME OTHER GUYS IN A CAR..
4-11
AS THEY TEAR AROUND A CORNER, THEY KNOCK OVER A FRUIT STAND, AND ORANGES FLY ALL OVER!
THEN, BOTH CARS GO ROARING OFF DOWN THE ROAD!
NO ONE EVER GOES BACK TO HELP PICK UP THE ORANGES..
SCHULZ

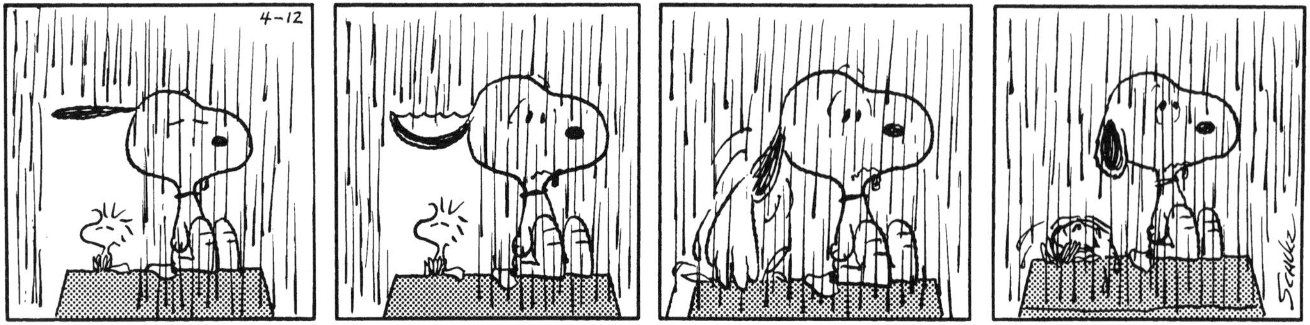
4-12
SCHULZ

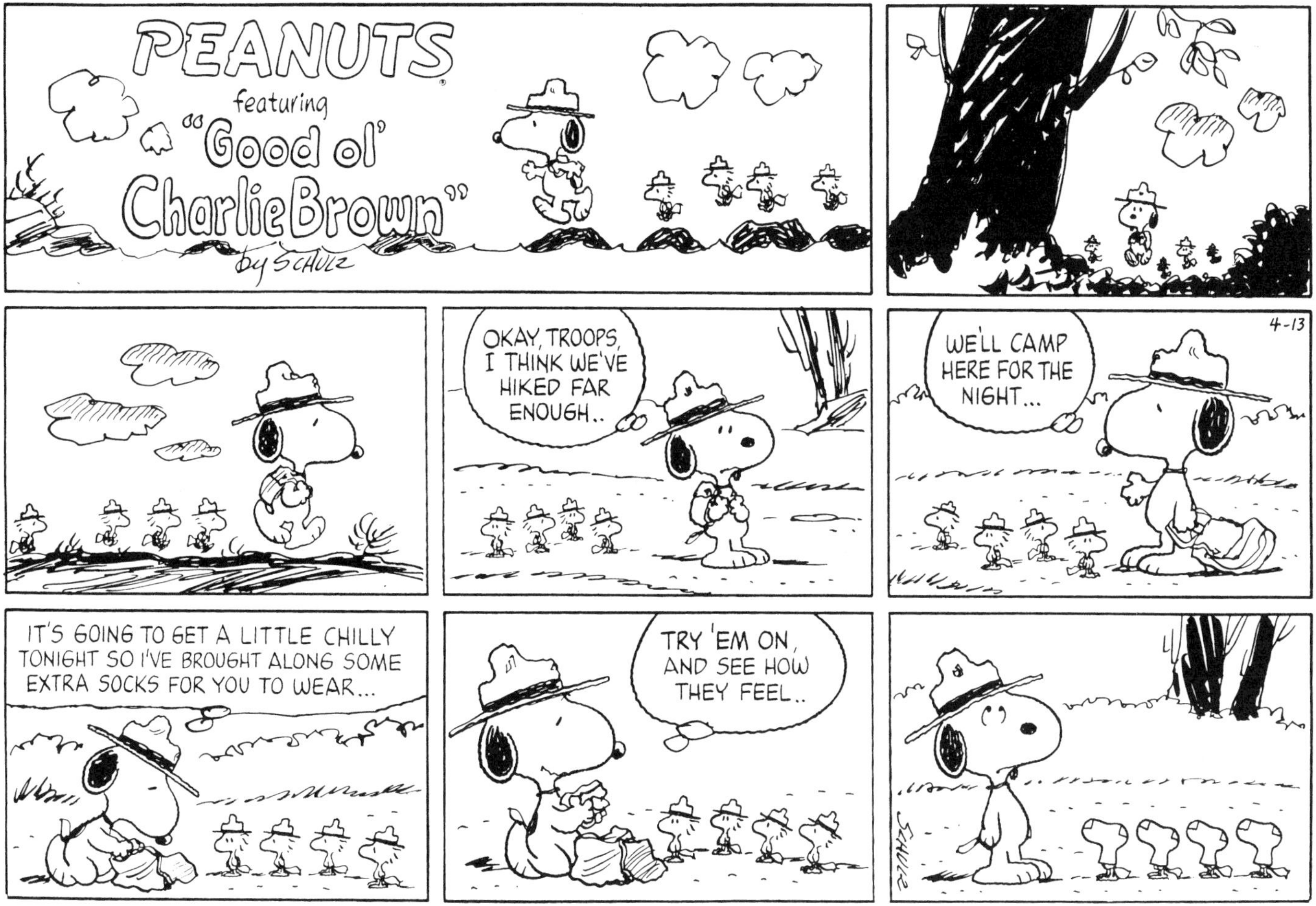
PEANUTS
featuring "Good ol' Charlie Brown"
by SCHULZ
OKAY, TROOPS, I THINK WE'VE HIKED FAR ENOUGH..
4-13
WE'LL CAMP HERE FOR THE NIGHT...
IT'S GOING TO GET A LITTLE CHILLY TONIGHT SO I'VE BROUGHT ALONG SOME EXTRA SOCKS FOR YOU TO WEAR...
TRY 'EM ON, AND SEE HOW THEY FEEL..
SCHULZ

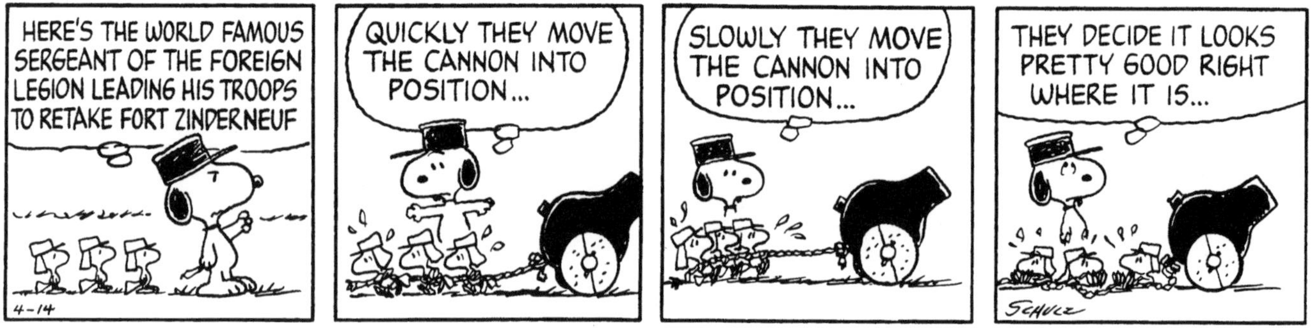
HERE'S THE WORLD FAMOUS SERGEANT OF THE FOREIGN LEGION LEADING HIS TROOPS TO RETAKE FORT ZINDERNEUF
4-14
QUICKLY THEY MOVE THE CANNON INTO POSITION...
SLOWLY THEY MOVE THE CANNON INTO POSITION...
THEY DECIDE IT LOOKS PRETTY GOOD RIGHT WHERE IT IS...

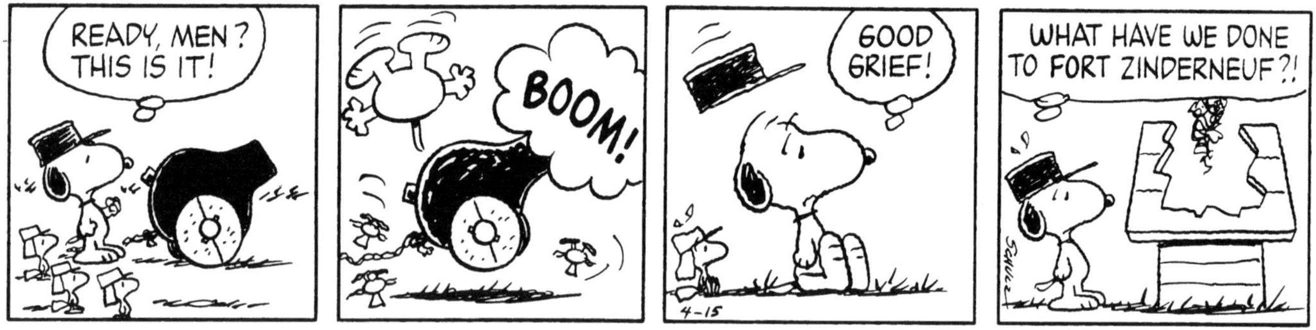
READY, MEN? THIS IS IT!
BOOM!
GOOD GRIEF!
4-15
WHAT HAVE WE DONE TO FORT ZINDERNEUF?!

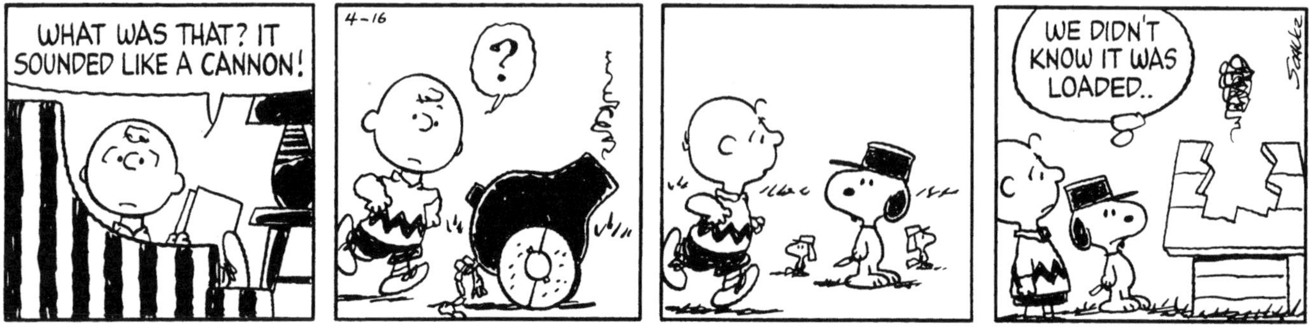
WHAT WAS THAT? IT SOUNDED LIKE A CANNON!
4-16
?
WE DIDN'T KNOW IT WAS LOADED..

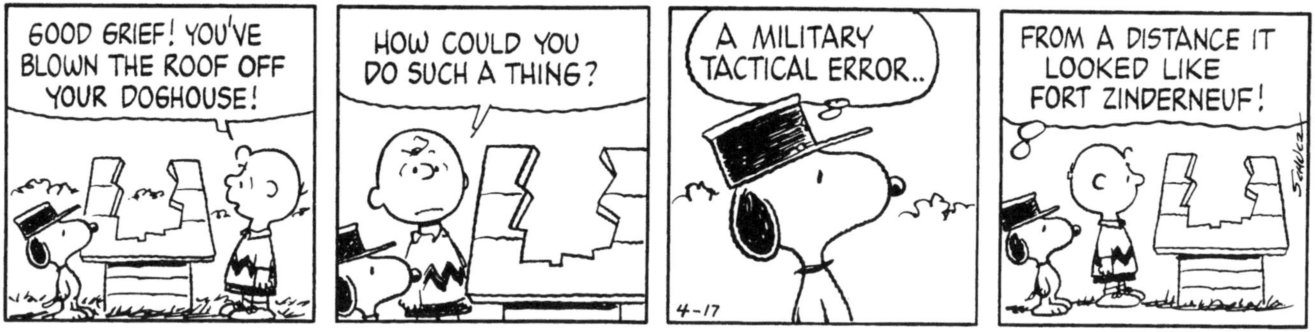
GOOD GRIEF! YOU'VE BLOWN THE ROOF OFF YOUR DOGHOUSE!
HOW COULD YOU DO SUCH A THING?
A MILITARY TACTICAL ERROR..
4-17
FROM A DISTANCE IT LOOKED LIKE FORT ZINDERNEUF!
SCHULZ

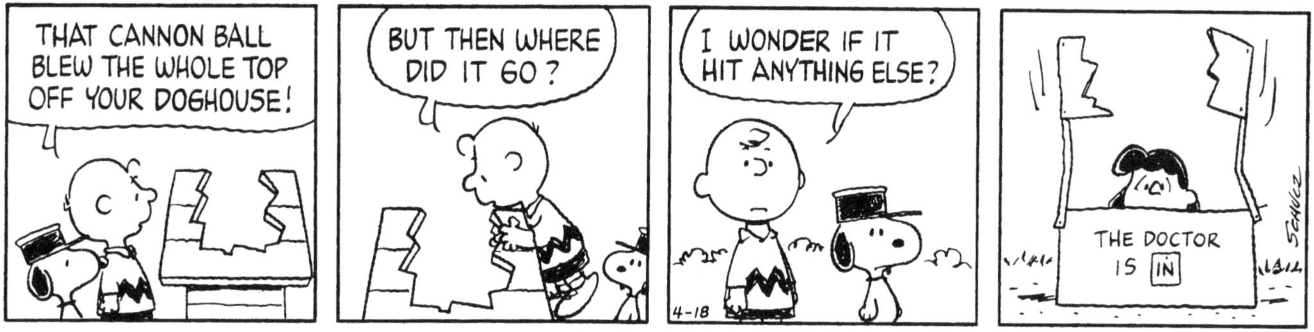
THAT CANNON BALL BLEW THE WHOLE TOP OFF YOUR DOGHOUSE!
BUT THEN WHERE DID IT GO?
I WONDER IF IT HIT ANYTHING ELSE?
4-18
THE DOCTOR IS IN
SCHULZ

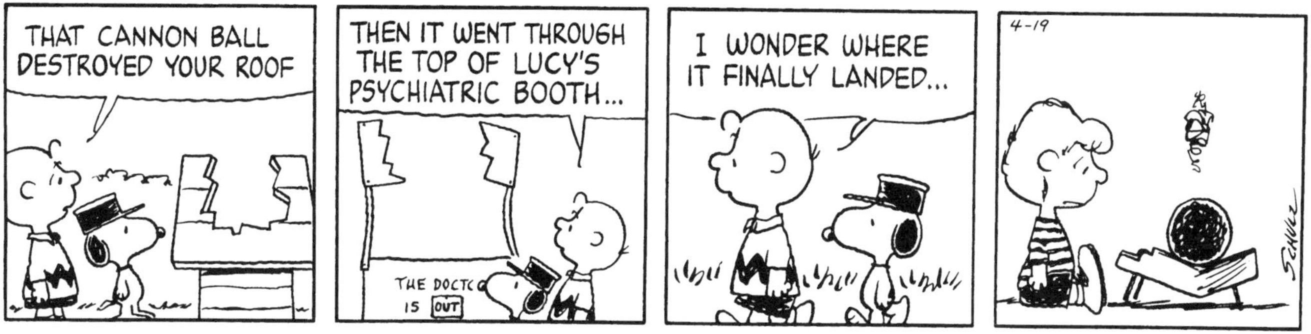
THAT CANNON BALL DESTROYED YOUR ROOF
THEN IT WENT THROUGH THE TOP OF LUCY'S PSYCHIATRIC BOOTH...
THE DOCTO
IS OUT
I WONDER WHERE IT FINALLY LANDED...
4-19
SCHULZ

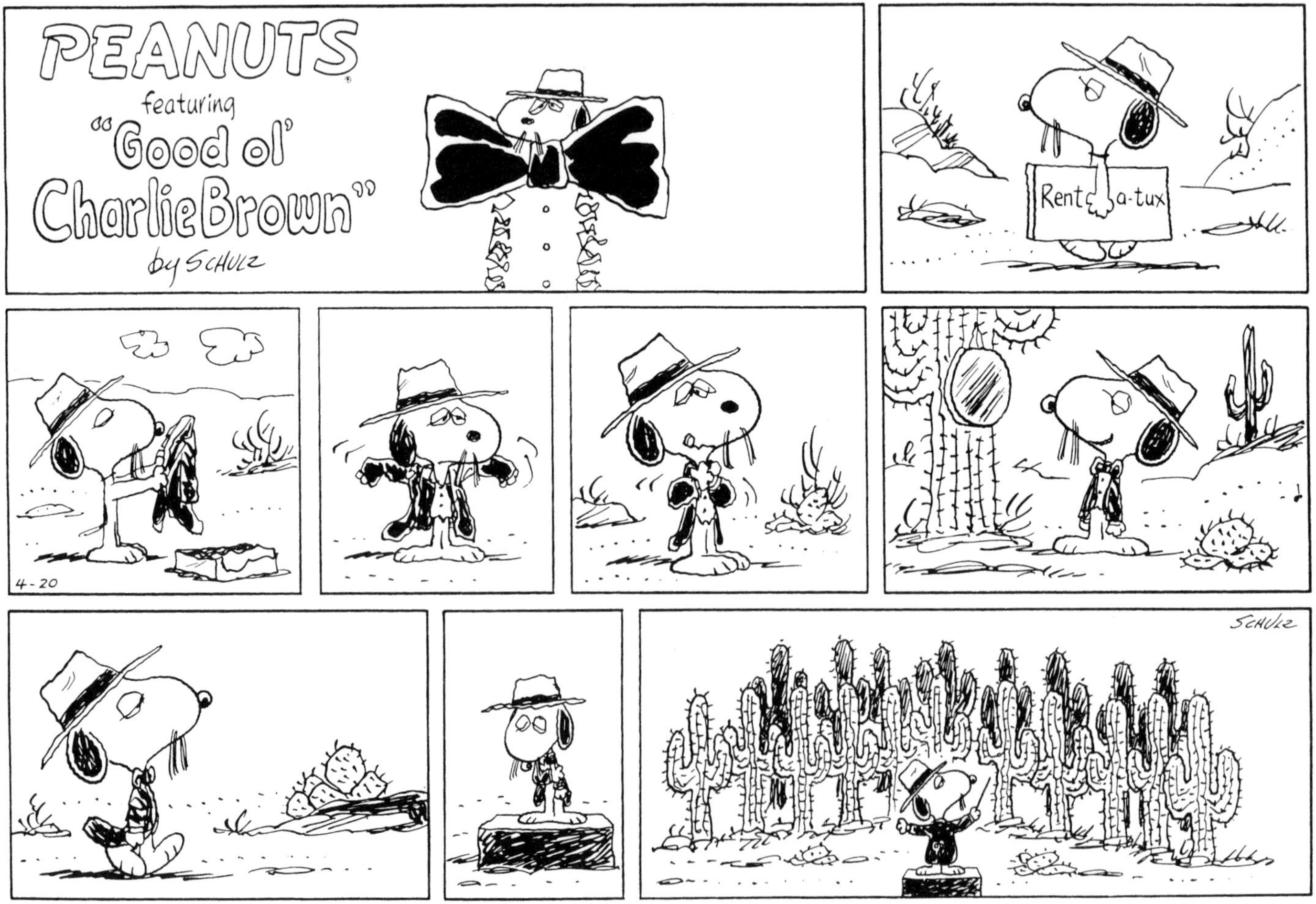
PEANUTS
featuring
"Good ol' Charlie Brown"
by SCHULZ
Rent-a-tux
4-20
SCHULZ

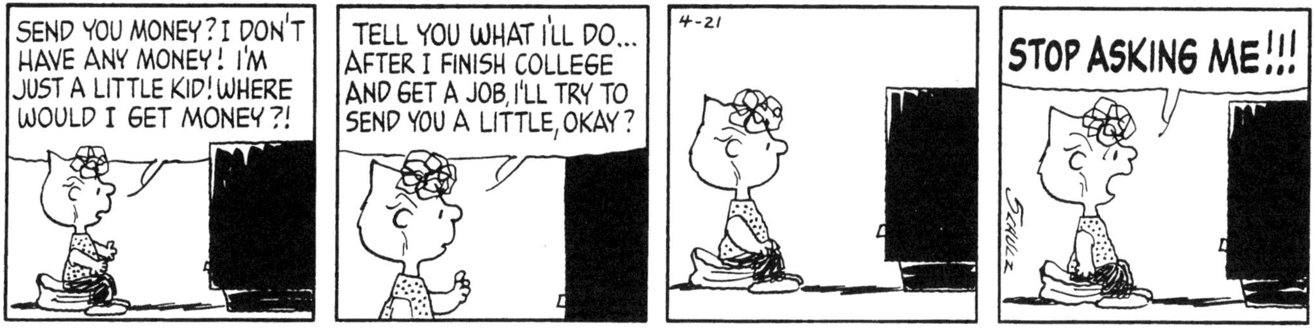
SEND YOU MONEY? I DON'T HAVE ANY MONEY! I'M JUST A LITTLE KID! WHERE WOULD I GET MONEY?!
TELL YOU WHAT I'LL DO... AFTER I FINISH COLLEGE AND GET A JOB, I'LL TRY TO SEND YOU A LITTLE, OKAY?
4-21
STOP ASKING ME!!!
SCHULZ

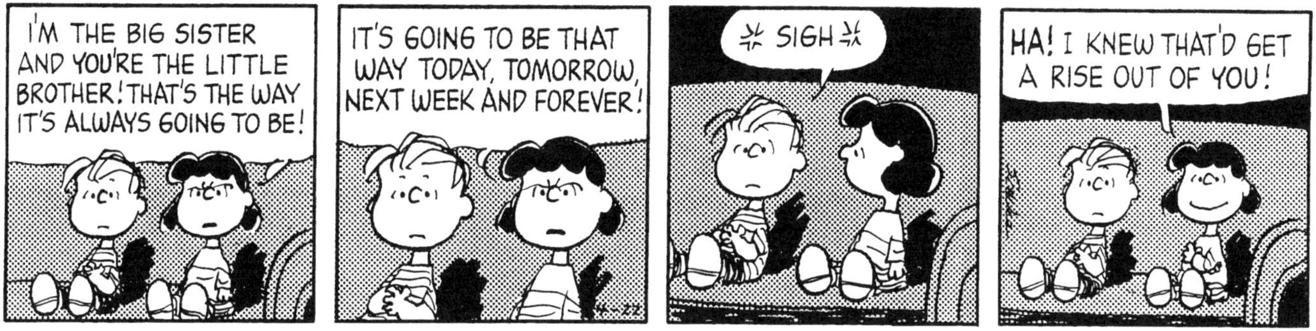
I'M THE BIG SISTER AND YOU'RE THE LITTLE BROTHER! THAT'S THE WAY IT'S ALWAYS GOING TO BE!
IT'S GOING TO BE THAT WAY TODAY, TOMORROW, NEXT WEEK AND FOREVER!
4-22
SIGH
HA! I KNEW THAT'D GET A RISE OUT OF YOU!

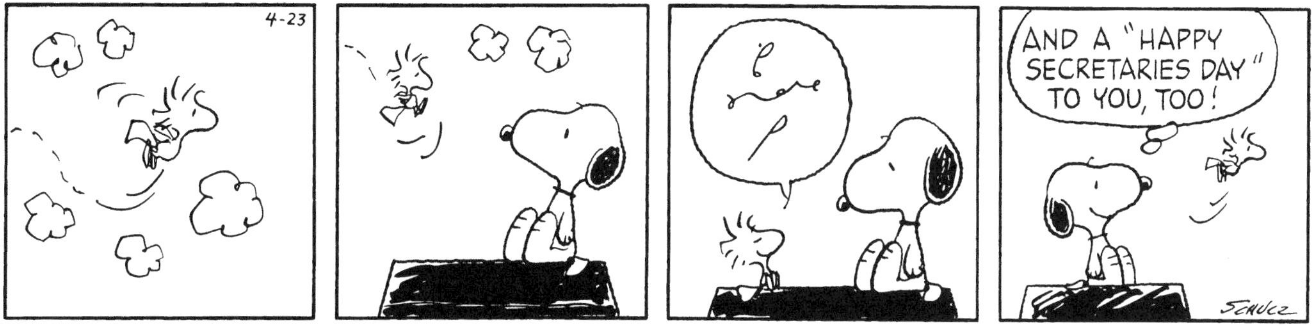
4-23
AND A "HAPPY SECRETARIES DAY" TO YOU, TOO!
SCHULZ

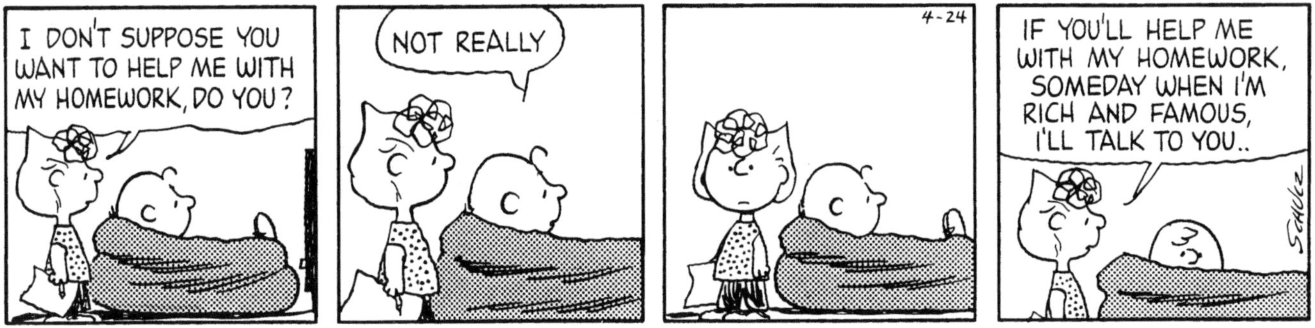
I DON'T SUPPOSE YOU WANT TO HELP ME WITH MY HOMEWORK, DO YOU?
NOT REALLY
4-24
IF YOU'LL HELP ME WITH MY HOMEWORK, SOMEDAY WHEN I'M RICH AND FAMOUS, I'LL TALK TO YOU..
SCHULZ

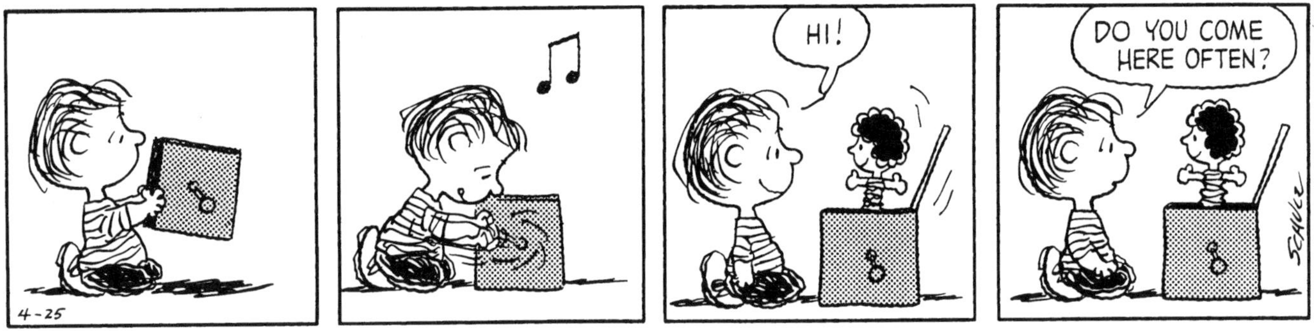
4-25
HI!
DO YOU COME HERE OFTEN?
SCHULZ

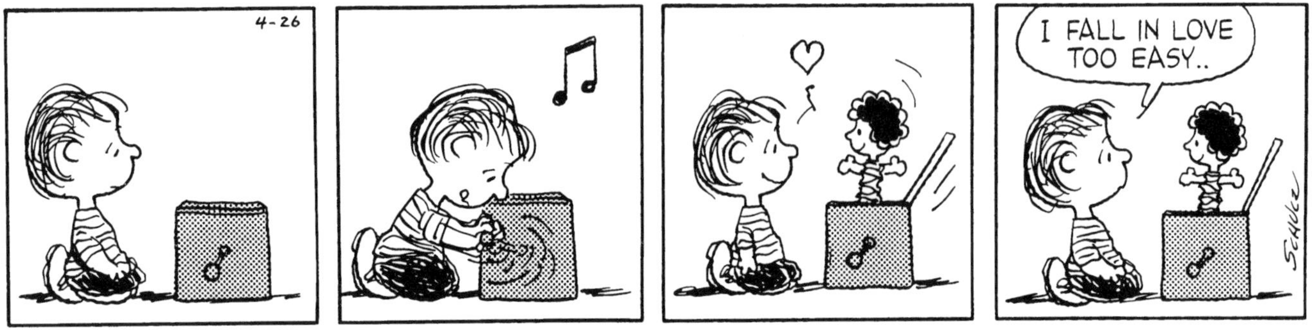
4-26
I FALL IN LOVE TOO EASY..
SCHULZ

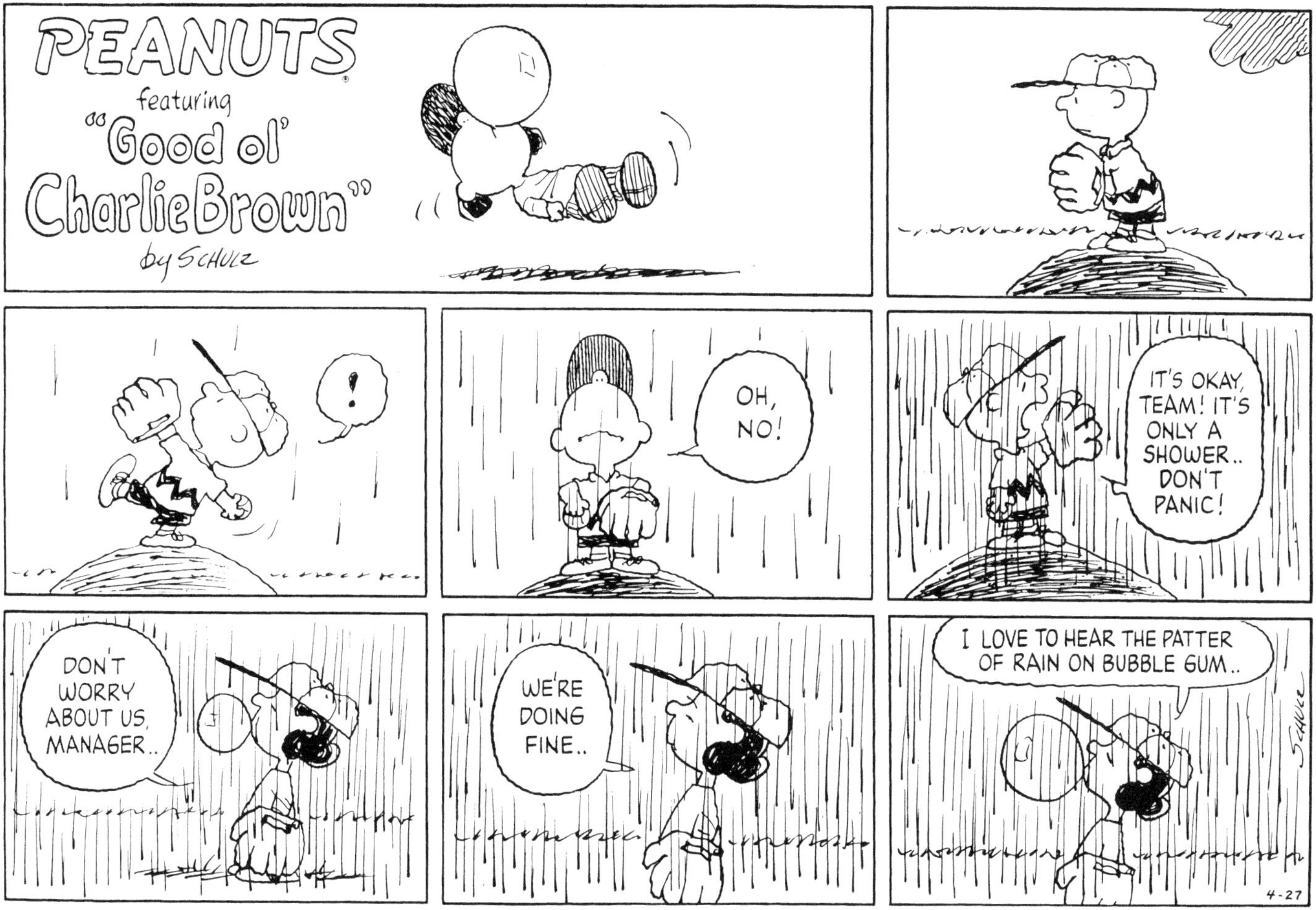
PEANUTS
featuring
"Good ol' CharlieBrown"
by SCHULZ
!
OH, NO!
IT'S OKAY, TEAM! IT'S ONLY A SHOWER.. DON'T PANIC!
DON'T WORRY ABOUT US, MANAGER..
WE'RE DOING FINE..
I LOVE TO HEAR THE PATTER OF RAIN ON BUBBLE GUM..
SCHULZ
4-27

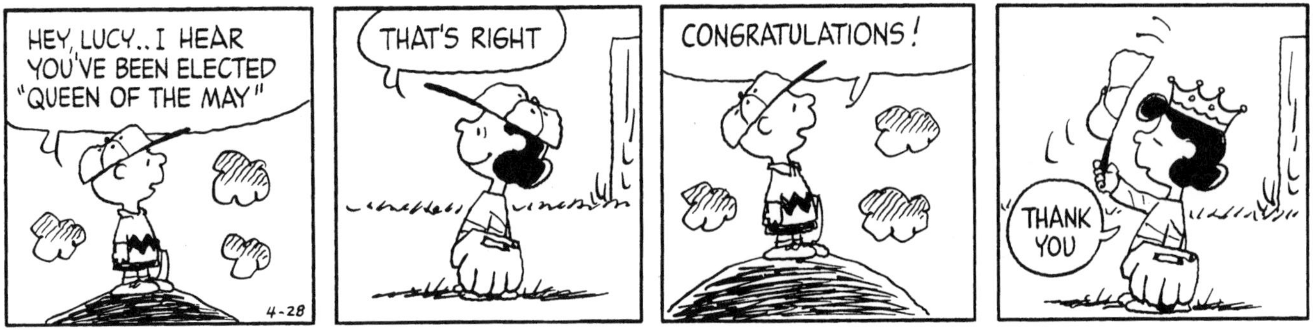
HEY, LUCY.. I HEAR YOU'VE BEEN ELECTED "QUEEN OF THE MAY"
4-28
THAT'S RIGHT
CONGRATULATIONS!
THANK YOU

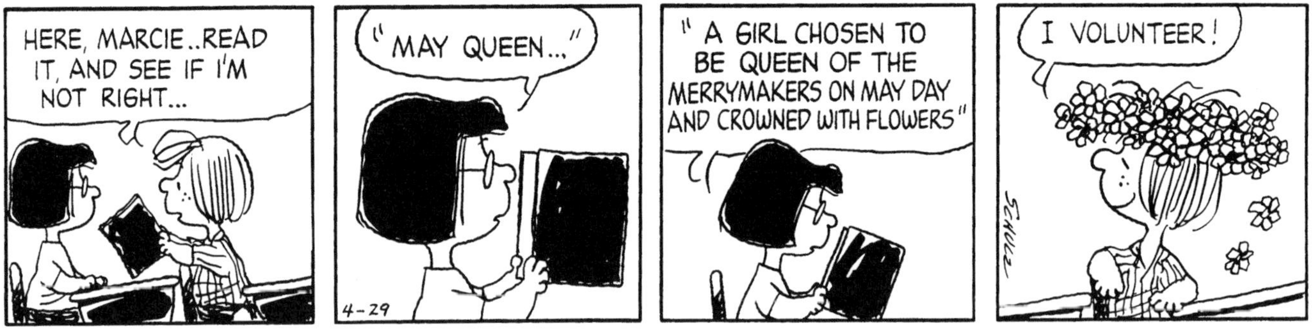
HERE, MARCIE..READ IT, AND SEE IF I'M NOT RIGHT...
"MAY QUEEN..."
4-29
" A GIRL CHOSEN TO BE QUEEN OF THE MERRYMAKERS ON MAY DAY AND CROWNED WITH FLOWERS"
I VOLUNTEER!
SCHULZ

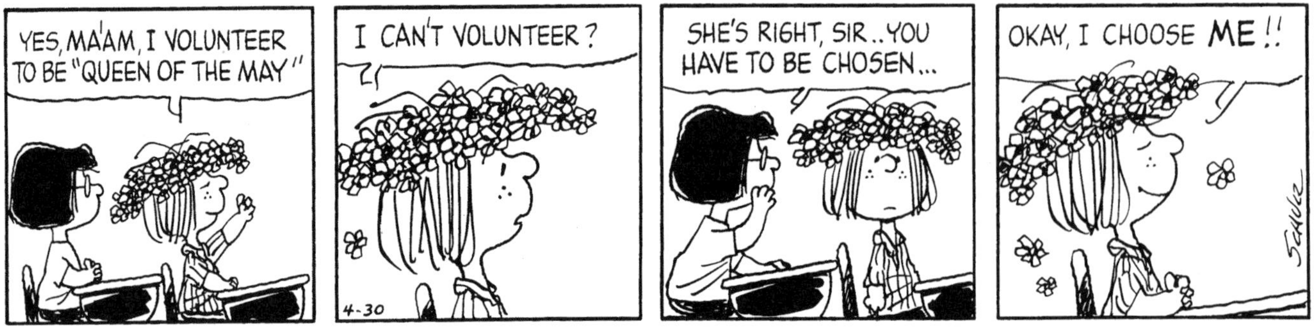
YES, MA'AM, I VOLUNTEER TO BE "QUEEN OF THE MAY"
I CAN'T VOLUNTEER?
4-30
SHE'S RIGHT, SIR..YOU HAVE TO BE CHOSEN...
OKAY, I CHOOSE ME!!
SCHULZ

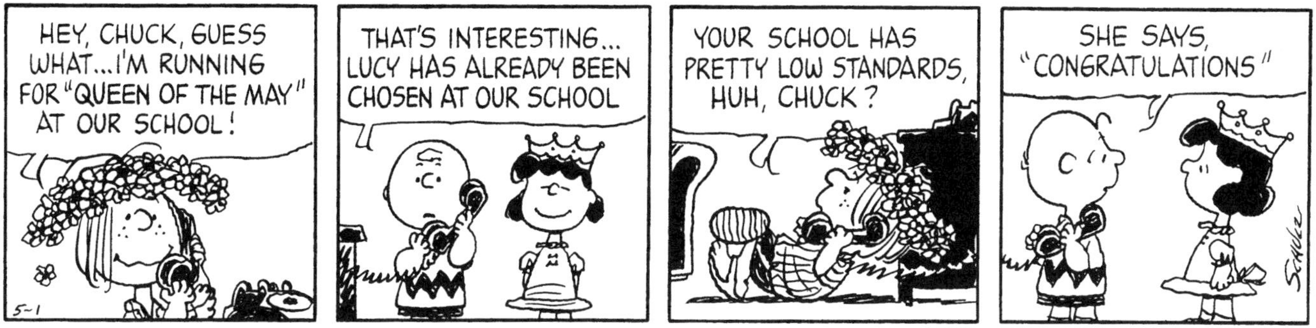
HEY, CHUCK, GUESS WHAT...I'M RUNNING FOR "QUEEN OF THE MAY" AT OUR SCHOOL!
5-1
THAT'S INTERESTING... LUCY HAS ALREADY BEEN CHOSEN AT OUR SCHOOL
YOUR SCHOOL HAS PRETTY LOW STANDARDS, HUH, CHUCK?
SHE SAYS, "CONGRATULATIONS"
SCHULZ

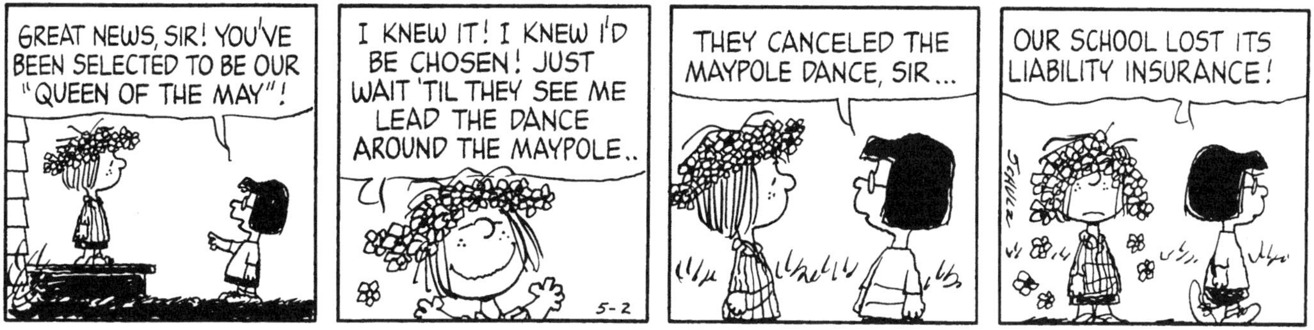
GREAT NEWS, SIR! YOU'VE BEEN SELECTED TO BE OUR "QUEEN OF THE MAY"!
I KNEW IT! I KNEW I'D BE CHOSEN! JUST WAIT 'TIL THEY SEE ME LEAD THE DANCE AROUND THE MAYPOLE..
5-2
THEY CANCELED THE MAYPOLE DANCE, SIR...
OUR SCHOOL LOST ITS LIABILITY INSURANCE!
SCHULZ

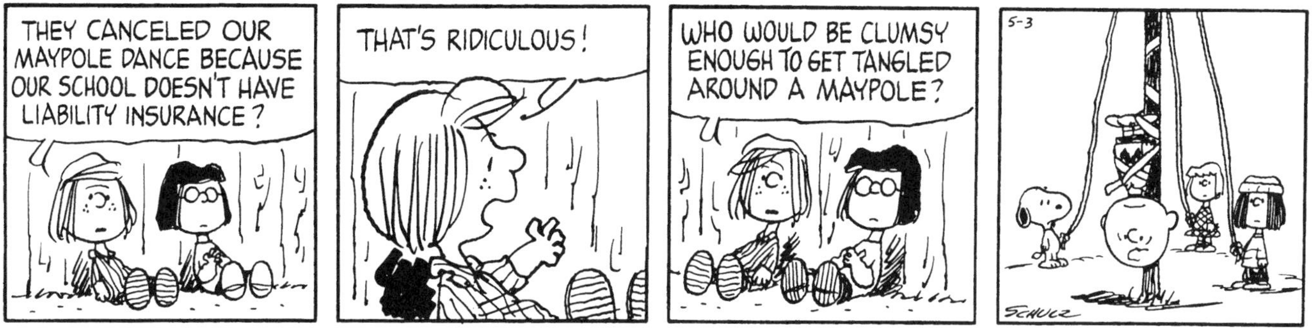
THEY CANCELED OUR MAYPOLE DANCE BECAUSE OUR SCHOOL DOESN'T HAVE LIABILITY INSURANCE?
THAT'S RIDICULOUS!
WHO WOULD BE CLUMSY ENOUGH TO GET TANGLED AROUND A MAYPOLE?
5-3
SCHULZ

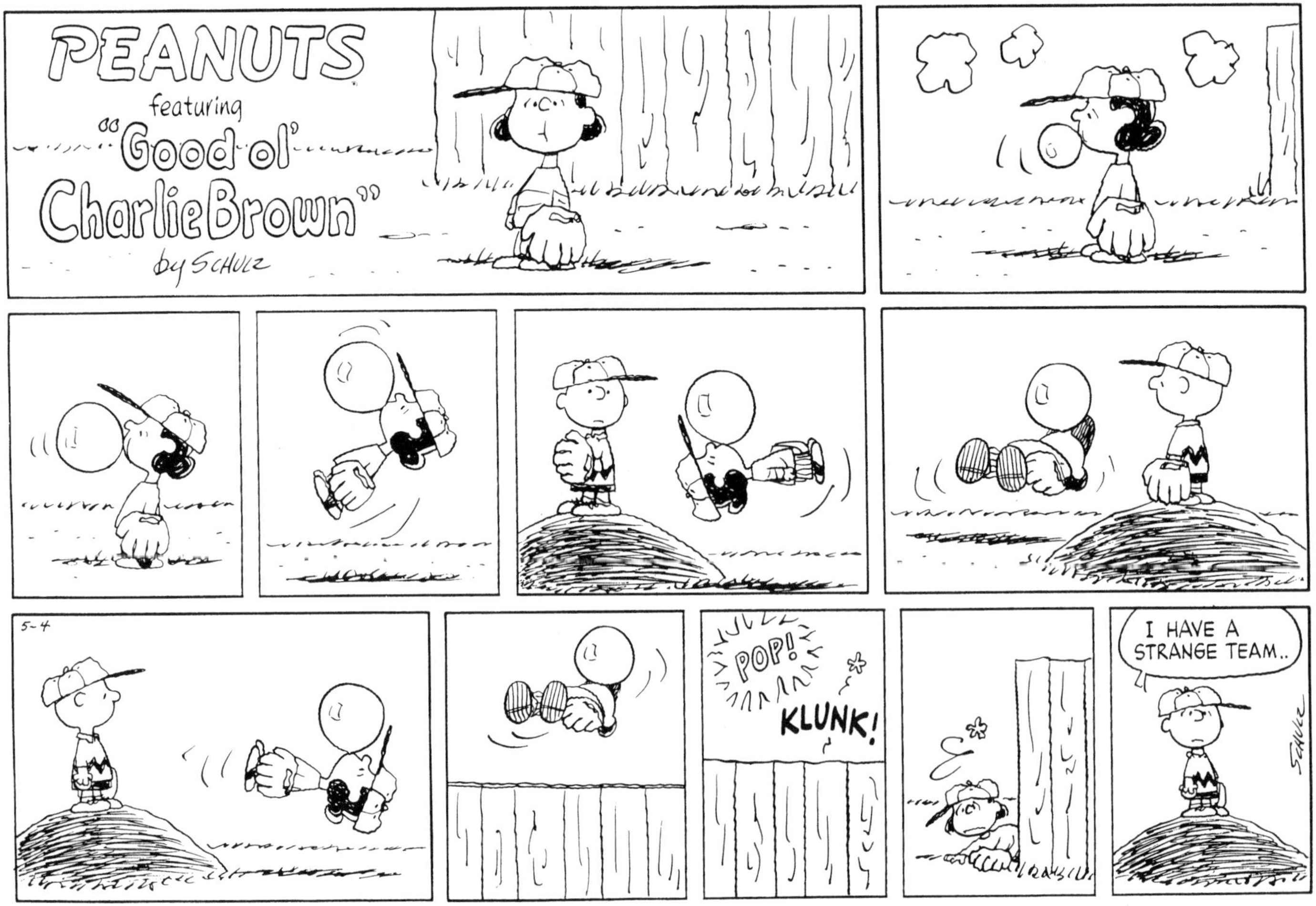
PEANUTS
featuring
"Good ol' Charlie Brown"
by SCHULZ
5-4
POP!
KLUNK!
I HAVE A STRANGE TEAM..
SCHULZ

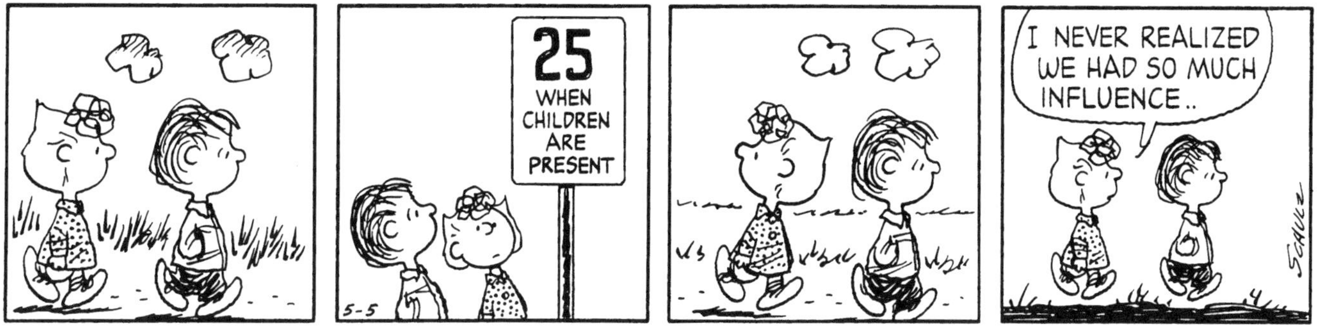
25 WHEN CHILDREN ARE PRESENT
5-5
I NEVER REALIZED WE HAD SO MUCH INFLUENCE..

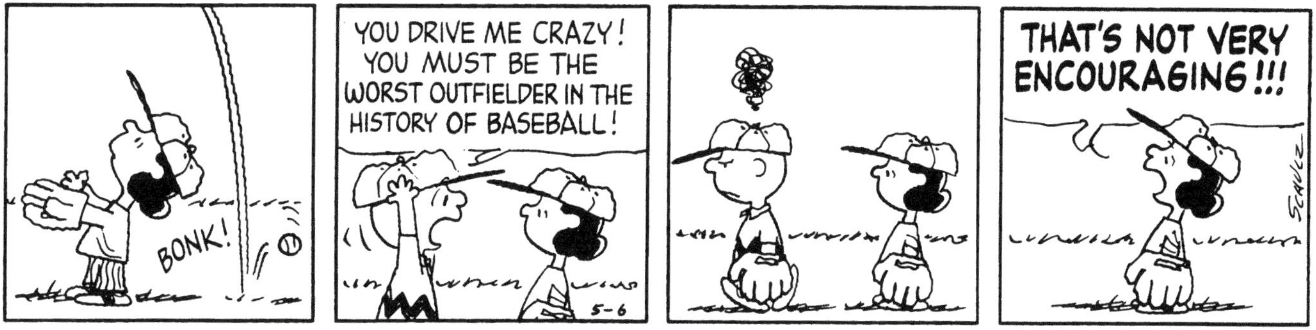
BONK!
YOU DRIVE ME CRAZY! YOU MUST BE THE WORST OUTFIELDER IN THE HISTORY OF BASEBALL!
5-6
THAT'S NOT VERY ENCOURAGING!!!

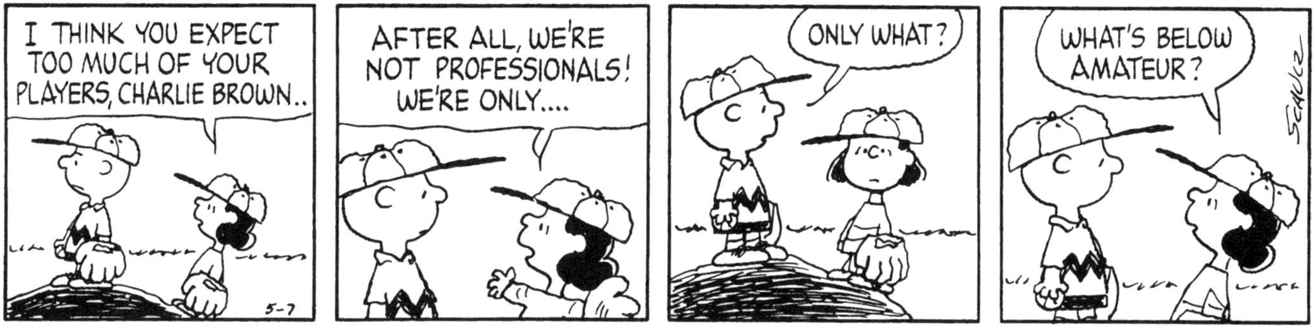
I THINK YOU EXPECT TOO MUCH OF YOUR PLAYERS, CHARLIE BROWN..
5-7
AFTER ALL, WE'RE NOT PROFESSIONALS! WE'RE ONLY....
ONLY WHAT?
WHAT'S BELOW AMATEUR?

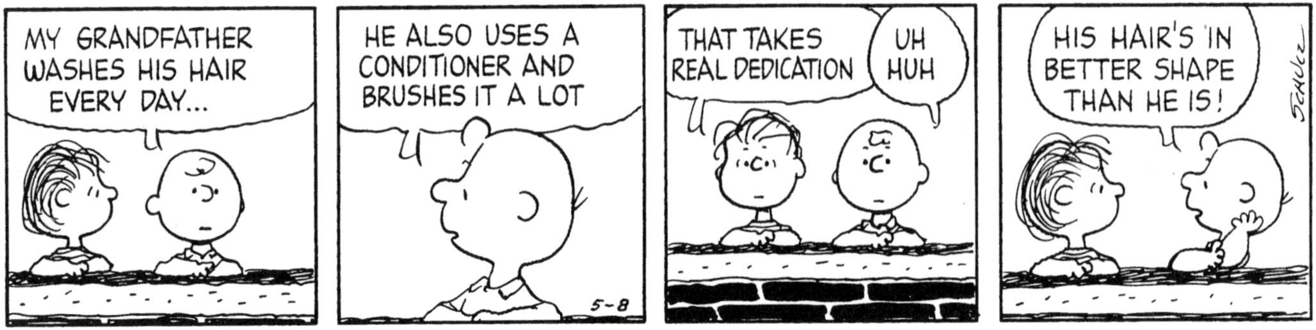
MY GRANDFATHER WASHES HIS HAIR EVERY DAY...
HE ALSO USES A CONDITIONER AND BRUSHES IT A LOT
THAT TAKES REAL DEDICATION
UH HUH
HIS HAIR'S IN BETTER SHAPE THAN HE IS!

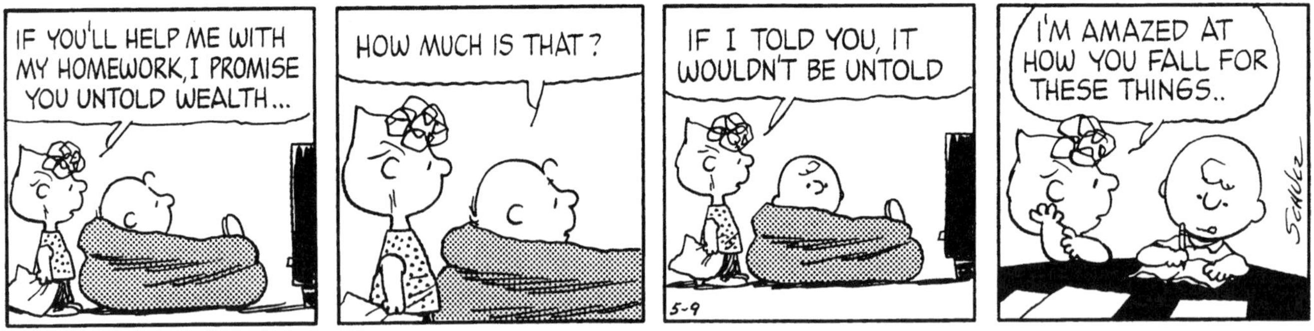
IF YOU'LL HELP ME WITH MY HOMEWORK, I PROMISE YOU UNTOLD WEALTH...
HOW MUCH IS THAT?
IF I TOLD YOU, IT WOULDN'T BE UNTOLD
I'M AMAZED AT HOW YOU FALL FOR THESE THINGS..

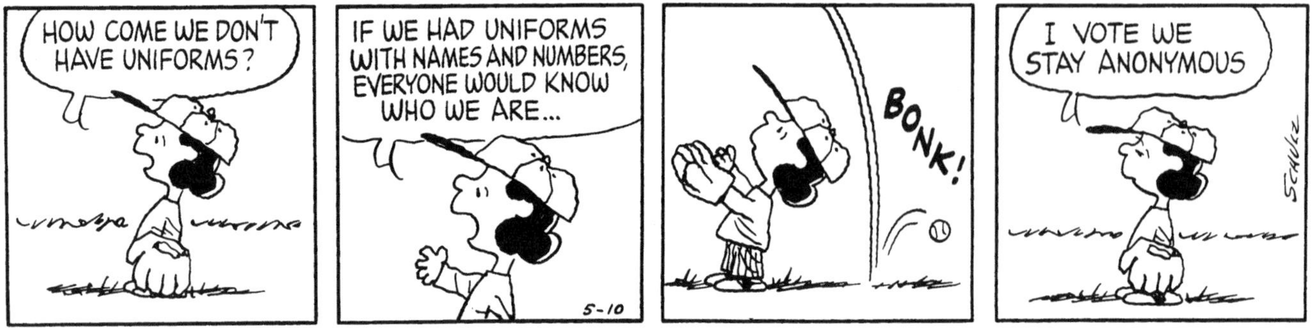
HOW COME WE DON'T HAVE UNIFORMS?
IF WE HAD UNIFORMS WITH NAMES AND NUMBERS, EVERYONE WOULD KNOW WHO WE ARE...
BONK!
I VOTE WE STAY ANONYMOUS

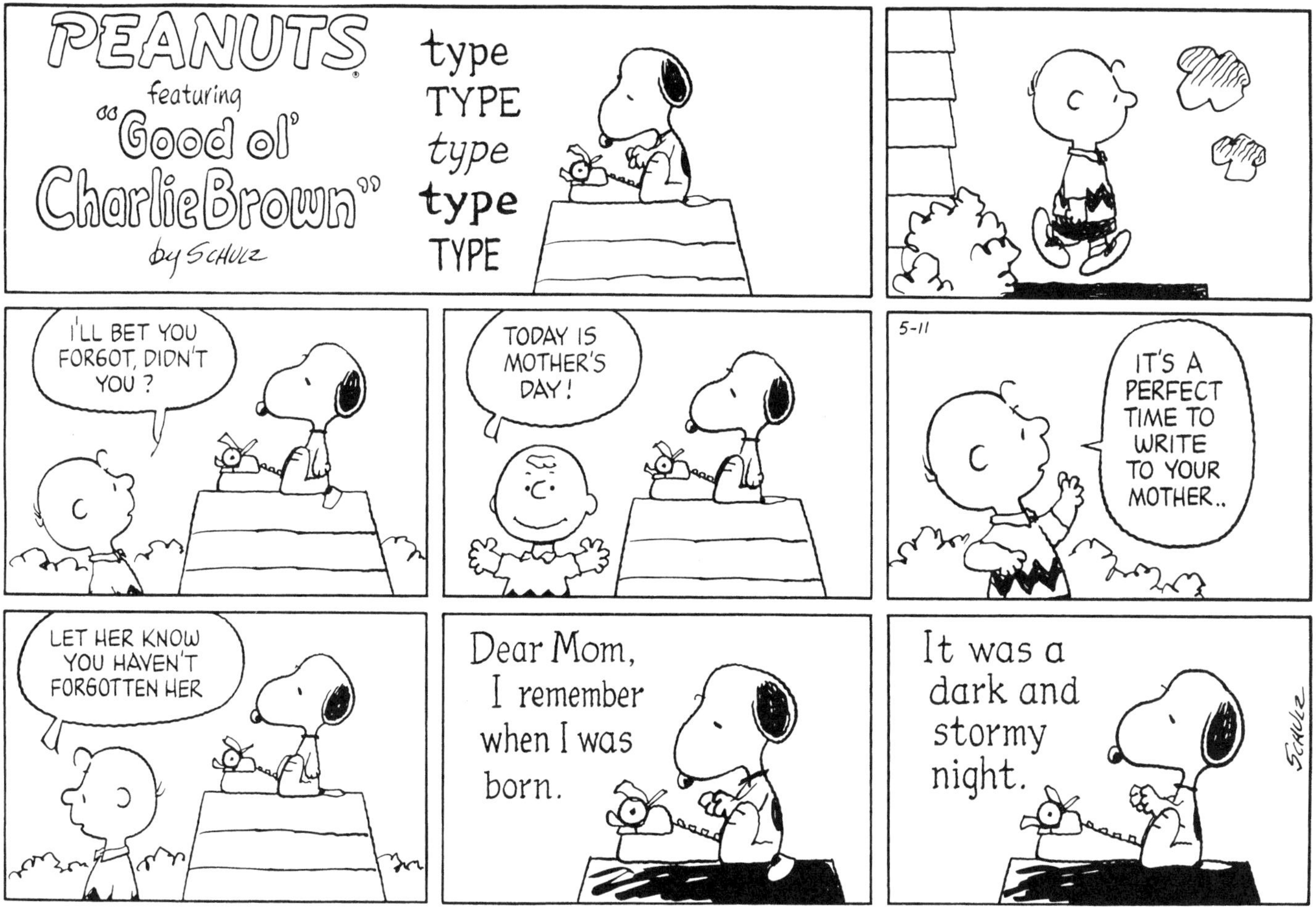
PEANUTS
featuring
"Good ol' Charlie Brown"
by SCHULZ
type
TYPE
type
type
TYPE
I'LL BET YOU FORGOT, DIDN'T YOU ?
TODAY IS MOTHER'S DAY!
5-11
IT'S A PERFECT TIME TO WRITE TO YOUR MOTHER..
LET HER KNOW YOU HAVEN'T FORGOTTEN HER
Dear Mom, I remember when I was born.
It was a dark and stormy night.
SCHULZ

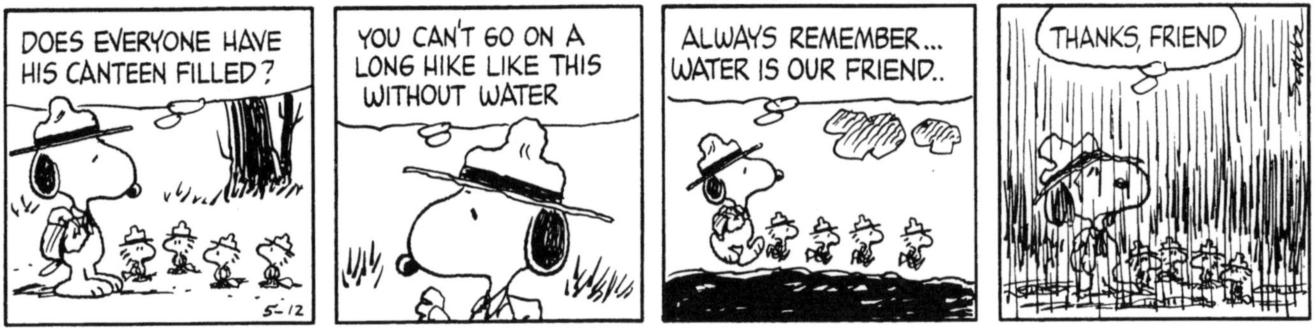
DOES EVERYONE HAVE HIS CANTEEN FILLED?
5-12
YOU CAN'T GO ON A LONG HIKE LIKE THIS WITHOUT WATER
ALWAYS REMEMBER... WATER IS OUR FRIEND..
THANKS, FRIEND
SCHULZ

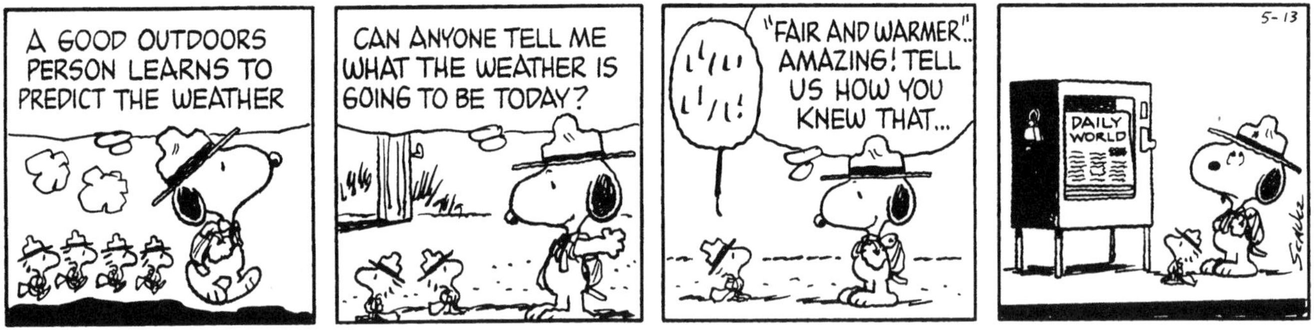
A GOOD OUTDOORS PERSON LEARNS TO PREDICT THE WEATHER
CAN ANYONE TELL ME WHAT THE WEATHER IS GOING TO BE TODAY?
"FAIR AND WARMER".. AMAZING! TELL US HOW YOU KNEW THAT...
5-13
DAILY WORLD
SCHULZ

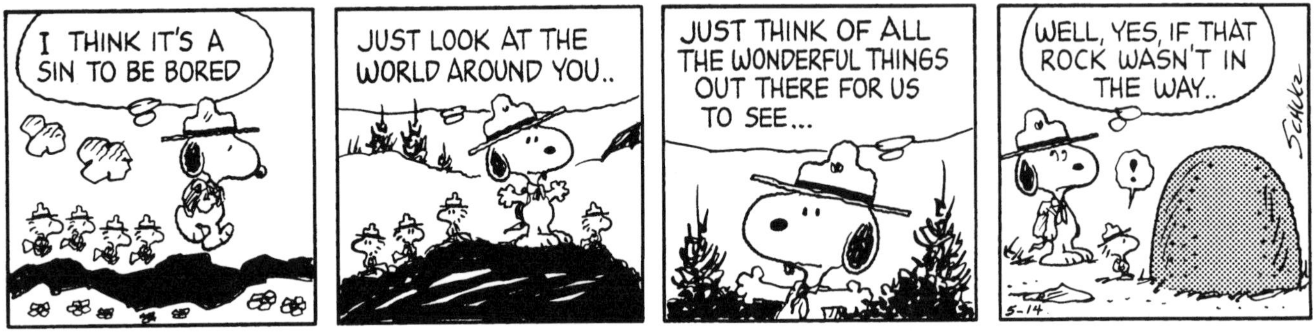
I THINK IT'S A SIN TO BE BORED
JUST LOOK AT THE WORLD AROUND YOU..
JUST THINK OF ALL THE WONDERFUL THINGS OUT THERE FOR US TO SEE...
WELL, YES, IF THAT ROCK WASN'T IN THE WAY..
!
SCHULZ
5-14

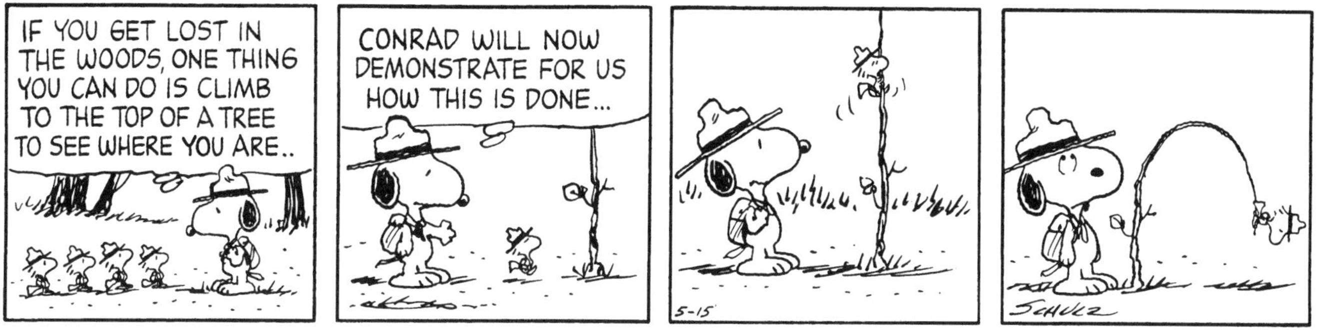
IF YOU GET LOST IN THE WOODS, ONE THING YOU CAN DO IS CLIMB TO THE TOP OF A TREE TO SEE WHERE YOU ARE..
CONRAD WILL NOW DEMONSTRATE FOR US HOW THIS IS DONE...
5-15
SCHULZ

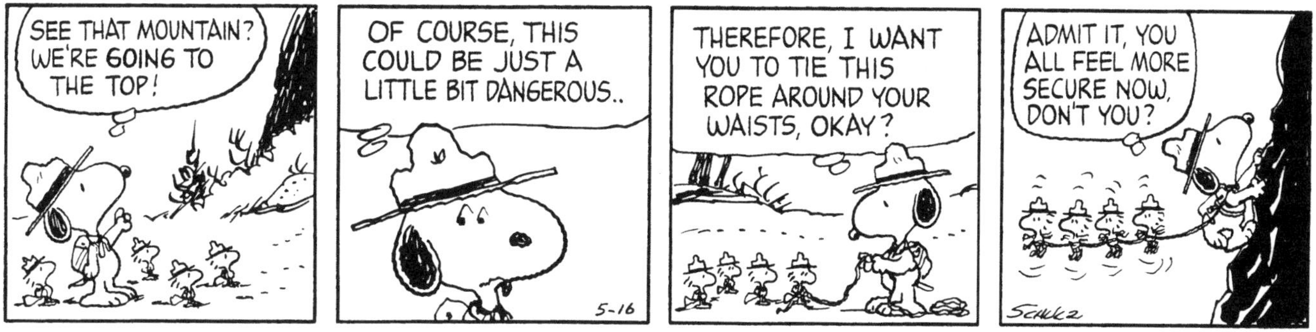
SEE THAT MOUNTAIN? WE'RE GOING TO THE TOP!
OF COURSE, THIS COULD BE JUST A LITTLE BIT DANGEROUS..
5-16
THEREFORE, I WANT YOU TO TIE THIS ROPE AROUND YOUR WAISTS, OKAY?
ADMIT IT, YOU ALL FEEL MORE SECURE NOW, DON'T YOU?
SCHULZ

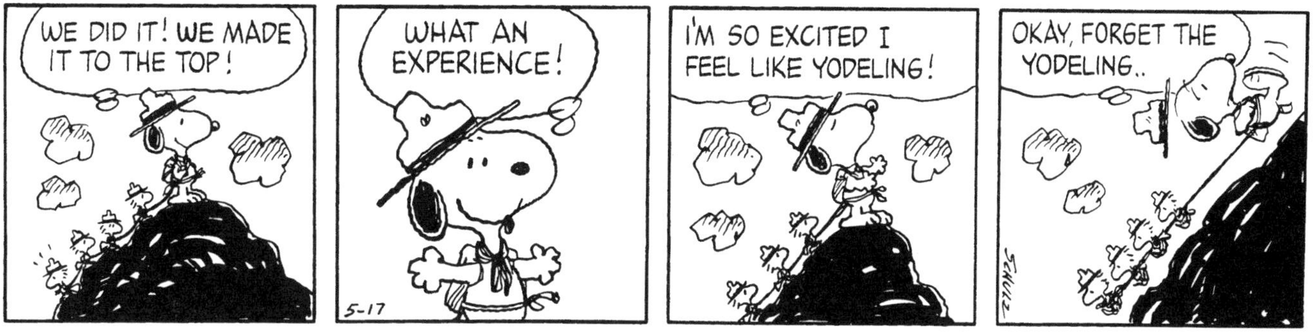
WE DID IT! WE MADE IT TO THE TOP!
WHAT AN EXPERIENCE!
5-17
I'M SO EXCITED I FEEL LIKE YODELING!
OKAY, FORGET THE YODELING..
SCHULZ

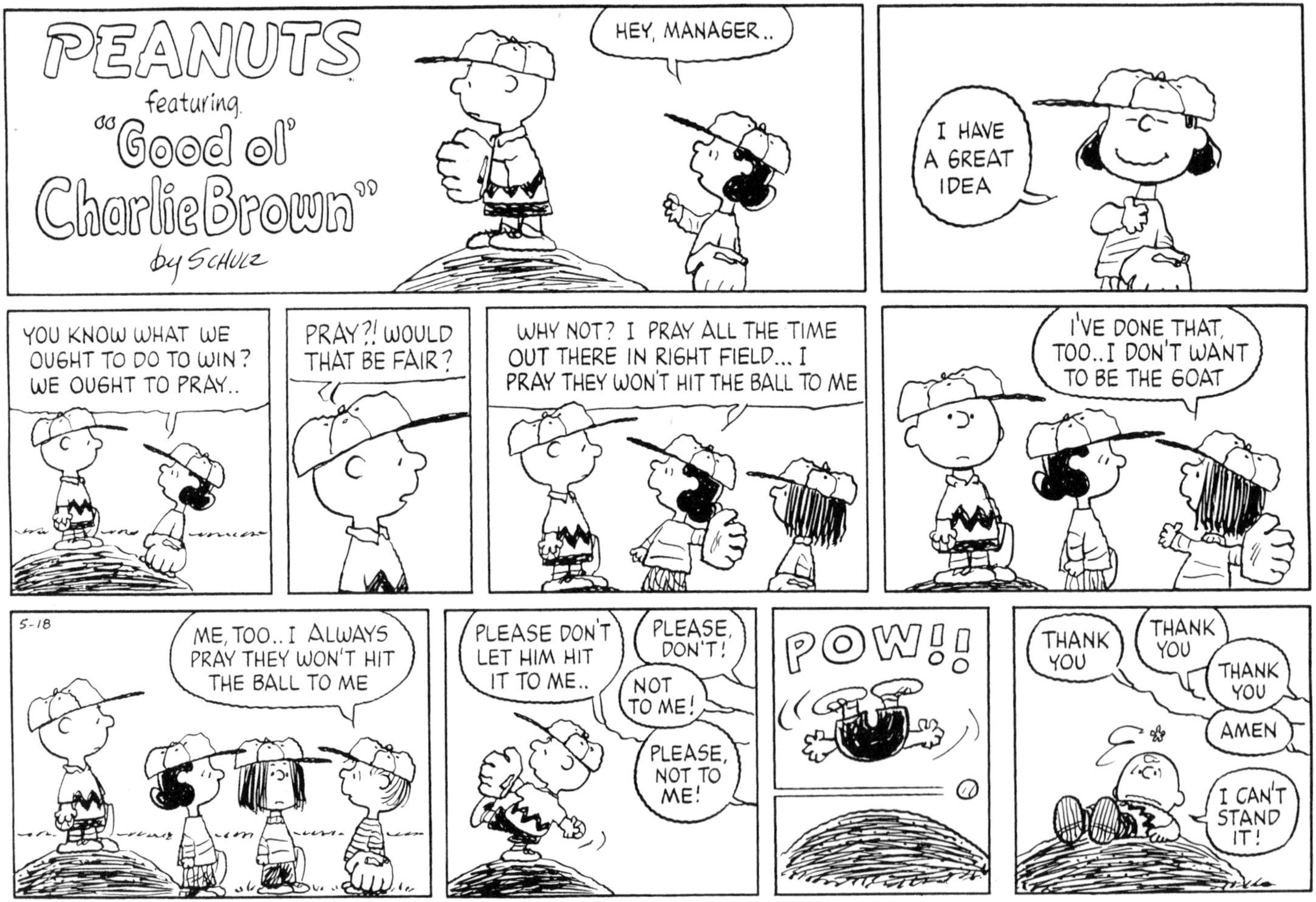
PEANUTS
featuring "Good ol' Charlie Brown"
by SCHULZ
HEY, MANAGER..
I HAVE A GREAT IDEA
YOU KNOW WHAT WE OUGHT TO DO TO WIN? WE OUGHT TO PRAY..
PRAY?! WOULD THAT BE FAIR?
WHY NOT? I PRAY ALL THE TIME OUT THERE IN RIGHT FIELD... I PRAY THEY WON'T HIT THE BALL TO ME
I'VE DONE THAT, TOO..I DON'T WANT TO BE THE GOAT
5-18
ME, TOO..I ALWAYS PRAY THEY WON'T HIT THE BALL TO ME
PLEASE DON'T LET HIM HIT IT TO ME..
PLEASE, DON'T!
NOT TO ME!
PLEASE, NOT TO ME!
POW!!
THANK YOU
THANK YOU
THANK YOU
AMEN
I CAN'T STAND IT!

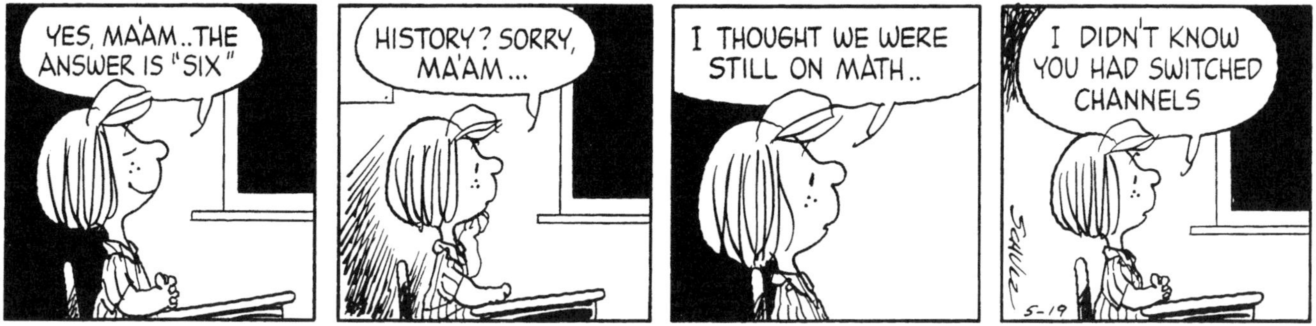
YES, MA'AM..THE ANSWER IS "SIX"
HISTORY? SORRY, MA'AM...
I THOUGHT WE WERE STILL ON MATH..
I DIDN'T KNOW YOU HAD SWITCHED CHANNELS
SCHULZ
5-19

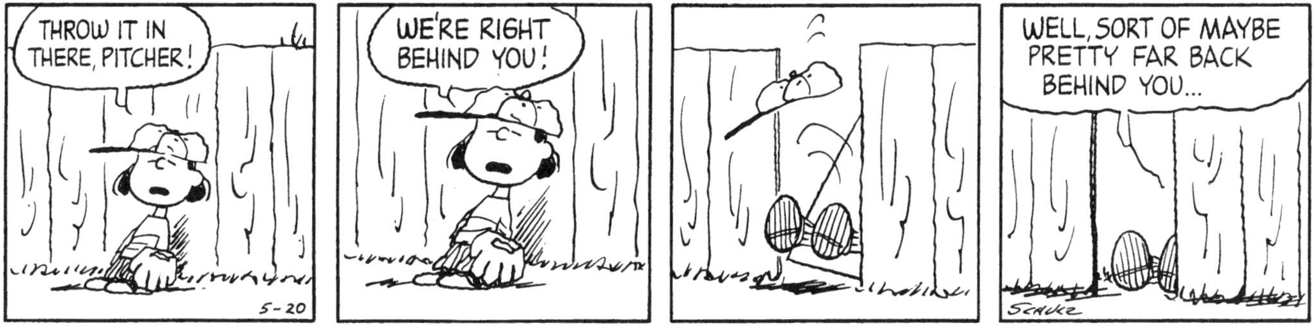
THROW IT IN THERE, PITCHER!
5-20
WE'RE RIGHT BEHIND YOU!
WELL, SORT OF MAYBE PRETTY FAR BACK BEHIND YOU...
SCHULZ

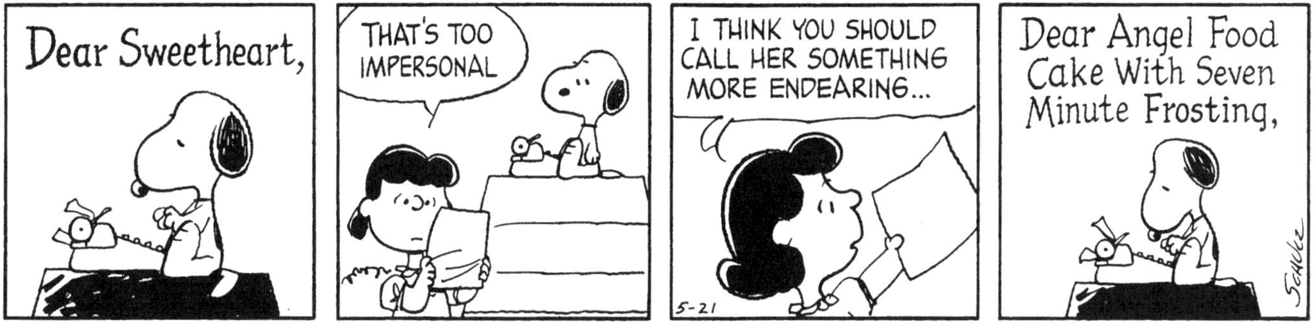
Dear Sweetheart,
THAT'S TOO IMPERSONAL
I THINK YOU SHOULD CALL HER SOMETHING MORE ENDEARING...
5-21
Dear Angel Food Cake With Seven Minute Frosting,
SCHULZ

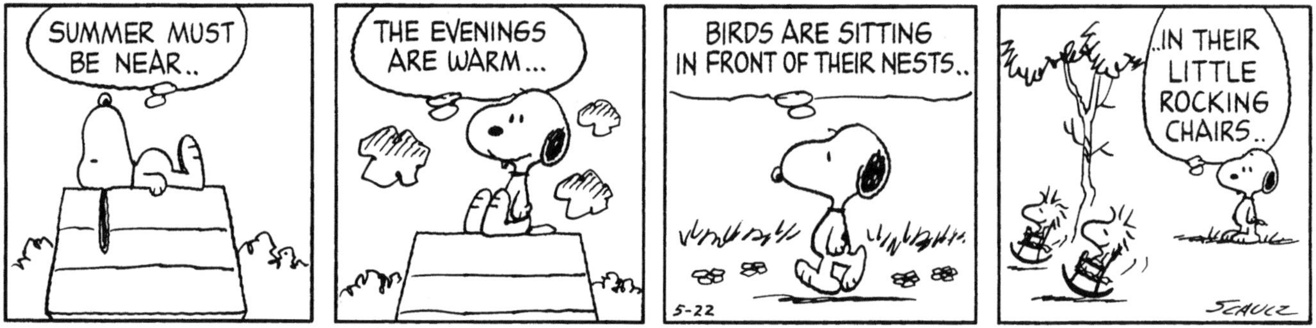
SUMMER MUST BE NEAR..
THE EVENINGS ARE WARM...
BIRDS ARE SITTING IN FRONT OF THEIR NESTS..
5-22
..IN THEIR LITTLE ROCKING CHAIRS..
SCHULZ

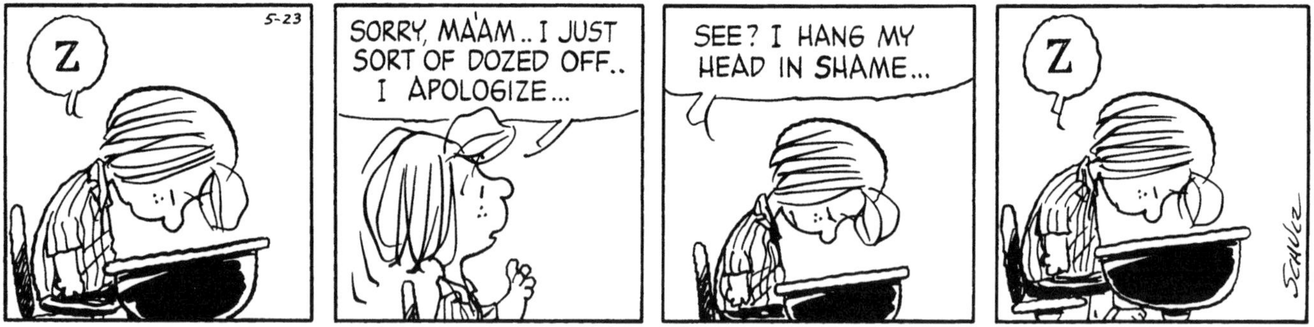
5-23
Z
SORRY, MA'AM.. I JUST SORT OF DOZED OFF.. I APOLOGIZE...
SEE? I HANG MY HEAD IN SHAME...
Z
SCHULZ

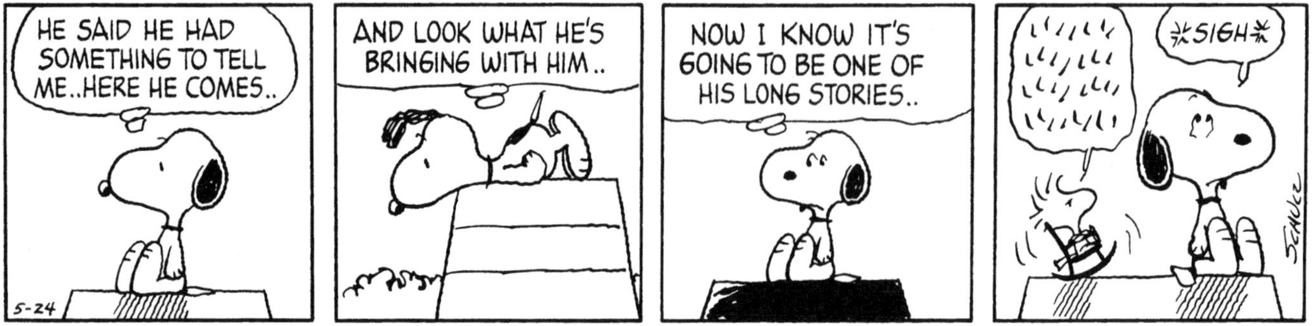
HE SAID HE HAD SOMETHING TO TELL ME..HERE HE COMES..
5-24
AND LOOK WHAT HE'S BRINGING WITH HIM..
NOW I KNOW IT'S GOING TO BE ONE OF HIS LONG STORIES..
SIGH
SCHULZ

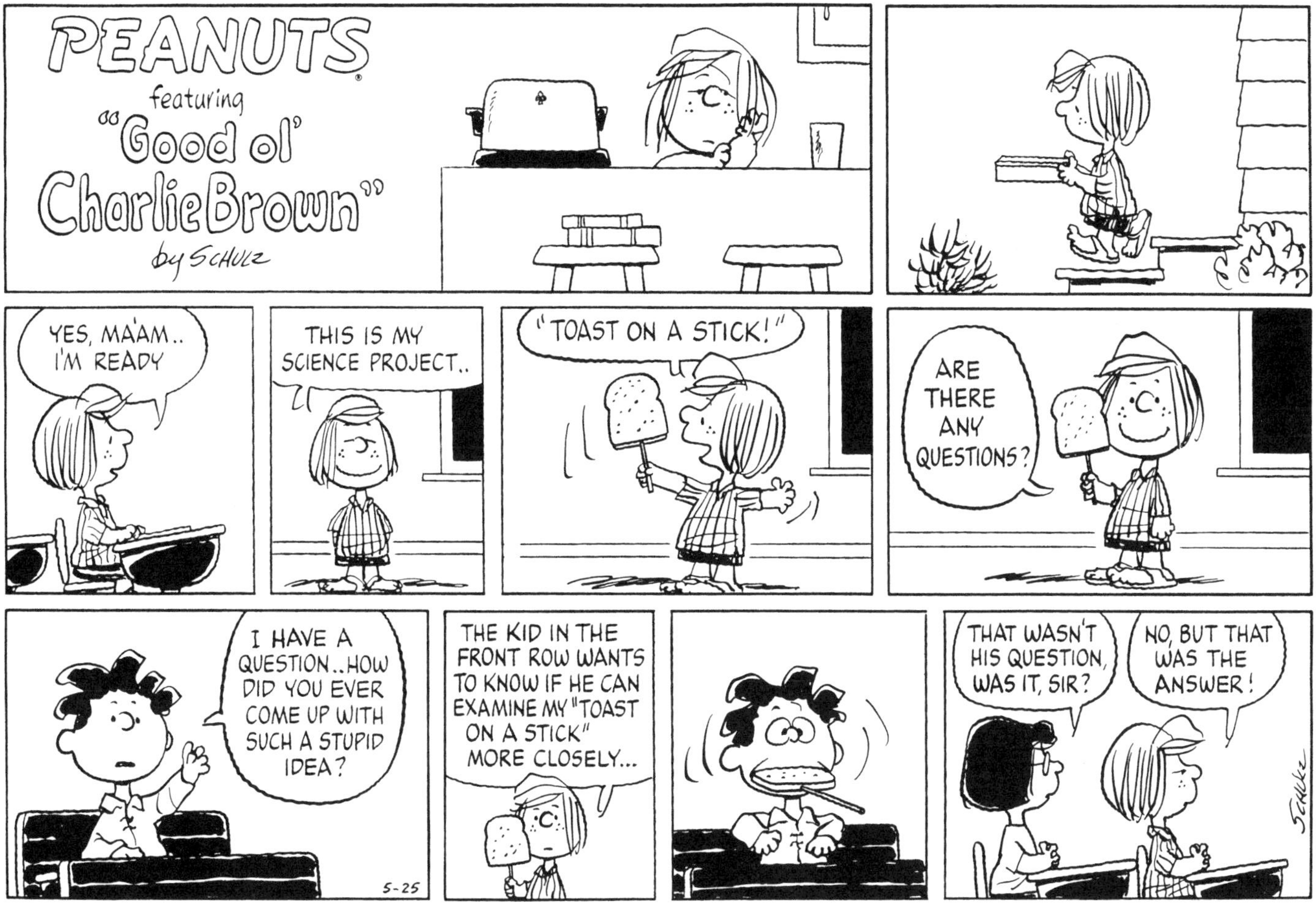
PEANUTS
featuring "Good ol' Charlie Brown"
by SCHULZ
YES, MA'AM.. I'M READY
THIS IS MY SCIENCE PROJECT..
"TOAST ON A STICK!"
ARE THERE ANY QUESTIONS?
I HAVE A QUESTION..HOW DID YOU EVER COME UP WITH SUCH A STUPID IDEA?
5-25
THE KID IN THE FRONT ROW WANTS TO KNOW IF HE CAN EXAMINE MY "TOAST ON A STICK" MORE CLOSELY...
THAT WASN'T HIS QUESTION, WAS IT, SIR?
NO, BUT THAT WAS THE ANSWER!
SCHULZ

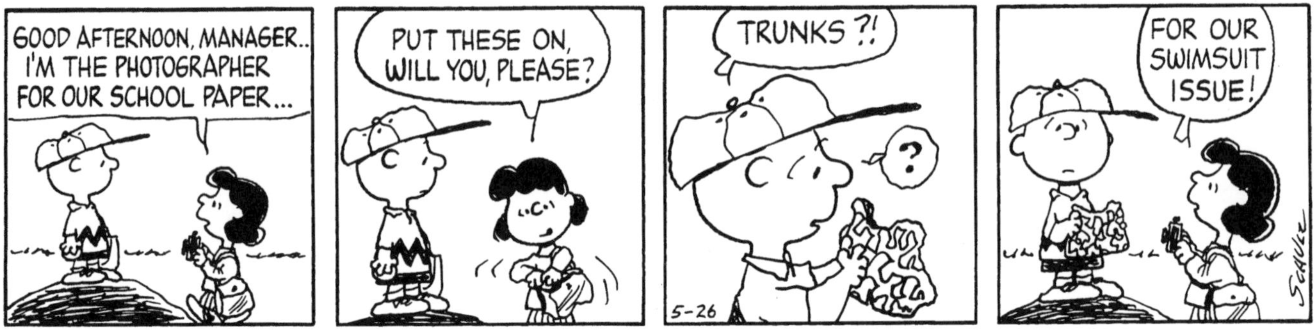
GOOD AFTERNOON, MANAGER.. I'M THE PHOTOGRAPHER FOR OUR SCHOOL PAPER...
PUT THESE ON, WILL YOU, PLEASE?
TRUNKS ?!
?
5-26
FOR OUR SWIMSUIT ISSUE!

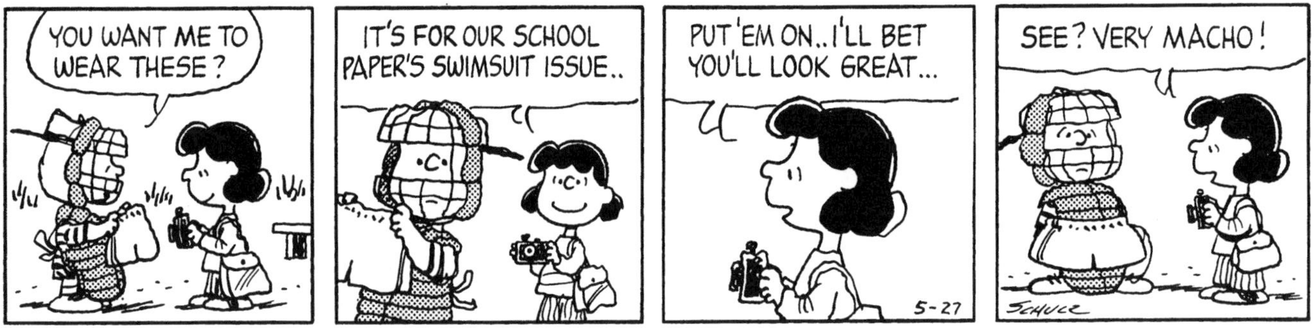
YOU WANT ME TO WEAR THESE?
IT'S FOR OUR SCHOOL PAPER'S SWIMSUIT ISSUE..
PUT 'EM ON.. I'LL BET YOU'LL LOOK GREAT...
5-27
SEE? VERY MACHO!

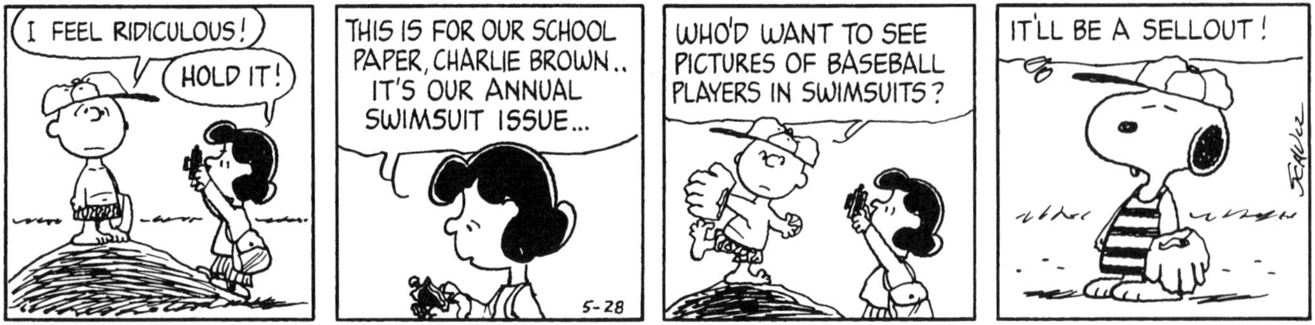
I FEEL RIDICULOUS!
HOLD IT!
THIS IS FOR OUR SCHOOL PAPER, CHARLIE BROWN.. IT'S OUR ANNUAL SWIMSUIT ISSUE...
5-28
WHO'D WANT TO SEE PICTURES OF BASEBALL PLAYERS IN SWIMSUITS?
IT'LL BE A SELLOUT!

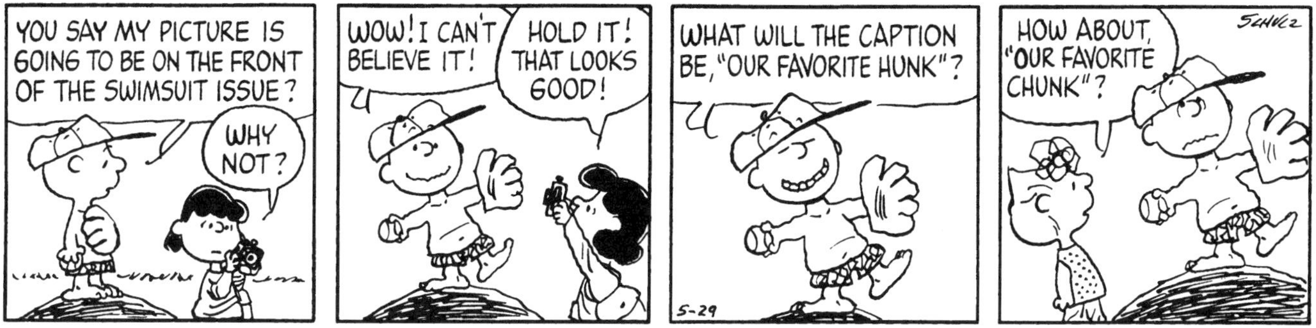
YOU SAY MY PICTURE IS GOING TO BE ON THE FRONT OF THE SWIMSUIT ISSUE?
WHY NOT?
WOW! I CAN'T BELIEVE IT!
HOLD IT! THAT LOOKS GOOD!
WHAT WILL THE CAPTION BE, "OUR FAVORITE HUNK"?
5-29
HOW ABOUT, "OUR FAVORITE CHUNK"?
SCHULZ

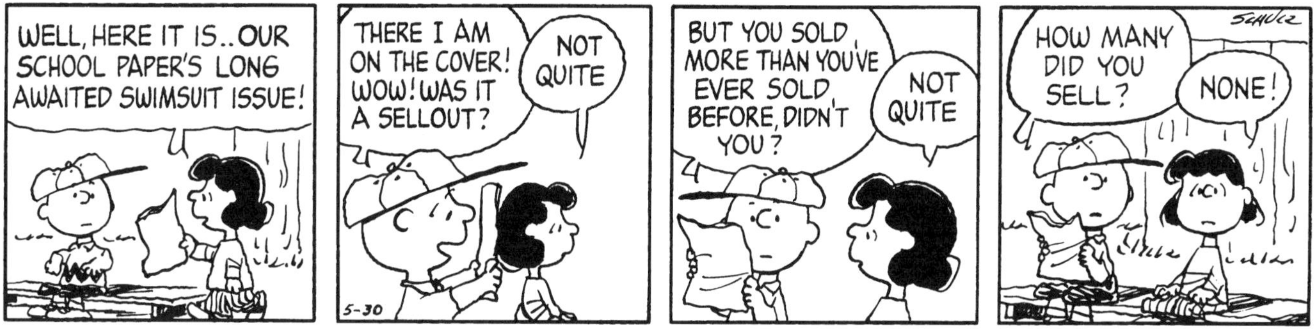
WELL, HERE IT IS..OUR SCHOOL PAPER'S LONG AWAITED SWIMSUIT ISSUE!
THERE I AM ON THE COVER! WOW! WAS IT A SELLOUT?
NOT QUITE
5-30
BUT YOU SOLD MORE THAN YOU'VE EVER SOLD BEFORE, DIDN'T YOU?
NOT QUITE
HOW MANY DID YOU SELL?
NONE!
SCHULZ

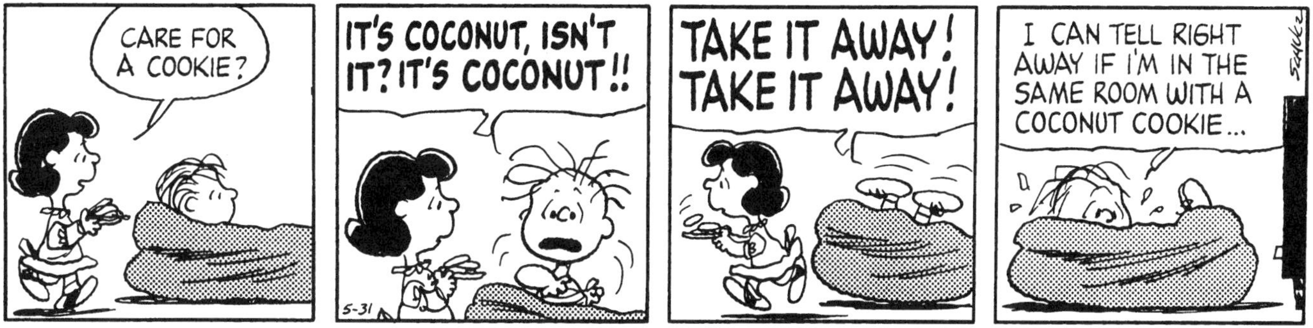
CARE FOR A COOKIE?
IT'S COCONUT, ISN'T IT? IT'S COCONUT!!
5-31
TAKE IT AWAY! TAKE IT AWAY!
I CAN TELL RIGHT AWAY IF I'M IN THE SAME ROOM WITH A COCONUT COOKIE...
SCHULZ

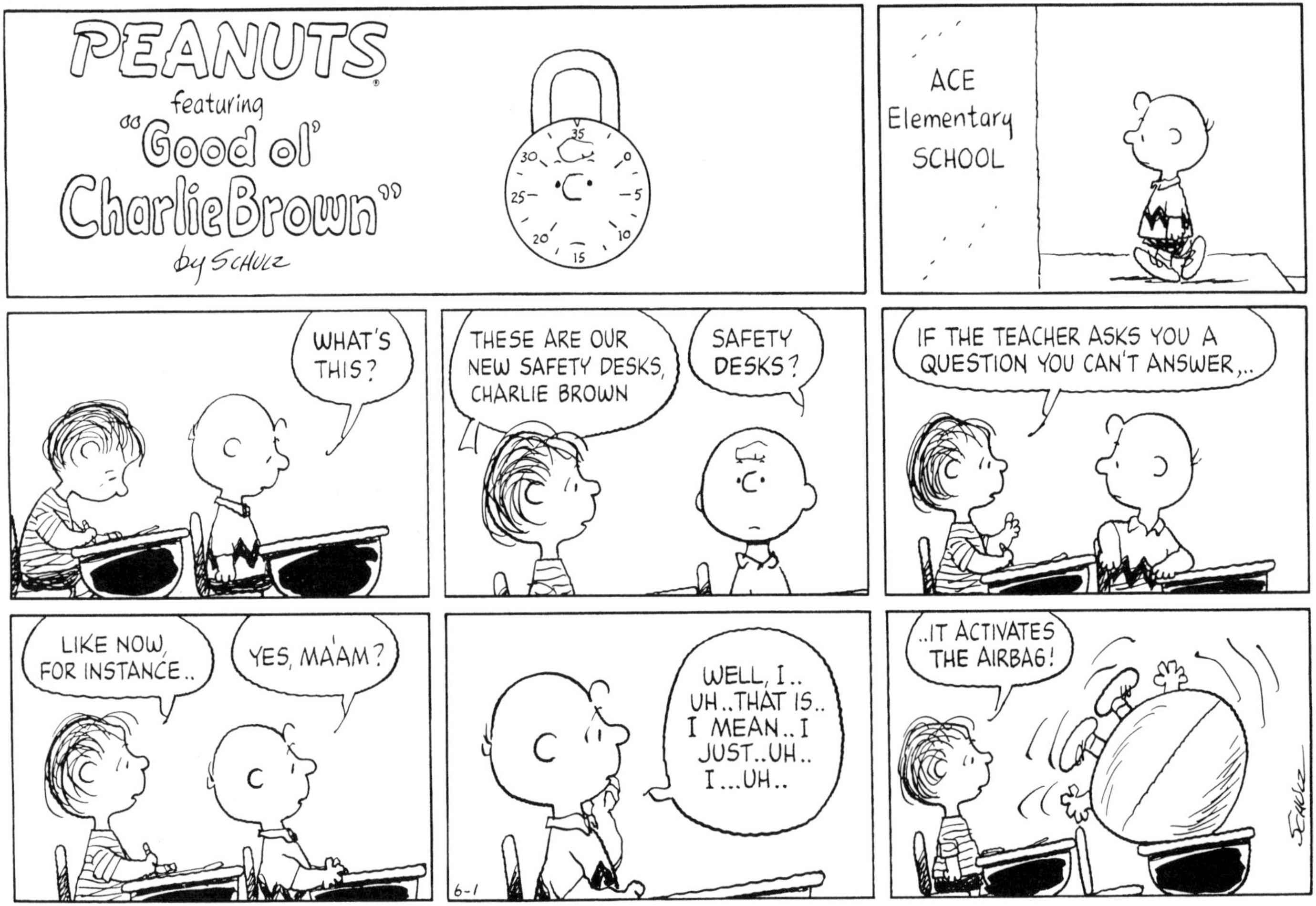
PEANUTS
featuring
"Good ol' Charlie Brown"
by SCHULZ
ACE Elementary SCHOOL
WHAT'S THIS?
THESE ARE OUR NEW SAFETY DESKS, CHARLIE BROWN
SAFETY DESKS?
IF THE TEACHER ASKS YOU A QUESTION YOU CAN'T ANSWER,..
LIKE NOW, FOR INSTANCE..
YES, MA'AM?
WELL, I.. UH..THAT IS.. I MEAN..I JUST..UH.. I...UH..
6-1
..IT ACTIVATES THE AIRBAG!
SCHULZ

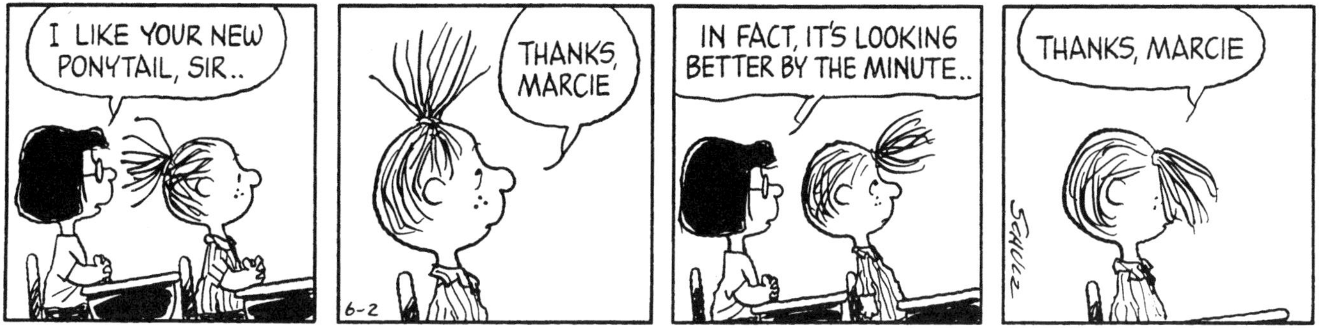
I LIKE YOUR NEW PONYTAIL, SIR..
THANKS, MARCIE
IN FACT, IT'S LOOKING BETTER BY THE MINUTE..
THANKS, MARCIE

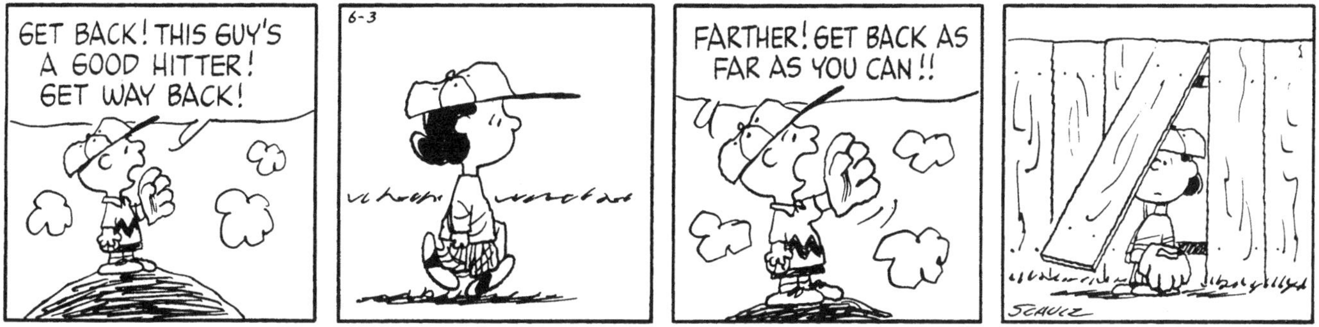
GET BACK! THIS GUY'S A GOOD HITTER! GET WAY BACK!
FARTHER! GET BACK AS FAR AS YOU CAN!!

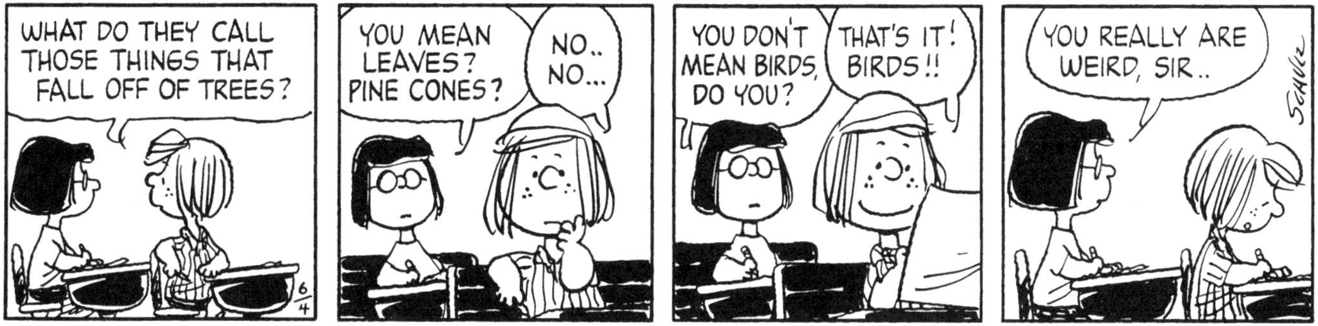
WHAT DO THEY CALL THOSE THINGS THAT FALL OFF OF TREES?
YOU MEAN LEAVES? PINE CONES?
NO.. NO...
YOU DON'T MEAN BIRDS, DO YOU?
THAT'S IT! BIRDS!!
YOU REALLY ARE WEIRD, SIR..

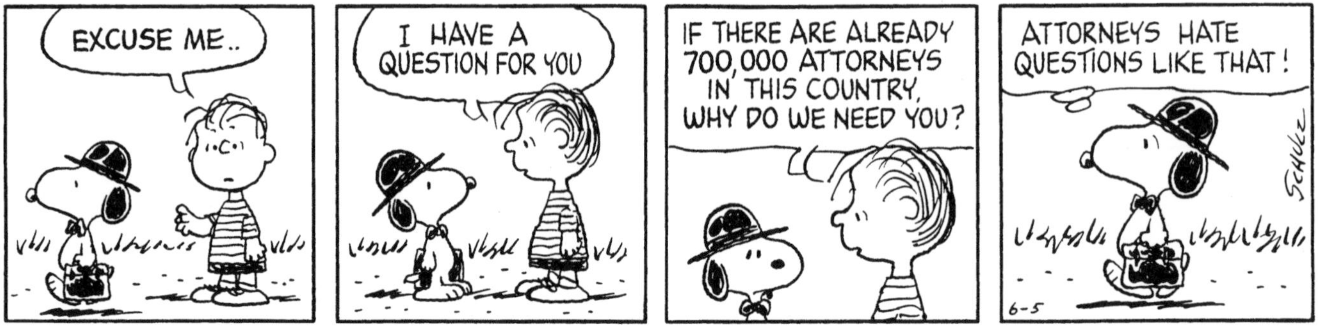
EXCUSE ME..
I HAVE A QUESTION FOR YOU
IF THERE ARE ALREADY 700,000 ATTORNEYS IN THIS COUNTRY, WHY DO WE NEED YOU?
ATTORNEYS HATE QUESTIONS LIKE THAT!
6-5

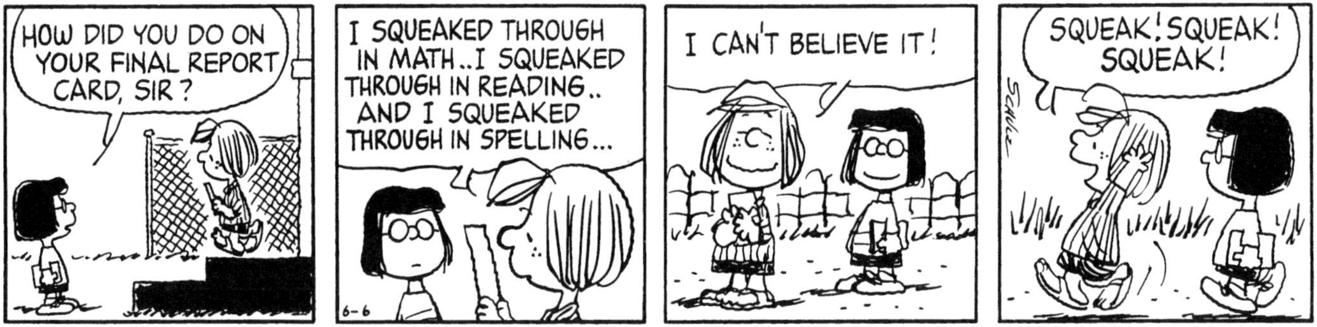
HOW DID YOU DO ON YOUR FINAL REPORT CARD, SIR?
I SQUEAKED THROUGH IN MATH..I SQUEAKED THROUGH IN READING.. AND I SQUEAKED THROUGH IN SPELLING...
6-6
I CAN'T BELIEVE IT!
SQUEAK! SQUEAK! SQUEAK!

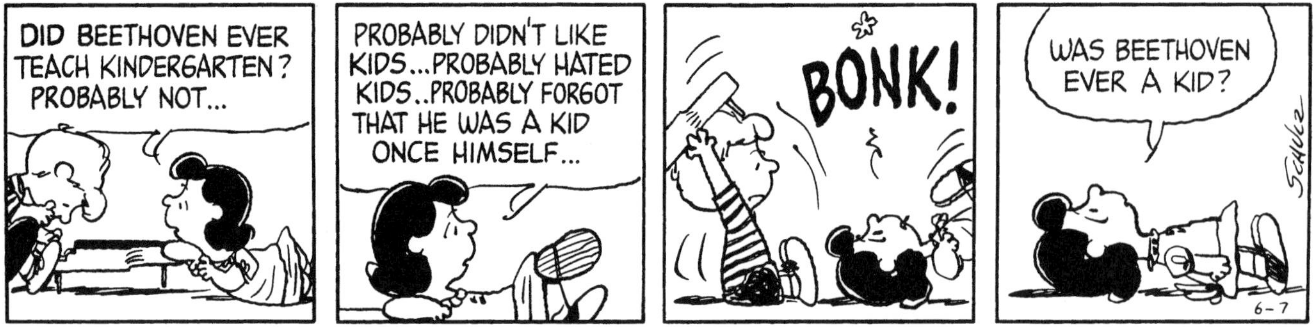
DID BEETHOVEN EVER TEACH KINDERGARTEN? PROBABLY NOT...
PROBABLY DIDN'T LIKE KIDS...PROBABLY HATED KIDS..PROBABLY FORGOT THAT HE WAS A KID ONCE HIMSELF...
BONK!
WAS BEETHOVEN EVER A KID?
6-7

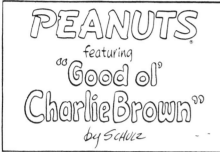

PEANUTS featuring "Good ol' CharlieBrown" by Schulz

FIVE TWO?

THIS IS SERIOUS..

LISTEN, PARTNER..WE'RE GONNA HAVE TO USE SOME STRATEGY HERE...

WE MAY HAVE TO STALL..

WHEN I GIVE YOU THE WORD, BEND OVER AND TIE YOUR SHOELACES

OKAY, PARTNER, NOW!

6-8

I DON'T HAVE ANY SHOELACES.. I DON'T EVEN HAVE ANY SHOES!

NOW, PARTNER! I SAID, "NOW!"

IT HURTS WHEN YOU TIE YOUR TOES TOGETHER!

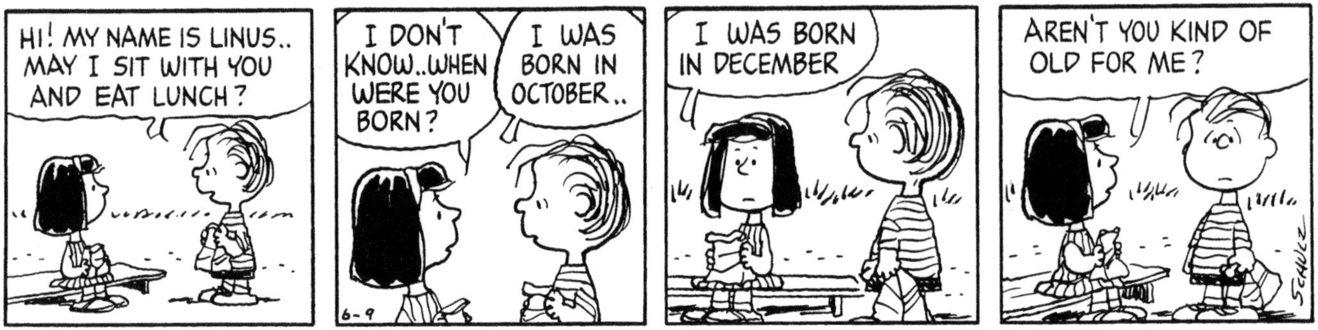
HI! MY NAME IS LINUS.. MAY I SIT WITH YOU AND EAT LUNCH?
I DON'T KNOW..WHEN WERE YOU BORN?
I WAS BORN IN OCTOBER..
I WAS BORN IN DECEMBER
AREN'T YOU KIND OF OLD FOR ME?
6-9
SCHULZ

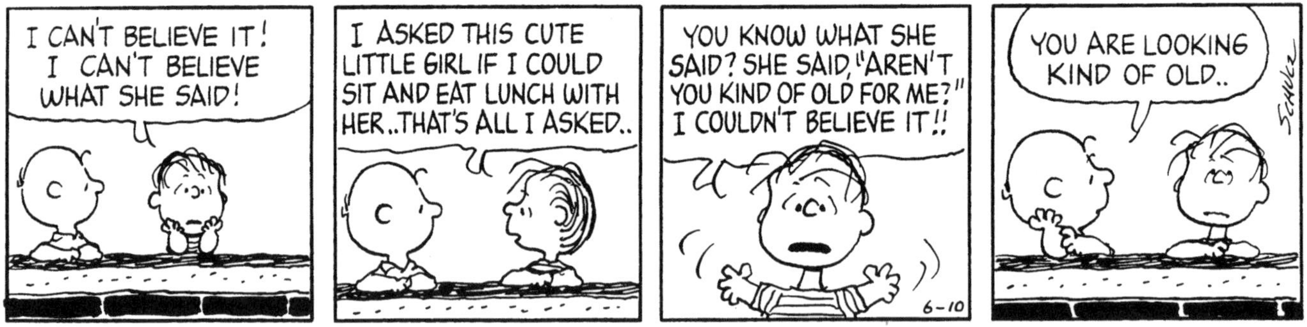
I CAN'T BELIEVE IT! I CAN'T BELIEVE WHAT SHE SAID!
I ASKED THIS CUTE LITTLE GIRL IF I COULD SIT AND EAT LUNCH WITH HER..THAT'S ALL I ASKED..
YOU KNOW WHAT SHE SAID? SHE SAID, "AREN'T YOU KIND OF OLD FOR ME?" I COULDN'T BELIEVE IT!!
YOU ARE LOOKING KIND OF OLD..
6-10
SCHULZ

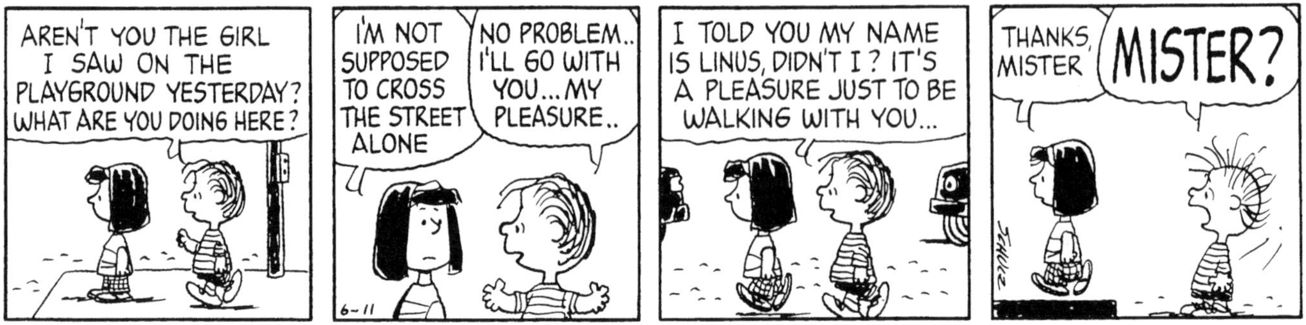
AREN'T YOU THE GIRL I SAW ON THE PLAYGROUND YESTERDAY? WHAT ARE YOU DOING HERE?
I'M NOT SUPPOSED TO CROSS THE STREET ALONE
NO PROBLEM.. I'LL GO WITH YOU... MY PLEASURE..
I TOLD YOU MY NAME IS LINUS, DIDN'T I? IT'S A PLEASURE JUST TO BE WALKING WITH YOU...
THANKS, MISTER
MISTER?
6-11
SCHULZ

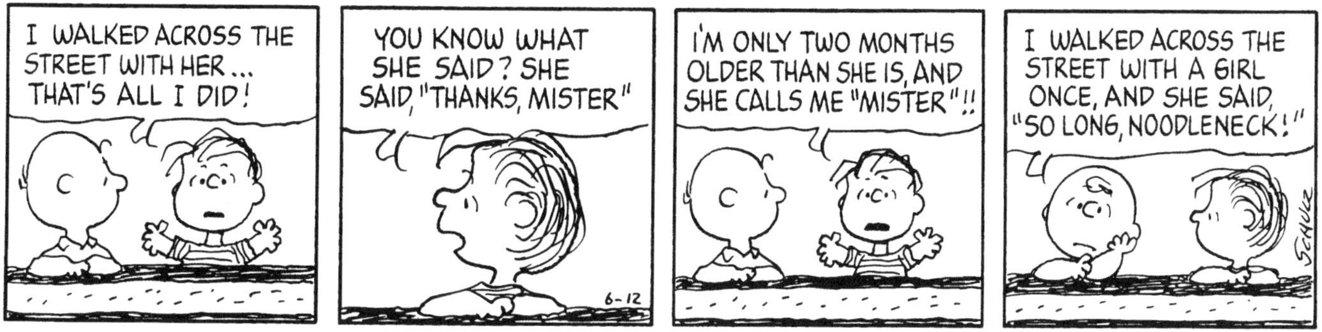
I WALKED ACROSS THE STREET WITH HER... THAT'S ALL I DID!
YOU KNOW WHAT SHE SAID? SHE SAID, "THANKS, MISTER"
6-12
I'M ONLY TWO MONTHS OLDER THAN SHE IS, AND SHE CALLS ME "MISTER"!!
I WALKED ACROSS THE STREET WITH A GIRL ONCE, AND SHE SAID, "SO LONG, NOODLENECK!"
SCHULZ

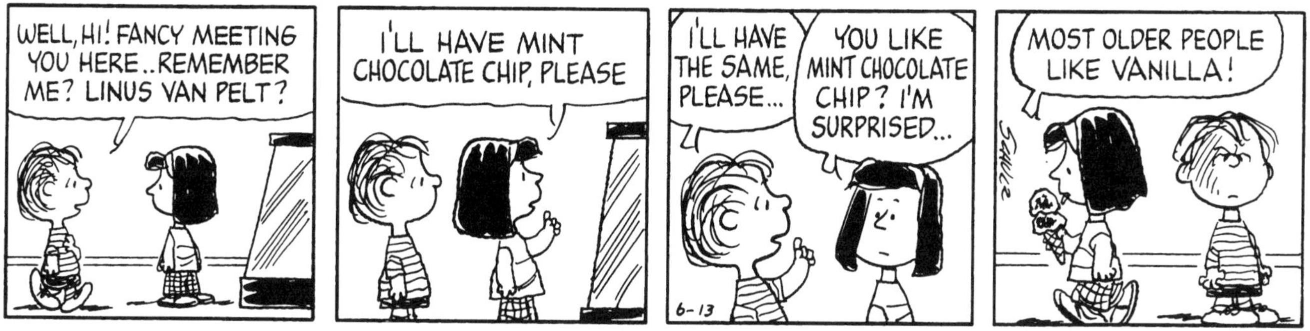
WELL, HI! FANCY MEETING YOU HERE..REMEMBER ME? LINUS VAN PELT?
I'LL HAVE MINT CHOCOLATE CHIP, PLEASE
I'LL HAVE THE SAME, PLEASE...
YOU LIKE MINT CHOCOLATE CHIP? I'M SURPRISED...
6-13
SCHULZ
MOST OLDER PEOPLE LIKE VANILLA!

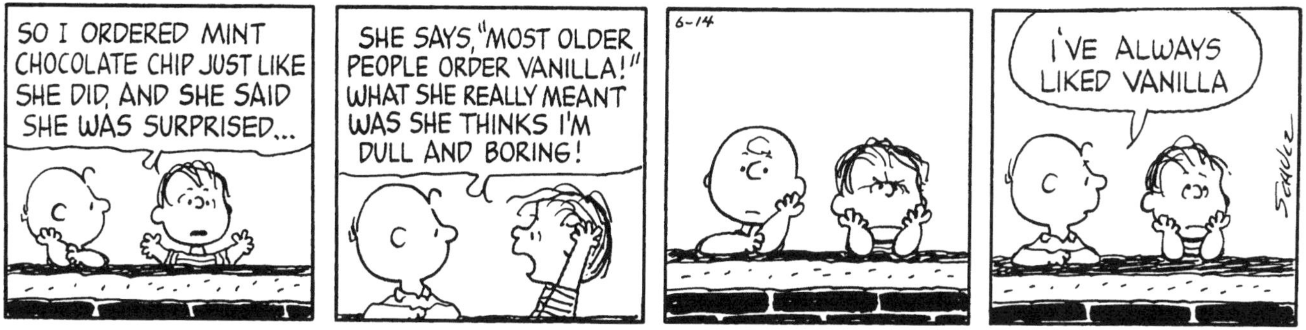
SO I ORDERED MINT CHOCOLATE CHIP JUST LIKE SHE DID, AND SHE SAID SHE WAS SURPRISED...
SHE SAYS, "MOST OLDER PEOPLE ORDER VANILLA!" WHAT SHE REALLY MEANT WAS SHE THINKS I'M DULL AND BORING!
6-14
I'VE ALWAYS LIKED VANILLA
SCHULZ

PEANUTS featuring "Good ol' Charlie Brown" by Schulz

June 15

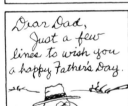
Dear Dad,
    Just a few lines to wish you a happy Father's Day.

I know you worry about me living alone out here on the desert, but I don't want you to worry about me.

Actually, some nice things have been happening...

Last week I was invited to sing in our local choir.

OWOOO!

And it's always exciting to work with my rock collection.

Anyway, Dad, have a happy Father's Day.
your son,
Spike

P.S. If you really want to, you can worry about me.

6-15

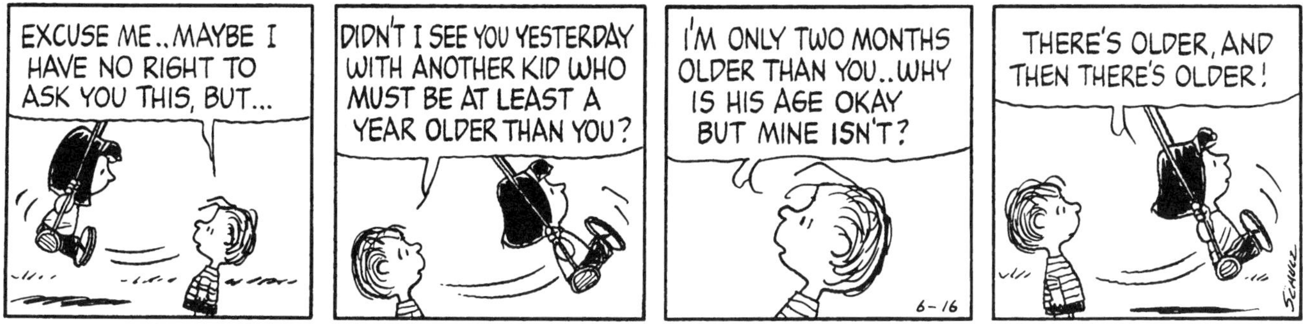
EXCUSE ME.. MAYBE I HAVE NO RIGHT TO ASK YOU THIS, BUT...
DIDN'T I SEE YOU YESTERDAY WITH ANOTHER KID WHO MUST BE AT LEAST A YEAR OLDER THAN YOU?
I'M ONLY TWO MONTHS OLDER THAN YOU.. WHY IS HIS AGE OKAY BUT MINE ISN'T?
6-16
THERE'S OLDER, AND THEN THERE'S OLDER!
SCHULZ

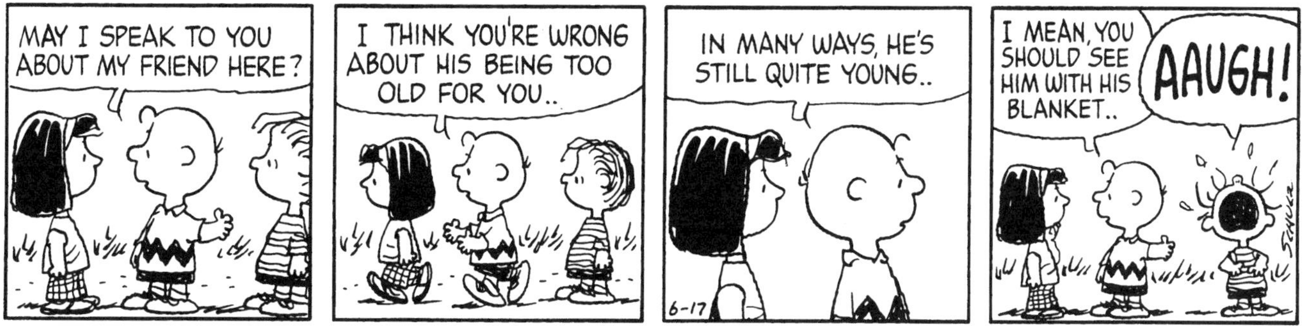
MAY I SPEAK TO YOU ABOUT MY FRIEND HERE?
I THINK YOU'RE WRONG ABOUT HIS BEING TOO OLD FOR YOU..
IN MANY WAYS, HE'S STILL QUITE YOUNG..
6-17
I MEAN, YOU SHOULD SEE HIM WITH HIS BLANKET..
AAUGH!
SCHULZ

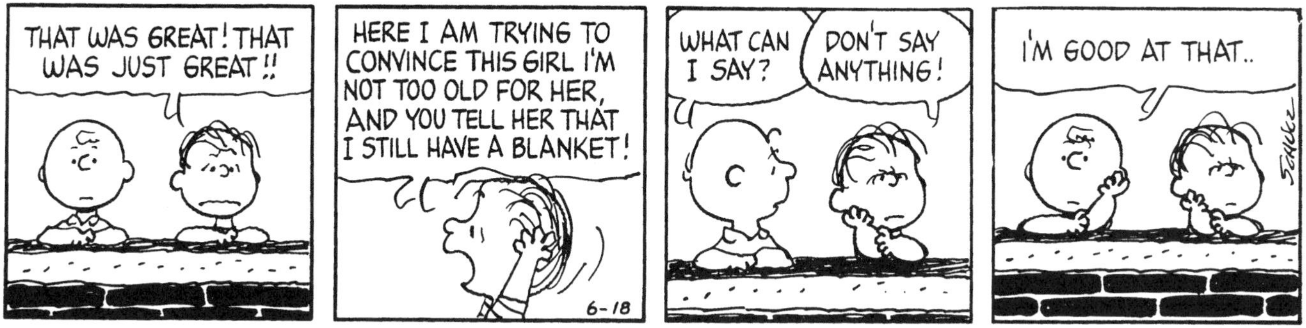
THAT WAS GREAT! THAT WAS JUST GREAT!!
HERE I AM TRYING TO CONVINCE THIS GIRL I'M NOT TOO OLD FOR HER, AND YOU TELL HER THAT I STILL HAVE A BLANKET!
6-18
WHAT CAN I SAY?
DON'T SAY ANYTHING!
I'M GOOD AT THAT..
SCHULZ

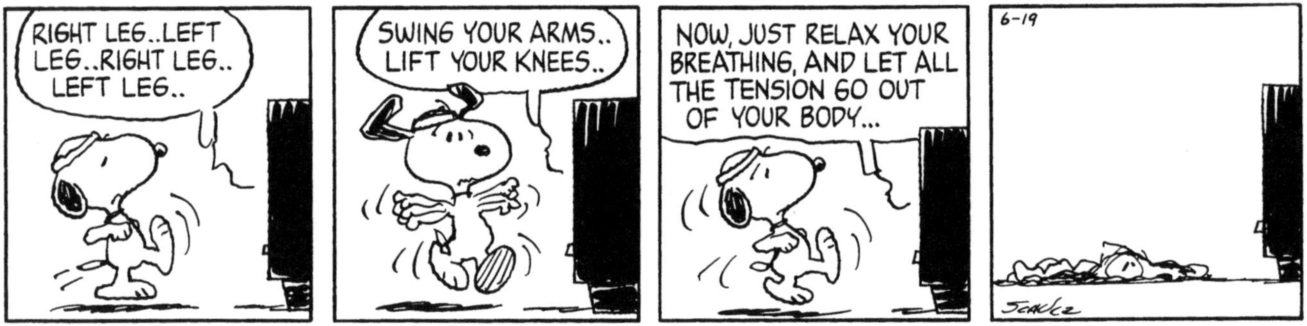
RIGHT LEG..LEFT LEG..RIGHT LEG.. LEFT LEG..
SWING YOUR ARMS.. LIFT YOUR KNEES..
NOW, JUST RELAX YOUR BREATHING, AND LET ALL THE TENSION GO OUT OF YOUR BODY...
6-19
SCHULZ

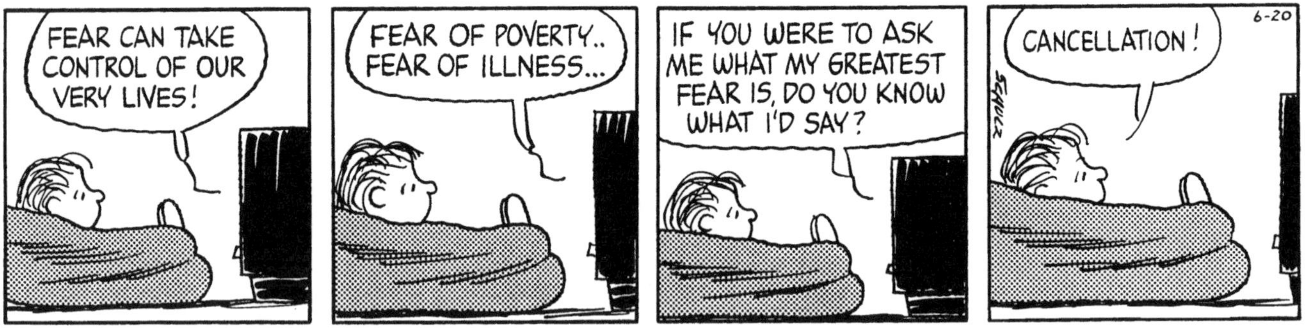
FEAR CAN TAKE CONTROL OF OUR VERY LIVES!
FEAR OF POVERTY.. FEAR OF ILLNESS...
IF YOU WERE TO ASK ME WHAT MY GREATEST FEAR IS, DO YOU KNOW WHAT I'D SAY?
6-20
SCHULZ
CANCELLATION!

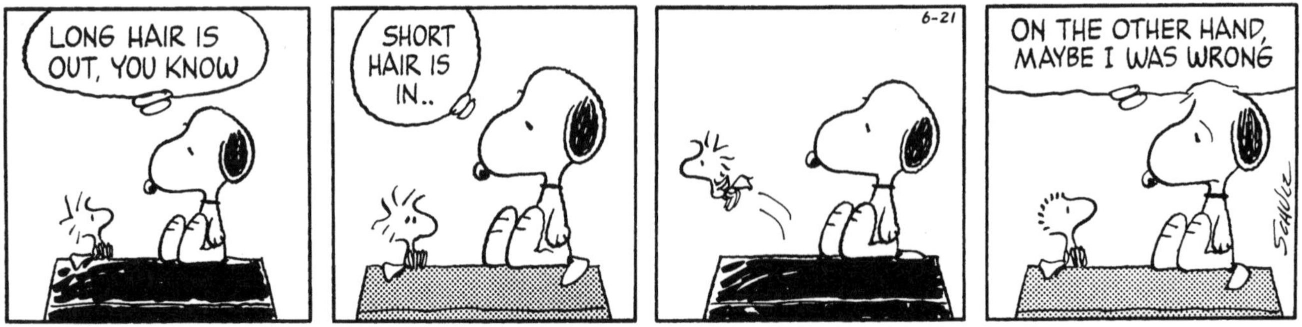
LONG HAIR IS OUT, YOU KNOW
SHORT HAIR IS IN..
6-21
ON THE OTHER HAND, MAYBE I WAS WRONG
SCHULZ

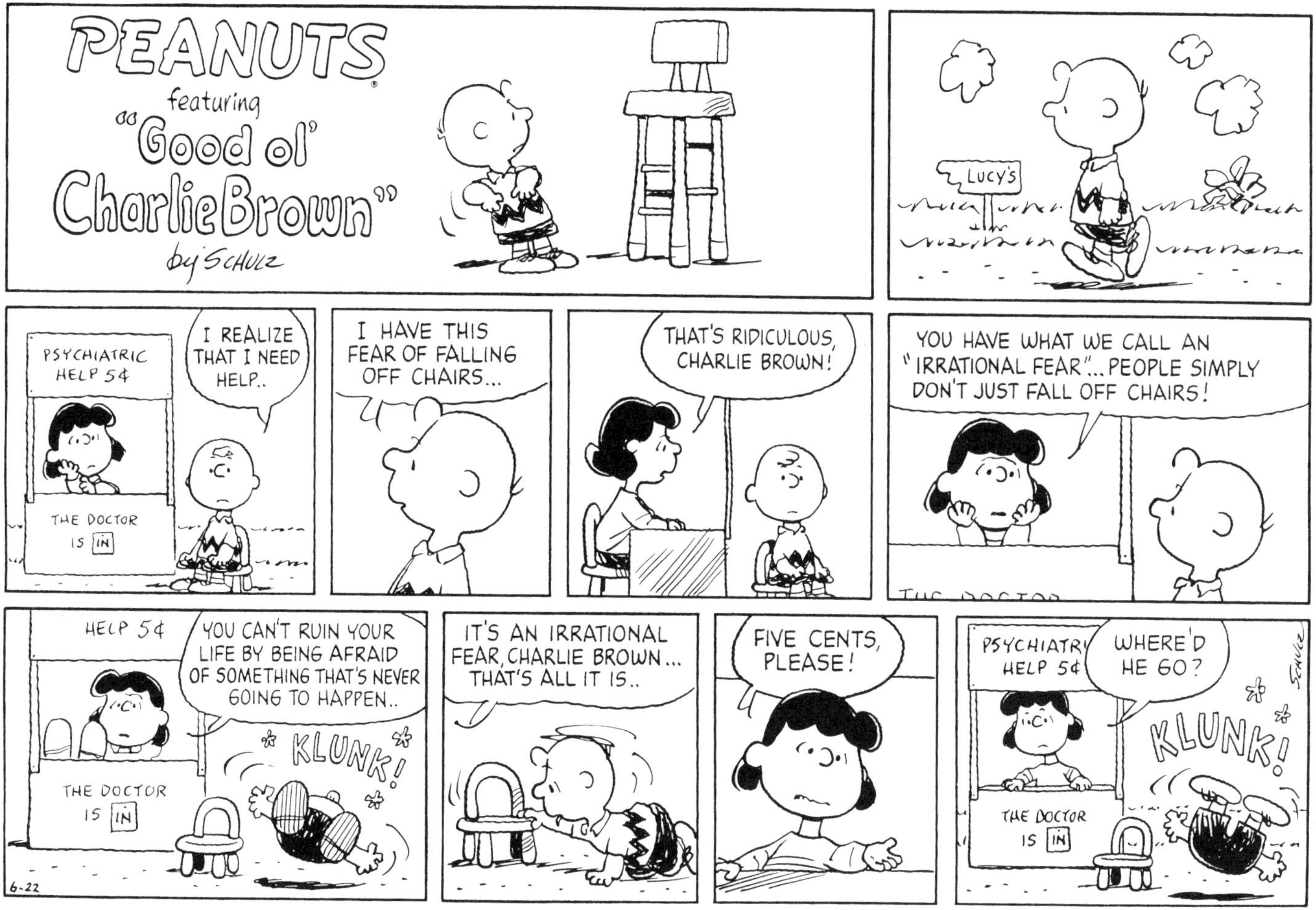
PEANUTS
featuring "Good ol' Charlie Brown"
by SCHULZ
LUCY'S
PSYCHIATRIC HELP 5¢
THE DOCTOR IS IN
I REALIZE THAT I NEED HELP..
I HAVE THIS FEAR OF FALLING OFF CHAIRS...
THAT'S RIDICULOUS, CHARLIE BROWN!
YOU HAVE WHAT WE CALL AN "IRRATIONAL FEAR"... PEOPLE SIMPLY DON'T JUST FALL OFF CHAIRS!
HELP 5¢
YOU CAN'T RUIN YOUR LIFE BY BEING AFRAID OF SOMETHING THAT'S NEVER GOING TO HAPPEN..
THE DOCTOR IS IN
KLUNK!
6-22
IT'S AN IRRATIONAL FEAR, CHARLIE BROWN... THAT'S ALL IT IS..
FIVE CENTS, PLEASE!
PSYCHIATRI HELP 5¢
WHERE'D HE GO?
SCHULZ
KLUNK!
THE DOCTOR IS IN

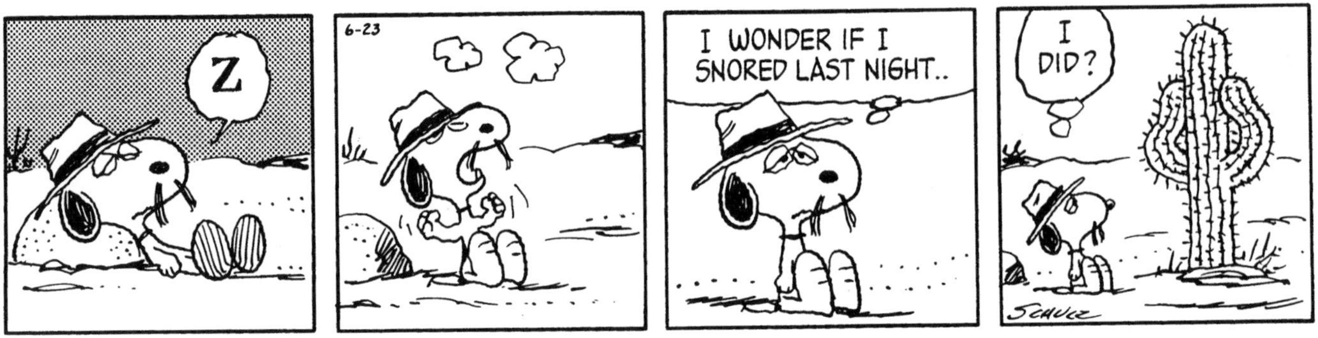
Z
6-23
I WONDER IF I SNORED LAST NIGHT..
I DID?
SCHULZ

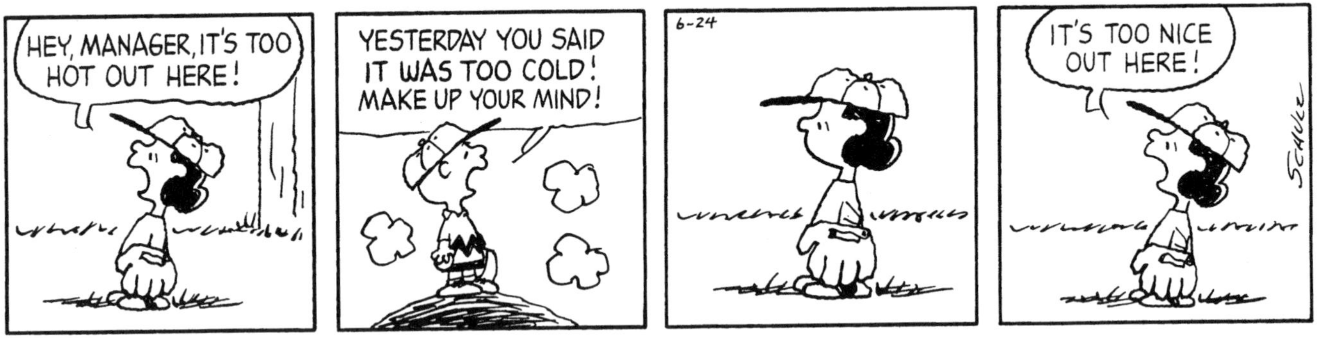
HEY, MANAGER, IT'S TOO HOT OUT HERE!
YESTERDAY YOU SAID IT WAS TOO COLD! MAKE UP YOUR MIND!
6-24
IT'S TOO NICE OUT HERE!
SCHULZ

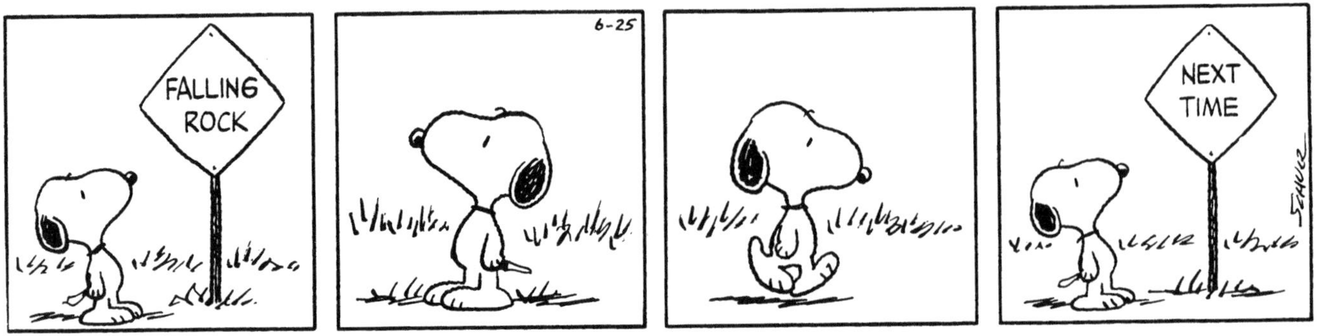
FALLING ROCK
6-25
NEXT TIME
SCHULZ

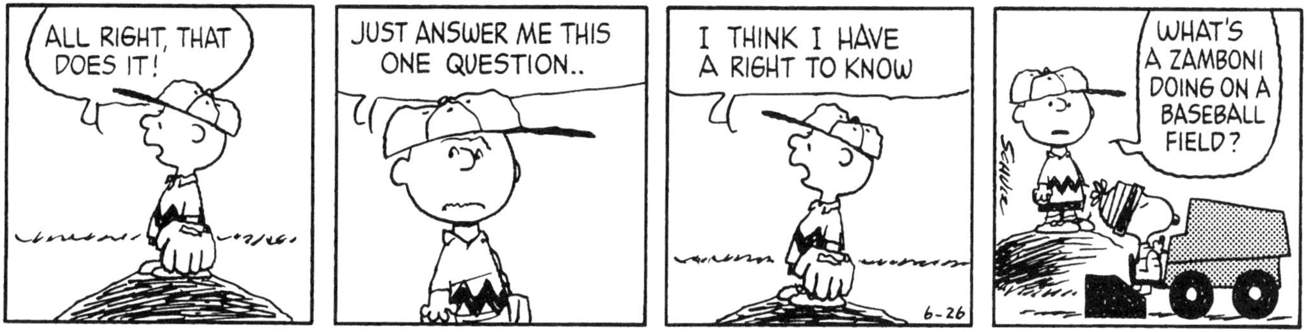
ALL RIGHT, THAT DOES IT!
JUST ANSWER ME THIS ONE QUESTION..
I THINK I HAVE A RIGHT TO KNOW
6-26
WHAT'S A ZAMBONI DOING ON A BASEBALL FIELD?
SCHULZ

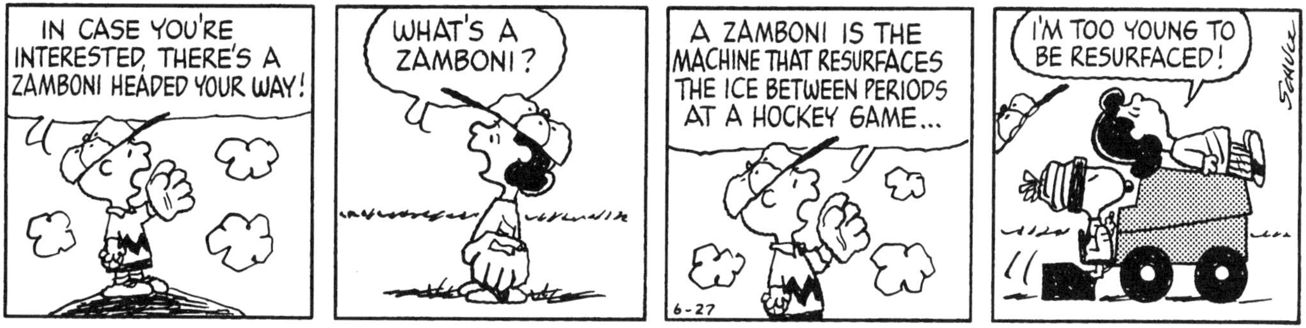
IN CASE YOU'RE INTERESTED, THERE'S A ZAMBONI HEADED YOUR WAY!
WHAT'S A ZAMBONI?
A ZAMBONI IS THE MACHINE THAT RESURFACES THE ICE BETWEEN PERIODS AT A HOCKEY GAME...
6-27
I'M TOO YOUNG TO BE RESURFACED!
SCHULZ

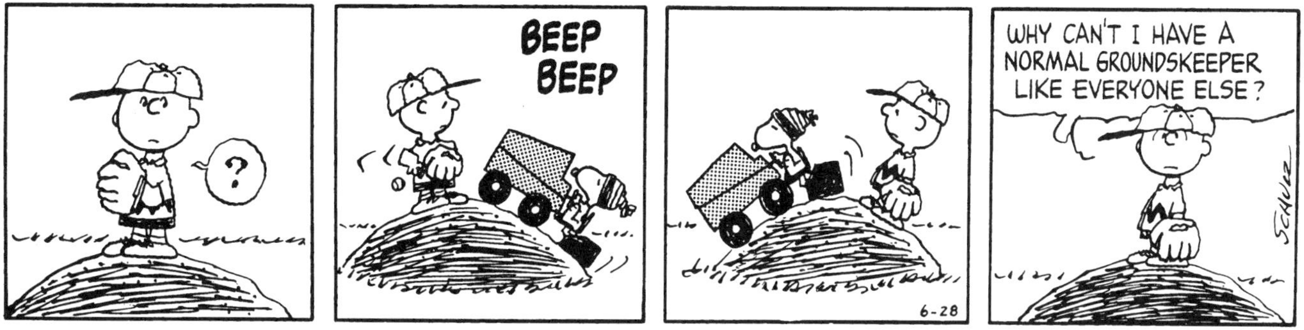
?
BEEP BEEP
6-28
WHY CAN'T I HAVE A NORMAL GROUNDSKEEPER LIKE EVERYONE ELSE?
SCHULZ

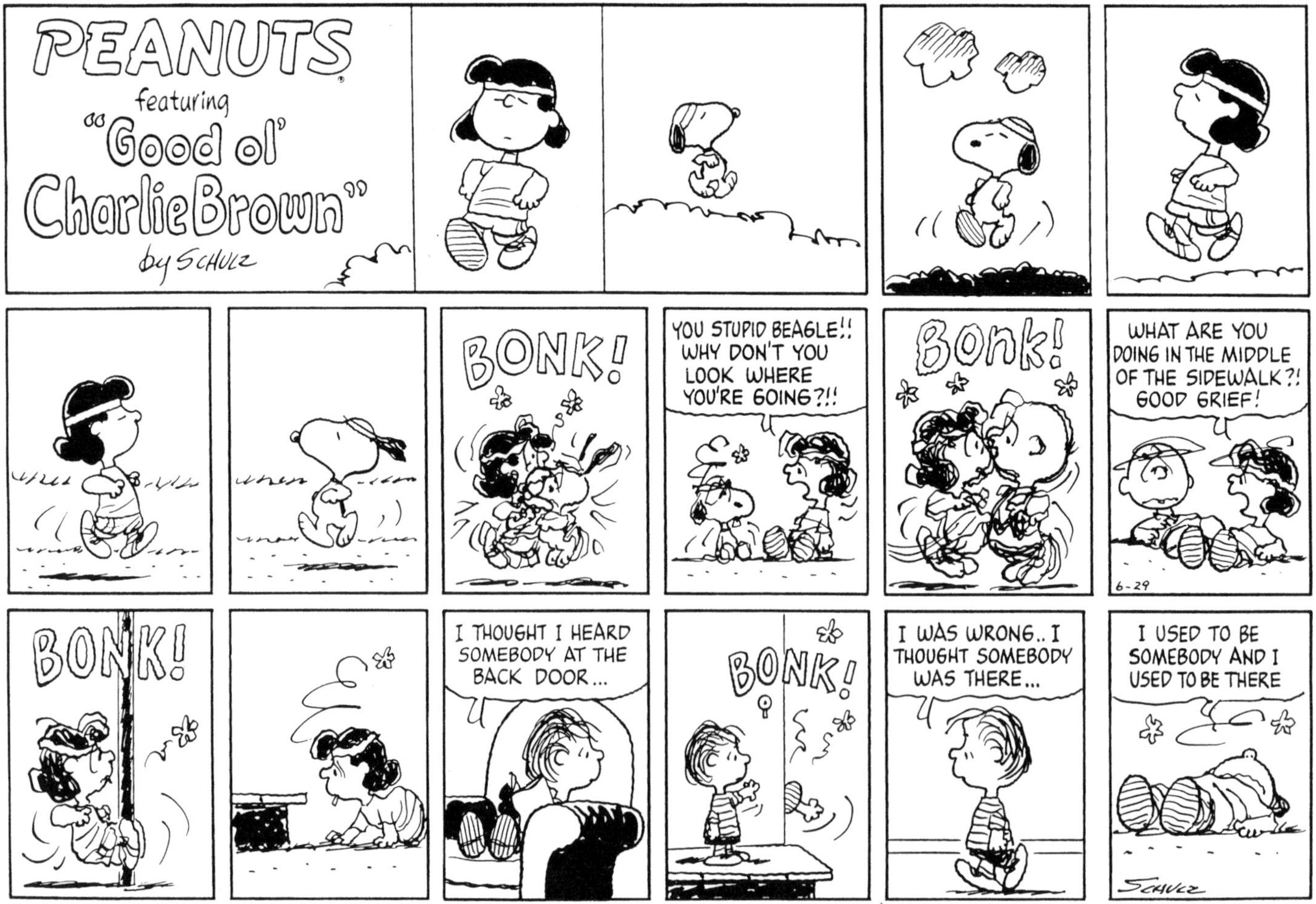
PEANUTS
featuring
"Good ol' Charlie Brown"
by SCHULZ
BONK!
YOU STUPID BEAGLE!! WHY DON'T YOU LOOK WHERE YOU'RE GOING?!!
BONK!
WHAT ARE YOU DOING IN THE MIDDLE OF THE SIDEWALK?! GOOD GRIEF!
6-29
BONK!
I THOUGHT I HEARD SOMEBODY AT THE BACK DOOR...
BONK!
I WAS WRONG.. I THOUGHT SOMEBODY WAS THERE...
I USED TO BE SOMEBODY AND I USED TO BE THERE
SCHULZ

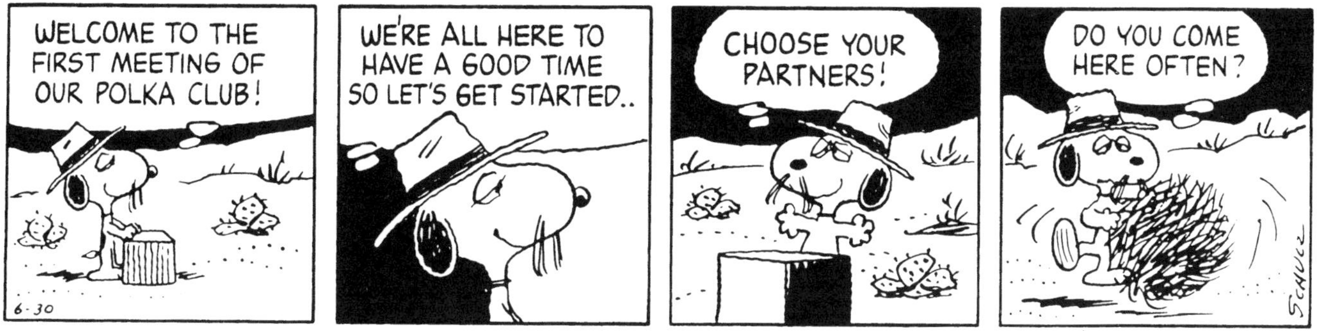
6-30
WELCOME TO THE FIRST MEETING OF OUR POLKA CLUB!
WE'RE ALL HERE TO HAVE A GOOD TIME SO LET'S GET STARTED..
CHOOSE YOUR PARTNERS!
DO YOU COME HERE OFTEN?
SCHULZ

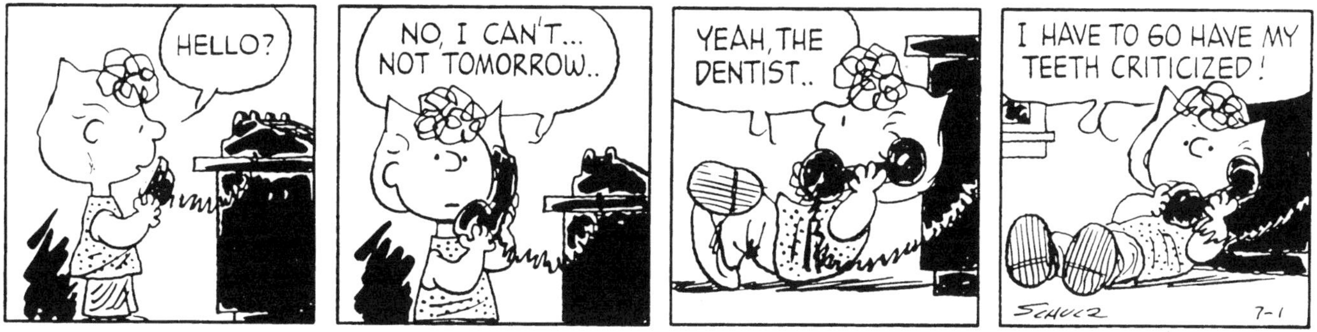
HELLO?
NO, I CAN'T... NOT TOMORROW..
YEAH, THE DENTIST..
I HAVE TO GO HAVE MY TEETH CRITICIZED!
SCHULZ
7-1

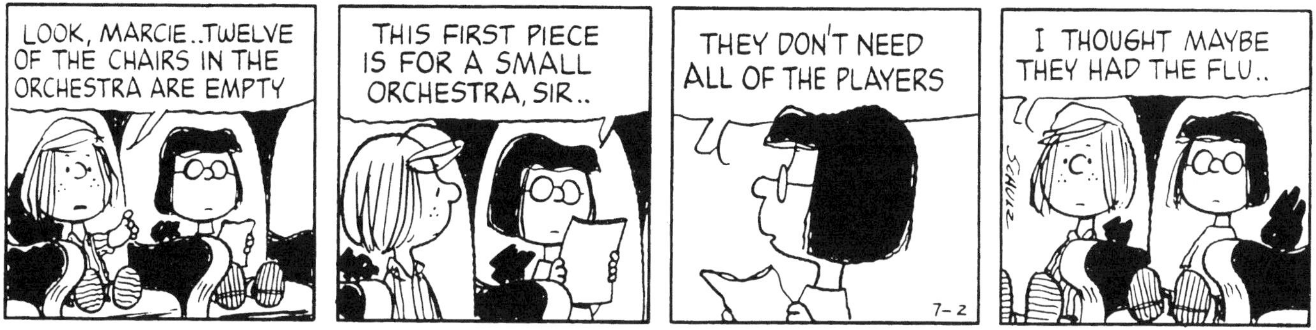
LOOK, MARCIE..TWELVE OF THE CHAIRS IN THE ORCHESTRA ARE EMPTY
THIS FIRST PIECE IS FOR A SMALL ORCHESTRA, SIR..
THEY DON'T NEED ALL OF THE PLAYERS
7-2
I THOUGHT MAYBE THEY HAD THE FLU..
SCHULZ

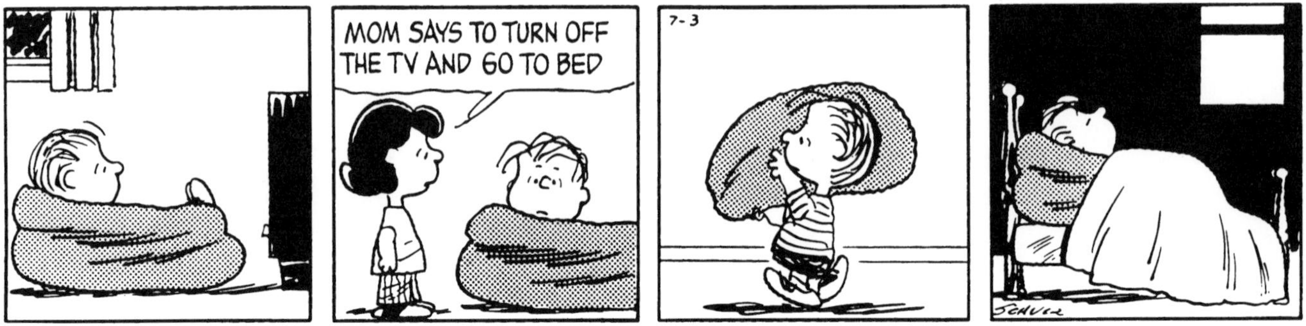
MOM SAYS TO TURN OFF THE TV AND GO TO BED
7-3
SCHULZ

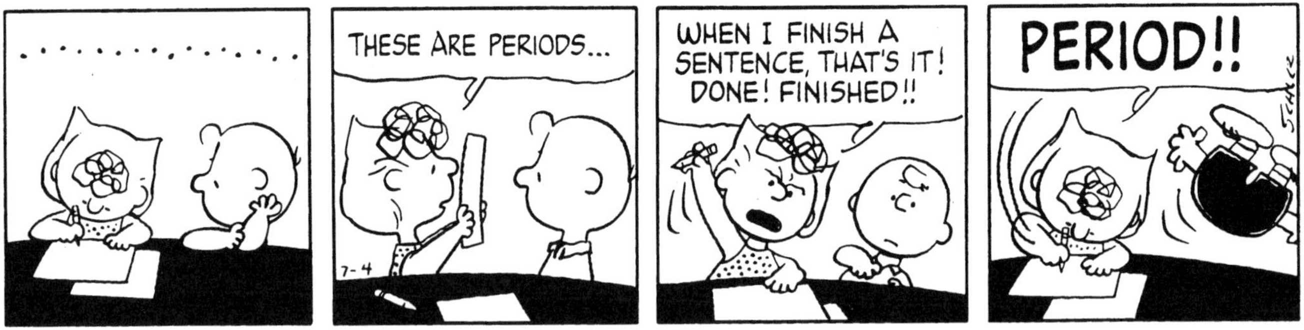
THESE ARE PERIODS...
7-4
WHEN I FINISH A SENTENCE, THAT'S IT! DONE! FINISHED!!
PERIOD!!
SCHULZ

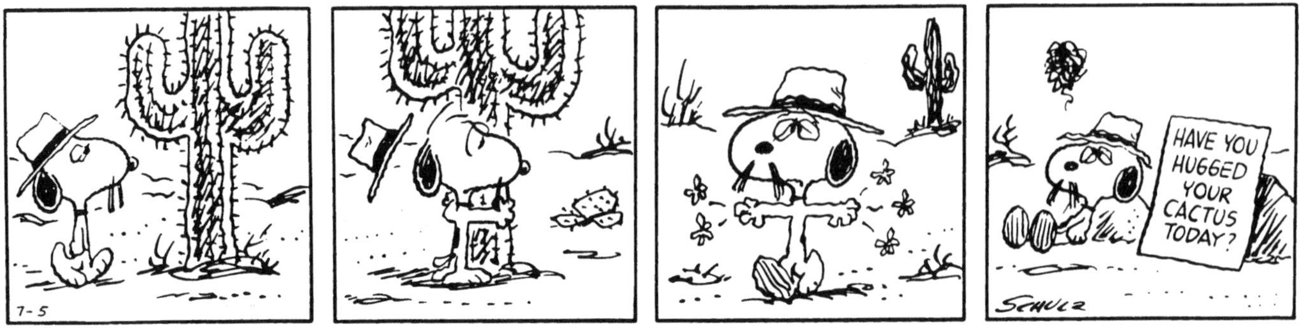
7-5
HAVE YOU HUGGED YOUR CACTUS TODAY?
SCHULZ

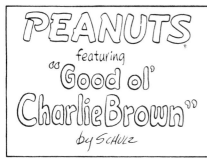

PEANUTS
featuring
"Good ol' CharlieBrown"
by Schulz

"DEAR DAD..WELL, HERE WE ARE AT CAMP REMOTE.."

I THINK THEY PRONOUNCE IT "REMOTAY," SIR

WHICH REMINDS ME, I HAVE A PROBLEM OF MY OWN..

I SWEAR, SIR, THAT I CAN HARDLY STAND IT!

I MAY JUST PUSH HIM IN THE LAKE OR SOMETHING!

AFTER ALL, I CAME TO CAMP TO HAVE A GOOD TIME, DIDN'T I?

7-6

WHY SHOULD I PUT UP WITH HIM?

LOOK! THERE HE IS...I'LL SHOW YOU..

HEY, KID!

WHAT?

THAT DID IT!!

AAUGH!!

SEE? HE KEEPS TALKING TO ME!

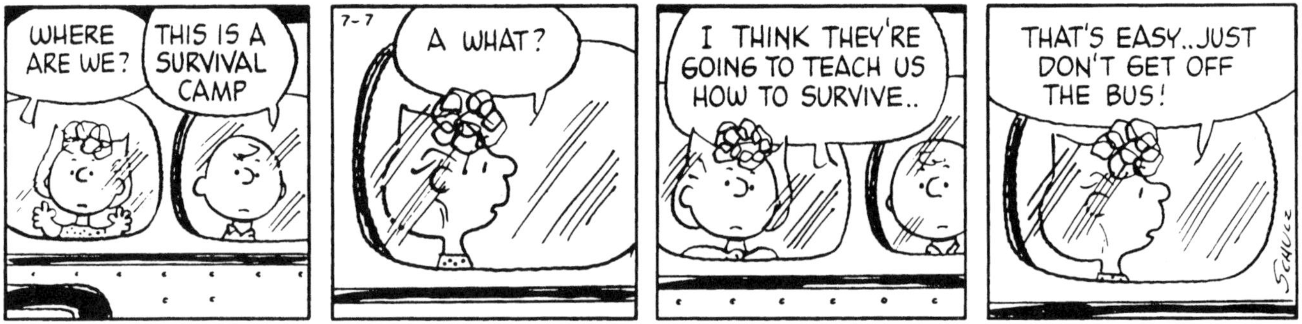
WHERE ARE WE?
THIS IS A SURVIVAL CAMP
7-7
A WHAT?
I THINK THEY'RE GOING TO TEACH US HOW TO SURVIVE..
THAT'S EASY..JUST DON'T GET OFF THE BUS!
SCHULZ

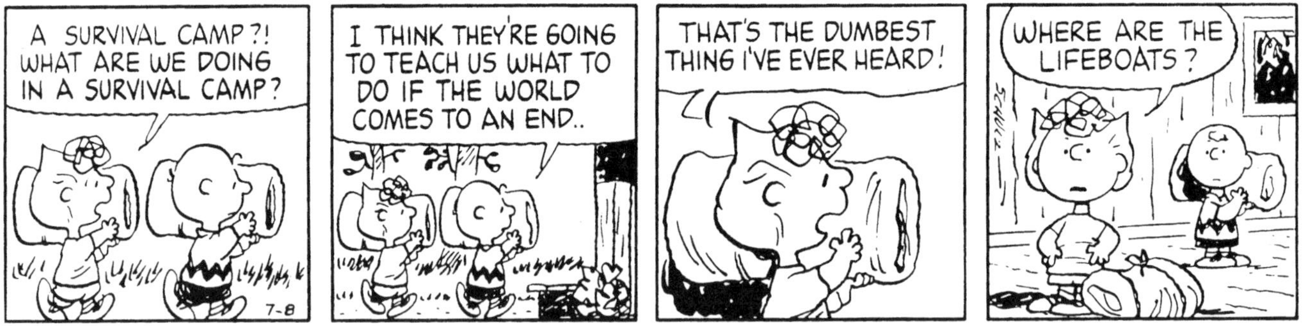
A SURVIVAL CAMP?! WHAT ARE WE DOING IN A SURVIVAL CAMP?
7-8
I THINK THEY'RE GOING TO TEACH US WHAT TO DO IF THE WORLD COMES TO AN END..
THAT'S THE DUMBEST THING I'VE EVER HEARD!
WHERE ARE THE LIFEBOATS?
SCHULZ

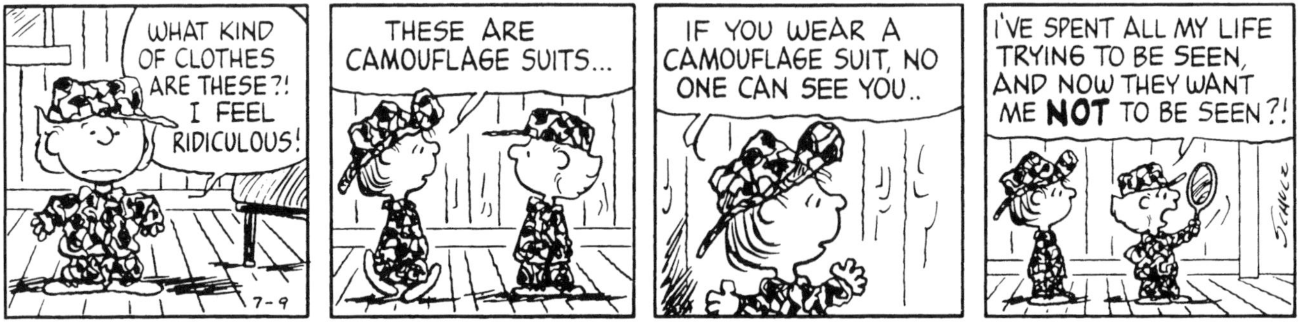
WHAT KIND OF CLOTHES ARE THESE?! I FEEL RIDICULOUS!
7-9
THESE ARE CAMOUFLAGE SUITS...
IF YOU WEAR A CAMOUFLAGE SUIT, NO ONE CAN SEE YOU..
I'VE SPENT ALL MY LIFE TRYING TO BE SEEN, AND NOW THEY WANT ME **NOT** TO BE SEEN?!
SCHULZ

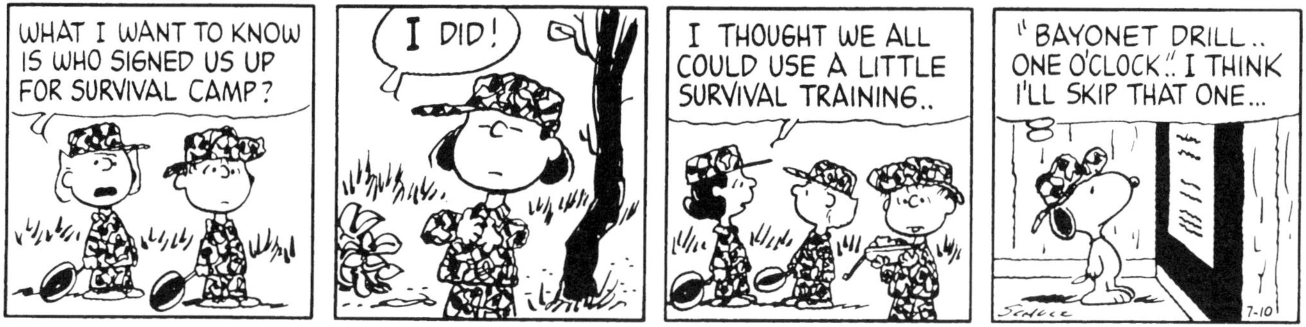
WHAT I WANT TO KNOW IS WHO SIGNED US UP FOR SURVIVAL CAMP?
I DID!
I THOUGHT WE ALL COULD USE A LITTLE SURVIVAL TRAINING..
"BAYONET DRILL.. ONE O'CLOCK." I THINK I'LL SKIP THAT ONE...
7-10

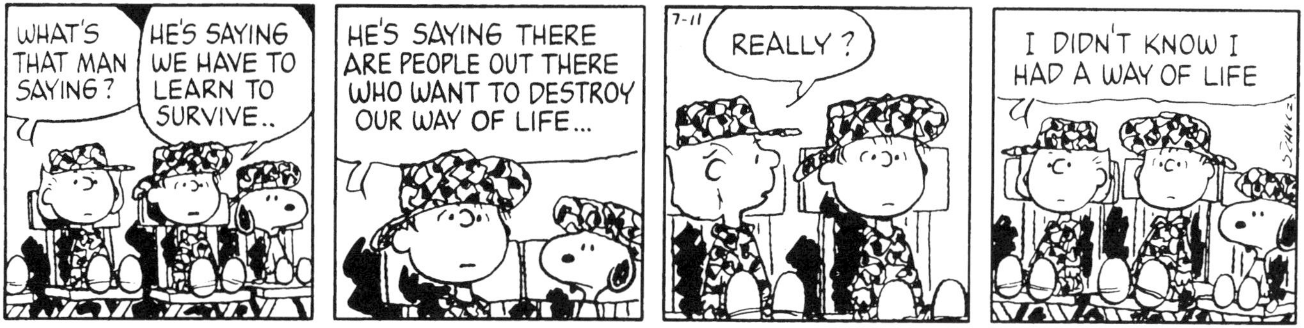
WHAT'S THAT MAN SAYING?
HE'S SAYING WE HAVE TO LEARN TO SURVIVE..
HE'S SAYING THERE ARE PEOPLE OUT THERE WHO WANT TO DESTROY OUR WAY OF LIFE...
7-11
REALLY?
I DIDN'T KNOW I HAD A WAY OF LIFE

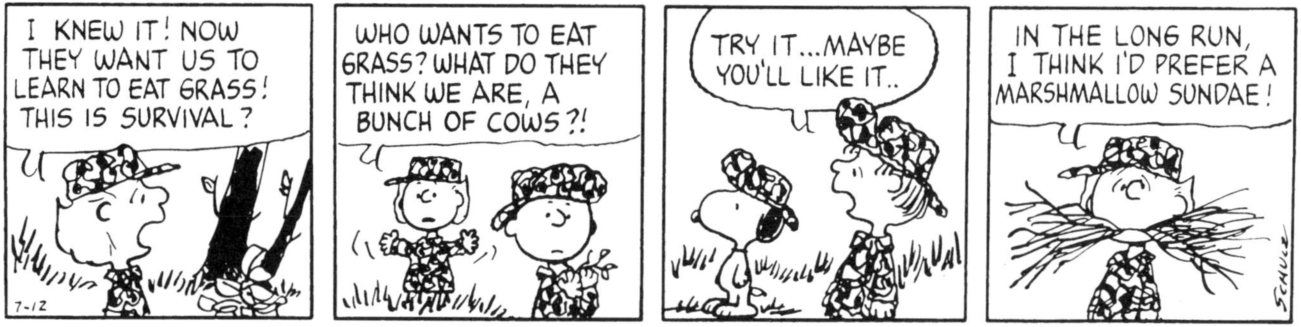
I KNEW IT! NOW THEY WANT US TO LEARN TO EAT GRASS! THIS IS SURVIVAL?
7-12
WHO WANTS TO EAT GRASS? WHAT DO THEY THINK WE ARE, A BUNCH OF COWS?!
TRY IT...MAYBE YOU'LL LIKE IT..
IN THE LONG RUN, I THINK I'D PREFER A MARSHMALLOW SUNDAE!

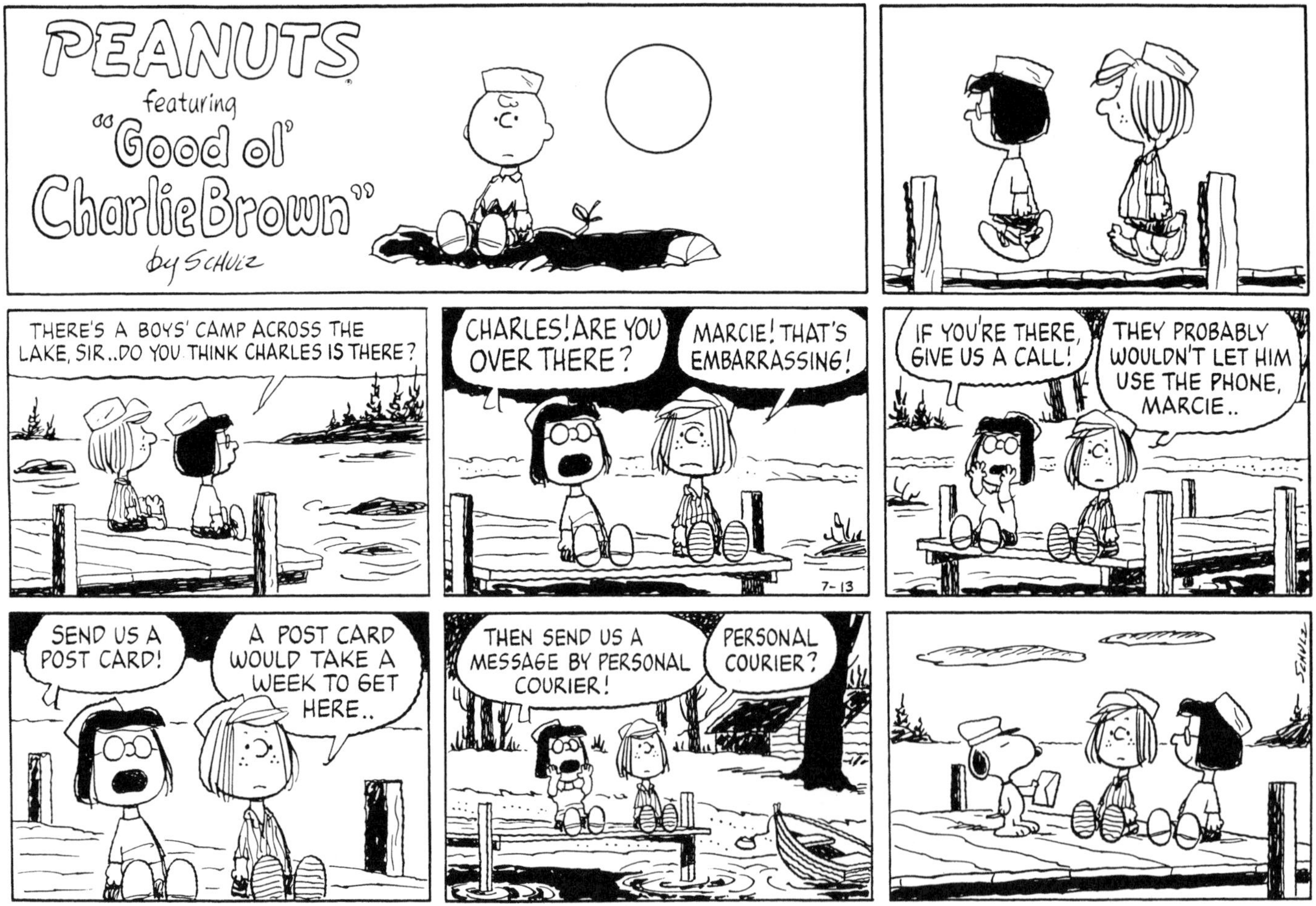
PEANUTS
featuring
"Good ol' Charlie Brown"
by SCHULZ
THERE'S A BOYS' CAMP ACROSS THE LAKE, SIR..DO YOU THINK CHARLES IS THERE?
CHARLES! ARE YOU OVER THERE?
MARCIE! THAT'S EMBARRASSING!
7-13
IF YOU'RE THERE, GIVE US A CALL!
THEY PROBABLY WOULDN'T LET HIM USE THE PHONE, MARCIE..
SEND US A POST CARD!
A POST CARD WOULD TAKE A WEEK TO GET HERE..
THEN SEND US A MESSAGE BY PERSONAL COURIER!
PERSONAL COURIER?
SCHULZ

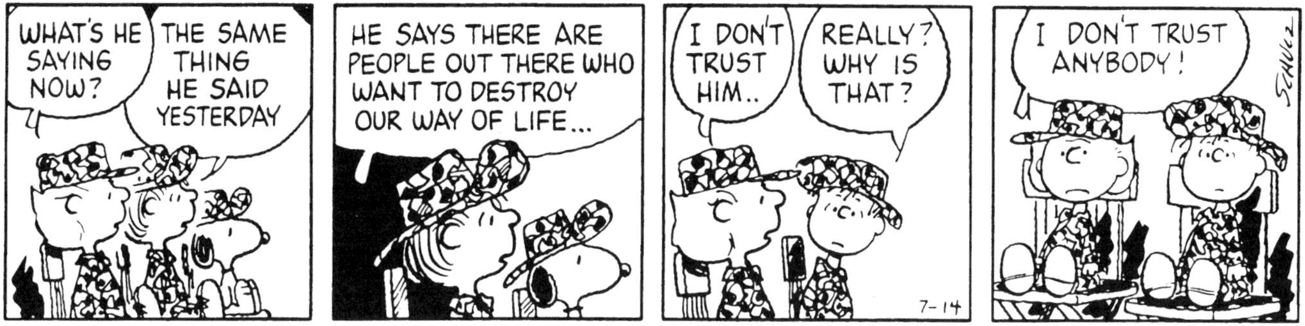
WHAT'S HE SAYING NOW?
THE SAME THING HE SAID YESTERDAY
HE SAYS THERE ARE PEOPLE OUT THERE WHO WANT TO DESTROY OUR WAY OF LIFE...
I DON'T TRUST HIM..
REALLY? WHY IS THAT?
7-14
I DON'T TRUST ANYBODY!
SCHULZ

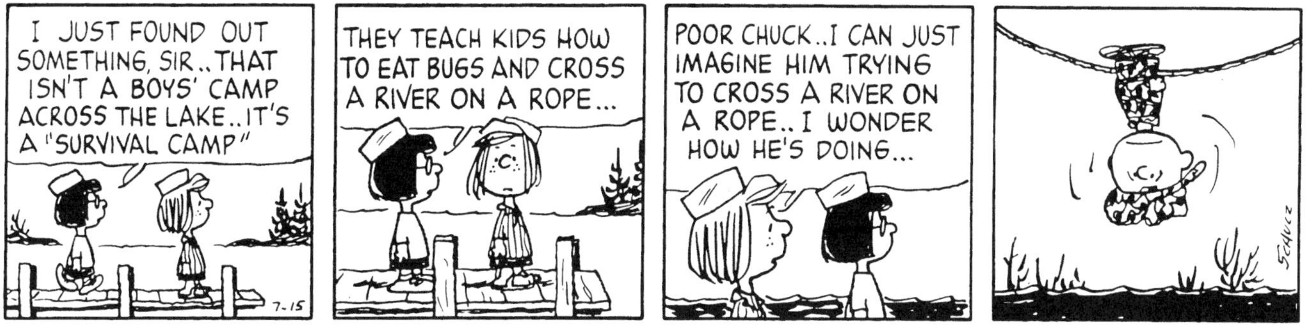
I JUST FOUND OUT SOMETHING, SIR.. THAT ISN'T A BOYS' CAMP ACROSS THE LAKE.. IT'S A "SURVIVAL CAMP"
7-15
THEY TEACH KIDS HOW TO EAT BUGS AND CROSS A RIVER ON A ROPE...
POOR CHUCK.. I CAN JUST IMAGINE HIM TRYING TO CROSS A RIVER ON A ROPE.. I WONDER HOW HE'S DOING...
SCHULZ

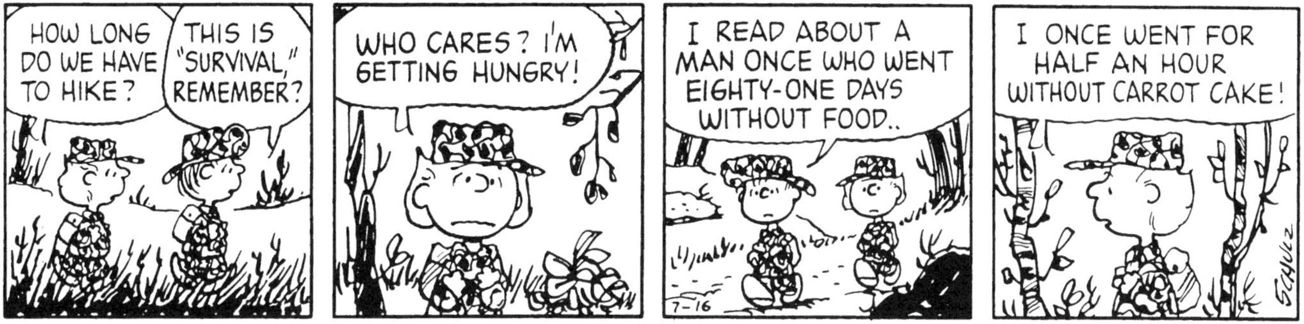
HOW LONG DO WE HAVE TO HIKE?
THIS IS "SURVIVAL," REMEMBER?
WHO CARES? I'M GETTING HUNGRY!
I READ ABOUT A MAN ONCE WHO WENT EIGHTY-ONE DAYS WITHOUT FOOD..
7-16
I ONCE WENT FOR HALF AN HOUR WITHOUT CARROT CAKE!
SCHULZ

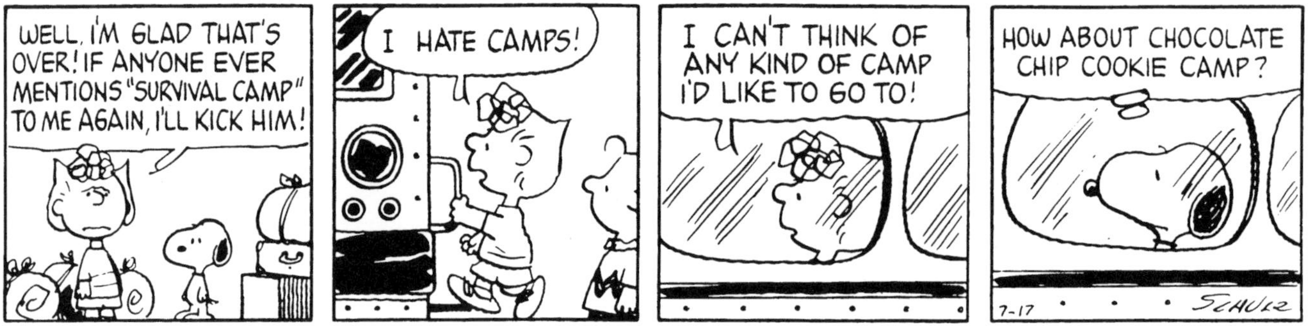
WELL, I'M GLAD THAT'S OVER! IF ANYONE EVER MENTIONS "SURVIVAL CAMP" TO ME AGAIN, I'LL KICK HIM!
I HATE CAMPS!
I CAN'T THINK OF ANY KIND OF CAMP I'D LIKE TO GO TO!
HOW ABOUT CHOCOLATE CHIP COOKIE CAMP?
7-17
SCHULZ

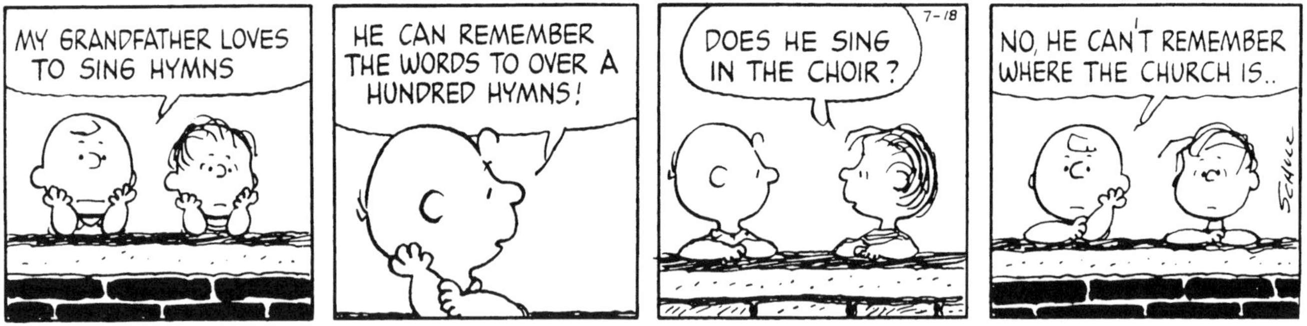
MY GRANDFATHER LOVES TO SING HYMNS
HE CAN REMEMBER THE WORDS TO OVER A HUNDRED HYMNS!
7-18
DOES HE SING IN THE CHOIR?
NO, HE CAN'T REMEMBER WHERE THE CHURCH IS..
SCHULZ

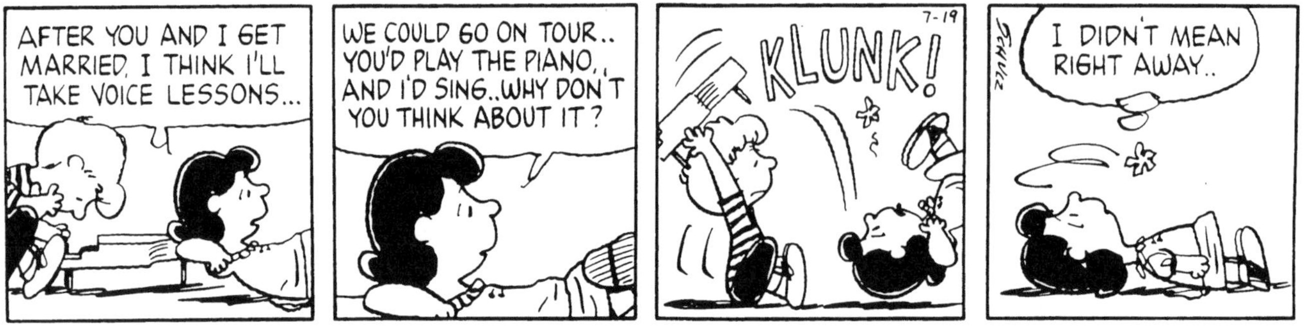
AFTER YOU AND I GET MARRIED, I THINK I'LL TAKE VOICE LESSONS...
WE COULD GO ON TOUR.. YOU'D PLAY THE PIANO, AND I'D SING..WHY DON'T YOU THINK ABOUT IT?
7-19
KLUNK!
SCHULZ
I DIDN'T MEAN RIGHT AWAY..

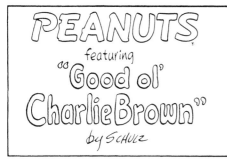

PEANUTS
featuring
"Good ol' CharlieBrown"
by SCHULZ

WATCH IT, BEAGLE! IF YOU TOUCH THIS BLANKET, I'LL DESTROY YOU!

I'LL DESTROY YOU AND ALL YOUR COUSINS, AND THE PLACE WHERE YOU WERE BORN AND ALL THE RECORDS AT THE COURT HOUSE! SMALL CRAFT WARNINGS WILL BE POSTED ALONG BOTH COASTS! I WILL POUNCE ON YOU LIKE THE LAST DAYS OF POMPEII!!

SO BACK OFF!

WHEN I BACK OFF, I BACK OFF!

7-20

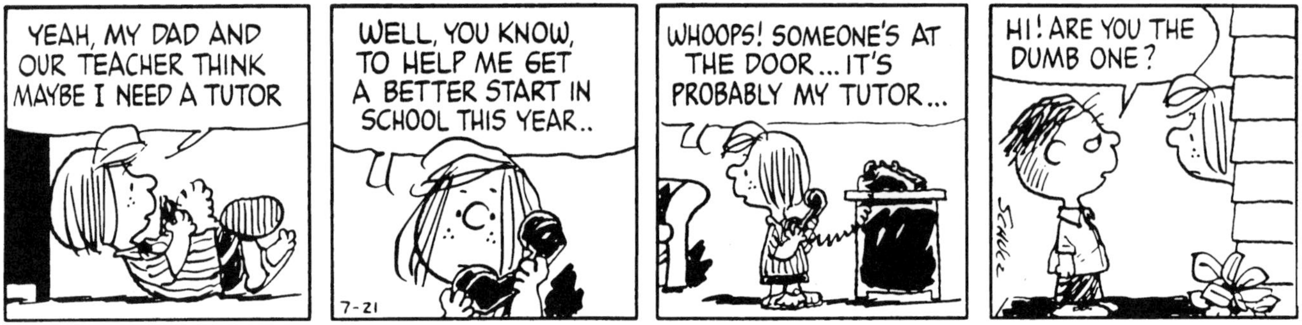
YEAH, MY DAD AND OUR TEACHER THINK MAYBE I NEED A TUTOR
WELL, YOU KNOW, TO HELP ME GET A BETTER START IN SCHOOL THIS YEAR..
7-21
WHOOPS! SOMEONE'S AT THE DOOR... IT'S PROBABLY MY TUTOR...
HI! ARE YOU THE DUMB ONE?
SCHULZ

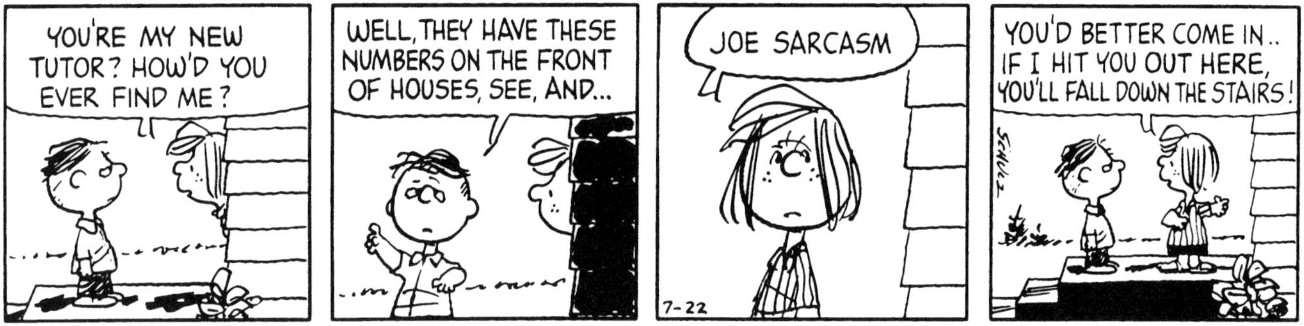
YOU'RE MY NEW TUTOR? HOW'D YOU EVER FIND ME?
WELL, THEY HAVE THESE NUMBERS ON THE FRONT OF HOUSES, SEE, AND...
JOE SARCASM
7-22
YOU'D BETTER COME IN.. IF I HIT YOU OUT HERE, YOU'LL FALL DOWN THE STAIRS!
SCHULZ

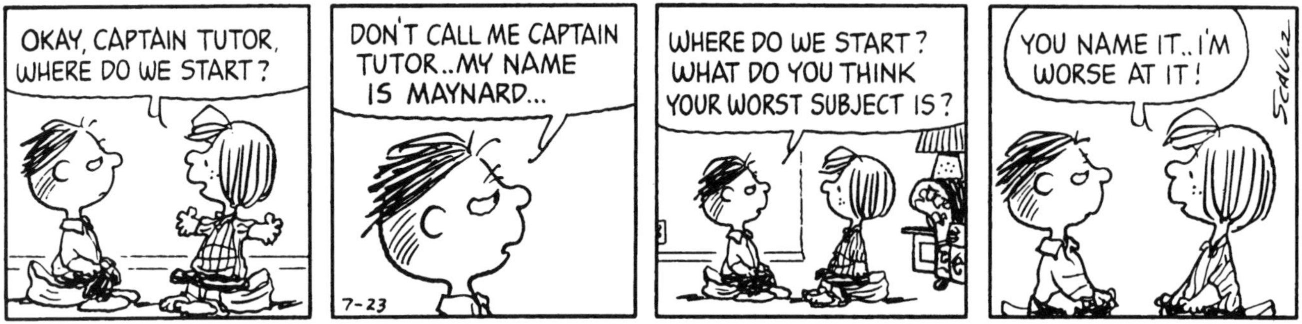
OKAY, CAPTAIN TUTOR, WHERE DO WE START?
DON'T CALL ME CAPTAIN TUTOR..MY NAME IS MAYNARD...
7-23
WHERE DO WE START? WHAT DO YOU THINK YOUR WORST SUBJECT IS?
YOU NAME IT..I'M WORSE AT IT!
SCHULZ

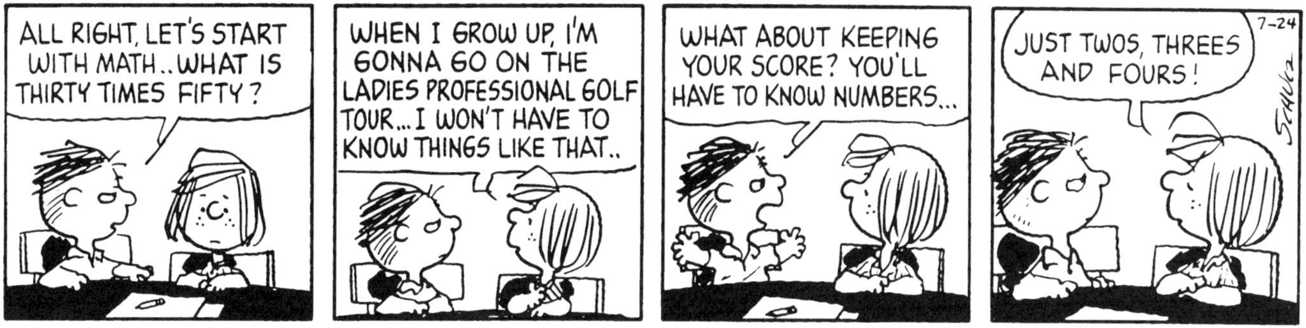
ALL RIGHT, LET'S START WITH MATH..WHAT IS THIRTY TIMES FIFTY?
WHEN I GROW UP, I'M GONNA GO ON THE LADIES PROFESSIONAL GOLF TOUR...I WON'T HAVE TO KNOW THINGS LIKE THAT..
WHAT ABOUT KEEPING YOUR SCORE? YOU'LL HAVE TO KNOW NUMBERS...
7-24
JUST TWOS, THREES AND FOURS!

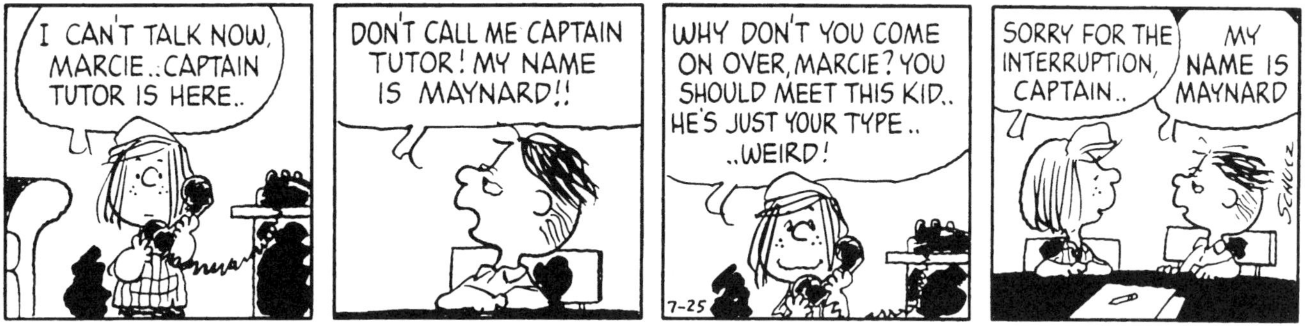
I CAN'T TALK NOW, MARCIE..CAPTAIN TUTOR IS HERE..
DON'T CALL ME CAPTAIN TUTOR! MY NAME IS MAYNARD!!
WHY DON'T YOU COME ON OVER, MARCIE? YOU SHOULD MEET THIS KID.. HE'S JUST YOUR TYPE.. ..WEIRD!
7-25
SORRY FOR THE INTERRUPTION, CAPTAIN..
MY NAME IS MAYNARD

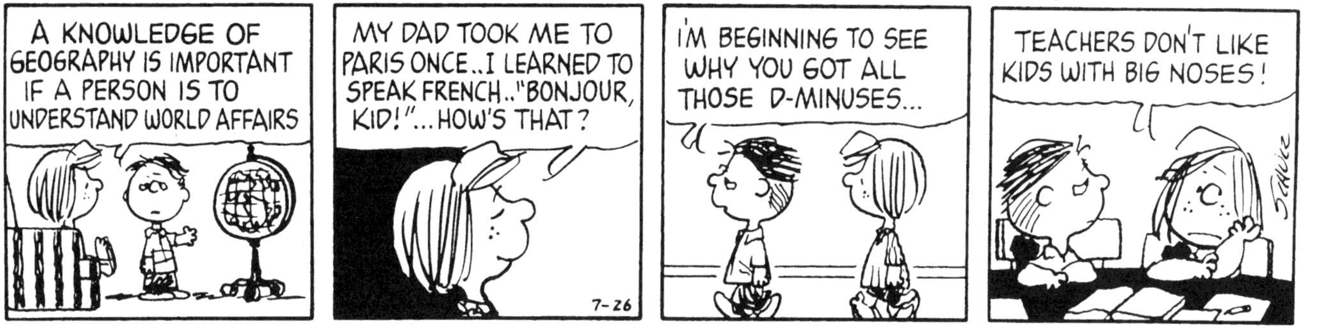
A KNOWLEDGE OF GEOGRAPHY IS IMPORTANT IF A PERSON IS TO UNDERSTAND WORLD AFFAIRS
MY DAD TOOK ME TO PARIS ONCE..I LEARNED TO SPEAK FRENCH.."BONJOUR, KID!"...HOW'S THAT?
7-26
I'M BEGINNING TO SEE WHY YOU GOT ALL THOSE D-MINUSES...
TEACHERS DON'T LIKE KIDS WITH BIG NOSES!

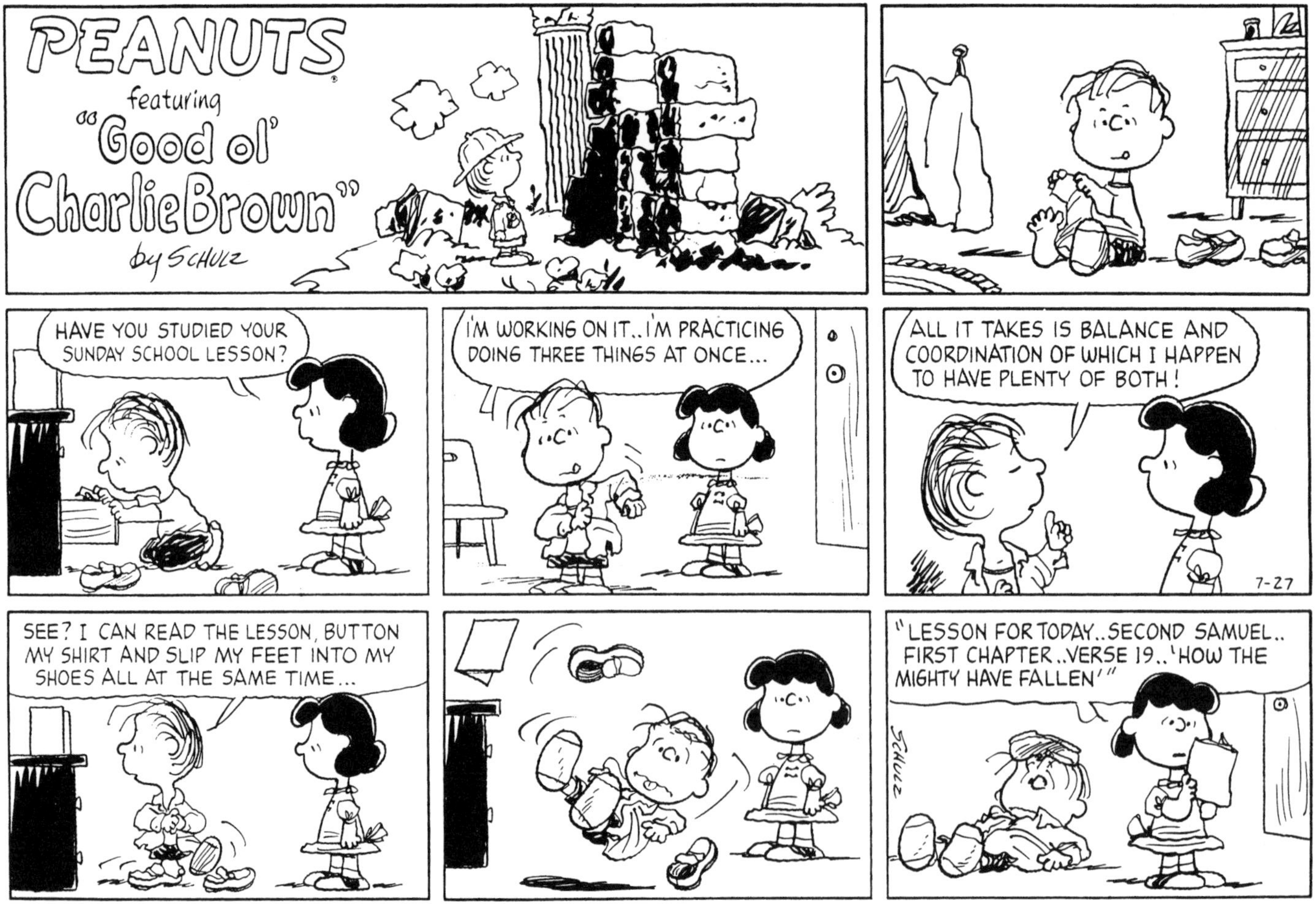
PEANUTS
featuring
"Good ol' CharlieBrown"
by SCHULZ
HAVE YOU STUDIED YOUR SUNDAY SCHOOL LESSON?
I'M WORKING ON IT.. I'M PRACTICING DOING THREE THINGS AT ONCE...
ALL IT TAKES IS BALANCE AND COORDINATION OF WHICH I HAPPEN TO HAVE PLENTY OF BOTH!
7-27
SEE? I CAN READ THE LESSON, BUTTON MY SHIRT AND SLIP MY FEET INTO MY SHOES ALL AT THE SAME TIME...
"LESSON FOR TODAY.. SECOND SAMUEL.. FIRST CHAPTER.. VERSE 19.. 'HOW THE MIGHTY HAVE FALLEN'"
SCHULZ

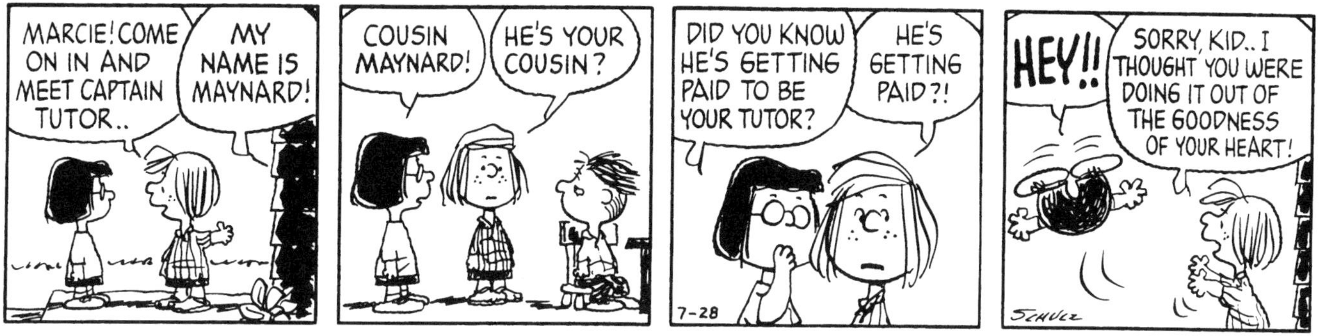
MARCIE! COME ON IN AND MEET CAPTAIN TUTOR..
MY NAME IS MAYNARD!
COUSIN MAYNARD!
HE'S YOUR COUSIN?
DID YOU KNOW HE'S GETTING PAID TO BE YOUR TUTOR?
HE'S GETTING PAID?!
7-28
HEY!!
SORRY, KID.. I THOUGHT YOU WERE DOING IT OUT OF THE GOODNESS OF YOUR HEART!
SCHULZ

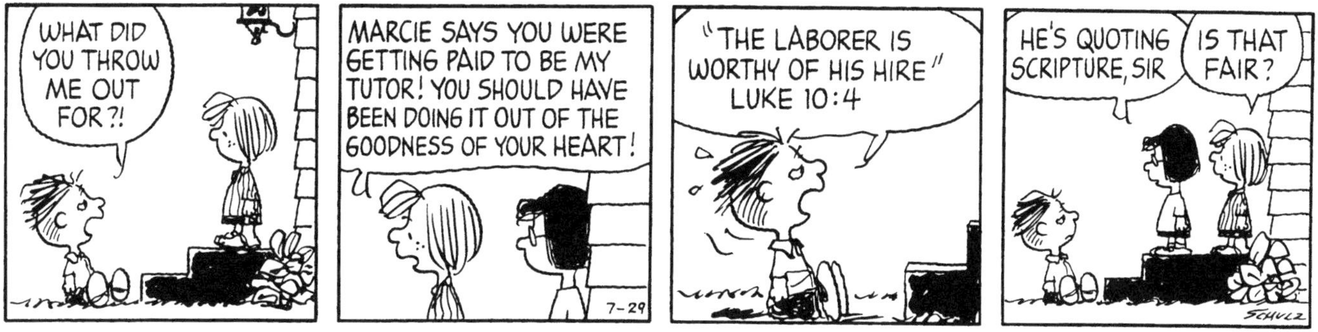
WHAT DID YOU THROW ME OUT FOR?!
MARCIE SAYS YOU WERE GETTING PAID TO BE MY TUTOR! YOU SHOULD HAVE BEEN DOING IT OUT OF THE GOODNESS OF YOUR HEART!
7-29
"THE LABORER IS WORTHY OF HIS HIRE" LUKE 10:4
HE'S QUOTING SCRIPTURE, SIR
IS THAT FAIR?
SCHULZ

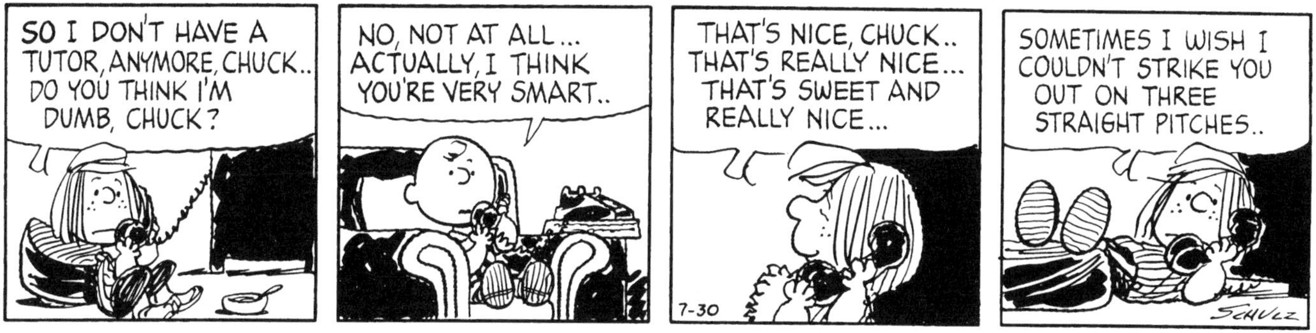
SO I DON'T HAVE A TUTOR, ANYMORE, CHUCK.. DO YOU THINK I'M DUMB, CHUCK?
NO, NOT AT ALL... ACTUALLY, I THINK YOU'RE VERY SMART..
THAT'S NICE, CHUCK.. THAT'S REALLY NICE... THAT'S SWEET AND REALLY NICE...
7-30
SOMETIMES I WISH I COULDN'T STRIKE YOU OUT ON THREE STRAIGHT PITCHES..
SCHULZ

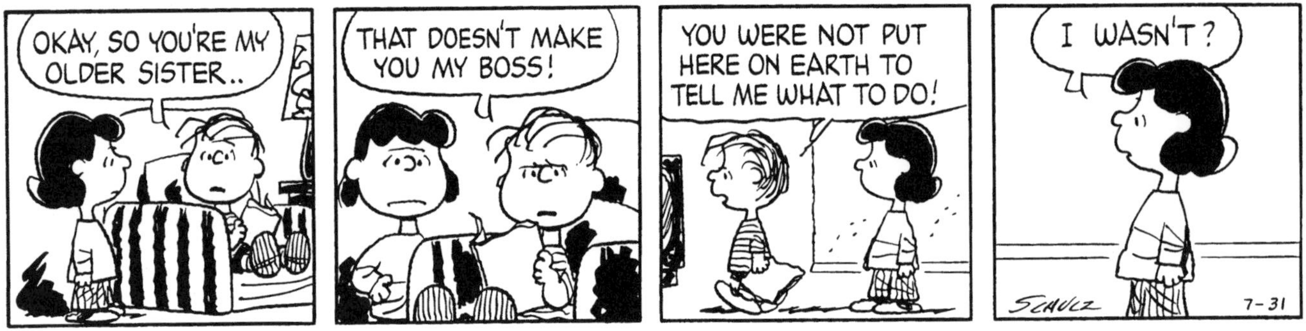
OKAY, SO YOU'RE MY OLDER SISTER..
THAT DOESN'T MAKE YOU MY BOSS!
YOU WERE NOT PUT HERE ON EARTH TO TELL ME WHAT TO DO!
I WASN'T?
SCHULZ
7-31

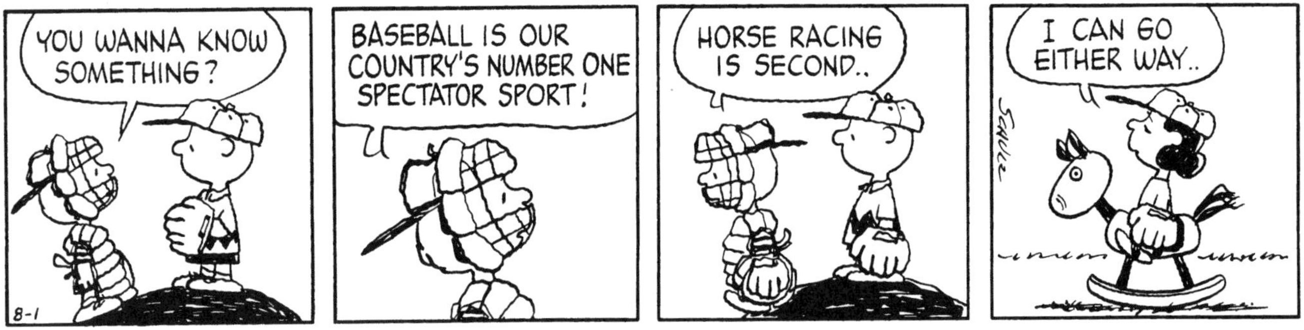
8-1
YOU WANNA KNOW SOMETHING?
BASEBALL IS OUR COUNTRY'S NUMBER ONE SPECTATOR SPORT!
HORSE RACING IS SECOND..
I CAN GO EITHER WAY..
SCHULZ

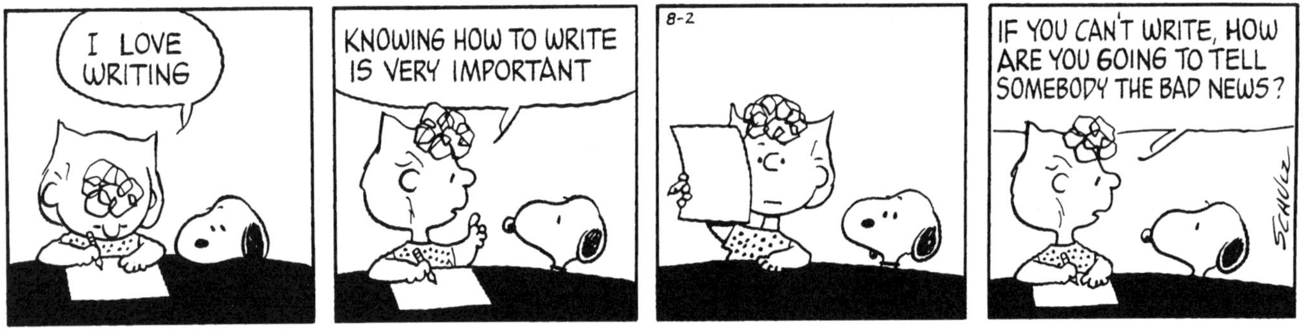
I LOVE WRITING
KNOWING HOW TO WRITE IS VERY IMPORTANT
8-2
IF YOU CAN'T WRITE, HOW ARE YOU GOING TO TELL SOMEBODY THE BAD NEWS?
SCHULZ

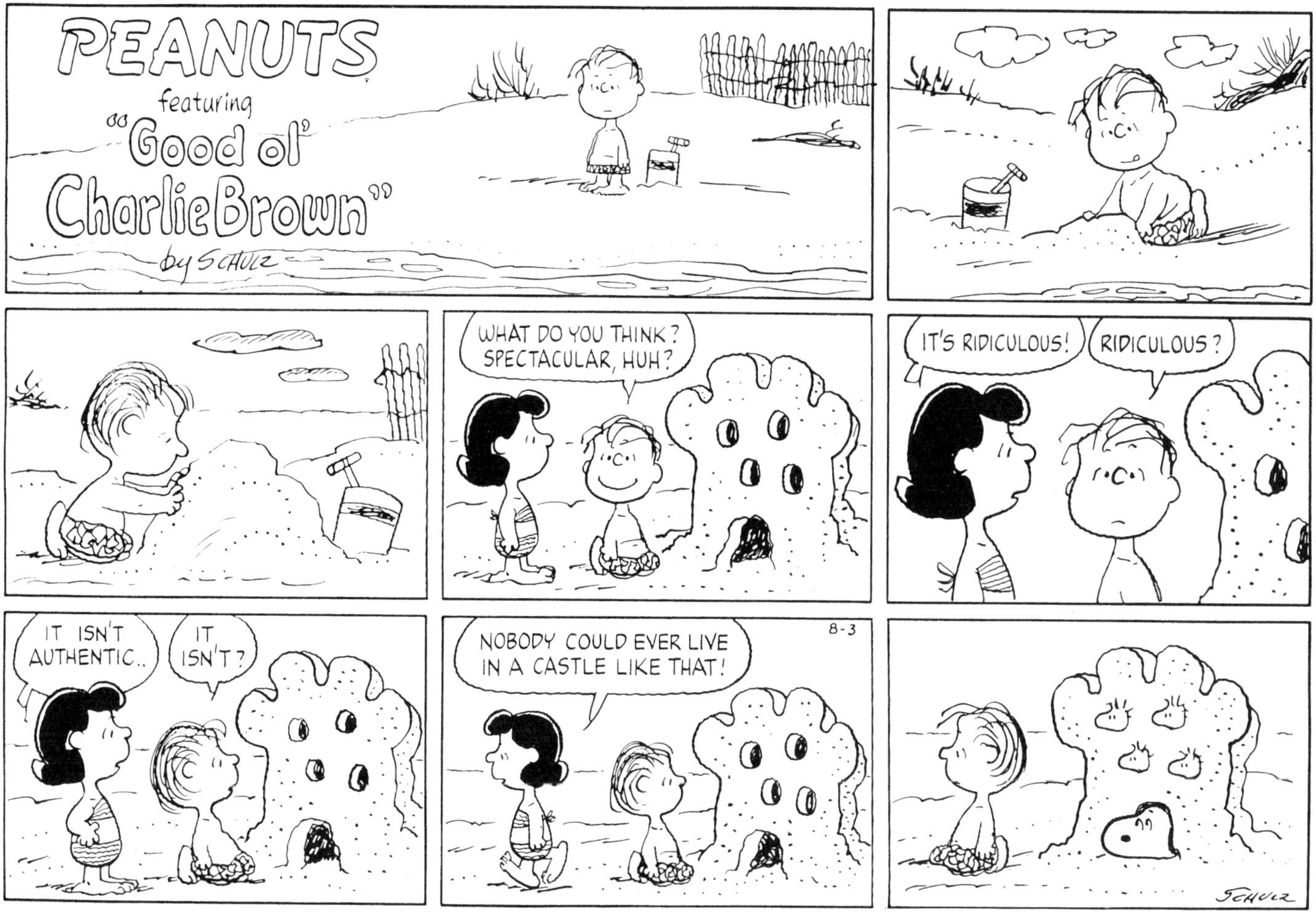
PEANUTS
featuring
"Good ol' Charlie Brown"
by SCHULZ
WHAT DO YOU THINK? SPECTACULAR, HUH?
IT'S RIDICULOUS!
RIDICULOUS?
IT ISN'T AUTHENTIC..
IT ISN'T?
8-3
NOBODY COULD EVER LIVE IN A CASTLE LIKE THAT!
SCHULZ

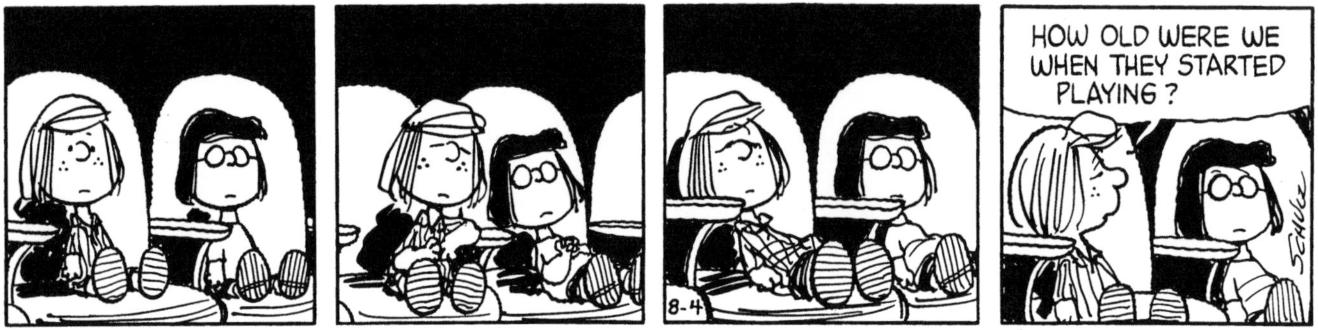
8-4
HOW OLD WERE WE WHEN THEY STARTED PLAYING?

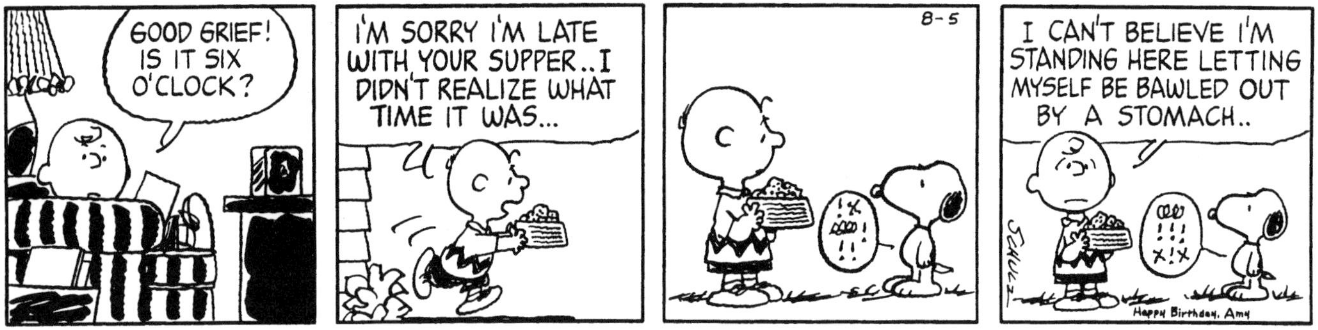
GOOD GRIEF! IS IT SIX O'CLOCK?
I'M SORRY I'M LATE WITH YOUR SUPPER.. I DIDN'T REALIZE WHAT TIME IT WAS...
8-5
I CAN'T BELIEVE I'M STANDING HERE LETTING MYSELF BE BAWLED OUT BY A STOMACH..
Happy Birthday, Amy

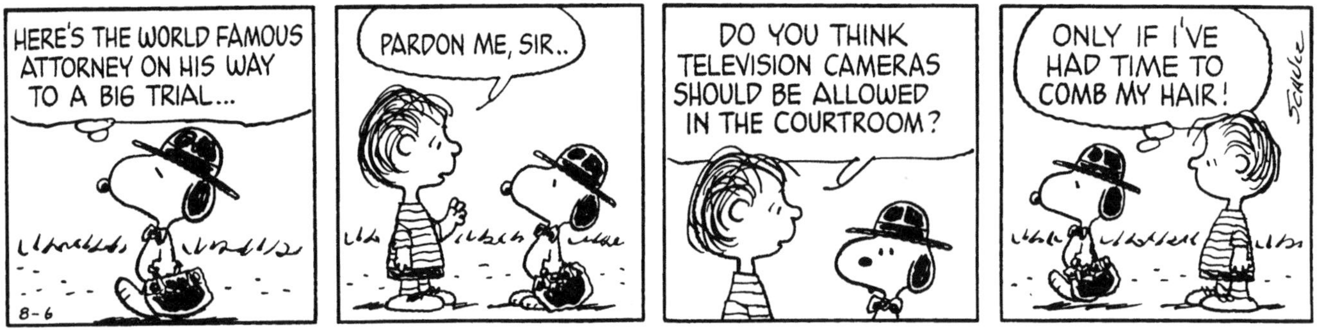
HERE'S THE WORLD FAMOUS ATTORNEY ON HIS WAY TO A BIG TRIAL...
8-6
PARDON ME, SIR..
DO YOU THINK TELEVISION CAMERAS SHOULD BE ALLOWED IN THE COURTROOM?
ONLY IF I'VE HAD TIME TO COMB MY HAIR!

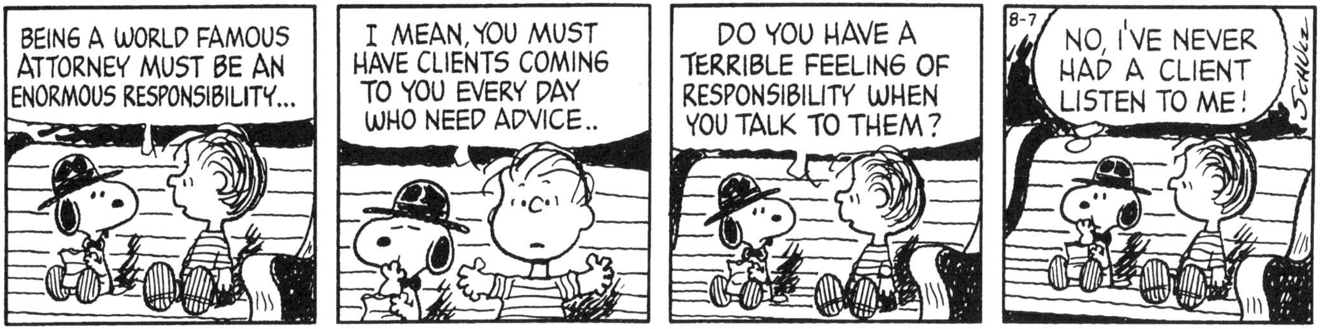
BEING A WORLD FAMOUS ATTORNEY MUST BE AN ENORMOUS RESPONSIBILITY...
I MEAN, YOU MUST HAVE CLIENTS COMING TO YOU EVERY DAY WHO NEED ADVICE..
DO YOU HAVE A TERRIBLE FEELING OF RESPONSIBILITY WHEN YOU TALK TO THEM?
8-7
NO, I'VE NEVER HAD A CLIENT LISTEN TO ME!
SCHULZ

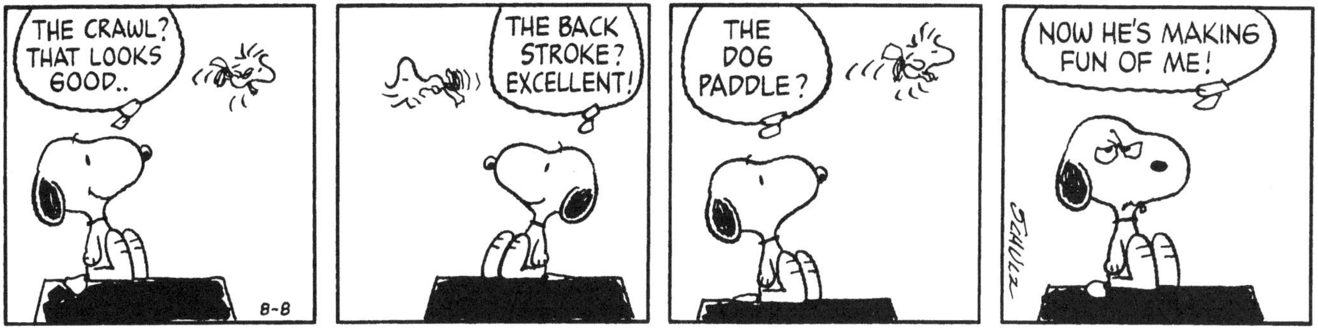
THE CRAWL? THAT LOOKS GOOD..
8-8
THE BACK STROKE? EXCELLENT!
THE DOG PADDLE?
NOW HE'S MAKING FUN OF ME!
SCHULZ

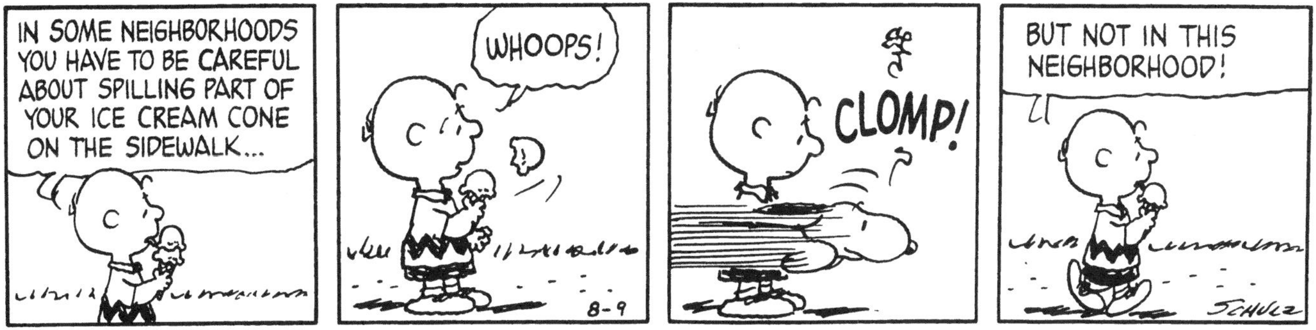
IN SOME NEIGHBORHOODS YOU HAVE TO BE CAREFUL ABOUT SPILLING PART OF YOUR ICE CREAM CONE ON THE SIDEWALK...
WHOOPS!
8-9
CLOMP!
BUT NOT IN THIS NEIGHBORHOOD!
SCHULZ

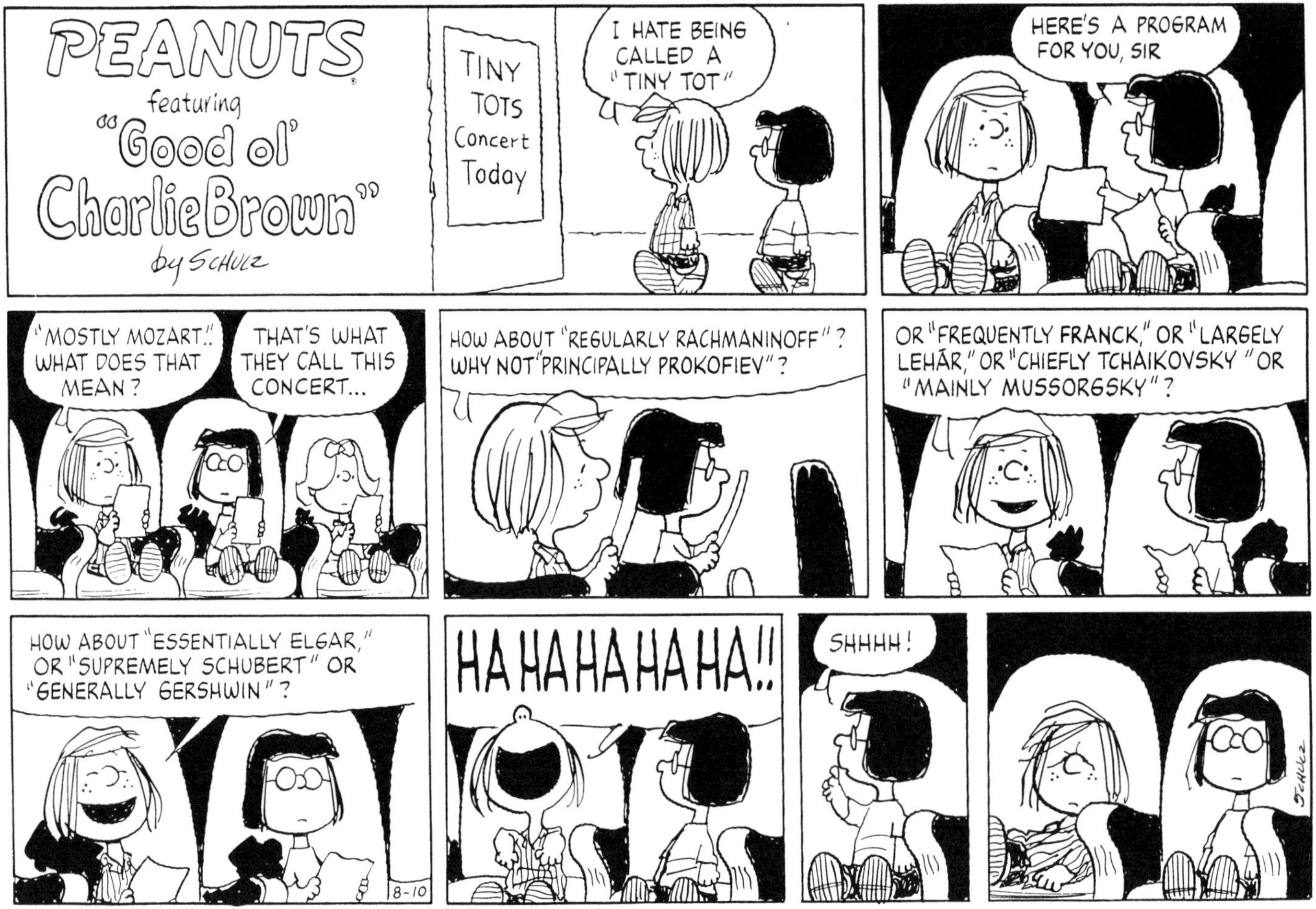
PEANUTS
featuring "Good ol' Charlie Brown"
by SCHULZ
TINY TOTS Concert Today
I HATE BEING CALLED A "TINY TOT"
HERE'S A PROGRAM FOR YOU, SIR
"MOSTLY MOZART." WHAT DOES THAT MEAN?
THAT'S WHAT THEY CALL THIS CONCERT...
HOW ABOUT "REGULARLY RACHMANINOFF"? WHY NOT "PRINCIPALLY PROKOFIEV"?
OR "FREQUENTLY FRANCK," OR "LARGELY LEHĀR," OR "CHIEFLY TCHAIKOVSKY" OR "MAINLY MUSSORGSKY"?
HOW ABOUT "ESSENTIALLY ELGAR," OR "SUPREMELY SCHUBERT" OR "GENERALLY GERSHWIN"?
8-10
HA HA HA HA HA HA!!
SHHHH!
SCHULZ

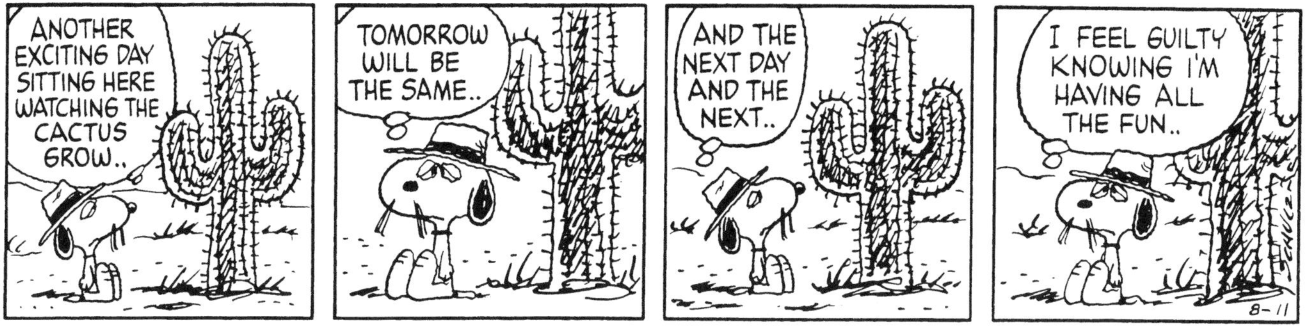
ANOTHER EXCITING DAY SITTING HERE WATCHING THE CACTUS GROW..
TOMORROW WILL BE THE SAME..
AND THE NEXT DAY AND THE NEXT..
I FEEL GUILTY KNOWING I'M HAVING ALL THE FUN..
SCHULZ
8-11

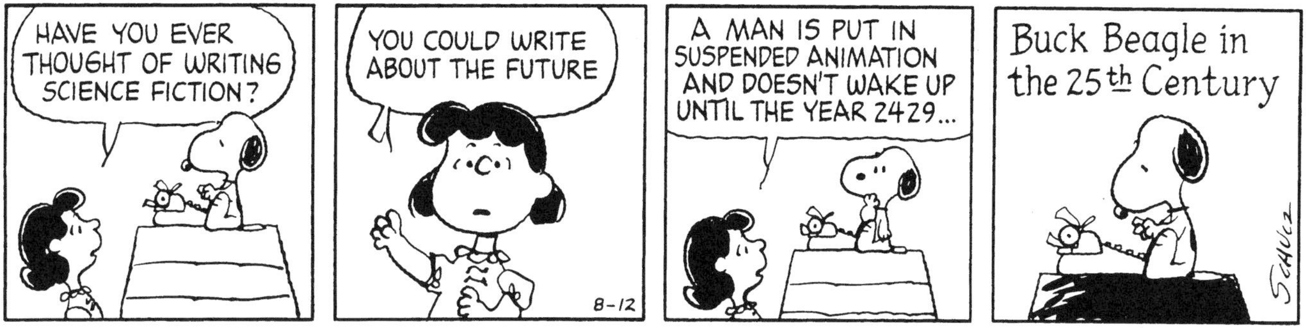
HAVE YOU EVER THOUGHT OF WRITING SCIENCE FICTION?
YOU COULD WRITE ABOUT THE FUTURE
8-12
A MAN IS PUT IN SUSPENDED ANIMATION AND DOESN'T WAKE UP UNTIL THE YEAR 2429...
Buck Beagle in the 25th Century
SCHULZ

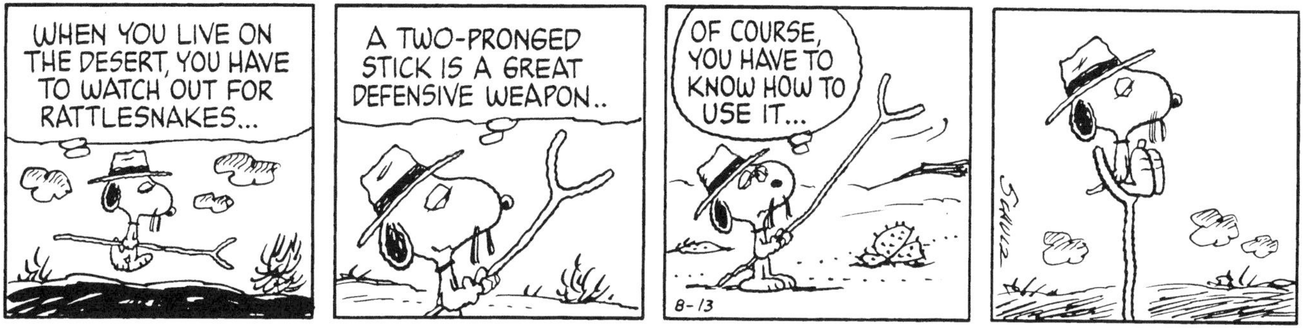
WHEN YOU LIVE ON THE DESERT, YOU HAVE TO WATCH OUT FOR RATTLESNAKES...
A TWO-PRONGED STICK IS A GREAT DEFENSIVE WEAPON..
OF COURSE, YOU HAVE TO KNOW HOW TO USE IT...
8-13
SCHULZ

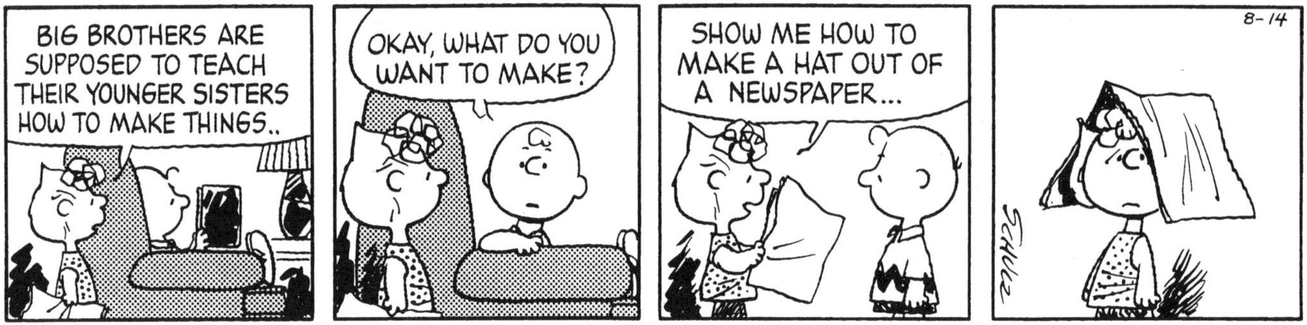
BIG BROTHERS ARE SUPPOSED TO TEACH THEIR YOUNGER SISTERS HOW TO MAKE THINGS..
OKAY, WHAT DO YOU WANT TO MAKE?
SHOW ME HOW TO MAKE A HAT OUT OF A NEWSPAPER...
8-14
SCHULZ

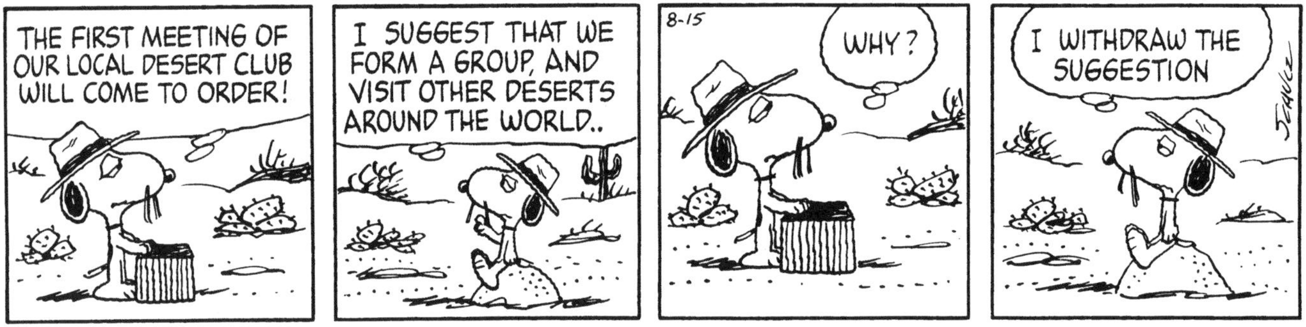
THE FIRST MEETING OF OUR LOCAL DESERT CLUB WILL COME TO ORDER!
I SUGGEST THAT WE FORM A GROUP, AND VISIT OTHER DESERTS AROUND THE WORLD..
8-15
WHY?
I WITHDRAW THE SUGGESTION
SCHULZ

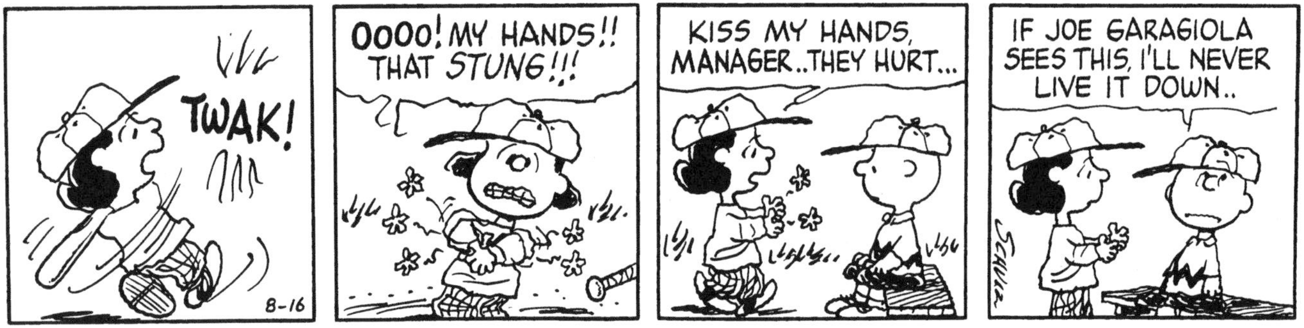
TWAK!
8-16
OOOO! MY HANDS!! THAT STUNG!!!
KISS MY HANDS, MANAGER..THEY HURT...
IF JOE GARAGIOLA SEES THIS, I'LL NEVER LIVE IT DOWN..
SCHULZ

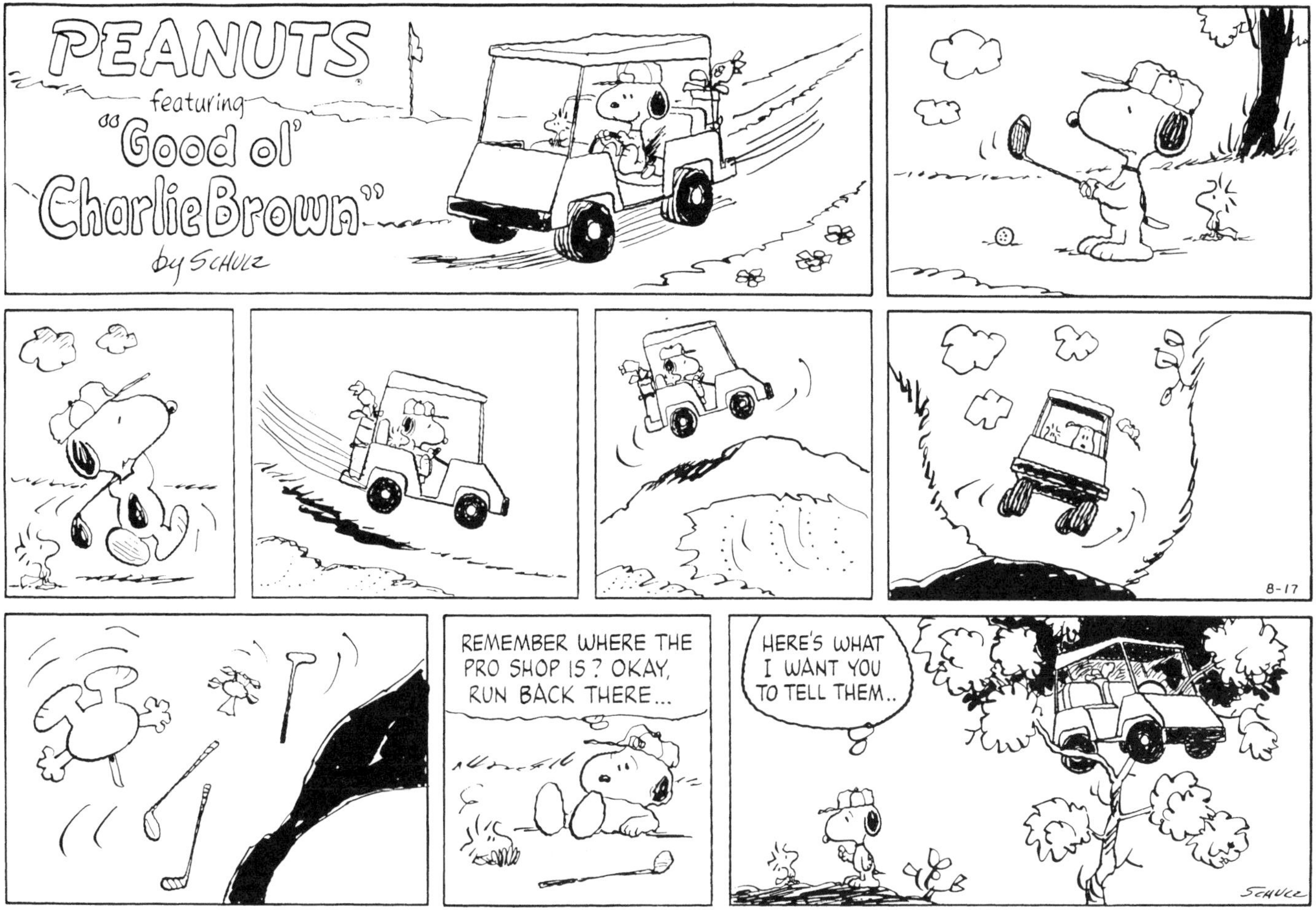
PEANUTS
featuring
"Good ol' Charlie Brown"
by SCHULZ
8-17
REMEMBER WHERE THE PRO SHOP IS? OKAY, RUN BACK THERE...
HERE'S WHAT I WANT YOU TO TELL THEM..
SCHULZ

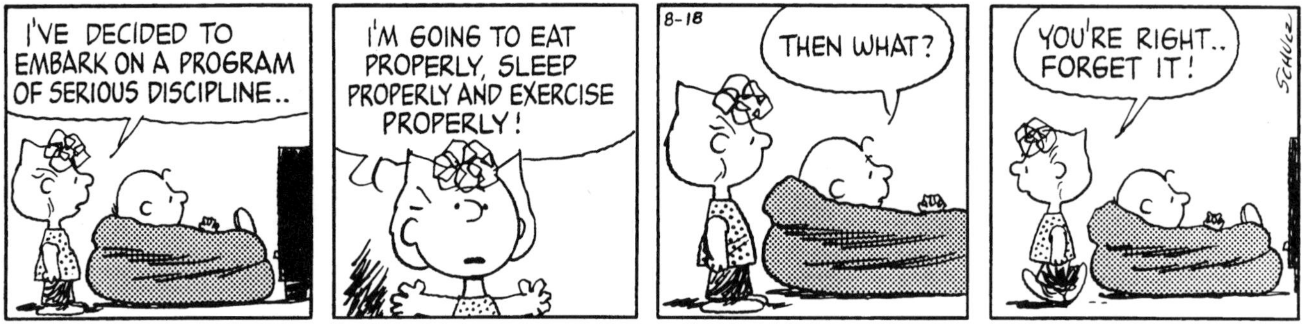
I'VE DECIDED TO EMBARK ON A PROGRAM OF SERIOUS DISCIPLINE..
I'M GOING TO EAT PROPERLY, SLEEP PROPERLY AND EXERCISE PROPERLY!
8-18
THEN WHAT?
YOU'RE RIGHT.. FORGET IT!

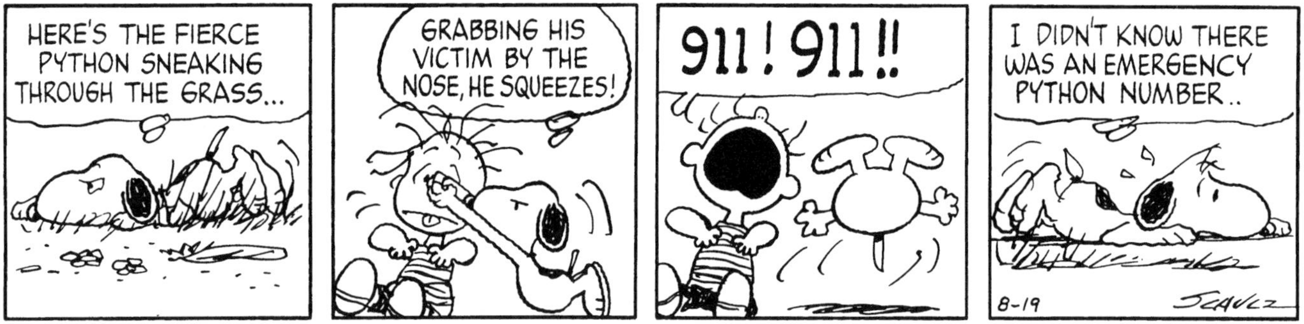
HERE'S THE FIERCE PYTHON SNEAKING THROUGH THE GRASS...
GRABBING HIS VICTIM BY THE NOSE, HE SQUEEZES!
911! 911!!
I DIDN'T KNOW THERE WAS AN EMERGENCY PYTHON NUMBER..
8-19

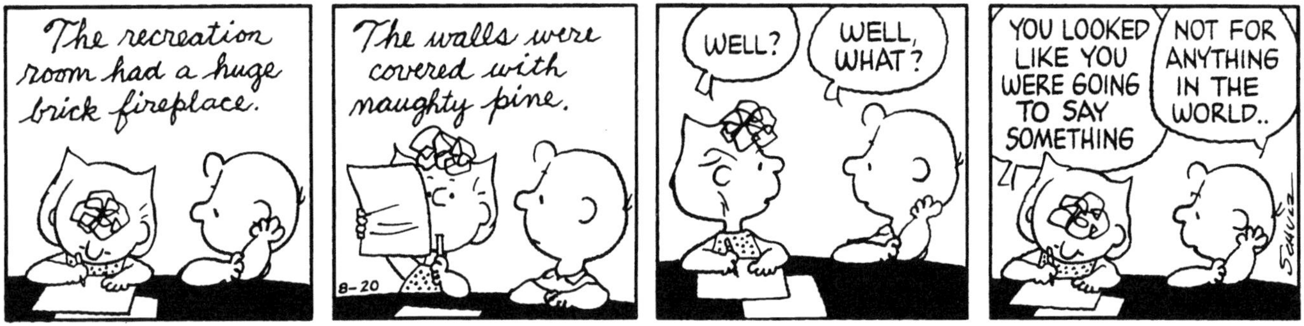
The recreation room had a huge brick fireplace.
The walls were covered with naughty pine.
8-20
WELL?
WELL, WHAT?
YOU LOOKED LIKE YOU WERE GOING TO SAY SOMETHING
NOT FOR ANYTHING IN THE WORLD..

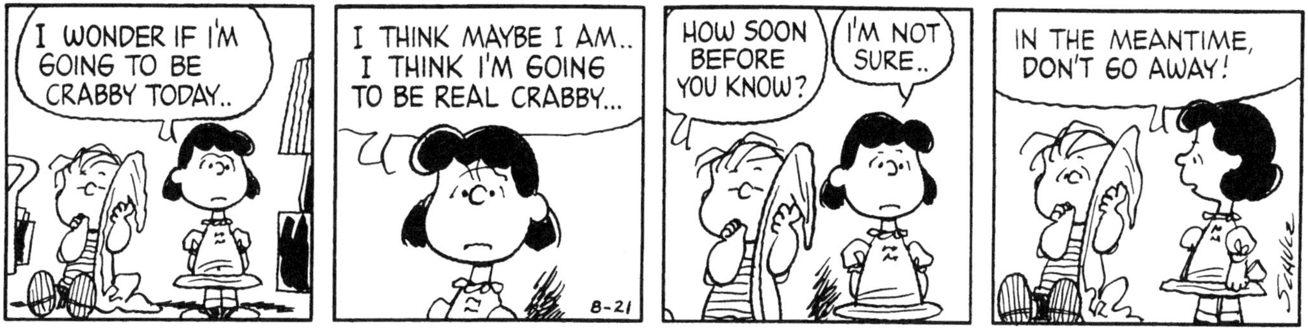
I WONDER IF I'M GOING TO BE CRABBY TODAY..
I THINK MAYBE I AM.. I THINK I'M GOING TO BE REAL CRABBY...
8-21
HOW SOON BEFORE YOU KNOW?
I'M NOT SURE..
IN THE MEANTIME, DON'T GO AWAY!
SCHULZ

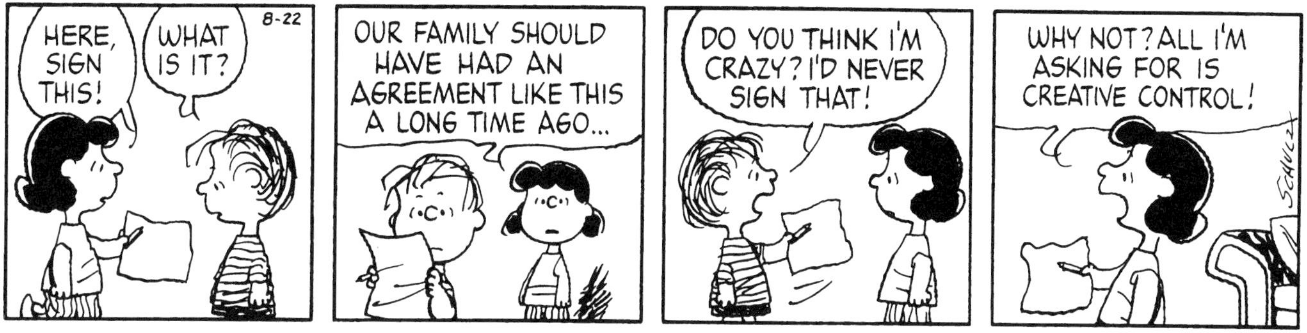
8-22
HERE, SIGN THIS!
WHAT IS IT?
OUR FAMILY SHOULD HAVE HAD AN AGREEMENT LIKE THIS A LONG TIME AGO...
DO YOU THINK I'M CRAZY? I'D NEVER SIGN THAT!
WHY NOT? ALL I'M ASKING FOR IS CREATIVE CONTROL!
SCHULZ

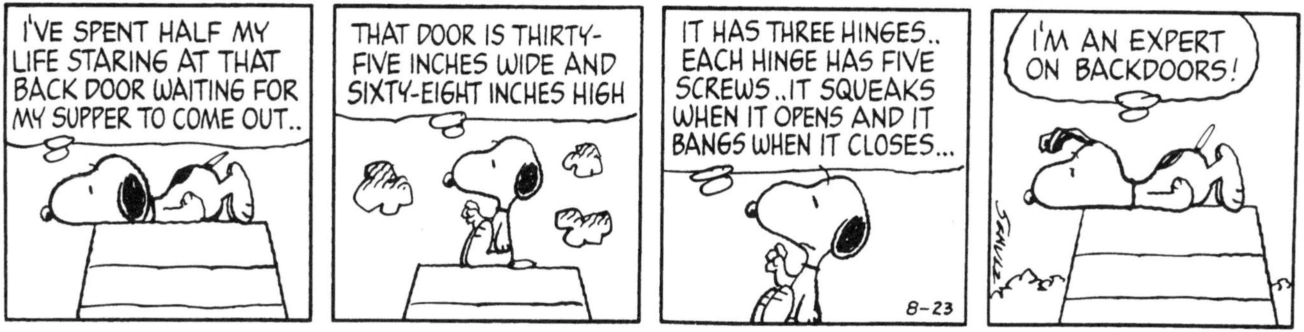
I'VE SPENT HALF MY LIFE STARING AT THAT BACK DOOR WAITING FOR MY SUPPER TO COME OUT..
THAT DOOR IS THIRTY-FIVE INCHES WIDE AND SIXTY-EIGHT INCHES HIGH
IT HAS THREE HINGES.. EACH HINGE HAS FIVE SCREWS.. IT SQUEAKS WHEN IT OPENS AND IT BANGS WHEN IT CLOSES...
8-23
SCHULZ
I'M AN EXPERT ON BACKDOORS!

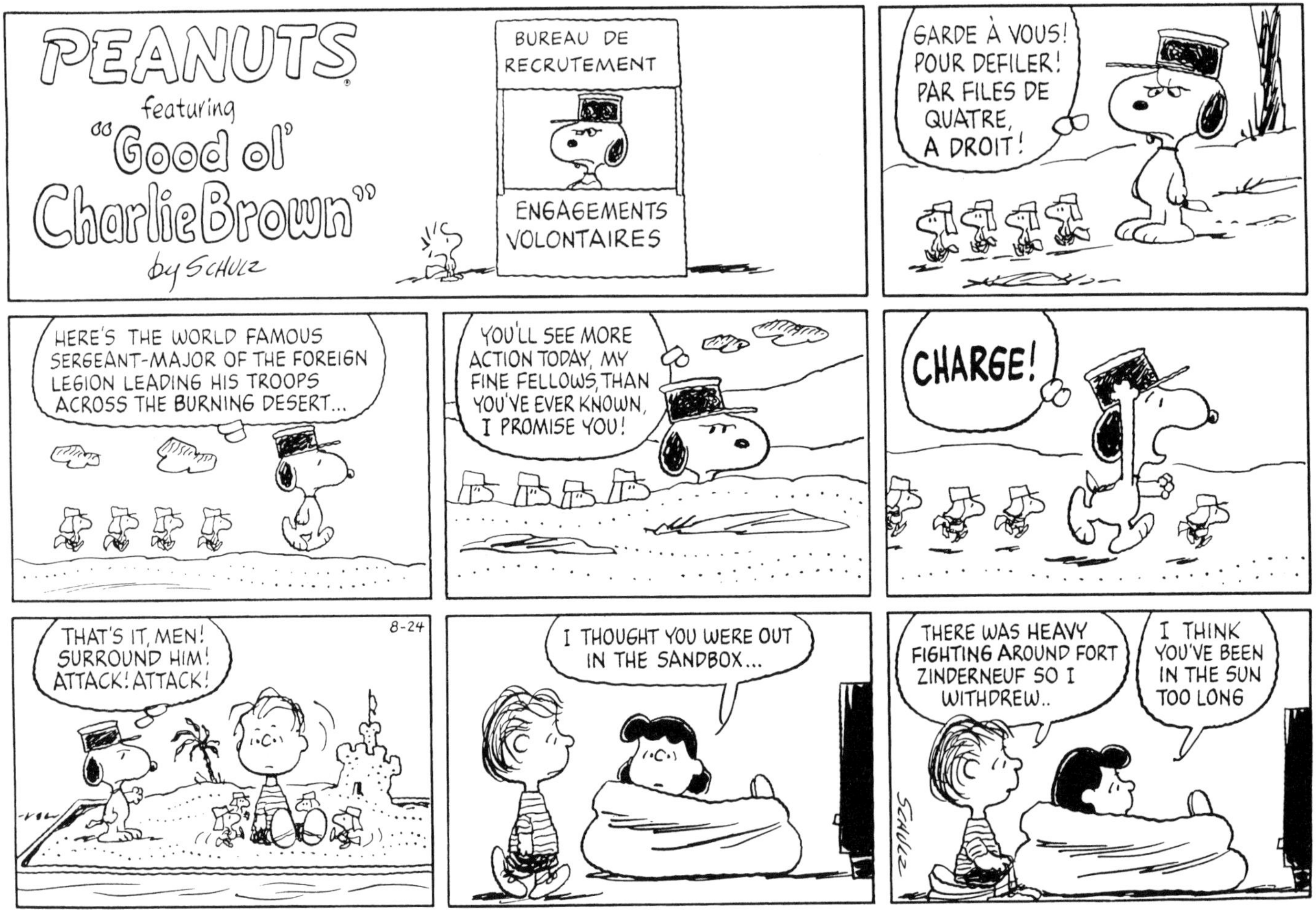
PEANUTS
featuring "Good ol' CharlieBrown"
by SCHULZ
BUREAU DE RECRUTEMENT
ENGAGEMENTS VOLONTAIRES
GARDE À VOUS! POUR DEFILER! PAR FILES DE QUATRE, A DROIT!
HERE'S THE WORLD FAMOUS SERGEANT-MAJOR OF THE FOREIGN LEGION LEADING HIS TROOPS ACROSS THE BURNING DESERT...
YOU'LL SEE MORE ACTION TODAY, MY FINE FELLOWS, THAN YOU'VE EVER KNOWN, I PROMISE YOU!
CHARGE!
THAT'S IT, MEN! SURROUND HIM! ATTACK! ATTACK!
8-24
I THOUGHT YOU WERE OUT IN THE SANDBOX...
THERE WAS HEAVY FIGHTING AROUND FORT ZINDERNEUF SO I WITHDREW..
I THINK YOU'VE BEEN IN THE SUN TOO LONG
SCHULZ

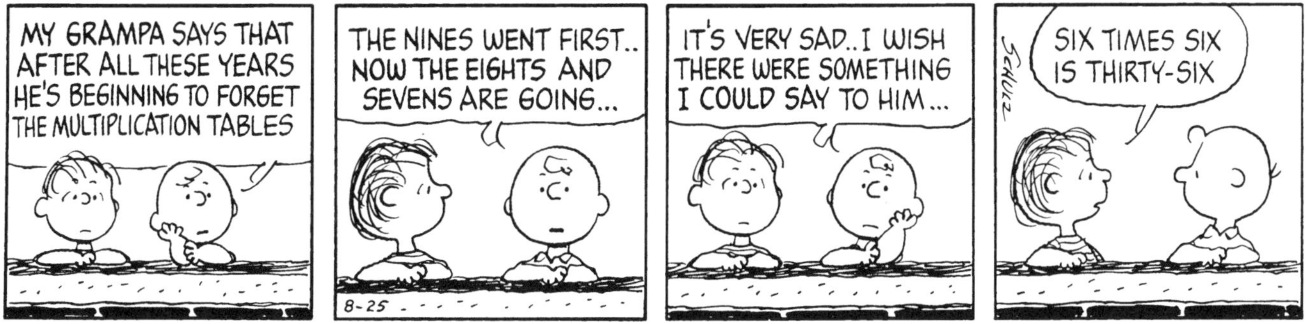
MY GRAMPA SAYS THAT AFTER ALL THESE YEARS HE'S BEGINNING TO FORGET THE MULTIPLICATION TABLES
THE NINES WENT FIRST.. NOW THE EIGHTS AND SEVENS ARE GOING...
8-25
IT'S VERY SAD..I WISH THERE WERE SOMETHING I COULD SAY TO HIM...
SCHULZ
SIX TIMES SIX IS THIRTY-SIX

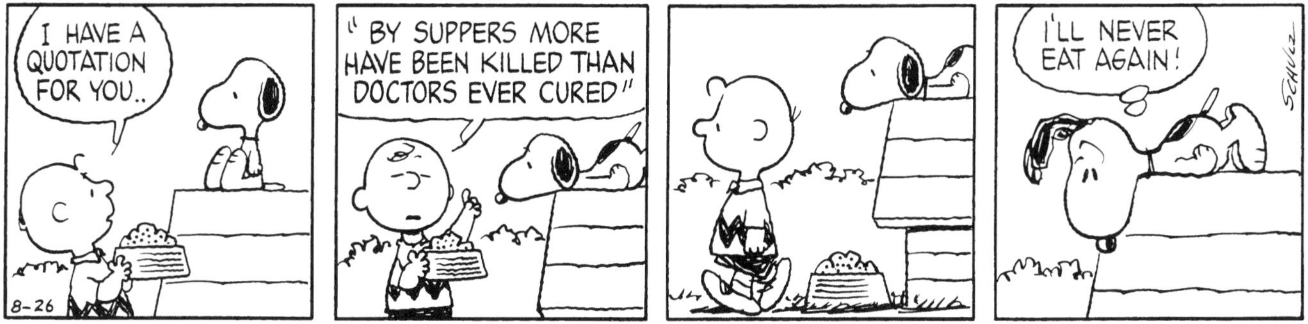
I HAVE A QUOTATION FOR YOU..
8-26
" BY SUPPERS MORE HAVE BEEN KILLED THAN DOCTORS EVER CURED"
I'LL NEVER EAT AGAIN!
SCHULZ

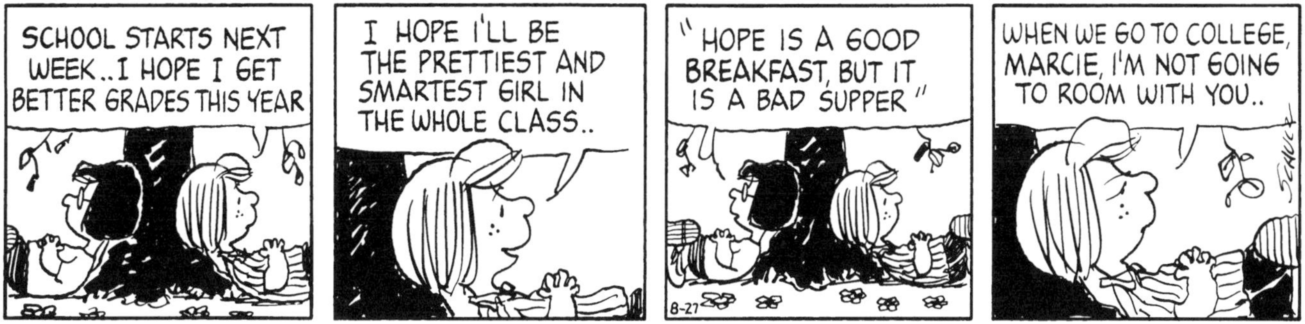
SCHOOL STARTS NEXT WEEK..I HOPE I GET BETTER GRADES THIS YEAR
I HOPE I'LL BE THE PRETTIEST AND SMARTEST GIRL IN THE WHOLE CLASS..
" HOPE IS A GOOD BREAKFAST, BUT IT IS A BAD SUPPER"
8-27
WHEN WE GO TO COLLEGE, MARCIE, I'M NOT GOING TO ROOM WITH YOU..
SCHULZ

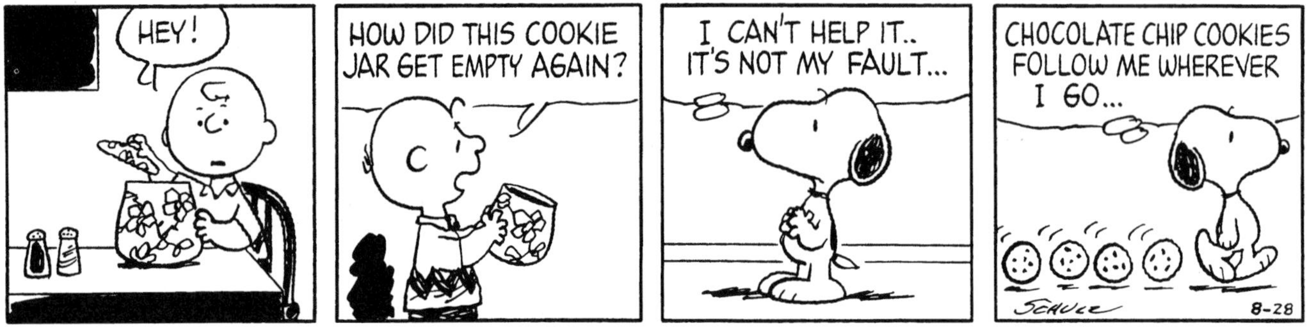
HEY!
HOW DID THIS COOKIE JAR GET EMPTY AGAIN?
I CAN'T HELP IT.. IT'S NOT MY FAULT...
CHOCOLATE CHIP COOKIES FOLLOW ME WHEREVER I GO...
SCHULZ
8-28

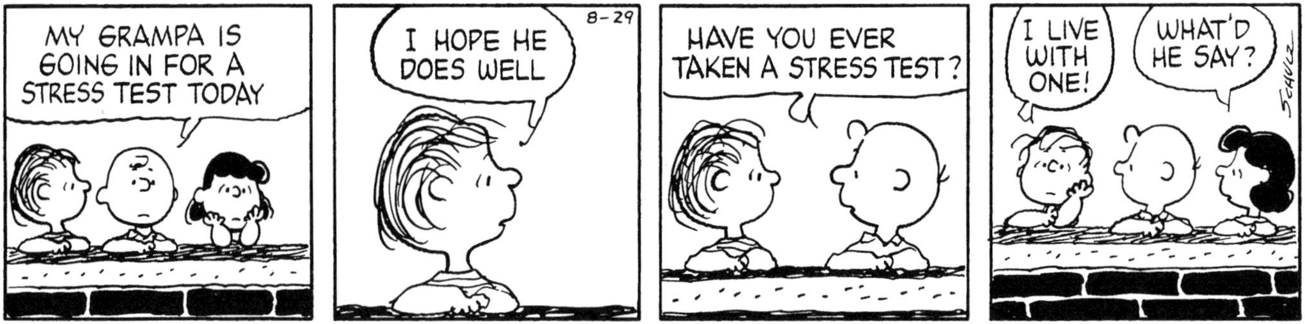
MY GRAMPA IS GOING IN FOR A STRESS TEST TODAY
8-29
I HOPE HE DOES WELL
HAVE YOU EVER TAKEN A STRESS TEST?
I LIVE WITH ONE!
WHAT'D HE SAY?
SCHULZ

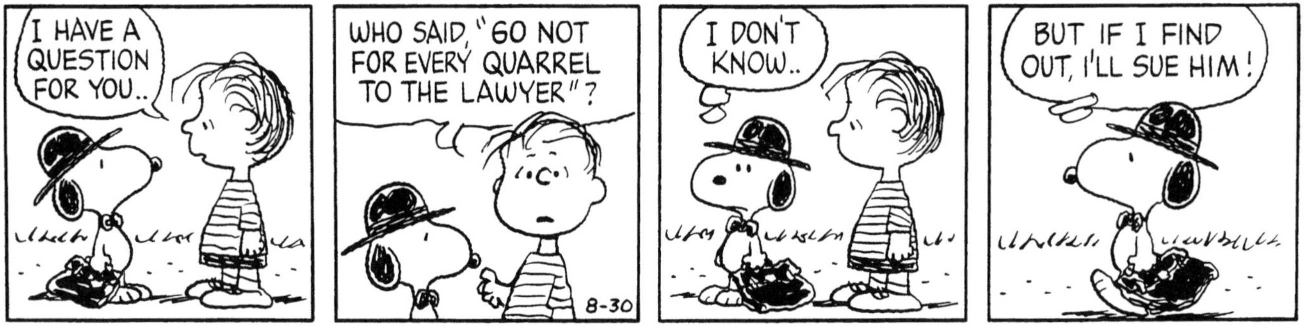
I HAVE A QUESTION FOR YOU..
WHO SAID, "GO NOT FOR EVERY QUARREL TO THE LAWYER"?
8-30
I DON'T KNOW..
BUT IF I FIND OUT, I'LL SUE HIM!

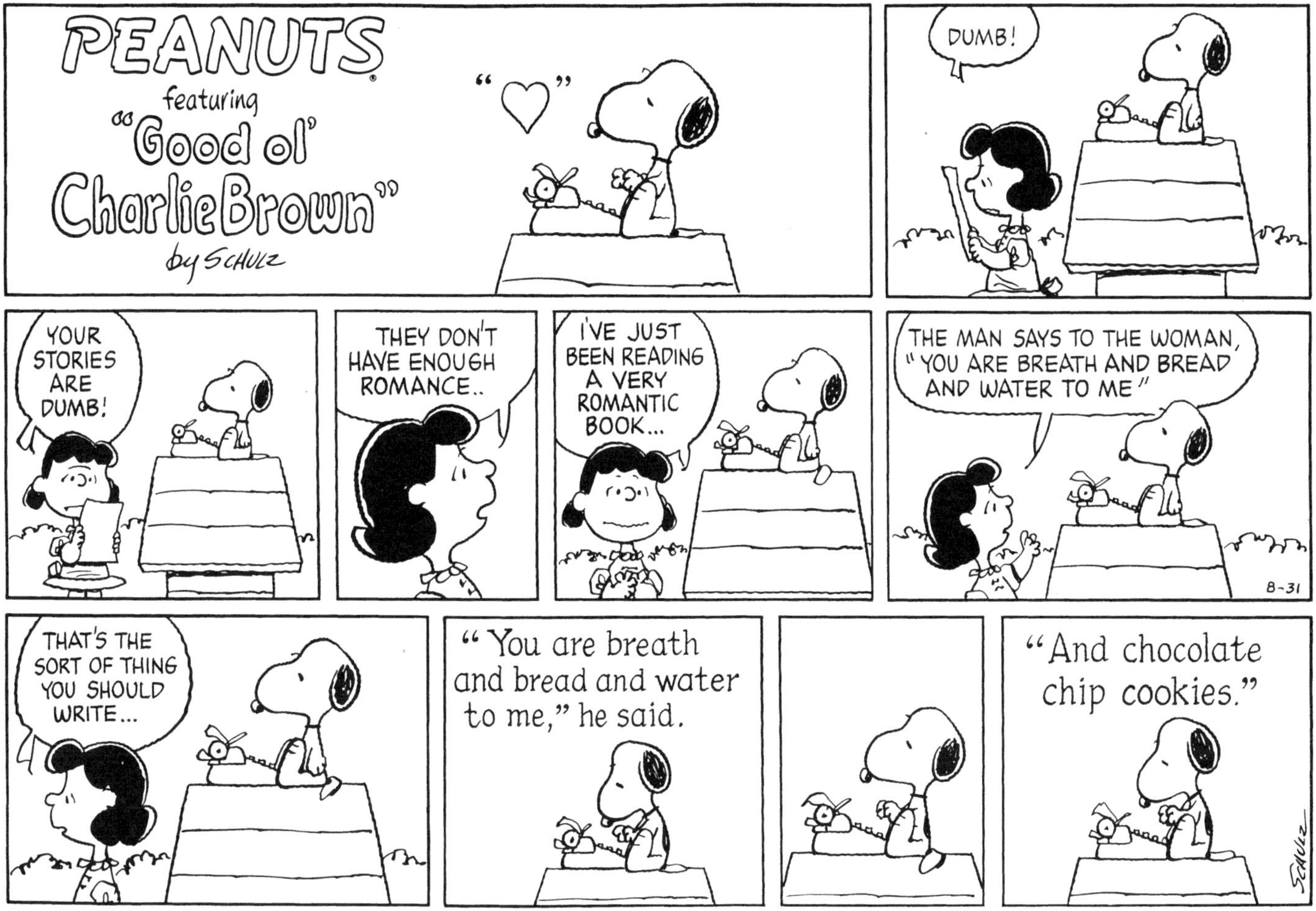
PEANUTS
featuring
"Good ol' Charlie Brown"
by SCHULZ
"♡"
DUMB!
YOUR STORIES ARE DUMB!
THEY DON'T HAVE ENOUGH ROMANCE..
I'VE JUST BEEN READING A VERY ROMANTIC BOOK...
THE MAN SAYS TO THE WOMAN, "YOU ARE BREATH AND BREAD AND WATER TO ME"
8-31
THAT'S THE SORT OF THING YOU SHOULD WRITE...
"You are breath and bread and water to me," he said.
"And chocolate chip cookies."
SCHULZ

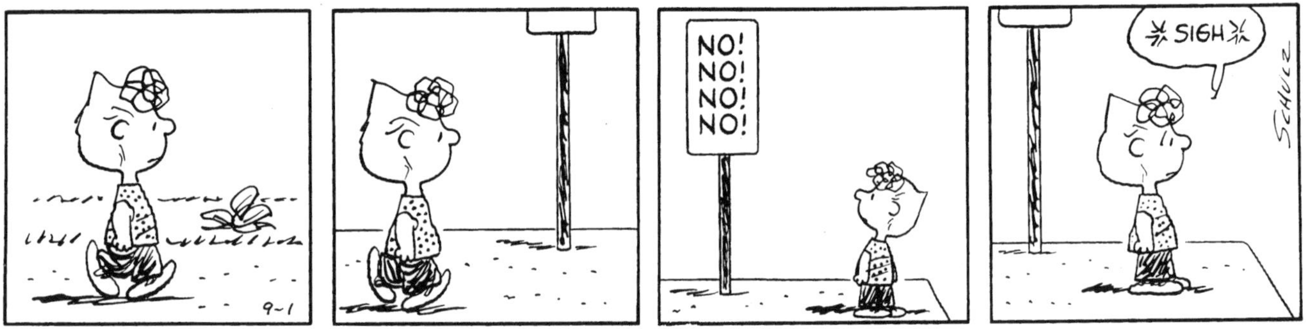
NO! NO! NO! NO!
SIGH

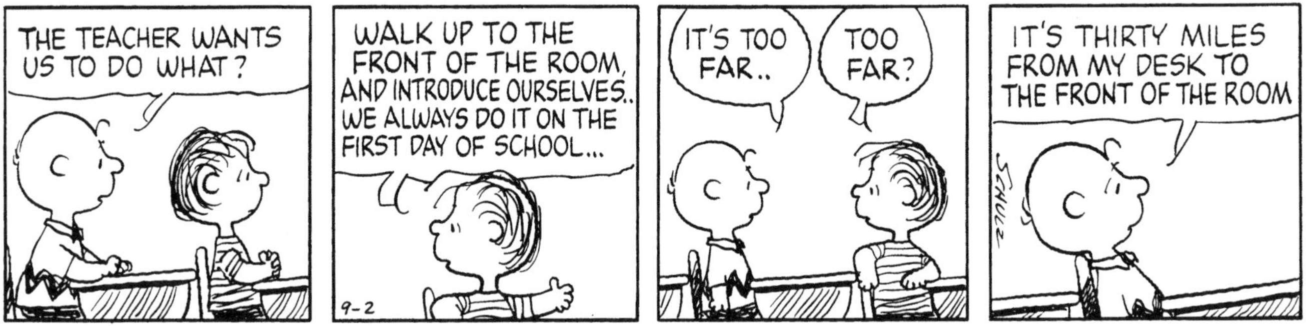
THE TEACHER WANTS US TO DO WHAT?
WALK UP TO THE FRONT OF THE ROOM, AND INTRODUCE OURSELVES.. WE ALWAYS DO IT ON THE FIRST DAY OF SCHOOL...
IT'S TOO FAR..
TOO FAR?
IT'S THIRTY MILES FROM MY DESK TO THE FRONT OF THE ROOM

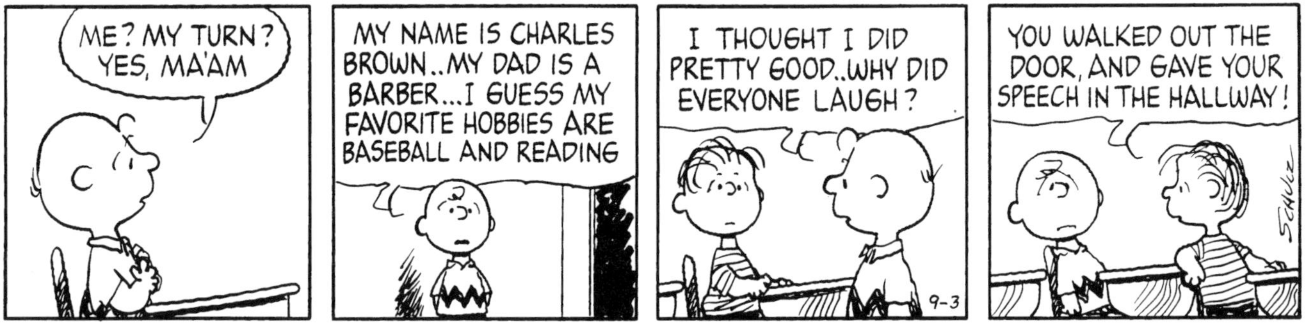
ME? MY TURN? YES, MA'AM
MY NAME IS CHARLES BROWN..MY DAD IS A BARBER...I GUESS MY FAVORITE HOBBIES ARE BASEBALL AND READING
I THOUGHT I DID PRETTY GOOD..WHY DID EVERYONE LAUGH?
YOU WALKED OUT THE DOOR, AND GAVE YOUR SPEECH IN THE HALLWAY!

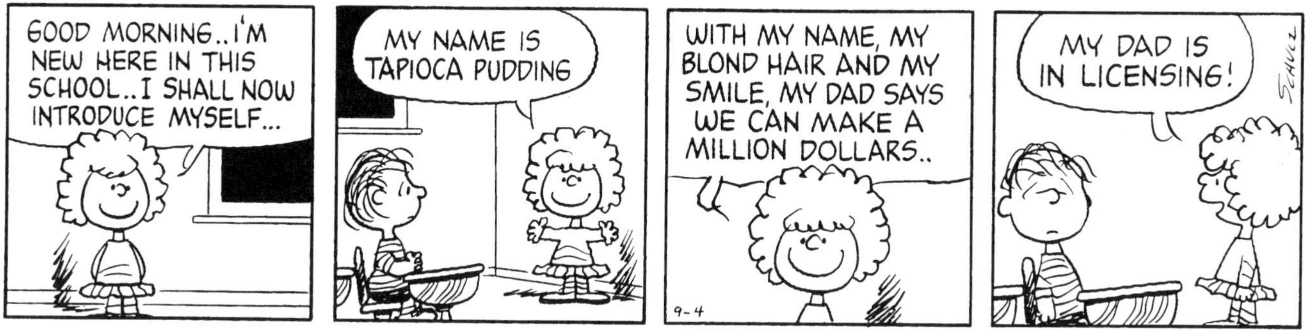
GOOD MORNING..I'M NEW HERE IN THIS SCHOOL..I SHALL NOW INTRODUCE MYSELF...
MY NAME IS TAPIOCA PUDDING
WITH MY NAME, MY BLOND HAIR AND MY SMILE, MY DAD SAYS WE CAN MAKE A MILLION DOLLARS..
MY DAD IS IN LICENSING!

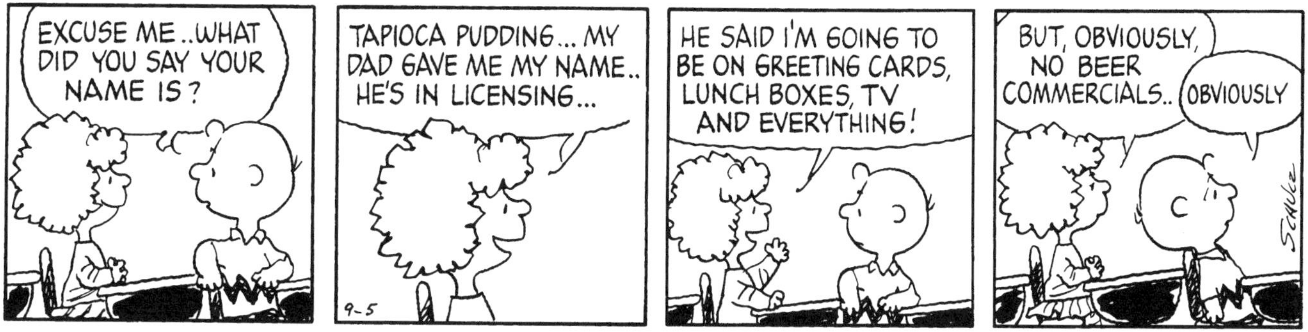
EXCUSE ME..WHAT DID YOU SAY YOUR NAME IS?
TAPIOCA PUDDING... MY DAD GAVE ME MY NAME.. HE'S IN LICENSING...
HE SAID I'M GOING TO BE ON GREETING CARDS, LUNCH BOXES, TV AND EVERYTHING!
BUT, OBVIOUSLY, NO BEER COMMERCIALS..
OBVIOUSLY

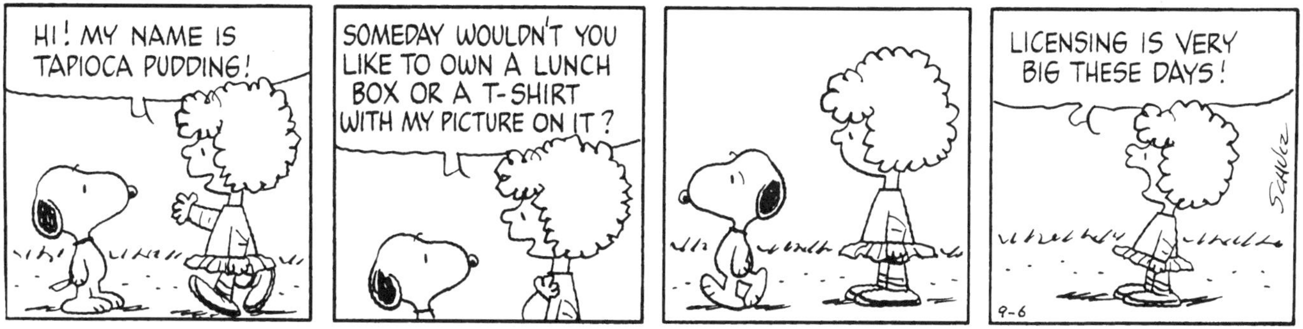
HI! MY NAME IS TAPIOCA PUDDING!
SOMEDAY WOULDN'T YOU LIKE TO OWN A LUNCH BOX OR A T-SHIRT WITH MY PICTURE ON IT?
LICENSING IS VERY BIG THESE DAYS!

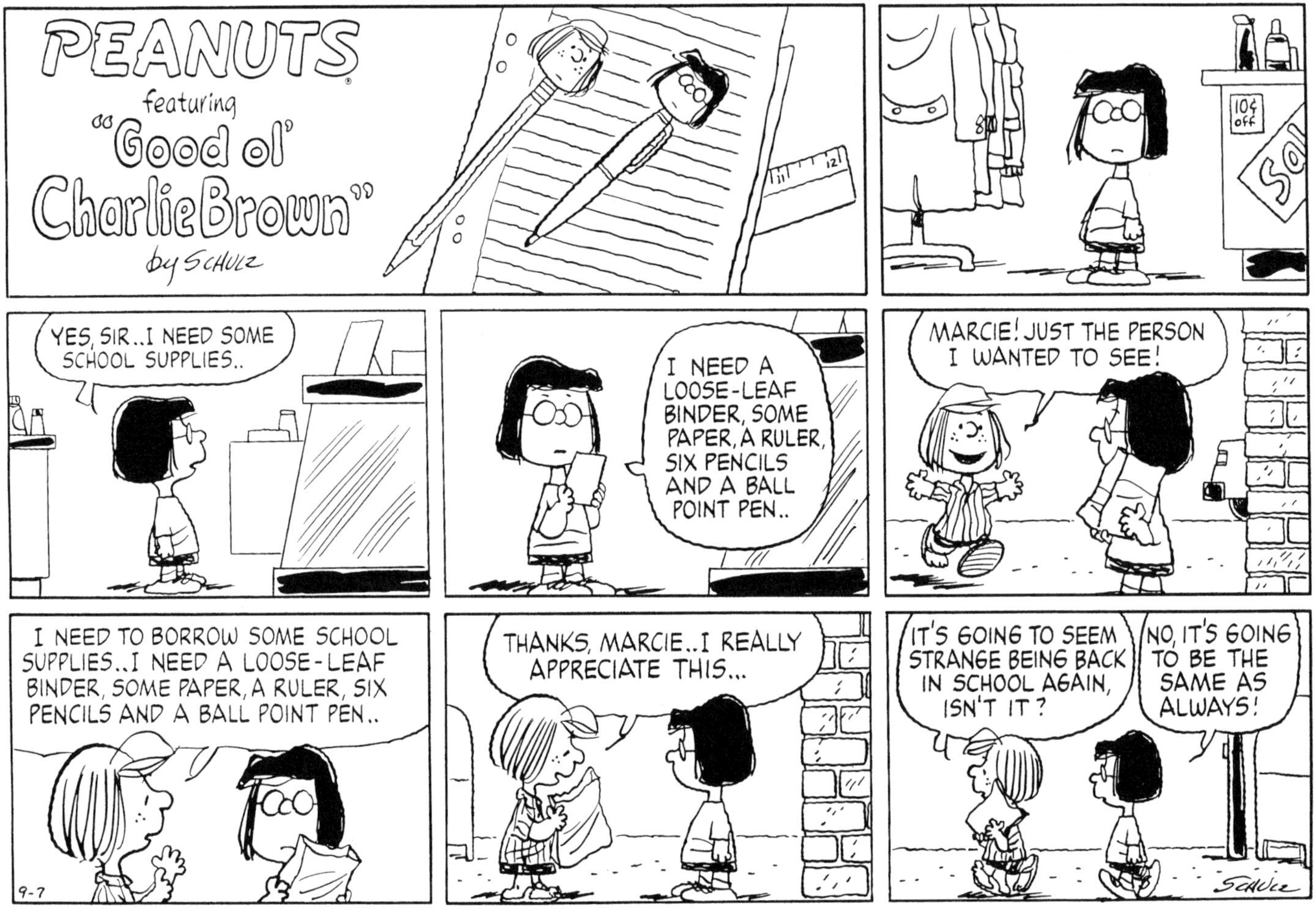
PEANUTS
featuring
"Good ol' CharlieBrown"
by SCHULZ
10¢ off
YES, SIR..I NEED SOME SCHOOL SUPPLIES..
I NEED A LOOSE-LEAF BINDER, SOME PAPER, A RULER, SIX PENCILS AND A BALL POINT PEN..
MARCIE! JUST THE PERSON I WANTED TO SEE!
I NEED TO BORROW SOME SCHOOL SUPPLIES..I NEED A LOOSE-LEAF BINDER, SOME PAPER, A RULER, SIX PENCILS AND A BALL POINT PEN..
9-7
THANKS, MARCIE..I REALLY APPRECIATE THIS...
IT'S GOING TO SEEM STRANGE BEING BACK IN SCHOOL AGAIN, ISN'T IT ?
NO, IT'S GOING TO BE THE SAME AS ALWAYS!
SCHULZ

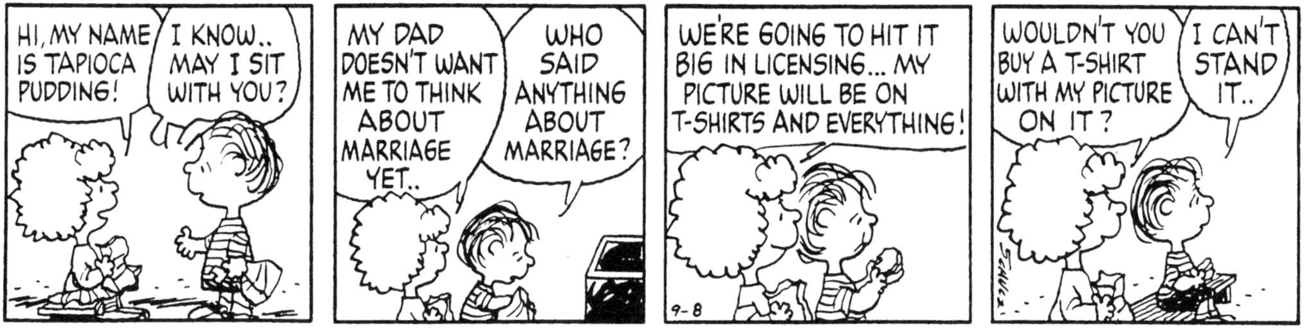
HI, MY NAME IS TAPIOCA PUDDING!
I KNOW.. MAY I SIT WITH YOU?
MY DAD DOESN'T WANT ME TO THINK ABOUT MARRIAGE YET..
WHO SAID ANYTHING ABOUT MARRIAGE?
WE'RE GOING TO HIT IT BIG IN LICENSING... MY PICTURE WILL BE ON T-SHIRTS AND EVERYTHING!
9-8
WOULDN'T YOU BUY A T-SHIRT WITH MY PICTURE ON IT?
I CAN'T STAND IT..

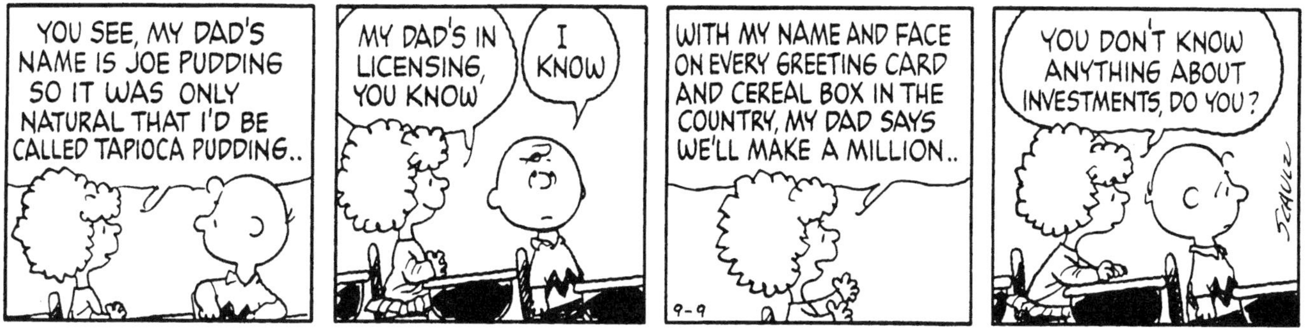
YOU SEE, MY DAD'S NAME IS JOE PUDDING SO IT WAS ONLY NATURAL THAT I'D BE CALLED TAPIOCA PUDDING..
MY DAD'S IN LICENSING, YOU KNOW
I KNOW
WITH MY NAME AND FACE ON EVERY GREETING CARD AND CEREAL BOX IN THE COUNTRY, MY DAD SAYS WE'LL MAKE A MILLION..
9-9
YOU DON'T KNOW ANYTHING ABOUT INVESTMENTS, DO YOU?
SCHULZ

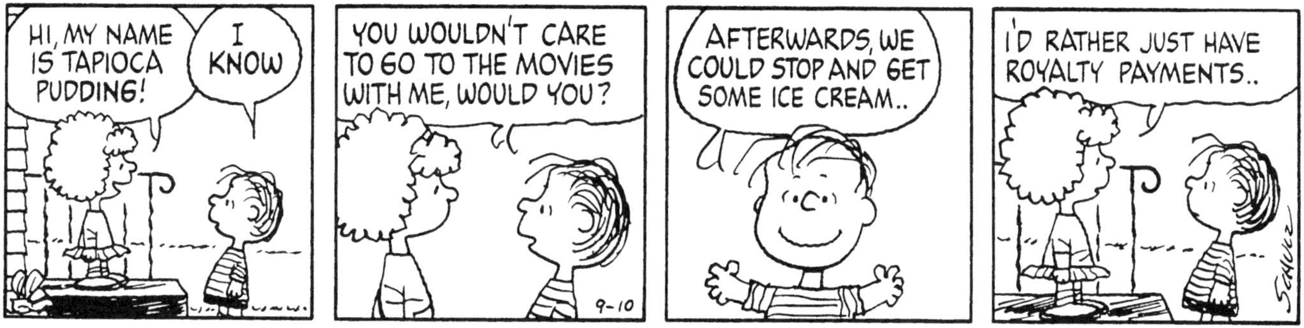
HI, MY NAME IS TAPIOCA PUDDING!
I KNOW
YOU WOULDN'T CARE TO GO TO THE MOVIES WITH ME, WOULD YOU?
9-10
AFTERWARDS, WE COULD STOP AND GET SOME ICE CREAM..
I'D RATHER JUST HAVE ROYALTY PAYMENTS..
SCHULZ

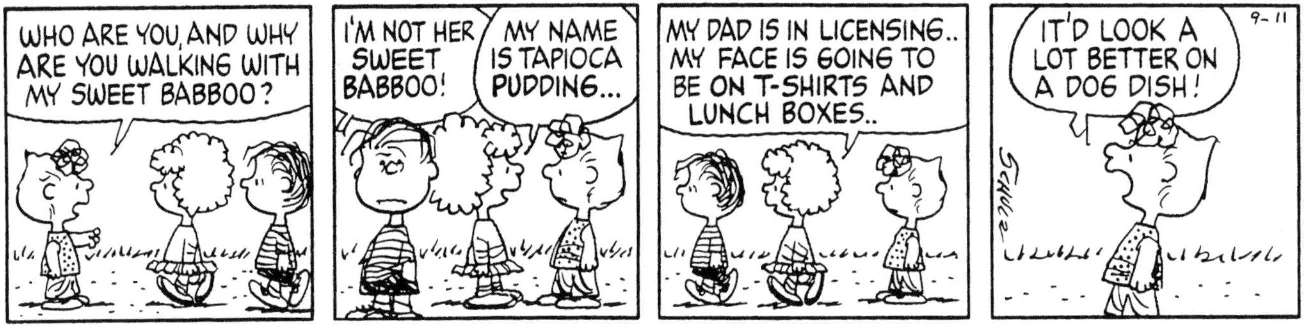
WHO ARE YOU, AND WHY ARE YOU WALKING WITH MY SWEET BABBOO?
I'M NOT HER SWEET BABBOO!
MY NAME IS TAPIOCA PUDDING...
MY DAD IS IN LICENSING.. MY FACE IS GOING TO BE ON T-SHIRTS AND LUNCH BOXES..
IT'D LOOK A LOT BETTER ON A DOG DISH!
9-11
SCHULZ

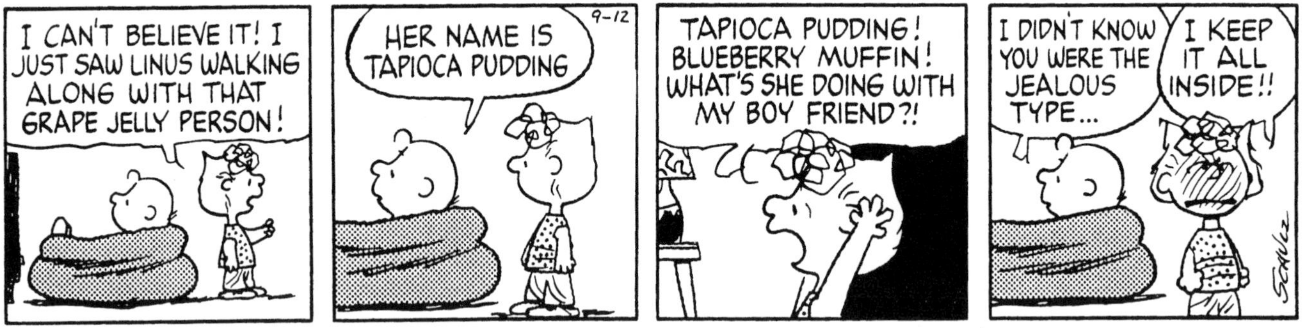
I CAN'T BELIEVE IT! I JUST SAW LINUS WALKING ALONG WITH THAT GRAPE JELLY PERSON!
9-12
HER NAME IS TAPIOCA PUDDING
TAPIOCA PUDDING! BLUEBERRY MUFFIN! WHAT'S SHE DOING WITH MY BOY FRIEND?!
I DIDN'T KNOW YOU WERE THE JEALOUS TYPE...
I KEEP IT ALL INSIDE!!
SCHULZ

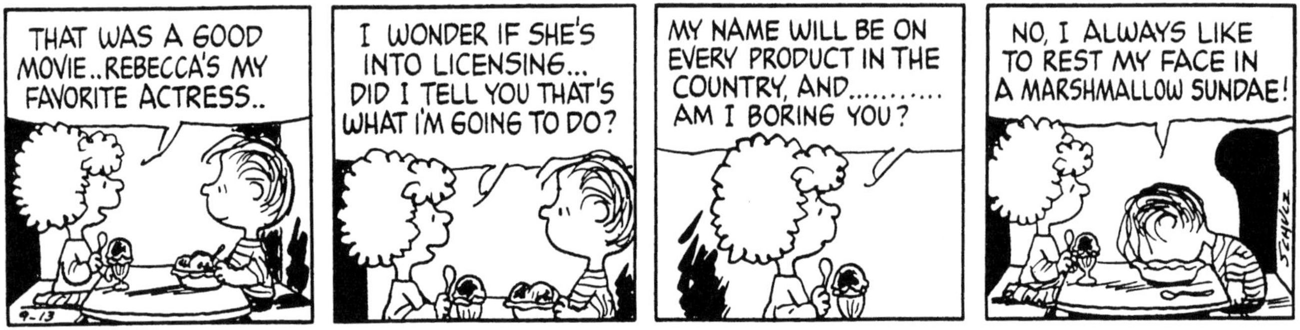
THAT WAS A GOOD MOVIE..REBECCA'S MY FAVORITE ACTRESS..
9-13
I WONDER IF SHE'S INTO LICENSING... DID I TELL YOU THAT'S WHAT I'M GOING TO DO?
MY NAME WILL BE ON EVERY PRODUCT IN THE COUNTRY, AND.......... AM I BORING YOU?
NO, I ALWAYS LIKE TO REST MY FACE IN A MARSHMALLOW SUNDAE!
SCHULZ

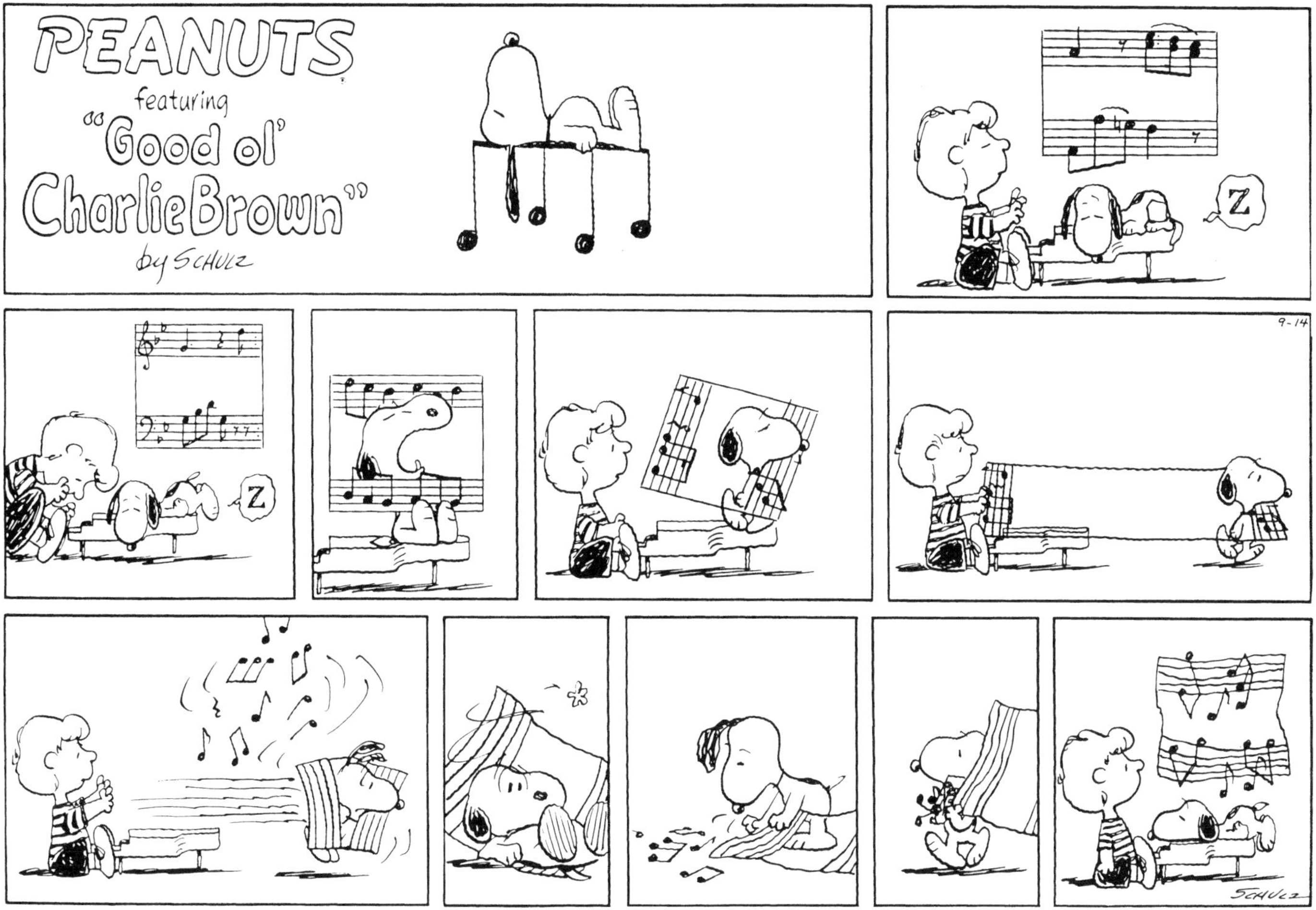
PEANUTS
featuring
"Good ol' Charlie Brown"
by SCHULZ
Z
Z
9-14
SCHULZ

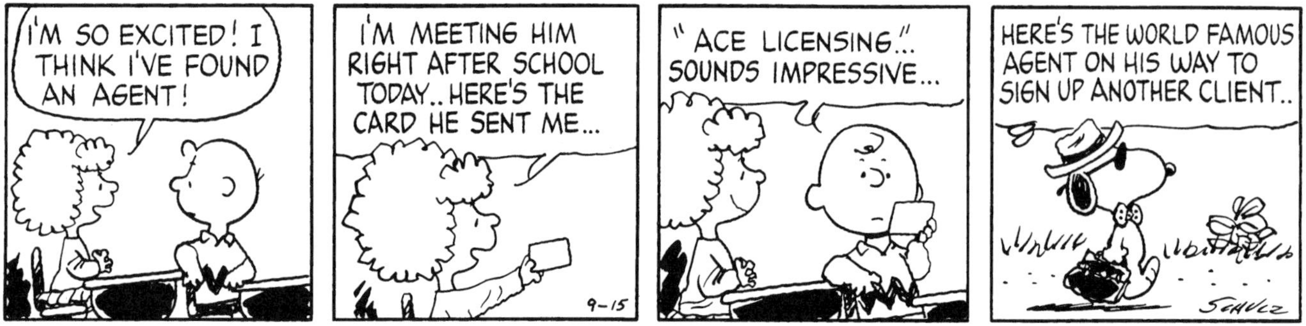
I'M SO EXCITED! I THINK I'VE FOUND AN AGENT!
I'M MEETING HIM RIGHT AFTER SCHOOL TODAY.. HERE'S THE CARD HE SENT ME...
9-15
"ACE LICENSING." SOUNDS IMPRESSIVE...
HERE'S THE WORLD FAMOUS AGENT ON HIS WAY TO SIGN UP ANOTHER CLIENT..
SCHULZ

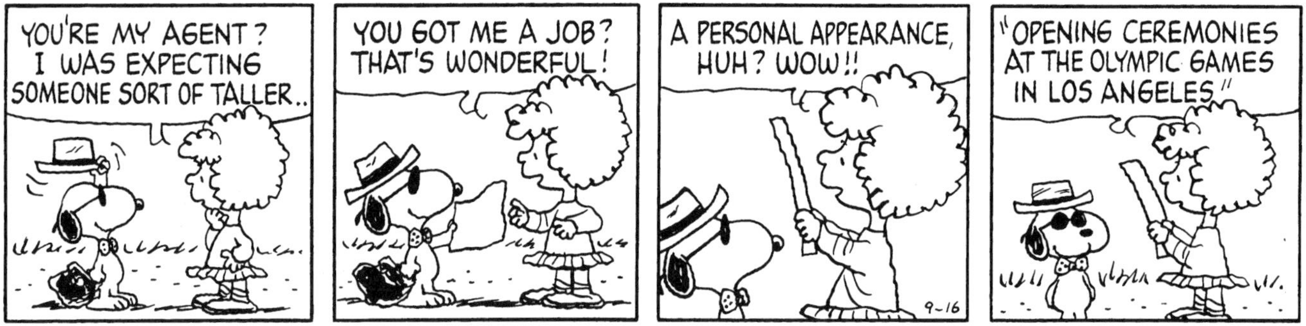
YOU'RE MY AGENT? I WAS EXPECTING SOMEONE SORT OF TALLER..
YOU GOT ME A JOB? THAT'S WONDERFUL!
A PERSONAL APPEARANCE, HUH? WOW!!
9-16
"OPENING CEREMONIES AT THE OLYMPIC GAMES IN LOS ANGELES"

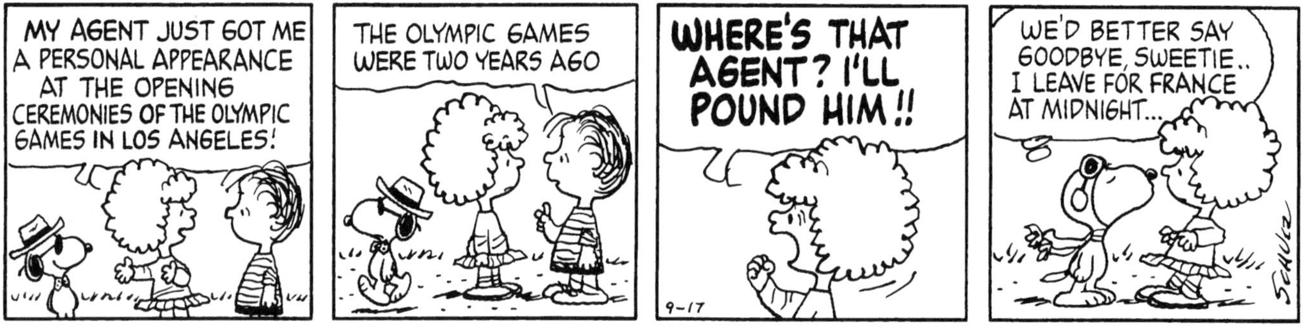
MY AGENT JUST GOT ME A PERSONAL APPEARANCE AT THE OPENING CEREMONIES OF THE OLYMPIC GAMES IN LOS ANGELES!
THE OLYMPIC GAMES WERE TWO YEARS AGO
WHERE'S THAT AGENT? I'LL POUND HIM!!
9-17
WE'D BETTER SAY GOODBYE, SWEETIE.. I LEAVE FOR FRANCE AT MIDNIGHT...
SCHULZ

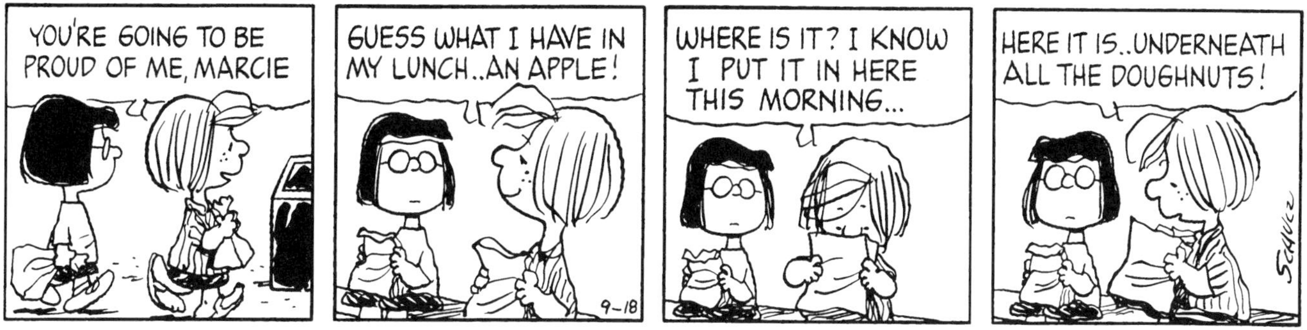
YOU'RE GOING TO BE PROUD OF ME, MARCIE
GUESS WHAT I HAVE IN MY LUNCH..AN APPLE!
9-18
WHERE IS IT? I KNOW I PUT IT IN HERE THIS MORNING...
HERE IT IS..UNDERNEATH ALL THE DOUGHNUTS!
SCHULZ

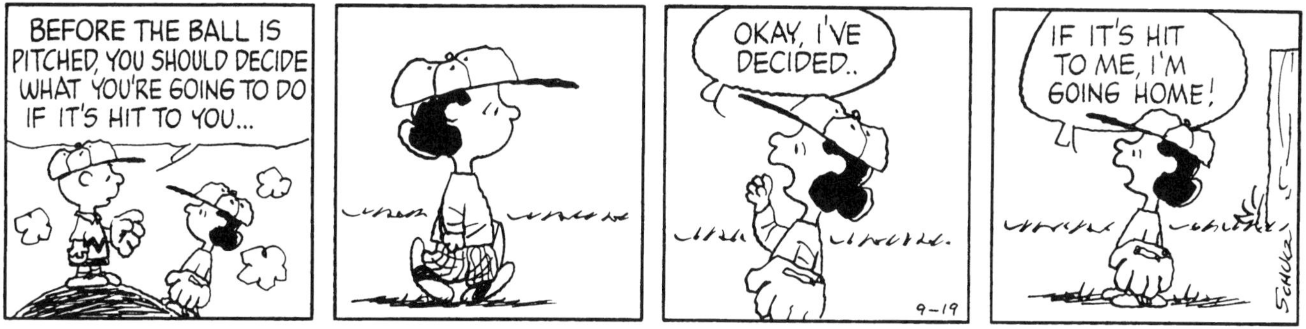
BEFORE THE BALL IS PITCHED, YOU SHOULD DECIDE WHAT YOU'RE GOING TO DO IF IT'S HIT TO YOU...
OKAY, I'VE DECIDED..
9-19
IF IT'S HIT TO ME, I'M GOING HOME!
SCHULZ

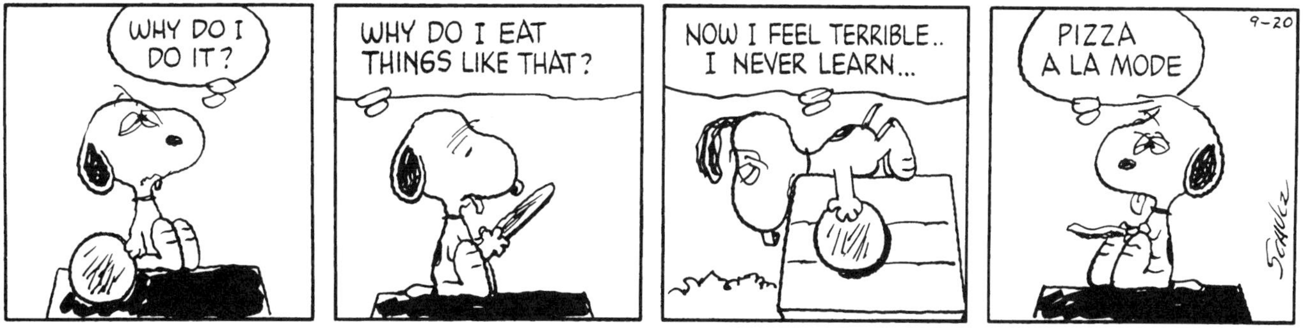
WHY DO I DO IT?
WHY DO I EAT THINGS LIKE THAT?
NOW I FEEL TERRIBLE.. I NEVER LEARN...
9-20
PIZZA A LA MODE
SCHULZ

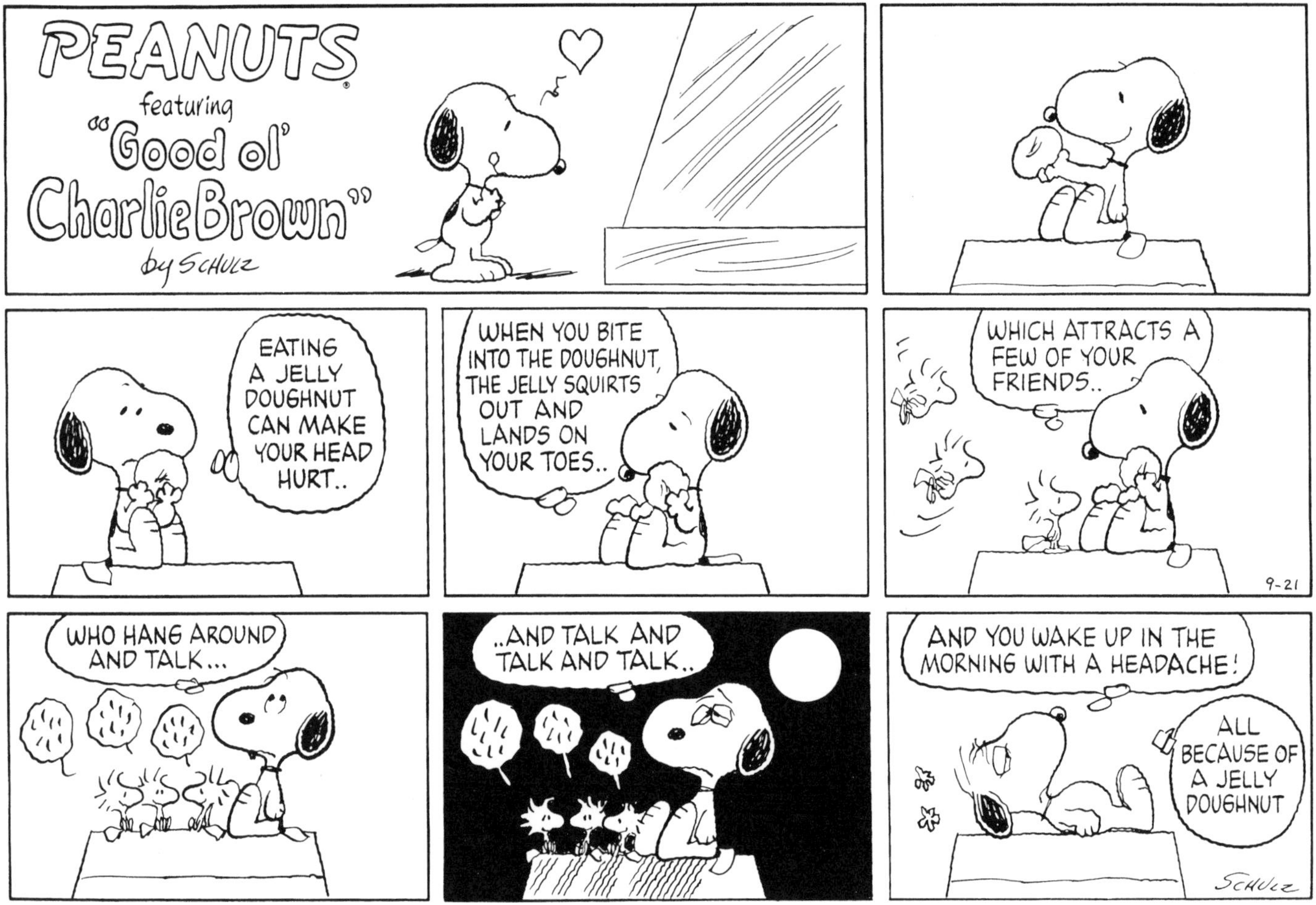
PEANUTS
featuring
"Good ol' CharlieBrown"
by SCHULZ
EATING A JELLY DOUGHNUT CAN MAKE YOUR HEAD HURT..
WHEN YOU BITE INTO THE DOUGHNUT, THE JELLY SQUIRTS OUT AND LANDS ON YOUR TOES..
WHICH ATTRACTS A FEW OF YOUR FRIENDS..
9-21
WHO HANG AROUND AND TALK...
..AND TALK AND TALK AND TALK..
AND YOU WAKE UP IN THE MORNING WITH A HEADACHE!
ALL BECAUSE OF A JELLY DOUGHNUT
SCHULZ

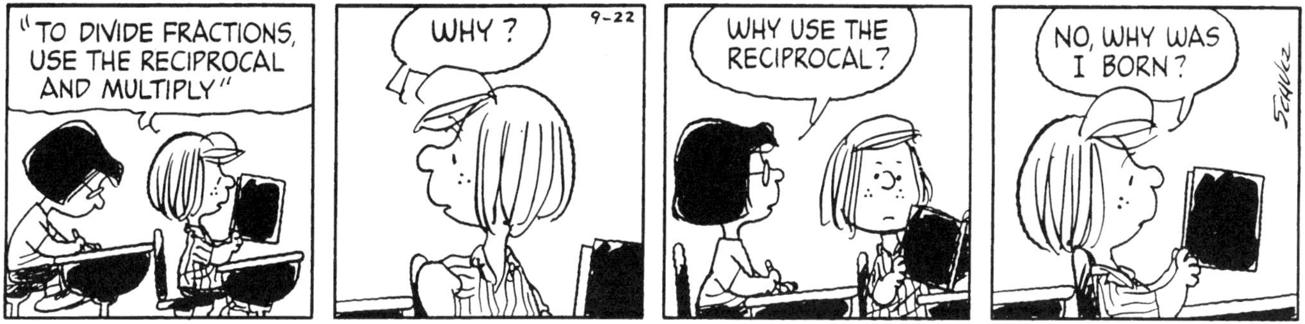
"TO DIVIDE FRACTIONS, USE THE RECIPROCAL AND MULTIPLY"
9-22
WHY ?
WHY USE THE RECIPROCAL ?
NO, WHY WAS I BORN ?

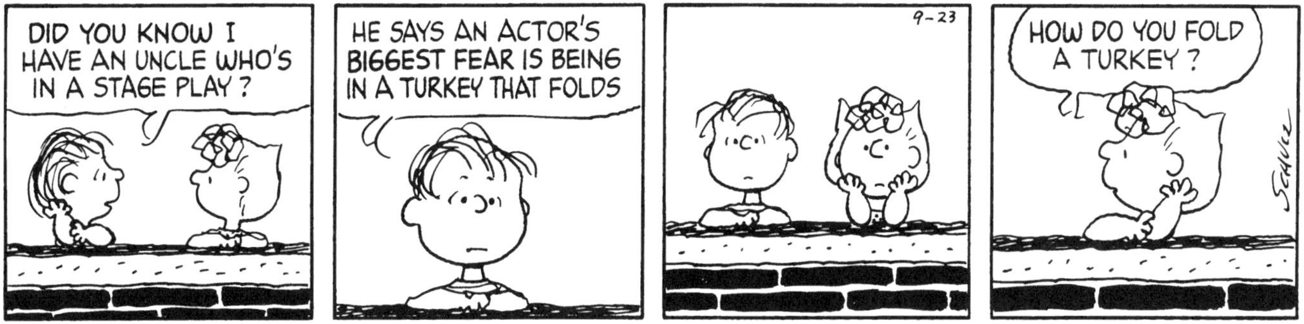
DID YOU KNOW I HAVE AN UNCLE WHO'S IN A STAGE PLAY ?
HE SAYS AN ACTOR'S BIGGEST FEAR IS BEING IN A TURKEY THAT FOLDS
9-23
HOW DO YOU FOLD A TURKEY ?

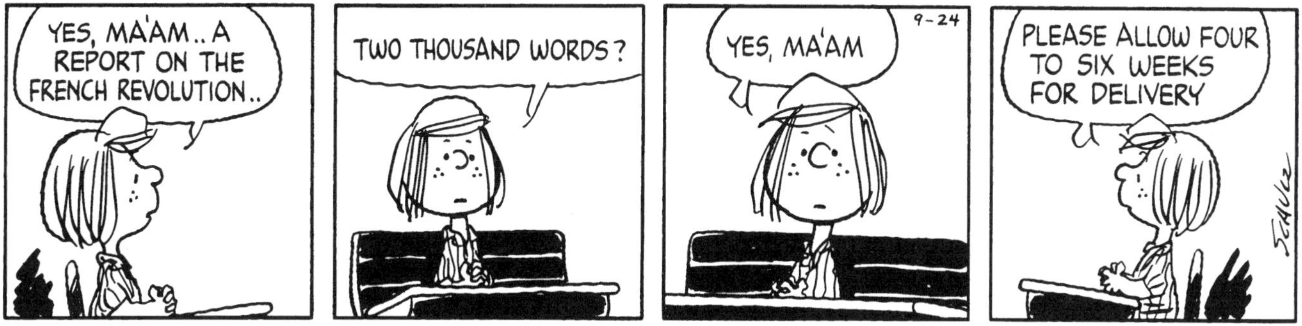
YES, MA'AM.. A REPORT ON THE FRENCH REVOLUTION..
TWO THOUSAND WORDS ?
9-24
YES, MA'AM
PLEASE ALLOW FOUR TO SIX WEEKS FOR DELIVERY

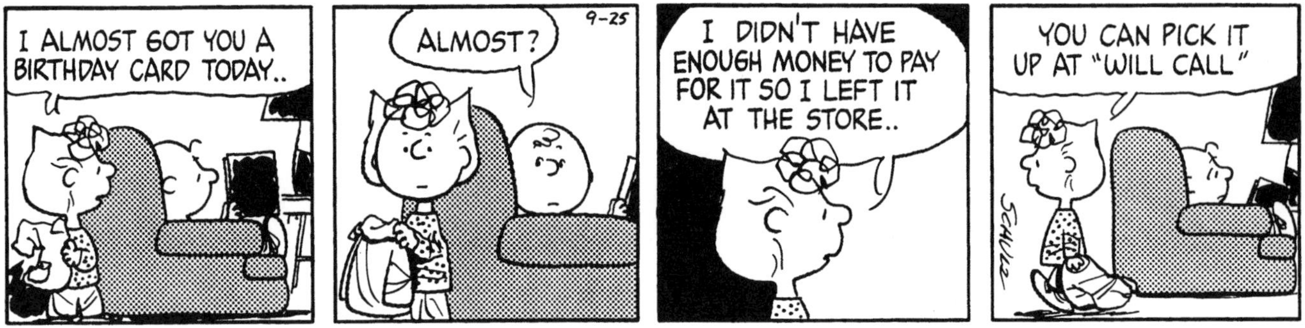
9-25
I ALMOST GOT YOU A BIRTHDAY CARD TODAY..
ALMOST?
I DIDN'T HAVE ENOUGH MONEY TO PAY FOR IT SO I LEFT IT AT THE STORE..
YOU CAN PICK IT UP AT "WILL CALL"
SCHULZ

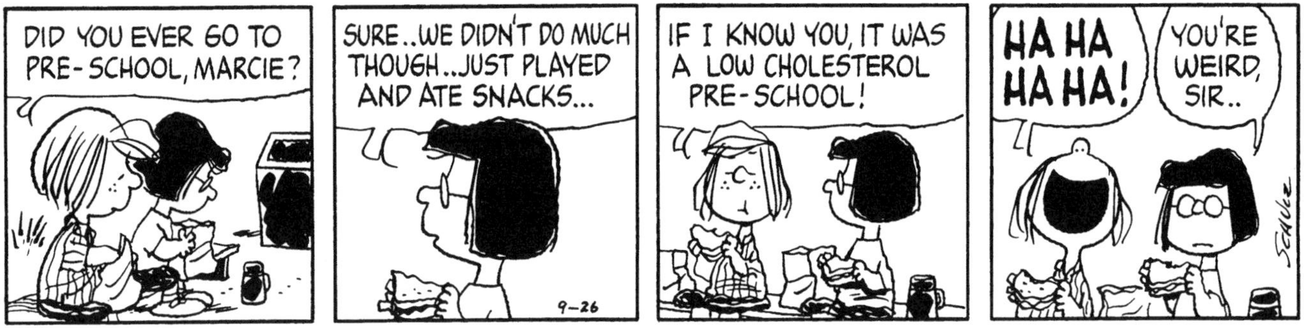
DID YOU EVER GO TO PRE-SCHOOL, MARCIE?
SURE..WE DIDN'T DO MUCH THOUGH..JUST PLAYED AND ATE SNACKS...
9-26
IF I KNOW YOU, IT WAS A LOW CHOLESTEROL PRE-SCHOOL!
HA HA HA HA!
YOU'RE WEIRD, SIR..
SCHULZ

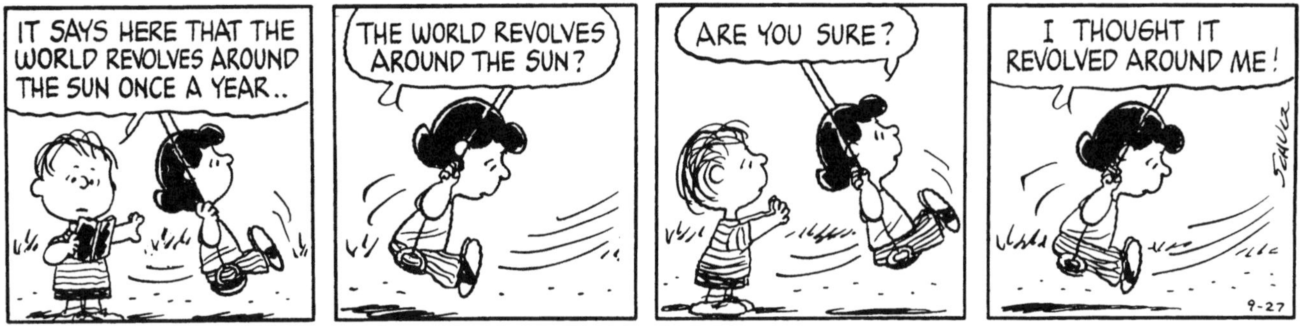
IT SAYS HERE THAT THE WORLD REVOLVES AROUND THE SUN ONCE A YEAR..
THE WORLD REVOLVES AROUND THE SUN?
ARE YOU SURE?
I THOUGHT IT REVOLVED AROUND ME!
SCHULZ
9-27

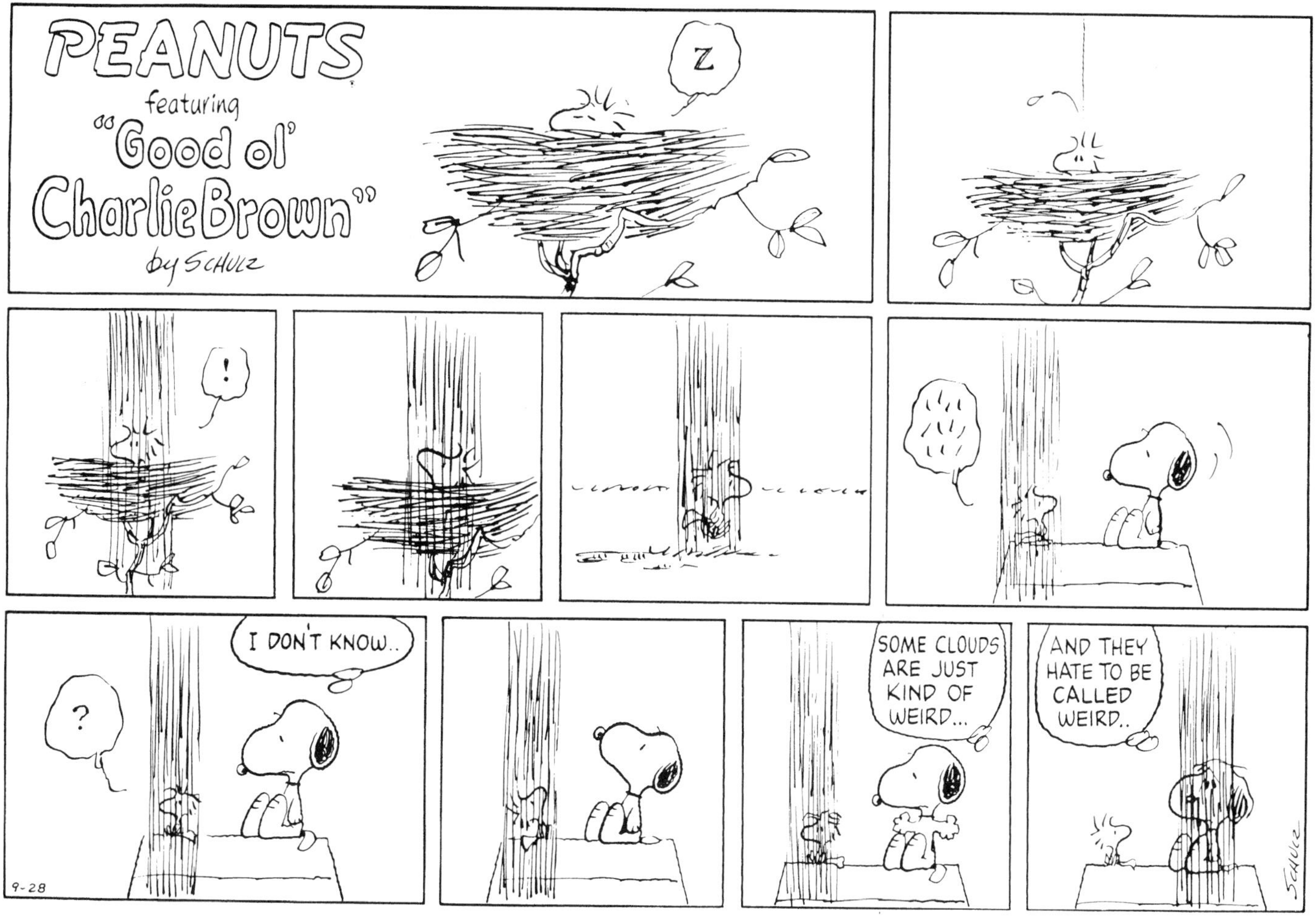
PEANUTS
featuring
"Good ol' CharlieBrown"
by SCHULZ
Z
!
?
I DON'T KNOW..
SOME CLOUDS ARE JUST KIND OF WEIRD...
AND THEY HATE TO BE CALLED WEIRD..
9-28
SCHULZ

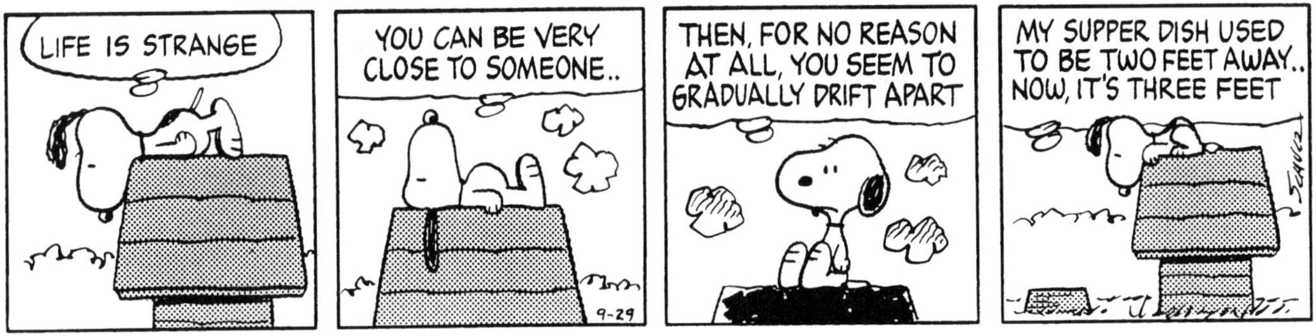
LIFE IS STRANGE
YOU CAN BE VERY CLOSE TO SOMEONE..
9-29
THEN, FOR NO REASON AT ALL, YOU SEEM TO GRADUALLY DRIFT APART
MY SUPPER DISH USED TO BE TWO FEET AWAY.. NOW, IT'S THREE FEET

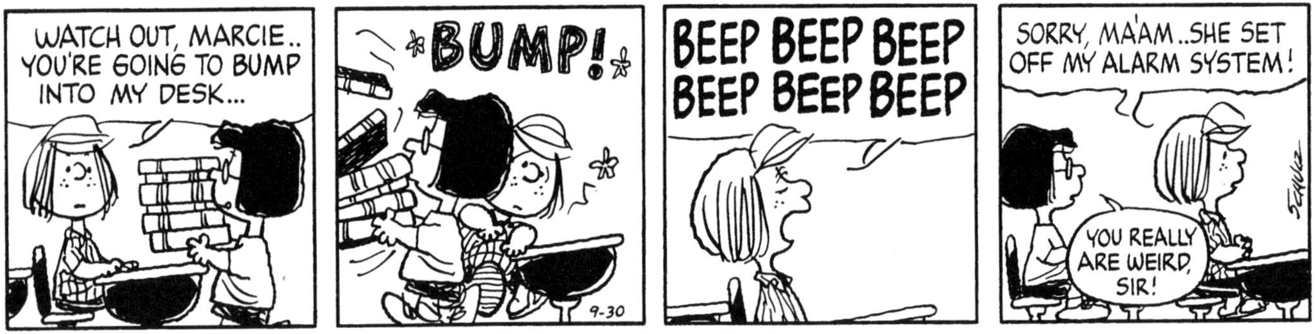
WATCH OUT, MARCIE.. YOU'RE GOING TO BUMP INTO MY DESK...
BUMP!
9-30
BEEP BEEP BEEP BEEP BEEP BEEP
SORRY, MA'AM..SHE SET OFF MY ALARM SYSTEM!
YOU REALLY ARE WEIRD, SIR!

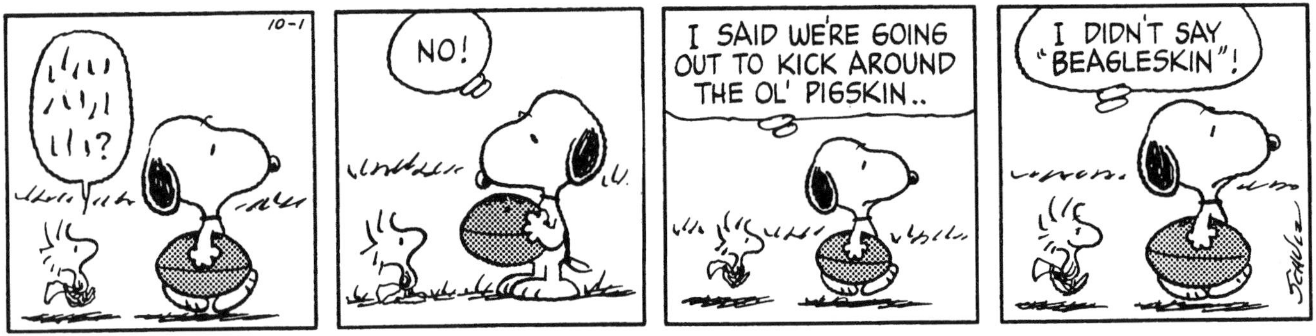
10-1
NO!
I SAID WE'RE GOING OUT TO KICK AROUND THE OL' PIGSKIN..
I DIDN'T SAY "BEAGLESKIN"!

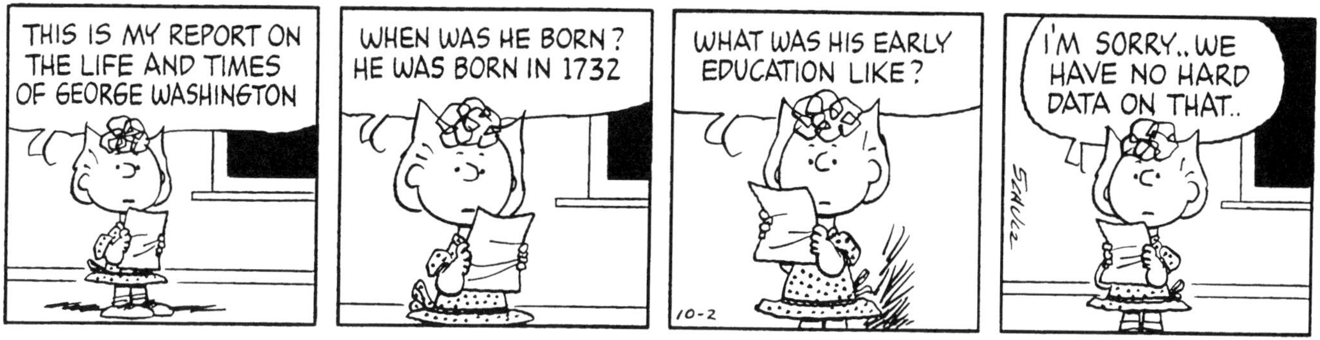
THIS IS MY REPORT ON THE LIFE AND TIMES OF GEORGE WASHINGTON
WHEN WAS HE BORN? HE WAS BORN IN 1732
WHAT WAS HIS EARLY EDUCATION LIKE?
10-2
I'M SORRY.. WE HAVE NO HARD DATA ON THAT..

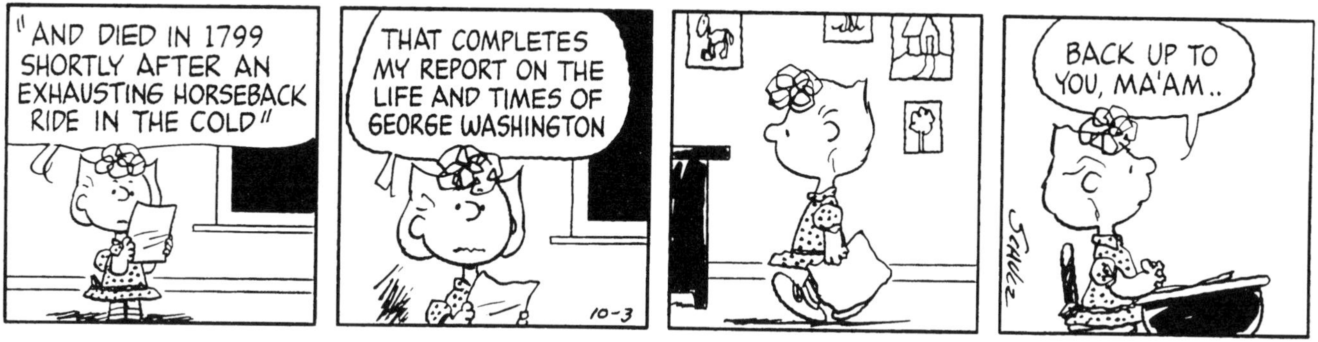
"AND DIED IN 1799 SHORTLY AFTER AN EXHAUSTING HORSEBACK RIDE IN THE COLD"
THAT COMPLETES MY REPORT ON THE LIFE AND TIMES OF GEORGE WASHINGTON
10-3
BACK UP TO YOU, MA'AM..

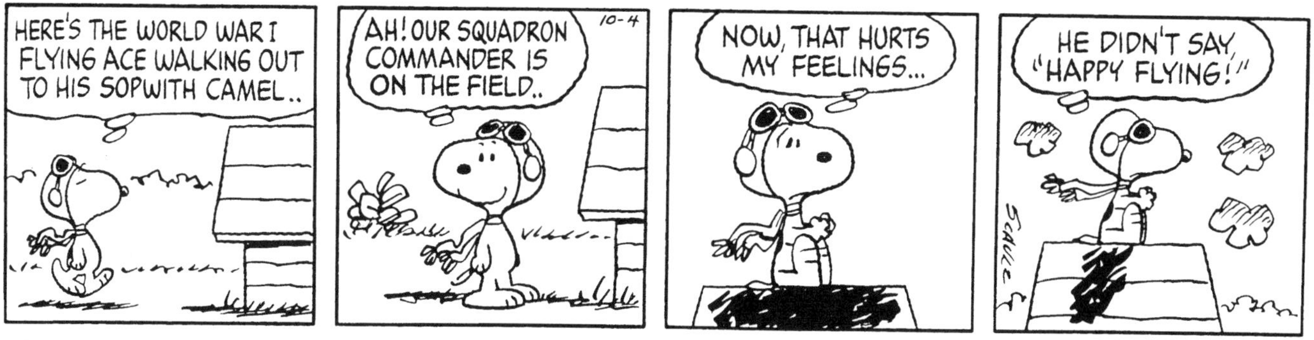
HERE'S THE WORLD WAR I FLYING ACE WALKING OUT TO HIS SOPWITH CAMEL..
10-4
AH! OUR SQUADRON COMMANDER IS ON THE FIELD..
NOW, THAT HURTS MY FEELINGS...
HE DIDN'T SAY, "HAPPY FLYING!"

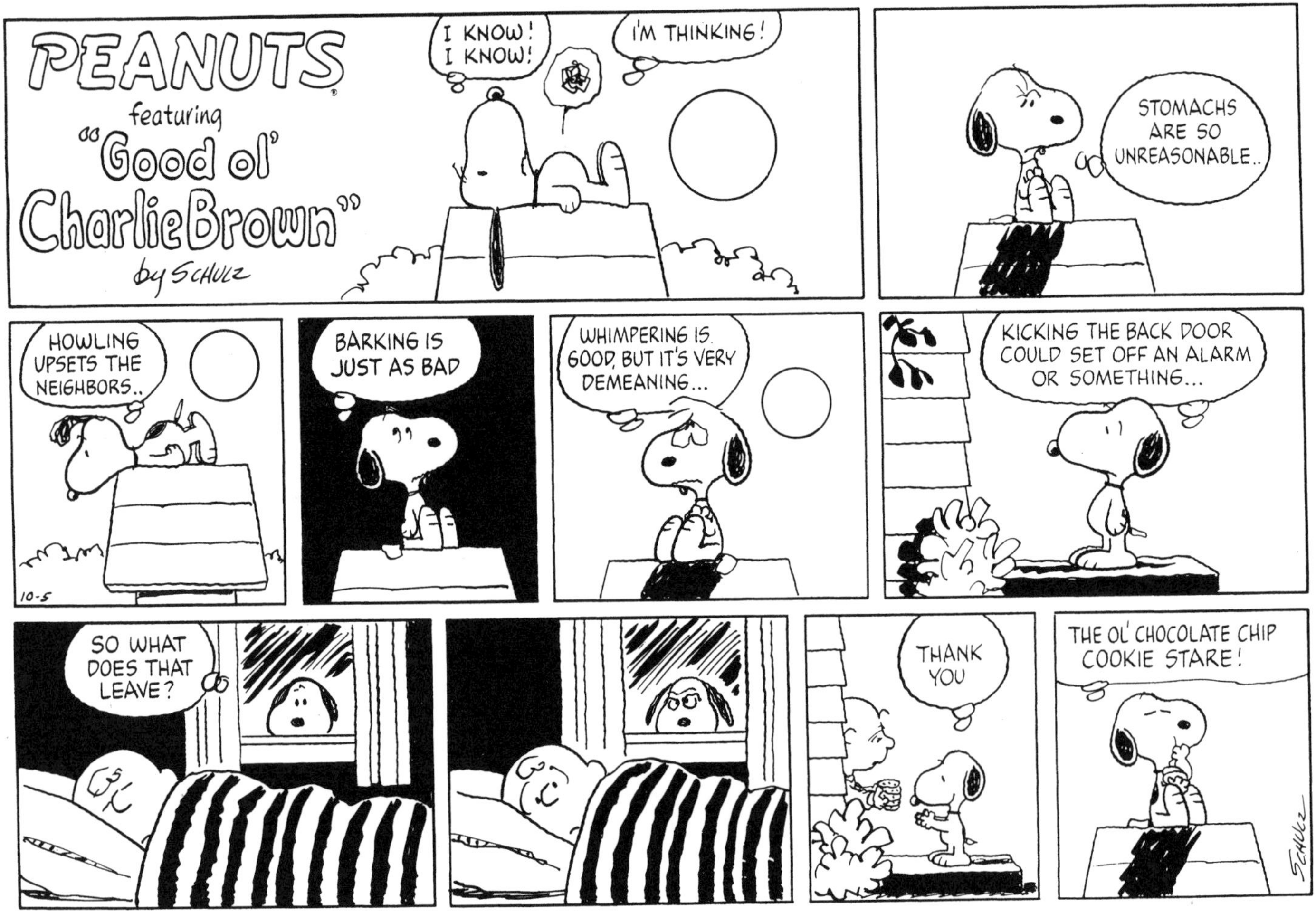
PEANUTS
featuring
"Good ol' Charlie Brown"
by SCHULZ
I KNOW! I KNOW!
I'M THINKING!
STOMACHS ARE SO UNREASONABLE..
HOWLING UPSETS THE NEIGHBORS..
10-5
BARKING IS JUST AS BAD
WHIMPERING IS GOOD, BUT IT'S VERY DEMEANING...
KICKING THE BACK DOOR COULD SET OFF AN ALARM OR SOMETHING...
SO WHAT DOES THAT LEAVE?
THANK YOU
THE OL' CHOCOLATE CHIP COOKIE STARE!
SCHULZ

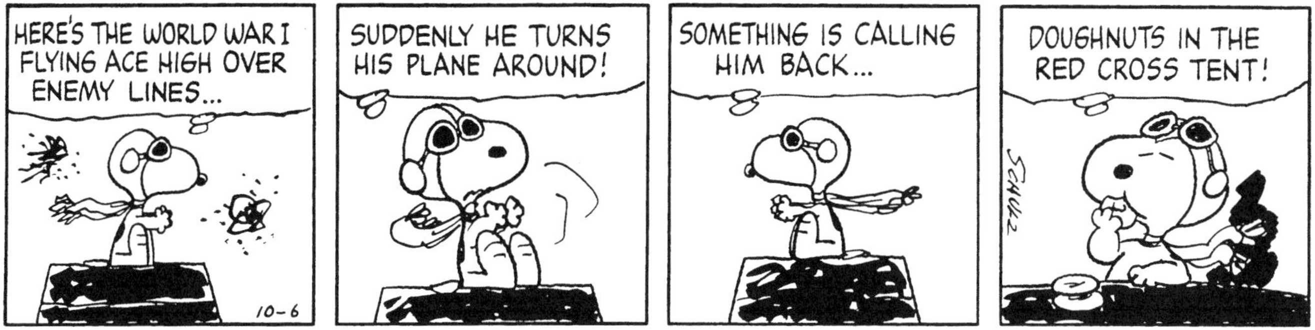
HERE'S THE WORLD WAR I FLYING ACE HIGH OVER ENEMY LINES...
SUDDENLY HE TURNS HIS PLANE AROUND!
SOMETHING IS CALLING HIM BACK...
DOUGHNUTS IN THE RED CROSS TENT!

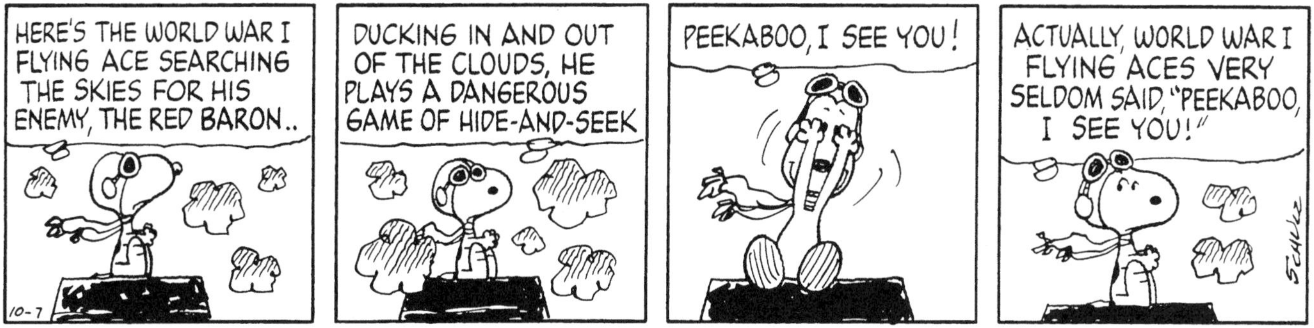
HERE'S THE WORLD WAR I FLYING ACE SEARCHING THE SKIES FOR HIS ENEMY, THE RED BARON..
DUCKING IN AND OUT OF THE CLOUDS, HE PLAYS A DANGEROUS GAME OF HIDE-AND-SEEK
PEEKABOO, I SEE YOU!
ACTUALLY, WORLD WAR I FLYING ACES VERY SELDOM SAID, "PEEKABOO, I SEE YOU!"

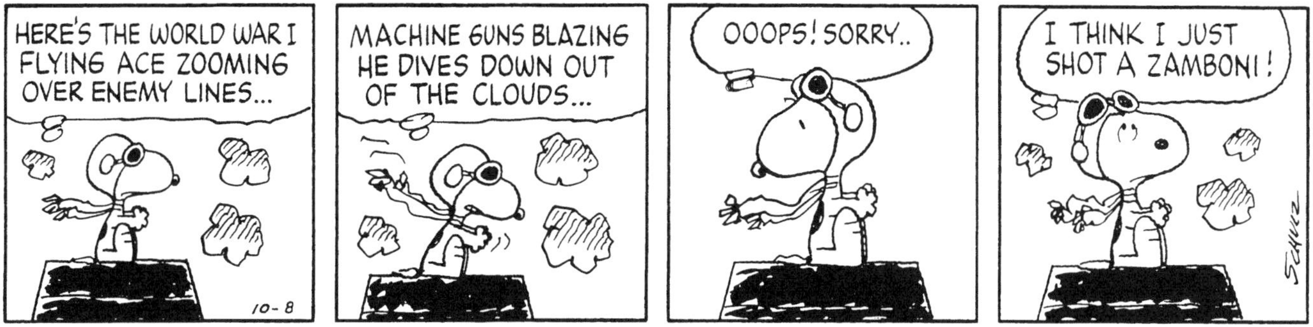
HERE'S THE WORLD WAR I FLYING ACE ZOOMING OVER ENEMY LINES...
MACHINE GUNS BLAZING HE DIVES DOWN OUT OF THE CLOUDS...
OOOPS! SORRY..
I THINK I JUST SHOT A ZAMBONI!

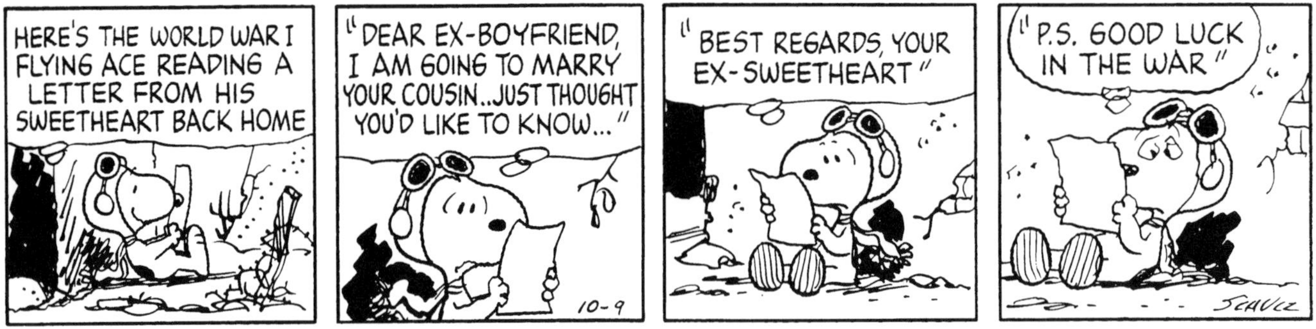
HERE'S THE WORLD WAR I FLYING ACE READING A LETTER FROM HIS SWEETHEART BACK HOME
"DEAR EX-BOYFRIEND, I AM GOING TO MARRY YOUR COUSIN...JUST THOUGHT YOU'D LIKE TO KNOW..."
10-9
"BEST REGARDS, YOUR EX-SWEETHEART"
"P.S. GOOD LUCK IN THE WAR"

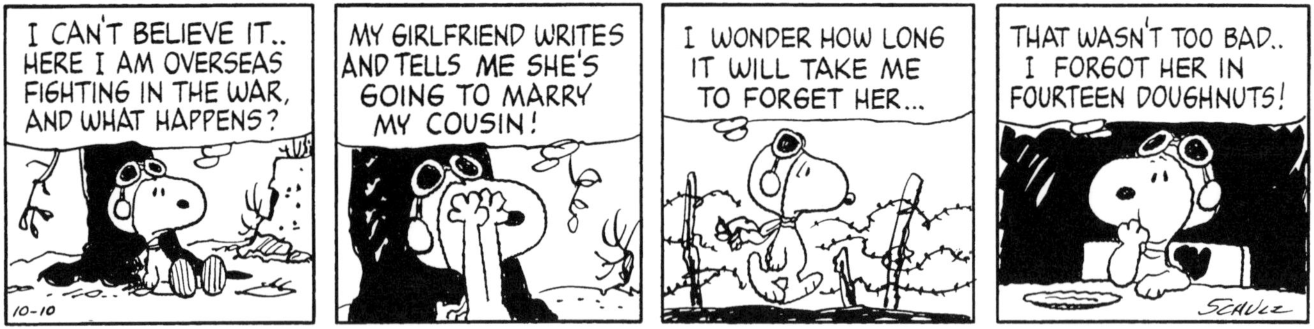
I CAN'T BELIEVE IT.. HERE I AM OVERSEAS FIGHTING IN THE WAR, AND WHAT HAPPENS?
10-10
MY GIRLFRIEND WRITES AND TELLS ME SHE'S GOING TO MARRY MY COUSIN!
I WONDER HOW LONG IT WILL TAKE ME TO FORGET HER...
THAT WASN'T TOO BAD.. I FORGOT HER IN FOURTEEN DOUGHNUTS!

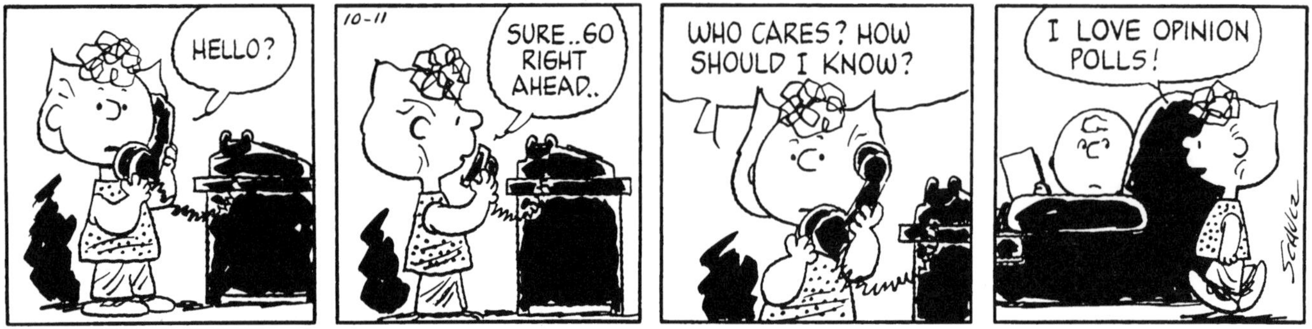
HELLO?
10-11
SURE..GO RIGHT AHEAD..
WHO CARES? HOW SHOULD I KNOW?
I LOVE OPINION POLLS!

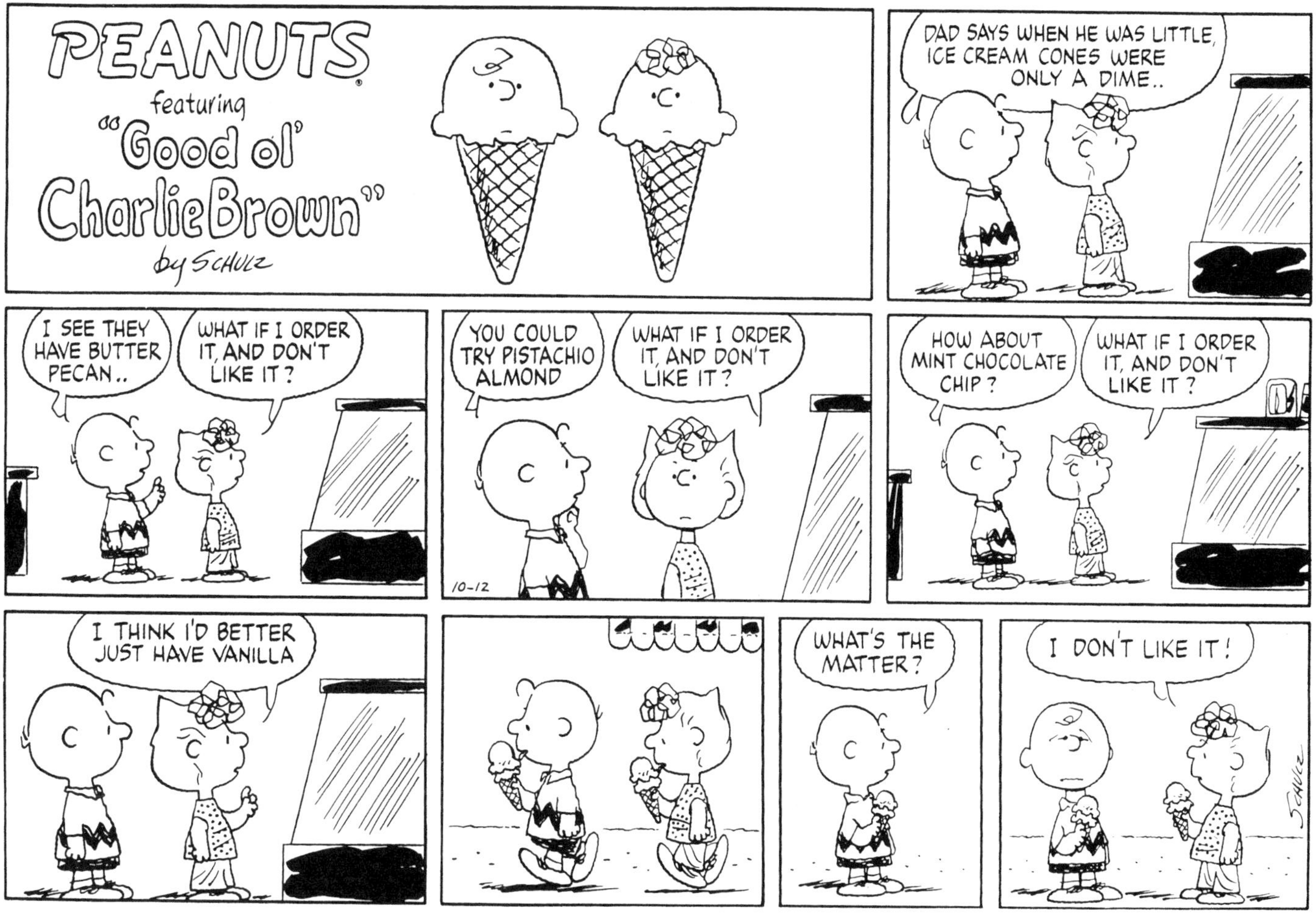
PEANUTS
featuring "Good ol' Charlie Brown"
by SCHULZ
DAD SAYS WHEN HE WAS LITTLE, ICE CREAM CONES WERE ONLY A DIME..
I SEE THEY HAVE BUTTER PECAN..
WHAT IF I ORDER IT, AND DON'T LIKE IT?
YOU COULD TRY PISTACHIO ALMOND
WHAT IF I ORDER IT, AND DON'T LIKE IT?
10-12
HOW ABOUT MINT CHOCOLATE CHIP?
WHAT IF I ORDER IT, AND DON'T LIKE IT?
I THINK I'D BETTER JUST HAVE VANILLA
WHAT'S THE MATTER?
I DON'T LIKE IT!
SCHULZ

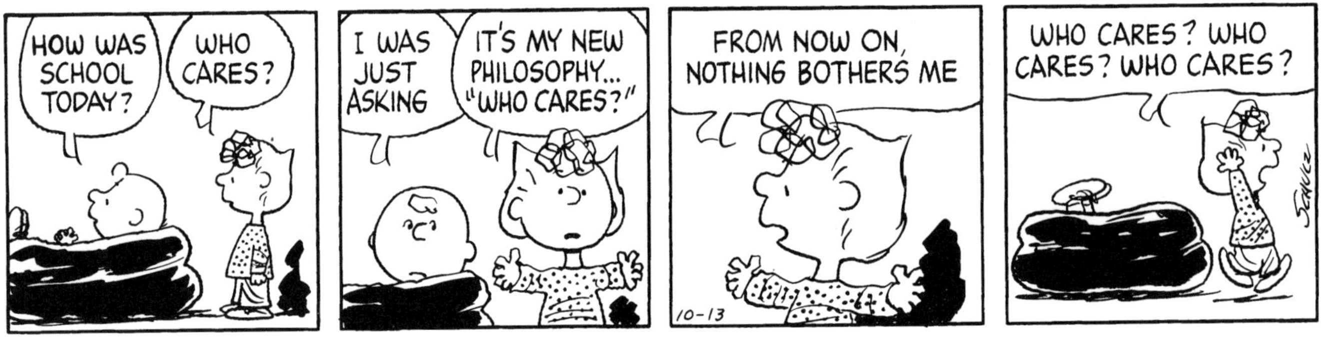
HOW WAS SCHOOL TODAY?
WHO CARES?
I WAS JUST ASKING
IT'S MY NEW PHILOSOPHY... "WHO CARES?"
FROM NOW ON, NOTHING BOTHERS ME
10-13
WHO CARES? WHO CARES? WHO CARES? WHO CARES?
SCHULZ

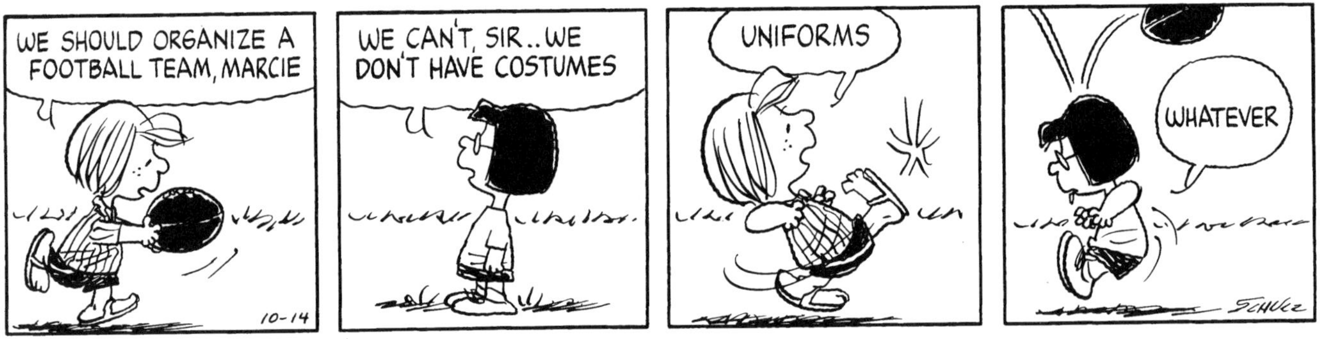
WE SHOULD ORGANIZE A FOOTBALL TEAM, MARCIE
10-14
WE CAN'T, SIR..WE DON'T HAVE COSTUMES
UNIFORMS
WHATEVER
SCHULZ

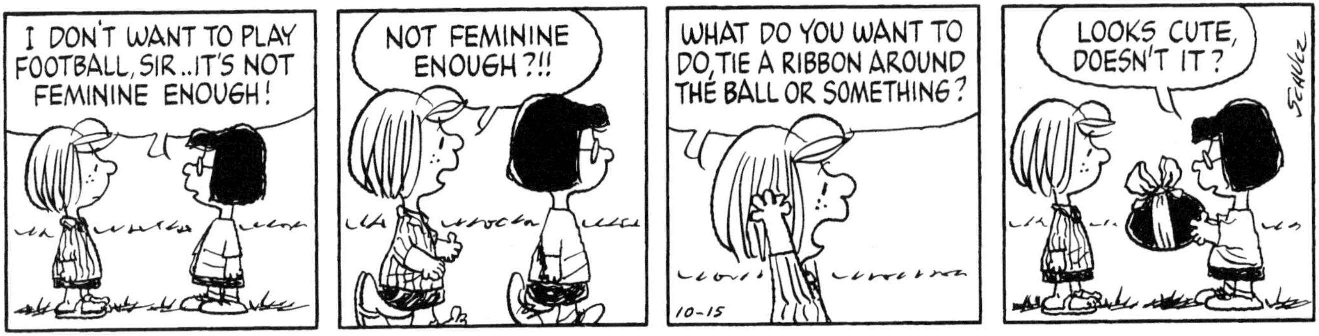
I DON'T WANT TO PLAY FOOTBALL, SIR..IT'S NOT FEMININE ENOUGH!
NOT FEMININE ENOUGH?!!
WHAT DO YOU WANT TO DO, TIE A RIBBON AROUND THE BALL OR SOMETHING?
10-15
LOOKS CUTE, DOESN'T IT?
SCHULZ

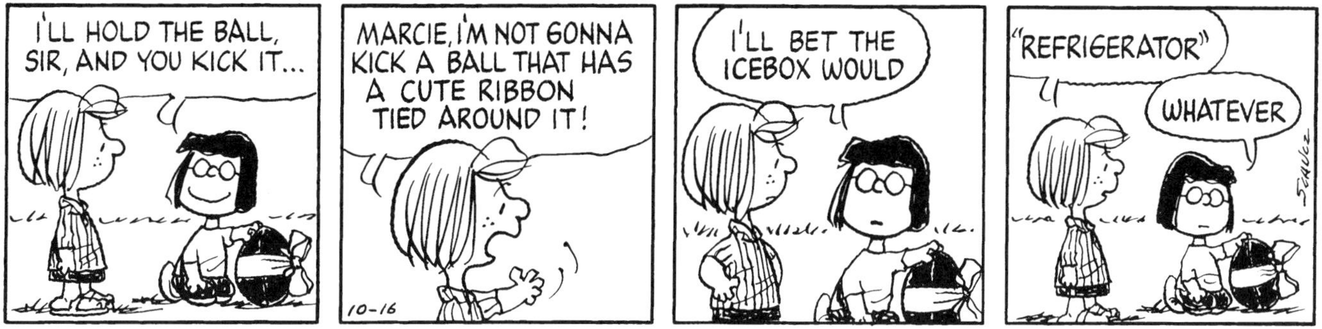
I'LL HOLD THE BALL, SIR, AND YOU KICK IT...
MARCIE, I'M NOT GONNA KICK A BALL THAT HAS A CUTE RIBBON TIED AROUND IT!
10-16
I'LL BET THE ICEBOX WOULD
"REFRIGERATOR"
WHATEVER
SCHULZ

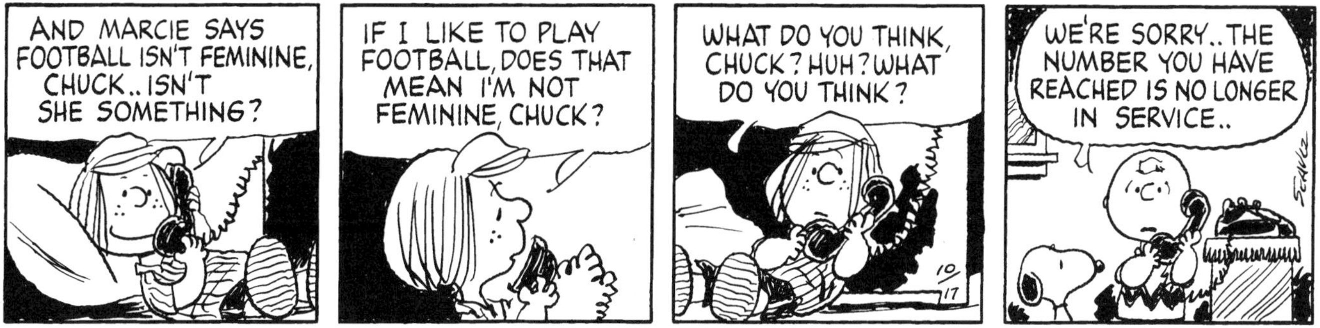
AND MARCIE SAYS FOOTBALL ISN'T FEMININE, CHUCK.. ISN'T SHE SOMETHING?
IF I LIKE TO PLAY FOOTBALL, DOES THAT MEAN I'M NOT FEMININE, CHUCK?
WHAT DO YOU THINK, CHUCK? HUH? WHAT DO YOU THINK?
10/17
WE'RE SORRY.. THE NUMBER YOU HAVE REACHED IS NO LONGER IN SERVICE..
SCHULZ

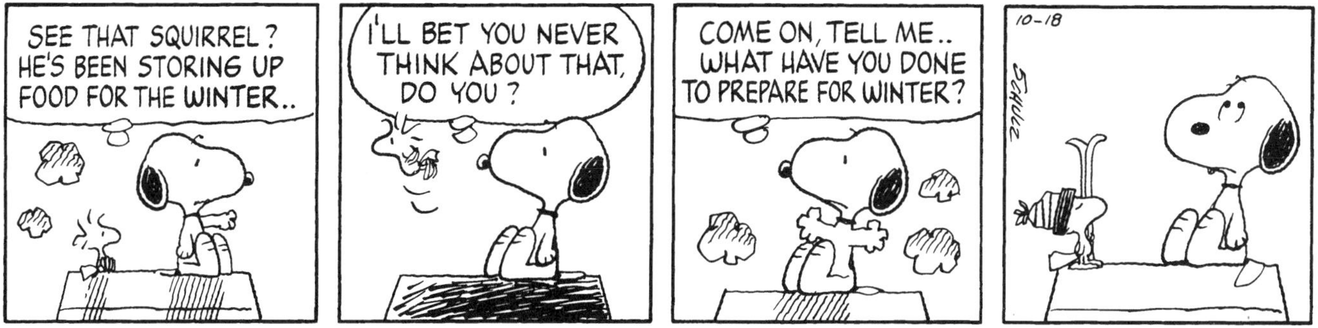
SEE THAT SQUIRREL? HE'S BEEN STORING UP FOOD FOR THE WINTER..
I'LL BET YOU NEVER THINK ABOUT THAT, DO YOU?
COME ON, TELL ME.. WHAT HAVE YOU DONE TO PREPARE FOR WINTER?
10-18
SCHULZ

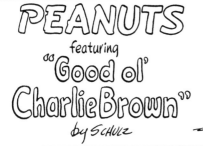

PEANUTS
featuring
"Good ol'
Charlie Brown"
by SCHULZ

ONCE A YEAR...JUST ONCE A YEAR..

CHARLIE BROWNNN.. ♫

CHARLIE BROWN, I'LL HOLD THE BALL, AND YOU COME RUNNING UP AND KICK IT!

SURE! SURE I WILL! YOU MUST THINK I'M REALLY STUPID!

10-19

PLEASE, CHARLIE BROWN..I LOOK FORWARD TO THIS SPECIAL MOMENT ALL YEAR...

I SUPPOSE IF SOMEONE LOOKS FORWARD TO SOMETHING, IT'S WRONG TO SPOIL IT..

THIS YEAR I'M GONNA KICK THAT BALL CLEAR TO BULLHEAD CITY!

AAUGH!

WHAM!

HOW DEPRESSING...YOU LOOK FORWARD ALL YEAR TO A SPECIAL MOMENT, AND BEFORE YOU KNOW IT, IT'S OVER!

IT'S SO DEPRESSING

I CAN'T STAND IT!

SCHULZ

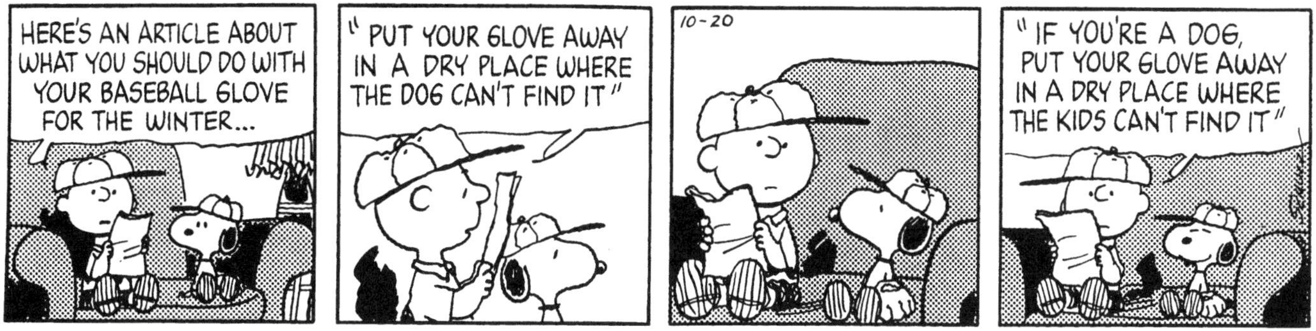
HERE'S AN ARTICLE ABOUT WHAT YOU SHOULD DO WITH YOUR BASEBALL GLOVE FOR THE WINTER...
" PUT YOUR GLOVE AWAY IN A DRY PLACE WHERE THE DOG CAN'T FIND IT "
10-20
" IF YOU'RE A DOG, PUT YOUR GLOVE AWAY IN A DRY PLACE WHERE THE KIDS CAN'T FIND IT "

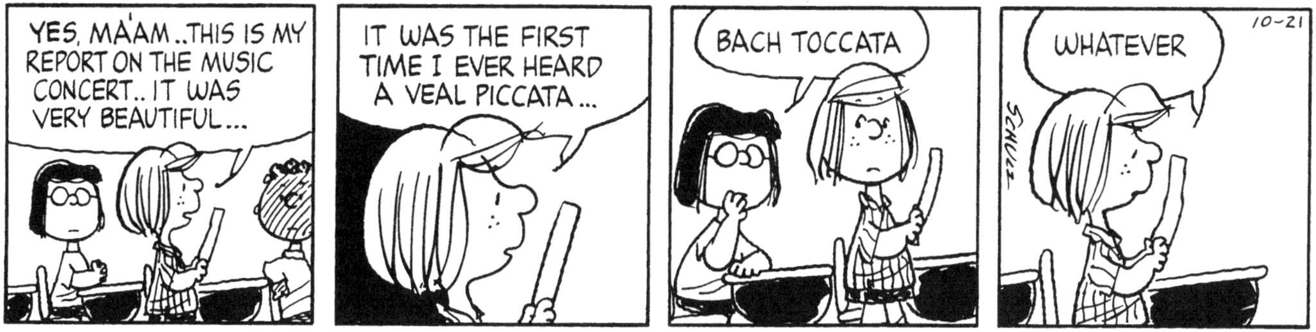
YES, MA'AM ..THIS IS MY REPORT ON THE MUSIC CONCERT.. IT WAS VERY BEAUTIFUL...
IT WAS THE FIRST TIME I EVER HEARD A VEAL PICCATA...
BACH TOCCATA
SCHULZ
WHATEVER
10-21

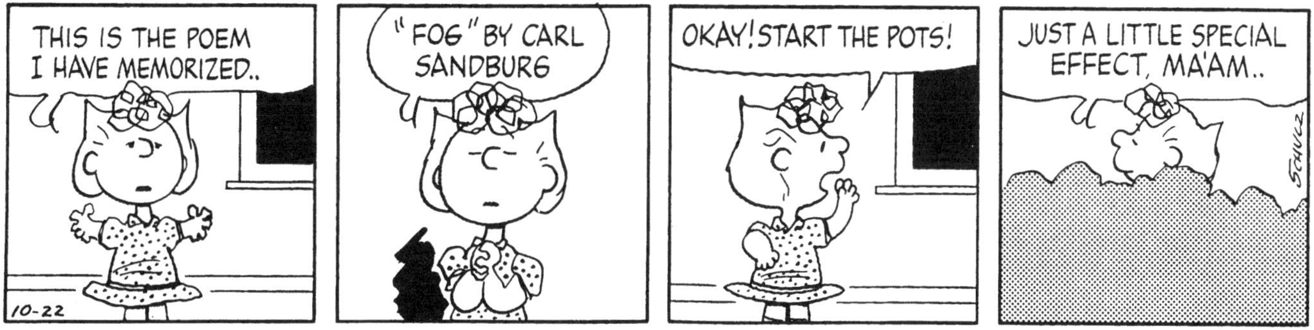
THIS IS THE POEM I HAVE MEMORIZED..
10-22
" FOG " BY CARL SANDBURG
OKAY! START THE POTS!
JUST A LITTLE SPECIAL EFFECT, MA'AM..
SCHULZ

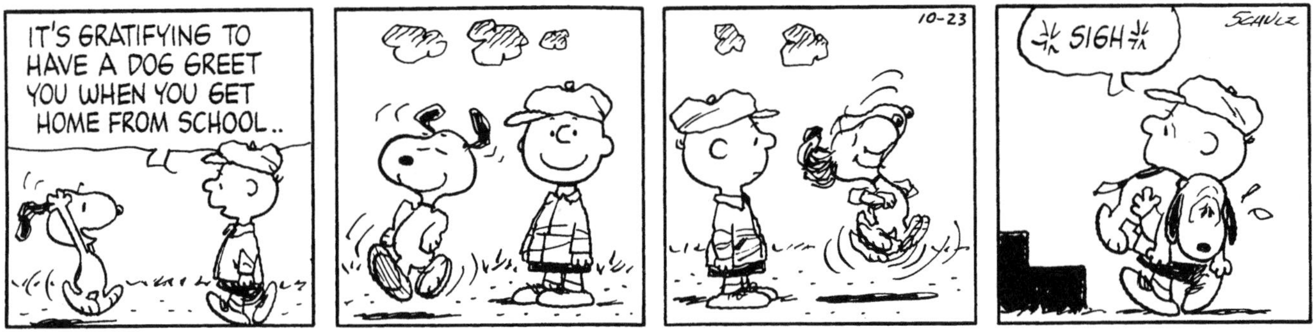
IT'S GRATIFYING TO HAVE A DOG GREET YOU WHEN YOU GET HOME FROM SCHOOL..
10-23
SIGH

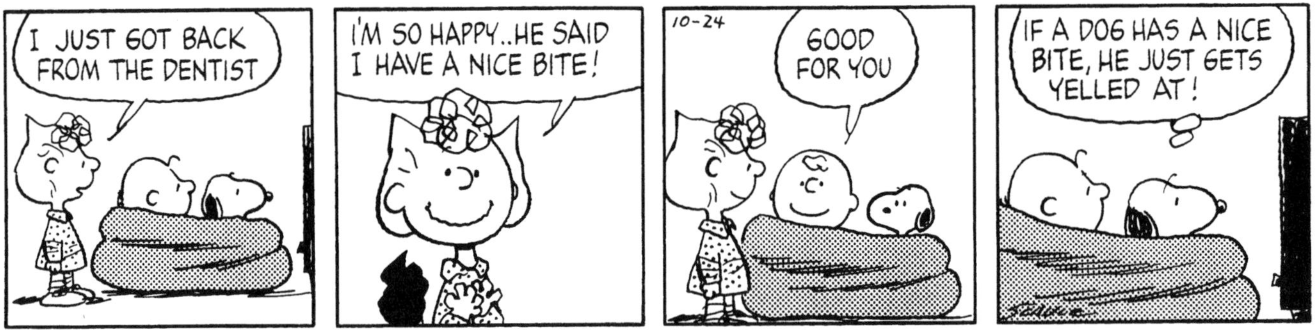
I JUST GOT BACK FROM THE DENTIST
I'M SO HAPPY..HE SAID I HAVE A NICE BITE!
10-24
GOOD FOR YOU
IF A DOG HAS A NICE BITE, HE JUST GETS YELLED AT!

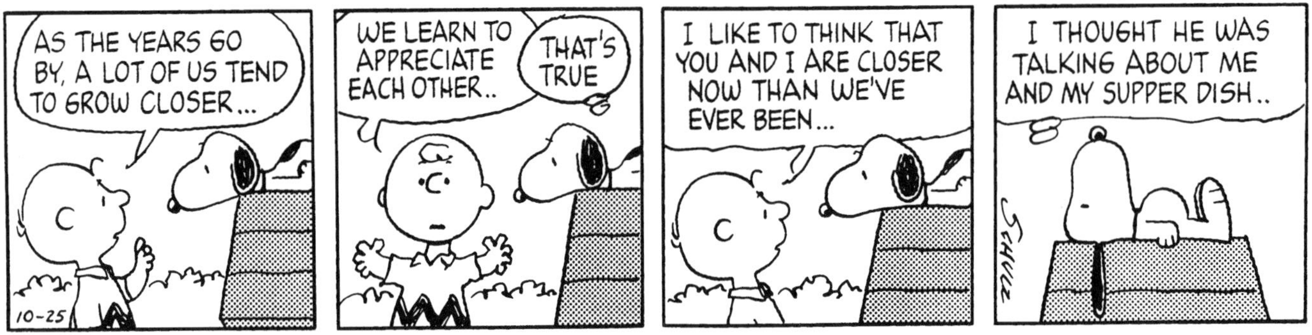
AS THE YEARS GO BY, A LOT OF US TEND TO GROW CLOSER...
10-25
WE LEARN TO APPRECIATE EACH OTHER..
THAT'S TRUE
I LIKE TO THINK THAT YOU AND I ARE CLOSER NOW THAN WE'VE EVER BEEN...
I THOUGHT HE WAS TALKING ABOUT ME AND MY SUPPER DISH..

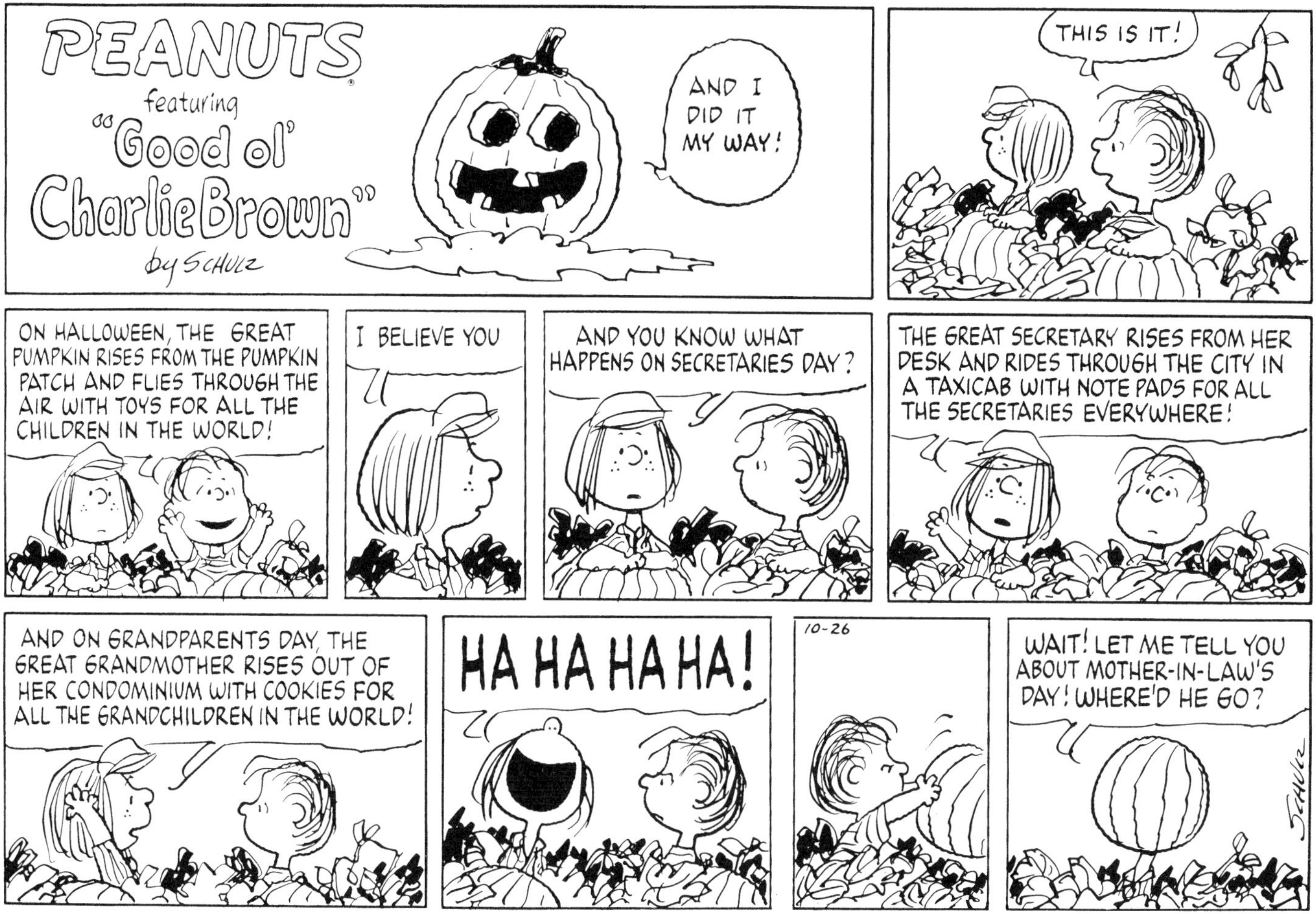
PEANUTS
featuring
"Good ol' CharlieBrown"
by SCHULZ
AND I DID IT MY WAY!
THIS IS IT!
ON HALLOWEEN, THE GREAT PUMPKIN RISES FROM THE PUMPKIN PATCH AND FLIES THROUGH THE AIR WITH TOYS FOR ALL THE CHILDREN IN THE WORLD!
I BELIEVE YOU
AND YOU KNOW WHAT HAPPENS ON SECRETARIES DAY?
THE GREAT SECRETARY RISES FROM HER DESK AND RIDES THROUGH THE CITY IN A TAXICAB WITH NOTE PADS FOR ALL THE SECRETARIES EVERYWHERE!
AND ON GRANDPARENTS DAY, THE GREAT GRANDMOTHER RISES OUT OF HER CONDOMINIUM WITH COOKIES FOR ALL THE GRANDCHILDREN IN THE WORLD!
HA HA HA HA HA!
10-26
WAIT! LET ME TELL YOU ABOUT MOTHER-IN-LAW'S DAY! WHERE'D HE GO?
SCHULZ

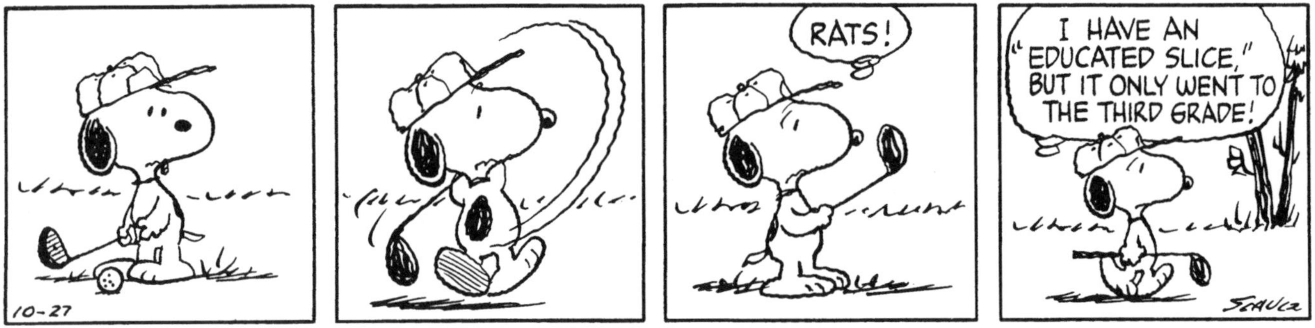
RATS!
I HAVE AN "EDUCATED SLICE," BUT IT ONLY WENT TO THE THIRD GRADE!
10-27

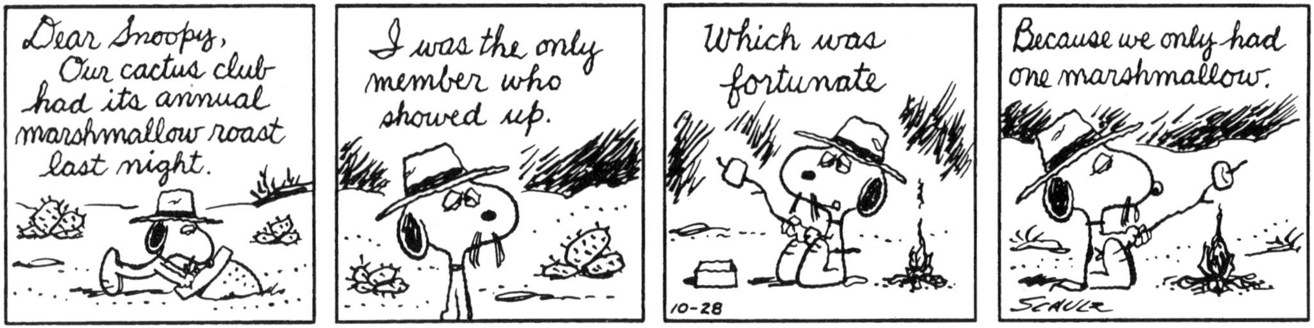
Dear Snoopy, Our cactus club had its annual marshmallow roast last night.
I was the only member who showed up.
Which was fortunate
Because we only had one marshmallow.
10-28

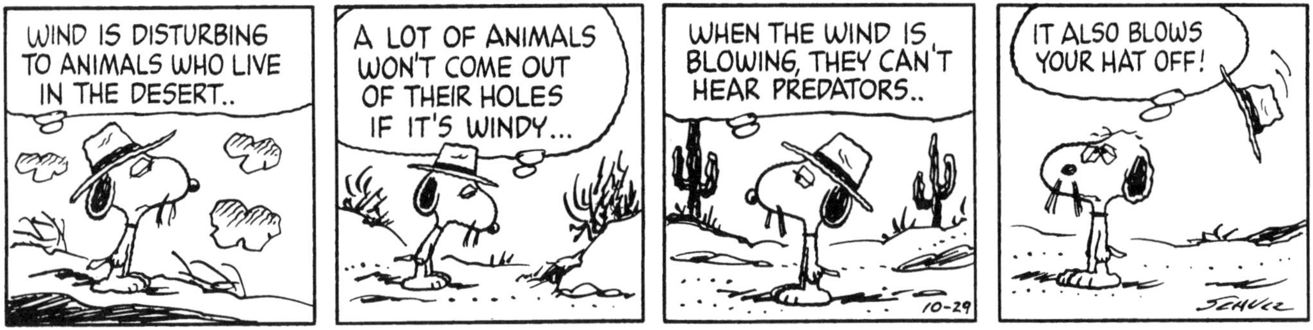
WIND IS DISTURBING TO ANIMALS WHO LIVE IN THE DESERT..
A LOT OF ANIMALS WON'T COME OUT OF THEIR HOLES IF IT'S WINDY...
WHEN THE WIND IS BLOWING, THEY CAN'T HEAR PREDATORS..
IT ALSO BLOWS YOUR HAT OFF!
10-29

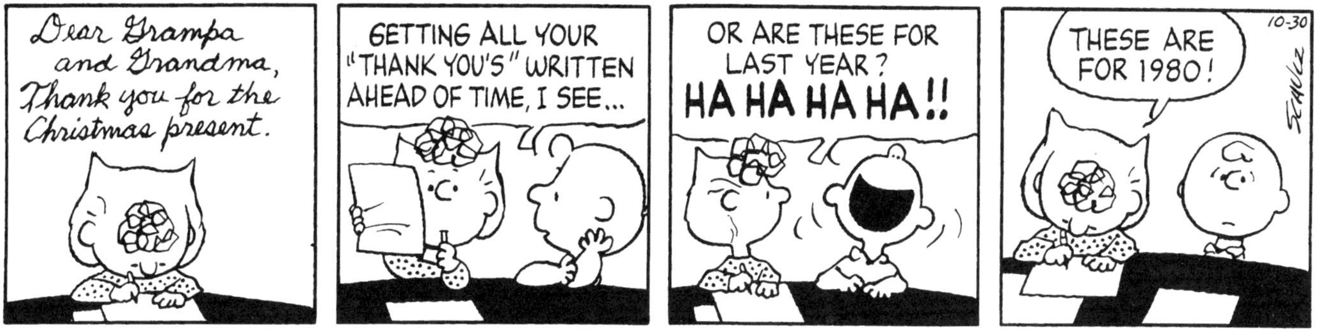
Dear Grampa and Grandma, Thank you for the Christmas present.
GETTING ALL YOUR "THANK YOU'S" WRITTEN AHEAD OF TIME, I SEE...
OR ARE THESE FOR LAST YEAR? HA HA HA HA!!
THESE ARE FOR 1980!
10-30
SCHULZ

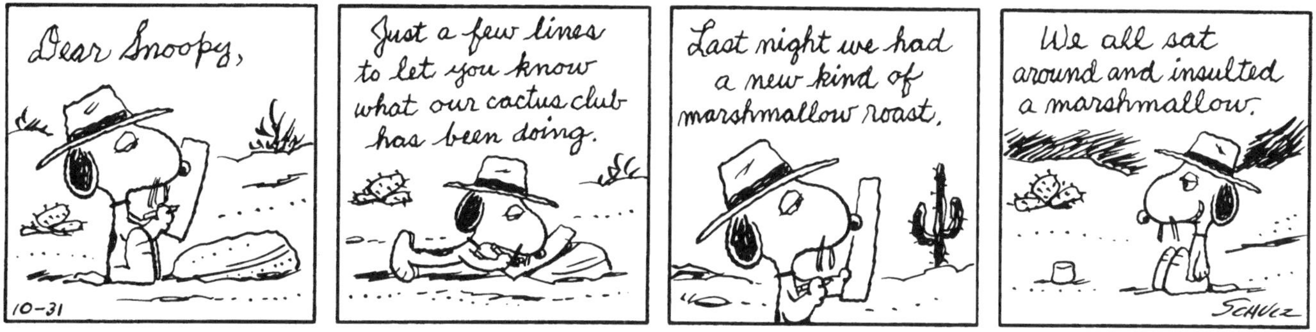
Dear Snoopy,
10-31
Just a few lines to let you know what our cactus club has been doing.
Last night we had a new kind of marshmallow roast.
We all sat around and insulted a marshmallow.
SCHULZ

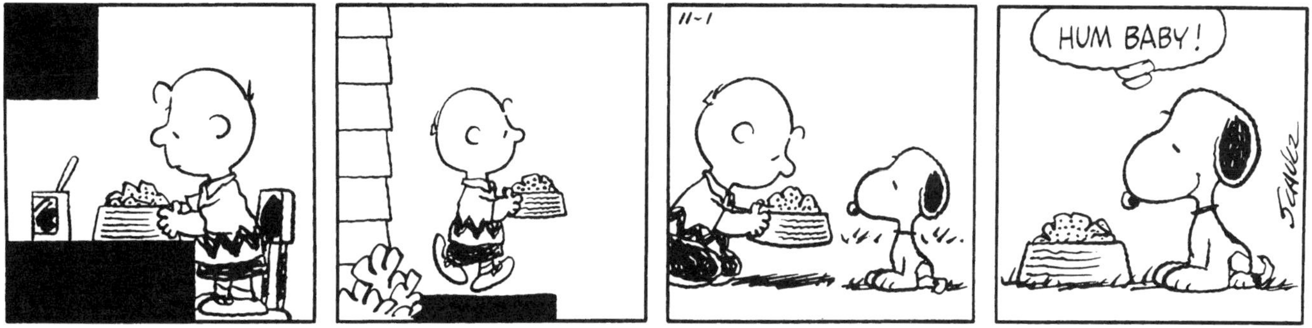
11-1
HUM BABY!
SCHULZ

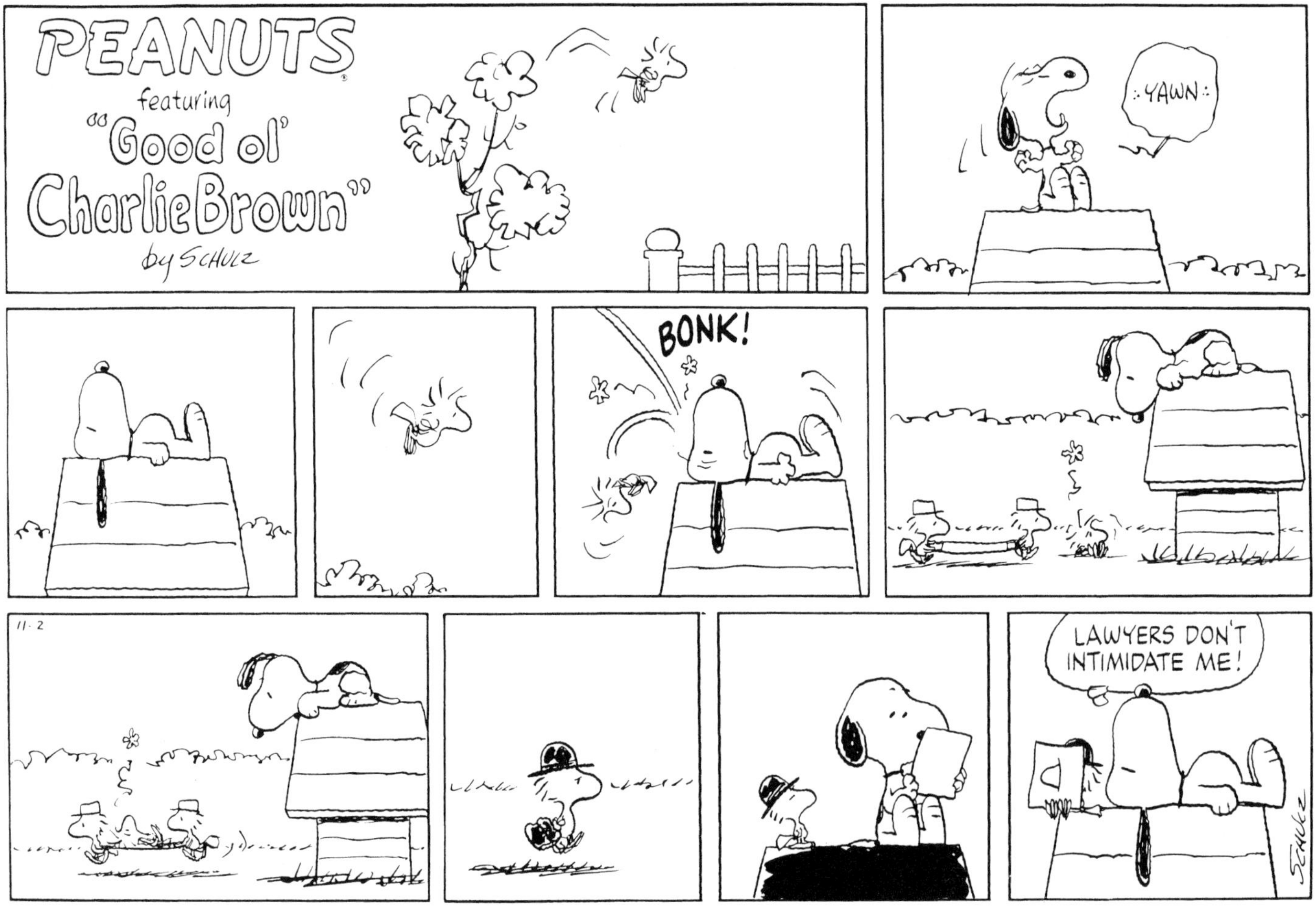
PEANUTS
featuring
"Good ol' Charlie Brown"
by SCHULZ
YAWN
BONK!
11-2
LAWYERS DON'T INTIMIDATE ME!
SCHULZ

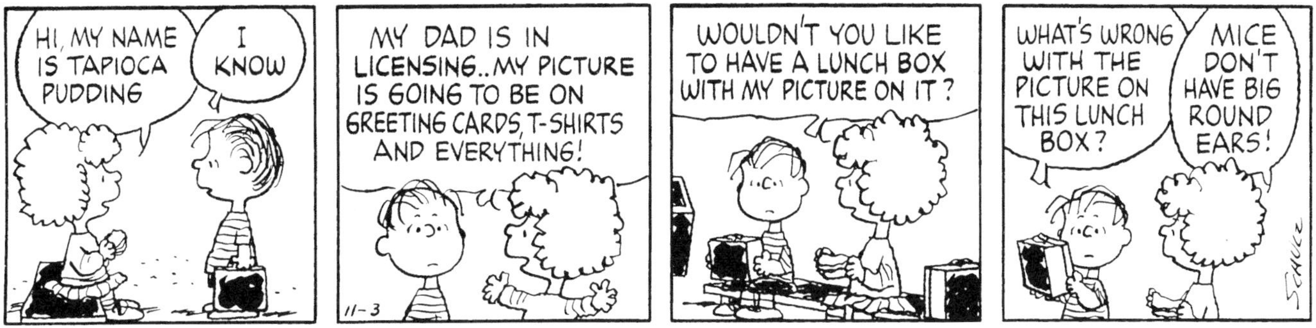
HI, MY NAME IS TAPIOCA PUDDING
I KNOW
MY DAD IS IN LICENSING.. MY PICTURE IS GOING TO BE ON GREETING CARDS, T-SHIRTS AND EVERYTHING!
11-3
WOULDN'T YOU LIKE TO HAVE A LUNCH BOX WITH MY PICTURE ON IT?
WHAT'S WRONG WITH THE PICTURE ON THIS LUNCH BOX?
MICE DON'T HAVE BIG ROUND EARS!
SCHULZ

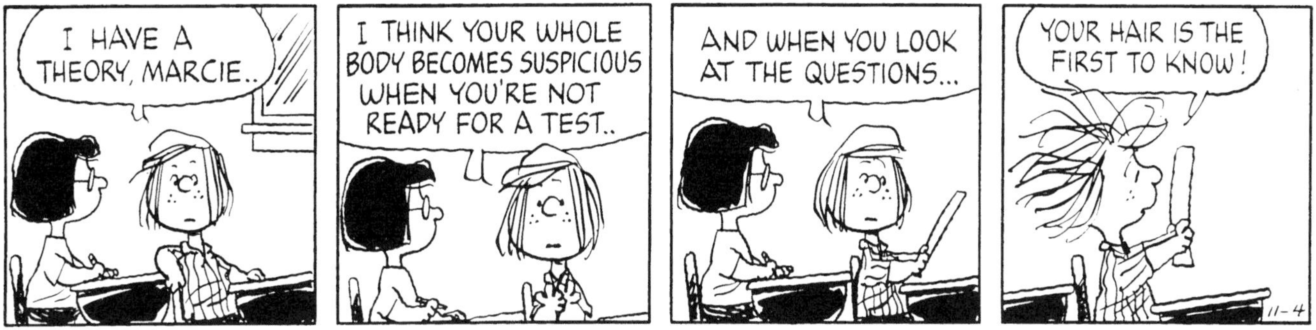
I HAVE A THEORY, MARCIE..
I THINK YOUR WHOLE BODY BECOMES SUSPICIOUS WHEN YOU'RE NOT READY FOR A TEST..
AND WHEN YOU LOOK AT THE QUESTIONS...
YOUR HAIR IS THE FIRST TO KNOW!
11-4

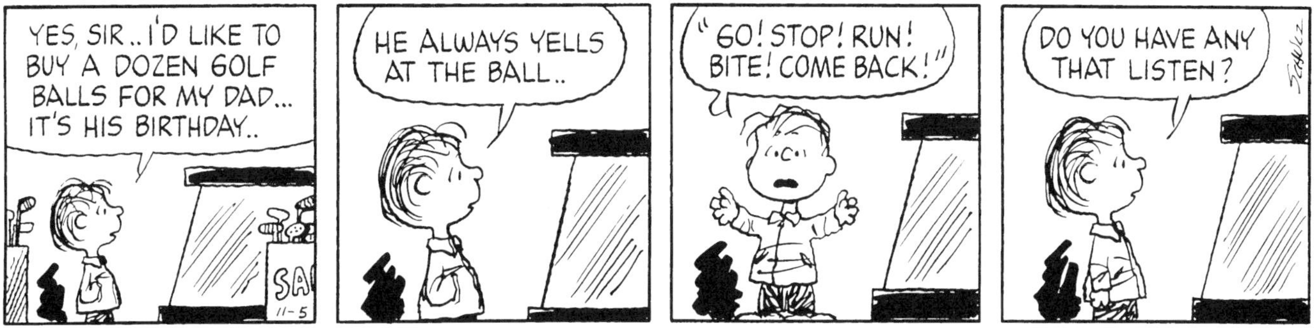
YES, SIR.. I'D LIKE TO BUY A DOZEN GOLF BALLS FOR MY DAD... IT'S HIS BIRTHDAY..
11-5
HE ALWAYS YELLS AT THE BALL..
"GO! STOP! RUN! BITE! COME BACK!"
DO YOU HAVE ANY THAT LISTEN?
SCHULZ

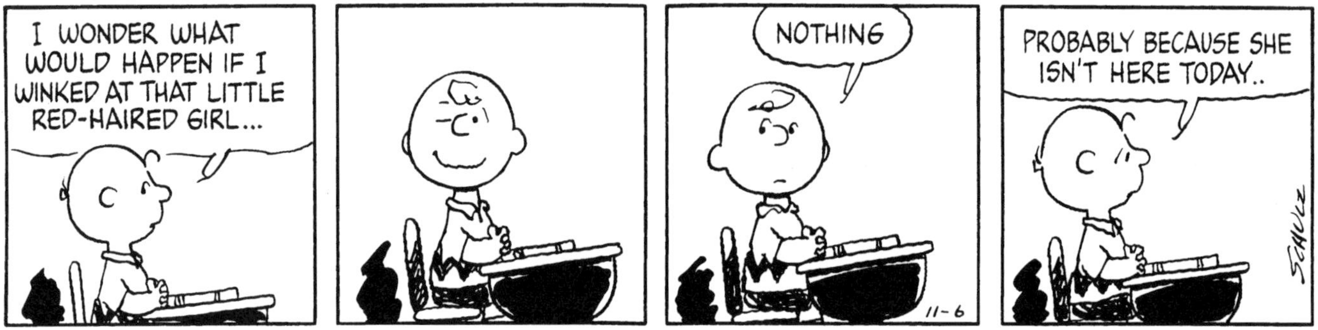
I WONDER WHAT WOULD HAPPEN IF I WINKED AT THAT LITTLE RED-HAIRED GIRL...
NOTHING
PROBABLY BECAUSE SHE ISN'T HERE TODAY..
11-6

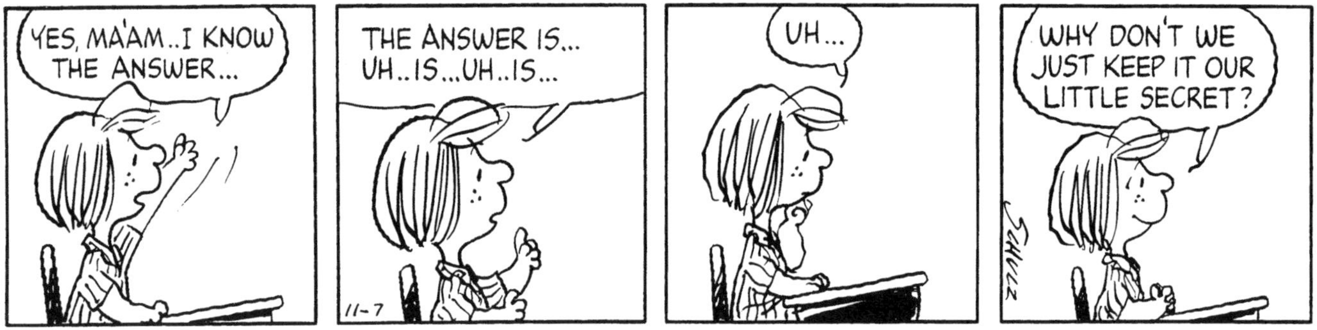
YES, MA'AM..I KNOW THE ANSWER...
THE ANSWER IS... UH..IS...UH..IS...
11-7
UH...
WHY DON'T WE JUST KEEP IT OUR LITTLE SECRET?

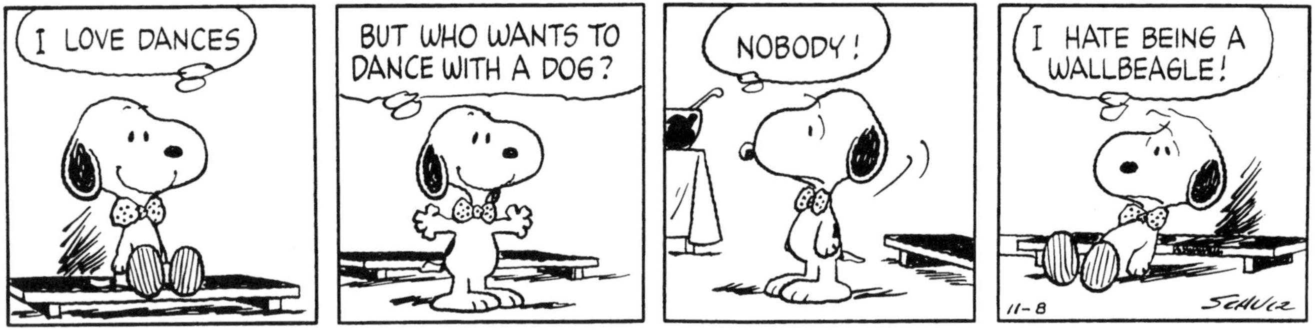
I LOVE DANCES
BUT WHO WANTS TO DANCE WITH A DOG?
NOBODY!
I HATE BEING A WALLBEAGLE!
11-8

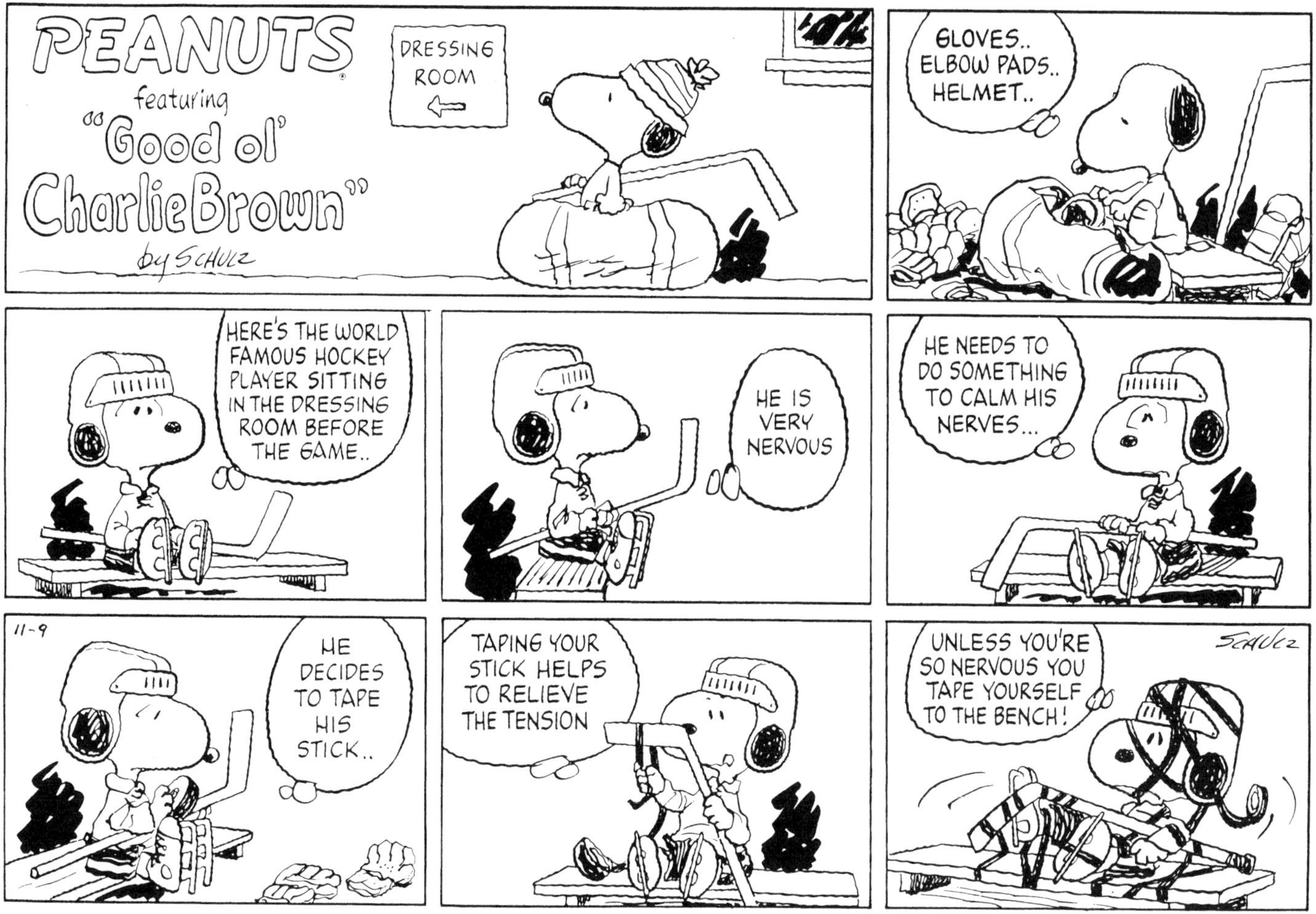
PEANUTS
featuring
"Good ol' Charlie Brown"
by SCHULZ
DRESSING ROOM
GLOVES.. ELBOW PADS.. HELMET..
HERE'S THE WORLD FAMOUS HOCKEY PLAYER SITTING IN THE DRESSING ROOM BEFORE THE GAME..
HE IS VERY NERVOUS
HE NEEDS TO DO SOMETHING TO CALM HIS NERVES...
11-9
HE DECIDES TO TAPE HIS STICK..
TAPING YOUR STICK HELPS TO RELIEVE THE TENSION
SCHULZ
UNLESS YOU'RE SO NERVOUS YOU TAPE YOURSELF TO THE BENCH!

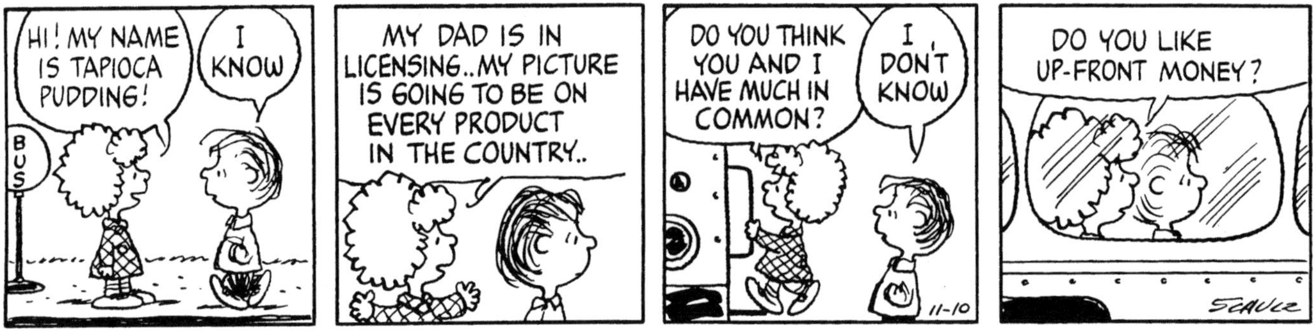
HI! MY NAME IS TAPIOCA PUDDING!
I KNOW
BUS
MY DAD IS IN LICENSING..MY PICTURE IS GOING TO BE ON EVERY PRODUCT IN THE COUNTRY..
DO YOU THINK YOU AND I HAVE MUCH IN COMMON?
I DON'T KNOW
11-10
DO YOU LIKE UP-FRONT MONEY?
SCHULZ

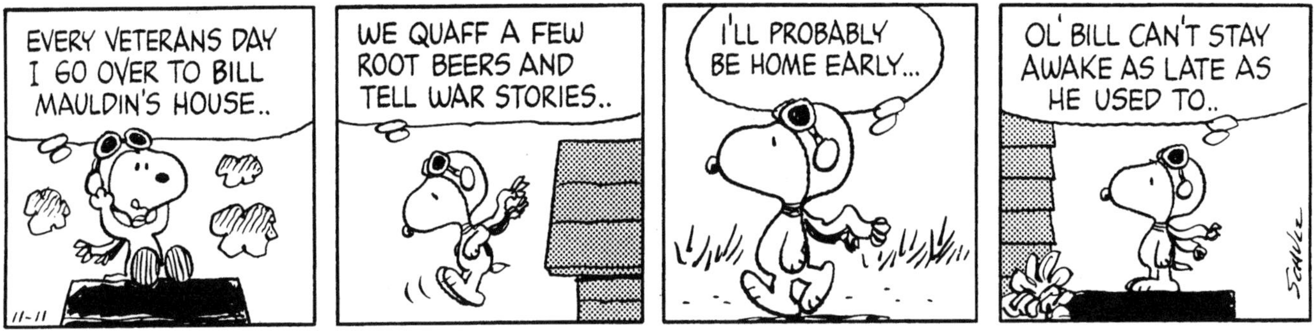
EVERY VETERANS DAY I GO OVER TO BILL MAULDIN'S HOUSE..
11-11
WE QUAFF A FEW ROOT BEERS AND TELL WAR STORIES..
I'LL PROBABLY BE HOME EARLY...
OL' BILL CAN'T STAY AWAKE AS LATE AS HE USED TO..
SCHULZ

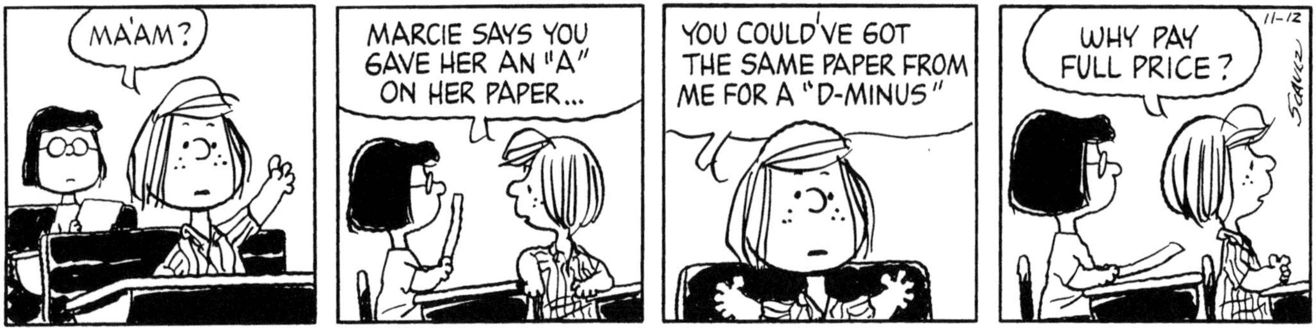
MA'AM?
MARCIE SAYS YOU GAVE HER AN "A" ON HER PAPER...
YOU COULD'VE GOT THE SAME PAPER FROM ME FOR A "D-MINUS"
11-12
WHY PAY FULL PRICE?
SCHULZ

SOME PEOPLE STAY IN THE SAME PLACE ALL THEIR LIVES

NOT ME.. WHEN I GROW UP, I'M GONNA MOVE ON!

YOU'RE NOT GONNA CATCH ME LIVING HERE FOR THE REST OF MY LIFE..

YOU DON'T LIKE IT HERE?

WHERE ARE WE?

PSYCHIATRIC HELP 5¢

THE DOCTOR IS IN

THINK ABOUT WHAT I'VE SAID, CHARLIE BROWN

IT'S REALLY ALL UP TO YOU..

THE DOCTOR IS IN

FIVE CENTS, PLEASE

THE DOCTOR IS IN

DO YOU TAKE BUBBLE GUM CARDS?

THE DOCTOR IS IN

EVERY NIGHT MY SUPPER COMES THROUGH THAT BACK DOOR..

SURPRISE!

TONIGHT I WENT OUT THE FRONT DOOR AND CAME AROUND THE SIDE OF THE HOUSE..

I'LL EAT FIRST, AND THEN I'LL CALL THE HUMANE SOCIETY!

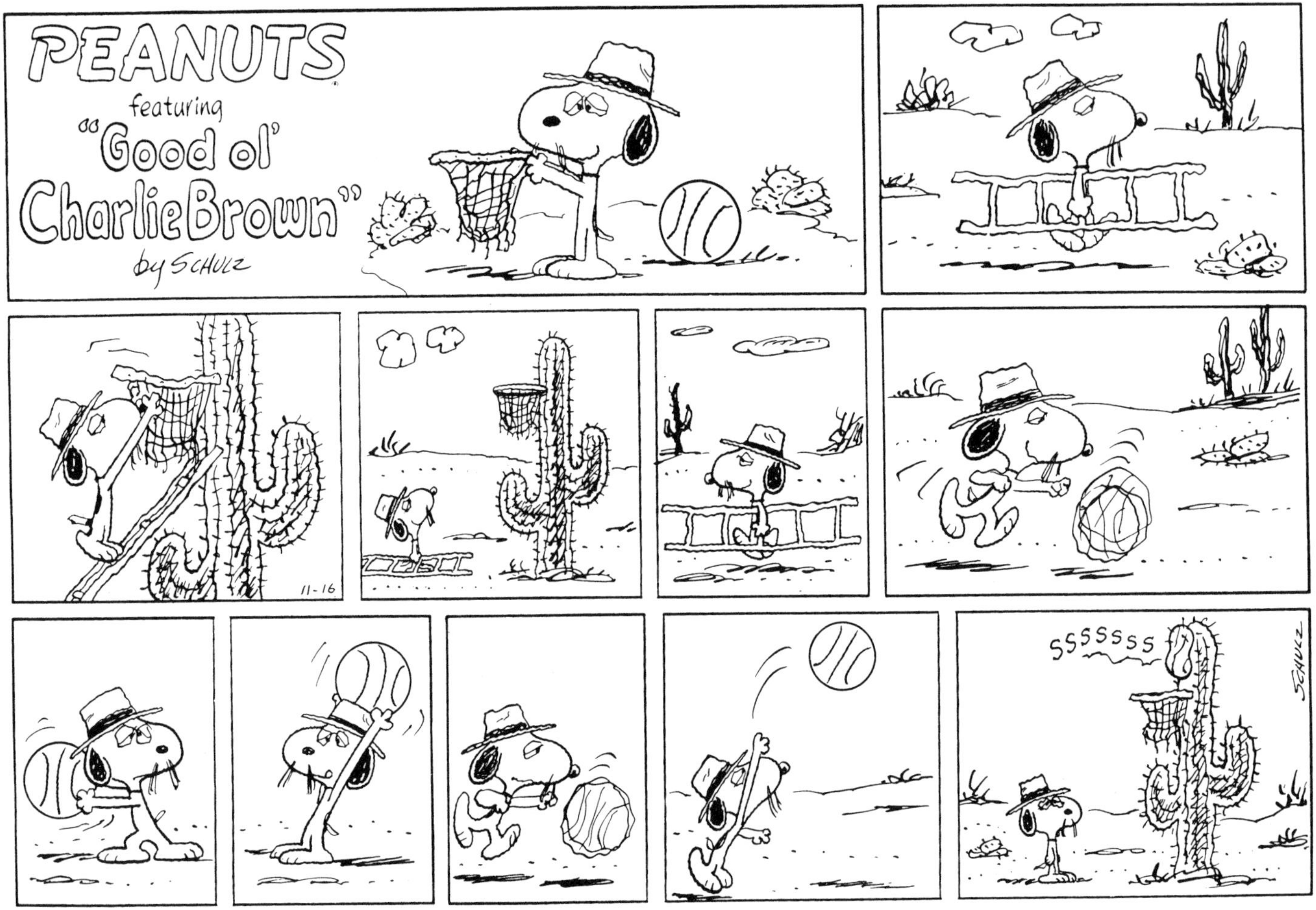
PEANUTS
featuring
"Good ol' Charlie Brown"
by SCHULZ
11-16
SSSSSSS
SCHULZ

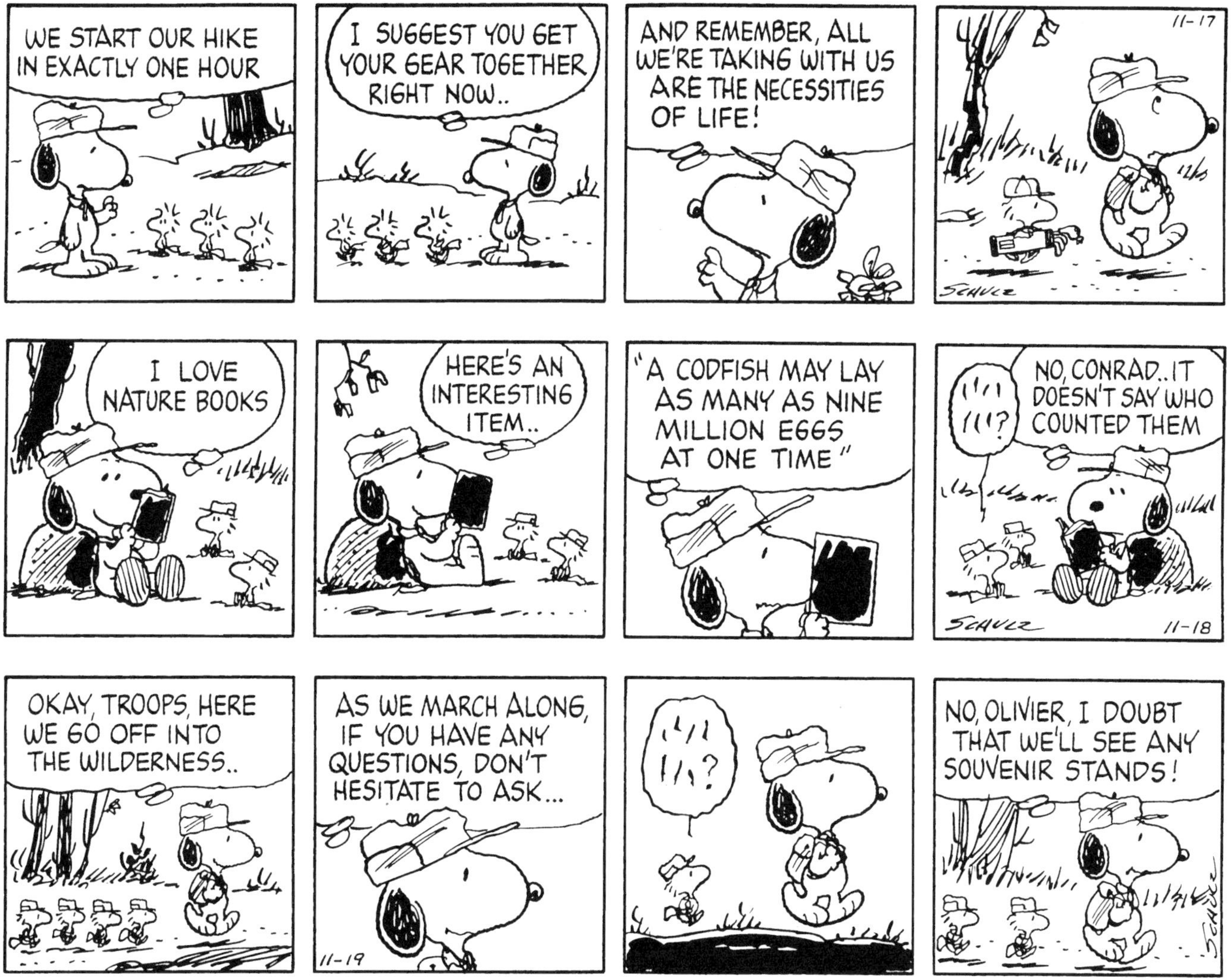
WE START OUR HIKE IN EXACTLY ONE HOUR
I SUGGEST YOU GET YOUR GEAR TOGETHER RIGHT NOW..
AND REMEMBER, ALL WE'RE TAKING WITH US ARE THE NECESSITIES OF LIFE!
11-17
SCHULZ
I LOVE NATURE BOOKS
HERE'S AN INTERESTING ITEM..
"A CODFISH MAY LAY AS MANY AS NINE MILLION EGGS AT ONE TIME"
?
NO, CONRAD..IT DOESN'T SAY WHO COUNTED THEM
SCHULZ
11-18
OKAY, TROOPS, HERE WE GO OFF INTO THE WILDERNESS..
AS WE MARCH ALONG, IF YOU HAVE ANY QUESTIONS, DON'T HESITATE TO ASK...
11-19
?
NO, OLIVIER, I DOUBT THAT WE'LL SEE ANY SOUVENIR STANDS!
SCHULZ

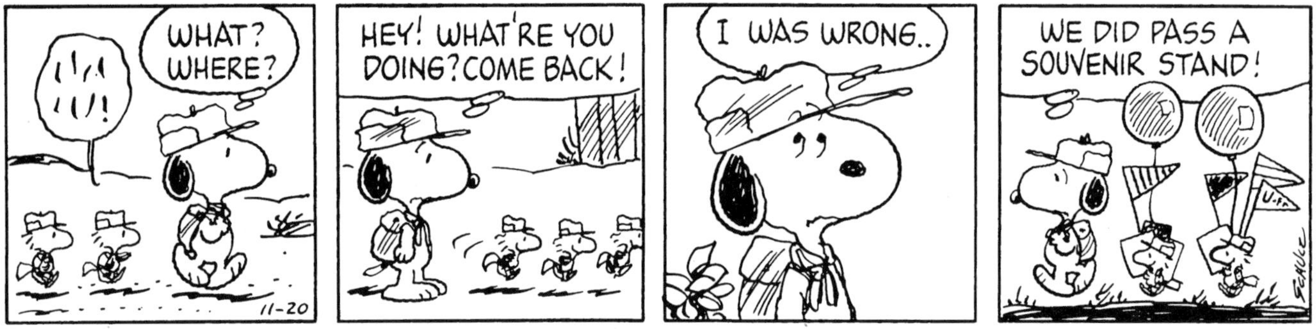
WHAT? WHERE?
HEY! WHAT'RE YOU DOING? COME BACK!
I WAS WRONG..
WE DID PASS A SOUVENIR STAND!

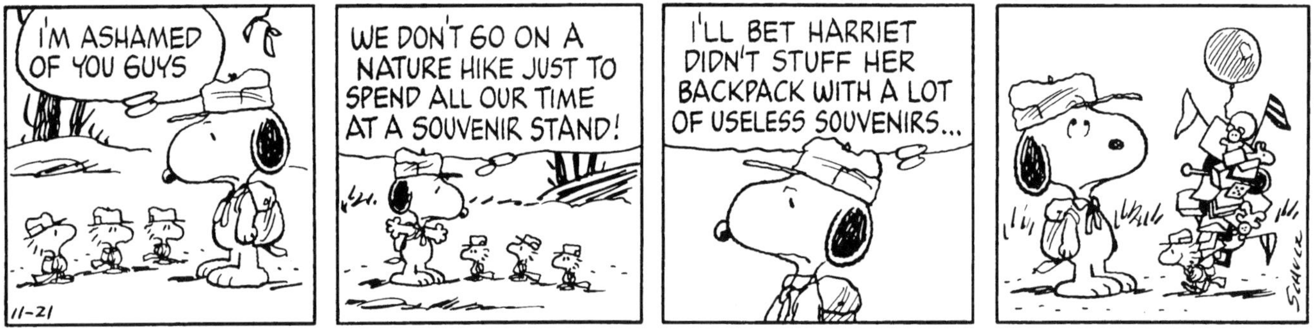
I'M ASHAMED OF YOU GUYS
WE DON'T GO ON A NATURE HIKE JUST TO SPEND ALL OUR TIME AT A SOUVENIR STAND!
I'LL BET HARRIET DIDN'T STUFF HER BACKPACK WITH A LOT OF USELESS SOUVENIRS...

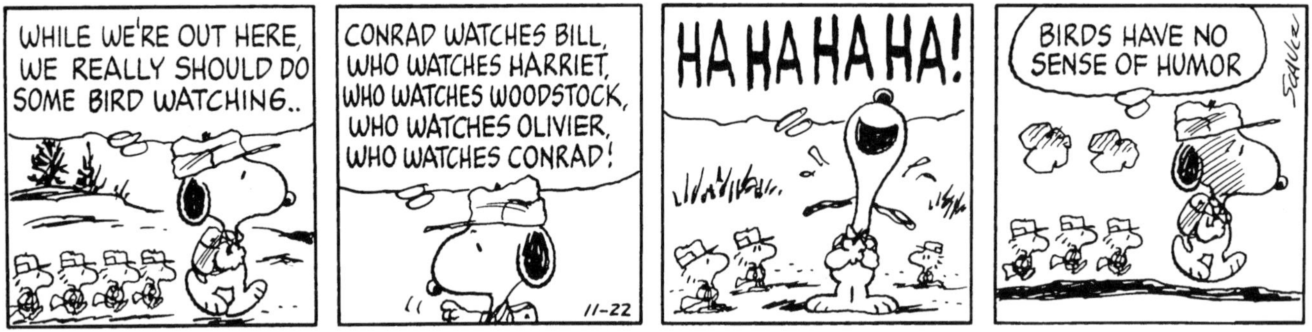
WHILE WE'RE OUT HERE, WE REALLY SHOULD DO SOME BIRD WATCHING..
CONRAD WATCHES BILL, WHO WATCHES HARRIET, WHO WATCHES WOODSTOCK, WHO WATCHES OLIVIER, WHO WATCHES CONRAD!
HA HA HA HA HA!
BIRDS HAVE NO SENSE OF HUMOR

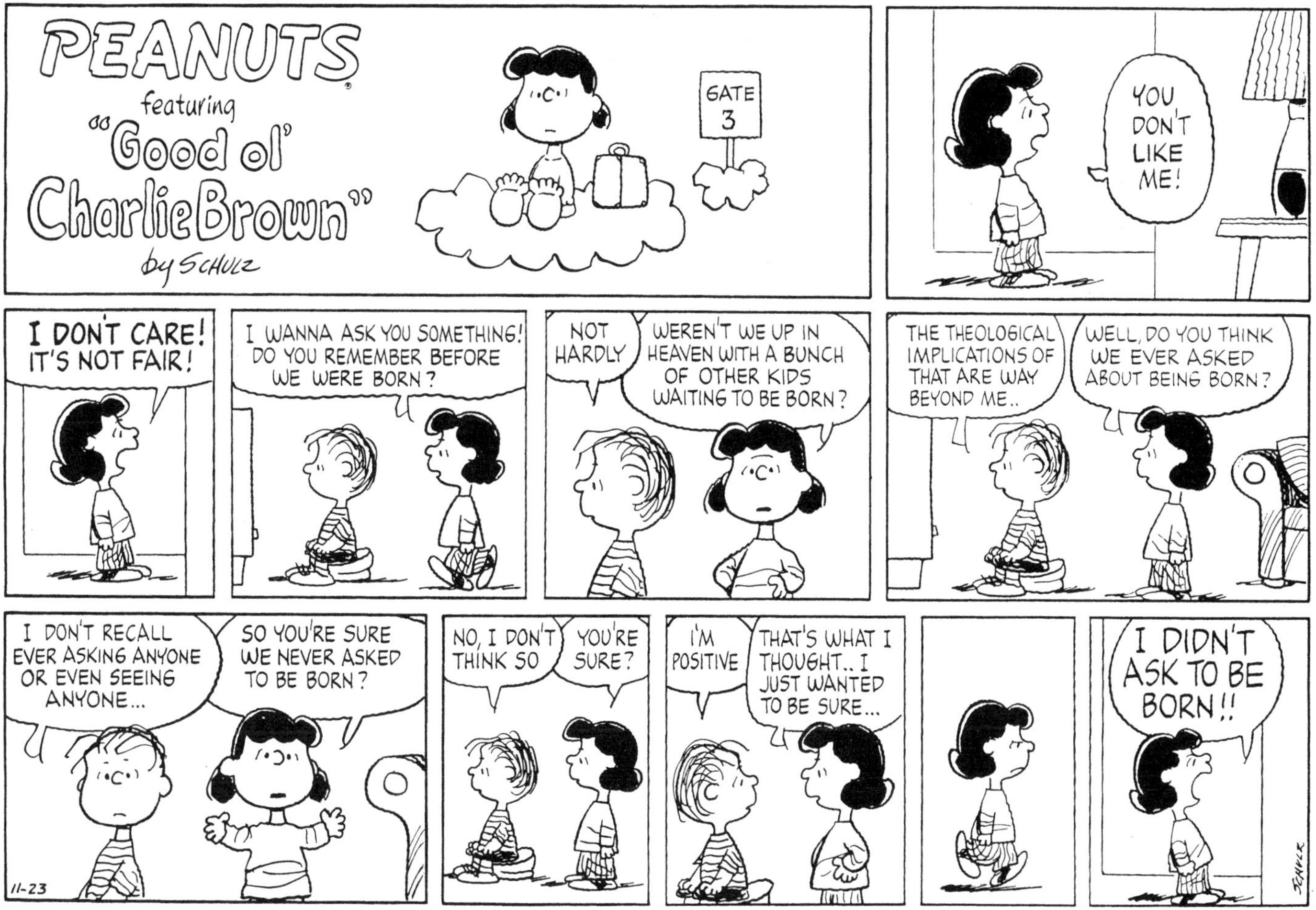
PEANUTS
featuring
"Good ol' Charlie Brown"
by SCHULZ
GATE 3
YOU DON'T LIKE ME!
I DON'T CARE! IT'S NOT FAIR!
I WANNA ASK YOU SOMETHING! DO YOU REMEMBER BEFORE WE WERE BORN?
NOT HARDLY
WEREN'T WE UP IN HEAVEN WITH A BUNCH OF OTHER KIDS WAITING TO BE BORN?
THE THEOLOGICAL IMPLICATIONS OF THAT ARE WAY BEYOND ME..
WELL, DO YOU THINK WE EVER ASKED ABOUT BEING BORN?
I DON'T RECALL EVER ASKING ANYONE OR EVEN SEEING ANYONE...
SO YOU'RE SURE WE NEVER ASKED TO BE BORN?
NO, I DON'T THINK SO
YOU'RE SURE?
I'M POSITIVE
THAT'S WHAT I THOUGHT.. I JUST WANTED TO BE SURE...
I DIDN'T ASK TO BE BORN!!
11-23
SCHULZ

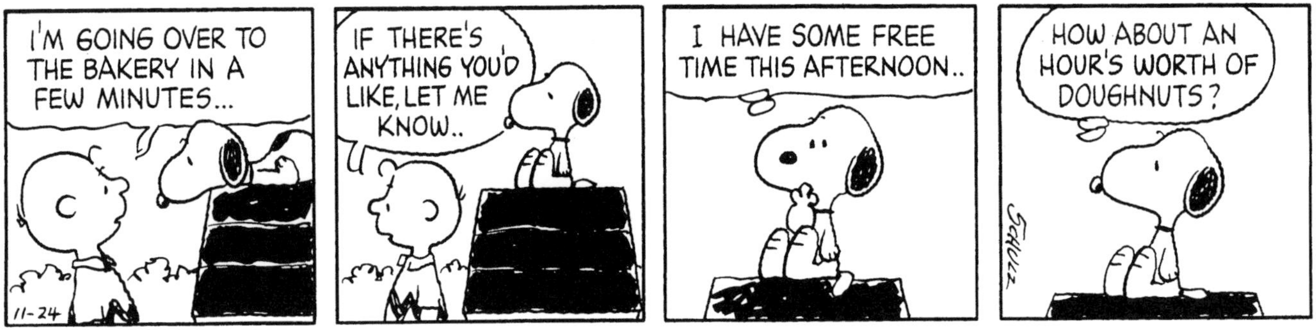
I'M GOING OVER TO THE BAKERY IN A FEW MINUTES...
11-24
IF THERE'S ANYTHING YOU'D LIKE, LET ME KNOW..
I HAVE SOME FREE TIME THIS AFTERNOON..
HOW ABOUT AN HOUR'S WORTH OF DOUGHNUTS?
SCHULZ

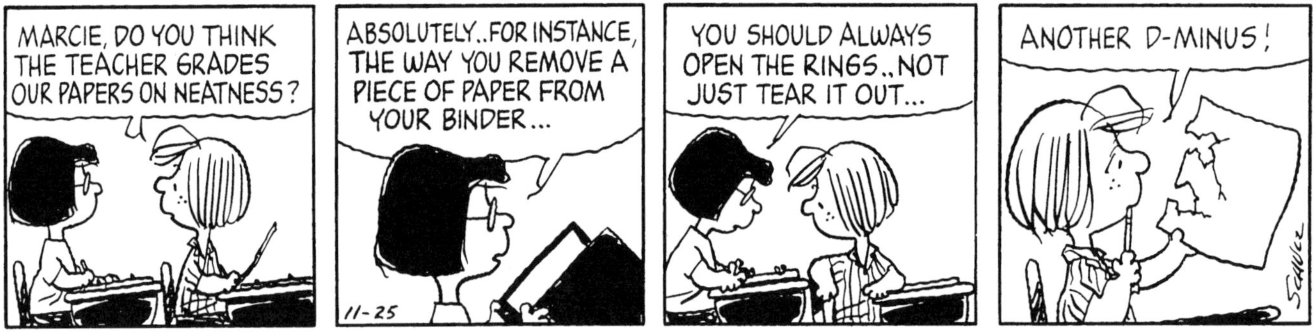
MARCIE, DO YOU THINK THE TEACHER GRADES OUR PAPERS ON NEATNESS?
ABSOLUTELY..FOR INSTANCE, THE WAY YOU REMOVE A PIECE OF PAPER FROM YOUR BINDER...
11-25
YOU SHOULD ALWAYS OPEN THE RINGS..NOT JUST TEAR IT OUT...
ANOTHER D-MINUS!
SCHULZ

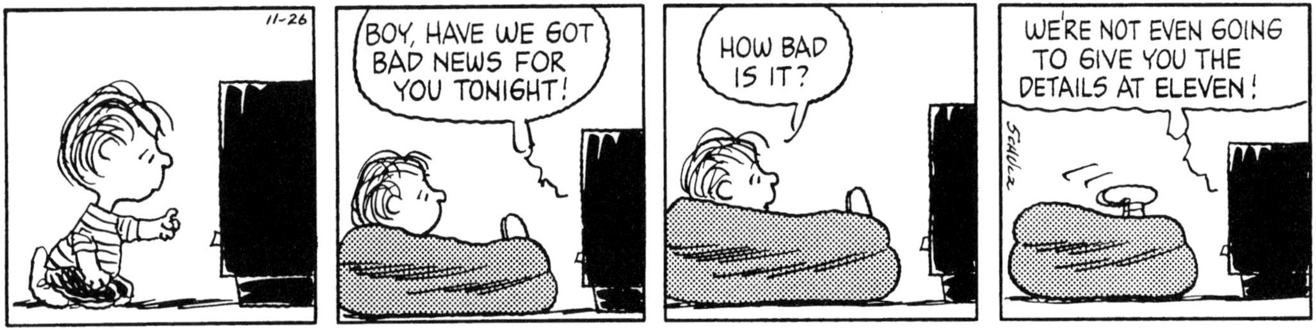
11-26
BOY, HAVE WE GOT BAD NEWS FOR YOU TONIGHT!
HOW BAD IS IT?
WE'RE NOT EVEN GOING TO GIVE YOU THE DETAILS AT ELEVEN!
SCHULZ

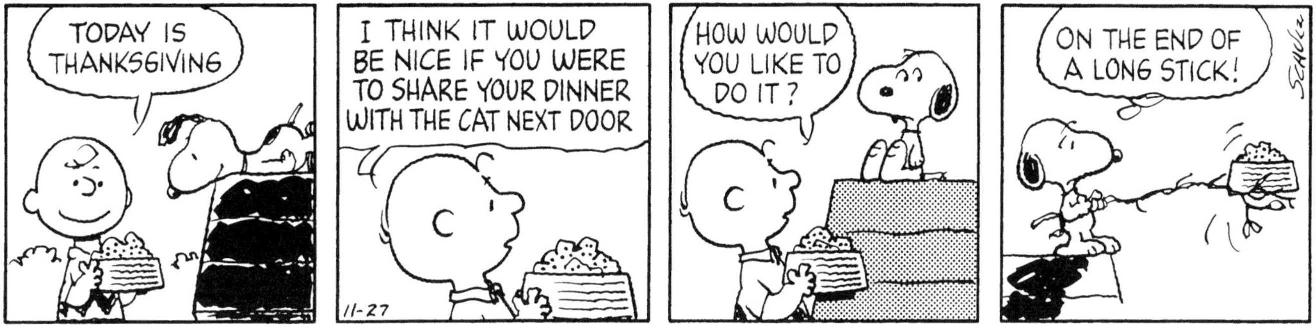
TODAY IS THANKSGIVING
I THINK IT WOULD BE NICE IF YOU WERE TO SHARE YOUR DINNER WITH THE CAT NEXT DOOR
11-27
HOW WOULD YOU LIKE TO DO IT?
ON THE END OF A LONG STICK!

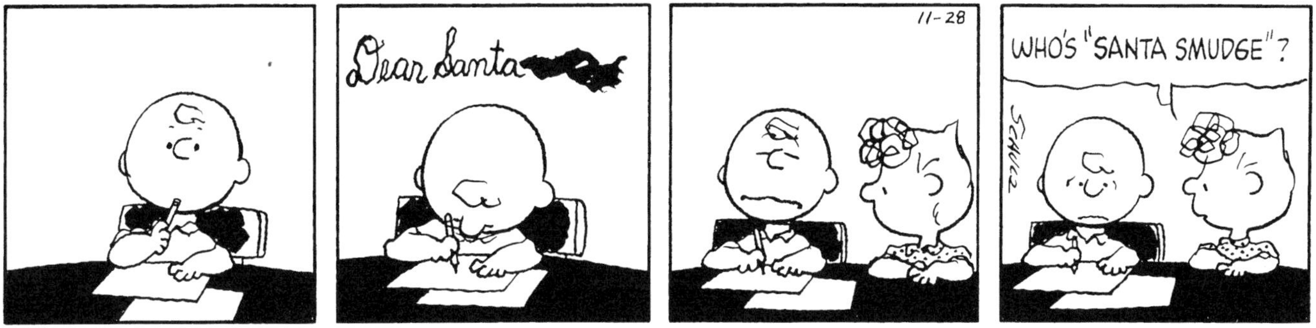
Dear Santa
11-28
WHO'S "SANTA SMUDGE"?

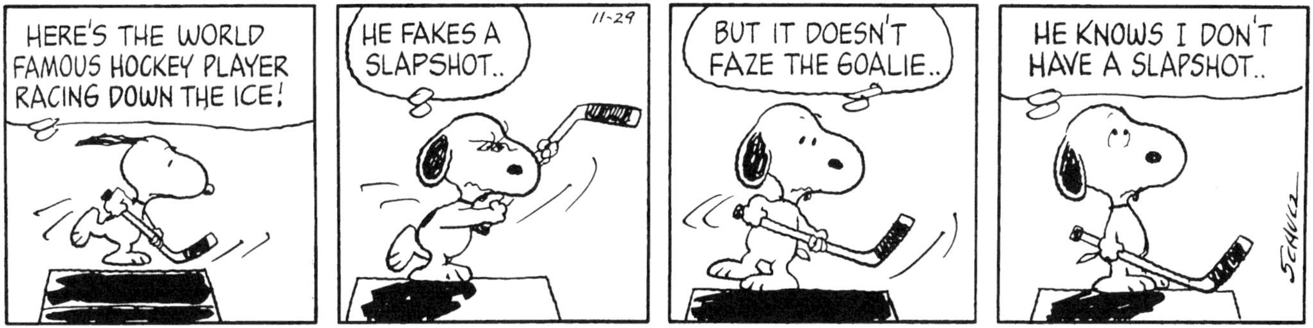
HERE'S THE WORLD FAMOUS HOCKEY PLAYER RACING DOWN THE ICE!
HE FAKES A SLAPSHOT..
11-29
BUT IT DOESN'T FAZE THE GOALIE..
HE KNOWS I DON'T HAVE A SLAPSHOT..

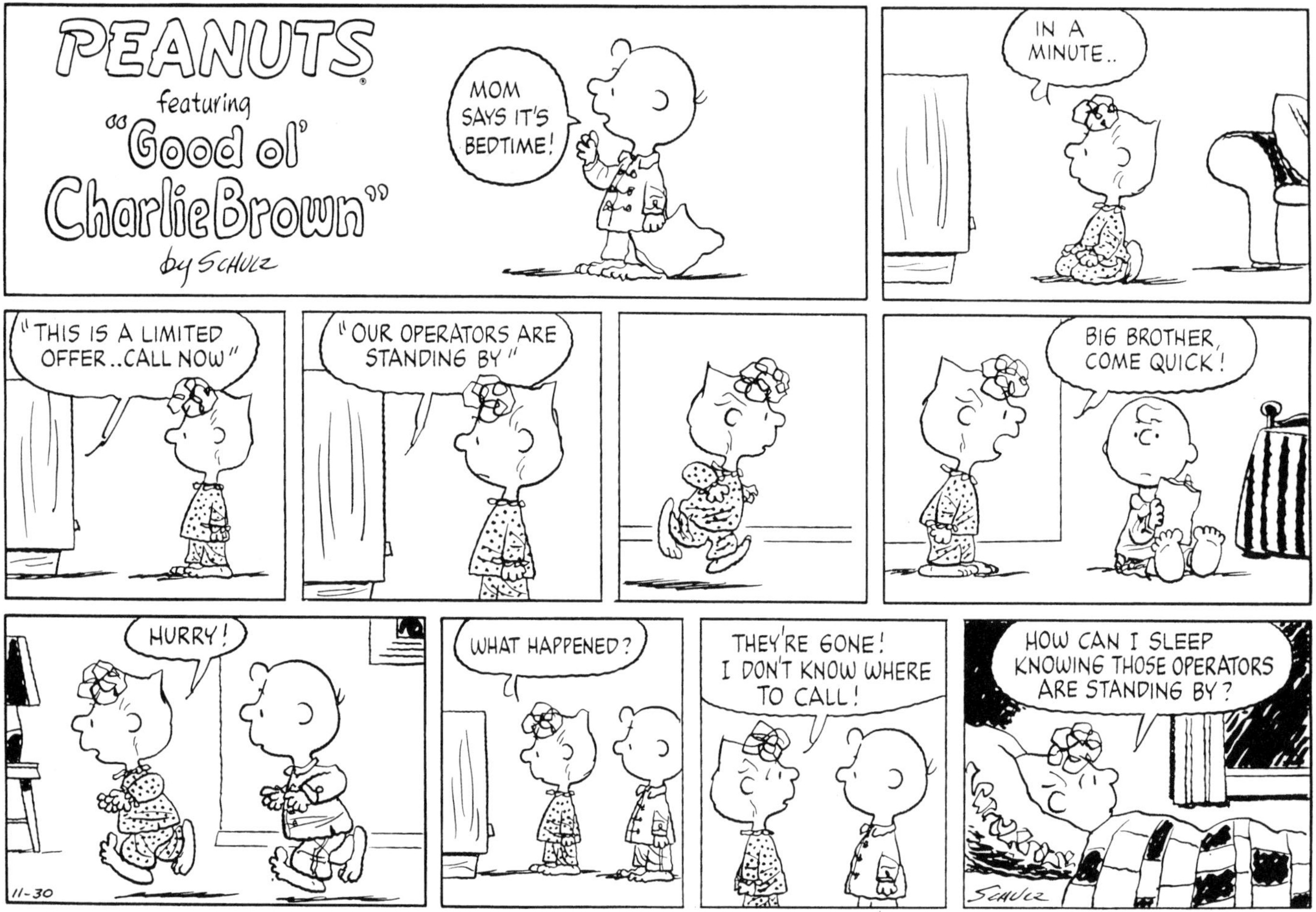
PEANUTS®
featuring "Good ol' CharlieBrown"
by SCHULZ
MOM SAYS IT'S BEDTIME!
IN A MINUTE..
"THIS IS A LIMITED OFFER..CALL NOW"
"OUR OPERATORS ARE STANDING BY"
BIG BROTHER, COME QUICK!
HURRY!
11-30
WHAT HAPPENED?
THEY'RE GONE! I DON'T KNOW WHERE TO CALL!
HOW CAN I SLEEP KNOWING THOSE OPERATORS ARE STANDING BY?
SCHULZ

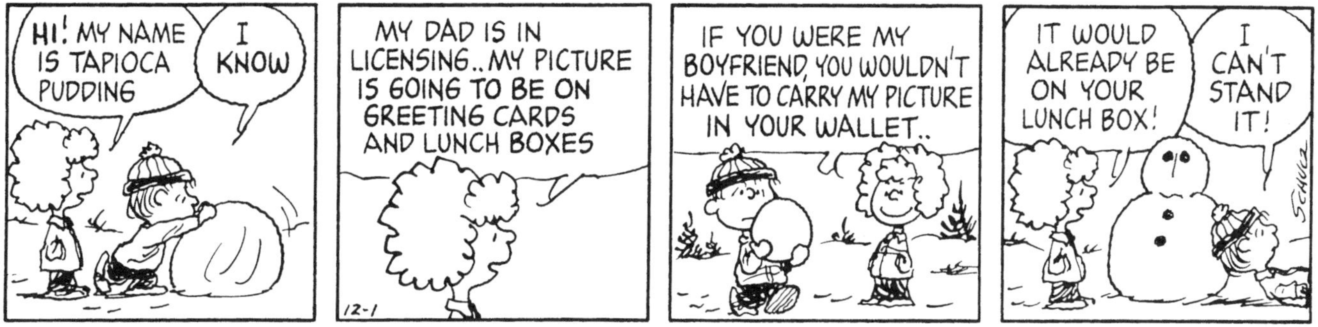
HI! MY NAME IS TAPIOCA PUDDING
I KNOW
MY DAD IS IN LICENSING.. MY PICTURE IS GOING TO BE ON GREETING CARDS AND LUNCH BOXES
12-1
IF YOU WERE MY BOYFRIEND, YOU WOULDN'T HAVE TO CARRY MY PICTURE IN YOUR WALLET..
IT WOULD ALREADY BE ON YOUR LUNCH BOX!
I CAN'T STAND IT!
SCHULZ

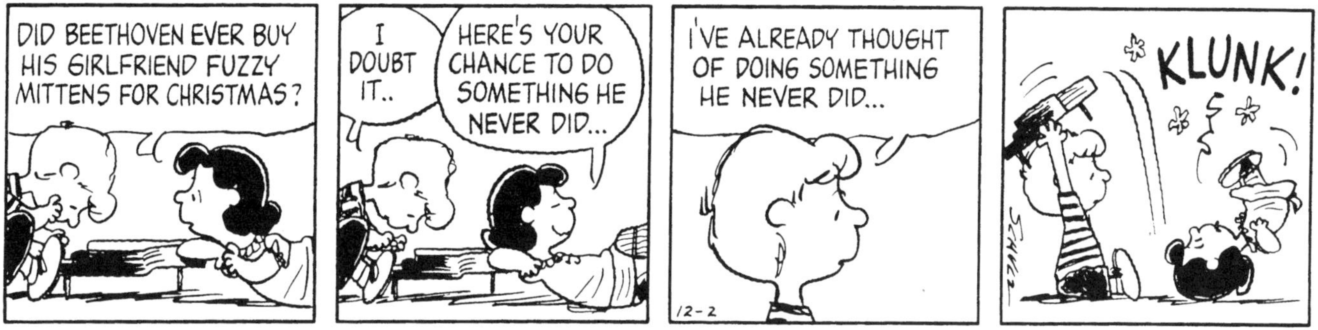
DID BEETHOVEN EVER BUY HIS GIRLFRIEND FUZZY MITTENS FOR CHRISTMAS?
I DOUBT IT..
HERE'S YOUR CHANCE TO DO SOMETHING HE NEVER DID...
I'VE ALREADY THOUGHT OF DOING SOMETHING HE NEVER DID...
12-2
KLUNK!
SCHULZ

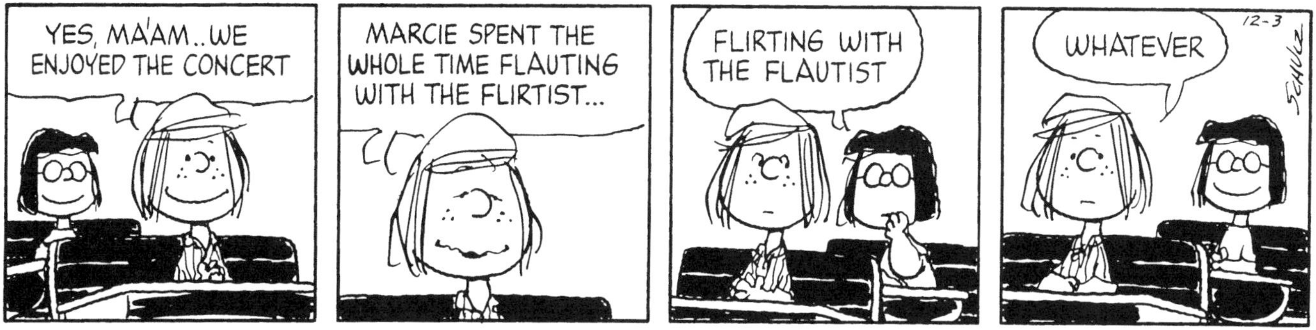
YES, MA'AM..WE ENJOYED THE CONCERT
MARCIE SPENT THE WHOLE TIME FLAUTING WITH THE FLIRTIST...
FLIRTING WITH THE FLAUTIST
WHATEVER
12-3
SCHULZ

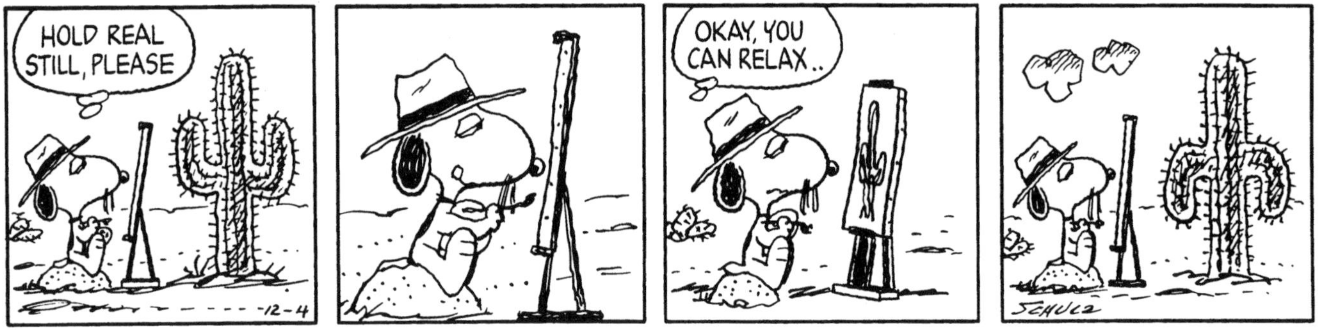
HOLD REAL STILL, PLEASE
OKAY, YOU CAN RELAX..

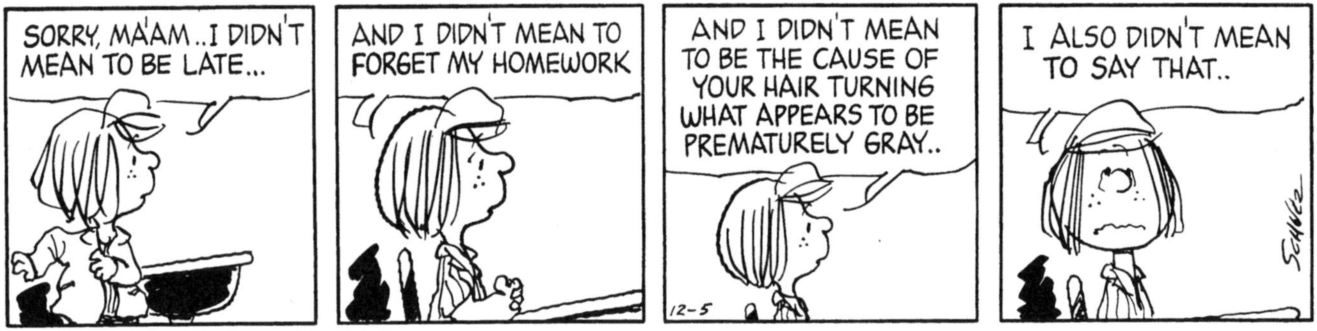
SORRY, MA'AM..I DIDN'T MEAN TO BE LATE...
AND I DIDN'T MEAN TO FORGET MY HOMEWORK
AND I DIDN'T MEAN TO BE THE CAUSE OF YOUR HAIR TURNING WHAT APPEARS TO BE PREMATURELY GRAY..
I ALSO DIDN'T MEAN TO SAY THAT..

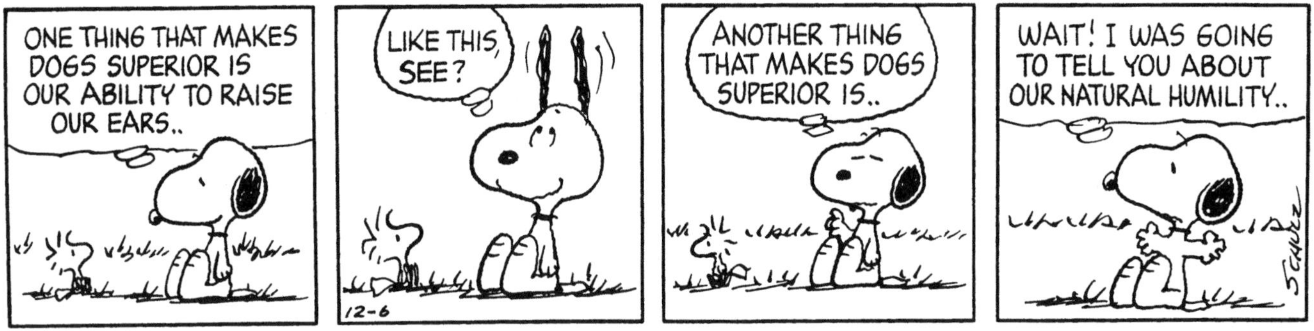
ONE THING THAT MAKES DOGS SUPERIOR IS OUR ABILITY TO RAISE OUR EARS..
LIKE THIS, SEE?
ANOTHER THING THAT MAKES DOGS SUPERIOR IS..
WAIT! I WAS GOING TO TELL YOU ABOUT OUR NATURAL HUMILITY..

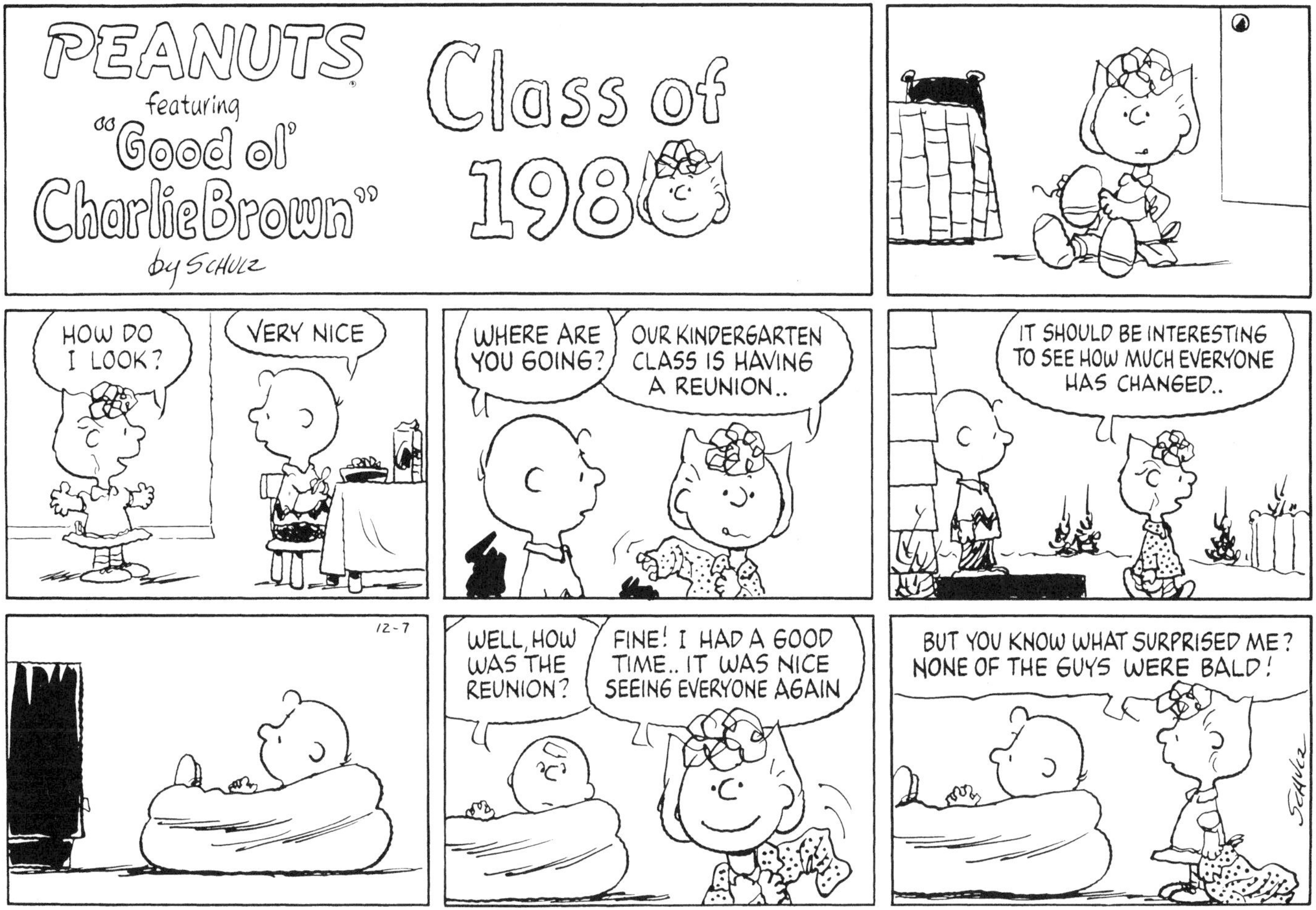
PEANUTS
featuring
"Good ol' Charlie Brown"
by SCHULZ
Class of 198
HOW DO I LOOK?
VERY NICE
WHERE ARE YOU GOING?
OUR KINDERGARTEN CLASS IS HAVING A REUNION..
IT SHOULD BE INTERESTING TO SEE HOW MUCH EVERYONE HAS CHANGED..
12-7
WELL, HOW WAS THE REUNION?
FINE! I HAD A GOOD TIME.. IT WAS NICE SEEING EVERYONE AGAIN
BUT YOU KNOW WHAT SURPRISED ME? NONE OF THE GUYS WERE BALD!
SCHULZ

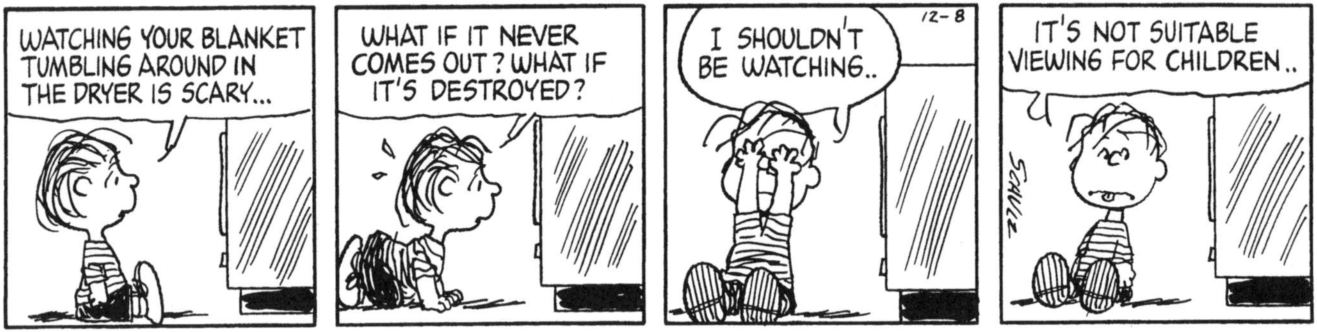
WATCHING YOUR BLANKET TUMBLING AROUND IN THE DRYER IS SCARY...
WHAT IF IT NEVER COMES OUT? WHAT IF IT'S DESTROYED?
12-8
I SHOULDN'T BE WATCHING..
IT'S NOT SUITABLE VIEWING FOR CHILDREN..
SCHULZ

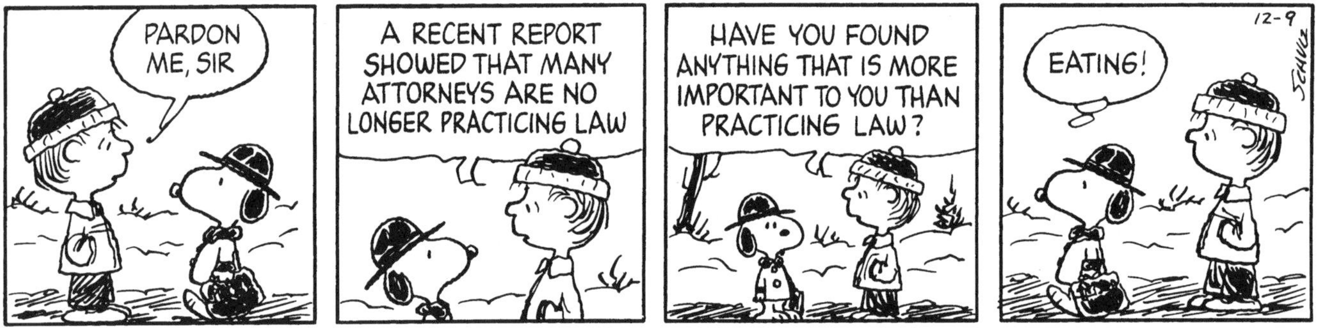
PARDON ME, SIR
A RECENT REPORT SHOWED THAT MANY ATTORNEYS ARE NO LONGER PRACTICING LAW
HAVE YOU FOUND ANYTHING THAT IS MORE IMPORTANT TO YOU THAN PRACTICING LAW?
12-9
EATING!
SCHULZ

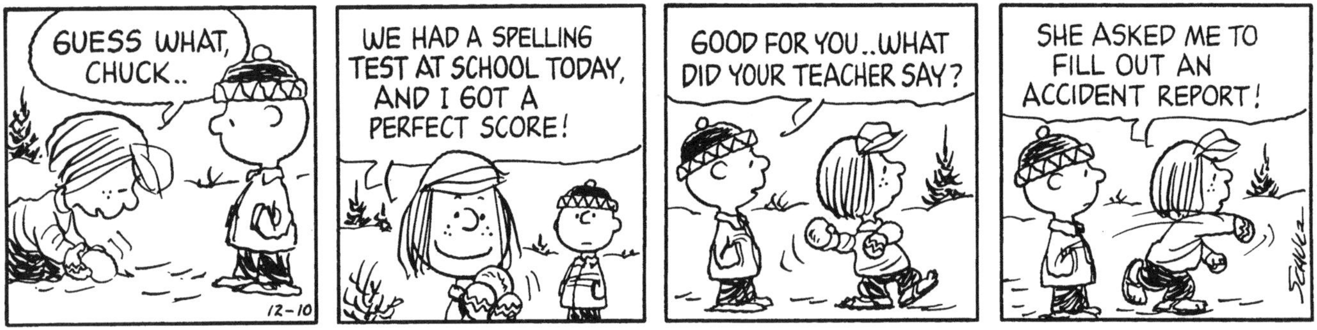
GUESS WHAT, CHUCK..
12-10
WE HAD A SPELLING TEST AT SCHOOL TODAY, AND I GOT A PERFECT SCORE!
GOOD FOR YOU..WHAT DID YOUR TEACHER SAY?
SHE ASKED ME TO FILL OUT AN ACCIDENT REPORT!
SCHULZ

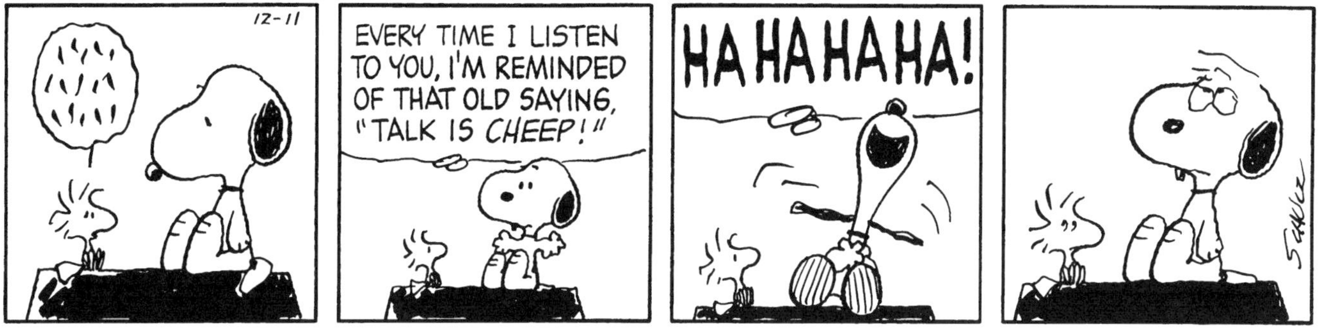
12-11
EVERY TIME I LISTEN TO YOU, I'M REMINDED OF THAT OLD SAYING, "TALK IS CHEEP!"
HAHAHAHA!

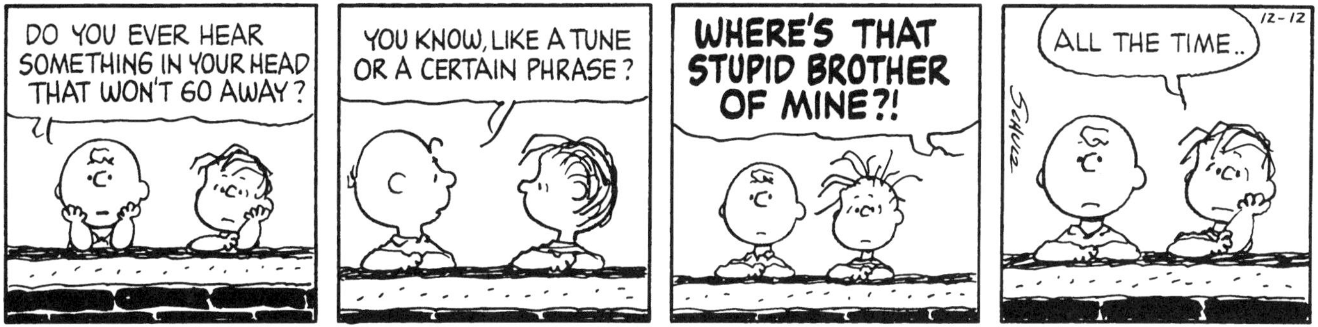
DO YOU EVER HEAR SOMETHING IN YOUR HEAD THAT WON'T GO AWAY?
YOU KNOW, LIKE A TUNE OR A CERTAIN PHRASE?
WHERE'S THAT STUPID BROTHER OF MINE?!
ALL THE TIME..
12-12

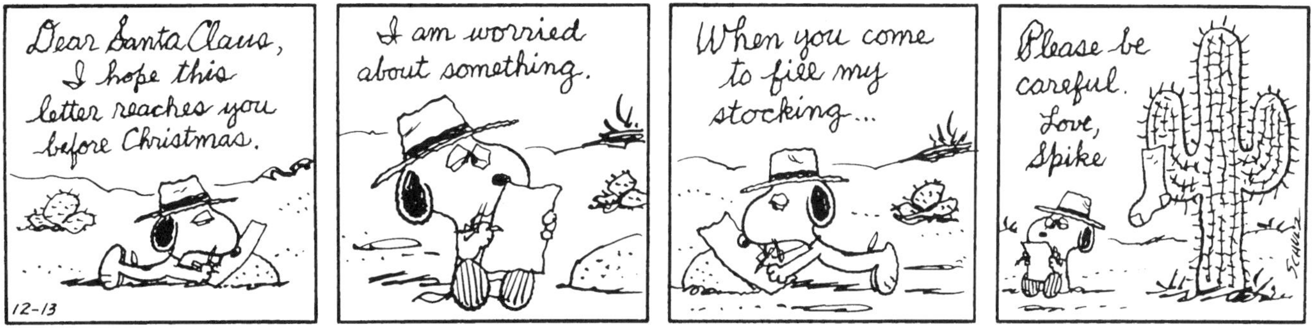
Dear Santa Claus, I hope this letter reaches you before Christmas.
12-13
I am worried about something.
When you come to fill my stocking...
Please be careful.
Love, Spike

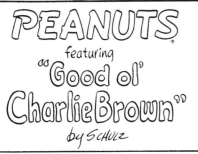

PEANUTS featuring "Good ol' Charlie Brown" *by Schulz*

I HEAR FOOTSTEPS

HEY, SNOOPY, LET'S GO FOR A WALK!

THIS IS THE WAY IT WAS MEANT TO BE

A BOY AND HIS DOG HIKING LIKE PERFECT COMRADES THROUGH THE WOODS

IF YOU SEE A SQUIRREL, OR A DEER, OR A PHEASANT OR A RABBIT, PLEASE FEEL FREE TO BARK AND HOWL AND PURSUE THEM MADLY OVER THE HILLS, THROUGH THE STREAMS AND ACROSS THE FIELDS!

12-14

I HATE IT WHEN HE LOOKS AT ME LIKE THAT..

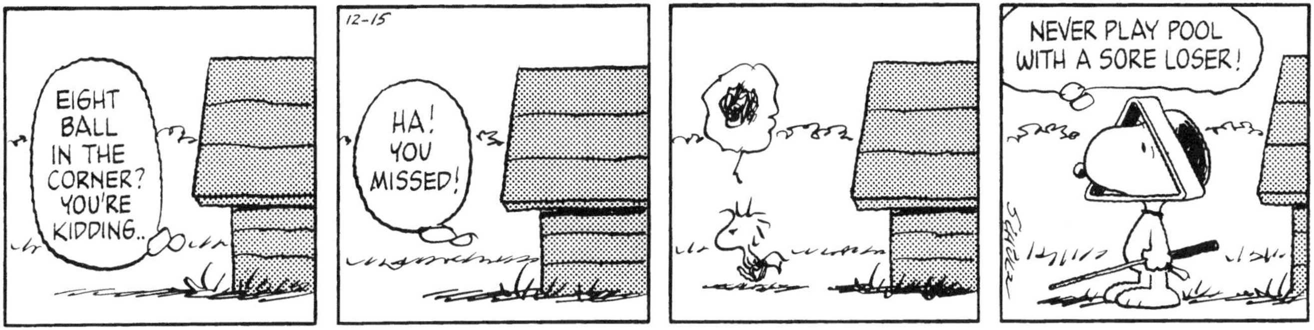
EIGHT BALL IN THE CORNER? YOU'RE KIDDING..
12-15
HA! YOU MISSED!
NEVER PLAY POOL WITH A SORE LOSER!
SCHULZ

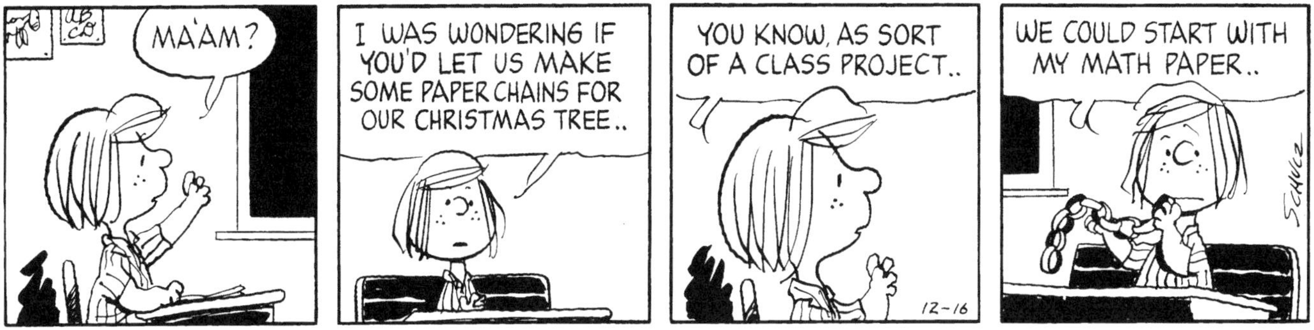
MA'AM?
I WAS WONDERING IF YOU'D LET US MAKE SOME PAPER CHAINS FOR OUR CHRISTMAS TREE..
YOU KNOW, AS SORT OF A CLASS PROJECT..
12-16
WE COULD START WITH MY MATH PAPER..
SCHULZ

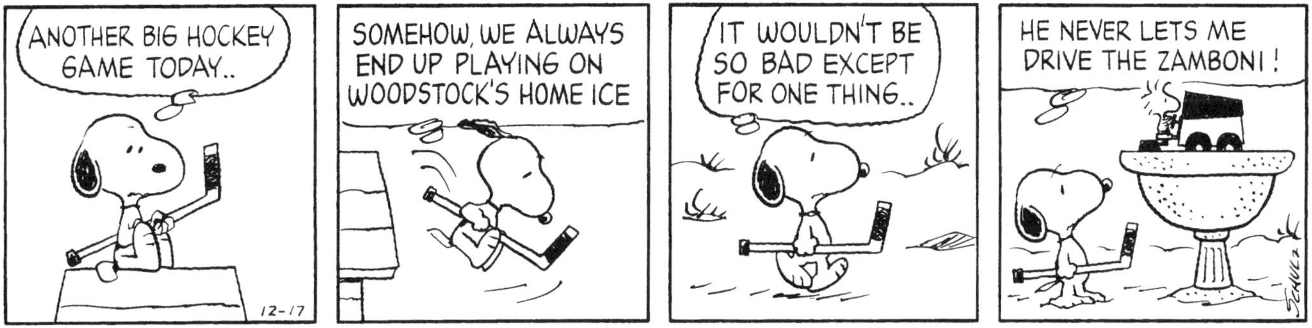
ANOTHER BIG HOCKEY GAME TODAY..
12-17
SOMEHOW, WE ALWAYS END UP PLAYING ON WOODSTOCK'S HOME ICE
IT WOULDN'T BE SO BAD EXCEPT FOR ONE THING..
HE NEVER LETS ME DRIVE THE ZAMBONI!
SCHULZ

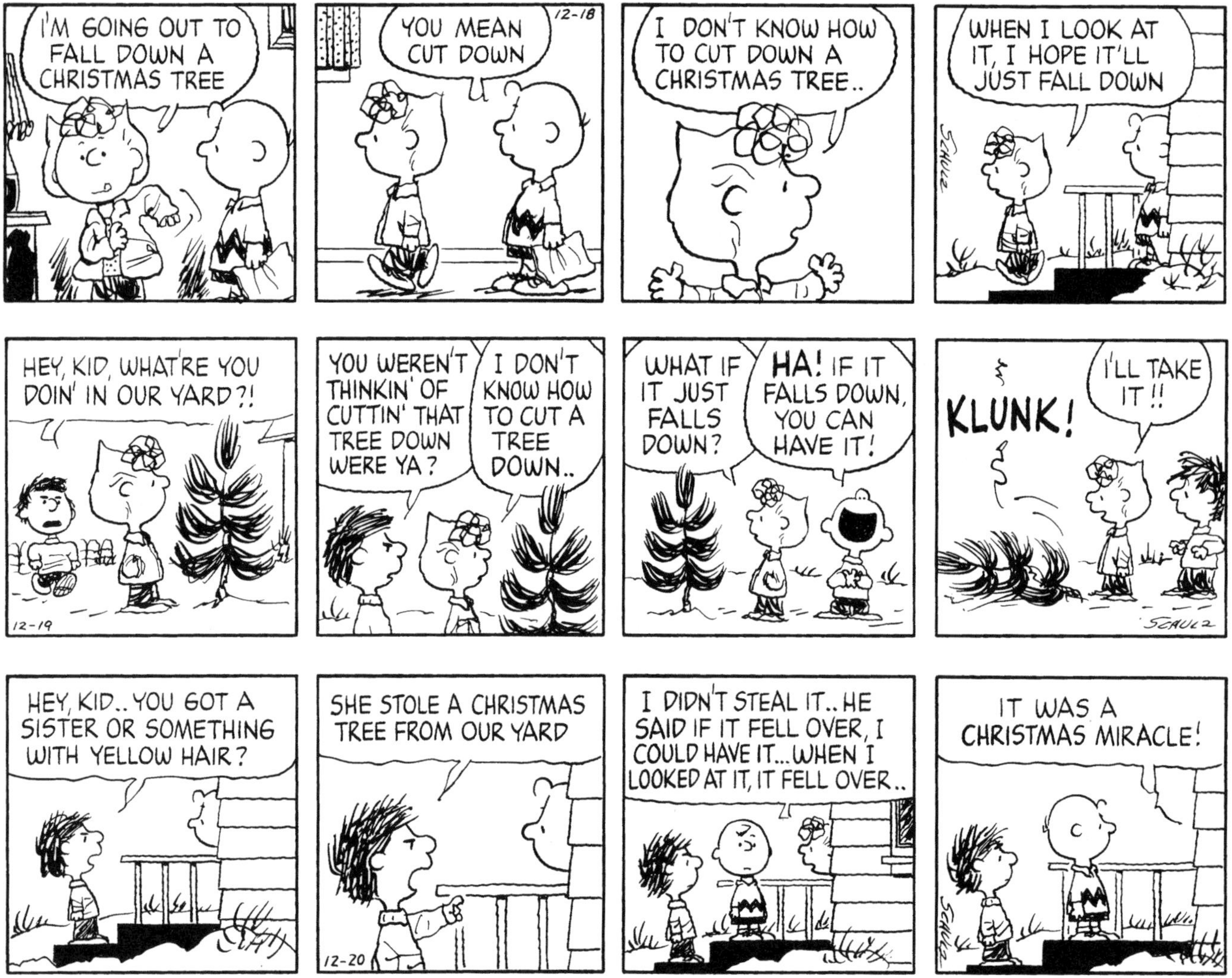
I'M GOING OUT TO FALL DOWN A CHRISTMAS TREE
12-18
YOU MEAN CUT DOWN
I DON'T KNOW HOW TO CUT DOWN A CHRISTMAS TREE..
WHEN I LOOK AT IT, I HOPE IT'LL JUST FALL DOWN
SCHULZ
HEY, KID, WHAT'RE YOU DOIN' IN OUR YARD?!
12-19
YOU WEREN'T THINKIN' OF CUTTIN' THAT TREE DOWN WERE YA?
I DON'T KNOW HOW TO CUT A TREE DOWN..
WHAT IF IT JUST FALLS DOWN?
HA! IF IT FALLS DOWN, YOU CAN HAVE IT!
KLUNK!
I'LL TAKE IT!!
SCHULZ
HEY, KID.. YOU GOT A SISTER OR SOMETHING WITH YELLOW HAIR?
SHE STOLE A CHRISTMAS TREE FROM OUR YARD
12-20
I DIDN'T STEAL IT.. HE SAID IF IT FELL OVER, I COULD HAVE IT... WHEN I LOOKED AT IT, IT FELL OVER..
IT WAS A CHRISTMAS MIRACLE!
SCHULZ

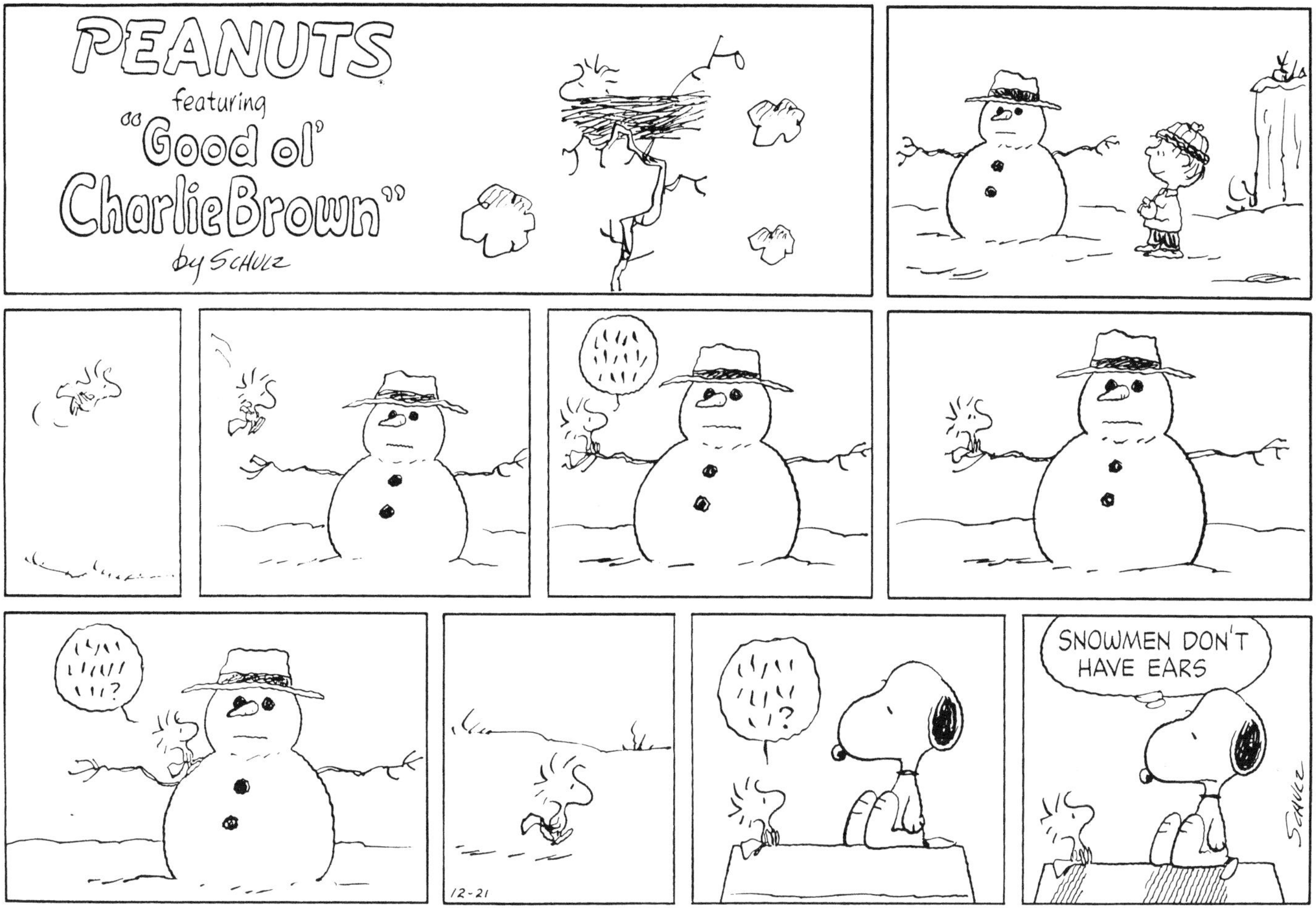
PEANUTS
featuring
"Good ol' Charlie Brown"
by SCHULZ
SNOWMEN DON'T HAVE EARS
12-21
SCHULZ

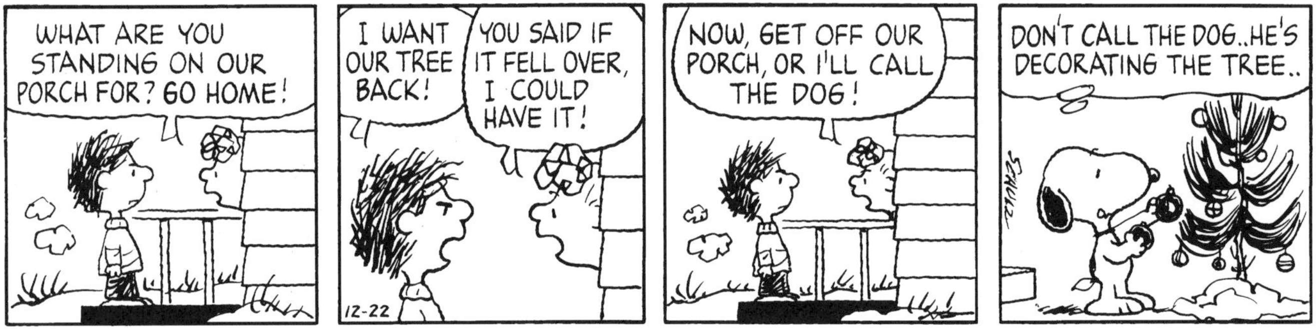
WHAT ARE YOU STANDING ON OUR PORCH FOR? GO HOME!
I WANT OUR TREE BACK!
YOU SAID IF IT FELL OVER, I COULD HAVE IT!
12-22
NOW, GET OFF OUR PORCH, OR I'LL CALL THE DOG!
DON'T CALL THE DOG..HE'S DECORATING THE TREE..

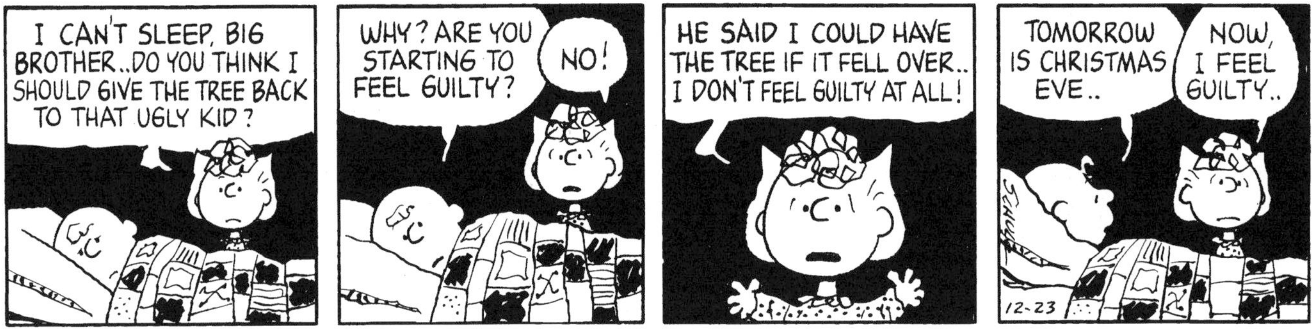
I CAN'T SLEEP, BIG BROTHER..DO YOU THINK I SHOULD GIVE THE TREE BACK TO THAT UGLY KID?
WHY? ARE YOU STARTING TO FEEL GUILTY?
NO!
HE SAID I COULD HAVE THE TREE IF IT FELL OVER.. I DON'T FEEL GUILTY AT ALL!
TOMORROW IS CHRISTMAS EVE..
NOW, I FEEL GUILTY..
12-23

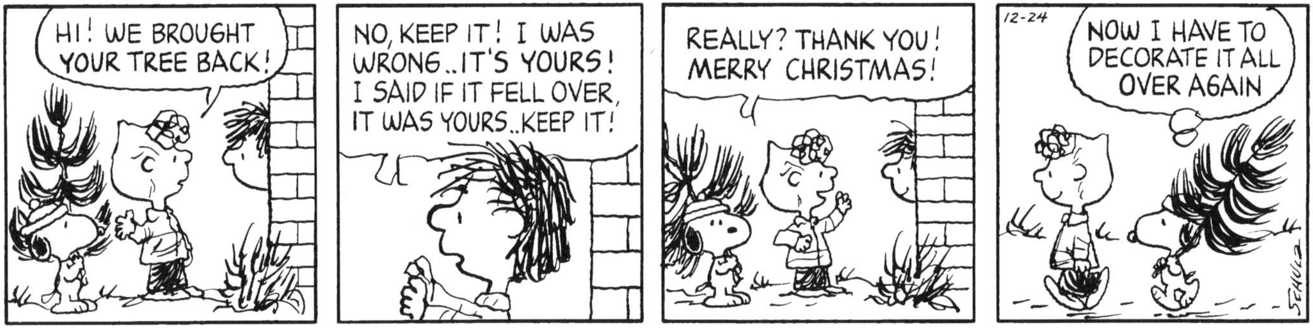
HI! WE BROUGHT YOUR TREE BACK!
NO, KEEP IT! I WAS WRONG..IT'S YOURS! I SAID IF IT FELL OVER, IT WAS YOURS..KEEP IT!
REALLY? THANK YOU! MERRY CHRISTMAS!
12-24
NOW I HAVE TO DECORATE IT ALL OVER AGAIN

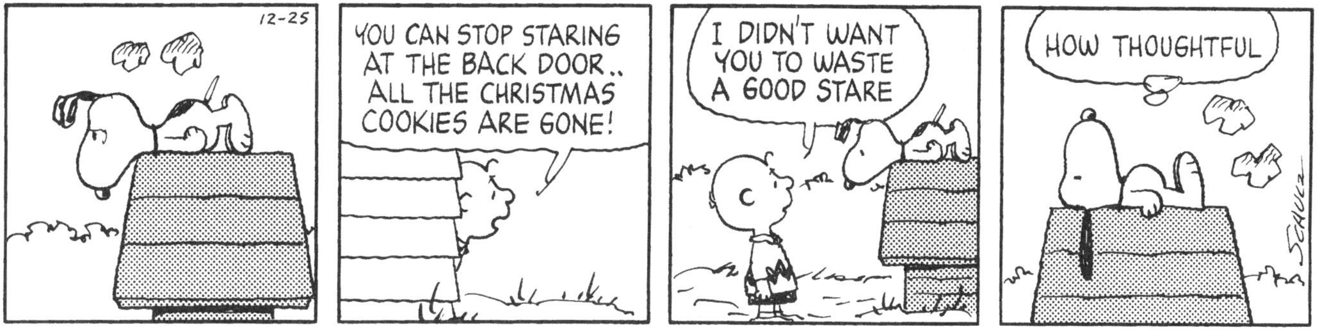
12-25
YOU CAN STOP STARING AT THE BACK DOOR.. ALL THE CHRISTMAS COOKIES ARE GONE!
I DIDN'T WANT YOU TO WASTE A GOOD STARE
HOW THOUGHTFUL
SCHULZ

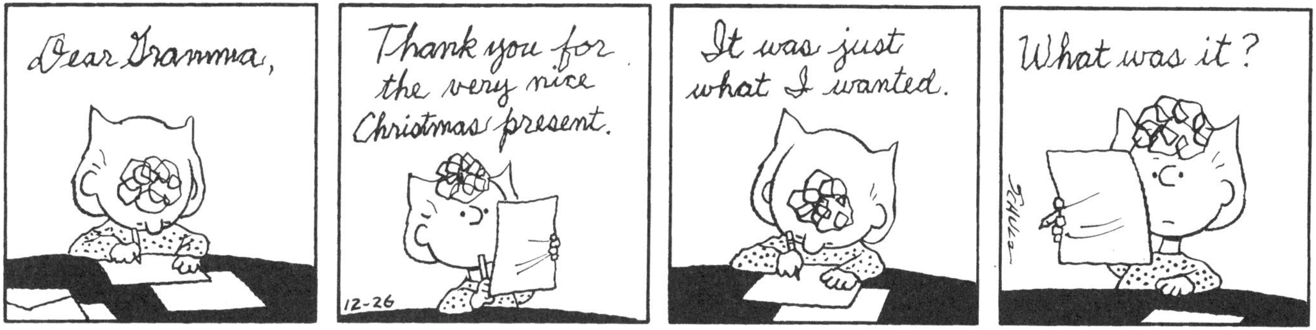
Dear Gramma,
Thank you for the very nice Christmas present.
12-26
It was just what I wanted.
What was it?
SCHULZ

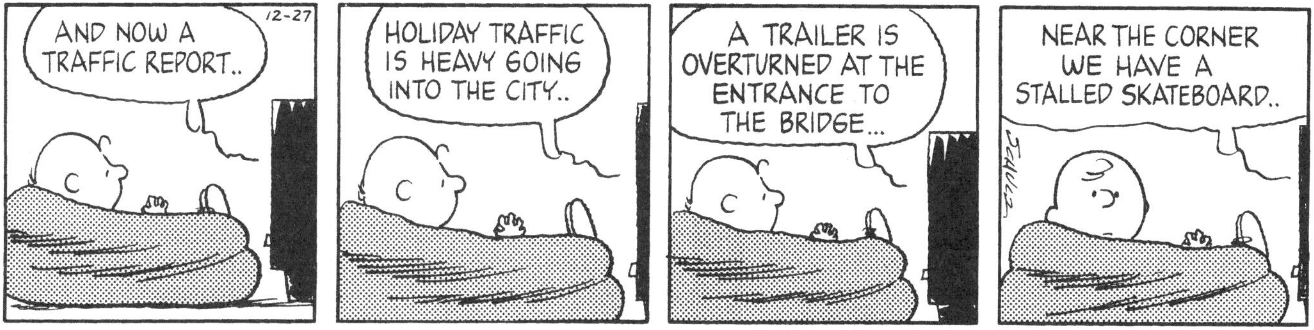
AND NOW A TRAFFIC REPORT..
12-27
HOLIDAY TRAFFIC IS HEAVY GOING INTO THE CITY..
A TRAILER IS OVERTURNED AT THE ENTRANCE TO THE BRIDGE...
NEAR THE CORNER WE HAVE A STALLED SKATEBOARD..
SCHULZ

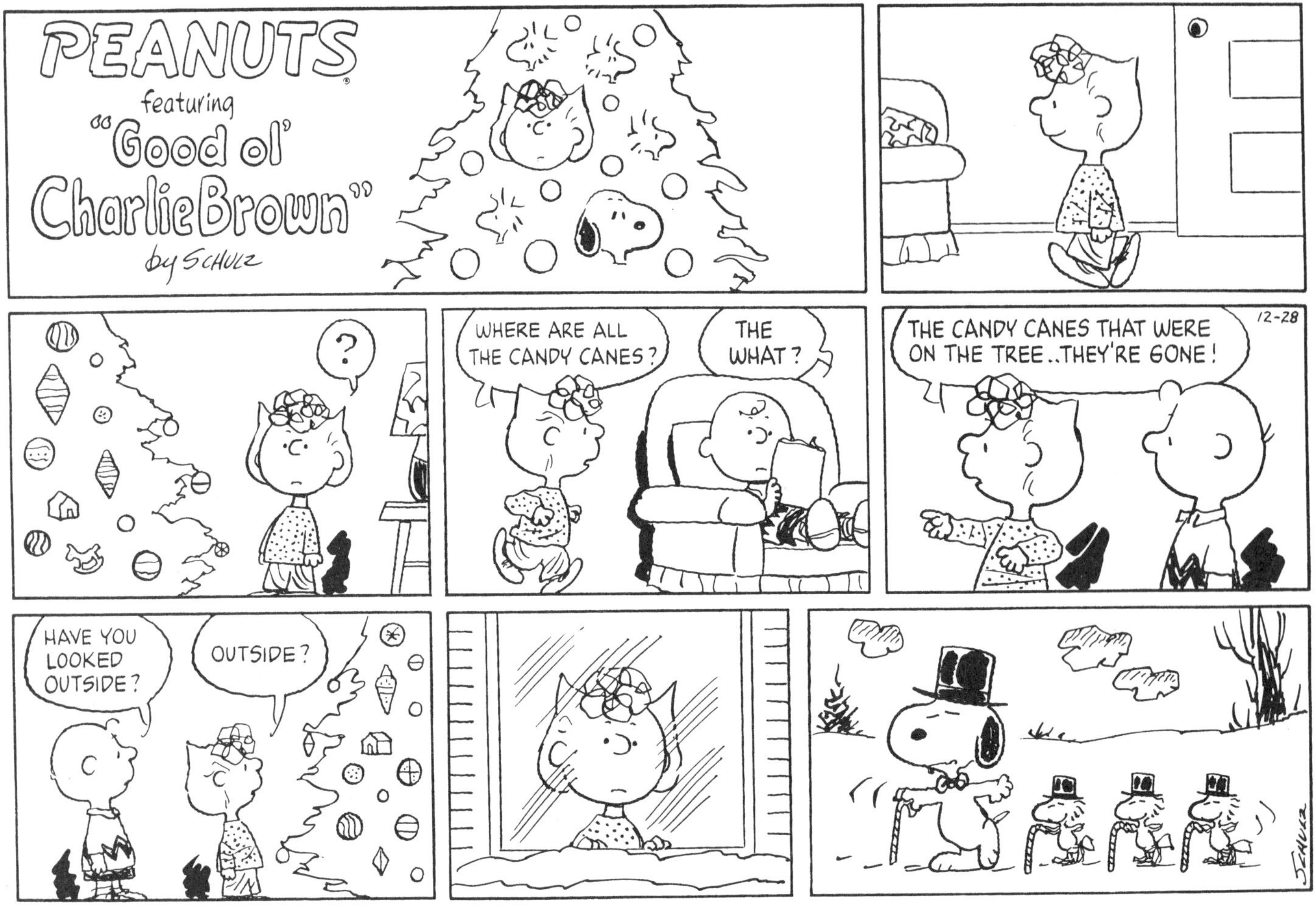
PEANUTS
featuring
"Good ol' CharlieBrown"
by SCHULZ
?
WHERE ARE ALL THE CANDY CANES?
THE WHAT?
12-28
THE CANDY CANES THAT WERE ON THE TREE..THEY'RE GONE!
HAVE YOU LOOKED OUTSIDE?
OUTSIDE?
SCHULZ

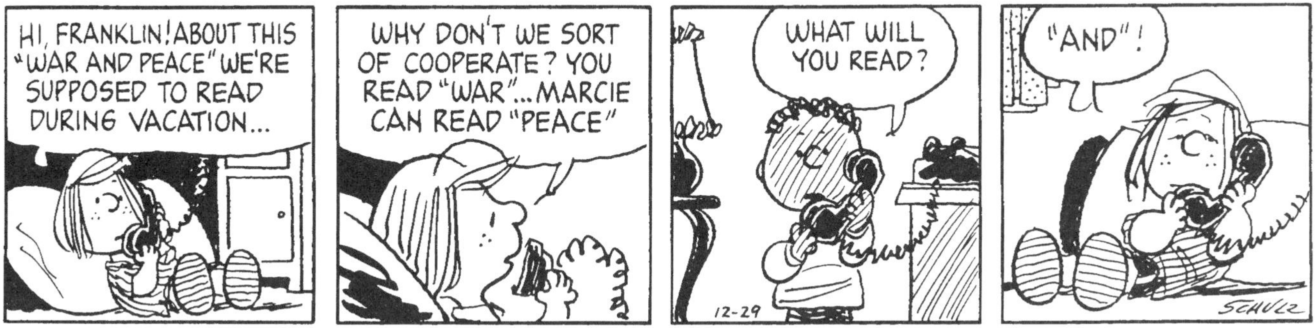
HI, FRANKLIN! ABOUT THIS "WAR AND PEACE" WE'RE SUPPOSED TO READ DURING VACATION...
WHY DON'T WE SORT OF COOPERATE? YOU READ "WAR"... MARCIE CAN READ "PEACE"
WHAT WILL YOU READ?
12-29
"AND"!
SCHULZ

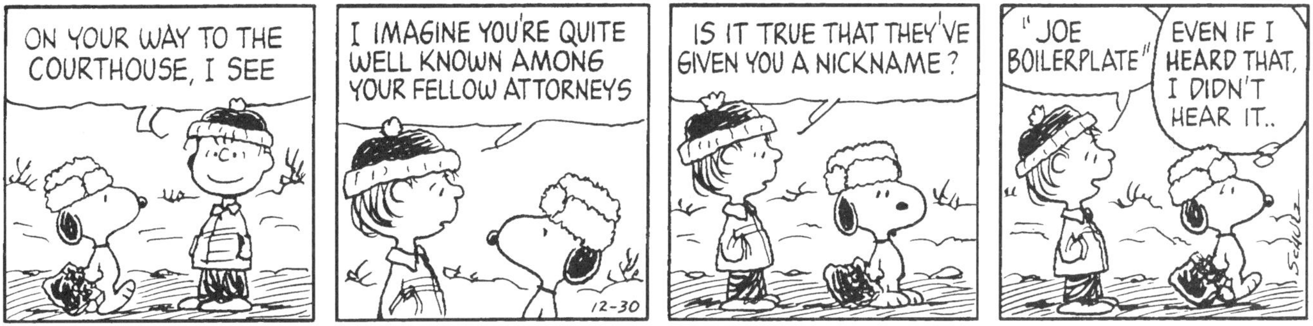
ON YOUR WAY TO THE COURTHOUSE, I SEE
I IMAGINE YOU'RE QUITE WELL KNOWN AMONG YOUR FELLOW ATTORNEYS
12-30
IS IT TRUE THAT THEY'VE GIVEN YOU A NICKNAME?
"JOE BOILERPLATE"
EVEN IF I HEARD THAT, I DIDN'T HEAR IT..
SCHULZ

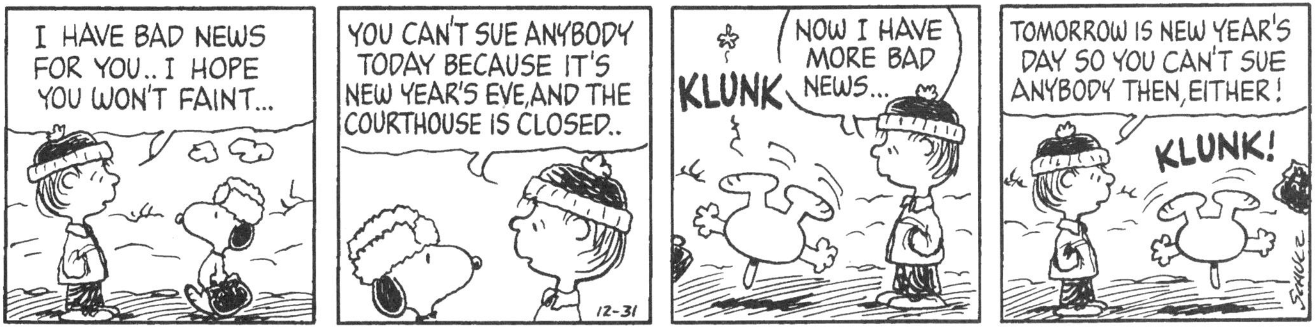
I HAVE BAD NEWS FOR YOU.. I HOPE YOU WON'T FAINT...
YOU CAN'T SUE ANYBODY TODAY BECAUSE IT'S NEW YEAR'S EVE, AND THE COURTHOUSE IS CLOSED..
12-31
KLUNK
NOW I HAVE MORE BAD NEWS...
TOMORROW IS NEW YEAR'S DAY SO YOU CAN'T SUE ANYBODY THEN, EITHER!
KLUNK!
SCHULZ

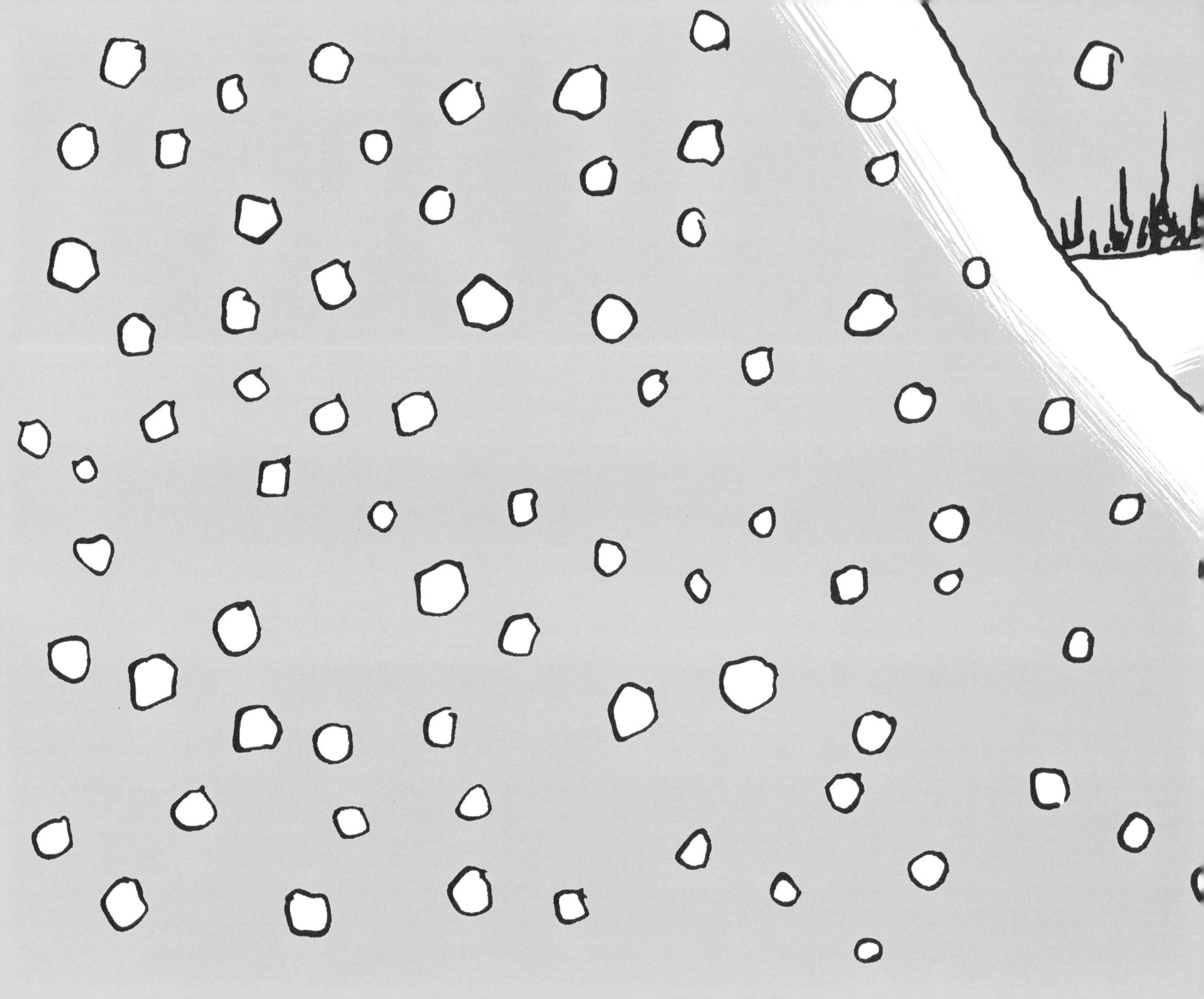

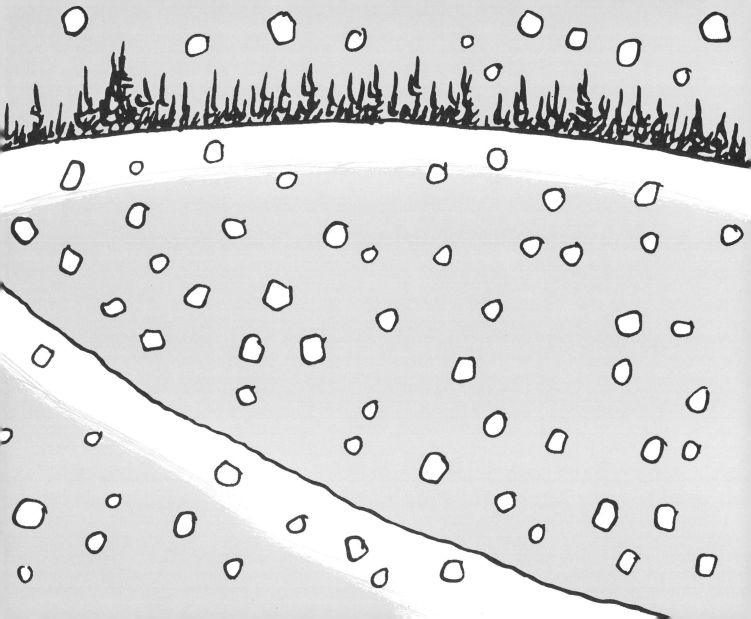

INDEX

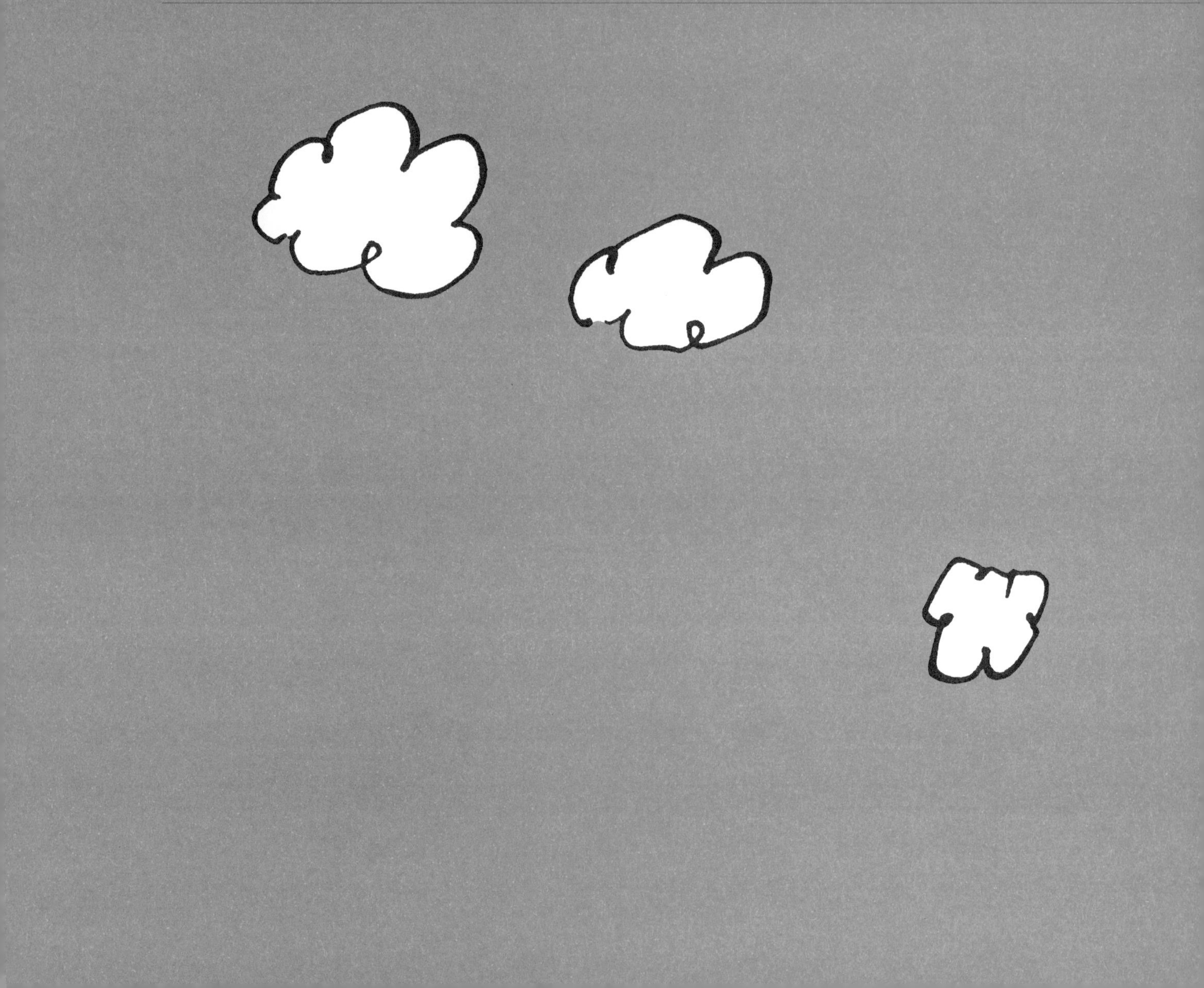

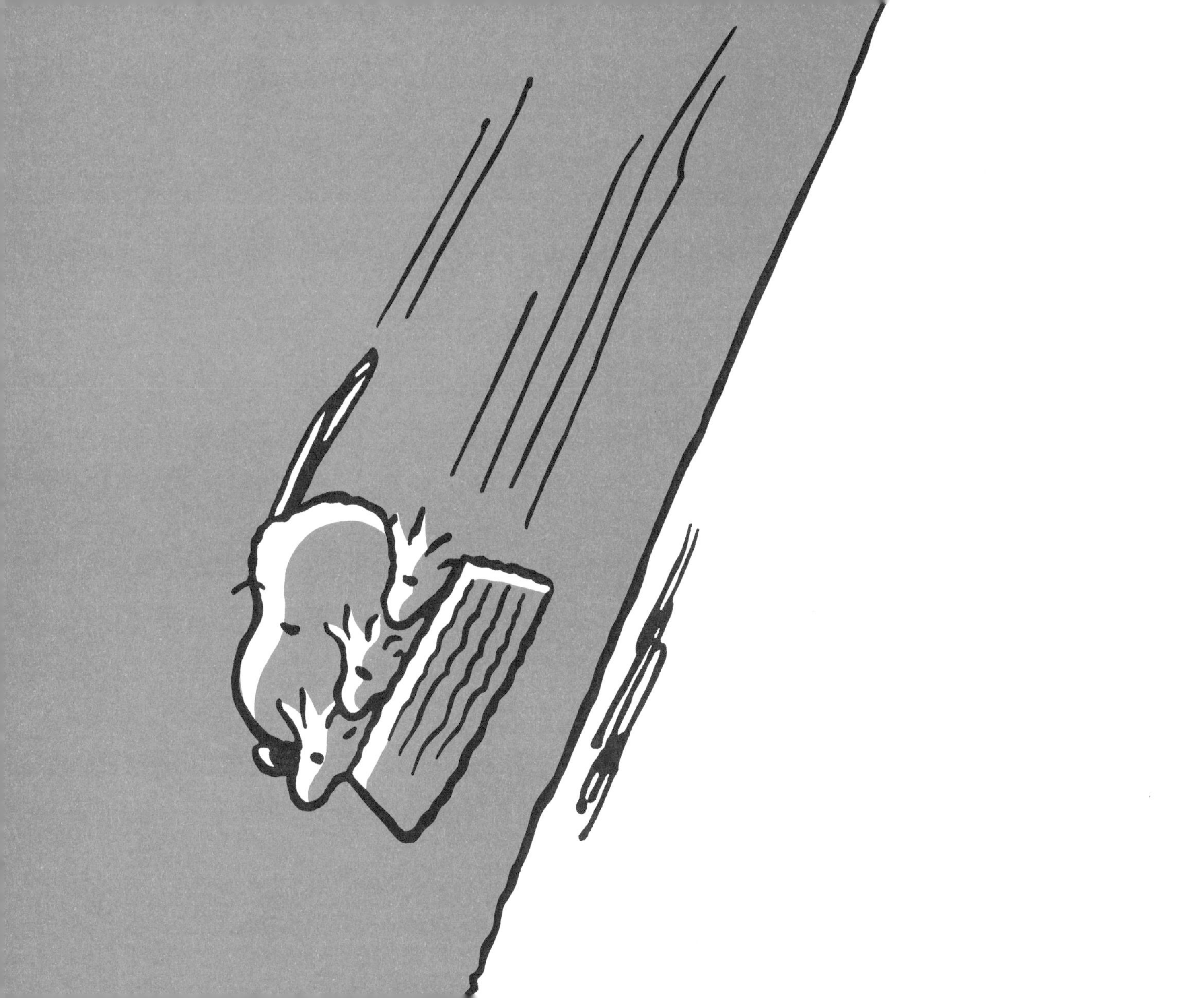

CHARLES M. SCHULZ · 1922 To 2000

Charles M. Schulz was born November 25, 1922 in Minneapolis. His destiny was foreshadowed when an uncle gave him, at the age of two days, the nickname Sparky (after the racehorse Spark Plug in the newspaper strip *Barney Google*).

Schulz grew up in St. Paul. By all accounts, he led an unremarkable, albeit sheltered, childhood. He was an only child, close to both parents, his eventual career path nurtured by his father, who bought four Sunday papers every week — just for the comics.

An outstanding student, he skipped two grades early on, but began to flounder in high school — perhaps not so coincidentally at the same time kids are going through their cruelest, most status-conscious period of socialization. The pain, bitterness, insecurity, and failures chronicled in *Peanuts* appear to have originated from this period of Schulz's life.

Although Schulz enjoyed sports, he also found refuge in solitary activities: reading, drawing, and watching movies. He bought comic books and Big Little Books, pored over the newspaper strips, and copied his favorites — *Buck Rogers*, the Walt Disney characters, *Popeye, Tim Tyler's Luck*. He quickly became a connoisseur; his heroes were Milton Caniff, Roy Crane, Hal Foster, and Alex Raymond.

In his senior year in high school, his mother noticed an ad in a local newspaper for a correspondence school, Federal Schools (later called Art

Instruction Schools). Schulz passed the talent test, completed the course and began trying, unsuccessfully, to sell gag cartoons to magazines. (His first published drawing was of his dog, Spike, and appeared in a 1937 *Ripley's Believe It Or Not!* installment.)

After World War II had ended and Schulz was discharged from the army, he started submitting gag cartoons to the various magazines of the time; his first breakthrough, however, came when an editor at *Timeless Topix* hired him to letter adventure comics. Soon after that, he was hired by his alma mater, Art Instruction, to correct student lessons returned by mail.

Between 1948 and 1950, he succeeded in selling 17 cartoons to the *Saturday Evening Post* — as well as, to the local *St. Paul Pioneer Press*, a weekly comic feature called *Li'l Folks*. It was run in the women's section and paid $10 a week. After writing and drawing the feature for two years, Schulz asked for a better location in the paper or for daily exposure, as well as a raise. When he was turned down on all three counts, he quit.

He started submitting strips to the newspaper syndicates. In the Spring of 1950, he received a letter from the United Feature Syndicate, announcing their interest in his submission, *Li'l Folks*. Schulz boarded a train in June for New York City; more interested in doing a strip than a panel, he also brought along the first installments of what would become *Peanuts* — and that was what sold. (The title, which Schulz loathed to his dying day, was imposed by the syndicate). The first *Peanuts* daily appeared October 2, 1950; the first Sunday, January 6, 1952.

Prior to *Peanuts*, the province of the comics page had been that of gags, social and political observation, domestic comedy, soap opera, and various adventure genres. Although *Peanuts* changed, or evolved, during the 50 years Schulz wrote and drew it, it remained, as it began, an anomaly on the comics page — a comic strip about the interior crises of the cartoonist himself. After a painful divorce in 1973 from which he had not yet recovered, Schulz told a reporter, "Strangely, I've drawn better cartoons in the last six months — or as good as I've ever drawn. I don't know how the human mind works." Surely, it was this kind of humility in the face of profoundly irreducible human question that makes *Peanuts* as universally moving as it is.

Diagnosed with cancer, Schulz retired from *Peanuts* at the end of 1999. He died on February 12th 2000, the day before his last strip was published (and two days before Valentine's Day) — having completed 17,897 daily and Sunday strips, each and every one fully written, drawn, and lettered entirely by his own hand — an unmatched achievement in comics.

—Gary Groth

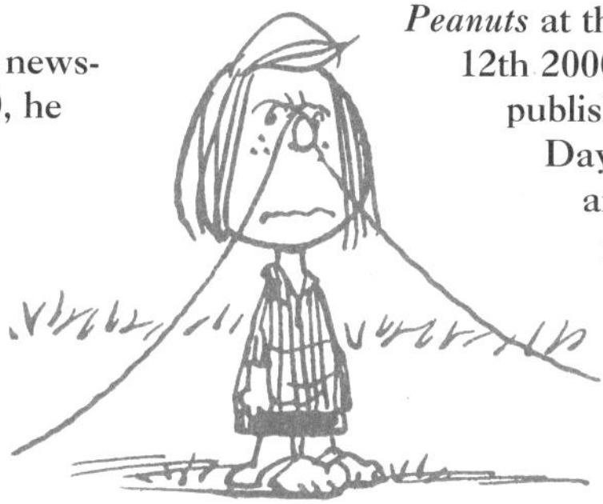

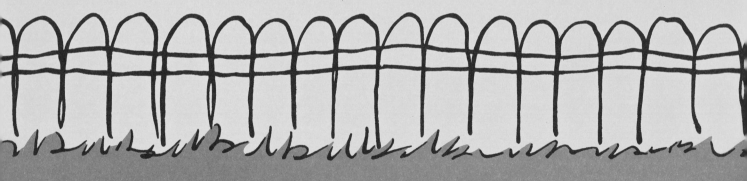

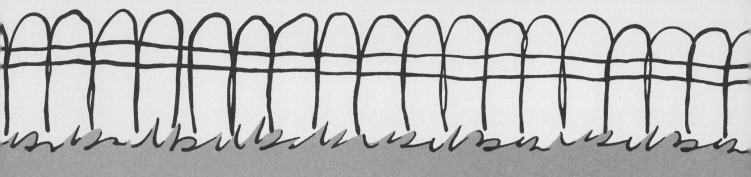

THE COMPLETE
PEANUTS

The definitive collection of
Charles M. Schulz's comic strip masterpiece

"An American treasure"
BARACK OBAMA

CANON‖GATE

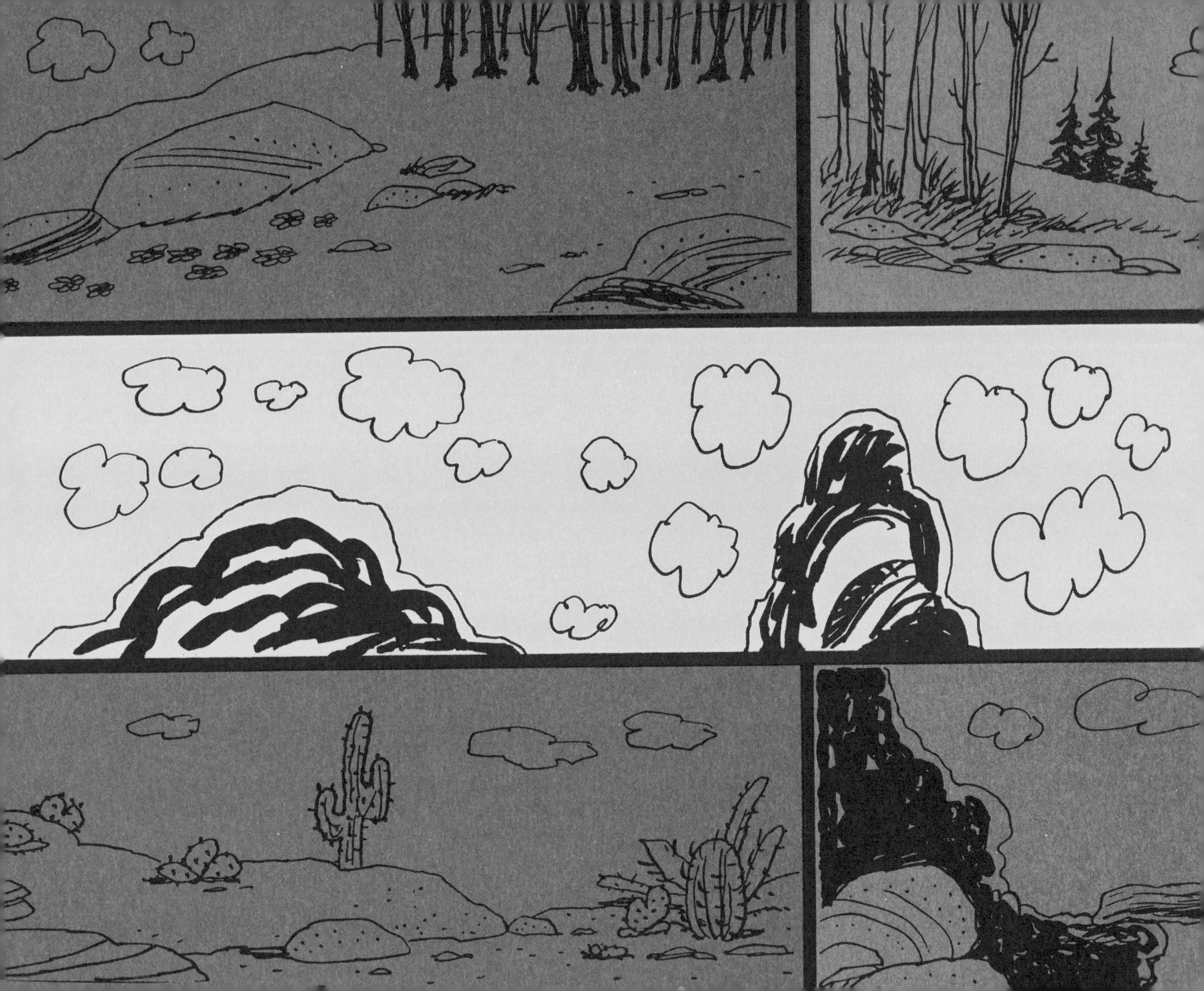